PUBLIC
SOCIOLOGY

John Germov is Associate Professor, Dean of Arts, and Deputy Head of the Faculty of Education and Arts at the University of Newcastle. He is the author and editor of 14 books including *Second Opinion* and *A Sociology of Food and Nutrition*.

Marilyn Poole is Honorary Associate Professor of Sociology at Deakin University. She is co-editor of *Sociology: Australian connections* and *A Certain Age*, and editor of *Family: Changing families, changing times*.

2ND EDITION

PUBLIC
SOCIOLOGY

An introduction to Australian society

EDITED BY

JOHN GERMOV & MARILYN POOLE

ALLEN&UNWIN

First edition published in 2007

This edition published in 2011

Allen & Unwin
83 Alexander Street
Crows Nest NSW 2065
Australia
Phone: (61 2) 8425 0100
Fax: (61 2) 9906 2218
Email: info@allenandunwin.com
Web: www.allenandunwin.com

Cataloguing-in-Publication details are available
from the National Library of Australia
www.trove.nla.gov.au

ISBN 978 1 74237 145 0

Internal design by Squirt Creative
Internal photographs by Maria Freij
Additional photographs by John Germov (Chapter 5), Getty Images (chapters 3, 17, and 19), and
Pedro Almeida (module openers)
Index by Maria Freij
Set in 11.5/14 pt Centaur MT by Midland Typesetters, Australia
Printed by South Wind Productions, Singapore

10 9 8 7 6 5 4 3 2

Contents

Tables and figures

Tables

Figures

Preface to the second edition

Welcome to the second edition of *Public Sociology*. We had a pleasing and positive response to our first edition, making it one of the foremost introductory sociology texts to be published in Australia. In this second edition, we have consolidated the strengths of the first edition in terms of the wide range of sociological topics presented in a user-friendly and accessible way.

We have taken the opportunity to carry out some extensive revisions, bringing the text up to date in a fast-changing social world. Even though it is only three years since the first edition was published, sociological debates have changed just as lifestyles and the political landscape have done. The increasingly rapid uptake of different forms of communication via the internet and the use of social networking sites are changing the ways in which we work and use our leisure time. Where appropriate, we have incorporated new information and ideas in order to provide a contemporary text that still makes links with, and builds upon, the major issues and theories in sociology.

New to the second edition

In addition to the new reader-friendly dual-colour format and many minor changes to bring chapters up to date, such as new citations to the scholarly literature and recent statistics, we have made the following changes to the second edition:

- Two new chapters have been added: 'Global risk and the surveillance state: A sociology of new terrorism', by Maria Freij and John Germov; and 'Religion and spirituality', by Andrew Singleton. The 'Environment' chapter from the previous edition no longer appears in the book, but is available on the book's website.
- Expanded material has been included on contemporary theorists and theories (Chapter 3). This includes information on Dorothy Smith and standpoint theory; Sylvia Walby and gender and the economy; Manuel Castells and network theory; Zygmunt Bauman and liquid modernity; and Raewyn Connell and Southern theory. There is also further discussion of public sociology (Chapter 1), levels of evidence (Chapter 4), youth transitions (Chapter 6), families and intimate relationships (Chapter 7), and the Global Financial Crisis (Chapter 11).

- There has been significant revision of the chapters on sporting life (Chapter 9), hybrid identities in a globalised world (Chapter 10), the gender order (Chapter 12), and media and popular culture (Chapter 21).
- An expanded book website is now available, with a wide range of extra resources for lecturers and students, such as access to chapter-specific YouTube clips, podcast summaries of chapter content, PowerPoint lecture slides for each book chapter (inclusive of book diagrams, illustrations, and tables), an online gallery of key theorists, updated online case studies, a list of chapter-specific essay topics, a test bank of multiple-choice questions, weblinks, and access to supplementary readings online from Allen & Unwin's back catalogue.

Why public sociology?

The first reaction of one of our colleagues upon seeing the outline for this book was, 'Not another introductory sociology textbook!' He even wondered with amusement whether there were 'statistics available on whether the total weight of the world's introductory sociology textbooks is greater than the total weight of the world's first-year sociology students'. While we have some sympathy with his view, we are convinced that our book offers a unique introduction to Australian sociology, and we chose the title *Public Sociology* to reflect this.

Public sociology—a reimagining of C. Wright Mills' notion of critical sociology—is premised on the principles of theoretical and methodological pluralism, and highlights the utility and relevance to Australian social life of an empirically grounded sociological perspective. It aims to encourage reflexivity among students so they can apply a sociological gaze to their own lives and the communities in which they live.

Sociology has many publics, and the theme of *Public Sociology* is that sociology must reach out beyond the academy—particularly to policy, business, community, and student audiences. All contributors to this book have addressed current public debates and highlighted the contribution of Australian sociological research wherever possible. Clearly, this book is primarily aimed at the student public, particularly the first-year student about to encounter sociology for the first time.

In keeping with the aim of both engaging our readers and meeting the needs of our student public, we have ensured that all contributors' chapters are accessible, topical, and lively. We have also included a broader range of foundational and topic-based chapters, such as two separate theory chapters (foundational and contemporary), a chapter that explains the main research methods used by sociologists and offers advice on how to evaluate research studies, and chapters on current social issues such as terrorism, globalisation, urbanisation and rurality, sport, consumption, contemporary Indigenous issues, ethnicity, youth, religion, and cultural hybridity.

We are also keenly aware of the need to supplement the text with pedagogic features that will aid not only the student, but also the academic public of tutors and lecturers.

For example, each chapter begins with a brief **'real-life' vignette** to grab the reader's interest and encourage a questioning and reflexive approach to the topic. **Key concepts** are highlighted in bold in the text and defined in separate margin paragraphs as well as appearing in a glossary at the end of the book. Each chapter also contains **Sociology Spotlight** breakout boxes that offer brief summaries of cutting-edge sociological empirical studies and debates. End-of-chapter material includes **Sociological Reflections** (brief self-directed or class-based icebreakers that help students apply their learning and highlight the relevance of sociological analysis), a **summary of main points**, as well as **discussion questions, recommended further reading**, and **chapter-specific websites, films, and documentaries**. The final module of the book provides students with skills and knowledge about developing their sociological imagination further, as well as advice on how to write and reference sociology essays.

Structure and content of the book

The book assumes no prior knowledge of sociology and is intended for undergraduate students. It is structured to provide a foundation in sociology in an Australian context. It is organised into the following learning modules:

- Module 1: Doing public sociology
- Module 2: Social identities
- Module 3: Social differences and inequalities
- Module 4: Social transformations
- Module 5: Future directions.

Suggestions and feedback

We are very interested in receiving feedback on the book and suggestions for future editions. You can contact us at <John.Germov@newcastle.edu.au> and <marp@deakin.edu.au>.

—*John Germov and Marilyn Poole*

Acknowledgments

First thanks must go to the contributors for producing chapters of such high quality.

Warm thanks are due to our publisher, Elizabeth Weiss, for encouraging us to produce this book and for her constructive feedback on all aspects of the writing process. We thank Dr Maria Freij for her expert editing of the entire manuscript, for managing the process of producing this book and its web material, and for the wonderful photos.

Thanks also to copyeditor Susan Jarvis, our in-house editor Ann Lennox, and designer Simon Rattray.

John would like to thank Sue Jelovcan for her support, patience, and good humour during the production of this book. He dedicates the book to their daughter, Isabella, already a budding sociologist!

Marilyn would like to thank Neil Swansson for his support and forbearance as she became immersed in the tasks of writing and editing.

Every effort has been made to trace and acknowledge the original sources for all material reproduced in this book. Where the attempt has been unsuccessful, the authors and publisher would be pleased to hear from the copyright holder concerned to rectify any omission.

Contributors

Janeen Baxter (PhD) is an Australian Research Council Professorial Fellow in the School of Social Science and the Institute for Social Science Research at the University of Queensland. Her research interests include gender, families, and inequality in comparative perspective. She is one of the chief investigators on the Negotiating the Lifecourse project, a member of the External Reference Group for the Households, Income and Labour Dynamics in Australia (HILDA) project, and a Fellow of the Academy of Social Sciences in Australia.

Neil Burdess (PhD) is a Senior Lecturer in Sociology at the Warrnambool campus of Deakin University. He teaches across a range of sociology units, including Introduction to Sociology, Sociology of Health, and Social Research. He is the author of several books, including *Good Study* (Pearson, 2007), and *Starting Statistics* (Sage, 2010). He has contributed chapters to a number of edited books, including *Health in Australia* (Pearson, 2004), and has written articles for a variety of journals, including *Policy, Organisation and Society*, the *Journal of Rural Studies*, and the *Electronic Journal of Australian and New Zealand History*.

Maria Freij (PhD) is a Lecturer and social researcher at the University of Newcastle. She is especially interested in private and public representations of identity. She combines her work in sociology with lecturing in Creative Writing; she is a poet in her other career and has published in *Meanjin, Blue Dog: Australian Poetry, Overland*, the *Mascara Literary Review*, and other literary journals. Her poems have won the Harri Jones Memorial Prize and been highly commended in the 2008 *Overland* Judith Wright Poetry Prize and the 2009 Bruce Dawe Poetry Prize. She also works as an editor and translates poetry between Swedish, English, and French.

John Germov (PhD) is Deputy Head of the Faculty of Education and Arts, Dean of Arts, Associate Professor of Sociology, and Head of the School of Humanities and Social Science at the University of Newcastle. He is currently the Secretary of the Australasian Council of the Deans of Arts, Social Science and Humanities (DASSH), and a former President of TASA: The Australian Sociological Association (2002–04), having served on its Executive for twelve years during which he established TASAweb and was its editor (1996–2005). He was an Editorial Board Member for the *Journal of Sociology* (2002–09), and a former Executive Board member of the International Sociological Association

(ISA) (2002–06). His research interests span the social determinants of food consumption and production, public health policy, workplace change, youth and health behaviour, and the history of sociology. John has published fifteen books, including *Get Great Marks for Your Essays, Reports, and Presentations* (Allen & Unwin, 2010), *Second Opinion: An Introduction to Health Sociology* (Oxford University Press, 2009), *A Sociology of Food and Nutrition: The Social Appetite* (Oxford University Press, 2008), *Australian Youth* (Pearson, 2007), and *Histories of Australian Sociology* (Melbourne University Press, 2005). In 2009, he completed the Australian Learning and Teaching Council (ALTC)-funded report *Teaching Sociology in Australia*.

Ian Gray (PhD) is an Associate Professor at Charles Sturt University in New South Wales and teaches sociology of community and the environment. He is an active member of several regional community organisations and professional associations. His research interests include community life, environmental issues, regionalism, and transport. Among his publications are *Politics in Place: Social Power Relations in an Australian Country Town* (Cambridge University Press, 1991) and *A Future for Regional Australia: Escaping Global Misfortune* (Cambridge University Press, 2001, with G. Lawrence). He has also published in the *Australian Journal of Social Issues*, *Sociologia Ruralis*, *Historic Environment*, *The Journal of Multi-disciplinary Engineering*, and *The Journal of Environmental Policy and Planning*.

Meredith Green (PhD) was a Postdoctoral Research Fellow at the Centre for Social Research at Edith Cowan University in Perth, Western Australia until 2007. Her research interests focus on Indigenous and non-Indigenous race relations in Australia, in particular issues of inequality and the notion of whiteness.

Tim Marjoribanks (PhD) is Professor of Management in the Graduate School of Management at La Trobe University. From 1997–2010, he taught and researched in sociology at The University of Melbourne. He has published widely in the area of media, including *News Corporation, Technology and the Workplace* (Cambridge University Press, 2000). He has also written journal articles and book chapters on media workplaces, news production and defamation law, representations of race in the media, and health and sport. He teaches and supervises in a range of undergraduate and postgraduate areas including media, organisations, qualitative methods, health, and work.

Vince Marotta (PhD) is a Senior Lecturer in Sociology at Deakin University. His research interests cover social theory, theories of identities, cosmopolitanism, multiculturalism, and multicultural cities. He is editor of the *Journal of Intercultural Studies* (Routledge) and has recently published a paper on intercultural subjectivity, and a chapter on the cosmopolitan stranger.

Tara Renae McGee (PhD) is a Senior Lecturer in the School of Criminology and Justice at Griffith University. Her teaching focuses on research methods and data analysis. Her main research interests are criminal careers and developmental criminology, neighbourhoods and crime, the history of Australian sociology, and longitudinal research methodology.

Julie McLeod (PhD) is an Associate Professor in the Melbourne Graduate School of Education at the University of Melbourne, where she is Convenor of the Strategic Research Program 'Education, Equity and Social Identities' and a member of the Melbourne Educational Research Institute (MERI). Her areas of research include gender and youth studies, and social and identity differences in relation to schooling. She is co-author (with Cherry Collins and Jane Kenway) of *Factors Influencing the Educational Performance of Males and Females at School and their Initial Destinations after Leaving School* (DETYA 2000), co-author (with Lyn Yates) of *Making Modern Lives: Subjectivity, Schooling and Social Change* (SUNY Press, 2006) and co-author with Rachel Thomson of *Researching Social Change: Qualitative Approaches* (Sage, 2009). Her current research includes a cross-generational study of the social and educational experiences of economically disadvantaged young women.

Peter Mewett (PhD) is a Senior Lecturer in Sociology at Deakin University. He received his first degree from the University of Hull, followed by postgraduate degrees from the universities of Manchester and Aberdeen. Originally he researched and published on British rural ethnography, having conducted his doctoral fieldwork on migration from the Isle of Lewis (Scotland). After moving to Australia, his interests shifted to the study of sport and he has engaged in research on professional running and the origins and development of sports training in modernity; he is currently researching women football fans.

Pam Nilan (PhD) is an Associate Professor in the Faculty of Education and Arts at the University of Newcastle. She has written two books on youth and is currently conducting funded research on youth and ambivalence in Indonesia. She leads a research project on masculinities and violence in Indonesia and India, and is currently collecting data for a research project on Muslim jobseekers in Australia. She is Treasurer of the Asia-Pacific Sociological Association.

Jan Pakulski (PhD) is Professor of Sociology and former Dean of Arts at the University of Tasmania and has research interests in the areas of class and social inequality. He is the author of *Globalising Inequalities* (Allen & Unwin, 2004) and co-author of *Postcommunist Elites and Democracy in Eastern Europe* (Palgrave Macmillan, 1998), *The Death of Class* (Sage, 1996), and *Postmodernization* (Sage, 1992).

Marilyn Poole (PhD) is an Associate Professor in Sociology in the School of History, Heritage and Society at Deakin University. Her research interests include the sociology of families, gender, and ageing. Although now retired and holding an honorary appointment, she continues to write and lecture. She works in a voluntary capacity in programs and services for older people. In addition to this book, she is co-editor of *Sociology Australian Connections* (Allen & Unwin, 3rd edition, 2003) and *A Certain Age: Women Growing Older* (Allen & Unwin, 1999), and the editor of *Family* (Allen & Unwin, 2005).

Sharyn Roach Anleu (PhD) is Professor of Sociology at Flinders University, Adelaide, a Fellow of the Australian Academy of Social Sciences, and a past president of The Australian Sociological Association (TASA). She was one of three editors of the *Journal of Sociology* (2001–04), and is the author of *Law and Social Change* (Sage, 2nd edition, 2010), and four editions of *Deviance, Conformity and Control* (Pearson, 4th edition, 2005), as well as numerous articles on deviance, legal regulation, and the criminal justice system. She is currently undertaking research (with Professor Kathy Mack) funded by the Australian Research Council on the judiciary and their courts.

Sherry Saggers (PhD) is Professor and Project Leader of Prevention, Early Intervention and Inequality at the National Drug Research Institute, Curtin University of Technology, Perth. She was formerly Foundation Professor of Applied Social Research and Director of the Centre for Social Research at Edith Cowan University. An anthropologist, she has worked with and for Indigenous communities throughout Australia for almost 30 years. She has published widely on Indigenous issues, including health, substance misuse, education, youth leadership, community development, and political economy.

Andrew Singleton (PhD) is a Senior Lecturer in Sociology at Monash University. His research interests include youth spirituality, alternative religions, and men and masculinity. Andrew has published extensively in these areas, both nationally and internationally, including the book *Spirit of Generation Y: Young People's Spirituality in a Changing Australia* (John Garratt, 2007, with M. Mason and R. Webber). He coordinates units on contemporary religion and spirituality; men, masculinity and society; and social research methods.

Zlatko Skrbis (PhD) is Professor of Sociology and Dean of the Graduate School at the University of Queensland. His publications include *Long-distance Nationalism* (Ashgate, 1999), *Constructing Singapore* (NIAS, 2008, with M. Barr), and *The Sociology of Cosmopolitanism* (Palgrave, 2009, with G. Kendall and I. Woodward). He is currently working on a manuscript titled *The Uses of Cosmopolitanism* (with I. Woodward, forthcoming, Sage).

Mark Western (PhD) is Director of the Institute for Social Science Research at the University of Queensland. His research interests include social inequality in capitalist societies, cultural change and the formation of social values and identities, the factors associated with individual and community vulnerability and resilience, and quantitative research methods.

Ian Woodward (PhD) is a Senior Lecturer in Cultural Sociology at Griffith University, and Deputy Director of Griffith's Centre for Public Culture and Ideas. He is also a Fellow of Yale University's Center for Cultural Sociology. In addition to publishing many papers on the cultural aspects of cosmopolitanism with his colleagues Zlatko Skrbis, Gavin Kendall, and Clive Bean, he has written extensively on consumption practices, subject-object relations, and material culture. He is the author of *Understanding Material Culture* (Sage, 2007), and co-author of *The Sociology of Cosmopolitanism* (Palgrave, 2009).

Grazyna Zajdow (PhD) has been teaching sociology, particularly feminist sociology, for over 25 years and has contributed to a number of textbooks. She is currently a Senior Lecturer at Deakin University. Her research interests are in drug and alcohol policy, the experience of addiction, and living with addiction. Her recent publications include articles in the *Journal of Sociology*, and a chapter in the book *The Politics of Illicit Drugs in Australia* (with Philip Mendes and James Rowe, Pearson, 2005). She is also the author of *Al-Anon Narratives: Women, Self-Stories and Mutual Aid* (Greenwood Press, 2002).

Abbreviations

ABC	Australian Broadcasting Corporation
ABSEG	Aboriginal Secondary Grants scheme
ABSTUDY	Aboriginal Study Grants Scheme
ACCC	Australian Competition and Consumer Commission
ACER	Australian Council for Educational Research
ACS	Australian Community Survey
ACTU	Australian Council of Trade Unions
AFP	Australian Federal Police
AGPS	Australian Government Publishing Service
AIC	Australian Institute of Criminology
AIDS	Acquired Immune Deficiency Syndrome
AIFS	Australian Institute of Family Studies
AIHW	Australian Institute of Health and Welfare
AIS	Australian Institute of Sport
ALP	Australian Labor Party
AMA	Australian Medical Association
ANOVA	Analysis of variance
ANTaR	Australians for Native Title and Reconciliation
ANZJS	*Australian and New Zealand Journal of Sociology*
ARCSHS	Australian Research Centre in Sex, Health and Society
ASADA	Australian Sports Anti-Doping Authority
ASEAN	Association of Southeast Asian Nations
ASIO	Australian Security Intelligence Organisation
ATSIC	Australian and Torres Strait Islander Commission
AWB	Australian Wheat Board
BBC	British Broadcasting Corporation
BPR	business process re-engineering
CCCS	Birmingham Centre for Contemporary Cultural Studies
CCTV	closed-circuit television
CIA	Central Intelligence Agency (US)
CNN	Cable News Network
DIAC	Department of Immigration and Citizenship
DIMIA	Department of Immigration and Multicultural and Indigenous Affairs

DIY	do it yourself
DZ	dizygotic
EOWA	Equal Opportunity for Women in the Workplace Agency
EU	European Union
FYA	Foundation for Young Australians
GDP	gross domestic product
GFC	Global Financial Crisis
GP	general practitioner
HIV	Human Immunodeficiency Virus
HNPCC	heredity nonpolyposis colorectal cancer
HREC	human research ethics committee
HREOC	Human Rights and Equal Opportunity Commission
ICT	information and communication technology
ILO	International Labour Organization
IMF	International Monetary Fund
IRA	Irish Republican Army
IVF	in-vitro fertilisation
JIT	just in time
JOS	*Journal of Sociology*
LSE	London School of Economics
MANAA	Media Action Network for Asian Americans
MMORPG	massively multiplayer online role-playing games
MOW	meaning of working
MZ	monozygotic
NACC	National Aboriginal Consultative Committee
NAFTA	North American Free Trade Agreement
NATO	North Atlantic Treaty Organization
NESB	non-English speaking background
NGO	non-governmental organisation
NHHRC	National Health and Hospitals Reform Commission
NHMRC	National Health and Medical Research Council
NILS	National Institute of Labour Studies (Flinders University)
NIMBY	'not in my backyard'
NTER	Northern Territory Emergency Response
OECD	Organisation for Economic Cooperation and Development
ONS	Office for National Statistics
PICT	Centre for Policing, Intelligence and Counter Terrorism
PIN	personal identification number
RACS	Royal Australasian College of Surgeons
RCT	randomised control trial

RSPCA	Royal Society for the Prevention of Cruelty to Animals
SAANZ	Sociological Association of Australia and New Zealand
SBS	Special Broadcasting Service
SCRGSP	Steering Committee for the Review of Government Service Provision
SES	socioeconomic status
SGY	Spirit of Generation Y
SPSS	Statistical Package for the Social Sciences
SRA	shared responsibility agreement
SSRC	Social Science Research Council
TAFE	Technical and Further Education
TASA	The Australian Sociological Association
TFR	total fertility rate
TNC	transnational corporation
TQM	total quality management
UN	United Nations
UNESCO	United Nations Educational, Scientific and Cultural Organization
UNFPA	United Nations Population Fund
VDHS	Victorian Department of Human Services
WEA	Workers' Education Association
WHO	World Health Organization
WMDs	weapons of mass destruction
WVS	World Values Survey
WYD08	World Youth Day 2008

Guided tour
Pedagogic features and supplementary resources

---

social structur
The recurring p
interaction thr
related to each

Key concepts highlighted in bold in the text and defined in separate margin paragraphs as well as appearing in a glossary at the end of the book

---

Introductory vignettes each chapter begins with a short 'real-life' vignette (or hypothetical) to grab the reader's interest, encourage a questioning and reflexive approach to the topic, and show the application of a sociological perspective

---

Sociology spotlight short boxed summaries of cutting-edge sociological empirical studies

---

Sociological reflection end-of-chapter self-directed or class-based icebreakers that help students apply their learning and highlight the relevance of sociological analysis

---

CrossLinks boxes related material cross-referenced in different chapters

---

Summary of main points

Discussion questions

References

Further reading short annotated list of key recommended readings

---

Recommended chapter-specific websites

Recommended chapter-specific films and documentaries

Online teaching and learning resources for lecturers and students
An expanded book website is now available, with a wide range of extra resources for lecturers and students, such as:

▶ access to chapter-specific YouTube clips and podcast summaries of chapter content
▶ PowerPoint lecture slides for each book chapter (inclusive of book diagrams, illustrations, and tables) (lecturers only)
▶ online biographies and photos of key theorists
▶ updated online case studies with discussion questions
▶ a list of chapter-specific essay topics (lecturers only)
▶ a test bank of multiple-choice questions (lecturers only)
▶ weblinks, and
▶ access to supplementary readings online from Allen & Unwin's back catalogue.

Module 1
Doing public sociology

This module aims to provide foundational knowledge on the discipline of sociology. It explores what sociology is and examines the contribution of Australian sociologists, as well as early and contemporary theories and theorists. It also offers understanding on how to evaluate social research.

The module contains the following chapters:

1   The sociological gaze: Linking private lives to public issues

2   Sociological foundations: Early theorists and theories

3   Contemporary sociological theorists and theories

4   Sociological investigations: Doing social research

CHAPTER 1

The sociological gaze:
Linking private lives
to public issues

John Germov and Marilyn Poole

Eating Skippy: The social origins of food habits

We often think of our food choices as an outcome of personal likes and dislikes, but there is a distinctly social flavour to our food habits. We can easily identify a range of national cuisines such as Italian, Thai, and Mexican, which clearly shows the impact of cultural differences on food preferences. No society consumes all the potential foods available in its environment; cultural values and traditions dictate what food is 'good to eat'. For some cultures, horse, dog, turtle, whale, and seal meat are highly valued, while other cultures can often view such practices as distasteful or even unethical. Some Indigenous Australians consume 'bush tucker' that white Australians may find objectionable, such as galahs, goannas, honey ants, and witchetty grubs. Food taboos and food morality are central features of all cultures, yet neither cultures nor food preferences are static. While many people around the world are familiar with the Australian TV series *Skippy: The Bush Kangaroo*, some are horrified to discover that you can consume kangaroo meat (literally 'eat Skippy') in a number of restaurants. Australia must be one of the few countries in the world to eat its national emblems: both the kangaroo and the emu are emblazoned on the national coat of arms and available on our dinner plates. While we will always have our personal taste preferences for certain foods and cuisines, notions of acceptable and unacceptable foods clearly vary over time and between cultures and subcultures. A sociological gaze helps to expose how our taken-for-granted and individualised view of the world—our personal behaviour and values—occurs within a social context, can have social origins, and can be a result of social relations.

Introducing the sociological enterprise

Sociology is a thing, which if it didn't exist, would have to be invented . . .
—**Leonard Broom (2005, p. 210)**

If you are new to sociology, and trying to get your head around exactly what it entails, you probably do not realise you have encountered it many times already. Sociological analyses feature regularly in media commentary and public debate, and concepts such as globalisation, economic rationalism, socialisation, class, social status, deviance, alienation, and lifestyle all have sociological origins. As the American sociologist Robert Merton noted some time ago, 'ours has become an age pervaded by sociology' and sociological concepts have 'drifted into our everyday language' (1981, p. 42). This familiarity with the subject matter of sociology—we are all members of society and thus by definition should be automatic experts on the topic—can too often lead to the dismissal of the sociological enterprise as mere common sense. As you will soon find out, it is not that simple.

Sociology involves a methodical study of human behaviours and societies (Macionis & Plummer 2008). It is the study of the relationship between the individual and society, investigating how human thought, action, and interaction shape and are shaped by society, or how 'we create society at the same time as we are created by it' (Giddens 1986, p. II). The 'sociological gaze' exposes the link between individual experience and the social context in which we live, work, and play. Many authors have offered definitions that attempt to capture the essence of the sociological enterprise. Some of the main definitions of sociology can be found in Sociology Spotlight I.I.

1.1: Defining sociology

Many sociologists have attempted to encapsulate the nature of sociology in a concise statement, and we reproduce some of the most commonly cited of these below. The word 'sociology' comes from the Latin *socius* meaning 'companion' and the Greek suffix *logie* meaning 'study of'. According to its Latin and Greek roots, sociology means the study of companionship—that is, the study of human relationships and, more generally, the study of society (Abercrombie 2004).

Charles Wright Mills

The sociological imagination enables us to grasp history and biography and the relations between the two within society . . . It is a quality of mind that seems most dramatically to promise an understanding of the intimate realities of ourselves in connection with larger social realities. (Mills 1959, pp. 6, 15)

Peter Berger

We see the puppets dancing on their miniature stage, moving up and down as the strings pull them around, following the prescribed course of their various little parts. We learn to understand the logic of this theatre and we find ourselves in its motions. We locate ourselves in society and thus recognize our own position as we hang from its subtle strings. For a moment we see ourselves as puppets indeed. But then we grasp a decisive difference between the puppet theatre and our own drama. Unlike the puppets, we have the possibility of stopping in our movements, looking up and perceiving the machinery by which we have been moved. In this act lies the first step towards freedom. (Berger 1963, pp. 140, 199)

Anthony Giddens

Sociology is the scientific study of human life, social groups, whole societies and the human world as such. It is a dazzling and compelling enterprise, as its subject-matter is our own behaviour as social beings. (Giddens 2009a, p. 6)

Zygmunt Bauman and Tim May

By examining that which is taken-for-granted, it has the potential to disturb the comfortable certitudes of life by asking questions no one can remember asking and those with vested interests resent even being asked . . . To think sociologically can render us more sensitive and tolerant of diversity. It can sharpen our senses and open our eyes to new horizons beyond our immediate experiences in order that we can explore human conditions, which, hitherto, have remained relatively invisible. Once we understand better how the apparently natural, inevitable, immutable, eternal aspects of our lives have been brought into being through the exercise of human power and resources, we shall find it much harder to accept that they are immune and impenetrable to subsequent actions, including our own. (Bauman & May 2001, pp. 10–11)

No such thing as society?

Any dictionary will somewhat unhelpfully define sociology as 'the study of society'. Expanding on this base, we can define sociology as the methodical study of the ways in which people construct and contribute to society, and how they, in turn, are influenced by society. When former UK Prime Minister Margaret Thatcher infamously said, 'there is no such thing as society' and went on to say that 'there are individual men and women, and there are families' (Thatcher, quoted in Keay 1987), she was making a (Conservative) political statement that reverberated around the world. The implication is that 'society' is just a collective term for a group of individuals occupying a particular geographic location, but we know it is much more than that. When we think of national cultures, languages, and traditions, we acknowledge the communal ties that bind them together. Many people speak of 'society' as an entity, reifying it as if it has a life of its own—particularly when media commentators state that society is dysfunctional or disintegrating. It is not uncommon to hear people ask, 'What is society coming to?' in response to gangland killings, youth drug-taking, or the exploitation of the aged by con artists. All of this implies that there is an entity called 'society' based on some shared cultural values, norms, practices, and institutions, and so on, that create a sense of cohesion and order in our daily lives, and these social factors are what represent the subject matter of sociology.

The structure–agency debate

Many of us believe that as individuals we are free agents making independent decisions about our lives. A sociologist will ask, 'How free are those choices?' Consider the choices you make about the clothes you wear, the music to which you listen, the movies you see, and the clubs, bars, and social events you frequent. Would those choices be the same if you lived on the other side of the world? If you were of the opposite sex? If your financial situation were different? While we all make our own decisions about how we live our lives—what sociologists refer to as human agency—we do not make them entirely free of social constraints and influences. Why do we buy certain consumer goods? Why do we find we must have some things? One of the important characteristics of a sociologist is to be curious, to look behind and beyond the familiar and the obvious

> **agency**
> The ability of people, individually and collectively, to influence their own lives and the society in which they live.

(Berger 1963). Thus a sociologist would study, for example, the impact of the marketing strategies that create demand for particular products. Our tastes and choices may be influenced by decisions made in corporate boardrooms or in advertising companies, and influenced by celebrity endorsements and peer-group pressure. Our individual choices, tastes, and behaviours are often shaped by external (social) influences, as the opening vignette on food habits showed. As Peter Berger (1963, p. 23) puts it, 'things are not what they seem', and sociology involves analysing the taken-for-granted world to identify 'the general in the particular'. By exposing social influences and social patterns, sociology helps to improve our understanding of why things are as they are, and offers the potential to consider how they could be otherwise.

Sociologists are concerned with patterned social relationships referred to as **social structures**, and they assume that social relationships are not determined solely by the idiosyncratic characteristics of the individuals involved. The **structure–agency debate** addresses an age-old philosophical question about the extent to which humans can exercise free will as opposed to their thoughts and actions being determined by external factors.

social structure
The recurring patterns of social interaction through which people are related to each other, such as social institutions and social groups.

structure–agency debate
A key debate in sociology over the extent to which human behaviour is determined by social structure.

social institutions
Formal organisations that address public needs such as education, health care, government, and welfare.

Sociologists see humans as social animals who are substantially influenced by the way their social environment is organised—that is, individuals are shaped by the social structures they inhabit, create, and reproduce. It is not difficult to imagine we are influenced by our cultural values and traditions, or that **social institutions** have a major impact on our lives, but how much agency do we actually have? There is no simple answer to this question, but sociologists maintain that structure and agency are interdependent and not mutually exclusive. That is, it is not a matter of preferring agency over structure, as simplistic media commentary often does when it characterises certain views as blaming the individual versus blaming society for various social ills. The point is that individuals both shape and are concurrently shaped by society. While we are born into a world that is not of our own personal making, and are socialised through a particular culture and exposure to various social institutions (such as education, religion, the legal system), we are not just 'puppets on strings'. As sentient (self-aware) beings, we have the capacity to think and act individually and collectively to change the society in which we live. As Anthony Giddens (1986) puts it, we have the ability to consider 'alternative futures'.

It is important not to conflate issues of structure and agency with positive or negative associations. For example, structures can be both constraining and enabling of human agency; laws, regulations, and social policies can facilitate our lives by protecting us from exploitation and providing support for health, education, and work. Social structures are thus an essential part of any society and can enable us to exercise our agency better; they also protect us from the unconstrained agency of others to potentially loot, harm, or exploit us. According to C. Wright Mills (1916–62), an individual 'contributes, however minutely, to the shaping of this society and to the course of its history, even as he is made by society and by its historical push and shove' (1959, p. 6). Interestingly, it is more than 50 years since Mills wrote that statement, and his use of the masculine pronoun 'he' now reads as dated and sexist—he was clearly a product of his time.

Sociological thinking

What does sociological analysis, or thinking sociologically, specifically entail? A useful starting point is the **sociological imagination**, a concept developed by Mills, who defined it as a 'quality of mind' that 'enables us to grasp history and biography and the relations between the two within society' (Mills 1959, pp. 6, 15). Mills suggested that sociologists aim to imagine the connection between individuals and larger social processes. He argued that no matter how personal or individual we may think our experiences are, they are significantly influenced by larger social forces, such as the political, economic, and cultural factors that set the social context in which individual experiences occur.

> **sociological imagination**
> A term coined by Mills to describe the sociological approach to analysing issues. We see the world through a sociological imagination, or think sociologically, when we make a link between personal troubles and public issues.

Mills considered the sociological imagination to be the distinction between *personal troubles* and *public issues*. As Mills (1959, p. 226) states, 'many personal troubles cannot be solved merely as troubles, but must be understood in terms of public issues . . . public issues must be revealed by relating them to personal troubles'. The well-known example given by Mills is that of unemployment. When one person is unemployed, that is a personal trouble and one may seek to explain it in terms of skills, motivation, and opportunities. Alternatively, within a nation, if hundreds of thousands of people are unemployed, unemployment is no longer a matter of personal failure; it becomes a public issue that requires economic and political interventions. This is what Mills meant by the distinctiveness of a sociological perspective—that is, the ability to imagine a link between the personal and public spheres.

There are many other examples connecting personal troubles and public issues, such as the impact of environmental pollution, workplace safety, and access to health care and education. In all these cases, individuals may face personal troubles, such as exposure to hazardous pollution from car exhausts or toxic chemicals at work, or the need to deal with the costs of personal ill-health and self-education. When personal troubles are experienced collectively, sociologists highlight underlying social patterns and social influences. Where social factors can be identified, social interventions may be possible to alleviate collectively experienced personal troubles, such as in the form of environmental, occupational, and health and education policies and regulations.

Mills did not mean that we should look at what happens to us fatalistically, as if we have no influence on the course of our own lives. Rather, if we are conscious of the impact of social forces on our own lives, then we are able to recognise that the solution to our personal problems is not just a matter of changing our situation, but changing what is happening in society. This is how social change occurs. In the late 1960s, second-wave feminism adopted the very sociological saying that 'the personal is political'. The personal rights for which many individual women were fighting, such as access to safe contraception, no-fault divorce, safety from domestic violence, protection from sex discrimination, and the need for affordable child care, along with maternity leave and equal pay, were also public issues that could be placed on the public agenda for political resolution. Indeed, the social reforms of the 1970s and 1980s, such as equal pay legislation, equal opportunity policies, and the *Sex Discrimination Act 1984* were clear acknowledgments of the linkages between private troubles and public issues—the sociological imagination in action.

The sociological imagination template: A model of sociological analysis

Many students ask, 'How do you do sociological analysis? What are its distinctive features?' Following the work of Mills (1959) and Giddens (1986), Australian sociologist Evan Willis (2004) suggests that the sociological imagination can be conceptualised as involving four interdependent sensibilities: historical, cultural, structural, and critical. To help operationalise the sociological imagination, we have envisaged it as a template, shown in Figure I.I.

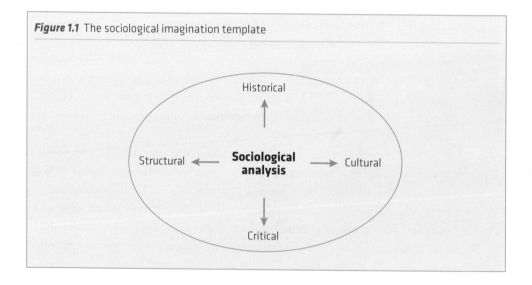

Figure 1.1 The sociological imagination template

When you want to remember what the sociological imagination entails and need to analyse a topic sociologically, recall this diagram and imagine applying its four features to your topic of study. 'Doing sociology' involves considering the role of the four factors and asking the following questions:

1. *Historical factors:* How have past events influenced the present?
2. *Cultural factors:* What influence do tradition, cultural values, and particular belief systems have on our behaviour and social interaction? In what ways has cultural change occurred? What subcultures exist? How does our own cultural background influence our sociological gaze?
3. *Structural factors:* How do various forms of social organisation and social institutions affect our lives? How do these vary over time and between countries and regions?
4. *Critical factors:* Why are things as they are? How could they be otherwise? Who benefits and who is disadvantaged by the status quo? What 'alternative futures' are possible? How do sociological insights relate to our own life experiences?

Clearly, a model such as this simplifies the practice of sociological analysis. As the remaining chapters in the first module of this book show, there are many theoretical and methodological issues that need to be considered when conducting sociological analysis. Furthermore, in reality, the four features of the model are interrelated and overlapping, so it is not always useful to differentiate historical factors from structural and cultural factors. Some aspects may feature more prominently than others, depending on what is being studied. Nonetheless, the sociological imagination template provides a handy starting point for sociological analysis and highlights the issues and questions that budding sociologists need to consider.

Adopting a sociological imagination or applying a sociological gaze to the world can often take us away from our comfort zones. It involves challenging the status quo and the taken-for-granted aspects of our lives. In this sense, it is important to be reflexive about sociological knowledge and to remember that the sociological gaze turns inwards as well as outwards. That is, it can challenge what we may personally believe, so we need to be open to questioning our own views and assumptions about the world. This type of thinking demands that we look at our place in the world and our role within the social structures and situations in which we exist. It requires that we look at ourselves and the ways in which we have been socialised, and how causes and effects interact with each other. As you make your way through the material in this book, keep in mind the following reflexive questions (Ruggiero 1996):

1. How do you react to an idea you have never heard of before? Do you wholeheartedly embrace it, resist it, or evaluate each side of an argument?
2. How do you form views on particular issues? Does your view depend on where it came from—for instance, from the media, the government, your parents, or your favourite celebrities?
3. How flexible are you about changing your views? When was the last time you changed your opinion about a significant issue? What made you change your mind?

Capturing the public (sociological) imagination

There is no single sociological theory of everything. In fact, sociology is a pluralistic discipline and as diverse as its subject matter. Therefore, sociologists do not speak with one voice, and their research can reflect different political and philosophical commitments. While sociology has as its primary concern a focus on the role of the 'social' (as opposed to the biological or psychological), it is neither inherently 'left' nor 'right' in terms of political philosophy. There are radical as well as conservative sociologists, though often these terms are not used by authors to describe themselves. It is true that sociology and socialism have often been conflated, in part due to the discipline's tendency to challenge the status quo (though it is fair comment to say that sociology has had its share of dogmatic ideological exponents). This book does not offer a particular political or ideological standpoint regarding the practice of sociology. Instead, our aim has been to expose readers to a wide array of theories, research methods, and empirical findings.

In recent times, there has been a renewed focus on 'public sociology' (Burawoy 2005)—that is, a commitment to highlighting the utility and application of sociology to audiences beyond the university community and professional (academic) sociologists. While sociology has many publics—students, academics, the mass media, government and non-government agencies, community and business groups—our primary concern in this book is with our student audience. With this in mind, we have structured the material in this book to facilitate a dialogue with the sociological issues presented and encourage the readers to reflect on the relevance of sociology to their own life experiences.

1.2: Michael Burawoy and Anthony Giddens—two very public sociologists

While **Michael Burawoy** (1948–   ) is most recently known for his promotion of public sociology, he is widely respected as a Marxist sociologist who has gone to great lengths to study the working lives of the working class in many different industries. He has done this by literally getting his hands dirty and spending months actually working in the places he studies. For example, in 1985 he took a job at the Lenin Steel Works in Hungary, working with a team responsible for melting pig iron in a large furnace. He has also worked as a personnel officer in a Zambian copper mine, in a Moscow rubber factory, and as a machine operator in a Chicago engine shop (Byles 2001). His engine shop experience became the basis for his most famous work *Manufacturing Consent* (Burawoy 1979), in which he explains the techniques management can use to gain the consent of workers to their own exploitation. No armchair sociologist, Burawoy is a fascinating example of using lived experience as the basis for sociological study and theory.

Anthony Giddens (1938–   ) is one of the most influential and widely cited of contemporary sociologists. He was the first member of his family to study at university and became a professor at Cambridge University in 1987, co-founded Polity Press in 1985 (a major sociology book publisher), and then went on to be Director of the London School of Economics (LSE) from 1997 until 2003. Not only has his influence on academic sociology been significant, he has also been a very public (sociology) intellectual, notably as an adviser to former British Prime Minister Tony Blair. His pro-motion of 'third-way' politics had a significant impact on the policies and electoral appeal of the British Labour Party. He was made a life peer in June 2004, given the title Baron, and made a member of the House of Lords, representing the Labour Party (Ritzer 2008). Now an Emeritus Professor, he continues to write and publish on topical issues, most recently *The Politics of Climate Change* (2009b), in addition to new editions of his popular textbook *Sociology* (Giddens 2009a).

All contributors to this book make use of topical issues and, while drawing on a wide global literature, have focused their attention on issues of relevance to Australian society. In doing this, they highlight Australian sociological analyses and empirical findings. Sociological analyses regularly make their way into public debate and impact on public policy. Our intention is to make the contribution of Australian sociology visible and show its engagement with public issues in the public arena. In this sense, we view 'public sociology' as an indigenous sociology whose theories and concepts are empirically grounded in the distinctive local and national characteristics of Australian society (Burawoy 2005; see also Connell 2007, 2005, 1997). It is also about showing the personal and career relevance of studying sociology.

On the utility of sociology, or avoiding 'doom and gloom' sociology

Much of this book is underpinned by a desire to provide an alternative version of sociology from the 'doom and gloom' school that exists in some quarters. 'Gloomy sociology' can be characterised by a sole focus on a critique of contemporary society that is always exposed as falling short of some ideal state, which often unintentionally promotes a defeatist stance of 'society is to blame' and the view that little can be done to change it (Wickham 2008; Marshall et al. 2009; Germov 2004). It is one thing to offer critique, but too much 'unengaged critique' in which 'modern Western governments . . . are always found wanting' can lead to a 'sit-on-the-sidelines-and-carp' mentality, as Gary Wickham (2008, p. 26) notes, which undermines the insights and utility of sociology. Peter Beilharz and Trevor Hogan (2006) refer to this tendency by some sociologists as 'miserablism', whereby students are bombarded with a critique of social life that exposes the injustices and inequalities that surround them, while tending to devalue their own experiences and interests in working towards possible solutions. Such gloomy sociology prioritises critique and resistance to the dominant structures of society, but offers little real hope for change or realistic alternative futures. As Stephen Crook (2003) states:

> Any hint that an application of sociology may be complicit with corporate or state power immediately condemns it. By contrast an application conducted in the name of 'resistance' is absolved of the need to meet any other criteria . . . We need to recognize more clearly that there is nothing inherently dishonourable about research that aims to enhance the

effectiveness of government programmes, or to restructure a corporate management, or to identify the market for a consumer product . . . We strengthen the case if we show that we can be 'useful' in quite narrow ways while at the same time encouraging sharp-edged and critical debates about social priorities and alternatives . . . now, more than ever, the pace and complexity of change processes require a strong sociological voice in public and policy debates about Australia's future. (pp. 13–14)

As Wickham states, what is needed is a turn 'towards the sort of responsible criticisms, descriptions, and assessments that actually assist modern Western governments' (2008, p. 31).

globalisation
The increased interconnectedness of the cultural, economic, and political aspects of social life; intensified circulation of capital, goods, information, and people across national boundaries; and increased interdependence of countries and regions of the world.

neo-liberalism
A philosophy based on the primacy of individual rights and minimal state intervention.

biological determinism
A belief that individual and group behaviours are the inevitable result of biology.

sociological determinism
A view that people's behaviour and beliefs are entirely shaped or determined by the social structure or social processes.

Unlike the straight career path that exists for economics and psychology graduates, there is no distinct professional occupation for those with sociology qualifications outside of universities. The career relevance of majoring in sociology is about the transferable skills and knowledge you develop that are applicable to a wide range of jobs and careers. Sociology graduates get jobs in fields such as journalism, teaching, administration and policy analysis, or as political advisers, program managers, welfare officers, community development officers, and research consultants (in government, community, welfare, and marketing agencies). The careers you pursue may partly reflect the courses you take at university. Rest assured, though, that sociological training is well regarded by employers—particularly your ability to conduct social analysis, find and evaluate information sources, scrutinise and conduct social research, and effectively communicate your understanding in written and oral forms. Module 5 of this book provides further resources to help you refine these skills.

As sociologists, we are in the unusual position of being both influenced by, and influential upon, that which we study (Berger 1963). Sociology is not vacuum-sealed from the social phenomena it studies; the social forces that come under its gaze, such as **globalisation** and **neo-liberalism**, also impact on the discipline itself (Crook 2003). Yet, just as sociology is critical of individualistic and **biologically deterministic** accounts, we need to be wary of **sociological determinism**. Sociology, despite what some early theorists once hoped, is not the 'mother science'. While it does address the 'big picture' and can help make sense of the world, it adds only one piece to help us understand the puzzle of life. The human condition is rightly the province of many academic disciplines—biology, psychology, and geography, to name a few. In highlighting the impact of 'the social', sociology plays an important part, and our hope is that it contributes to improving the quality of human existence.

A brief history of Australian sociology

Sociology is a relatively young academic discipline. Auguste Comte coined the term in 1839 and the first book with the word 'sociology' in its title, *The Study of Sociology*, was published in 1874 by Herbert Spencer. The first university Department of Sociology was established at the University of Chicago in 1892, though technically the University of Kansas had founded its Department of History and Sociology in 1891. The first academic journal, the *American Journal of Sociology*, began in 1895 and continues to this day. In the same year, the University of Bordeaux established the first European Department of Sociology, led by Émile Durkheim, who also founded *L'Année sociologique* (the sociology annual) in 1896. The first British Sociology Department was established at the LSE in 1904.

In Australia, sociology is an even more recent phenomenon. While sociology courses and publications appeared from the early 1900s onwards, the first professorial chair and Department of Sociology were established in 1959 at the University of New South Wales. Four years later, in 1963, the Sociological Association of Australia and New Zealand (SAANZ) was founded, and two years after that, in 1965, it established the *Australian and New Zealand Journal of Sociology* (*ANZJS*). SAANZ changed its name to The Australian Sociological Association (TASA) in 1988 (with New Zealand members forming their own independent association), and ten years later, in 1998, the *ANZJS* was renamed the *Journal of Sociology* (*JOS*).

Even though the discipline had a rather late start in Australia, it grew rapidly and continues to be one of the largest academic fields in the social sciences (Germov & McGee 2005). It is difficult to predict what the future holds for Australian sociology, though it is likely to remain a significant contributor to Australian social science research, teaching, social policy, and publication for years to come.

Preliminary conclusions

In this chapter, we have only sketched out a brief introduction to what sociology entails. As you work through the remainder of the book, you will find yourself developing your own sociological imagination. Sociology is a means by which we can enhance our understanding of the complexity of social life. It takes us beyond biological and individualistic assumptions, and enables us to explore the connections between our individual experiences and our social environment. With a sociological imagination in mind, we can apply our sociological gaze to see private problems as public issues. Above all, sociology enables us to understand what is happening in our daily lives.

Summary of main points

▶ Sociology challenges individualistic and biological accounts of social life and human behaviour by focusing on how society influences our lives and how social change occurs.

▶ The sociological imagination, or sociological analysis, involves four interrelated features: historical, cultural, structural, and critical sensibilities.

▶ The structure–agency debate concerns the extent to which humans are influenced by social structures. Keeping this debate in mind, it is important to remember that structure and agency are interdependent, and that they can be both enabling and constraining of human behaviour and social interaction.

▶ Sociology itself influences and is influenced by the things it studies. It is thus important to be a reflexive practitioner of sociology by considering the relevance of sociological insights to your own life and by adopting a questioning stance towards why things are the way they are, who benefits from present arrangements, and what alternatives exist to the status quo.

▶ In adopting a sociological perspective, beware of its limits and the potential for sociological determinism, and be open to theoretical and methodological pluralism.

SOCIOLOGICAL
REFLECTION

1.1 A sociological autobiography

This exercise asks you to apply the sociological imagination to understand the person you have become. Apply the four parts of the sociological imagination template to yourself by briefly noting some of the major influences on your beliefs, interests, and behaviour. In other words, write a short sociological autobiography by considering the following:

▶ *Historical factors:* How has your family background or key past events and experiences shaped the person you are?

▶ *Cultural factors:* What role have cultural background, traditions, and belief systems played in forming your opinions and influencing your behaviour?

▶ *Structural factors:* How have various social institutions influenced you?

▶ *Critical factors:* In what ways have your values and opinions about what you consider important changed over time?

If you are doing this in a tutorial setting, you might want to use these questions to interview one of your classmates and use your sociological understanding to report your findings to your classmates.

SOCIOLOGICAL
REFLECTION

1.2 Going up or down? A social experiment

The elevator experiment is a classic example of exposing the taken-for-granted social nature of our daily lives. Next time you go into an elevator, instead of facing the doors and ignoring all the occupants as social norms dictate, do the opposite. Stand in front of the doors, face everyone and attempt to make eye contact—and see what happens.

▶ How did other elevator occupants react?

▶ What feelings did you experience by breaking such social conventions?

Discussion questions

1.1 What is the sociological imagination? In providing your answer, think of some examples that make a link between private troubles and public issues.

1.2 As a budding sociologist, how would you respond to the statement, 'There is no such thing as society'?

1.3 In what ways do conservative groups attempt to transform public issues into private problems?

1.4 What arguments would a sociologist make to counter the view that 'biology is destiny'?

1.5 To what extent can you relate the structure–agency debate to your own life? Think of specific examples of the influence of social structure and your own agency in providing your answer.

1.6 What are the benefits and limitations of a sociological perspective?

Further reading

Module 5 of this textbook provides an extensive list of further resources and advice on writing and referencing sociology essays. Below we list some recommended reading that supplements the content in this chapter and the remainder of the book.

Short introductions to sociology

Bauman, Z. & May, T. 2001, *Thinking Sociologically*, 2nd edn, Blackwell, Oxford.

Bruce, S. 1999, *Sociology: A Very Short Introduction*, Oxford University Press, Oxford.

Willis, E. 2004, *The Sociological Quest*, 4th edn, Allen & Unwin, Sydney.

Comprehensive introductions to sociology

Fulcher, J. & Scott, J. 2007, *Sociology*, 3rd edn, Oxford University Press, Oxford.

Giddens, A. 2009, *Sociology*, 6th edn, Polity Press, Cambridge.

Macionis, J.J. & Plummer, K. 2008, *Sociology: A Global Introduction*, 4th edn, Pearson Education, Harlow.

van Krieken, R., Habibis, D., Smith, P., Hutchins, B., Haralambos, M. & Holborn, M. 2006, *Sociology: Themes and Perspectives*, 3rd edn, Pearson Education, Sydney.

Advanced reading

Connell, R. 2007, *Southern Theory: The Global Dynamics of Knowledge in Social Science*, Allen & Unwin, Sydney.

Crook, S. 2003, 'Change, uncertainty and the future of sociology', *Journal of Sociology*, vol. 39, no. I, pp. 7–I4.

Denemark, D., Meagher, G., Wilson, S., Western, M. & Philips, T. (eds) 2007, *Australian Social Attitudes 2: Citizenship, Work and Aspirations*, UNSW Press, Sydney.

Germov, J. & McGee, T.R. (eds) 2005, *Histories of Australian Sociology*, Melbourne University Press, Melbourne.

Marshall, H., Robinson, P., Germov, J. & Clark, E. 2009, *Teaching Sociology in Australia: A Scoping Study*, report to the Australian Learning and Teaching Council, ALTC, Canberra.

Ritzer, G. 2008, *Sociological Theory*, 7th edn, McGraw-Hill, New York.

Wilson, S., Meagher, G., Gibson, R., Denemark, D. & Western, M. (eds) 2005, *Australian Social Attitudes: The First Report*, UNSW Press, Sydney.

On public sociology

For more discussion of the notion of public sociology, go to the book website for relevant weblinks.

Study aids

Germov, J. 20II, *Get Great Marks for Your Essays, Reports, and Presentations*, 3rd edn, Allen & Unwin, Sydney.

Williams, L. & Germov, J. 200I, *Surviving First Year Uni*, Allen & Unwin, Sydney.

Sociology dictionaries

Abercrombie, N., Hill, S. & Turner, B.S. 2006, *The Penguin Dictionary of Sociology*, 5th edn, Penguin, Melbourne.

Jary, D. & Jary, J. 2005, *Collins Dictionary of Sociology*, 4th edn, HarperCollins, Glasgow.

Scott, J. & Marshall, G. (eds) 2005, *A Dictionary of Sociology*, 3rd edn, Oxford University Press, Oxford.

Websites

- Michael Burawoy—Public Sociology: <http://burawoy.berkeley.edu/PS.Webpage/ps.mainpage.htm>. Michael Burawoy's personal website contains a section devoted to public sociology on which he keeps an updated and extensive list of publications on public sociology, all accessible from this site.
- SocioSite: <www.sociosite.net>. One of the best and longest-running sociology portal websites, it includes links to many high-quality resources.

- TASA—The Australian Sociological Association: <www.tasa.org.au>. The premier website for Australian sociology, with plenty of free resources and helpful links, including a Public Access Sociology section that provides a range of online papers and information briefs about the discipline. Students thinking of majoring in sociology should consider joining TASA as student members.

Films/documentaries

- *Introducing Sociology*, 1998, DVD, Halovine Video. A well-produced and straightforward introduction to sociology for beginning and prospective students. <www.onlineclassroom.tv/sociology>.
- *Understanding Sociology*, 1998, DVD, three volumes, Halovine Video. Volume I: Theory and methods (Classical sociology: Positivism, interpretivism, and realism); Volume 2: Making sense of sociological theory (Marxism, functionalism, and interactionism); Volume 3: From modernity to post-modernity. <www.onlineclassroom.tv/sociology>.
- *Core Concepts in Sociology (Short Cuts)*, n.d., DVD, Halovine Video. Examines the concepts of culture, socialisation,and identity. <www.onlineclassroom.tv/sociology>.
- *Doing Sociological Research*, n.d., DVD, Halovine Video. Interviews, surveys, and observational research methods. <www.onlineclassroom.tv/sociology>.

Visit the *Public Sociology* book website to access topical case studies, weblinks, YouTube clips, and extra readings.

References

Abercrombie, N. 2004, *Sociology*, Polity Press, Cambridge.

Bauman, Z. & May, T. 2001, *Thinking Sociologically*, 2nd edn, Blackwell, Oxford.

Beilharz, P. & Hogan, T. 2006, 'Introduction', in P. Beilharz & T. Hogan (eds), *Sociology: Place, Time & Division*, Oxford University Press, Melbourne, pp. xv–xxii.

Berger, P. 1963, *Invitation to Sociology: A Humanistic Perspective*, Penguin, Harmondsworth.

Broom, L. 2005, 'Sociology, anyone?', in J. Germov & T. McGee (eds), *Histories of Australian Sociology*, Melbourne University Press, Melbourne.

Burawoy, M. 2005, 'For public sociology, 2004 presidential address', *American Sociological Review*, vol. 70, February, pp. 4–28.

—— 1979, *Manufacturing Consent: Changes in the Labor Process under Monopoly Capitalism*, University of Chicago Press, Chicago.

Byles, J. 2001, 'Tales of the Kefir furnaceman', *The Village Voice*, 10 April <www.villagevoice.com/2001–04–10/arts/tales-of-the-kefir-furnaceman> (accessed 23 February 2010).

Connell, R. 1997, 'Why is classical theory classical?', *American Journal of Sociology*, vol. 102, no. 6, pp. 1511–57.

—— 2005, 'Australia and world sociology', in J. Germov & T.R. McGee (eds), *Histories of Australian Sociology*, Melbourne University Press, Melbourne.

—— 2007, *Southern Theory: The Global Dynamics of Knowledge in Social Science*, Allen & Unwin, Sydney.

Crook, S. 2003, 'Change, uncertainty and the future of sociology', *Journal of Sociology*, vol. 39, no. 1, pp. 7–14.

Germov, J. 2004, 'On the everyday life of a significant sociologist: The life-work of Stephen Crook', TASA 2003 Presidential Address: A Symposium on the Life and Work of Stephen Crook, *Journal of Sociology*, vol. 40, no. 3, pp. 205–12.

Germov, J. & McGee, T. 2005, 'Australian sociology: Recent trends and prospects', in J. Germov & T. McGee (eds), *Histories of Australian Sociology*, Melbourne University Press, Melbourne.

Giddens, A. 1986, *Sociology: A Brief but Critical Introduction*, 2nd edn, Macmillan, London.

—— 2009a, *Sociology*, 6th edn, Polity Press, Cambridge.

—— 2009b, *The Politics of Climate Change*, Polity Press, Cambridge.

Keay, D. 1987, 'Margaret Thatcher, extract from interview for *Woman's Own* ("no such thing as society")', Margaret Thatcher Foundation website, <www.margaretthatcher.org/document/106689> (accessed 9 August 2010).

Macionis, J.J. & Plummer, K. 2008, *Sociology: A Global Introduction*, 4th edn, Pearson Education, Harlow.

Marshall, H., Robinson, P., Germov, J. & Clark, E. 2009, *Teaching Sociology in Australia: A Scoping Study*, report to the Australian Learning and Teaching Council, ALTC, Canberra.

Merton, R.K. 1981, 'Our sociological vernacular', *Columbia*, November, pp. 42–4.

Mills, C.W. 1959, *The Sociological Imagination*, Oxford University Press, New York.

Ritzer, G. 2008, *Sociological Theory*, 7th edn, McGraw-Hill, New York.

Ruggiero, V.R. 1996, *A Guide to Sociological Thinking*, Sage, Thousand Oaks, CA.

Wickham, G. 2008, 'High society: Are our social sciences as relevant to government as they might be?' *Australian Universities Review*, vol. 50, no. 2, pp. 25–32.

Willis, E. 2004, *The Sociological Quest*, 4th edn, Allen & Unwin, Sydney.

CHAPTER 2

Sociological foundations: Early theorists and theories

Marilyn Poole and John Germov

It's okay in theory, but . . .

A common misconception about the term 'theory' is that it refers to something merely speculative, with little basis in real-life facts or evidence. While theories are often viewed as removed from reality, we actually use them every day of our lives in order to make sense of the world. When people advance opinions about why Australian public transport is so poor, argue that we pay too much tax, worry about the influence of reality TV on youth, or express concern about the impact of the internet on our lives, they are basically theorising about why things are the way they are. Commonsense theories of everyday life, such as those noted above, tend to reflect personal prejudices and are often based on anecdotal, rather than systematic and reliable, evidence. This is where sociological theories can help. Sociologists differentiate between what they consider to be empirical investigations (or a collection of facts about something) and theories that answer the 'how' and 'why' questions about those facts. The early or classical sociologists discussed in this chapter lived in a world of massive social change, a world that had been turned upside down by the onset of the Industrial Revolution. The early sociologists wanted to know why social change occurred, and how it impacted on social life. You may ask why we should study the classical theorists of sociology, of people from a different era than our own. They too were struggling with a period of massive social upheaval and the changing relationships between individuals and their social world. Some of their insights are still relevant today, and have influenced contemporary sociological theories. Therefore, it is necessary to appreciate the origins of sociological theory in order to provide a basis for greater understandings of our own social world.

Introduction

This chapter introduces you to the foundational theorists and theories that represent the birth of sociology as an academic discipline. We cover only a selection of key theorists; we acknowledge that this is not an exhaustive list. In providing this overview, rather than offering an in-depth evaluation, we highlight some of the key ideas of each theorist. Our aim is to help you gain an awareness of the range of foundational sociological theories you are likely to encounter in the wider literature.

Often referred to as 'classical sociology', the theories of Auguste Comte, Herbert Spencer, Karl Marx, Émile Durkheim, Max Weber, and Georg Simmel are generally regarded as those of the 'founding fathers' of the discipline. You will note the masculine bias here—the foundational theorists are all men. According to recent feminist writing, the 'traditional telling of the history of sociological theory has been shaped by a politics of gender that tends to emphasize male achievement and erase female contributions' (Lengermann & Niebrugge-Brantley 2004, p. 271). The absence of women is assumed to be a reflection of the relative status and position of men and women in society during the 1800s, when sociology first developed. Few women received a formal education in this era; most girls were educated at home. Even accomplished women had to struggle for recognition and appreciation of their work. Recent sociological writing has attempted to address the gender imbalance in the telling of the history of sociology by incorporating women whose work has been overlooked or forgotten, such as early sociologist and feminist Harriet Martineau, among others (see Abbott, Wallace & Tyler 2005; Lengermann & Niebrugge-Brantley 2004).

Sociological beginnings: Birth of a discipline

The term 'sociology' was coined by Auguste Comte in 1839 to mean the scientific study of society. This is not to suggest there was no interest in the study of society before this; people have always asked questions about the 'how' and 'why' of society and human relationships. Important questions regarding society and human nature were raised in the influential writing of English philosopher Thomas Hobbes (1588–1679), in which he addressed the question that is now perceived as fundamental to sociology: 'How is society possible?' In his book *Leviathan* (1651), Hobbes argued that the foundation of every society was a social contract in which all citizens implicitly agreed on certain rights and obligations in exchange for social order and protection from violence. To make his point, he suggested a hypothetical 'state of nature' (anarchy) where humans faced with an environment of scarce resources would violently defend their self-interest, leading to constant conflict and a 'war of all against all' so that life was 'solitary, poor, nasty, brutish, and short' (Hobbes 1651, Ch. 13). According to Hobbes, a society evolves when individuals realise their best interests are served through peace and collective organisation by entering into a social contract, subsuming their individual freedoms to the state and the rule of law. While Hobbes offers a pessimistic account of human nature, his attempt to theorise the basis of why societies come into existence laid the foundation for the discipline of sociology (Williams 2006). In particular, his notion of the social contract exposes the tension between individual freedoms and social obligations that continues to this day. Many sociological theories reflect Hobbesian notions of social order, either in terms of conceptualising human nature as self-interested and competitive, or in terms of viewing social order as a human creation and subject to human transformation.

Sociology as a discipline, in terms of society being studied in a systematic and purposeful way, arose only in the nineteenth century. The following social and political developments had an impact on the beginnings of sociology:

- The development of the **Enlightenment** thought during the eighteenth century signalled the decline of organised religion and the rise of secular society based on a commitment to rationality, reason, and science.

- The French Revolution of 1789 had a major influence throughout the world in promoting notions of democracy and individual liberty. Coupled with the American War of Independence in 1776, these events laid the foundations for the liberal-democratic nation-state.

Enlightenment
A period in European history that lasted from the seventeenth century to the eighteenth century, also known as the Age of Reason. Enlightenment thinkers advocated the power of reason over the authority of the church to reach a true understanding of nature and society.

Industrial Revolution
Beginning in England in the late eighteenth century, the Industrial Revolution introduced major changes to work processes and everyday life that resulted in social and political transformations in society. Agrarian economies and lifestyles gave way to a wage-labour system, the separation of home from work, and the urbanisation of the population.

- The **Industrial Revolution** began in England in the late eighteenth century and provided the impetus for significant social change. Machines, technology, and new forms of energy (steam and coal initially) transformed work and everyday existence. Agrarian economies and lifestyles gave way to urbanisation in towns and cities, the development of a wage labour force, and the separation of work and home.
- The internationalisation of trade, particularly through the colonisation of Africa, the Middle East, and Asia, brought Third World societies into contact with industrial economies through the supply of raw materials and products. In turn, these societies changed their cultures and social systems.

As a result of these changes, new ways of understanding the world emerged and new ideas forced people to think about society in different ways. Sociological thinking began during this time of change. The early sociologists were particularly interested in how societies developed and progressed.

Auguste Comte and positivism: Sociology as science

August Comte (1798–1857) was born in Montpellier, France and grew up in the turbulent period following the French Revolution. Like many others living in troubled times, Comte wanted to know how society operated and why societies developed in different ways. Comte considered that societies could be studied in a rational and scientific way, and he wished to apply scientific methods (originally developed in the natural sciences such as physics, chemistry, and biology) to the study of society. Comte was a proponent of what he initially termed 'social physics', but later called sociology. He believed that sociology could be modelled on the 'hard sciences' as a means of understanding the world through scientific and empirical study (Ritzer 2000).

Comte's approach had an evolutionary focus: it was his view that societies passed through major epochs or stages. The first stage or epoch was theological: supernatural beliefs were paramount and people believed that events were the result of God's will. The second was metaphysical: events were viewed as natural rather than supernatural, and organised religion prevailed. The third and final stage was scientific: people sought to understand their world based on science and scientific facts. In this final or positivistic stage, people would seek the laws that regulated and governed the world (Ritzer 2000).

Comte was a proponent of **positivism** in sociology—that is, the development of laws about society and social life that can be tested by the collection of **empirical** data.

Herbert Spencer and social evolution

The notions of social progress and the development of societies through different stages articulated by Comte were shared by Herbert Spencer (1820–1903), who was born in Derby, England. Spencer, an engineer and social scientist, was an early proponent of the theory of the evolution of society. He formulated the view that societies progress from the simple to the complex. In his model, societies evolve from simple organisms to highly complex and differentiated structures 'in which the individual parts, while becoming more autonomous and specialised, nevertheless come increasingly to depend on each other' (Swingewood 2000, p. 23).

Spencer's work was very influential in the nineteenth century, and he was one of the most widely read writers of his day. His views on social evolution preceded the theory of evolution developed by Charles Darwin in *On the Origin of Species by Means of Natural Selection* (1859). Spencer was something of a rival of Darwin's, and coined the term 'survival of the fittest'—by which he meant that superior groups are likely to be the most successful in society. This view is referred to as **social Darwinism**. Spencer argued that the poor and the sick should be left to fend for themselves and should not receive assistance from governments. His views and influence still echo today when we hear politicians arguing that welfare policies should be cut on the basis that assistance to the poor, the sick, and the needy discourages self-reliance and is detrimental to the well-being of society as a whole.

Spencer was very much a product of his time, and believed not only in social evolution but also that some social forms and societies—such as those of Western Europe—were superior to others. In his view, the greater complexity of modern societies was a key factor in their ability to adapt and to survive (Allan 2005).

positivism
A contested view in sociology that social phenomena should be studied in the same way as the natural world, by focusing only on observable and quantifiable events through which causal connections and universal laws can be determined.

empirical
Empirical knowledge is derived from, and can be tested by, the gathering of data or evidence.

social Darwinism
The application of evolutionary laws of natural selection to human societies to 'explain' social processes and behaviours. Spencer coined the term 'survival of the fittest' (often misattributed to Darwin) to describe how Darwin's ideas about natural selection in nature could be used to explain social processes and behaviours.

Karl Marx: Class conflict, alienation, and Marxism

Karl Marx (1818–83) was born in Trier, Prussia and as a university student joined the Young Hegelians, who were critical of Prussian society. Because of his political affiliations and writings critical of the Prussian government, he fled Germany and moved first to Paris in 1843, from where he was expelled (due to pressure from the Prussians on the

French government), then to Brussels in 1845, and eventually to London in 1849, where he lived for the remainder of his life (Ritzer & Goodman 2004). Although Marx was not, strictly speaking, a sociologist, his impact on sociological thought has continued to the present day. Like many other social scientists of the nineteenth century, Marx also believed in social evolution. He was interested in the major changes brought about by the Industrial Revolution and argued that the way in which goods are produced in society affects everything else. Marx considered that 'people must first be able to supply themselves with food and drink, and clothing and habitation' in order to survive, and that 'any analysis of history must first begin by studying the production of the means to satisfy these needs' (cited in Cheal 2005, p. 89). This approach is called **historical materialism.**

> **historical materialism**
>
> A view of society, developed by Marx, which asserts that material conditions of a particular era (ways in which people supply themselves with food, shelter, and clothing) provide the basis for all social arrangements.

> **capitalism**
>
> An economic system based on the private ownership of natural resources and the means of production, in which commodities are sold for a profit.

Marx believed that societies evolved progressively according to different stages of economic production. His interest was on one of the later stages—**capitalism**—as it was the 'mode of production of his own time' (Cheal 2005, p. 89).

Control over the labour process, exploitation, and alienation

In capitalism, according to Marx (see Marx & Engels 1948), there are two classes of people: the workers and the capitalists (which he terms the proletariat and the bourgeoisie respectively). The relationship between these classes involves a division of labour. The capitalists supply the capital, such as the raw materials and machinery necessary to organise production and control the labour process. The workers supply their labour, which turns those raw materials into commodities—goods and services that can be bought and sold (Cheal 2005). One of the most important aspects of this relationship, according to Marx, is that of domination. The workers sell their labour to capitalists for a wage. The capitalists in turn control the workers' conditions and the hours they work. Employers tell their workers what to do. Marx argued that this relationship was one of domination and unequal power. In large-scale enterprises, many workers are employed by a small number of capitalists with the power to control workers. In turn, specialised workers or managers are hired to manage the workers and ensure that the work is done according to the wishes of the employers. Most business enterprises and large-scale employers have a hierarchy of positions, with the owners or capitalists at the top, the supervisors or managers in the middle, and the mass of workers at the bottom.

> **alienation**
>
> A term used by Marx to denote the estrangement of workers from the products of their labour and the loss of control felt by workers under capitalism.

A key concept of Marx's, **alienation** refers to the relationship between people and their labour and the fact that, under capitalism, workers are separated from the things they produce, which thus have no meaning for them. Instead of the products of people's labour being something creative and of value, the workers are 'impoverished' because their work is appropriated and commodified by capitalists. As more products are produced by machines, the greater the alienation experienced by the workers (Cheal 2005).

Class inequality

Based on his experiences in Europe and in nineteenth-century industrial England where he spent the latter years of his life, Marx was concerned about the **class** inequalities created by industrial capitalism. He believed that the differences between the opulent lifestyles of the rich compared with the poverty and squalor of the working class were not only unfair, but would result in class conflict. Marx argued that conflict between the two classes—the bourgeoisie and the proletariat—was inevitable and would result in an overthrow of capitalism from which a new social order would arise. Eventually capitalism would be replaced by **socialism** and ultimately **communism**. Conflict between the classes was the vehicle of change in society.

Marx was not just a social theorist but was politically active, and his writings with friend, benefactor, and collaborator Friedrich Engels (1820–95) were responsible for political movements worldwide. In 1848, Marx and Engels published *Manifesto of the Communist Party*—often referred to as *The Communist Manifesto*—a major critique of capitalism and a call for its replacement by communism. The influence of communist ideology has been profound, and was responsible for revolutions and the introduction of new social orders in countries such as Russia, China, and Cuba.

Marxism continues to influence the social sciences, and is sometimes referred to as 'conflict theory' in general terms or more specifically as neo-Marxism. Conflict theory arose in the 1950s and 1960s, in part as a reaction to **structural functionalism**, and highlights inequalities in society. Working within this perspective, sociologists identify certain groups of people who benefit from the unequal distribution of money, power, and status in society and those who, for reasons of class, gender, age, ethnicity, or race, may not. This perspective highlights the conflict between the 'haves' and the 'have-nots' in society (Macionis & Plummer 2005, p. 27). Another offshoot of Marxism is 'critical theory', a term used to describe the work of a diverse collection of theorists such as Herbert Marcuse (1898–1979), Jürgen Habermas (1929–   ) and Douglas Kellner (1943–   ), who extended Marxist-influenced analyses to the topics of culture, psychoanalysis, critiques of positivism, and critiques of communist regimes (Ritzer & Goodman 2004).

class/social class
A central but contested term in sociology that refers to a position in a system of structured inequality based on the unequal distribution of wealth, power, and status.

socialism
A political ideology with numerous variations, but with a core belief in the creation of societies in which private property and wealth accumulation are replaced by state ownership and distribution of economic resources. See also *communism*.

communism
A utopian vision of society based on communal ownership of resources, cooperation, and altruism to the extent that social inequality and the state no longer exist. Sometimes used interchangeably with *socialism* to refer to societies ruled by a communist party.

(structural) functionalism
A theoretical perspective in sociology in which society is seen as consisting of many complex and interdependent parts that contribute to consensus and social stability. Prominent theorists include Durkheim, Merton, and Parsons.

Émile Durkheim: Social facts, social cohesion, and anomie

The issues of order, structure, integration, and function in society arose with the work of Émile Durkheim (1858–1917), who was born in Épinal, France. Durkheim became the first Professor of Sociology at the University of Bordeaux in 1887. This is seen as the beginning of sociology as an academic discipline, though as mentioned in Chapter 1, it took a few more years for the first Sociology Department to be established in a university (in 1892 at the University of Chicago). The work of Durkheim contributed to the establishment of sociology as a discipline distinct from others that studied human behaviour, such as psychology.

Durkheim agreed with Comte that society should be studied on a scientific basis, and he considered that the proper subject matter of sociology should be the study of

social facts. By this, Durkheim meant that sociology should not be the study of individuals or individual behaviour, but rather those aspects of social life that shape our actions as individuals, such as religion or the economy (Giddens 2001). Social facts are external to the individual and constrain or restrict individual behaviour. In all of his work, Durkheim argued against an individual approach to social analysis, and

social facts
A term coined by Durkheim to refer to the subject-matter of sociology; social facts are seen as social forces external to the individual.

thus rejected psychological explanations of social behaviour. He insisted that it was not possible to study human beings without studying the forces that construct and constrain them. According to Durkheim, individuals are not born knowing how to behave but are taught by others. Morals, laws, and codes of behaviour are handed down through the generations.

Division of labour

Much of Durkheim's work studies how societies maintain **social cohesion** and social order. He assumed that social and moral solidarity was a prerequisite for any society; otherwise,

life would be chaotic and unpredictable. Durkheim, like many social theorists in the nineteenth century, was interested in how social stability was maintained amidst the massive social changes brought about by the Industrial Revolution, particularly in terms of the increasing specialisation of work.

social cohesion
The degree to which people feel they are part of a wider society made up of people whom they can generally trust.

Durkheim tended to stress those conditions that favoured the smooth running of society. He was interested in what he termed solidarity. Social solidarity refers to 'how people get along together, how they cooperate with one another and ultimately how societies hold together without being torn apart by conflict' (Cheal 2005, p. 17). In *The Division of Labour in Society* (1893), Durkheim suggests that two types of solidarity occurred during different historic periods:

1. *Mechanical solidarity* occurred in traditional societies where people had similar occupations and were bound together by communal values and beliefs. This kind

collective conscience
A term used by Durkheim to refer to the norms and values held by a group or a society.

of society had what Durkheim termed a **collective conscience**, which occurs when people share patterns of thinking or consensus such as in religious beliefs.

2. *Organic solidarity* emerged with the progression from pre-industrial (traditional) societies to industrial, urbanised (modern) societies. It occurred in larger and more secular populations that enabled a greater degree of individual freedom. Industrialisation had led to the specialisation and differentiation of tasks. Durkheim argued that solidarity was achieved in this situation not so much by communal and traditional ties but by economic interdependence. The more specialised our work has become, the more we depend on others to provide goods and services; as such, social consensus in modern societies is achieved by 'economic reciprocity and mutual dependency' (Giddens 2001, p. 10).

Durkheim believed that societies change over time from mechanical to organic solidarity. During this process, the collective conscience becomes weaker. Durkheim attributed the decline in the collective conscience in France and other European countries to the decline in religious belief (Cheal 2005). Marx, Weber, and Durkheim all experienced the impact of industrialisation, rapid population growth, and urbanisation at first hand. Although Durkheim expressed confidence in organic solidarity, he was aware that a condition he termed **anomie** could arise. In periods of rapid social change, social connectedness can diminish, leaving individuals with a lack of meaning in their lives and no sense of knowing what is expected of them (Ritzer 2003, p. 20).

anomie
A concept used by Durkheim for a societal condition in which individuals feel aimless and lack guidance in social norms. Anomie means to be without laws or norms.

Suicide

One of Durkheim's best-known works is *Suicide*, first published in 1897. In this statistical study, Durkheim illustrates how a very personal and individual act such as suicide is linked to social relationships and social integration. Durkheim argues that those who commit suicide are the people who are least well integrated into society and that, generally speaking, the higher the social integration in society, the less likelihood of suicide.

Durkheim identifies a number of different kinds of suicide:

- *Egoistic suicide* is where levels of integration in society are low. In situations where moral constraints break down, or at times of rapid social change, people may lose a sense of meaning in their lives. Those embedded in families are less likely to commit suicide than those who are single. It is interesting to note that in times of war, or national emergency, suicide rates fall as these are periods when people feel more connected to each other within a community that is facing an external threat.

- *Altruistic suicide* is a form with which we have become all too familiar in recent years. It occurs when integration levels are high and an individual feels they are acting for the common good or for shared goals. Islamic suicide bombings in the Middle East are an example of altruistic suicide, as were the acts of Japanese Kamikaze pilots during World War II.
- *Anomic suicide* occurs in times of social upheaval and when people no longer know how to behave. Durkheim refers to anomie, or normlessness, as a period of time in people's lives when they feel a sense of despair and do not see the point in continuing. Difficult personal times such as divorce or bankruptcy may lead to anomic suicide.
- *Fatalistic suicide* occurs when the individual is over-regulated in society—for example, in repressive conditions such as detention centres, prisons, or concentration camps.

Durkheim had a major impact on sociology that continues to this day. In 1896 he initiated the publication of a scholarly journal, *L'Année sociologique*, which not only disseminated sociological ideas but also promoted the establishment of sociology as a discipline (Ritzer 2000, p. 20).

Max Weber: Rationalisation, the Protestant ethic, and social stratification

Max Weber (1864–1920) was born in Erfurt, Germany and, like other early sociologists, was interested in the development of modern capitalism and its impact on society. Weber sought the reasons for social change. His writing and interests were diverse, ranging from the law, history, and religion to economics, and the study of different cultures.

Rationalisation

Weber considered that one of the chief characteristics of an industrial society was the process of **rationalisation**, epitomised by the growth in bureaucratic organisations. Given the preoccupation with efficiency and probity via conformity to standardised procedures, bureaucratic organisations appeared the best way to organise work in complex societies, so much so that Weber correctly predicted that the 'future belongs to bureaucratisation' (1968/1921, p. 1401). Both Weber and Marx recognised the efficiency of industrial capitalism, and both also recognised some of the problems that accompanied it. Weber felt that bureaucracies treated individuals in a dehumanising way, which could lead to 'disenchantment with the world' (Macionis & Plummer 2005, p. 91). In this regard, Weber agreed with Marx that alienation was a characteristic of modern society; however, he believed that alienation was not necessarily due to capitalism alone.

rationalisation
A tendency to apply reason, to think and act in a calculative manner (as opposed to an emulative or traditional manner). It is seen by *Weberian* scholars as the key aspect of modernisation and as the synonym of detraditionalisation.

The Protestant ethic

Weber disagreed with the views of Marx about the importance of economics, and felt that ideas and values were significant contributors to social change. In fact, he considered that charismatic religious authority could be a potent force for social change and could transform an economic system. In perhaps his best-known work, *The Protestant Ethic and the Spirit of Capitalism* (1958/1904–05), Weber examined the relationship between certain forms of Protestantism (Calvinism in particular) and the rise of capitalism. While Marx considered capitalism to be the product of economic conditions and forces, Weber considered that ideas—particularly certain religious ideas—also played a major role in the rise of capitalist society. For Weber, 'the spirit of capitalism was a derivation from Protestant asceticism as it came into existence in Europe in the sixteenth century' (Cheal 2005, p. 78). Notably, within early Protestantism, money earned was not spent; rather, it was used for further investment, and work was considered a duty and an obligation that produced a hard-working workforce. According to Weber, the relationship between ascetic Protestantism and capitalism meant that it produced entrepreneurs who invested their capital rather than spending it on personal goods or luxuries, and this commitment to investment drove the economy. It was this emphasis on capital accumulation—on making more and more money—that 'gave capitalism its characteristic obsession with growth and which has made it such a dynamic system' (Cheal 2005, p. 77).

Social stratification: Class, status, and party

The sociology of Max Weber is often at odds with the views of Marx. Weber rejected Marx's views 'of the centrality of class antagonism' and 'revised the key tenets of class theory' (Pakulski 2004, p. 58), acknowledging the importance of the middle class and other bases of social inequality. According to Weber, the markets rather than class were the basis for class stratification, and 'class positions reflected differential market capacities and graded life chances' (Pakulski 2004, p. 58). Class theory, according to Weber, was a reflection of 'differential market opportunities, status privileges and hierarchies of authority' (Pakulski 2004, p. 58). Weber's view on class differed from that of Marx in that he saw class divisions not just as a reflection of economic divisions, but also of social standing in society. He referred to this as status. Usually status is a reflection of people's job or their economic position in society, as well as the prestige accorded to them by society, but wealth alone does not confer high status. In Australia, for example, we can think of a number of wealthy business people who have attained wealth by rather dubious means. These people have lower status than those who may be less wealthy but have more prestigious occupations, such as judges or surgeons. For Weber, status groups share common interests and lifestyles, and tend to reflect professional, ethnic, and religious group membership. Status group membership is not open to all, and in fact is often restricted through what Weber termed **social closure**. People who belong to the

social closure
A term first used by Weber to describe the way power is exercised to exclude outsiders from the privileges of social membership (in *social classes*, professions, or status groups).

powerful and ruling groups in society share a sense of belonging and community with each other, and may well attempt to restrict access to others whom they regard as outsiders. According to Weber, a further basis for social division could be found in 'parties': groups that can wield power, such as unions, professional bodies, political parties, and various interest/pressure groups. Weber continues to influence the work of sociologists, and can be seen in Australian studies of social inequality produced by Sol Encel (1970) and Ron Wild (1978, 1974).

Georg Simmel and social interaction

Georg Simmel (1858–1918), a German social theorist and a contemporary of Max Weber, was born in Berlin. He is noted for introducing an emphasis on social interaction as a central issue in sociology, which had a major influence on the development of the sociological perspective of **symbolic interactionism** (see Chapter 3). He wrote on many diverse topics, such as music, fashion, and urban life. A defining feature of his work was his view of society not as an external structure imposed on passive individuals, but rather the result of a patterned web of interactions. For Simmel, society simply constituted groups of interacting individuals and, while patterned structures such as the nation-state, the city, and the family seemingly endured beyond individuals, they were still conceived as an outcome of ongoing social interaction—or 'sociation'.

symbolic interactionism
A theoretical framework first developed by Mead that places strong emphasis on the importance of language and on social interactions as key components in the development of a sense of *self*.

Simmel's study of social interaction focused on 'form' rather than 'content'. He realised that the world was made up of never-ending events and interactions, so rather than the actual details of individual interactions (the 'content'), what mattered were the patterns underpinning those social interactions (the 'form'). In other words, Simmel sought to define the common features of a range of particular interactions. Rather than imposing these forms on social reality, Simmel was careful to ground them in empirical study. Moreover, he did not propose a unifying theory of social interaction like Marx or Durkheim, but rather tried to make sense of the complexity of social life by exposing its underlying order (Ritzer & Goodman 2004). For example, in one of his major works, *The Philosophy of Money* (1907), he focused on the subjective experience of consumption, which he viewed as a means by which people redressed the drudgery of work.

CrossLink:
For more on
Simmel's
influence, see
Chapter 8.

Harriet Martineau: An early (feminist) sociologist

Harriet Martineau (1802–76) was born in Norwich, England. As was common for women in that era, she was educated at home and going to university was not an option (Allan 2005).

Martineau belongs to the same generation of sociologists as Comte, Spencer, and Marx. She independently undertook a scientific study of society, and between 1832 and 1834 published a series of 'didactic novels' intended to teach 'the principles of the new science of society' (Lengermann & Niebrugge-Brantley 2004, p. 273). Between 1834 and 1836, Martineau travelled around America, interviewing people ranging from former US President James Madison to people living in poverty (Henslin 2005). Her research, an analysis of American society, was published in *Society in America* (1837). Martineau is best known for her translation of Comte's *Positive Philosophy*, which she also revised and condensed. She considered this introduction of French positivism into English thought one of her great intellectual contributions (Hoecker-Drysdale 2003).

Harriet Martineau subscribed to the view articulated by Comte that a science of society would be a 'key to understanding societal change and the uncertainties of the age' (Hoecker-Drysdale 2003, p. 41). She published extensively, and her writing was translated into a number of different languages. She was influential not only in England and America, but in many other countries (Hoecker-Drysdale 2003). Her writing ranged from political and moral philosophy to advocacy for anti-slavery campaigns and improving the status of women. She worked in a number of social reform movements on behalf of women, such as the suffrage movement, and advocated women's education and women's right to work for a decent wage (Hoecker-Drysdale 2003).

Although Martineau's contributions to sociology were neglected for many years, it is now recognised that she made a significant impact. Not only was she a keen observer of the morals and manners of society, but she was also one of the first sociologists to examine women and what she termed the 'domestic state'. She believed that the way society treated women was one of the key measures for understanding the 'universal law of happiness' that she considered a basic and inalienable human right (Allan 2005, p. 271).

Conclusion

While it is important to understand sociology's foundational authors and theories, particularly given their continuing influence on many contemporary writers, it is equally important to acknowledge the social and historical context in which these early works were produced (see Sociology Spotlight 2.1). Invariably, as societies change, so, too, do sociological theories as new insights, capabilities, and knowledge are added to the sociological enterprise. As this chapter has shown, different theories aim to find answers to diverse questions, and often use different levels of analysis and focus on different sets of issues. Therefore, it is not uncommon to find that most sociological theories can add to our sociological understanding. For this reason, among others, they should not automatically be viewed as oppositional, but rather in terms of the potential they have to expand our sociological imagination. That said, it should be stressed that sociology also involves a contest of ideas that results in vigorous debate and disagreement among sociologists over the most appropriate concepts and theories to explain social phenomena.

In response to contemporary social issues and environments, new sociological theories have developed and are the subject of the next chapter. At this stage of your sociological journey, it is enough to appreciate the range of theories that exists and some of the reasons for their diversity; you are not expected to understand or remember every aspect of the sociological theories covered here. You can always return to the theory chapters and dip into various parts to shed further light on the concepts and theories you will come across in the various chapters of this book. Moreover, the further reading and web resources recommended at the end of this chapter can be used to extend your own theoretical foundations.

SOCIOLOGY SPOTLIGHT

2.1: Sociology's imperial gaze

Most sociology textbooks will introduce students to an overview of 'classical' theories—often the 'big three' of Marx, Weber, and Durkheim are singled out for special attention as the 'founding fathers' of the discipline. In recent years, some textbooks have included a wider collection of authors, such as those in this chapter, including feminist writers and, in some cases, non-Western authors (see Connell 1997). It is generally assumed that the 'big three' founded the discipline through their analyses of the social transformation of European society in the eighteenth and nineteenth centuries. According to internationally acclaimed Australian sociologist Raewyn Connell, this canon—or 'privileged set of texts, whose interpretation and reinterpretation defines a field' (1997, p. 1512)—was actually invented in the mid-twentieth century, most notably by Talcott Parsons and his followers in the United States, in an attempt to gain professional legitimacy for a relatively young academic discipline. It quickly became institutionalised as the official history of sociology through the power of US sociology publishing. For Connell (1997), so successfully has the canon become entrenched that even though classical theories are no longer relevant, they continue to be paid due deference as a symbolic rite of passage for professional and student sociologists alike.

Connell makes a persuasive case that the key theme in the work of many of the founding authors centred on notions of social progress. For Connell, sociology has its roots in **imperialism** and social evolution. Foundational sociologists were significantly influenced by the era of 'rule over indigenous peoples, and the creation of plantation economies and colonies of settlement' (Connell 1997, p. 1522). While not all were racist, according to Connell the 'imperial gaze' biased their views towards attempting to explain the ascent of Western civilisation. Early sociologists were concerned primarily with documenting and analysing encounters with the colonised world, making comparisons between so-called 'primitive' societies and their own 'progressive' societies. Sociology, as the 'science of society', attempted to identify laws of social progress, underpinned by **eugenic** ideas and the potential for social engineering. Therefore, sociology's heritage lay less in understanding the impact of industrialisation and urbanisation (though these were explored) and had more to do with imperial notions of race, gender, and culture. The lesson to be learnt from this alternative story of the history of sociology is that, rather than focusing on the canons,

imperialism
A term originally used to describe the political aspirations of Napoleon III of France, and now generally used to describe the domination of developed countries over the developing world. See also *colonialism*.

eugenics
A term coined in 1883 by Francis Galton, who applied the principles of agricultural breeding to humans based on the unproven assumption that selective breeding could improve the intellectual, physical, and cultural traits of a population.

abstracted from their historical and social context, we should attempt to include a diverse and inclusive view of sociological theory (Connell 1997). Moreover, rather than worshipping a few heroic founding fathers, we need to empirically ground theories in the local and national characteristics of particular societies under study.

Summary of main points

► Comte coined the term sociology. Although many others had studied society, Comte was influential in society being studied in a systematic way.

► The key sociological thinkers who helped establish sociology are Comte, Spencer, Marx, Durkheim, Weber, and Simmel, though some commentators would suggest a much wider group. The ideas of these key thinkers are still influential today.

► In the male-dominated era of the nineteenth century, the work of women was rarely recognised.

► The founders of sociology saw profound transformations in society following the French Revolution and with the advent of the Industrial Revolution. They had interpretations of these transformations; however, most believed in, and were committed to, social progress—albeit from a mostly imperialist worldview.

► Durkheim was a reformist whose work explained social solidarity and social cohesion.

► Marx believed that the economic base of society affected and underpinned all aspects of social life.

► Weber believed that one of the chief characteristics of an industrial capitalist society was rationalisation, exemplified by the growth of bureaucracies.

► There are a number of theoretical approaches in sociology and the discipline is not tied to one theoretical viewpoint.

2.1 What is your theory?

After reading about the foundational sociological theorists in this chapter, which one most appeals to you? Reflect on the reasons for your answer.

Discussion questions

2.1 In what ways do Durkheim's notion of anomie and his work on suicide still have relevance today?

2.2 Marx believed that the economic base of society determined all other aspects of social life. What evidence would you cite to support, refute, or modify this view?

2.3 To what extent do you agree with Weber's prediction that social life would increasingly become bureaucratised?

2.4 What are some of the reasons that gender issues were largely neglected by foundational sociological theorists?

2.5 Which, if any, of the theories and concepts addressed in this chapter do you think have contemporary relevance?

2.6 What are some examples of the limitations of adopting one theoretical approach and ignoring others?

Further reading

Best, S. 2003, *A Beginner's Guide to Social Theory*, Sage, London.

Connell, R. 1997, 'Why is classical theory classical?', *American Journal of Sociology*, vol. 102, no. 6, pp. 1511–57.

—— 2005, 'Australia and world sociology', in J. Germov & T.R. McGee (eds), *Histories of Australian Sociology*, Melbourne University Press, Melbourne.

Cuff, E.C., Sharrock, W.W. & Francis, D.W. 2005, *Perspectives in Sociology*, 5th edn, Routledge, London.

Ritzer, G. 2003, *The Blackwell Companion to Major Classical Social Theorists*, Blackwell, Malden, MA.

—— (ed.) 2005, *Encyclopedia of Social Theory*, 2 vols, Sage, Thousand Oaks, CA.

Ritzer, G. 2008, *Sociological Theory*, 7th edn, McGraw-Hill, New York.

Scott, J. 2006, *Social Theory: Central Issues in Sociology*, Sage, London.

Swingewood, A. 2000, *A Short History of Sociological Thought*, 3rd edn, St Martin's Press, New York.

Websites

- Dead Sociologists Society: <http://media.pfeiffer.edu/lridener/DSS/DEADSOC.HTML>. Online summaries of and biographical information about some key social theorists.
- The Émile Durkheim Archive: <http://durkheim.itgo.com>. An in-depth, informative source of information on Émile Durkheim.
- Feminist Majority Foundation: <www.feminist.org>. A vast United States-based activist-oriented website.
- Sociology Timeline from 1600 by Ed Stephan: <www.edstephan.org/timeline.html>. This site has a comprehensive timeline of sociological developments.

- Marx and Engels' Writings: <http://marx.eserver.org>. The collected works of these authors available online.
- Marxist Internet Archive: <www.marxists.org>. A vast website covering many aspects of Marxism, including key writers and a digital library of main reference works, as well as overviews of historical and political aspects of Marxism.
- SocioSite—Sociological Theories and Perspectives: <www.sociosite.net/topics/theory/php>. This site includes links to many high-quality resources.
- Theory: <www. theory.org.uk>. An introductory site covering a wide range of foundational and contemporary social theories.

Films/documentaries

- *Understanding Sociology*, 1998, DVD, three volumes, Halovine Video. Volume 1: Theory and methods (Classical sociology: Positivism, interpretivism, and realism); Volume 2: Making sense of sociological theory (Marxism, functionalism, and interactionism; Volume 3: From modernity to post-modernity. For details see, <www.onlineclassroom.tv/sociology>.

Visit the *Public Sociology* book website to access topical case studies, weblinks, YouTube clips, and extra readings.

References

Abbott, P., Wallace, C. & Tyler, M. 2005, *An Introduction to Sociology: Feminist Perspectives*, 3rd edn, Routledge, London.

Allan, K. 2005, *Explorations in Classical Sociological Theory: Seeing the Social World*, Pine Forge Press, Thousand Oaks, CA.

Cheal, D. 2005, *Dimensions of Sociological Theory*, Palgrave Macmillan, Basingstoke.

Connell, R. 1997, 'Why is classical theory classical?', *American Journal of Sociology*, vol. 102, no. 6, pp. 1511–57.

——— 2007, *Southern Theory: The Global Dynamics of Knowledge in Social Science*, Allen & Unwin, Sydney.

Darwin, C. 1859, *On the Origin of Species by Means of Natural Selection, or the Preservation of Favoured Races in the Struggle for Life*. Online edition, <www.literature.org/authors/darwin-charles/the-origin-of-species> (accessed 3 August 2009).

Durkheim, É. 1964 [1893], *Division of Labour in Society*, Free Press, New York.

Encel, S. 1970, *Equality and Authority: A Study of Class, Status and Power in Australia*, Cheshire, Melbourne.

Giddens, A. (with the assistance of Birdsall, K.) 2001, *Sociology*, 4th edn, Polity Press, Cambridge.

Henslin, J.M. 2005, *Sociology: A Down-to-Earth Approach*, 7th edn, Pearson, Boston.

Hobbes, T. 1651, *Leviathan*, Printed for Andrew Crooke, at the Green Dragon in St Paul's Churchyard, London.

Hoecker-Drysdale, S. 2003, 'Harriet Martineau', in G. Ritzer (ed.), *The Blackwell Companion to Major Classical Social Theorists*, Blackwell, Oxford, pp. 41–68.

Lengermann, P.M. & Niebrugge-Brantley, J. 2004, 'Early women sociologists and classical sociological theory: 1830–1930', in G. Ritzer & D.J. Goodman (eds), *Classical Sociological Theory*, 4th edn, McGraw-Hill, Boston, pp. 271–303.

Macionis, J.J. & Plummer, K. 2005, *Sociology: A Global Introduction*, 3rd edn, Pearson/ Prentice Hall, Harlow, Essex.

Martineau, H. 1962 [1837], *Society in America*, Anchor Books, New York.

Marx, K. & Engels, F. 1948 [1848], *Manifesto of the Communist Party*, International Publishers, New York.

Pakulski, J. 2004, *Globalising Inequalities: New Patterns of Social Privilege and Disadvantage*, Allen & Unwin, Sydney.

Ritzer, G. 2000, *Modern Sociological Theory*, 5th edn, McGraw-Hill, Boston.

—— 2003, *Contemporary Sociological Theory and Its Classical Roots: The Basics*, McGraw-Hill, New York.

Ritzer, G. & Goodman, D.J. 2004, *Sociological Theory*, 6th edn, McGraw-Hill, New York.

Simmel, G. 1978 [1907], *The Philosophy of Money*, Routledge & Kegan Paul, London.

Swingewood, A. 2000, *A Short History of Sociological Thought*, 3rd edn, St Martin's Press, New York.

Weber, M. 1968 [1921], *Economy and Society*, Bedminster, New York.

—— 1958 [1904–05], *The Protestant Ethic and the Spirit of Capitalism*, Scribner, New York.

Wild, R. 1974, *Bradstow*, Angus & Robertson, Sydney.

—— 1978, *Social Stratification in Australia*, George Allen & Unwin, Sydney.

Williams, G. 2006, 'Thomas Hobbes', in *The Internet Encyclopedia of Philosophy*, <www. iep. utm.edu> (accessed 13 August 2006).

CHAPTER 3

Contemporary sociological theorists and theories

Marilyn Poole and John Germov

Facebook theory

The world in which we live is one of rapid communication through instant messaging, mobile phones, emails, YouTube, and social networking sites such as Facebook, Twitter, and MySpace. Facebook is arguably the most popular social networking site, with millions of users worldwide. So how can we use some of the sociological theories in this chapter to analyse Facebook?

Manuel Castells (2001) argues that new social structures predominantly focused on networks had emerged by the end of the twentieth century. This new network-based informational economy has permeated the ways in which we conduct our lives through work, leisure, and social interactions. Both Ulrich Beck (2009) and Anthony Giddens (2001) believe that we live in a world of late modernity, characterised by a break with traditions and replaced by a world of risk and uncertainty. It is a world in which individual identity has become more important and one in which individuals write their own biographies—a manifestation of this can be as online identities on, for example, Facebook where one of the first tasks when registering an account is to create a profile made up of text, photographs, video, and other markers with which to construct an online identity. Information posted on the site may be shared with others so that contact can be facilitated. Managing a profile on Facebook can be seen as an example of what sociologist Erving Goffman (1959) called 'impression management', and the work undertaken to maintain an online identity could be viewed, using his term, 'backstage work'.

Introduction: On theoretical pluralism and the contest of ideas

The aim of this chapter is to provide you with a basic understanding of some of the key theorists, theories, and concepts in contemporary sociology. In doing this, we trust that you will gain an appreciation of the reasons for the diversity and differences among sociological theories today. We adopt a position of 'theoretical pluralism'—that is, an assumption that many theories can have something to offer. Inevitably, different theories will focus on different levels of analysis, ask different questions, and be concerned with different topics of investigation. While most theories contribute to our sociological understanding, in the final analysis, competing theories are vying for supremacy, so it is up to you to decide which theories have greater explanatory power.

CrossLink: See Chapter 2 for more on Marx, Weber, and Durkheim

The 'classical' thinkers in sociology—the modernists of their day, particularly Karl Marx, Émile Durkheim, and Max Weber—were 'engaged in an analysis and critique of modern society' (Ritzer 2000, p. 422). All were interested in the changes brought about by the

Enlightenment

A period in European history that lasted from the seventeenth century to the eighteenth century, also known as the Age of Reason. Enlightenment thinkers advocated the power of reason over the authority of the church to reach a true understanding of nature and society.

Industrial Revolution

Beginning in England in the late eighteenth century, the Industrial Revolution introduced major changes to work processes and everyday life that resulted in social and political transformations in society. Agrarian economies and lifestyles gave way to a wage-labour system, the separation of home from work, and the urbanisation of the population.

modernity

The historical period from the mid-eighteenth century until the late twentieth century whereby traditional agrarian societies were transformed into industrialised, urbanised, and secular nation states based on the rule of law, science, and reason.

globalisation

The increased interconnectedness of the cultural, economic, and political aspects of social life; intensified circulation of capital, goods, information, and people across national boundaries; and increased interdependence of countries and regions of the world.

Enlightenment and the **Industrial Revolution**. All of them saw that **modernity** was a result of these changes and tried to analyse the problems they perceived to be associated with it. For Marx, the problem was the development of a capitalist economy that accompanied industrialisation; for Weber, the problem was the 'expansion of rationality'; for Durkheim, it was the weakening of the collective conscience or common values so that people found themselves in a life without meaning in the modern world (Ritzer 2000). Contemporary theorists, while influenced by this tradition, necessarily explore different forms of social change, such as the impact of information and communication technologies (ICTs) and the social implications of **globalisation.**

This chapter begins by discussing the earlier but influential sociological contributions of symbolic interactionists George Herbert Mead and Charles Horton Cooley, and then focuses on the more contemporary work of Erving Goffman and Arlie Hochschild. It then discusses the ideas of Talcott Parsons and Robert Merton and the perspective of structural functionalism, which rose to prominence in the mid-twentieth century. This is followed by a discussion of feminist perspectives, focusing on the work of Dorothy Smith and Sylvia Walby. The chapter then turns to postmodern social theory, particularly the work of Michel Foucault. It then explores the contemporary theories of Anthony Giddens, Ulrich Beck, Manuel Castells, George Ritzer, Pierre Bourdieu, Zygmunt Bauman, and Raewyn Connell. A hallmark of these authors' work is their attempt to synthesise ideas from various perspectives—notably the first generation of sociologists such as Marx, Weber, and Durkheim—as well as to produce theories that endeavour to integrate notions of structure and agency.

At the outset, it should be noted that this chapter aims to provide an awareness of the breadth of contemporary sociological theories and concepts, but does not attempt a comprehensive overview or offer in-depth evaluations of each theory covered. Some colleagues would no doubt include other theorists, but we are confident that the chapter allows you to develop an appreciation of the benefits of theoretical pluralism in sociology.

George Mead: The self, and symbolic interactionism

The origins of symbolic interactionism owe a great deal to the writings of the philosopher George Herbert Mead (1863–1931), particularly conveyed through his book *Mind, Self and Society* (1962), and his colleague Charles Horton Cooley (1864–1929). Mead and Cooley were interested in how people used symbols in order to make sense of the world, particularly through the interaction between individuals and small groups—an approach Herbert Blumer (1900–87) coined 'symbolic interactionism' in 1937 (see Blumer 1969). Mead did not accept the biological basis of human behaviour, but believed that human behaviour was learnt as an outcome of social interaction. The concept of the **self**—developed by Mead—is a key component of symbolic-interactionist thought. According to Mead (1962), the self develops through social relationships that make possible the ability to engage in reflexivity, whereby individuals are able to view themselves from the perspective of another person. By imagining ourselves from the viewpoint of others, we can attempt to evaluate ourselves objectively, and potentially modify our attitudes and behaviors. As Mead (1962, p. 134), states:

(the) self
The reflexive condition of all humans in which they can view themselves objectively as unique individuals by imagining themselves from the standpoint of others.

> It is by means of reflexiveness . . . that the social process is thus brought into the experience of the individuals involved in it; it is by such means, which enable the individual to take the attitude of the other toward himself [sic], that the individual is able consciously to adjust himself to that process . . .

*CrossLink:
See Chapter 5
for more
discussion
of Mead and
Cooley.*

Cooley (1964/1902) defined this process as the 'looking-glass self'.

Given the focus on small-scale social relations, symbolic-interactionist theorists, such as Goffman (discussed below), Anselm Strauss (1916–96), and Howard Becker (1928–   ), reject a 'grand theory' that orders the world—in contrast to the sociology of Marx, Weber, and Durkheim (Adams & Sydie 2002).

Erving Goffman and the sociology of everyday life

Erving Goffman (1922–82) was born in Canada and completed his postgraduate study at the University of Chicago. He remains the leading exponent of symbolic interactionism in what is referred to as his 'sociology-of-everyday-life' approach. In his seminal work, *The Presentation of Self in Everyday Life* (1959), he develops the view that social life can be seen as a theatrical production in which individuals are the actors giving performances on a stage—an approach referred to as **dramaturgy.**

---

dramaturgical analysis/dramaturgy
The term used by Goffman to describe how people take on social roles, just as actors do in the theatre.

Goffman believes that we are continuously involved in performances, which he terms the 'presentation of self', in order to influence others to see us in a particular way. For Goffman, the self is not so much a product of being an actor; rather, the self is developed 'as the product of the dramatic interaction between actor and audience' (Ritzer & Goodman 2004, p. 358). In his book, Goffman assumes that when people interact they wish to present a certain aspect of self. Just as actors on the stage must be aware of audience reactions, so we as individuals need to be attuned to our audiences—a notion he refers to as **impression management** (Ritzer & Goodman 2004). Goffman (1959) suggests the notion of identity as a series of performances, where we use impression management to portray ourselves appropriately in different environments.

impression management
A concept used by Goffman to describe individuals' presentation of self as they try to create a specific impression in their interactions with others.

One of Goffman's (1982) key concerns was the 'interaction order', or what we do in the presence of others. He suggested that one of the most important aspects of social interaction was 'maintenance of face'—it is very important for individuals to present themselves in a way that is socially desirable, what Goffman refers to as acting out a 'line'. It was Goffman's belief that individuals work hard in presenting their performances and wish to live up to the face that they consider to be theirs (Cheal 2005). These are so-called 'front stage' areas where we put on our performances. Performances also need props and settings, just as in theatrical productions. For example, think of someone giving a sociology lecture with the podium, microphone, whiteboard, and screens as their props in a lecture hall (Cheal 2005). Just as actors go back stage when they have finished their performances, so we all relax 'back stage' where we are not seen or where we prepare for our performances. Many of us do this when we get home from work: we relax and perhaps change into more comfortable clothes or wash off the makeup we have worn to the office.

There is growing interest in applying the insights of Goffman to electronic forms of communication, such as online social networking sites, personal web pages, and blogs (Miller & Arnold 2001). Just as we use clothes and other 'props' in face-to-face interactions, so the internet can be used as a vehicle for self-expression to represent ourselves and to interact with others. Sherry Turkle (1995), in her pioneering study of constructing identity in cyberspace, states:

> In cyberspace, we can talk, exchange ideas and assume personae of our own creation. We have the opportunity to build new kinds of communities, virtual communities, in which we participate with people from all over the world with whom we converse daily, people with whom we may have fairly intimate relationships but whom we may never physically meet. (pp. 9–10)

Goffman was also interested in understanding why most social interactions are cooperative and orderly. He 'did not attribute this to culture and socialization, nor to agencies of social control, but to the structure of social interaction' (Cheal 2005, p. 146). Goffman referred to the 'ground rules'—the social norms that govern our behaviour—by which people interact with each other. He used the example of traffic signals that regulate the flow of traffic on roads as a metaphor for the rules that govern our social interactions. People stop at a red light because they know that running the light puts them in danger of crashing into another car. They obey traffic signals because they know that, when this is done, the flow of traffic is likely to be orderly.

Goffman referred to the 'situational proprieties' that apply when we initiate a conversation, such as the manner of talking and the topics to be covered, which will vary depending on to whom we are talking and the reason for and context of the conversation. Within all conversations there are openings and closings—just like green and red traffic signals—conveyed by standard greetings such as 'hello' or 'goodbye' (Cheal 2005).

These ground rules also apply to non-verbal communication and the way in which people behave in public (Goffman 1959). Goffman was interested in how we acknowledge others by means of 'civil inattention' in public places. For example, when we are in crowded situations with strangers, such as on public transport or in a lift, while we are aware of their presence, we tend to avoid eye contact. In other social situations, such as in clubs or at a party, we may glance at or 'catch the eye' of someone we do not know, and in this way initiate social contact.

Arlie Russell Hochschild and emotion work

Arlie Hochschild's (1940–) theoretical work on the sociology of emotions has extended Goffman's work. Just as Goffman's work explores the outward manifestations of emotions such as shame and embarrassment, Hochschild examines the 'inner emotional life of the self' (Adams & Sydie 2002, p. 180). One of the important differences between Hochschild and Goffman is that Hochschild 'is interested in "how people try to feel" rather than "how people try to appear to feel"' (Adams & Sydie 2002, p. 180).

Hochschild's first major work, *The Managed Heart: Commercialization of Human Feeling* (1983), examines the **emotional labour** required of two different occupations: flight attendants (mostly women), and bill collectors (mostly men). Flight attendants were expected to feel 'sympathy, trust and good will' towards their clients, while bill collectors were generally expected to feel the opposite (1983, p. 137). Hochschild suggests that strain appears when people in occupations that require emotional labour feel differences between the emotion they are really experiencing and the one they are supposed to feel. She labels the strain that is produced **emotional dissonance** (Wallace & Wolf 2006).

emotional labour
A term used by Hochschild to describe the commodification of feelings experienced by workers in personal service occupations and the use of feelings by employees as part of their paid work (such as nurses caring for patients).

emotional dissonance
The strain felt by people between the emotions they really feel and those they are supposed to feel.

In *The Second Shift: Working Parents and the Revolution at Home* (1989) and *The Time Bind: When Work Becomes Home and Home Becomes Work* (1997), Hochschild highlights the importance of emotions in understanding the sociology of everyday life. In these two books, which are studies of interactions in the home, Hochschild applies Goffman's dramaturgical analysis in terms of 'the front stage ideals as to how parents are expected to deal with their children, and the backstage reality' of how people manage amid all the pressures to which they are subject (Wallace & Wolf 2006, p. 252).

Talcott Parsons and structural functionalism

CrossLink:
See Chapter 2
for more on
Durkheim
and Weber.

In *The Structure of Social Action* (1937), American sociologist Talcott Parsons (1902–79) constructed a major theoretical work—that of structural functionalism—based on the ideas of Durkheim and Weber. This perspective uses an analogy—referred to as the organic analogy—viewing society as an organism made up of interrelated parts in the same way the human body is made up of components such as the skeleton, heart, and lungs. Parsons viewed society as consisting of component parts such as the family, the education system, religion, and the like, which make up the whole. The different parts of society are seen as interdependent and must work together if society is to function smoothly. The contribution made by each component to the whole is called the function.

More recent sociologists see society as a system rather than an organism; nevertheless, they are interested in how parts of the system relate together. The perspective has been influential in the analysis of public policy and organisational management, and in these arenas is often referred to as 'systems theory'. It is also known as 'consensus theory' because of its focus on the maintenance of social order.

Parsons wanted to explain the integration of culture, structure, and personality. He argues that in most Western societies there are hierarchies, and that this stratification is based on hard work, ambition, motivation, and so on. The functionalist view of social stratification is that it is appropriate for people in responsible jobs to be paid more and have greater status in society than those doing less-responsible work. In other words, functionalists legitimate stratification in society on the grounds that for the good of society as a whole, those in responsible positions should be well rewarded. In order for society to function smoothly, there must be an allocation of roles and commensurate rewards.

CrossLink:
See Chapter 7
for further
discussion of
Parsons' work
on the family.

Parsons is well known for his work on the family. In his view, the most important functions of the family are the socialisation of children and meeting the emotional needs of the adults. According to Parsons, these functions are met when men and women have separate but complementary roles within the family. He argues that women should take on the nurturing roles of wife and mother, providing warmth and emotional support for their husband and children, while men should be the main breadwinners of the family. According to Parsons, this division of roles between the sexes underpins a stable family (Parsons & Bales 1956)—an argument that many feminist sociologists (discussed below) were later to contest.

Robert Merton on deviance: Manifest and latent functions

deviance
Behaviours or activities that violate
social expectations about what is
normal.

Robert Merton (1910–2003) was an American sociologist influenced by Parsons' work on structural functionalism. He is best known for his work on **deviance**, published in his widely cited book *Social Theory and Social Structure* (1968). By adapting

Durkheim's concept of **anomie**, he devised a typology of five categories of deviance. Merton argued that value systems could become the source of social conflict. For example, when a society promotes social ends that cannot be achieved by socially approved means, the result can be crime and rebellion. If society promotes the social values of money and high-value consumer goods, it is not surprising that those who cannot achieve these goals through socially approved means, such as highly paid jobs, will turn to fraud and theft. Rising expectations may well result in rebellion and dissent in society if those expectations are not met (Pakulski 2004).

anomie
A concept used by Durkheim for a societal condition in which individuals feel aimless and lack guidance in social norms. Anomie means to be without laws or norms.

CrossLink:
See Chapter
16 for more
on deviance.

Merton (1968) produced a more refined and nuanced version of structural functionalist theory, maintaining that functionalist analysis can operate at various levels—societal, institutional, and group. Rather than Parsons' focus on grand theory, which attempted to explain all forms of social organisation from a macro-societal viewpoint, Merton preferred what he termed mid-range theories of social life that concerned the operation of social institutions and social groups (Ritzer & Goodman 2004). He developed the distinction between **manifest** and **latent functions**. Manifest functions are those we perform knowingly with observed outcomes; latent functions are those which have either unintended outcomes or outcomes of which we are unaware. For example, the prohibition of alcohol in the United States between 1920 and 1933 had the manifest function of stopping the production and sale of alcohol (though interestingly it did not actually ban alcohol consumption), which resulted in the latent function of 'bootlegging'—the widespread illegal production and continued consumption of alcohol.

manifest functions
Functions that are obvious and purposeful.

latent functions
Functions that may be hidden.

Merton also developed the concept of **dysfunction**. An underlying assumption of functionalism is social order, whereby all the key social structures perform positive functions to ensure a smooth-running society. Merton noted that there are aspects of a society that may produce strains and tensions, and that 'not all parts of a social system or its culture are integrated, or work together for the good of the whole' (Adams & Sydie 2002, p. 26). For example, racial and sexual discrimination is clearly dysfunctional, but nonetheless persists because it can be functional for those who benefit from it, particularly white males (Adams & Sydie 2002).

dysfunction
An institution is dysfunctional when one of its activities impedes the workings of another institution.

Functionalist theories have been the subject of extensive criticism in sociology due to their inherently conservative approach of focusing on how social stability and consensus are maintained, thereby marginalising issues of conflict and social change (Ritzer & Goodman 2004). American sociologist Jeffrey Alexander (1947–) attempted to address many of these criticisms by developing the perspective of 'neofunctionalism' (Alexander 1998), though it is fair to say it has had little impact on the discipline to date.

Feminist sociology

Feminism refers to a broad social, political, and intellectual movement that seeks to explain and address all forms of social inequality and discrimination experienced by women. Contemporary feminism arose with the second wave of the women's movement in the 1960s and 1970s, a period of intense social change. Feminist theories and perspectives were initially divided into a number of competing strands:

- liberal feminism
- Marxist/socialist feminism, and
- radical feminism.

---

liberal feminism
Liberal feminism maintains that women should have the same *citizenship rights* as men and focuses on equal rights and anti-discrimination.

Marxist/socialist feminism
Draws on the work of Marx and Engels in order to explain women's inequality, focusing on unpaid labour in the home, wage differentials between women and men, and barriers to women in employment. Since the 1980s, dual systems theory has developed, which argues the necessity to articulate Marxist class theory with *radical feminist* theories of *patriarchy*.

---

radical feminism
Radical feminism defines *patriarchy* as the cause of women's oppression and argues that all women are oppressed, focusing on issues such as sexual assault and prostitution.

Each had different intellectual and historic origins, and all tried to explain gender inequalities through social processes. The impact of feminist scholarship on sociology brought the recognition that men and women experience the world in different ways, together with the understanding that gender differences are socially constructed, and that the gender order is hierarchical. According to Sarah Delamont (2003), underlying feminist sociology was the desire to make the discipline of sociology better reflect women's lives and concerns. Feminist sociologists critiqued what they termed 'malestream' sociology, based on the view that:

- sociological research had been focused on men, and as a result sociological theories applied primarily to men's lives
- research tended to be based on all male (or predominantly male) samples and incorrectly generalised to the population as a whole, and
- those areas of concern and of primary interest to women were overlooked or designated as relatively unimportant (Abbott, Wallace & Tyler 2005).

Today, there are many diverse feminist sociological theories; below, two theorists who have had a major impact on the discipline are introduced.

Dorothy Smith and standpoint theory

Dorothy Smith (1926–   ) was born in England, graduated from the University of London, and emigrated to the United States where she obtained her doctoral degree in sociology from the University of California. She held a number of academic appointments in the United States, the United Kingdom, and Canada, and is now Professor Emerita at the University of Toronto. She explains that her sociological theorising was initially derived from her personal experiences of being a doctoral student and her responsibilities as a single parent. She writes that she began to 'attend to the university and my work there from the "standpoint" of my home subjectivity. I started to notice what I had not seen before.' (Smith 2005, p. 12). She found that,

> '[t]he profession of sociology has been predicated on a universe grounded in men's experience and relationships and still largely appropriated by men as their "territory". Sociology is part of the practice by which we are all governed; that practice establishes its relevance.' (Smith 1990, pp. 13–14)

materialism
A style of sociological analysis that places emphasis on modes of economic production as the key determinant of everything else in society and culture.

ethno-methodology
Coined by Garfinkel to refer to the methods people use to describe and understand their everyday life.

patriarchy
A system of power through which males dominate households. It is used more broadly by feminists to refer to society's domination by patriarchal power, which functions to subordinate women and children.

Smith is a highly regarded contemporary feminist sociologist who is synonymous with standpoint theory, which 'emerged in the 1970s and 80s' and 'had an earlier history in Marxian thought, upon which most of the earlier feminist theories explicitly drew' (Harding 2004, p. 2). Smith's standpoint theory has its origins in the **materialism** of Marx and the **ethno-methodology** of Harold Garfinkel (1917–   ). Standpoint as a concept is based on the idea that what we do shapes our perspectives on the world. Smith treats as problematic the taken-for-granted experiences of women's everyday lives, and argues that, as women are mostly powerless in a **patriarchal** society, 'women experience a line of fault between what they know and experience in their everyday/everynight lives, and what is official knowledge, as expressed in the symbols, images, vocabularies and concepts of the patriarchal culture' (Wallace & Wolf 2006, p. 294). This fault line—the different ways in which women know and experience the world—is what she terms a 'bifurcated consciousness'. In other words, women's experiences and generally subordinated position in the world provide them with a different perspective—a standpoint—that challenges conventional (male) worldviews. A major focus of Smith's standpoint theory is what she calls 'relations of ruling'—that is, not just the state, but the administration and governance of the 'professions that organize, lead and regulate contemporary societies' (Wallace & Wolf 2006, p. 295). In *The Conceptual Practices of Power: A Feminist Sociology of Knowledge* (1990), Smith questions whether it is sufficient that gender issues are addressed in sociology, and proposes a sociology for, rather than about, women.

Sylvia Walby: Gender, globalisation, and a new conceptual toolkit for sociology

Sylvia Walby is currently United Nations Educational, Scientific and Cultural Organization (UNESCO) Chair in Gender Research and Professor of Sociology at the University of Lancaster, England. She is an exponent of dual systems theory in order to explain gender inequalities and the oppression of women by men. This theory attempts to combine the insights of Marxist class theory with radical feminist theories of patriarchy

(Abbott, Wallace & Tyler 2005). In *Theorising Patriarchy* (1990), Walby argues that there are six key interrelated sites of patriarchy in a capitalist society:

1. household production
2. paid employment
3. the state
4. violence
5. sexuality, and
6. cultural institutions.

In these six social structures and practices, men dominate, oppress, and exploit women. Walby argues that as these structures interrelate in a dynamic way, a change in one generates a change in others and that, while all societies are patriarchal to some extent, there is great variation from one society to another.

In *Gender Transformations* (1997), Walby discusses how the transformation of gender relations in contemporary Western countries has 'affected the economy and all forms of social relations', and argues that the driving force behind these changes has been the increase in women's education and employment, together with 'new forms of political representation of women's interests' (p. 1). As women have moved out of the private sphere of home and family and into the public sphere, so gender relations have changed. Although the lives of women altered greatly in the latter half of the twentieth century and new opportunities were available to them, new forms of inequality have since developed. For example, although women are almost as likely as men to be employed, the rewards are disproportionate in terms of pay and pensions, job security, and access to skilled work (Walby 1997).

More recently, Walby has focused on the implications on gender inequality of globalisation, particularly the deregulation and deindustrialisation of capitalist economies. She states that 'much of the interest in globalisation and inequalities in the economy has focused on class relations to the exclusion of other forms of social inequalities', such as those based on gender and ethnicity (Walby 2003, p. 6), and argues that complexity theory is a means of offering a new and innovative set of conceptual tools to sociology in order to better understand 'modernities and how they inter-relate' (2003, p. 10). Walby comments that the classical sociology of Marx, Durkheim, and Weber was about large-scale social processes, yet points out that in recent decades, due to the influence of postmodernism, sociology as a discipline has seen the 'privileging of issues of particularity, of difference' (2003, p. 10). Now, with the growing interest in sociology in global processes, Walby believes it is time to address issues on a larger scale. She shares the view of a number of other globalisation theorists that globalisation has made a significant difference to the idea of separate societies and the neatly bounded nation state, and that a new agenda for sociological analysis is required in order to understand and explain the complexities of the globalised world.

Continuing with her discussion that sociology needs a new conceptual toolkit, in *Globalization and Inequalities* (2009) she writes that complexity theory 'comprises a collection

of work that addresses fundamental questions on the nature of systems and their changes'
(Walby 2009, p. 47).

Complexity theory, now a trans-disciplinary development, introduces the central ideas
of chaos theories originating in the physical and mathematical sciences and involves a
fundamental rethinking of the nature of systems (Walby 2003). It is an approach to
analysis that views whole systems based upon the links and interactions between the
component parts and their relationships with each other and the environment within which
they exist (Cham & Johnson 2007). Walby considers that 'social theory is challenged to
take account of complex inequalities beyond class' (2009, p. 1), and that it has particular
difficulty in simultaneously analysing social inequalities. In her view, complexity theory
allows sociology simultaneously to analyse those inequalities associated with gender,
ethnicity, age, disability, sexual orientation, nation, and religion, particularly where they
intersect (2009).

Postmodern social theory

The terms 'post-structuralism' and 'postmodernism' are often used interchangeably
(Ritzer 1997), and even though historical distinctions can be made between the two, in
sociology at least they have become virtually identical and the term postmodernism is
now the more commonly used (with or without a hyphen). Drawing on Ritzer (1997), we
can make the following useful distinctions between postmodernity, postmodernism, and
postmodern social theory:

1. *Postmodernity* refers to an alleged new historical epoch following that of modernity.
2. *Postmodernism* refers to the culture of postmodernity (art, architecture, movies, and
   beliefs); in fact, Fredric Jameson (1991) defines it as the 'cultural logic of late
   capitalism'.
3. *Postmodern social theory* refers to a particular way of conceptualising and explaining
   social life. It is a social theory, rather than a sociological theory, because most of
   its exponents are actually not sociologists.

Postmodern social theory refers to a diverse range of interdisciplinary theories, most of
which, to a greater or lesser degree, share the following main characteristics:

- *The relativity of knowledge and truth-claims*: Postmodernists reject the idea of universal
  truths about the world, instead suggesting that reality is a social construction.
  Therefore, all knowledge is merely a claim to truth, reflecting the subjectivity
  of those involved. Postmodernists focus on how truth-claims about the world
  are socially constructed. Thus there is no single reality or ultimate truth, only
  versions or interpretations of what is 'real', 'true', 'normal', 'right', or 'wrong'.
- *The rejection of grand theories or meta-narratives*: Postmodern perspectives are critical of
  structuralist approaches such as functionalism and Marxism, which suggest that

meta-narratives

The 'big picture' analysis that frames and organises observations and research on a particular topic.

deconstruction

An approach that aims to expose the multiple and contradictory interpretations of meaning contained within any text.

intertextuality

A term used to describe when one text (written or visual) references or interacts with another text; while still existing in its own right, it also exists in relationship to all other texts. The term is also used to recognise the expectations an audience brings to interpreting a text.

there is an overriding logic of social organisation based on an assumption of social progress. They dispute the existence or importance of **meta-narratives**, unifying trends, universal concepts, social laws, and structural determinants such as class, patriarchy, or rationalisation.

- *An emphasis on pluralist discourses*: Postmodernists adopt a pluralist approach and claim that social life is characterised by fragmentation, differentiation, indeterminacy, and subjectivity, reflecting people's difference in terms of their culture, lifestyle, and vested interests. Such a perspective supports tolerance of diversity and focuses on local narratives of social experience, **deconstruction** and **intertextuality**, but can imply that 'almost anything goes' (Best & Kellner 1991; Ritzer 1997).

The term postmodernity is an oxymoron, as it implies that something has come after (or post) the present (modernity)— clearly what comes after the current historical period is another current historical period (Denzin 2005). In this sense, it is a pity that the term has stuck, given that defining a postmodern condition or epoch by reference to what it is not tends to obscure rather than illuminate. As many critics have pointed out, the view that there are no meta-narratives, or universal concepts and trends, or that knowledge is relative, are all truth-claims and represent a (postmodern) grand narrative itself. These philosophical conundrums aside, it is clear that postmodern social theorists share common sensibilities, and there is general agreement that the following authors are the main exponents: Michel Foucault (1926–84), Jean-Francois Lyotard (1924–98), Jean Baudrillard (1929–2007), and Fredric Jameson (1934–   ).

Michel Foucault and disciplinary society

Michel Foucault was born in Poitiers, a provincial region of France. He was not a sociologist, though his work has had a significant influence in sociology—especially the historical analyses of asylums, prisons, and sexuality found in his books *Madness and Civilization* (1965), *Discipline and Punish* (1979), and *The History of Sexuality* (1980). He was a social historian, philosopher, and public intellectual.

governmentality

The control and regulation of people through practices and knowledges developed within the human sciences and applied to different social institutions, such as schools and prisons.

Foucault was concerned with how power and knowledge were exercised to regulate and control the behaviour of various social groups, such as prisoners, the mentally ill, and sexually active citizens. He originally coined the concept of 'power/knowledge' to convey how knowledge and power were inextricably linked, but in later works replaced it with the concept of **governmentality**. The government of populations—or the 'conduct of conduct', in Foucault's (1982) words—involves much more than the formal exercise of power through the institutions of the nation-state, such as the military, police, and legal system. As Foucault insightfully pointed out, the government of human conduct involves any means by which human behaviour is subject to modification, such as in schools, hospitals, or via cultural ideals (Dean 2010). Such government of conduct can also be self-imposed.

Foucault's (1979) study of the prison as a setting in which surveillance of prisoners was paramount led to his conceptualisation of the panopticon as a metaphor for a theory of surveillance and social control, which has been a major legacy of his work. The panopticon (all-seeing place) was developed by Jeremy Bentham (1748–1832) in the eighteenth century as an architectural design for a prison or any social institution, consisting of a central observation tower surrounded by circles of cells so that every cell could be observed simultaneously. According to Foucault:

> All that is needed, then, is to place a supervisor in a central tower and to shut up in each cell a madman, a patient, a condemned man, a worker, or a schoolboy . . . [resulting in] a state of consciousness and permanent visibility that assures the automatic functioning of power . . . in short, that the inmates should be caught up in a power situation of which they themselves are the bearers. (1979, pp. 200–1)

Therefore, control could be maintained by the assumption of being constantly under surveillance, so that individuals subjected to the disciplinary gaze are 'totally seen without ever seeing, whilst the agents of discipline see everything, without ever being seen' (Foucault 1979, p. 202). The idea that social control of people's behaviour can be exerted in such an indirect and self-induced way has been a significant insight. Foucault viewed the panopticon as the basis for 'a whole type of society' that he believed was emerging: the disciplinary society (1979, p. 216). For example, the thin ideal of female beauty in Western cultures can have panoptic effects, whereby women are under constant body surveillance and social pressure to be thin, resulting in their undertaking numerous activities to discipline their bodies, such as dieting, exercise, and possibly cosmetic surgery (Williams & Germov 2008).

agency
The ability of people, individually and collectively, to influence their own lives and the society in which they live.

structure (or social structure)
The recurring patterns that occur in social life, in particular the rules and resources that give similar social practices systematic form.

structuration
A theory developed by Giddens to denote the two-way process by which individuals shape their social world and in turn are shaped by social processes.

Anthony Giddens and the juggernaut of late modernity

Anthony Giddens (1938–) was born in North London. He is one of the most widely read of contemporary social theorists and was the most cited scholar in the social sciences between 2000 and 2009.

Many sociological theories focus on either the large-scale structures of society or on the micro-levels of everyday life. More recently, there have been attempts to integrate micro and macro issues. One of the key debates in sociology in the latter half of the twentieth century concerned the relationship between

agency and **structure**. Giddens' work on **structuration** theory proved to be an important development in debates regarding the relationship between agency and structure in that it draws upon a number of different theoretical perspectives. Giddens examined a wide range of theories: some began with the individual (or agent), such as symbolic interactionism, while some, such as Marxism, began with society and large social structures (Ritzer & Goodman 2004). The key to structuration theory is the relationship between agency and structure. Agency refers to the choices individuals make, and the ways in which they interpret the world, rather than the assumption that they are passively shaped by it. Structure consists of the 'rules and resources recursively implicated in the reproduction of social systems' (Wallace & Wolf 2006, p. 188). Rules are observed because they make for an orderly society: there are informal rules governing our everyday interactions and formal and public rules that govern areas such as elections and professional conduct (Swingewood 2000). Structuration refers to the two-way process in which individuals 'make and remake social structure during the course of their everyday activities' (Giddens 2001, p. 668)—that is, the 'rules' informing what people do. Structuration attempts to place individuals as 'active agents who construct their own lives, but not always under conditions of their own choosing' (Cheal 2005, p. 162).

CrossLink:
For more on
Giddens see
Chapter 1

By the 1990s, Giddens had developed an interest in what he calls **late modernity**. He rejects the idea that we have entered an era of postmodernity. Instead, Giddens believes that modernity has reached a kind of high point, which he originally referred to as high modernity and subsequently termed late modernity (Cheal 2005; Ritzer 2000). Giddens sees modernity as a juggernaut, something that pushes everything out of its path—'a runaway engine of enormous power which, collectively as human beings, we can drive to some extent but which also threatens to rush out of our control' (Giddens 1990, p. 139).

---

late modernity (or high modernity)
A period reached towards the end of the twentieth century that refers to the advanced state of industrialisation and capitalism.

Late modernity is a characteristic of a society that is pluralistic, constantly changing, and insecure. It is a world where people are surrounded by risks, many of them global threats such as those from Swine Flu, HIV/AIDS, genetically modified food, and terrorism. Risks may stem from our global interdependence, where economic factors in one part of the world create crises elsewhere—such as the rising price of oil or failures in financial markets. Traditions have been replaced by experts and, although we might trust the experts, the juggernaut is always threatening to spiral out of control (Ritzer 2003).

Ulrich Beck and risk society

Ulrich Beck (1944–   ) is a German sociologist who is currently Professor of Sociology at the University of Munich and who also holds a professorial appointment at the London School of Economics. He was the sixth most cited scholar in the social sciences in the period 2000–09. His sociological interests have focused on the **risk society**, which is the consequence of late modernity, **individualisation**, and globalisation.

risk society
A term coined by Beck to describe the centrality of risk calculations in people's lives in Western society, whereby the key social problems today are unanticipated (or manufactured) hazards, such as the risks of pollution, food poisoning, and environmental degradation.

individualisation
A trend towards the primacy of individual choice, freedom, and self-responsibility.

CrossLink: See Chapter 7 for the implications of individualisation on families.

Beck argues in *Risk Society: Towards a New Modernity* (1992), and more recently in *World at Risk* (2009), that in the period of classical modernity—the historical period when industrialisation occurred—most social conflicts concerned the distribution of economic resources. The preoccupation in late modernity is how to avoid, prevent, minimise, control, and manage risks such as flu pandemics, nuclear accidents, pollutants, and terrorism.

In an era in developed societies when the majority of people are living longer and are healthier, people are now preoccupied with external threats. The risks of society in a period of late modernity are often 'global in scope and outside the control of state agencies: pollution is borderless; radiation ignores national boundaries. They also defy time limits: harmful effects extend to future generations' (Pakulski 2004, p. 137). For example, the nuclear disaster that occurred in Chernobyl, Russia over twenty years ago still casts a long shadow. Not only are people still dying from the effects of radiation, but even today sheep grazing on the hillsides in Wales thousands of miles away have to be tested for radiation levels before being sold to market (Macalister & Carter 2009). According to Beck, a new form of class hierarchy has occurred as a result of risks, with those in lower class positions more likely to be exposed to pollutants, toxins, and industrial accidents.

Beck and Elisabeth Beck-Gernsheim (2002) argue that one of the features of late modernity is increasing individualisation, whereby '[t]he ethic of individual self-fulfillment and achievement is the most powerful current in modern society' (p. 22). Living an 'individualised' life reflecting one's own choices is risky: failure can no longer be attributed to social forces and thus people have to take responsibility for both personal success and personal misfortune. In the past, it was easier to fall back on custom and ritual; now, managing individual biographies has become a balancing act incorporating a higher level of risk in that 'there is greater danger of collapse if attempts to reach agreement are not successful' (2002, p. 98).

Manuel Castells and the network society

Manuel Castells (1942–   ) was born in Spain and is currently Professor of Communication Technology and Society at the University of Southern California and Professor Emeritus at the University of California at Berkeley. He was the fifth most cited scholar in the social sciences in the period 2000–09. Castells' earlier work was on urbanism and the study of cities, but he is best known for his study of the social impact of communications technologies. His magnum opus trilogy *The Information Age—The Rise of the Network Society* (1996), *The Power of Identity* (1997), and *End of Millennium* (1998)—details the rise of the information-based society that drives the economy, culture, and social relations. Castells argues that in the last quarter of the twentieth century, an Information Technology Revolution has ushered in a new kind of society, one that has seen the transformation of industrial society to an informational society—what he prefers to term the 'network society'.

Castells uses the term network society to encapsulate the changes made from advances in microelectronics and telecommunications, and the introduction of the internet:

> As a historical trend, dominant functions and processes in the information age are increasingly organized around networks. Networks constitute the new social morphology of our societies, and the diffusion of networking logic substantially modifies the operation and outcomes in processes of production, experience, power and culture. (1996, p. 469)

According to Castells, the Information Technology Revolution has substantially modified all domains of human life on a global scale:

> Information technology is to this revolution what new sources of energy were to the successive Industrial Revolutions, from the steam engine to electricity to fossil fuels, and even nuclear power, since the generation and distribution of energy was the key element underlying the industrial society. (1996, p. 31)

Just as the technological developments of steam power and electricity were the drivers of the Industrial Revolution, beginning in the late eighteenth century, so information technology is seen as responsible for changes in the social structures, work organisation, and social relationships beginning in the late twentieth century.

By way of explanation, in *The Internet Galaxy* (2001, p. 2), Castells argues that the new social structure of networks emerged from the convergence of three independent processes:

1. 'The need for management flexibility and for the globalization of capital, production and trade'
2. 'The demands of society in which the values of individual freedom and open communication became paramount', and
3. 'The extraordinary advances in computing and telecommunications made possible by the microelectronics revolution'.

Under these three processes, the internet became 'the lever for the transition to a new form of society, the network society—and with it a new economy' (p. 2).

Castells (2001) argues that networks provide the most flexible organisational form for business in an information economy. In what he terms the 'network enterprise', or 'a lean agency of economic activity, built around specific business projects, which are enacted by networks of various composition and origin: the network is the enterprise' (p. 67). The network enterprise model was initially taken up with great success in the electronics industry by companies such as Nokia, IBM, and Hewlett Packard, but expanded quickly into other sectors. For example, there are now purely online companies that rely on the internet for the organisation of production, management, and distribution (Castells 2001). Perhaps more important in the new global economy is the development of 'a global, interdependent financial market, operated by computer networks, with a new set of rules for capital investment and the valuation of stocks, and of securities in general' (2001, p. 79). As we know, national regulations may differ, but with electronic trading, capital can flow 'in and out of securities and currencies across markets . . . at an accelerated pace' (2001, p. 81). The global financial crash of 2008 and the subsequent global recession provide us with an important illustration of the effects of global financial interdependence.

George Ritzer and the McDonaldization of society

George Ritzer (1940–) was born in New York and is currently Distinguished University Professor at the University of Maryland. Writing in the last decade of the twentieth century, Ritzer (1993) coined the term **McDonaldization**, based on Weber's theories of rationalisation. While Weber viewed bureaucracy as the classic example of rationalisation, Ritzer uses McDonald's to represent the epitome of contemporary rationalisation. McDonaldization is '*defined as the process by which the principles of the fast-food restaurant are coming to dominate more and more sectors of American society, as well as the rest of the world*' (Ritzer 2003, p. 138, original italics).

McDonaldization
A term coined by Ritzer to refer to the standardisation of work processes by rules and regulations. It is based on increased monitoring and evaluation of individual performance, akin to the uniformity and control measures used by fast-food chains.

The success of McDonald's, according to Ritzer, lies in its ability to standardise the production and consumption of its products through four central mechanisms:

1. calculability (extreme quantification of all features of productive activity)
2. efficiency (prioritising the cheapest means of achieving any designated outcomes)
3. predictability (a focus on standardisation so that a process always operates in the same way), and
4. control (use of managerial strategies and technology to minimise employee autonomy).

*CrossLink:
See Chapter 2
for more
on Weber's
theory of
rational-
isation.*

So successful have McDonald's fast-food outlets become that other organisations (that are quite dissimilar to the fast-food industry) have adopted their organisational model, such as Toys'R'Us, Starbucks, Officeworks, and Bunnings, to name but a few. Ritzer's McDonaldization thesis is that the McDonald's model of intensified rationalisation based on its four core principles is increasingly affecting more aspects of social life, to the extent that we are moving steadily towards Weber's predicted 'iron cage of rationality'. Unchecked, the 'irrationality of rationality' may triumph, with individuality, diversity, and creativity becoming rare features of social life across the globe.

Pierre Bourdieu: Field, capital, and habitus

Pierre Bourdieu (1930–2002) was born in southwest France and was the founder and director of the Centre for European Sociology and a Professor of Sociology at the Collège de France. Bourdieu was a regular political commentator in France and was considered one of its foremost public intellectuals. He is widely cited around the globe in a range of academic disciplines, making him possibly the most influential of contemporary French sociologists.

One of the guiding principles of Bourdieu's work was to overcome the 'opposition between the individual and society' (cited in Ritzer & Goodman 2004, p. 387). His was an integrative theoretical approach that incorporated both agency and structure (Cheal 2005) by means of three fundamental concepts: **field** (distinct social settings), capital (resources), and **habitus** (personal dispositions).

Bourdieu analysed society in terms of fields—social settings where people struggle over social resources (such as higher education, the economy, or politics), competing and cooperating as needed (Cheal 2005). According to Bourdieu, fields are analogous to games, and people develop various strategies to play the game to their personal benefit. Individuals' locations in a field are the result of the interaction of their habitus, capital, and the 'rules of the game'.

Bourdieu was interested in hierarchies and how positions of superiority and inferiority, or domination and subordination, are structured and maintained (Cheal 2005). While class was central to his analysis, he nevertheless did not accept the Marxist view that society could be analysed solely in terms of social classes and class-determined interests (Wallace & Wolf 2006). Reworking Marx's notion of capital from being one that is only economically based, Bourdieu used the terms **cultural capital**, **social capital**, and **symbolic capital** in addition to economic capital. Cultural capital is important, as it gives us an understanding of how class structures and hierarchies are maintained in society. It is acquired through the socialisation of children in families and in schools, and its transmission is a hidden means of ensuring that 'class positions are passed on from one generation to the next' (Cheal 2005, p. 156).

According to Bourdieu, knowledge and tastes are stratified; there are hierarchies of taste in classical or popular music, in art, in clothing, and even in food (Cheal 2005). Bourdieu maintains that tastes are not superficial, but in fact serve to unify certain classes of people (Ritzer 2003). Bourdieu's major interest was in class reproduction and how cultural capital is

field
This refers to an area of social activity, for example sport, in which people's dispositions predispose them to construct characteristic social actions that reflect their *habitus*.

habitus
Refers to socially learnt dispositions or taken-for-granted sets of orientations, skills, and ways of acting that shape behaviour. People are the product and creators of their habitus.

cultural capital
A term to indicate cultural competencies, such as the taste preferences and lifestyle, that differentiate one social class from another and are transmitted through the generations and via the education system.

social capital
A term used to refer to social relations, networks, norms, trust, and reciprocity between individuals that facilitate cooperation for mutual benefit.

symbolic capital
A sub-category of *cultural capital* denoting the honour and prestige accorded to certain individuals.

transmitted through the education system. He explained this by saying that children from privileged homes possess certain attitudes and cultural knowledge that tend to make them feel comfortable and at home in school. As a result, they are generally more likely to succeed in education.

Social capital 'is the sum of the resources, actual or virtual, that accrue to an individual or a group by virtue of possessing a durable network of more or less institutionalised relationships of mutual acquaintance and recognition' (Bourdieu & Wacquant 1992, p. 119). In other words, social capital is a question of whom you know and the social ties made by individuals. Social capital underlines the importance of group membership and of meeting people, particularly those who themselves possess economic and cultural capital. Symbolic capital can be viewed as a sub-category of cultural capital, and refers to the honour and prestige accorded to certain individuals, usually reflecting their economic or cultural capital (Bourdieu & Wacquant 1992).

Bourdieu also uses the concept of habitus—the mental or cognitive structures: dispositions or properties through which people deal with the world. Habitus is seen by Bourdieu as the key to class reproduction because it 'generates repeated practices that make up social life' (Wallace & Wolf 2006, p. 116). Habitus may be internalised, but it is acquired in practice through the activities and experiences of everyday life. In this sense, habitus is seen to be an important part of socialisation in that it is a 'pattern of dispositions' (Cheal 2005, p. 150), and those acquired when young take priority over later experiences. Although habitus is an internalised structure, it does not determine what people do—it simply suggests to them what they should do, underpinning the principles by which people make choices (Ritzer 2003).

Zygmunt Bauman and liquid modernity

liquid modernity
A term coined by Bauman to refer to the constantly changing nature of social conditions in contemporary society so that individuals live with uncertainty and flux, undermining the formation of routines and habits to guide actions and beliefs.

Polish-born Zygmunt Bauman (1925–) is Emeritus Professor of Sociology at the Universities of Leeds and Warsaw. He has been a prolific and influential author, initially concerned with postmodernity, and subsequently developing his own perspective of **liquid modernity** through books such as *Liquid Modernity* (2000), *Liquid Life* (2005), and *Liquid Times* (2007). Bauman's work has synergies with that of Beck and Giddens, though there are distinct differences. Bauman (2005, p. 1) argues that life in a liquid modern society is one 'in which the conditions under which its members act change faster than it takes the ways of acting to consolidate into habits and routines . . . liquid life is a precarious life, lived under conditions of constant uncertainty'. For Bauman (2007), liquid times have fundamentally been driven by the rise of consumerism, which facilitates individuals' ability to create their identity and lifestyle, but nonetheless poses a number of major challenges never before faced:

1. Social structures and routines of behaviour change so often that they 'cannot serve as frames of reference for human actions and long-term life strategies' (2007, p. 1).
2. The decline of the power of nation states and their political institutions to address the needs of citizens increasingly leads to the private provision of public services and 'unpredictable market forces' (p. 2).
3. The withdrawal and diminution of welfare support and legislative protections by the state undermine collective action, social solidarity, and community bonds, whereby 'exposure to the vagaries of commodity-and-labour markets inspires and promotes division, not unity; it puts a premium on competitive attitudes, while degrading collaboration' (pp. 2–3).
4. Life is increasingly fragmented and disjointed, underpinned by 'the collapse of long-term thinking, planning and acting, and the disappearance or weakening of social structures in which thinking, planning and acting could be inscribed' (p. 3), so that past success or experience can no longer be relied upon to guide future actions.
5. The resultant individualisation of social life means people are 'now expected to be "free choosers" and to bear in full the consequences of their choices . . . The virtue proclaimed to serve the individual's interest best is not *conformity* to rules . . . but *flexibility*: a readiness to change tactics and style at short notice, to abandon commitments and loyalties without regret' (pp. 3–4, original italics).

Raewyn Connell and Southern theory

Professor Raewyn Connell (1944–   ), formerly Robert William (Bob) Connell, holds a University Chair at the University of Sydney and is perhaps Australia's most famous sociologist, with a world-renowned reputation in the fields of social theory, gender studies, sexuality, education, intellectual labour, and class. She is a recipient of the American Sociological Association's award for distinguished contribution to the study of sex and gender, and The Australian Sociological Association's (TASA) award for distinguished service to sociology in Australia. In 2003, TASA conducted a survey to identify the most influential books in Australian sociology (Skrbis & Germov 2004), in which four of Connell's books were in the top ten, including the number one ranked book, *Ruling Class, Ruling Culture* (1977), along with *Gender and Power* (1987), *Masculinities* (1995), and the co-authored *Making the Difference* (1982).

In her recent book, *Southern Theory* (2007), which was awarded the Stephen Crook Memorial Prize for the best monograph in Australian sociology (2005–07), Connell challenges the orthodox history of the discipline (discussed in Chapter 2) and challenges the universality of mainstream theories by highlighting their bias to the viewpoints and issues that concern what she calls the 'metropole' of the 'global North' (the major urban centres of Europe and North America). For Connell, there is an uncritical assumption that 'Northern theory'—through concepts such as globalisation (not to mention risk society, individualisation, and liquid modernity)—is universally applicable to all societies, irrespective of culture, history, and place. Thus the dominant social theories that are widely published, and subsequently taught through university curricula, perpetuate the worldview of the affluent and powerful minority of the metropole.

Connell (2007) identifies four major limitations of social theory from the metropole:

1. *The claim of universality*: Social theories tend to assume that they are universally relevant and applicable to all societies, whereby '[i]t is assumed that all societies are knowable, and they are knowable in the same way and from the same point of view' (p. 44).

2. *Reading from the centre*: Professional academia requires that theories are situated within the existing literature, and that literature is always of the metropole, whose worldview is the filter through which existing literature and issues are read and analysed.

3. *Gestures of exclusion*: Literature and theories arising from the colonised world—the periphery, in Connell's terms—are generally excluded from reference and discussion by theorists of the metropole. While the periphery may serve as the source of data and exotic examples, ideas, concepts, and theories from the periphery are rarely addressed.

4. *Grand erasure*: Social theory draws upon empirical research that is conducted in the metropole, which addresses the issues and problems of the metropole. The rest of the world—its viewpoints, experiences, and social thought—is effectively erased from consideration. As Connell (2007, p. 47) notes:

> *Terra nullius*, the coloniser's dream, is a sinister presupposition for social science. It is invoked every time we try to theorise the formation of social institutions and systems from scratch, in a blank space. Whenever we see the words 'building block' in a treatise of social theory, we should be asking who used to occupy the land.

As an alternative, Connell makes a persuasive case for 'Southern theory'—that is, indigenised social theories that develop from the periphery, rather than Europe and North America. Such theories already exist, and Connell introduces the reader to a range of them, arguing that they need to be taken as seriously as the views of Giddens, Beck, or Bauman. Southern theory, then, is a catch-all term for theories derived from Africa, Indigenous Australia, India, the Middle East, and Latin America—it is a call to include the voices and issues of the periphery within the dialogue of sociology and the wider social sciences. For Connell, location matters, and Southern theory is a way to challenge the dominance of metropolitan worldviews. This is not to say that metropolitan sociology is bunk. As Connell notes:

> It has profound insights, well-honed methods, well-defined concepts and lots of skilled practitioners ... But its theorising is vitiated whenever it refuses to recognise its

ethno-sociological being—or, to put it another way, its situation in the world and its history in the world . . . They result not in minor omissions but in major incompleteness, and a profound problem about the truthfulness of arguments framed as universal generalisations. (2007, p. 226)

Connell is not arguing that generalisations are impossible, but rather that they need to be situated in the social contexts from which they emerge and to which they are applied. Rather than 'universal generalisations' and 'pure general theory', Connell suggests we employ 'dirty theory', whereby:

The goal of dirty theory is not to subsume, but to clarify; not to classify from outside, but to illuminate a situation in its concreteness . . . Our interest as researchers is to maximise the wealth of materials that are drawn into the analysis and explanation . . . That includes multiplying the local sources of our thinking. (2007, p. 207)

Conclusion

The existence of so many sociological theories can be daunting at first, but it is testimony to the fact that social change inevitably brings with it new ideas, concepts, and social theories. We have only been able to sketch an outline of some of the major contemporary sociological theories in this chapter. In so doing, it should be noted that we have not attempted to critically evaluate them, but rather have aimed to give you an appreciation of their diversity and the contributions they have made to the understanding of social life. Further detail on these theories can be found by consulting the Further reading and Web resources sections at the end of this chapter. That said, we are firmly of the view that the best way to study theories is through their application to real-world issues, which is what you will encounter in the remainder of this book.

Summary of main points

▶ There are many contemporary sociological theories, making it difficult to synthesise, categorise, and comprehend them all. We have only touched on some of the main theories to give you a 'taster' of the different questions, levels of analysis, and insights provided by various theories. While you may be attracted to particular theories, we hope you have an appreciation of the potential that all theories have to increase our sociological understanding.

▶ Feminist sociological theories, such as Smith's standpoint theory and Walby's work on gender and the economy, have highlighted the gendered nature of social life and present an ongoing challenge to other sociological theories that marginalise issues of gender inequality and sexuality.

▶ Postmodern social theories present a challenge to the sociological enterprise by rejecting grand over-arching theories and instead emphasising pluralist accounts that reflect the subjectivity of social life.

▶ The sociological theories of Giddens, Beck, Castells, Ritzer, Bourdieu, and Bauman reflect a synthesis of various foundational perspectives and integrate notions of structure and agency to explore contemporary social issues.

▶ The Australian sociologist Raewyn Connell challenges much of contemporary sociological theory by highlighting its metropolitan ('Northern') bias and instead encourages a dialogue with 'Southern' theories of the periphery.

SOCIOLOGICAL
REFLECTION

3.1 Imagining Southern theory

Review the arguments made by Connell regarding Northern and Southern theory.

▶ What would an Australian Southern theory of social inequality need to consider?

▶ What issues would be distinctly different from those developed in the metropole?

Discussion questions

3.1 Which sociological theories appealed to you in this chapter? Why?

3.2 What aspects of your life do you think contemporary sociological theory does not address?

3.3 What are some examples of the way contemporary theorists have addressed the structure–agency debate?

3.4 In what ways do you practise Goffman's presentation of the self?

3.5 Are we living in postmodern times? Why or why not?

3.6 To what extent are we living in a risk society? Provide some examples.

3.7 How applicable is Bourdieu's concept of cultural capital in explaining the reproduction of social inequality in contemporary Australia?

3.8 In what ways have information and communication technologies transformed social interaction? Are we living in a network society?

3.9 What are the overlaps and differences between the concepts of late modernity, risk society, and liquid modernity?

3.10 Do you agree with Walby that it is necessary to analyse social inequalities such as gender, ethnicity, and age where they intersect rather than in isolation?

Further reading

Best, S. 2003, *A Beginner's Guide to Social Theory*, Sage, London.

Connell, R. 2007, *Southern Theory: The Global Dynamics of Knowledge in Social Science*, Allen & Unwin, Sydney.

Holmes, M. 2007, *What is Gender? Sociological Approaches*, Sage, London.

Miles, S. 2001, *Social Theory in the Real World*, Sage, London.

Ritzer, G. 2008, *Sociological Theory*, 7th edn, McGraw-Hill, New York.

Wallace, R.A. & Wolf, A. 2006, *Contemporary Sociological Theory: Expanding the Classical Tradition*, 6th edn, Pearson Prentice Hall, Englewood Cliffs, NJ.

Websites

- Feminist Majority Foundation: <www.feminist.org>. A vast United States-based activist-oriented website.
- Society for the Study of Symbolic Interaction: <www.espach.salford.ac.uk/sssi/index.php>. The Society for the Study of Symbolic Interaction (SSSI) is an international professional organisation of scholars interested in the study of a wide range of social issues with an emphasis on identity, everyday practice, and language.
- SocioSite: A premier indexing site for high-quality sociology resources:
  - Sociological Theories and Perspectives: <www.sociosite.net/topics/theory.php>.
  - Famous sociologists: <www.sociosite.net/topics/sociologists.php>.
- Southern Perspectives: <www.southernperspectives.net>. A primarily Australian and New Zealand site dealing with a wide range of social and cultural issues by promoting ideas and discussion from outside the transAtlantic metropolitan regions.
- Theory: <www.theory.org.uk>. An introductory site covering a wide range of foundational and contemporary social theories.

Films/documentaries

Understanding Sociology, 1998, DVD, three volumes, Halovine Video. Volume 1: Theory and methods (Classical sociology: Positivism, interpretivism, and realism); Volume 2: Making sense of sociological theory (Marxism, functionalism, and interactionism; Volume 3: From modernity to post-modernity. For details see, <www.onlineclassroom.tv/sociology>.

Visit the *Public Sociology* book website to access topical case studies, weblinks, YouTube clips, and extra readings.

References

Abbott, P., Wallace, C. & Tyler, M. 2005, *An Introduction to Sociology: Feminist Perspectives*, 3rd edn, Routledge, London.

Adams, B.N. & Sydie, R.A. 2002, *Contemporary Sociological Theory*, Pine Forge Press, Thousand Oaks, CA.

Alexander, J. 1998, *Neofunctionalism and After*, Blackwell, Oxford.

Bauman, Z. 2000, *Liquid Modernity*, Polity Press, Cambridge.

—— 2005, *Liquid Life*, Polity Press, Cambridge.

—— 2007, *Liquid Times*, Polity Press, Cambridge.

Beck, U. 1992, *Risk Society: Towards a New Modernity*, Sage, London.

—— 2009, *World at Risk*, Polity Press, Cambridge.

Beck, U. & Beck-Gernsheim, E. 2002, *Individualization: Institutionalized Individualism and Its Social and Political Consequences*, Sage, London.

Best, S. & Kellner, D. 1991, *Postmodern Theory: Critical Interrogations*, Guilford Press, New York.

Blumer, H. 1969, *Symbolic Interactionism: Perspective and Method*, Prentice-Hall, Englewood Cliffs, NJ.

Bourdieu, P. & Wacquant, L. 1992, *An Invitation to Reflexive Sociology*, Polity Press, Cambridge.

Castells, M. 1996, *The Information Age: Economy, Society and Culture. Volume 1: The Rise of the Network Society*, Blackwell, Cambridge, MA.

—— 1997, *The Information Age: Economy, Society and Culture. Volume 2: The Power of Identity*, Blackwell, Cambridge, MA.

—— 1998, *The Information Age: Economy, Society and Culture. Volume 3: End of Millennium*, Blackwell, Cambridge, MA.

—— 2001, *The Internet Galaxy: Reflections on the Internet, Business and Society*, Oxford University Press, London.

Cham, K. & Johnson, J. 2007, 'Complexity theory: A science of cultural systems?' *m/c journal*, vol. 10, no. 3, <http://journal.media-culture.org.au/0706/08-cham-johnson.php> (accessed 12 December 2009).

Cheal, D. 2005, *Dimensions of Sociological Theory*, Palgrave Macmillan, Basingstoke.

Cooley, C.H. 1964 [1902], *Human Nature and the Social Order*, Scribner's, New York.

Connell, R. 1977, *Ruling Class, Ruling Culture: Studies of Conflict, Power and Hegemony in Australian Life*, Cambridge University Press, Cambridge.

—— 1987, *Gender and Power: Society, the Person, and Sexual Politics*, Allen & Unwin, Sydney.

—— 1995, *Masculinities*, Allen & Unwin, Sydney.

—— 2007, *Southern Theory: The Global Dynamics of Knowledge in Social Science*, Allen & Unwin, Sydney.

Connell, R., Ashenden, D.W., Kessler, S. & Dowsett, G.W. 1982, *Making the Difference: Schools, Families and Social Division*, Allen & Unwin, Sydney.

Delamont, S. 2003, *Feminist Sociology*, Sage, London.

Dean, M. 2010, *Governmentality: Power and Rule in Modern Society*, 2nd edı

Denzin, N.K. 2005, 'Postmodernism', in G. Ritzer (ed.), *Encyclopedia o)*
  2 vols, Sage, Thousand Oaks, CA.

Foucault, M. 1965, *Madness and Civilization: A History of Insanity in the Age o)*   ...ıtage,
  New York.

—— 1979, *Discipline and Punish: The Birth of the Prison*, Penguin, Harmondsworth.

—— 1980, *The History of Sexuality, Volume 1: An Introduction*, Vintage, New York.

—— 1982, 'The subject and the power', in H.A. Dreyfus & P. Rabinow *Michel Foucault:
  Beyond Structuralism and Hermeneutics*, 2nd edn, University of Chicago Press, Chicago,
  pp. 208–26.

Giddens, A. 1990, *The Consequences of Modernity*, Stanford University Press, Stanford, CN.

Giddens, A., with the assistance of K. Birdsall 2001, *Sociology*, 4th edn, Polity Press,
  Cambridge.

Goffman, E. 1959, *The Presentation of Self in Everyday Life*, Doubleday, Garden City.

—— 1982, 'The interaction order', *American Sociological Review*, vol. 48, pp. 1–17.

Harding, S. 2004, 'Introduction: Standpoint theory as a site of political, philosophic
  and scientific debate', in S. Harding (ed.), *Feminist Standpoint Theory Reader: Intellectual and
  Political Controversies*, Routledge, New York, pp. 1–15.

Hochschild, A.R. 1983, *The Managed Heart: Commercialization of Human Feeling*, University of
  California Press, Berkeley, CA.

—— 1989, *The Second Shift: Working Parents and the Revolution at Home*, Viking, New York.

—— 1997, *The Time Bind: When Work Becomes Home and Home Becomes Work*, Henry Holt and
  Co., New York.

Jameson, F. 1991, *Postmodernism, or the Cultural Logic of Late Capitalism*, Duke University
  Press, Durham, NC.

Macalister, T. & Carter, H. 2009, 'Britain's farmers still restricted by Chernobyl
  nuclear fallout', *Guardian* (online edition), 12 May, <www.guardian.co.uk/
  environment/2009/may/12/farmers-restricted-chernobyl-disaster> (accessed
  6 January 2010).

Mead, G.H. 1962 [1934], *Mind, Self and Society: From the Standpoint of a Social Behaviorist*,
  University of Chicago Press, Chicago.

Merton, R.K. 1968 [1949], *Social Theory and Social Structure*, The Free Press, New York.

Miller, H. & Arnold, J. 2001, 'Self in web home pages: Gender, identity and power in
  cyberspace', in G. Riva & C. Galimberti (eds), *Cyberpsychology: Mind, Cognition and Society
  in the Internet Age*, IOS Press, Amsterdam, pp. 74–93.

Pakulski, J. 2004, *Globalising Inequalities: New Patterns of Social Privilege and Disadvantage*, Allen
  & Unwin, Sydney.

Parsons, T. 1937, *The Structure of Social Action*, McGraw-Hill, New York.

Parsons, T. & Bales, R.F. 1956, *Family Socialization and Interaction Process*, Routledge & Kegan
  Paul, London.

Ritzer, G. 1997, *Postmodern Social Theory*, McGraw-Hill, New York.

—— 2000, *Modern Sociological Theory*, 5th edn, McGraw-Hill, Boston.

—— 2003, *Contemporary Sociological Theory and Its Classical Roots: The Basics*, McGraw-Hill, Boston.

Ritzer, G. & Goodman, D.J. 2004, *Sociological Theory*, 6th edn, McGraw-Hill, Boston.

Skrbis, Z. & Germov, J. 2004, 'The most influential books in Australian sociology, 1963–2003', *Journal of Sociology*, vol. 40, no. 3, pp. 283–302.

Smith, D. 1990, *The Conceptual Practices of Power*, University of Toronto Press, Toronto.

—— 2005, *Institutional Ethnography: A Sociology for People*, Altamira Press, Oxford.

Swingewood, A. 2000, *A Short History of Sociological Thought*, 3rd edn, Macmillan, Basingstoke.

Turkle. S. 1995, *Life on the Screen: Identity in the Age of the Internet*, Simon & Schuster, New York.

Walby, S. 1990, *Theorising Patriarchy*, Blackwell, Oxford.

—— 1997, *Gender Transformations*, Routledge, London.

—— 2003, 'Modernities/globalisation/complexities', Department of Sociology, Lancaster University, <www.comp/lancs/ac.uk/sociology/papers> (accessed 13 November 2009).

—— 2009, *Globalization & Inequalities: Complexity and Contested Modernities*, Sage, London.

Wallace, R.A. & Wolf, A. 2006, *Contemporary Social Theory: Expanding the Classical Tradition*, 6th edn, Pearson Prentice Hall, Upper Saddle River, NJ.

Williams, L. & Germov, J. 2008, 'Constructing the female body: Dieting, the thin ideal and body acceptance', in J. Germov & L. Williams (eds), A *Sociology of Food and Nutrition: The Social Appetite*, 3rd edn, Oxford University Press, Melbourne, pp. 329–62.

CHAPTER 4

Sociological investigations: Doing social research

Tara Renae McGee

A sociological controversy

Laud Humphreys (1970) became famous as a sociologist for his doctoral research on impersonal sexual encounters between males in public restrooms. The starting point for his research was a recognition that arrests in public restrooms accounted for the majority of arrests for homosexual behaviour. Given this, he decided to immerse himself in this subculture to observe and record what was going on. His role became that of 'watch queen', where on the approach of police or a stranger he would cough loudly to alert the people inside the public restroom. This type of immersion in the environment that is being studied is known as 'participant observation'. Humphreys also combined the information he recorded while using participant observation techniques with data from interviews he conducted one year later.

Locating the men later in order to interview them was a somewhat devious undertaking by Humphreys. While keeping lookout at the public restroom, he recorded the vehicle licence plate numbers of those he observed. Then, with the help of a police officer, he gained access to their address details. One year later, disguised and posing as a government interviewer, he went to their houses to ask a range of socio-demographic questions. He found that only 14 per cent of those he had observed were members of the gay community and interested in homosexual relationships (Humphreys 1970).

While the findings of this research challenged many of the stereotypes surrounding impersonal sex in public restrooms, and may have led to changes in police practices, it also caused public outrage and created division among staff in the department where Humphreys studied (Sieber 1977). This was in part because Humphreys did not protect the identity of the research subjects and risked the social standing of people who were non-voluntary subjects of the research. In fact, such research today would be considered unethical and would be illegal under privacy legislation. His adviser had his research funding blocked and tensions were high among academic staff in the department. Culminating in a physical fight over the research, during which Professor Alvin Gouldner assaulted and hospitalised Humphreys, the controversy resulted in the closure of the Sociology Department at Washington University (Berry 2004). While not all sociological research is as controversial as Humphreys' work, it does attempt to answer questions or challenge assumptions about the social world. This chapter will provide you with an overview of the main aspects of the sociological research enterprise.

Introduction

Students of sociology often mistakenly think that studying sociology is about learning a bunch of dusty old theories and memorising a stack of 'social facts'. While such knowledge is a foundational requirement of any discipline, including sociology, what sociologists really do is study the social world in a systematic way—that is, they conduct social research. Social research draws on various theoretical frameworks and also on the studies that other sociologists have conducted. It is one of the most enjoyable aspects of sociology, and while it may be a number of years until you conduct your own research projects, throughout your studies you will need to be able to locate, understand, and critically evaluate the research work of sociologists. The aim of this chapter is to provide you with an overview of the social research process. It considers the impact of the researcher and the place of theory and previous research findings in the research process. This will be followed by a quick overview of research design and how sociologists go about finding the people they want to research. Finally, it takes a look at the standard structure of journal articles and some of the techniques of analysis employed by sociologists.

The social research process

There are a number of steps that most sociologists go through when conducting their social research. The first thing they usually do is develop research questions. These are based either on observations of the social world or on a systematic review of the existing literature on the topic under investigation. A literature review lets the researcher ascertain what is already known about that topic and assists in identifying the gaps in the research—that is, it tells the researcher what needs to be looked at further or in more detail to extend knowledge on that topic. There are a number of ways in which researchers can tackle their research questions and they usually develop a plan of how they will do it. This plan is known as the **research design**. In social research, there is often a distinction drawn between *quantitative* research that focuses on numerical data, and *qualitative* non-numerical research (these will be discussed in more detail later in the chapter).

research design

A research design is the plan that researchers develop for conducting their research, and includes the rationale for the study, the theoretical framework/s informing the study, the research questions, the methods of data collection and analysis, and the sampling strategy.

Depending on the state of knowledge about a particular topic, the nature of the research design will vary. If very little is known about the topic, the research will be *exploratory* in nature. In this type of research, the aim is to gather foundational knowledge on the topic. More established topics of research may require detailed *descriptive* research, where the aim is to describe a particular process or pattern of human relationships in detail. When researchers are seeking to explain the origins or causes of a particular social phenomenon, they conduct *explanatory* research. A single research design can focus on one or a combination of these purposes.

The research design is also influenced by other factors, including the time and funding available, the skills of the researcher, the research designs used in previous research on the same topic, and the theoretical framework employed by the researcher. The central position of theory in the social research process is the reason why learning sociological theory is important to your training as a sociologist. Theory provides the framework for research and guides the researcher in relation to the object of investigation, the types of research questions asked, and the research design.

Once specified, the research design will also guide the selection of the research participants, such as who should be studied, how many people will be included in the study, and how to recruit or access these participants. The researcher then uses data-collection techniques to gather information from the research participants (for example, questionnaires, interviews, or **participant observation**), which is then systematically coded using one or more data-analysis techniques so that the researchers can develop answers to their research questions. Social research is a cumulative process, in that each piece of research adds to the knowledge gained from previous research. In order for social research to be cumulative, sociologists need to communicate to others about what they have found out in their research. To do this, sociologists present their research at academic conferences and publish it in academic journals.

participant observation
Participant observation is a data-collection technique that involves participating at some level in a social environment, while observing and recording experiences in that environment.

Before researchers' findings appear in an academic journal, their work is reviewed by their peers (other researchers in the same field). Academic journals are often published by professional associations, other scholarly institutions such as universities, or specialist commercial publishers. Journal articles are written in a formal academic style and include the credentials of the author and a reference list of the sources upon which the author has based the arguments.

*CrossLink:
See
Chapter 25
for advice on
key databases
and effective
search
strategies.*

Examples of sociological journals are the *Journal of Sociology* (*JOS*), the *American Sociological Review*, and the *British Journal of Sociology*. You should locate where the sociological journals, increasingly accessed in electronic form, are kept in your library and familiarise yourself with those to which your university library subscribes, most of which will be indexed and accessible via online journal databases, such as *Sociological Abstracts*. As a sociology student, you will undoubtedly be required to use such databases to find relevant journal articles as information sources for your assessment items. Journal databases allow you to use a range of search options to locate articles about a particular topic. (Your librarian can provide you with advice on using databases and locating journals.) You can then use the findings of these articles to support the arguments in your assignments. Before further exploring the stages of the research process, let us first consider the impact that the researcher has on this process.

The impact of the researcher

Social research is never truly objective, and sociologists influence their research through their own personal values and the assumptions that are inherent in their research paradigms and theoretical frameworks. The way in which people view the social world is referred to as their *ontological* position—the assumptions or worldview through which we seek to make sense of the world and explain social reality (Mason 1998). For example, an evolutionary psychologist might view human behaviour as being shaped by biology and would look to the biological characteristics of the individual to examine what may or may not cause a particular behaviour. Alternatively, a sociologist would probably view human behaviour as largely influenced by social structures, and to gain further insight would thus investigate social factors such as the family or the community in which an individual lives.

Values and objectivity

Research is influenced to differing degrees by the values and background of the researcher. Values are our deeply held ideals, beliefs, and customs, and often operate as taken-for-granted assumptions that guide our thinking and go unnoticed until someone with different values challenges them. Max Weber (1864–1920) argued that research should be at once 'value neutral' in that it pursues truth, and 'value relevant' in that it has direct relevance to practical values (Hammersley 2000, p. 18). Value neutrality is particularly characteristic of the **positivist** tradition, where objectivity and freedom of interference from the researcher are seen to increase the scientific accuracy of the research. While these researchers are expected to conduct research in a way that is value neutral, this is an ideal, and there is recognition that there will still be bias due to the values of the researcher (Hammersley 2000).

positivism
A contested view in sociology that social phenomena should be studied in the same way as the study of the natural world, by focusing only on observable and quantifiable events through which causal connections and universal laws can be determined.

Box 4.1: Levels of evidence

Think about a scenario where it was your responsibility to advise a policy-maker on the choice of bullying prevention program to be implemented in schools across Australia. What would you say? Which evidence would you base your advice on? There are lots of different types of studies and some are considered to be 'stronger' forms of evidence than others—hence the term 'levels of evidence'. Back to our example: in conducting your research on bullying prevention, you discover some research titled 'Best Practices for Preventing or Reducing Bullying in Schools' (Whitted & Dupper 2005). On reading it, you discover that it contains advice from experts in the field on how to prevent bullying. You also discover a report titled 'Effectiveness of Programmes to Reduce

School Bullying' (Ttofi, Farrington & Baldry 2008). This report is a systemic review of findings from a number of studies using a statistical technique known as a meta-analysis. Which one should you consider to be more reliable? Understanding 'levels of evidence' enables you to answer this question. In Australia, many researchers refer to the levels of evidence that are published by the National Health and Medical Research Council (NHMRC 2008; see <www.nhmrc.gov.au>). Systematic reviews of **randomised controlled trials (RCTs)** are placed at the top of the list as the most reliable form of evidence. This is followed by individual RCTs, retrospective cohort studies, case-control studies, and case series studies. At the bottom of the hierarchy is expert opinion. So when examining the bullying research you found, which is the item to which you would give more weight? The systematic review, of course—because it is at the top of the list. It is important to note that the NHMRC levels of evidence only apply to quantitative research and thereby exclude qualitative studies from consideration as 'evidence'—a similar schema for evaluating the strength of qualitative research is yet to eventuate.

randomised control trials (RCTs)
A research procedure commonly used in health research to evaluate the effectiveness of particular interventions, whereby participants are randomly assigned to an experimental ('trial') group or a control group (which receives a placebo or no treatment and is used for comparison).

interpretivism
A view in sociology that understanding social phenomena cannot be achieved by emulating the natural sciences, but instead requires a focus on the interpretation of people's meanings, reasons, and actions.

paradigm
A paradigm is a framework for understanding the social world. In the context of social research, a paradigm determines what aspects of the social world will be investigated, the types of research questions that will be asked, and how the results of the research will be interpreted.

At the other end of the spectrum are **interpretivist** approaches, which allow multiplicity of meaning, experience, and interpretation. Some of these researchers immerse themselves not only in the research process but also in the reporting of their research. They disclose their own position and values in relation to the research and include their own 'voice' and those of their participants in the reporting of their findings (Hertz 1997). Regardless of the level of disclosure and use of voice in the research, all researchers have different values that will impact on the research they conduct and the interpretations they make of the information they collect. The dual concerns of explanatory rigour and interpretive judgments in social research are inseparable (Gewirtz & Cribb 2006). Still, researchers' values usually fit well within the chosen sociological **paradigm** that guides their research.

Paradigms

Sociologists usually work within a particular paradigm or tradition of social research. In the natural sciences, paradigms usually move through a succession from true to false. For example, before Copernicus proposed that Earth was one of the many planets to orbit the sun, it was believed that Earth was stationary at the centre of all other planetary

(structural) functionalism
A theoretical perspective in sociology in which society is seen as consisting of many complex and interdependent parts that contribute to consensus and social stability. Prominent theorists include Durkheim, Merton, and Parsons.

feminism/feminist
A broad social and political movement based on a belief in equality of the sexes and the removal of all forms of discrimination against women. A feminist is one who makes use of, and may act upon, a body of theory that seeks to explain the subordinate position of women in society.

CrossLink: See Chapter 3 for more on structural functionalism and feminism.

movements. This change in thinking is what is known as a paradigm shift (Kuhn 1970). In the social sciences, paradigm has a slightly different meaning: it refers to the framework that affects the way in which we perceive reality and also how we respond to that perception. Examples of paradigms include positivism, **structural functionalism**, and **feminism**. These sociological paradigms change in popularity but tend not to move through the same succession from 'true' to 'false' that is observed in the natural sciences (Babbie 1998). Researchers' epistemological positions influence their alignment with a particular paradigm. Epistemology, or the study of knowledge, concerns the assumptions and criteria we use to determine whether our knowledge about the world is valid and accurate. People's epistemological position will affect what they consider to be knowledge or evidence of things in the social world. An epistemological framework also provides the principles and rules by which a researcher decides whether and how aspects of the social world can be identified and how this knowledge is shared with others (Mason 1998).

Sociology provides a plethora of explanations about the nature of the social world. These paradigms and epistemological positions are never 'right' or 'wrong', although some sociologists will argue the supremacy of a particular perspective over others. What they offer the sociologist is a particular way of looking at the world. Researchers' paradigms will ultimately guide their research design and the types of research questions that are developed. For example, researchers examining criminality within a feminist paradigm have examined the combined impact of 'liberation' and 'economic marginality' on female offending (Hunnicutt & Broidy 2004). Others have examined patterns of offending with a focus on social class differences (Dunaway et al. 2000). (To discover what these researchers found, you will have to locate and read these articles yourself.)

As you become more aware of the various sociological paradigms, you will undoubtedly decide that some make more sense and have more value than others. These decisions represent the culmination of a range of influences, including your training, your own life experiences, and your personal values. As a student of sociology, you need to understand that various and often competing paradigms exist. As a consumer of social research, you need to understand how differences in research design and sometimes even the findings of research can be affected by the paradigm within which the researcher is operating. Paradigms are also closely related to theoretical perspectives, and the following section discusses the central position of theory in the research process.

theory (social)
A theory is a statement that explains the nature of relationships between aspects of the social world.

The importance of theory

Theories are statements about the way the world is believed to work. All theories can be positioned within a particular paradigm, and therefore a researcher's values, and the paradigms that are commensurate with those values will also guide the theories that a researcher supports or examines. The previous two chapters in this textbook have provided you with a brief overview of some of the main theories within sociology. Sociologists usually end up adopting one of these theories, or a combination, as a framework for their sociological research. In the context of social research, theories provide us with expectations about the nature of relationships between **variables** in the social world. Variables are any phenomena that have measurable attributes, and the range of variables that is open for investigation is limitless—such as gender, age, class, income, and ethnicity, to name a few.

variable
Any phenomenon with measurable attributes.

atheoretical research
Research that does not use a theoretical framework as the starting point for the research.

Although theory allows findings to be generalised to a wider variety of settings (Champion 2006), it is important to note that some approaches to social research are atheoretical. **Atheoretical research** does not use theory as a framework for the research process and is exemplified in some types of evaluation research and action research. This research is usually qualitative in nature. It focuses on incorporating the participants of research to effect change. For example, action research techniques have been used to explore barriers faced by immigrant and Indigenous groups in accessing health care (Gibson et al. 2005) and immigrant women's understandings of domestic violence (Bhuyan et al. 2005). The aspect common to all action research is the inclusion of participants in a cyclic process of action and critical reflection.

Evaluation research, in simple terms, is social research conducted to assess the success or viability of a particular strategy or program. Research that assesses the success of an anti-smoking media campaign in reducing smoking (Goldman & Glantz 1998), or an assessment of the success of neighbourhood watch programs in enhancing partnerships with police (Fleming 2005) are examples of evaluation research. Although theoretical perspectives can be incorporated into this research, most evaluation research is concerned with answering practical rather than theoretical questions.

The role of the literature review in the research process

Irrespective of whether theory guides the research, sociologists need to know what other researchers have already found out about the topic and the methods they have used to carry out this research. To do this, they conduct a thorough review of the existing literature on the topic of research. When researchers review literature, they focus mainly on scholarly sources of information and these are usually contained in academic journals and books. After they have gathered all the information together, they present it in a synthesised, critical manner. It is important to realise that a literature review is not just a summary or descriptive list of previous research. There are many other sources that can provide you with detailed instruction on how to conduct and write a literature review (see Hart 1998, for example); this chapter concentrates instead on the place of the literature review in the social research process.

When researchers begin their literature review, they already have a fairly good idea of what it is that they are going to be researching. A review can have varying purposes depending on the type and stage of research. The aim of the literature review is to help the researcher refine ideas. This is particularly important for new researchers who may not be fully aware of the body of literature on a particular topic. A systematic literature review allows the researcher to gain an understanding of the current state of knowledge on their topic. The knowledge gained from the literature review will highlight which variables are important to study and what others have found when looking at the same topic.

A perfect match: Research questions and research design

Earlier in this chapter, we looked at exploratory, descriptive, and explanatory research designs. In this section, we will look at the research design process in a little more depth and examine its relationship to research questions. The types of questions a researcher attempts to answer will determine the research design.

case study
Case study research focuses on one person or group of people as the object of study. The purpose is to gain an in-depth understanding of the concepts under investigation.

deductive research
Research that begins with hypotheses based on a theoretical framework and previous empirical literature. The aim of the research process is to test the hypotheses and interpret the research findings in the context of the theory and literature on which the hypotheses were based.

inductive research
Starting with an observation about the social world, this approach then compares this observation with other observations, and eventually leads to the generation of a theory.

If the research is attempting to uncover information about large groups of people or populations, then a quantitative survey research design is likely to be the most appropriate. If the research is exploratory in nature, and is attempting to record information about individual experiences in depth, or experiences of minority groups for example, a qualitative **case study** approach using interviews may be the best research design. Quantitative research is most commonly associated with surveys and **deductive research**, and qualitative research is most commonly associated with case studies and **inductive research**. It should be noted that these are generalisations; in reality, you will see some variation in these relationships.

To compare surveys and case studies, we will consider two examples. If a researcher is interested in exploring community attitudes to domestic violence (Carlson & Pollitz Worden 2005), a small-scale case study research design will be unable to capture 'community attitudes' and a large-scale survey would be most appropriate. In this type of study, the researcher would most probably collect quantitative data. On the other hand, if a researcher is interested in children who kill other children (Asquith 1996), case studies would probably be the most appropriate approach for studying this relatively rare phenomenon. In this type of investigation, the researcher is more likely to collect qualitative information. The most important consideration is that the research design matches the research questions.

Some sociologists see the choice between qualitative and quantitative research designs as much more controversial than this. The position presented here is that the choice between quantitative and qualitative research designs depends on the questions the researcher is attempting to answer. It is also important to remember, however, that the type of research questions that the researcher will develop very much depends on the paradigm, theoretical tradition, and previous research on which the researcher is relying. For some, the theoretical foundation of their research precludes them from using a quantitative approach because they believe that reduction techniques that aggregate individuals are inappropriate, as each individual's experiences are unique. For others, the scientific paradigm within which they operate precludes them from doing in-depth case study research because there is an expectation that they will conduct large-scale surveys in an attempt to uncover universal 'truths' about populations.

While qualitative/quantitative and positivist/interpretivist debates are essentially unproductive (Miles & Huberman 1994; Weber 2004), these epistemological differences are often the basis of tension and ongoing disputes between sociologists. Increasingly, though, researchers are using mixed-method designs that incorporate both qualitative and quantitative methods into the one research project. The methodological practices within each of these traditions influence the way research is conducted at each stage of the social research process, including from whom and from how many people the researcher gathers information, the type of information that is collected, and the way in which the information is processed and presented. The following sections of this chapter consider each of these methodological procedures in turn.

Finding the people

Once a research design has been chosen and research questions have been developed, the next step is to find the people who can provide the information needed to answer the questions. First, the researcher needs to identify which group of people she or he is interested in researching. This group is known in research terms as the **population**. A population can vary depending on the topic of interest. For example, it can be as broad as all the people residing in a particular city, or people of a particular gender or ethnic group, or as narrowly defined as a class of university students, or a group of incarcerated juveniles. Researchers usually do not have the time or financial resources to talk to everyone in a population, so they talk to a smaller selection of people from the population they want to study. This is referred to as a **sample**.

There are a number of techniques that researchers can use in order to identify their sample. These techniques can be divided into **probability** and **non-probability** samples. Probability samples are based on random selection, which

population
A population is the group of people about which the researcher is interested in finding more information.

sample (probability and non-probability)
The sample is the part of the population that the researcher examines. Samples can be selected from the population using probability and non-probability techniques.

ensures that the sample is representative of the population from which it has been drawn. In order to identify a probability sample, the researcher must know all the elements in a population and must be able to employ some technique of random selection. This method of selection allows researchers to make generalisations from their sample-based research findings back to the broader population. Probability samples are also often a prerequisite for quantitative data-analysis techniques.

If random selection and generalisability to the population are not necessary or appropriate for the research, researchers use non-probability sampling techniques. Non-probability sampling techniques are used in both quantitative and qualitative research. Some common methods include:

- *snowball sampling:* asking one respondent to identify other respondents who may be able to provide information relevant to the researcher
- *convenience sampling:* using whoever is available to the researcher to participate in the research, and
- *purposive sampling:* targeting particular respondents because some characteristic they possess makes them of interest to the researcher.

The other major decision the researcher needs to make in relation to sampling is the size of the sample. A general rule of thumb for probability samples is 10 per cent of the population. Qualitative researchers using non-probability samples often use a guideline of *saturation*, where they stop adding new members to the sample when no new information is being gained. Once the sample has been identified, the researcher needs to develop a tool for collecting information from the members of the sample.

Data collection

There are many data-collection options available to a researcher. We will look at two main types: questionnaires and interviews. You are probably familiar with questionnaires and have undoubtedly filled out a questionnaire at least once.

Questionnaires allow for the collection of information from large numbers of people with relatively little time expenditure. Questionnaires are usually used in social research to collect information about people's attitudes or behaviours. The two main ways of administering a questionnaire are via a mailout to members of the sample and face to face in a particular setting, such as a classroom or a prison. They can contain closed-ended questions where the respondents have to select from a finite list of options, or open-ended questions where the respondent is given space to write a response to the question. Closed-ended questions are easier to code and analyse, but open-ended questions provide richer and sometimes unexpected information.

questionnaire
A data-collection device that includes a set of written questions for the respondent to answer.

interviews (structured and unstructured)
Interviews vary from structured to unstructured. More structured interviews tend to be associated with quantitative research, whereas unstructured interviews are more commonly associated with qualitative research.

Rich information can also be gathered using interviews. **Interviews** can vary in nature from being very **unstructured** and taking the form of a natural conversation to being so **structured** that they are virtually the verbal administration of a questionnaire with closed-ended questions. Unstructured interviews require the researcher to have good communication skills and the ability to ask questions that will elicit the information needed for the research. Interviewing is very demanding in terms of the time and energy taken to conduct the interview, and to collate and process the information obtained.

What does it all mean? Analysis, interpretation, and reporting

It is all well and good to go out and collect masses of data, but until the information is collated, analysed, and interpreted it is meaningless. In this section we will look briefly at different techniques that researchers use to analyse and interpret their data. The final part of this section describes the standard format of an academic journal article. This quick overview will assist you in understanding how and where the various aspects of the social research process are reported within an article.

Analysis and interpretation

The analysis techniques used by a researcher, like everything else in the research process, are very much dependent on the paradigm and theoretical tradition within which the researcher is working. Those who have conducted quantitative research are going to have predominantly numerical data that need to be systematically coded and summarised. In order to do this, the data first need to be 'cleaned' (of any errors) and coded so that they can be entered into a dataset. A dataset is usually structured so that each line of information relates to an individual and each column of data relates to a variable. The dataset is usually created in a computerised statistical analysis program. Those commonly used by social researchers are SPSS (Statistical Package for the Social Sciences), SAS statistical software, and Stata. If you go on to study statistics, you will no doubt learn how to use one or more of these programs to analyse data.

Quantitative techniques, although at times complementary to qualitative techniques, are very different from those used by researchers operating within a qualitative research paradigm. The data collected by qualitative researchers tend to be textual. Such data come in many forms, including interview transcripts, field notes, personal diaries, and photographs. There are many techniques that can be employed in the analysis of qualitative data; examples include thematic coding and pile sorts. Often this analysis takes place throughout the data-collection process rather than after all the data have been collected. As with quantitative analysis, there are computer programs that can be used to analyse qualitative data. Some researchers prefer to code their data using a basic word-processing program. A more sophisticated and commonly used Australian program is Nvivo, and students studying qualitative research methods often learn to use this program.

Irrespective of whether the analysis is quantitative or qualitative in nature, the findings have little value unless they are interpreted and reported in the context of the theoretical framework and previous findings on the topic. In interpreting their results, researchers discuss what the findings mean for the theoretical framework in which they are positioned and how their results compare with those studies that have also examined the same topic. The interpretation of results also involves the researcher identifying the limitations of their research and what they think needs to be done in the future by researchers examining the same topic.

Reporting

Once data have been collated, analysed, and interpreted, they need to be presented in a report or journal article. One of the key reasons for doing this is to ensure that the knowledge the researcher has gathered is shared with other sociologists and has the opportunity to feed into and guide future research. Depending on the methodologies they have employed, researchers may use a variety of formats to report their research. What follows is a description of a standard structure used for reporting research. You will see this format in many of the empirical journal articles that you read.

The *introduction* provides a brief history and background to the research. The rationale and purpose of the study are made clear in the introduction; therefore, by reading it you should know what the study is about and why the researchers think the topic is important. This is followed by the *literature review*, which contains a synthesised and critical summary of the theoretical framework and previous empirical research on the topic and closely related topics. In the literature review, the researcher defines the parameters of the research and demonstrates how their research builds on previous empirical knowledge. This background material leads to logically deduced research questions and, where applicable, hypotheses that spell out the expectations for the relationships between variables. Once this background information has been documented, the methods the researcher has used in their own research are reported.

The *methodology* section of the paper describes the steps the researchers took to collect and analyse their data. This includes describing the sampling procedure, characteristics of the sample, and measures used. The methodology section also includes details of the data-collection techniques, how the data were collated, and the data-analysis techniques used. Reporting the methodology is important because it allows the consumer of the research to make determinations about the quality of the research practices, as well as the subsequent validity and reliability of the results. It also allows future researchers examining the same topic to see what has been done previously and to replicate or extend the research.

The methodology is usually followed by a summary of the *results*. The results section does not include all the information that was collected; instead, it provides summary tables of data, selected sections of text, quotations from interviews, or other summary data that may be related to the research questions. In qualitative studies, the discussion of the results is usually interwoven with the presentation of the summary data, but in quantitative research the *discussion* of the results usually appears in a new section. The discussion focuses on interpreting the results of the research in the context of the theoretical and empirical information presented in the literature review. The discussion is also where the researcher highlights the limitations of the research and the implications of these limitations for the findings. The research report usually finishes with a summary or *conclusion* that answers the research questions asked by the researcher and also discusses directions for future research.

SOCIOLOGY
SPOTLIGHT

4.1: Understanding common statistical tests reported in journals

Sociologists who collect quantitative data can end up with large datasets of numerical informa-tion. To make sense of the information they have collected, they use statistical procedures to analyse their data. To help you interpret the results sections of quantitative journal articles you read while studying sociology, we have provided an explanation of commonly used statistical procedures reported by social scientists:

- *Measures of association* tell us how strongly one variable is related to another. They also tell us the direction of the relationship—whether, as the value of one goes up, the value of the other goes up (positive association) or down (negative association). The most common measure of association is a correlation coefficient. Generally, measures of association range from zero to one. Zero means there is no association between the variables and a value of one means there is a perfect association.

- *Statistical significance (p value)* refers to how likely it is that an event or association would occur according to chance. Common levels of significance are 5 per cent and 1 per cent. If you read 'p<.05' it means that the result has a 95 per cent chance of being true. It is important to note that, when using large samples, relationships that are statistically significant should be inter-preted with caution. Something that is highly significant is not necessarily highly important.

- *Chi-square* is one of the most common tests used with *categorical data* (i.e. data grouped in categories such as 'religion' or 'education'). It tests whether two variables are independent or related. If a chi-square value is significant, it indicates that there is a statistically significant relationship between the two variables.

- The *t-test* is a test that assesses whether the arithmetic means of two groups are statistically different from each other. The significance value of a *t*-test reports a probability that the two sample means are greater than would be expected by chance.

- *Analysis of variance (ANOVA)* is used to test hypotheses about differences between two or more means. ANOVA statistically compares the group means, testing whether the means of the groups are different enough not to have occurred by chance.

- *Multiple regression (R^2)* examines the relationship between several independent variables and a dependent variable. The R^2 value tells you how much variation is explained by the regression equation or, put differently, how well the model fits the data. The R^2 value varies between one and zero and a value close to zero indicates the independent variables are not doing a good job of predicting the dependent variable—that is, the model is not a good fit for the data.

Ethics and research

Sociologists, like all researchers, should never conduct themselves in a way that could harm the people they are researching. Therefore, researchers must always consider the ethical implications of the research that they propose. Australian research involving human subjects needs to be conducted in a manner that complies with the National Health and Medical Research Council (NHMRC) ethical guidelines (NHMRC 2007). These guidelines are interpreted within universities by human research ethics committees (HRECs), whose purpose is to ensure that research meets ethical standards. There is not always agreement regarding the content of ethical guidelines, the role of HRECs in the research process, or HRECs' interpretations of ethical guidelines (Israel 2004; TASA 2005; van den Hoonaard 2001).

The perceived necessity of HRECs originates in part from the many cases of harm that researchers have caused in the absence of ethics committees. It is now almost taken for granted that research must be conducted in an ethically responsible way, but in the 1970s there was still debate about whether it may in fact be necessary or appropriate to conduct unethical research, and discussion regarding whether the findings of unethical research should be published in academic journals (discussed in DeBakey 1974). Nor is unethical research altogether a thing of the past. One study exploring the practices of researchers from both the natural and social sciences suggests that questionable research practices are quite widespread (discussed in Martinson, Anderson & de Vries 2005).

In the name of science, cancer patients have been exposed to extreme doses of radiation (discussed in Stephens 2002), pregnant women have been exposed to radiation (discussed in Sea 1994), mentally disabled boys have been fed radioactive ions in their breakfast cereal and infected with hepatitis (discussed in Rothman & Rothman 1984), prisoners have been used to test anything from cosmetics to chemical weapons (discussed in Hornblum 1998), and poor black men have had treatment for syphilis withheld (discussed in Jones 1993; Reverby 2000). Still, this type of unethical research is not always recognised as such (discussed in Kmietowicz 1998). The similarity among most unethical research is that the victims are members of marginalised groups in society who are least able to protect themselves. The research in these examples was not undertaken by rogue scientists; rather, it was conducted and funded by universities and government departments. Unfortunately, social scientists are equally guilty of conducting unethical research.

The work by Laud Humphreys discussed at the beginning of this chapter is an excellent example of the type of research that was able to be conducted in the absence of HRECs. Other examples include Stanley Milgram's (1963) electric shock experiments on obedience to authority, and the Stanford University Prison Experiment on the dehumanising effect of the prison environment (Haney, Banks & Zimbardo 1973). The other way in which researchers can act in unethical ways is to publish fraudulent research results by fabricating data and/or results. Stem cell research data have been fabricated in South Korea (see Hwang et al. 2004), oral cancer data were fabricated in Norway (see Sudbø 2005), and obesity research data have been fabricated in the United States (see Poehlman, Toth & Gardner 1995). These studies were all reviewed by experts and published in the most prestigious journals. While all of these examples have been discovered, there are undoubtedly others that have not. The onus is always on the individual researcher to act in an ethical manner.

Conclusion

Now that you have read this chapter, you will have a basic understanding of what sociologists do when they undertake social research. Social research is influenced by the values of the researcher, the paradigm and theoretical framework within which the research is positioned, and the investigations that other social researchers have previously conducted on the topic. Research questions guide research and, depending on the approach adopted, these will be derived from observations of the social world or theory and previous research.

Social researchers must also consider whom they are going to research, and which sampling procedures and data-collection methods they are going to use to find these people and obtain information from them. Two common methods of data collection examined in this chapter were questionnaires and interviews. Once the data are collected, the researchers must then analyse and interpret the information they have collected.

The final stage of the social research process is reporting the findings. It is crucial that sociologists tell each other about their research, and to do this they publish their findings as articles in peer-reviewed academic journals. As a student of sociology, you need to be able to locate, read, and understand these journal articles. This chapter has provided you with a background to the social research process and information on what is contained in a research article so that you can now go forth and use social research with confidence.

Summary of main points

▶ Sociologists study the social world. Social research is guided by the values of the researcher, theoretical traditions, and previous empirical research.

▶ There is considerable debate among sociologists regarding qualitative and quantitative approaches to research. It is important to consider which approach is best for the research questions under investigation.

▶ Depending on the requirements of the research, people are selected from populations using either probability or non-probability sampling techniques.

- ▶ Information is gathered in many ways, but the most common are questionnaires and interviews.
- ▶ Qualitative data are usually analysed using coding techniques and quantitative data are usually analysed using statistical techniques.
- ▶ Research must be conducted in an ethical manner. In Australia, HRECs provide guidance on the ethical conduct of researchers working with human subjects.

SOCIOLOGICAL **REFLECTION**

4.1 Doing your own social research

Does the thought of doing your own social research seem exciting? Most people are budding social researchers, particularly sociology students. That is because they are interested in finding out more about why the social world is the way it is. As you now understand from reading this chapter, true social science research has a number of set procedures that need to be followed. To become a social researcher, you will have to study research methods classes in your degree at university. Until then, you can begin to develop research questions in relation to the topics you study in your courses and the things you observe in the world around you.

Activity 4.1

(a) On a sheet of paper, write down some of the things that you have observed in the world around you. Examples of observations include: the proportion of male to female police officers; the socioeconomic backgrounds of university students; or the way in which the media construct 'ethnicity' and 'youth crime'.

(b) For each of the observations you have identified, think back to the theories presented in the previous chapters and consider what contribution they could make to understanding your observation.

(c) Have a go at developing some research questions based on your observation. What needs to be researched and what questions need to be asked to better understand what you have observed?

(d) What types of information need to be collected to answer these research questions? Where are you going to go to collect this information? From whom are you going to collect this information?

Discussion questions

4.1 Can social research be truly value free? In what ways might the paradigm that guides the researcher influence the social research process?

4.2 What are your core values? How do they differ from those of other people in your class, in your street, and in your city? In what ways do you think your values could affect the social research that you conducted?

4.3 What are the differences between qualitative and quantitative research? Do you think the two approaches are incompatible?

4.4 Can you think of an example of a quantitative research project that you would like to conduct? What about a qualitative research project?

4.5 Which type of research do you think would be easier to conduct: a questionnaire-based survey of 1000 households in a city or in-depth interviews with 50 home owners in the same city. What do you think would be the benefits and drawbacks of each data-collection technique?

4.6 To what extent do you think human research ethics committees (HRECs) have a role to play in the research process? Why? Are there any instances where the harm to participants outweighs the benefits to society? What would you do if an HREC prevented you from conducting the research that you wanted to do?

Further reading

Agresti, A. & Finlay, B. 2009, *Statistical Methods for the Social Sciences*, 4th edn, Prentice Hall, Upper Saddle River, NJ.

Babbie, E. 2007, *The Practice of Social Research*, 11th edn, Wadsworth, Belmont, CA.

Israel, M. & Hay, I. 2006, *Research Ethics for Social Scientists: Between Ethical Conduct and Regulatory Compliance*, Sage, London.

Kellehear, A. 1993, *The Unobtrusive Researcher: A Guide to Methods*, Allen & Unwin, Sydney.

Neuman, W.L. 2006, *Social Research Methods: Qualitative and Quantitative Approaches*, 6th edn, Pearson/Allyn and Bacon, Boston.

Walter, M. (ed.) 2006, *Social Research Methods: An Australian Perspective*, Oxford University Press, Melbourne.

Websites

- Social Research Methods: <www.socialresearchmethods.net>. A resource for information on all aspects of the social research process. Contains a great tool for deciding what type of analysis to undertake, as well as online tutorials.
- Laud Humphreys: <www.glbtq.com/social-sciences/humphreys_1.html>. Read more about Laud Humphreys' background and research on this online *Encyclopedia of Gay, Lesbian, Bisexual, Transgender, and Queer Culture*.
- World Values Survey: <www.worldvaluessurvey.org>. This website contains research using large-scale surveys of people's values around the world.

- NHMRC Ethical Guidelines: <www.nhmrc.gov.au/health_ethics/research/index.htm>. This is the government website of the NHMRC and provides guidelines on how to conduct ethical research.
- Stanford Prison Experiment: <www.stanford.edu/dept/news/pr/97/970108 prisonexp.html>. The person responsible for calling a stop to the Stanford Prison Experiment discusses the ethical issues involved in social research of this nature.
- The lie of the Stanford Prison Experiment: <www.stanforddaily.com/cgi-bin/?p=1017752>. This short article by Carlo Prescott outlines his involvement in the project as an informant regarding prison practices. He argues that the 'guards' in the Stanford Experiment did not invent the punishments, but were instructed by the experimenters on how to behave.
- TASA Ethical Guidelines: <www.tasa.org.au/ethical-guidelines>. This web page contains the ethical guidelines to which all members of The Australian Sociological Association are expected to adhere.

Films/documentaries

- *Quiet Rage: The Stanford Prison Study*, 1991, documentary, directed by K. Musen, Insight Media. This film includes flashback footage taken during the experiment in 1971 as well as interviews with the subjects of the experiment conducted twenty years later. Unlike earlier versions of documentary footage on this study, *Quiet Rage* discusses the very serious ethical implications of this research and describes the way in which the researchers became blind to the harm they were causing. Most university libraries keep a copy of this film in their collections.
- *Obedience: A Re-enactment*, 1996, documentary, produced by S. Milgram, San Diego State University Department of Telecommunications and Film. This film presents segments from a re-enactment of Stanley Milgram's classic experiment on obedience to authority. It raises questions about the ethics of psychological experimentation with human subjects.

Visit the *Public Sociology* book website to access topical case studies, weblinks, YouTube clips, and extra readings.

References

Asquith, S. 1996, 'When children kill children: The search for justice', *Childhood*, vol. 3, no. 1, pp. 99–116.

Babbie, E. 1998, *The Practice of Social Research*, 8th edn, Wadsworth, Belmont, CA.

Berry, D.M. 2004, 'Internet research: Privacy, ethics and alienation—an open source approach', *Internet Research*, vol. 14, no. 4, pp. 323–32.

Bhuyan, R., Mell, M., Senturia, K., Sullivan, M. & Shiu-Thornton, S. 2005, '"Women must endure according to their karma": Cambodian immigrant women talk about domestic violence', *Journal of Interpersonal Violence*, vol. 20, no. 8, pp. 902–21.

Carlson, B.E. & Pollitz Worden, A. 2005, 'Attitudes and beliefs about domestic violence: Results of a public opinion survey', *Journal of Interpersonal Violence*, vol. 20, no. 10, pp. 1197–1218.

Champion, D.J. 2006, *Research Methods for Criminal Justice and Criminology*, 3rd edn, Pearson Prentice Hall, Upper Saddle River, NJ.

DeBakey, L. 1974, 'Ethically questionable data: Publish or reject?', *Clinical Research*, vol. 22, no. 3, pp. 113–21.

Dunaway, R.G., Cullen, F.T., Burton, V.S. & Evans, T.D. 2000, 'The myth of social class and crime revisited: An examination of class and adult criminality', *Criminology*, vol. 38, no. 2, pp. 589–632.

Fleming, J. 2005, *'Working Together': Neighbourhood Watch, Reassurance Policing and the Potential of Partnerships*, Trends and Issues in Crime and Criminal Justice No. 303, Australian Institute of Criminology, Canberra.

Gewirtz, S. & Cribb, A. 2006, 'What to do about values in social research: The case for ethical reflexivity in the sociology of education', *British Journal of Sociology of Education*, vol. 27, no. 2, pp. 141–55.

Gibson, N., Cave, A., Doering, D., Ortiz, L. & Harms, P. 2005, 'Socio-cultural factors influencing prevention and treatment of tuberculosis in immigrant and aboriginal communities in Canada', *Social Science and Medicine*, vol. 61, no. 5, pp. 931–42.

Goldman, L.K. & Glantz, S.A. 1998, 'Evaluation of antismoking advertising campaigns [Special Communications]', *Journal of the American Medical Association*, vol. 279, no. 10, pp. 772–7.

Hammersley, M. 2000, *Taking Sides in Social Research: Essays on Partisanship and Bias*, Routledge, London.

Haney, C., Banks, C. & Zimbardo, P.G. 1973, 'Interpersonal dynamics in a simulated prison', *International Journal of Criminology and Penology*, vol. 1, pp. 69–97.

Hart, C. 1998, *Doing a Literature Review: Releasing the Social Science Research Imagination*, Sage, London.

Hertz, R. (ed.) 1997, *Reflexivity and Voice*, Sage, Thousand Oaks, CA.

Hornblum, A.M. 1998, *Acres of Skin: Human Experiments at Holmesburg Prison—A Story of Abuse and Exploitation in the Name of Medical Science*, Routledge, New York.

Humphreys, L. 1970, *Tearoom Trade: Impersonal Sex in Public Places*, Aldine, Chicago.

Hunnicutt, G. & Broidy, L.M. 2004, 'Liberation and economic marginalization: A reformulation and test of (formerly?) competing models', *Journal of Research in Crime and Delinquency*, vol. 41, no. 2, pp. 130–55.

Hwang, Woo Suk, Young June Ryu, Jong Hyuk Park, Eul Soon Park, Eu Gene Lee,

Ja Min Koo, Hyun Yong Jeon, Byeong Chun Lee, Sung Keun Kang, Sun Jong Kim, Curie Ahn, Jung Hye Hwang, Ky Young Park, Cibelli, J.B. & Shin Yong Moon 2004. 'Evidence of a pluripotent human embryonic stem cell line derived from a cloned blastocyst', *Science*, vol. 303, pp. 1669–74.

Israel, M. 2004, *Ethics and the Governance of Criminological Research in Australia*, New South Wales Bureau of Crime Statistics and Research, <www.lawlink.nsw.gov.au/bocsar1. nsf/files/r55.pdf/$file/r55.pdf> (accessed 12 June 2006).

Jones, J.H. 1993, *Bad Blood: The Tuskegee Syphilis Experiment*, Free Press, New York.

Kmietowicz, Z. 1998, 'MRC cleared of unethical research practices', *British Medical Journal*, vol. 316, p. 1625.

Kuhn, T. 1970, *The Structure of Scientific Revolutions*, University of Chicago Press, Chicago.

Martinson, B.C., Anderson, M.S. & de Vries, R. 2005, 'Scientists behaving badly', *Nature*, vol. 435, no. 7043, pp. 737–8.

Mason, J. 1998, *Qualitative Researching*, Sage, London.

Miles, M.B. & Huberman, A.M. 1994, *Qualitative Data Analysis: An Expanded Sourcebook*, Sage, Thousand Oaks, CA.

Milgram, S. 1963, 'Behavioral study of obedience', *Journal of Abnormal and Social Psychology*, vol. 67, pp. 371–8.

National Health and Medical Research Council (NHMRC) 2007, *National Statement on Ethical Conduct in Human Research*, National Health and Medical Research Council, <www.nhmrc.gov.au/guidelines/ethics/human_research/index.htm> (accessed 31 August 2009).

—— 2008, *NHMRC Additional Levels of Evidence and Grades for Recommendations for Developers of Guidelines: STAGE 2 Consultation: Early 2008–End June 2009*, National Health and Medical Research Council, Canberra, <www.nhmrc.gov.au/guidelines/_files/ Stage%202%20Consultation%20Levels%20and%20Grades.pdf> (accessed 31 August 2009).

Poehlman, Eric T., Toth, M.J. & Gardner, A.W. 1995, 'Changes in energy balance and body composition at menopause: A controlled longitudinal study', *Annals of Internal Medicine*, vol. 123, pp. 673–5.

Reverby, S.M. (ed.) 2000, *Tuskegee's Truths: Rethinking the Tuskegee Syphilis Study*, University of North Carolina Press, Chapel Hill, NC.

Rothman, S.M. & Rothman, D. 1984, *The Willowbrook Wars*, Harper & Row, New York.

Sea, G. 1994, 'The radiation story no one would touch', *Columbia Journalism Review*, <http://archives.cjr.org/year/94/2/radiation.asp> (accessed 12 June 2006).

Sieber, J. 1977, *Laud Humphreys and the Tearoom Sex Study*, University of Missouri-Columbia, <http://web.missouri.edu/~philwb/Laud.html> (accessed 12 June 2006).

Stephens, M. 2002, *The Treatment: The Story of Those Who Died in the Cincinnati Radiation Tests*, Duke University Press, Durham, NC.

Sudbø, J. 2005. 'Non-steroidal anti-inflammatory drugs and the risk of oral cancer: A nested case-control study', *Lancet*, vol. 366, pp. 1359–66.

TASA 2005, *Submission to the Review of the National Statement on Ethical Conduct in Research Involving Humans (1999)*, The Australian Sociological Association, Brisbane.

Ttofi, M.M., Farrington, D.P. & Baldry, A. 2008, *Effectiveness of Programmes to Reduce School Bullying*, Brå—The Swedish National Council for Crime Prevention, Stockholm.

van den Hoonaard, W.C. 2001, 'Is research-ethics review a moral panic?', *The Canadian Review of Sociology and Anthropology*, vol. 38, no. 1, pp. 19–36.

Weber, R. 2004, 'The rhetoric of positivism versus interpretivism: A personal view—editor's comments', *MIS Quarterly*, vol. 28, no. 1, pp. iii–xii.

Whitted, K.S. and Dupper, D.R. 2005, 'Best practices for preventing or reducing bullying in schools', *Children and Schools*, vol. 27, pp. 167–75.

Module 2
Social identities

In this module, we turn our attention to some of the major social experiences that influence the person we become in life. Chapters consider the latest developments in the long-running 'nature versus nurture' debate, the rise and impact of youth culture, the significant changes to family life in Australia in recent decades, the increasing importance of consumption-based lifestyles, the central role of sport in Australian culture, and notions of hybrid identities in the context of multicultural Australia.

The module contains the following chapters:

5 Socialisation and the new genetics

6 Youth transitions and youth culture

7 Families and intimate relationships

8 Consumption and lifestyles

9 Sporting life

10 Hybrid identities in a globalised world

CHAPTER 5

Socialisation and the new genetics

Marilyn Poole

Finding out about yourself: how much do genes count?

Are you curious about the future? Would you like to know whether you are likely to develop Alzheimer's disease, or find out your risks of developing cancer, schizophrenia, rheumatoid arthritis, or diabetes? Predictive direct-to-the-consumer gene-testing services or personal genomics are relatively cheap, and it is easy for the customer to provide a DNA sample (usually saliva) for analysis. The gene-testing service analyses the sample and provides a report on conditions and traits for which there are genetic associations based on 'a series of risk assessments keyed to the findings in the most current scientific literature' (Reilly 2008, p. 275).

Personal genomics are causing a great deal of controversy. There is concern that some laboratories are unregulated, that they may not have adequate facilities, and that the results they provide are of debatable quality. There is a view among some health professionals that direct-to-the-consumer gene testing offers little of value and that it can potentially cause anxiety and harm.

On the other hand, individuals feel empowered by gaining knowledge about their own potential health risks and may make lifestyle changes as a result (Reilly 2008, p. 277). For example, if you carry the HNPCC gene variant, you have a high lifetime risk of developing colorectal (colon or bowel) cancer. If so, you might consider initiating screening processes before you develop symptoms. If you carry two copies of the gene variant ApoE4, you may be susceptible to late-onset Alzheimer's disease (Reilly 2008, p. 276). This information might not seem terribly relevant if you are in your twenties and have a lifetime ahead of you, but if you are in your sixties or seventies it might make you consider putting your financial affairs in order, taking that long trip you have always planned, or making a will.

There is little doubt that genetic factors are important, but genes are not destiny—we should not forget the interaction between genes and the environment. For example, heart disease and diabetes are a result of the complex interactions between multiple genes, environmental factors, and lifestyle factors such as diet and exercise.

Introduction

Socialisation is the process through which we learn to fit into society. Socialisation begins at birth and continues throughout our lives. Through the socialisation process,

ms

…nared expectations of how people ought to behave or act. They can take the form of laws, regulations, guidelines, conventions, expectations, understandings, or other rules.

culture

The values, assumptions, and beliefs shared by a group of people that influence the behaviour of group members.

agency

The ability of people, individually and collectively, to influence their own lives and the society in which they live.

social identity

The idea that people develop an identity, an understanding of themselves, that is conditioned by social processes and becomes key to their own understanding of themselves and how others see them—for example, as an environmentalist, a committed Christian, a *feminist*, an Australian, and so on.

late modernity (or high modernity)

A period reached towards the end of the twentieth century that refers to the advanced state of industrialisation and capitalism.

we learn the **norms** or rules of society and the patterns of our **culture**; we internalise society's values, and play out a variety of social roles in life. It enables us to fit into social groups and make adjustments to new situations. Learning to become a member of society is not a one-way process. While we are shaped and moulded by our social environment, in turn we interpret and give meaning to our environment. We have what is termed **agency**. We do not simply replicate our social roles but rather redefine them. Socialisation is one of the means by which cultural values are transmitted and reproduced across the generations, and it enables these values to continue over a period of time.

Socialisation plays a major role in shaping our identities. The concept of identity has become a very important one in sociology. Our identity is how we see ourselves, how we define ourselves, and how others see us. 'Identity is about belonging, about what you have in common with some people and what differentiates you from others' (Weeks 1991, p. 88). We might see ourselves as a student, Asian, wife, Catholic, footballer, and so on. These are all social markers of who we are. Socialisation plays a part in forming our identities through our interactions within our families or with friends, at school, in workplaces, or during leisure activities. **Social identities** often 'have a collective dimension. They mark the ways that individuals are "the same" as others' (Giddens 2001, p. 29). As Anthony Giddens notes, shared identities are based on common goals or interests, such as those shared by the supporters of social or political movements such as Republicans, environmentalists, or unionists.

In pre-modern times, identities tended to be fixed and integrated into the community. Identity was defined by markers like religion, social class, and occupation. Today, in **late modernity**, there is an emphasis on individualism and we are faced with many choices (usually based on lifestyle) about how to build a personal identity.

Nature and nurture: How we become who we are

How do we become who we are? Human babies are helpless at birth. So how do we develop as individuals? Is the development of our personality and our behaviour due to *nature*? Or should we attribute these things to *nurture* and our social environment? There are no simple answers to these questions, and for years the relative importance of nature or nurture in human development has been the subject of intense and sometimes acrimonious debate.

One of the major themes of this chapter is what it means to be a human being. This is not a new question, but one that has been debated for centuries, and this seems a particularly good time to revisit the issue. The Human Genome Project was completed in 2003 and since then advances in genetics and molecular biology have been rapid. This chapter will address the increasingly prominent role given to our biology, specifically our genes and **DNA** (deoxyribonucleic acid). Many of our individual characteristics are increasingly being explained by our genetic inheritance. Although many of these explanations are hotly debated, evidence has nevertheless been found to support claims for the genetic basis of characteristics such as intelligence, musical talent, sporting prowess, health, and aggression (Hinchliffe & Woodward 2000).

DNA (deoxyribonucleic acid)
The molecule within cells that transmits hereditary information.

In *On the Origin of Species by Means of Natural Selection*, Charles Darwin (1859) argued that each species evolves over many generations during which genetic variations occur. These variations can be passed down from one generation to the next by means of heredity. Through a process of 'natural selection' that acts as a kind of filter, those biological traits that enhance survival of the species are passed down the generations. Classical Darwinian theory described how organisms adapt to their environment, gradually developing new traits, and evolving into new species. Traits that foster survival and enhance reproduction are said to be *adaptive* (Lippa 2002). In 1865, Gregor Mendel 'turned the study of the way traits are inherited into a science' (Pilnick 2002, p. 8). Following Mendel's work, genetic science began to develop, although it was not until 1909 'that the term *gene* was coined to describe Mendelian units of heredity' (Pilnick 2002, pp. 9–10).

Herbert Spencer (1961) was also interested in evolution, defining 'the study of Sociology as the study of Evolution in its most complex form' (cited in Ritzer & Goodman 2004, p. 112). He formed a viewpoint of 'the survival of the fittest', also referred to as **social Darwinism**, as an explanation of individual and social progress rather than how 'living things adapt to an ecological niche' (Pinker 2002, p. 15).

social Darwinism
The application of evolutionary laws of natural selection to human societies to 'explain' social processes and behaviours. Spencer coined the term 'survival of the fittest' (often misattributed to Darwin) to describe how Darwin's ideas about natural selection in nature can be used to explain social processes and behaviours.

Francis Galton, Charles Darwin's cousin and friend, was influenced by Darwin's theories. Galton applied the principles of agricultural breeding to humans and suggested that evolution needed some kind of helping hand by discouraging less fit individuals from breeding, a policy he named 'eugenics' in 1883 (Pinker 2002, p. 16). In fact, it was Galton himself who coined the alliteration 'nature and nurture', the saying that has fuelled debate for well over a century: 'The phrase "nature and nurture" is a convenient jingle of words, for it separates under two distinct heads the innumerable elements of which personality is composed' (Galton 1874, p. 12).

The influence of Galton's ideas was widespread. In the first decades of the twentieth century, laws were passed in a number of countries that called for the involuntary sterilisation of 'delinquents' or the 'feeble-minded'. Eugenics was only really questioned when the policies of the National Socialist Party in Germany began in the 1930s and culminated in the murder of thousands of Jews, Gypsies, homosexuals, and other so-called 'undesirables' in Nazi Germany and in German-occupied Europe (Pilnick 2002). Since the Holocaust, there has been a sense of revulsion towards theories of human nature that seek to explain and justify racism, sexual differences, and social inequalities in society, in biological terms.

Still, the concept and discourse of eugenics remain. Couples facing the information that their offspring have a high risk of inheriting a severe genetic disorder may well take up the option of pre-implantation genetic diagnosis. The couple can use in-vitro fertilisation (IVF) techniques to create embryos and then use genetic testing to ascertain which of them are free of the disease in question. Some children are conceived deliberately so that they can be bone-marrow donors to existing siblings who are seriously ill; these babies are popularly known as 'saviour children' (Reilly 2008, p. xv).

There seem to be good reasons why social scientists should distrust biological explanations of human behaviour. Simon Williams, Lynda Birke, and Gillian Bendelow (2003, p. 2) suggest that biological explanations have 'too often served dubious ends: called upon to legitimate inequalities and to limit freedoms. So why invoke the biological, we might ask? Surely social and cultural change outstrips biological evolution by far?'

The case for nature

Why should we invoke the biological in order to explain who we are? Darwin accumulated a great deal of evidence from his expeditions and 'from discussions with domestic animal breeders in order to develop his ideas of evolution through selection' (Hinchliffe & Woodward 2000, p. 13), but it was not until the mid-twentieth century that important evidence on inheritance was provided. In 1952, it was established that genes were made of DNA, and in 1953 Francis Crick and James Watson discovered the double-helix structure of DNA, a basic structure held by all organisms (Pilnick 2002). The genetic material in all humans is 99.9 per cent identical but that tiny difference of one-tenth of 1 per cent of DNA accounts for the differences between individuals, which are larger than those between groups. We know that people who share the same ancestry are likely to have genes more similar to each other than to those who are not related. For example, the gene linked to Tay Sachs disease has been identified in Ashkenazi Jews. We also know that, when looking at the medical history of families, certain people can be identified as being likely to develop heart disease, some cancers, and diabetes; however, these diseases are not always the product of a single gene, nor of the interaction of multiple genes; rather, they represent a complex combination of genetic factors, lifestyle choices, and the environment.

Genes are inherited from both parents; however, children from the same family inherit a different mix of genes. It was considered that the answer to questions about the importance of heredity and environment might lie with the study of identical twins.

Identical twins—also known as monozygotic (MZ) twins—are always the same sex and share an identical genetic inheritance. Since MZ twins share the same genetic background, any differences in their behaviour, intelligence, or other characteristics might be attributed to environmental and social factors. Studies were attempted on those identical twins who had been separated at birth, but this proved rather limiting due to the research population being rather small (Pilnick 2002). More commonly, MZ twins have been compared with non-identical, dizygotic (DZ) twins. Twin studies tend to give rather similar results: '[i]dentical twins reared apart are highly similar; identical twins reared together are more similar than non-identical (DZ) twins reared together, biological siblings are far more similar than adoptive siblings' (Pinker 2002, p. 374).

While this seems to support the case for heredity, interestingly, twin studies do give us insights into the effects of environment. For example, there is the shared environment of parents and their children: our homes, grandparents, and neighbourhoods. There is also the unique environment of each person—who has perhaps suffered an illness or accident, did not get along so well at school, or had a different set of friends (Pinker 2002). Taking all this into account, the findings are that 'identical twins are no more similar than one would expect from the effects of their shared genes' (Pinker 2002, p. 379). In other words, the unique environment that each twin experiences has a significant impact, over and above their shared environment and their biological sameness.

The concept of the genetic self

The concept of a person as an individual is increasingly being defined in terms of their genetic makeup—their 'genetic self' (Petersen & Bunton 2002, p. 13). Supporters of the 'new genetics' argue that the reductionism present in earlier biological determinist arguments has been superseded, that today the interplay of genetics and the environment is taken very seriously (Kerr 2004). Others, such as Alison Pilnick (2002, p. 36), disagree and point out that the major advances in genetic science at the end of the twentieth century have made the gene a kind of 'cultural icon and has given rise to genetic essentialism, where individuals and their traits and characteristics are reduced to genes'.

The Human Genome Project identified the 30 000 genes that make up human DNA. Diagnostic gene testing is becoming common for a range of diseases, as are predictive self-administered direct-to-the-consumer DNA kits that test for various conditions or traits ranging from baldness to blindness. Advances are being made in pharmacogenomics (which studies how an individual's genetic inheritance affects responses to drug therapy) in order to develop personalised therapeutic drugs rather than the current 'one size fits all', thus making the treatment of diseases much more effective.

The availability of information on our genetic makeup presents both individuals and society with problems. Let us consider for a moment the concept of 'private troubles' and 'public issues' in C. Wright Mills' *The Sociological Imagination* (1959). If we have information about genetic conditions that predispose people to certain kinds of hereditary breast or ovarian cancer (such as those associated with the inherited gene mutations BRCAI and BRCA2), or to Huntington's disease, or sickle-cell conditions, what do we do? What decisions do we make? In early 2009, the first British baby genetically screened as an embryo to be free of the gene BRCAI (that renders a person highly susceptible to breast cancer) was born (Quinn 2009). If we can free babies from heredity conditions such as cystic fibrosis or Huntington's disease, should we go down the route of embryonic screening? Another example to consider is the HNPCC (heredity nonpolyposis colorectal cancer) gene mutation (Vasen et al. 1999). Although people carrying this gene account for a small percentage of all colorectal cancer cases, those who do carry it have a high lifetime probability of developing colorectal cancer. Should genetic testing be carried out on people with a family history of colorectal cancer? What other screening measures should be put into place? What decisions should be made by individuals, insurance companies, or governments in the case of known inherited risk factors?

Prenatal screening and testing present other dilemmas. It is routine for pregnant women to have at least one ultrasound scan. Serum testing at Weeks 15 to 18 of the pregnancy may be used to estimate the risk of foetal abnormalities such as Down syndrome and spina bifida. Alison Pilnick (2002, p. 72) comments that 'prenatal testing fundamentally involves contested choices and rights. At the forefront of these are: a woman's right to choose; the civil rights of people with disabilities; the postulated rights of the unborn child; and the rights of the individual versus the rights of society.'

Twin studies have provided us with some interesting ideas about the differential effects of genes and the environment. Take as an example the case of schizophrenia. Until the 1960s, schizophrenia was thought to be environmental in origin and various theories were put forward, many of them blaming mothers and poor parenting for its onset. Schizophrenia runs in families, but this was considered to be supportive of environmental causes rather than genetics. However, 'twin and adoption studies successfully changed this view' (Plomin & Asbury 2005, p. 2). If one member of a pair of MZ twins is schizophrenic, the risk is 45 per cent that the other twin also will be. For DZ twins, the chances are 17 per cent; however, the important point is that the concordance rate for schizophrenia for identical twins is only 45 per cent. The discordance cannot simply be explained genetically: 'it must be due to environmental factors' (Plomin & Asbury 2005, p. 2). This example demonstrates the effects of both genetic inheritance and environment.

There seems to be little doubt that our genetic background counts. We are not born a 'blank slate'. Stephen Pinker (2004, p. 7) points out that 'the existence of environmental mitigations doesn't make the effects of the genes inconsequential. On the contrary, the genes specify what kinds of environmental manipulations will have what kinds of effects and with what costs.' We know that children often resemble their parents in such aspects as hair-, eye-, and skin colour. We know that certain talents run in families. If you come from a family with a history of sporting prowess, you might have the genetic endowment to excel at endurance sports (such as marathon running) or speed sports (running and jumping). Genetic screening is already in place for elite athletes; however, you still need the right social environment for your talents to develop. You still need the motivation to practise and the determination to succeed. It is not a question of nature versus nurture; rather, it is nature and nurture together—there is an interplay of genetics and environment.

The case for nurture: Theories of socialisation

social construction/ism
Refers to the socially created characteristics of human life based on the idea that people actively construct reality, meaning it is neither 'natural' nor inevitable. Therefore, notions of normality/abnormality, right/wrong, and health/illness are subjective human creations that should not be taken for granted.

Social scientists in the past generally supported the concept that our sense of self and our identities are **socially constructed**. They 'sought to explain all customs and social arrangements as the product of socialisation of children by the surrounding culture: a system of words, images and stereotypes, role models and contingencies of reward and punishment' (Pinker 2004, p. 6). Socialisation is a complex process, and important contributions to our understanding of the processes involved have been detailed by a number of theorists.

Cooley and Mead: The development of self

One of the key issues in the socialisation process is how we produce a sense of self. As we saw in Chapter 3, Charles Horton Cooley (1864–1929), an American sociologist, used the term 'looking-glass self' (Cooley 1902/1964, p. 184) to explain how we use others as a kind of mirror in order to construct a self-image.

Our self-concept develops through our interactions with others. If we are defined as 'ugly' or 'fat' or 'stupid', then we may begin to see ourselves in that way and behave accordingly.

The philosopher George Herbert Mead (1863–1931), who spent most of his working life at the University of Chicago, is regarded as the founder of a branch of sociology called symbolic interactionism. It was Mead's belief that the sense of self is developed from our very first social interactions, and that the acquisition of language is essential for the development of self (Mead 1934). He suggests that babies learn a repertoire of behaviours and gestures that produce certain responses. For example, they may learn that crying brings the presence of a parent and results in being held in the parent's arms. Smiling often produces smiling responses in others. Through symbolic interaction, children learn what behaviours to expect in others and to adjust their own accordingly. Mead (1934) suggests that the self has two parts: the 'I' and the 'me'. The 'I' is the impulsive, uncontrolled, and unsocialised self, whereas the 'me' is, in a certain sense, the censor—it is the *social self* or the self in a specific social role. Mead (1934) maintains that we 'talk' to ourselves, holding a sort of internal conversation in which we develop a sense of ourselves and how others see us. Only when we learn to differentiate between the 'I' and the 'me' do we achieve self-consciousness and self-awareness. According to Mead, the development of a sense of self is essential to our becoming human beings.

**CrossLink:
See Chapter 3
for more on
symbolic
inter-
actionism.**

Mead (1934) uses three stages of child development to explain how this sense of self develops. The first stage is a kind of preparatory or 'pre-play stage', in which children imitate the actions of family members or others who are important to them. Mead stresses that at this stage children are merely imitating, without understanding the meaning or social relationships of the roles they adopt. Later, at about age three or four, they enter the 'play stage', in which they give meaning to these actions and roles. For example, they may take on the role of parents when playing with dolls or soft toys. One of the most important aspects of socialisation is that of role-taking. Mead explains that when children take on roles they are not simply playing or imitating others; role-taking enables them to adopt another's perspective, and through these activities they become aware of their own sense of self and learn to see themselves through the eyes of others. The development of what Mead terms the concept of the **generalised Other** occurs in the final stage of development—the 'game stage'. In the game stage, school-age children can be involved in organised, complex games, such as team sports like football or netball, in which it is necessary to anticipate, understand, and take on the roles and attitudes of others.

generalised Other
Occurs in the final stage of the development of *self* when a child can take on and understand the roles and attitudes of others.

The work of both Cooley and Mead is important in that they explain how our sense of self emerges. Mead has been criticised for his view that the development of the self is social—a result of our social interactions and experiences—rather than being based on biological foundations.

Piaget and the four stages of cognitive development

Jean Piaget (1896–1980), a Swiss psychologist, was influential due to his studies of children's cognitive development. His work has influenced those concerned with the education of young children. Many concepts such as 'discovery learning', 'learning through play', and 'reading readiness' were developed with reference to his work (Hinchliffe & Woodward 2000, p. 30). Piaget was interested in how children think and how their thinking is different from that of adults. Piaget noted that the very young children he observed took little notice of other children's speech; he termed their speech 'egocentric speech'. This refers to the fact that young children tend to see the world from their own viewpoint and as centred around themselves (Hinchliffe & Woodward 2000). Based on his observations of children and their language patterns, Piaget identified four major stages of cognitive development that also reflected biological maturation and chronological age (Piaget & Inhelder 1969). Although there may be some variation in the ages of the child at various stages, the stages themselves always follow the same sequence:

1. the *sensorimotor stage* from birth to age two, when the world is experienced through the senses such as touching, sucking, and biting
2. the *preoperational stage* from two to seven years, which sees the development of language and symbolic play

3. the *concrete operational stage* from ages seven to eleven, the time when children can logically connect causes and events. They lose their egocentric outlook and see the world from the point of view of others, and

4. the *formal operational stage*, which occurs after the child reaches the age of twelve. It involves the ability to engage in abstract thoughts and complex activities.

It was Piaget's view that all human beings proceed through these sequential stages, irrespective of their culture and social background—although he conceded that not all children reach the final formal stage.

According to both Piaget and Mead, children pass through developmental stages. Both stressed the importance of the acquisition of language, and believed that once they reach the final stage of development, children are able to think in an abstract, complex, and logical manner. Like Mead, Piaget believed that individuals have the power to shape their social world.

Goffman and social interaction

Erving Goffman (1922–82), a symbolic-interaction theorist, extended role theory in *The Presentation of Self in Everyday Life* (1959). As we saw in Chapter 3, Goffman likened the individual to an actor 'who puts on a performance in order to communicate to others a certain kind of impression of himself or herself' (Cheal 2005, p. 146). Goffman was interested in how we interact in the presence of others, and he used what he termed **dramaturgical analysis** to investigate how we behave in social situations. According to Goffman, people take on social roles just as actors perform roles in the theatre. The interactions we have with others are a kind of dramatic production in which we present ourselves in the best possible light. Goffman's insights can also be applied to electronic communications with others (Miller 1995). Although the presentation of self electronically is obviously not done as face-to-face interaction, Goffman's concept of self and the ways in which we choose and present that self nevertheless seems relevant in the context of popular social networking sites such as Facebook, or when people play interactive computer games—especially when they use 'avatars' (online characters) and 'handles' (screen names) to represent themselves.

dramaturgical analysis/dramaturgy
The term used by Goffman to describe how people take on social roles, just as actors do in the theatre.

Learning gender

gender
Refers to the socially constructed categories of feminine and masculine (the cultural values that dictate how women and men should behave), as opposed to the categories of biological *sex* (female or male).

How do we learn how to behave in an appropriate way as a man or a woman? Debates about whether our **gender** roles are biologically or culturally produced have continued over the last 30 or so years. Is our behaviour as a man or a woman innate and biologically determined, or does the culture of a society exert pressure on individuals to behave in certain socially acceptable ways? Many sociologists believe that gender roles are socially constructed, in that we learn how to be a man or a woman in our society—or, more specifically, how to be masculine or feminine. Both gender differences and gender dominance are often explained as '*differential socialization*—the *nurture* side of the equation' (Kimmel 2004, p. 3, original italics).

Let us take an example: a couple is expecting a baby and starts planning for the birth of their child. At birth (or more commonly following a prenatal ultrasound scan), the first question is, 'Is it a girl or a boy?' Names, type and colour of clothes, decoration of the child's room, and toys are predicated on whether the child is male or female. The biological sex of the child is used as one of the major sorting mechanisms on which to base the future allocation of roles within the social structure of society.

Children learn their gender roles at an early age: they identify with and imitate the same-sex parent, and the parents often reinforce gender-stereotypical behaviour through clothes, books, and games. From birth, girls are often dressed in 'pretty' clothing while boys' clothes are more practical and rugged. Even children's dress-ups reflect this: girls wear fairy dresses with spangled, wispy skirts, but when boys dress up it can be as anything from Superman to Spiderman. Boys are given building sets, electronic toys, balls, cars, and train sets—toys that are activity oriented and technical. Girls, on the other hand, are still given toys that reflect the sexual division of labour in many households, such as dolls, miniature household appliances (vacuum cleaners or stoves), and toy prams—toys that lead to a quieter kind of play. Despite the level of awareness of the gendered social world of children, a visit to a toyshop or the toy section of a department store, or a glance at toy catalogues, reveals marked differentiation between what are considered toys for boys and toys for girls.

Are boys and girls treated differently by their parents? Certainly there are differences in the kinds of toys children are given. There is also evidence that fathers in particular tend to play in a rougher and much more physical way with their sons than with their daughters. Other studies indicate that fathers react negatively when they see their sons engage in what might be termed 'cross-gender play'. Fathers also seem to expect their sons to be tougher, both physically and emotionally, than their daughters; however, in such areas as 'affection and everyday speech with infants and toddlers', few differences in parental interactions have been revealed (Wharton 2005, pp. 125–7).

Young children are the targets of socialisation from parents and others, but sociali-sation is a two-way process and children are active agents in learning 'appropriate' gender roles (2005). Although parents play a major role in the socialisation of young children, children themselves are 'very skilled at de-coding gender messages from the world around them' (2005, p. 127). As soon as children can identify themselves as male or female and acquire a gender identity, they very quickly learn to apply these labels to others. Wharton (2005, p. 127) points out that as early as age three, when young children are asked to sort things as male or female, they will pick out shirts, ties, razors, shaving cream, and footballs as being male and items such as cosmetics, handbags, vacuum cleaners, and pots and pans as female. In fact, children learn very quickly to apply gender labels to objects, which is sometimes referred to as 'gender-centric reasoning'.

Many studies indicate that young children prefer to play with a child of the same sex. This preference for gender-segregated interaction manifests itself as early as the age of three and continues strongly until at least age eleven (Stockard 2006). The years from five until eight have been described as the most 'sexist' period of life, when children view any deviation from a gender label as not just misguided but 'wrong' (cited in Wharton 2005, p. 128).

Early writings on socialisation tended to ignore the importance of peers for younger children. Today, most children in Australia attend playgroups, kindergarten, or childcare centres before they begin primary school. In these settings, they have the opportunity to play with other children their own age. From an early age—around two or three—many children seek out and seem to prefer same-sex playmates and choose to play with different toys (Stockard 2006, p. 218).

ethnography/ethnographic
A research method based on the direct observation of the social interaction and culture of a particular social group, involving detailed description and evaluation of behaviours, activities, and events.

Voluntary sex-segregation of children means that boys tend to socialise with other boys and girls seem to prefer to socialise with girls. **Ethnographic** studies of children and adolescents document the nature of gender-segregated peer groups and reveal the importance of interactions with others of the same sex in enabling children to develop 'their gender identity and definitions of appropriate gender roles, as children actively discuss and develop definitions of masculinity and femininity' (Stockard 2006, p. 221).

Many Australian children participate in organised sport through a school, club, or association outside of school hours. In the survey year 2005–06, 63.5 per cent of children aged five to fourteen participated in sport outside of school hours, with those aged between nine and eleven years having the highest participation rate (70.2 per cent) (ABS 2006). The Australian Bureau of Statistics (ABS) 2006 figures show that, across all age groups, boys had a higher participation rate (68.9 per cent) than girls (58 per cent). For boys, the most popular sports were outdoor soccer, swimming, and Australian Rules football; for girls, the two most popular sports were netball and swimming. Although boys had a higher participation rate in organised sport, girls had a high participation rate in organised dancing (23.1 per cent). The participation rate of boys in dancing was a low 2.4 per cent (ABS 2006).

Boys also tend to have a higher participation rate than girls in non-organised physical recreation activities such as bike riding and skateboarding/rollerblading: 'For both activities, a higher percentage of boys (73.4 per cent and 29.2 per cent respectively) participated than did girls (61.9 per cent and 17.6 per cent)' (ABS 2006).

Participation in sporting activities is another means by which self-socialisation occurs. In Australia, as in many countries, boys are expected to participate in sports and it is through this participation that boys' status groups are formed. Team sports enhance physical skills, but also teach values. Boys in particular often find a sense of identity through sports and 'learn that to achieve in sports is to gain stature in masculinity' (Henslin 2005, p. 83). According to Connell (2005), when boys begin playing 'competitive sport they are not just learning a game . . . Only a tiny minority reach the top as professional athletes, yet the production of masculinity throughout the sports world is marked by the hierarchical, competitive structure of the institution' (2005, p. 35).

Agencies of socialisation

To understand better how the socialisation process works we must consider where and how it occurs. Those sites and institutions that have an impact on our socialisation are termed agencies of socialisation.

The family

In many cultures, the **primary socialisation** agent is the family. Initially, children are dependent on caregivers (usually parents), who meet their immediate needs. The bond that develops between a baby and its primary caregiver (often the mother) is usually viewed as the first and most intense part of the socialisation process. The family is a child's first reference group. Yet families are diverse, and their styles of parenting reflect cultural, class, ethnic, and religious differences. The pervasive influence of the family in the socialisation process may have diminished somewhat as other agencies of socialisation, such as child care, kindergartens, schools, peer groups, and the media, have taken over or increased their impact.

primary socialisation
Refers to the socialisation of babies and young children, and mainly occurs within the family.

The school

The period in which children attend school is usually referred to as **secondary socialisation**. In this context, other children, teachers, and the wider social world begin to influence the child. Schools have what are termed **manifest functions**—that is, their purpose is to teach knowledge and skills and to prepare students for the world of work and adult life; however, schools also teach what are described as **latent functions**—attitudes and values. This question of 'values' is quite contentious in Australia, where many children are taught within the private sector of education. Parents select private schools that reflect their social situation and religious background. Social class is, of course, a significant factor in the selection of a private or state school. More affluent parents may well select a private school where their children will learn the 'skills and values that match their higher position', whereas less affluent, working-class parents send their children to the local state school (Henslin 2005, p. 81).

secondary socialisation
Refers to the socialisation of children by their peers and by institutions such as schools.

manifest functions
Functions that are obvious and purposeful.

latent functions
Functions that may be hidden.

The peer group

As we have seen, Mead, Cooley, and Goffman stress the importance of social interactions, which often occur via the peer group. Children and young people use peer groups to develop social skills when they are beginning to separate from their families and seek an identity of their own. The importance of socialisation through peer groups has grown. In the past, peer-group socialisation tended to be geographically based in terms of neighbourhoods, schools, or universities, or interest based—focused on aspects such as sports, hobbies, and leisure activities. Within the last decade or so, social interactions within peer groups have changed markedly.

According to the *Mobile Me* report conducted in 2007 with eleven- to fifteen-year-old children in New South Wales public schools, most (between 66 and 82 per cent) owned a mobile phone (NSW Commission for Children & Young People, 2007). Not only is mobile phone ownership by children and young people increasing rapidly, but the age at which they have a mobile phone is falling (and this is expected to continue to fall). Children in mid-primary school are now acquiring mobile phones. There is a gender difference in mobile phone ownership, which perhaps says something about how parents view the relative needs of boys and girls. For example, at age eleven, boys were 30 per cent less likely than girls to have a mobile, but by age fifteen they were about as likely as girls to own one (NSW Commission for Children & Young People 2007).

What is interesting about the use of mobile phones is that communication is fast, easy, and flexible, enabling young people to keep in touch with friends, and with parents who may be at work, as well as to maintain family relationships—such as with grandparents over a distance (NSW Commission for Children & Young People 2007). They change the processes of communication. Texting and voice communication alone (even with video augmentation) is not the same as face-to-face interaction. Those non-verbal cues of body language and tone of voice are missing. Children using mobile phones are aware of this and comment that a lack of non-verbal cues can lead to misunderstandings and even deceit (NSW Commission for Children & Young People 2007).

5.1: Cyber kids

Children today have used computers and accessed the internet from an early age. Of these 'digital natives', almost two-thirds use computers and access the internet for web surfing, chatting, and gaming as well as for assistance with their homework and educational studies (ABS 2008). The differences in computer use vary by both gender and age. Boys and younger children (aged eight to eleven) are more likely to access the internet at home for entertainment such as games, websites, and music, while girls and older children (aged twelve and thirteen) tend to use the internet for email and instant messaging (NetRatings Australia 2005, p. 37).

The most common internet-based activities undertaken by children (in age cohorts) at home are:

▶ Five- to eight-year-olds play online games and use the internet for educational or school activities (62 per cent each) followed by leisure activities (38 per cent).

▶ Nine- to eleven-year-olds use the internet for school and educational activities (86 per cent) and 54 per cent use it to play online games, while 44 per cent access the internet for leisure activities, and 42 per cent for email or online messaging.

▶ Twelve- to fourteen-year-olds access the internet for school or educational purposes (90 per cent), 68 per cent for emailing or messaging, 52 per cent for leisure, 43 per cent for playing online games and 40 per cent for downloading music from internet sites (ABS 2008).

Parents report that over one-third of children with a home internet connection access it daily, and a further third do so at least two or three times per week (NetRatings 2005, p. 15). Older children (in the eight to thirteen years age range) are more likely to be daily users than younger children; however, these older children spend half as much time using the internet at home as do teenagers (aged fourteen to seventeen) (ABS 2008).

Just as mobile phone usage gives children and young people a greater means of communicating independently with others, so does access to the internet. The work of Sarah Holloway and Gill Valentine (2003, pp. 130–1) indicates that children and young people use email to keep in touch with friends who live locally. It enables girls to talk to boys, or boys to girls, with whom they might feel embarrassed if they spoke face to face. It is also a means of binding dislocated families together. While access to the internet allows children and young people to extend existing social relationships, it also allows them to 'develop new forms of interaction on-line and social relationships' (2003, p. 132). Interactive computer technology allows users to construct online 'alternative' identities (2003, p. 132). Manuel Castells (2001, p. 118) comments that 'teenagers are the people who are in the process of discovering their identity, of experimenting with it, of finding out who they really are or who they would like to be'. He writes that: '[r]ole playing and identity-building as the basis of online interaction are a tiny proportion of Internet-based sociability, and this kind of practice seems to be heavily concentrated among teenagers' (2001, p. 118).

The social interactions of the peer group across the lifespan, from young people to the elderly, have been transformed in the last decade or so through the almost ubiquitous use of mobile phones and access to the internet. Whereas in the past sociability and connectivity were governed by proximity and geographic location, now we have peer group socialisation in a globalised context, based on mutual interests.

Mass media

Most children in Australia are exposed to the media in the form of radio, television, comics, magazines, books, DVDs, video games, advertising, the internet, and newspapers. The term 'mass media' usually refers to communication to mass audiences. The most significant of these is television. Watching television, DVDs, or videos outside of school hours is still the most common recreational activity for children aged five to fourteen years, 'with an average of 22 hours over a fortnight during a school term' (ABS 2006, p. 7). The *Children's Participation in Cultural and Leisure Activities* survey (ABS 2006) indicates that 97 per cent of children in the five to fourteen years age group watch television or DVDs outside school hours. Many families have home entertainment centres, and in Australia it is common for older children to have a television in their bedroom.

One often-debated question is the impact of media violence on children. Just because children watch violent programs on television or DVDs does not necessarily mean they will imitate them. Other factors are involved. Patricia Edgar (2005) comments that: '[w]hile media violence may not be a major factor in explaining individual acts of violence and bullying, it may be a very important factor at the societal level.' She goes on to say that: '[t]he media depict a very violent world and the media exploit that violence in news programs as well as in sport and fictional drama.' Viewing violent images, whether on news or fictional programs, encourages people to adopt aggressive attitudes and to believe that problems can be solved through violence. Edgar comments that in the past media content contained more tales of justice and retribution—bad people got their 'just deserts'. She reminds us of a past 'when the hero drew his gun only when provoked', and always for good reason. This has changed, though, and anti-social behaviour has become glamorised to the extent that the differences between right and wrong have become blurred.

Socialisation throughout the life course

Socialisation in adult life is sometimes referred to as **tertiary socialisation**. We take on new identities through paid work, interactions with new friends and colleagues, and changes in our personal lives. We learn how to become parents and grandparents and later to become senior citizens. Adulthood has many transitions, some of which are negotiated more successfully than others. **Resocialisation** occurs when we learn new norms and values that match our new situation in life. Many young adults go through a resocialisation process when they leave high school and go to university. Resocialisation occurs for students who are training for a particular profession. Education students must learn that they are expected to take on the characteristics and behaviour of a teacher rather than those of a student.

tertiary socialisation
Processes of socialisation that occur in adulthood.

resocialisation
Part of the socialisation process; it occurs during our adult years.

total institutions
A term used by Goffman to refer to institutions such as prisons and asylums in which life is highly regulated and subjected to authoritarian control to induce conformity.

Much of resocialisation builds on existing norms, roles, and values. Sometimes the transitions are more abrupt. In *Asylums* (1961), Erving Goffman describes controlled environments that he defines as **total institutions**. These are usually military camps, prisons, psychiatric hospitals, nursing homes, or religious institutions such as convents, which totally regulate the life of the individual, attempt to strip the individual of identity, and require the internalisation of new norms, roles, attitudes, and values. Within a total institution, individuals are usually cut off from the outside world and have limited access to their family and friends. As Cooley and Mead pointed out, we form our sense of self and self-image from our interactions with others—we see ourselves as a 'good bloke', a 'nice guy', or a 'good friend', which often mirrors how others see us. These reflections may be denied us in a total institution; the sense of self we know is absent. Goffman indicates that one of the ways in which we maintain our sense of identity is through appearance—clothes, hairstyle, or personal possessions (such as the kind of car we drive and the house in which we live). Removal of these—which is part of the admission procedure of many total institutions—strips the individual of identity. Goffman terms many of these procedures a 'mortification of self' (1961). The self is systematically degraded and humiliated. For example, someone becoming a prison inmate may be searched, undressed, bathed, disinfected, fingerprinted, forced to wear a uniform, and given a number rather than their name. They may be forced to become obedient to prison warders or other prisoners, and to conform to prison rules and regulations. They are confined, and contact with the outside world may be contingent on good behaviour. Despite all this, Goffman claims that for most inmates there is not a permanent change of self, as they adapt to the institution and often resist it in a variety of ways.

Conclusion

In the past, socialisation was seen as deterministic, in that social interactions and social forces constantly shape us within our culture. This view ignores agency—that is, the ways in which individuals mediate, interpret, and adapt the messages they receive from others and resist the pressure to conform. Rapid advances in genetics have provided us with information on the interplay of genetics and environment in making us who we are. Technological advances in electronic communications have had an impact on our peer group socialisation and the ways in which we interact with others. Perhaps the most interesting aspect of socialisation is our flexibility, and the fact that we are always changing as we encounter different life situations. At each stage in our life process, we adapt to produce a distinctive and unique sense of self.

Summary of main points

▶ Socialisation is a lifelong process.

▶ Nature and nurture reflect our biological heritage and our social environment.

▶ Any understanding of socialisation must also take account of the potential influence of genetic predisposition, varied personal experiences, and the exercise of agency to resist or modify socialisation processes.

▶ Many writers believe that there are stages of development in the socialisation of children.

▶ Childhood socialisation theories stress the acquisition of language and social interaction.

▶ Agencies of socialisation are the sites or contexts in which socialisation occurs.

▶ Gender socialisation is the process through which we acquire a gender identity.

▶ Peer group socialisation has been transformed in recent decades through the extensive use of mobile phones and the internet.

5.1 What made me?

▶ Would you be interested in using predictive direct-to-the-consumer gene testing services? Why or why not? What are the risks and benefits?

▶ In what ways have you resisted or challenged the socialisation processes you have encountered?

▶ To what extent do you believe the person you have become is a result of nature or nurture?

▶ Have you explored using alternative identities such as avatars in massively multiplayer online role-playing games (MMORPGs), such as Second Life?

Discussion questions

5.1 Do you think that our behaviour and characteristics come more from our genetic background (nature) or from our social environment (nurture)?

5.2 An old Jesuit adage is, 'Give me a child until he [sic] is seven and I will give you the man.' Is early childhood socialisation still so powerful, or have other forms of socialisation become more important?

5.3 Why are some commentators and parents concerned about the influence of the internet and video games on children? In what ways might these forms of mass media be different from traditional media such as TV, books, magazines, and newspapers?

5.4 Some diseases have a heredity component—for example, susceptibility to some forms of breast and ovarian cancer, prostate cancer, heart disease, diabetes, and schizophrenia. Consider these from the viewpoint of C. Wright Mills' concept of 'private troubles' and 'public issues'. Discuss some of the issues.

5.5 What are some of the ways in which young children learn to 'do gender'?

5.6 Discuss the idea of conceiving a child for a purpose. This can be to save a seriously ill sibling, to create a child free from serious genetic disease, or even to create a child who is an elite athlete.

Further reading

Giddens, A. 1991, *Modernity and Self-identity: Self and Society in the Late Modern Age*, Stanford University Press, Stanford, CA.

Goffman, E. 1959, *The Presentation of Self in Everyday Life*, Doubleday, Garden City.

Pilnick, A. 2002, *Genetics and Society: An Introduction*, Open University Press, Buckingham.

Wharton, A. 2005, *The Sociology of Gender: An Introduction to Theory and Research*, Blackwell, Oxford.

Williams, S.J., Birke, L. & Bendelow, G.A. (eds) 2003, *Debating Biology: Sociological Reflections on Health, Medicine and Society*, Routledge, London.

Websites

- Feral Children: <www.feralchildren.com/en/index.php>. A fascinating site documenting the myths and evidence for so-called 'feral children' or 'wolf-children', who have grown up isolated from human contact.
- The Mead Project 2.0: <http://spartan.ac.brocku.ca/~lward>. Everything you ever wanted to know about George Herbert Mead.
- Society for the Study of Symbolic Interaction: <www.espach.salford.ac.uk/sssi/index.php>. Links to the journal *Symbolic Interaction* and contains information about its conferences and discussion forums on the sociological perspective that has most influenced our understanding of socialisation.
- 23andMe <www.23andme.com>. A personal genomics-predictive gene testing service that was *Time* magazine's 2008 invention of the year.

Films/documentaries

- *Seven Up!*, 1964–2004, television documentary (ongoing series), directed by M. Apted, Granada Television, DVD distributed by First Run Features (USA, 2004). A series of documentaries beginning in 1964 that traces the lives of fourteen British children. The children were of different socio-economic backgrounds and the documentary was based on the adage, 'Give me a child until he [sic] is seven and I will give you the man.' The participants (those who are still willing and available) are filmed every seven years. The next filming (*56 Up*) is planned for 2011–12.
- *L'Enfant Sauvage (The Wild Child)*, 1970, motion picture, directed by F. Truffaut, distributed by Les Artistes Associés, France. A famous French film that tells the story of a child found living like an animal in a forest, who then became the socialisation project of a physician.

Visit the *Public Sociology* book website to access topical case studies, weblinks, YouTube clips, and extra readings.

References

Australian Bureau of Statistics (ABS) 2006, *Children's Participation in Cultural and Leisure Activities*, cat. no. 4901.0, ABS, Canberra.

——— 2008, *Australian Social Trends: Internet Access at Home*, cat. no. 4102, ABS, Canberra.

Castells, M. 2001, *The Internet Galaxy: Reflections on the Internet, Business and Society*, Oxford University Press, Oxford.

Cheal, D. 2005, *Dimensions of Sociological Theory*, Palgrave, Basingstoke, Hampshire.

Connell, R. 2005, *Masculinities*, 2nd edn, Allen & Unwin, Sydney.

Cooley, C.H. 1902/1964, *Human Nature and the Social Order*, Transaction, New York.

Darwin, C. 1859, *On the Origin of Species by Means of Natural Selection, or the Preservation of Favoured Races in the Struggle for Life*, online edition, <www.literature.org/authors/darwin-charles/the-origin-of-species> (accessed 3 August 2009).

Edgar, P. 2005, 'TV violence: The good and bad for our children', *The Age*, 4 April, <www.theage.com.au/articles/2005/04/10/1113071849363.html> (accessed 21 May 2009).

Galton, F. 1874, *English Men of Science: Their Nature and Nurture*, Macmillan, London.

Giddens, A. (with the assistance of Birdsall, K.) 2001, *Sociology*, 4th edn, Polity Press, Cambridge.

Goffman, E. 1959, *The Presentation of Self in Everyday Life*, Doubleday, Garden City.

—— 1961, *Asylums: Essays on the Social Situations of Mental Patients and Other Inmates*, Penguin, Harmondsworth.

Henslin, J.M. 2005, *Sociology: A Down-to-Earth Approach*, 7th edn, Pearson, Boston.

Hinchliffe, S. & Woodward, K. 2000, *The Natural and the Social: Uncertainty, Risk and Change*, Routledge in association with the Open University, London.

Holloway, S.L. & Valentine, G. 2003, *Cyberkids: Children in the Information Age*, Routledge, London.

Kerr, A. 2004, *Genetics and Society: A Sociology of Disease*, Routledge, London.

Kimmel, M.S. 2004, *The Gendered Society*, 2nd edn, Oxford University Press, New York.

Lippa, R.A. 2002, *Gender, Nature and Nurture*, Lawrence Erlbaum, Mahwah, NJ.

Mead, G.H. 1934, *Mind, Self and Society*, University of Chicago Press, Chicago.

Miller, H. 1995, 'The presentation of self in electronic life: Goffman on the internet', paper presented at Embodied Knowledge and Virtual Space conference, Goldsmiths College, University of London, June 1995, <www.ntu.ac.uk/soc/psych/miller/goffman.htm> (accessed 25 May 2009).

NetRatings Australia 2005, 'Kidsonline@home Internet Use in Australian Homes', prepared by NetRatings Australia Pty Ltd for the Australian Broadcasting Authority and NetAlert Ltd, Sydney.

New South Wales Commission for Children and Young People 2007, *Ask the Children: Mobile Me—Kids Speak Out about Mobile Phones*, report prepared by the Commission and the University of Sydney and the University of Technology, Sydney.

Petersen, A. & Bunton, R. 2002, *The New Genetics and Public Health*, Routledge, London.

Piaget, J. & Inhelder, B. 1969, *The Psychology of the Child*, trans. H. Weaver, Basic Books, New York.

Pilnick, A. 2002, *Genetics and Society: An Introduction*, Open University Press, Buckingham.

Pinker, S. 2002, *The Blank Slate: The Modern Denial of Human Nature*, Viking Penguin, New York.

—— 2004, 'Why nature & nurture won't go away', *Daedalus*, Fall, pp. 1–13.

Plomin, R. & Asbury, K. 2005, 'Nature and nurture: Genetic and environmental influences on behavior', *Annals of the American Academy of Political and Social Science*, vol. 86, pp. 52–67.

Quinn, B. 2009, 'Cancer gene test stirs ethics debate', *The Age*, 11 January.

Reilly, P.R. 2008, *The Strongest Boy in the World: How Genetic Information is Reshaping Our Lives*, Cold Spring Harbour Laboratory Press, Cold Spring Harbour, NY.

Ritzer, G. & Goodman, D.J. 2004, *Classical Sociological Theory*, 4th edn, McGraw-Hill, New York.

Stockard, J. 2006, 'Gender socialization', in J. Salzman Chafetz, *Handbook of the Sociology of Gender*, Springer Science & Business Media, New York, pp. 215–27.

Spencer, H. 1961 [1873], *The Study of Sociology*, University of Michigan Press, Ann Arbor, MI.

Vasen, H.F., Watson, P., Mecklin, J.P. & Lynch, H.T. 1999, 'New clinical criteria for hereditary nonpolyposis colorectal cancer (HNPCC, Lynch syndrome) proposed by the International Collaborative group on HNPCC', *Gastroenterology*, vol. 116, no. 6, pp. 1453–6.

Weeks, J. 1991, *Against Nature: Essays on History, Sexuality and Identity*, Rivers Oram Press, London.

Wharton, A. 2005, *The Sociology of Gender: An Introduction to Theory and Research*, Blackwell, Oxford.

Williams, S.J., Birke, L. & Bendelow, G.A. 2003, 'Introduction: Debating biology', in S.J. Williams, L. Birke & G.A. Bendelow (eds), *Debating Biology: Sociological Reflections on Health, Medicine and Society*, Routledge, London, pp. 1–12.

Wright Mills, C. 1959, *The Sociological Imagination*, Oxford University Press, New York.

CHAPTER 6

Youth transitions and youth culture

Pam Nilan

Friday night

Thomas is eighteen years old and comes from a professional family. He has just left his last afternoon class at the exclusive single-sex boys' school he attends. He jumps into his sporty Mazda with three friends to go to rowing practice for a few hours. Thomas wants to study commerce and become a stockbroker. Although he studies hard, on Friday night after rowing practice he drinks with his mates. When they arrive, the bar is packed with well-dressed young professionals. After a few hours of drinking their favourite James Boag beer, they move on to a popular dance club where they drink spirits. Thomas does not remember much, but he does recall (vaguely) the girl he was with before he got home. His mates have sent incriminating visual evidence to his iPhone. After a day of recovery he picks up his girlfriend, who also attends a private school. They eat at a restaurant and go to see a film. Thomas has an early night because he has a rowing competition on Sunday, then he studies until late on Sunday night.

At 5.00 p.m., nineteen-year-old Fatima leaves work, a hardware shop owned by her uncle. From a Lebanese-Australian family, she left high school in Year 11 to work for her uncle. She texts her friend Sophia to meet at their favourite café. They use Sophia's laptop to read emails and check Facebook. Fatima keeps her internet activity separate from home. It is after six o'clock so she hurries for the bus. When Fatima arrives home, she removes her head scarf, helps her mother serve dinner to her father and five siblings, then washes up. The family watches a rented movie. Fatima is in bed by 11.00 p.m. because she starts work at eight. Fatima's parents want to arrange her marriage, but she refuses. She believes she can find a Lebanese boyfriend her parents will accept. She chats to young male customers, and is making clandestine use of online resources to meet a suitable boy.

Introduction

The two contrasting profiles of young Australians above invite us to think about **youth transitions**, communication technology, leisure practices, gender, class, and ethnicity in the lives of young people. In 2007, there were 2.9 million Australians aged fifteen to 24 years—14 per cent of the population (ABS 2008). This chapter examines some important sociological debates around youth issues.

youth transitions
The sequence of major life events through which full adult social status is achieved.

What is youth?

It may seem a large claim, but there is actually no such thing as youth. In human history there were only adults and children. While puberty always signalled the change from child to adult—and still does—the ten- to fifteen-year period of 'youth' is a modern, socially constructed category. In fact, adolescence was invented during the Industrial Revolution in Europe, at the same time as the steam engine (Musgrove 1964). The long period of youth is characterised by distinct patterns of leisure, consumption, social bonding, and courting. Applying a sociological lens, a number of factors emerge. The first is the extended human lifespan (see Nilan, Julian & Germov 2007). The second is the upward credentialling of the labour force (see DiPrete & Grusky 1990). A third factor is youth identified as a demographic category in legislation and policy (Lamb & Mason 2008). A fourth is the expanded range of consumer choices and leisure options in the global economy (Nilan, Julian & Germov 2007).

Youth transitions

During the extended period of 'youth', young people undergo the transition to adult-hood. There are five transitions that mark adult status: 'completing schooling, beginning full-time work, financial independence, getting married, and becoming a parent' (Aronson 2008, p. 60). This means moving from education to work, from living in the family home to independent living, and from having the closest relationship with family and siblings to an intimate relationship with a partner (Furlong & Cartmel 1997). A short, straightforward process in the past, youth transitions now take much longer and are much less predictable. Some describe this process as 'emerging adulthood' (Arnett 2006) because it takes a long time to reach full adult status. For instance, some young people are working but still at school and living at home. Other youth live independently but are neither at school nor working. Young people in their twenties may be living in independent de facto relationships, and may even be parents, but may not be employed. Legally, young Australians can have sex and drive a motor vehicle at the age of seventeen but cannot vote or drink alcohol. Banks are reluctant to lend money to people under 25, yet much younger people get a credit card. In other words, while youth-to-adult transition might once have been a straight line, it is now more of a zigzag.

A dramatic change has taken place in the relationship between youth, education, and the labour force (Wyn & Woodman 2006; Shah & Burke 2006). Significantly, com-pletion of full-time education no longer guarantees entry to the labour market. Over the last fifteen years, the proportion of Australian school-leavers not in full-time activity six months after leaving school has been slightly less than a third (Dusseldorp Skills Forum 2007). Furthermore, we have seen a 'long-term fall in full-time teenage job opportunities. Structural changes to the Australian economy have gradually changed the number of jobs available to young people' (Lamb & Mason 2008, p. 37). Year 12 or TAFE qualifications are now required even for relatively undemanding jobs, especially when unemployment rates are high. For well-paid jobs, young people need tertiary qualifications, along with expert grooming and self-presentation. This is the upward credentialling of the labour market. Young people who leave school early—especially young women—find it very hard to get a job (Lamb & Mason 2008).

Moreover, nearly a quarter of young Australians aged between twenty and 34 are continuing to live with their parents (ABS 2009, p. 24). They may still consider themselves reasonably independent because they have a job and a permanent partner. And many Australian youth are working part time, even while they are still at school (Ferguson 2007). In short, while some aspects of youthful lives are adult-like early on, in other ways child-like dependency on family is extended. Jeffrey Arnett (2006) reports that when he asked young people aged eighteen to 25 in North America whether they had reached adulthood, most responded both yes *and* no (2006).

Class, gender, and ethnic factors greatly affect transition experiences and outcomes (Aronson 2008), as we saw for Thomas and Fatima above. For example, Harry Savelsberg and Bonnie Martin-Giles (2008, p. 29) found that, for socially excluded young Australians, the 'cumulative effects of socio-economic deprivation and policy failure resulted in feelings of resentment, anger, cynicism, isolation, alienation and even shame and relegation to the margins of society'. The young people they studied could not sustain themselves economically during the transition to adulthood, even through welfare payments. In their study of what it means to be adult, Janel Benson and Frank Furstenberg (2007) found that becoming a parent was important for females but not for males.

To grasp the complexity of contemporary youth transitions in multicultural Australia, we need to acknowledge that youth itself is understood differently in some ethnic cultures. Youth may not be understood as a transitional life stage characterised by leisure and socialising with peers. Rather, adulthood may be recognised only when a young person leaves the family home for marriage (Francis & Cornfoot 2007). Finally, Indigenous Australian youth face particularly significant challenges in youth-to-adult transitions (Wyn 2008). In summary, not all young Australians 'face the same constraints and the choices available are far from equal' (Wyn & Woodman 2006, p. 507).

individualisation
A trend towards the primacy of individual choice, freedom, and self-responsibility.

In sociological circles, it is argued that, for the post-1970s generation (see Wyn & Woodman 2006; Mannheim 1952), youth transitions have been increasingly shaped by **individualisation.** In the neo-liberal state, the emphasis is on the individual, not the family or community (see Giddens 1991; Beck 1992; Beck & Beck-Gernsheim 2002), so each young person is under pressure to consciously tailor-make her or his own life trajectory towards successful adult citizenship (Furlong & Cartmel 1997; Ball, Maguire & Macrae 2000; Harris 2004; Kelly 2006). Individuals are subject to a range of uncertainties as the number of choices in their lives increases (Giddens 1991). Achieving a legitimate social identity has become more complex and confusing. Young Australians may feel 'overwhelmed and bewildered by the seemingly endless array of choices available to them' (Huntley 2006, p. 170). Another factor is **detraditionalisation**—the withering away of old forms of social collectivity and associated patterns of behaviour (Giddens 1994). A strong primary identity is no longer gained from place, kinship, religion, or social class membership, so 'each phase of transition tends to become an identity crisis' (Giddens 1991, p. 148). The 'self' becomes something to be consciously worked on by the young person to create a successful biography (Hendersen et al. 2007), achieved through the 'right' choices (Brannen & Nilsen 2007).

detraditionalisation
From the 1970s on, old traditions, loyalties, and rituals progressively lost their meanings. People no longer define themselves in traditional terms in the family or in the community. While this is a good thing in some ways, it carries the danger that people can become more confused about their identity, and more isolated, than in previous eras.

In everyday social practice, identities legitimate within youth culture can be established by selective consumption (or even sometimes rejection) of consumer goods and fashion trends. In social psychology terms, this process expresses the need for the young person to find 'ontological security' (Giddens 1991, p. 44)—a symbolic position of safety and certainty. This takes us to youth culture, a social arena for identity construction that lies outside the constraints of family and school.

Youth culture

Youth culture includes constructing an identity, socialising, consumption, claims to legitimacy and adult power, creativity, **hybridity**, and resistance to dominant structures. Youth in Australia bring creativity, enthusiasm, and sometimes despair to the business of dealing with an increasingly competitive education and work environment, in a world saturated with global popular culture, and the message to consume (or die socially). Youth culture, along with the peer groups and **subcultures** associated with it, provides important informal social structures offering psychological reassurance and stability (ontological security) during the transition to adult citizenship. Yet, conversely, peer groups and subcultures demand demonstrations of conformity and loyalty that can be counter-productive.

hybridity
Where two or more cultural forms are combined to form something new that has not existed before—a mutual grafting that creates an original product.

subculture
A smaller cultural group of people sharing the same tastes and ideas, nested inside a larger, less well-defined 'culture'. Examples include goths, ferals, and skinheads.

Young people derive considerable satisfaction and enjoyment from being part of an identified group—for instance, a recognisable group of friends who come from the same suburb, or ethnic peers, or young drinkers at the same pub, or a sporting club or church youth group. In youth culture, global products such as music, language, and fashion are transformed into local resources (Willis 1990). This transformation process is always located within the cultural circumstances of the young person in question. As Thomas and Fatima illustrate above, class, gender, and ethnicity are very important aspects of how youth culture may be experienced and expressed differently.

Sociological debates about youth culture

deviance
Behaviours or activities that violate social expectations about what is normal.

moral panic
An exaggerated reaction by the mass media, politicians, and community leaders to the actions and beliefs of certain social groups or individuals, which are often minor and inconsequential, but are sensationally represented to create anxiety and outrage among the general public.

Before the 1970s, youth cultures meant **deviance,** a threat to public order (e.g. Cohen 1955). In the 1950s, Australia saw a media-driven outcry over gangs of 'bodgies' (male) and 'widgies' (female), who dressed in black, wore pointy shoes, listened to 'beat' music, danced the jive, and hung about on the streets (Stratton 1993). In his 1967 study of Mods and Rockers in Britain, Stan Cohen argues that the media labelling of loosely knit groups as 'gangs' created a **moral panic** about youth as 'folk devils'. Moral panics about youth culture are with us still in twenty-first century Australia, as we saw in the media hysteria over the Cronulla race riots in 2005 (Poynting 2006).

Youth subcultures

The idea of youth *subcultures* came from early studies of youth deviance. Howard Becker's famous **ethnographic** study of the 'subculture' of marijuana smokers (1973) is an early example. Research on UK subcultures was carried out at the Birmingham Centre for Contemporary Cultural Studies (CCCS). Stuart Hall and Tony Jefferson (1976), Dick Hebdige (1979, 1988), Paul Willis (1977, 1990), and Angela McRobbie (1991) collectively made use of Antonio Gramsci's theory of **hegemony** (1971) to advance the following theory of youth cultures:

ethnography/ethnographic
A research method based on the direct observation of the social interaction and culture of a particular social group, involving detailed description and evaluation of behaviours, activities, and events.

hegemony
The operation of one powerful group over others, such that the consensus of the subordinated groups is not achieved by physical force, but rather by convincing people it is in their interests to agree with and follow the dominant group's ideas.

high culture
The cultural products and practices (such as classical music, poetry, opera, ballet, or abstract art) associated with the educated and relatively wealthy elite of society.

- Marginal or working-class youth are located outside the dominant cultural structures of society by virtue of their age, and their stigmatised socioeconomic and/or racial position. They are remote in all ways from **high culture** such as English literature, modern art, and classical music.
- As a reaction, youth collectively create instances of 'common culture' (Willis 1990) from the very substance of their lives. Punk and grunge arose in just this way, later to be commercialised.
- Youth subcultures implicitly express opposition (resistance) to dominant groups in society that have created and defined hegemonic culture to support and enhance their powerful social position.
- Youth subcultures challenge the status quo because they create new cultural forms and practices that disturb and shock the older generation in the 'theatre of struggle' that characterises class relations in late modernity.

The CCCS analysis of youth cultures has been criticised strongly, particularly the idea of resistance. Jonathon Epstein (1998) points out that, far from challenging the status quo, delinquent and destructive activities of youth within subcultures have the greatest negative effect on young people themselves. Stephen Miles (2000) maintains that, even though 'young people's lives actively reflect their relationship to dominant power structures' (p. 6), the extent to which this relationship is in any way resentful and oppositional will depend on the characteristics of very different youth groups and trends. Contemporary youth cultures are therefore not inherently forms of resistance. The real picture is much more complicated. For example, youth in the popular clean-living 'straight edge' trend say yes to music and fashion but no to cigarettes, drugs, and alcohol. Even when there is a moral panic about the apparent threat posed by a particular youth subculture, we must be careful about assuming that subcultural practice expresses resistance in any real sense. For example, the popular youth cultural practice of binge drinking really poses a risk to the health and well-being of the young people themselves rather than representing a challenge to the wider status quo. This is especially so when we acknowledge that youth drinking cultures mimic adult drinking cultures.

Despite criticism, the term 'subculture' remains popular. Using Max Weber's theories, David Muggleton (2000) finds subculture a useful term because subcultures offer young people a place to construct an alternative identity that challenges the adult-defined, limited versions of identity offered to them by school, work, gender, and status/class boundaries. Elsewhere, the term subculture has been replaced by *neotribes* (Bennett 1999), *lifestyles* (Miles 2000), *post-subcultures* (Muggleton & Weinzierl 2003), *cybercultures*, and so on.

With regard to gender, the original CCCS analysis of youth subcultures sadly left young women out. McRobbie first resurrected girls in her 1970s and 1980s research (collected in 1991), and many compelling investigations of female youth culture have been carried out since then (for example, Kearney 1998; Driscoll 2002; Harris 2004). Riot grrrl subculture provides an interesting example of an international youth culture that relies on technology. Riot grrrl is a 1990s feminist-inspired female youth network. It developed after members of the US bands Bratmobile and Bikini Kill sought to challenge sexism in the underground music scene and spread rapidly internationally:

> Female audience members began by challenging the traditional division of the gig environment into gendered spaces, where women were largely absent from front of stage. Other grrrls formed bands, wrote zines, arranged meetings and organised events to introduce girls to music making. (Leonard 1998, p. 103)

These activities took place not only not in real space and time, but in the virtual reality of the internet through websites, chatrooms, and 'e-zines'.

Youth cultures in Australia

Australia has many urban youth 'tribes' (Maffesoli 1996), just like any developed country, but the youth cultural landscape is different. Australia has fewer punks and even fewer skinheads, but more (a lot more) 'surfies'. We have pockets of 'gothic' subculture, and very public and political 'ferals'. There are 'emos' in the inner city and 'skaties' in the suburbs. Beyond such identifiable subcultures, though, Australian young people from widely varied ethnic groups and cultural backgrounds participate in a very broad sense in youth culture (White & Wyn 2004). Drinking alcohol together is an established practice in most Australian youth cultures.

6.1: Youth and alcohol

Youth researcher Jo Lindsay offers an informative account of the alcohol-drinking practices of young Australians against a media-driven moral panic about youth binge drinking in 2007. Lindsay conducted two qualitative studies of the drinking patterns of young people. She found that young people drink for pleasure, fun, sociability, and escape. The positive effects of being drunk were stressed, such as alcohol-enhanced relaxation, happiness, social confidence, and the ability to socialise. Yet there were also negative consequences. Drinking could cause trouble with friends and other people. Participants talked about vomiting, falling over, hangovers, and depression (Lindsay 2009).

normalising
The sociological meaning comes from Foucault, and refers to processes of regulation and surveillance used to normalise (record and treat in standardised forms) persons and populations so they are more easily 'governed'.

The young drinkers staged their intoxication to 'enhance pleasure and minimise pain from their consumption' (2009, p. 376). They decided when they drank, what they drank, with whom, and in what circumstances. Nights out were planned so as to manage the risks. They knew about drinking laws and regulations, and the health promotion literature that emphasises individual self-control. Participants stressed control. For example, a 'big night out' meant drinking rapidly for intoxication and then exercising self-control (2009). Binge-drinking patterns of young people are heavily influenced by **normalising** cultural expectations and avid marketing by alcohol companies in the popular press, in televised sport, and at sporting events.

Battles over the culture of drinking alcohol have been a feature of Australian life since colonisation (Lindsay 2009). Currently, state governments encourage intensive development of bars, pubs, and clubs that invite young people to drink to excess, even while attempting to curb excessive drinking and public intoxication through curfews, giving police greater powers and even rezoning. In other words, mixed messages are being presented to young people. The Australian media foster a moral panic about youth binge drinking—one that ignores the fact that drinking behaviour is learned from parents and older members of the community. Consuming alcohol continues to be viewed as central to adulthood and an indispensable element in socialising and celebrating, while at the same time young 'binge drinkers' are demonised (Lindsay 2009).

Within this contradictory set of circumstances, the young drinkers studied by Lindsay staged intoxication and excess in certain contexts and controlled their alcohol consumption in other contexts. Self-control certainly was an important aspect of the way in which they viewed their alcohol consumption, but mainly after getting drunk. Lindsay concludes that individual self-control has only a limited role to play in curbing public intoxication and binge drinking, so it is unrealistic to depend on it as the major strategy for limiting the associated risks and dangers.

Lindsay's study (see Sociology Spotlight 6.1) draws our attention to key contradictions between the messages of the state and the actions of the state in regard to young people. It serves as an example of the claim made by Johanna Wyn and Dan Woodman (2006) that 'young people's actions, attitudes and priorities reveal disjunctures between their lives and the assumptions about youth made by state policies' (2006, p. 497).

Woodman (2004) studied concepts of well-being among young Australians aged sixteen and seventeen. He found that they were optimistically attempting to keep a balance in their lives between engagement with the social world driven by the need to build a successful life trajectory, and ensuring that they did not miss out on leisure and pleasure. Woodman identified computer games, physical activities, and music as ways by which young people stepped away from their highly engaged preoccupation with building a life. They prized autonomy in both spheres. Steven Threadgold (see Threadgold & Nilan 2004) studied young Australians in the same age group. He also found a generally optimistic outlook; still, most indicated a disengagement from politics despite a strengthened government focus on youth as a category. The young people felt that youth were not recognised or represented in political debate. They trusted neither politicians nor the state to look after their interests. Political engagement was signalled primarily in the young people's consumption choices—for example, by listening to music produced by musicians working outside the commercial music industry, or by not buying products that exploited workers or animals.

Both studies indicate that young Australians are actively engaged in making their own social worlds within a context of individualised pressure to work towards making a successful transition to adulthood. This must be understood against the historical circumstances of their lives that are markedly different from the pre-1970s generation. Today's youth have experienced quite different economic circumstances amid a proliferation of choices enhanced by a rapidly transforming technology sector in the fields of education, work, and leisure. At the level of the state, the post-1970s emphasis on youth as a problem category has seen a great increase in regulations that govern education, health, welfare, labour market participation, and the criminal justice system in relation to young people. Regulations and policies appear to be protective and beneficial, but they are very often at odds with the way young people see themselves and their social worlds. There is really very little effective dialogue between young people and political decision-makers. At the same time, the media play a dually manipulative role. Young people are the primary target of the consumer industries that sponsor the media through advertising, yet the media also foster moral panic about what young people do with the massive array of consumer and lifestyle choices presented to them, as we saw above in the example of the Australian drinking culture.

Conclusion

From a sociological perspective, we need to analyse youth issues in ways that avoid a normative idea of youth-to-adult transitions being imposed on all youth, regardless of their circumstances. While young people do control and manage their own lives to a certain extent, they do not enjoy a completely free set of choices. As Karl Marx said, while people make their own lives, 'they do not make it as they please; they do not make it under self-selected circumstances, but under circumstances existing already, given and transmitted from the past' (1978, p. 595). Future possibilities look quite different for Thomas and Fatima. We might see Fatima as a kind of victim because the constraints in her life are so obvious, yet she views the future with considerable optimism because she has taken control of whom she will marry. We might see Thomas as much freer than Fatima, yet he too is under strong parental expectations: for a professional career. He is also expected to conform to exhausting normative expectations of masculine drinking culture, but still achieve excellent exam grades. Finally, both of them are positioned within the changing circumstances of the Australian labour market. Thomas' future as a stockbroker may be less secure, in the end, than Fatima's job in her uncle's hardware shop. On the other hand, given his privileged family background, it is probable that Thomas will enjoy greater protection from a variety of health and socioeconomic risks.

Taking up Marx's quote, circumstances 'existing already' for young people in contemporary Australia include class or socioeconomic status (SES), personal or family income, gender, ethnicity, religion, and rural or urban location. Circumstances 'transmitted from the past' include their deep understandings of life, meaning, culture, and social interaction, which come from their families and communities—what sociologist Pierre Bourdieu (1998) calls their **habitus**.

habitus
Refers to socially learnt dispositions or taken-for-granted sets of orientations, skills, and ways of acting that shape behaviour. People are the product and creators of their habitus.

Habitus is a useful concept for understanding young people's decision-making and choices in the fields of education, work, personal relationships, and leisure. Habitus is not only people's outlook towards society according to where they grew up, whom they grew up with, and their family class background, but it also expresses the way in which individuals 'become themselves', and engage in various practices. Habitus is the set of regulating principles and dispositions that generate and organise our daily interaction and social practice, 'enabling agents to cope [or not cope] with unforeseen and ever-changing situations' (Bourdieu 1998, p. 72). Habitus comprises deeply held values that are long lasting and can be applied to many situations. Since habitus allows for improvisation, it permits us to follow and respond to cultural rules and contexts with a certain degree of flexibility. Habitus is not entirely fixed—yet it is not free. How a young person sees the world is greatly influenced by the worldview of significant others in the process of growing up. Applying this notion, we can say that the kind of life chances and choices young people see for themselves will depend a lot on their 'habitus'—that which feels most familiar and easy according to that young person's sociocultural and socioeconomic background. That is one reason why there has been so little change in the class and gender composition of the Australian labour market over the last two decades.

Young people are not robots. They actively and creatively engage with the possibilities around them. That means we can never predict exactly what a young person will do in adult life. Upward social mobility is always possible, as is downward social mobility. Fatima might marry a rich man, or start a small business, and leave the hardware shop far behind. In the stressful world of financial investment, Thomas might turn to drugs and end up ragged on the street, disowned by his family. The first principle for developing a sociological perspective on young people is to look beyond the narrow category of youth as a fixed developmental age group, and see young people as active social agents who would have been counted as fully adult during earlier periods of human history when the normal lifespan ended at 40. If we try to understand young people in this way, we will see the need for mutually respectful dialogue rather than top-down regulation.

Summary of main points

- ▶ Youth is a socially constructed category rather than a developmental stage.
- ▶ The idea of youth transitions describes the process of moving towards adulthood. This process is now very different for young people compared with that of the past.
- ▶ Class, gender, and ethnicity are important aspects of how different youth transition processes take place, and the way they are experienced by young people.
- ▶ Youth culture membership constructs a collective identity that bolsters individual identity for young people in the globalised modern world.
- ▶ CCCS theorists argued that marginalised youth formed subcultures that directly and implicitly expressed resistance to dominant groups. Few contemporary youth cultures can actually be described as resistant.
- ▶ Applying Bourdieu's ideas, we can say that the way young people engage with the world will depend a lot on their 'habitus'—that which feels most familiar and easy according to their sociocultural and socioeconomic background.

SOCIOLOGICAL **REFLECTION**

6.1 In search of habitus

After reading this chapter, turn to the paragraphs at the beginning describing Thomas and Fatima. Make a list of their differences according to the following headings:

▶ Gender
▶ Ethnicity
▶ Class
▶ Transition (use sketches with labels if you like).

Then see whether you can apply Bourdieu's ideas about 'habitus' to their contrasting lifestyles and situations. Finally, see whether you can extend this to analysing yourself and your friends according to Bourdieu's notion of habitus.

Discussion questions

6.1 Are young people in their twenties who live at home with their parents less independent? What are the main reasons why young people stay in the family home or leave it?

6.2 What are some of the problems for young women in youth culture? Are there any all-female youth subcultures that you know about?

6.3 Why do so many people make a link between youth culture and criminal behaviour? Why do you think the media are so keen to create moral panics about youth?

6.4 What is the role of mobile phones, text messages and photos, email, blogs, Facebook, Twitter, and so on in the social construction of contemporary youth cultural identities?

6.5 What roles do fashion, music, and dance play in the everyday lives of young people?

Further reading

France, A. 2007, *Understanding Youth in Late Modernity*, Open University Press, London.

Nayak, A. & Kelihy, M. 2008, *Gender, Youth and Culture: Young Masculinities and Femininities*, Palgrave Macmillan, London.

Nilan, P. & Feixa, P. (eds) 2006, *Global Youth? Hybrid Identities, Plural Worlds*, Routledge, London.

Nilan, P., Julian, R. & Germov, J. 2007, *Australian Youth: Social and Cultural Issues*, Pearson, Melbourne.

Wierenga, A. 2009, *Young People Making a Life*, Palgrave Macmillan, Melbourne.

White, R. & Wyn, J. 2008, *Youth and Society: Exploring the Social Dynamics of Youth Experience*, Oxford University Press, Melbourne.

Websites

- International Childhood and Youth Research Network: <www.icyrnet.net>. A site where you can find articles on youth research from around the world.
- Australian Youth Research: <www.edfac.unimelb.edu.au/yrc>. You can find information about current Australian research on young people here.
- Australian Clearinghouse for Youth Studies: <www.acys.utas.edu.au>. This site offers lots of information and links relevant to youth studies and youth work.
- The Australian Youth Forum: <www.youth.gov.au/ayf>. Run by the Australian government as a communication channel between the government, young people and the organisations that work with, for, and on behalf of young people.

Films/documentaries

- *Puberty Blues* 1981, motion picture, directed by B. Beresford, Limelight Productions. Follows in detail the efforts of two girls from Cronulla to make it in the local surf and drugs scene. They later recognise the sexist emptiness of that subculture.
- *The Year My Voice Broke*, 1987, motion picture, directed by J. Duigan, Kennedy Miller Productions. A quirky coming-of-age story in rural Australia that depicts small-town hypocrisy and sexual repression.
- *Romper Stomper*, 1992, motion picture, directed by G. Wright, Seon Films. Anglo-Australian skinheads clash with Australian-Vietnamese youth and defend their 'territory' in urban Melbourne.
- *Looking for Alibrandi*, 1999, motion picture, directed by K. Woods, Village Roadshow. An amusing and endearing film adaptation of the widely read novel about the life of seventeen-year-old Josie, an Australian teenager of Italian descent dealing with the culture clash experienced by the children of first-generation migrants
- *My Big Fat Greek Wedding*, 2002, motion picture, directed by J. Zwick, IFC Films. US comedy about the culture clash that occurs when a Greek woman decides to marry a non-Greek man.
- *Candy*, 2006, motion picture, directed by N. Armfield, Candy Productions. Two young people believe their love to be enhanced by the euphoric effects of heroin but they are on a downward spiral involving theft, prostitution, despair, and denial.
- *The Black Balloon*, 2007, motion picture, directed by E. Down, Black Balloon Productions. A humorous but dark story that combines coming-of-age romantic comedy and the dilemmas of life in a family dealing with disability.

• *Samson & Delilah*, 2009, motion picture, directed by W. Thornton, Scarlett Pictures and CAAMA Productions. Explores issues of love and survival for two ostracised teenagers from a remote Indigenous community in Central Australia.

Visit the *Public Sociology* book website to access topical case studies, weblinks, YouTube clips, and extra readings.

References

Australian Bureau of Statistics (ABS) 2008, *Australian Social Trends 2008*, cat. no. 4102.0, Australian Bureau of Statistics, Canberra, <www.abs.gov.au/AUSSTATS> (accessed 11 August 2009).

—— 2009, *Australian Social Trends 2009*, cat. no. 4102.0, Australian Bureau of Statistics, Canberra, <www.abs.gov.au/AUSSTATS> (accessed 11 August 2009).

Arnett, J.J. 2006, 'Emerging adulthood in Europe: A response to Bynner', *Journal of Youth Studies*, vol. 9, no. 1, pp. 111–23.

Aronson, P. 2008, 'The markers and meanings of growing up: Contemporary young women's transition from adolescence to adulthood', *Gender & Society*, vol. 22, no. 1, pp. 56–82.

Ball, S., Maguire, M. & Macrae, S. 2000, *Choice, Pathways and Transitions Post-16: New Youth, New Economies in the Global City*, Routledge/Falmer, London.

Beck, U. 1992, *Risk Society: Towards a New Modernity*, Sage, London.

Beck, U. & Beck-Gernsheim, E. 2002, *Individualization: Institutionalised Individualism and Its Social and Political Consequences*, Sage, London.

Becker, H. 1973, *Outsiders: Studies in the Sociology of Deviance*, Collier Macmillan, London.

Bennett, A. 1999, 'Subcultures or neo-tribes? Rethinking the relationship between youth, style and musical taste', *Sociology*, vol. 33, no. 3, pp. 599–617.

Benson, J. & Furstenberg, F. 2007, 'Entry into adulthood: Are adult role transitions meaningful markers of adult identity?', in R. MacMillan (ed.), *Constructing Adulthood: Agency and Subjectivity in Adolescence and Adulthood*, JAI Press, Amsterdam.

Bourdieu, P. 1998 [1977], *Outline of a Theory of Practice*, trans. R. Nice, Cambridge University Press, Cambridge.

Brannen, J. & Nilsen, A. 2007, 'Young people, time horizons and planning: A response to Anderson et al.' *Sociology*, vol. 41, no. 1, pp. 153–60.

Cohen, A.K. 1955, *Delinquent Boys: The Culture of the Gang*, Free Press, Glencoe, IL.

DiPrete, T. & Grusky, D. 1990, 'Structure and trend in the process of stratification for American men and women', *The American Journal of Sociology*, vol. 8, no. 1, pp. 107–43.

Driscoll, C. 2002, *Girls: Feminine Adolescence, Popular Culture and Cultural Theory*, Columbia University Press, New York.

Dusseldorp Skills Forum 2007, *How Young People are Faring in Australia*, DSI

Epstein, J. 1998, 'Introduction: Generation X, youth culture and identity (ed.), *Youth Culture: Identity in a Postmodern World*, Blackwell, Malden and Oxford.

Ferguson, J. 2007, *Skilling Young Australians: Young People's Views on Improving Skills, Training and Welfare*, Youth Action and Policy Association, <www.yapa.org.au/yapa/policy/skilling.pdf> (accessed 11 August 2009).

Francis, S. & Cornfoot, S. 2007, *Multicultural Youth in Australia: Settlement and Transition*, Australian Research Alliance for Children & Youth, Melbourne.

Furlong, A. & Cartmel, F. 1997, *Young People and Social Change: Individualization and Risk in Late Modernity*, Open University Press, Buckingham.

Giddens, A. 1991, *Modernity and Self-Identity*, Polity Press, Cambridge.

—— 1994, 'Living in a post-traditional society', in U. Beck, A. Giddens & S. Lash (eds), *Reflexive Modernization: Politics, Tradition and Aesthetics in the Modern Social Order*, Polity Press, Cambridge.

Gramsci, A. 1971, *Selections from the Prison Notebooks*, Lawrence and Wishart, London.

Hall, S. & Jefferson, T. (eds) 1976, *Resistance Through Rituals: Youth Subcultures in Post-war Britain*, Routledge, London.

Harris, A. 2004, *Future Girl: Young Women in the Twenty-first Century*, Routledge, London.

Hebdige, D. 1979, *Subculture: The Meaning of Style*, Methuen, New York.

—— 1988, *Hiding in the Light*, Routledge, London.

Henderson, S., Holland, J., McGrellis, S., Sharpe, S., Thomson, R. with Grigoriou, T. 2007, *Inventing Adulthoods: A Biographical Approach to Youth Transitions*, Sage, London.

Huntley, R. 2006, *The World According to Y*, Allen & Unwin, Sydney.

Kearney, M.C. 1998, '"Don't need you": Rethinking identity politics and separatism from a grrrl perspective', in J. Epstein (ed.), *Youth Culture: Identity in a Postmodern World*, Blackwell, Oxford.

Kelly, P., 2006, 'The entrepreneurial self and "youth at-risk": Exploring the horizons of identity in the twenty-first century', *Journal of Youth Studies*, vol. 9, no.1, pp. 17–32.

Lamb, S. & Mason, K. 2008, *How Young People are Faring '08: An Update about the Learning and Work Situation of Young Australians*, The Foundation for Young Australians, Melbourne.

Leonard, M. 1998, 'Paper planes: Travelling the new grrrl geographies', in T. Skelton & G. Valentine (eds), *Cool Places: Geographies of Youth Cultures*, Routledge, London.

Lindsay, J. 2009, 'Young Australians and the staging of intoxication and self-control', *Journal of Youth Studies*, vol. 12, no. 4, pp. 371–84.

Maffesoli, M. 1996, *The Time of the Tribes: The Decline of Individualism in Mass Society*, Sage, London.

Mannheim, K. 1952[1928], 'The problem of generations', in P. Kecskemeti (ed.), *Essays on the Sociology of Knowledge by Karl Mannheim*, Routledge & Kegan Paul, New York.

Marx, K. 1978 [1852], 'The eighteenth brumaire of Louis Bonaparte', in R.C. Tucker (ed.), *The Marx-Engels Reader*, 2nd edn, W.W. Norton, New York.

McRobbie, A. 1991, *Feminism and Youth Culture*, Macmillan, Basingstoke.

Miles, S. 2000, *Youth Lifestyles in a Changing World*, Open University Press, Buckingham.

Muggleton, D. 2000, *Inside Subculture: The Postmodern Meaning of Style*, Berg, Oxford.

Muggleton, D. & Weinzierl, R. (eds), 2003, *The Post-Subcultures Reader*, Berg, London.

Musgrove, F. 1964, *Youth and the Social Order*, Routledge & Kegan Paul, London.

Nilan, P., Julian, R. & Germov, J. 2007, *Australian Youth: Social and Cultural Issues*, Pearson, Melbourne.

Poynting, S. 2006, 'What caused the Cronulla riot?', *Race & Class*, vol. 48, no. 1, pp. 85–92.

Savelsberg, H. & Martin-Giles, B. 2008, 'Young people on the margins: Australian studies of social exclusion', *Journal of Youth Studies*, vol. 11, no. 1, pp. 17–31.

Shah, C & Burke, G. 2006, *Qualifications and the Future of the Labour Market in Australia*, CEET, National Training Forum Taskforce, Canberra.

Stratton, J. 1993, 'Bodgies and widgies', in R. White (ed.), *Youth Subcultures*, National Clearinghouse for Youth Studies, Hobart.

Threadgold, S. & Nilan, P. 2004, 'Young people, habitus and opinions about politics', *Melbourne Journal of Politics*, no. 29, pp. 96–113.

White, R. & Wyn, J. 2004, *Youth and Society: Exploring the Social Dynamics of Youth Experience*, Oxford University Press, London.

Willis, P. 1977, *Learning to Labour*, Saxon House, London.

—— 1990, *Common Culture*, Westview, Boulder, CO.

Woodman, D. 2004, 'Responsibility and time for escape: The meaning of wellbeing to young Australians', *Melbourne Journal of Politics*, no. 29, pp. 82–95.

Wyn, J. 2008, *The Changing Context of Australian Youth and its Implications for Social Inclusion*, Social Inclusion and Youth Workshop Proceedings, Melbourne, Youth Research Centre and Brotherhood of St Laurence, <www.bsl.org.au/pdfs/Wyn_paper_29Oct08.pdf> (accessed 11 August 2009).

Wyn, J. & Woodman, D. 2006, 'Generation, youth and social change in Australia', *Journal of Youth Studies*, vol. 9, no. 5, pp. 495–514.

CHAPTER 7

Families and intimate relationships

Marilyn Poole

DNA paternity testing

What is termed DNA identity testing was first developed in 1984 for use as a forensic tool in crime investigations. In Australia, DNA identity testing was only used more widely in the 1990s when the Child Support Scheme was introduced and the Family Court ordered DNA testing when non-custodial fathers denied biological paternity. Since that time, the number of DNA testing laboratories has increased and test results are 99.9 per cent accurate. Although there is not a great deal of evidence, it is believed that the testing laboratories undertake about 3000 paternity tests per year in Australia (Turney & Wood 2007).

Why test for paternity? In the past, paternity was assumed either by marriage or registration at the birth of a child. Well-publicised court cases of 'paternity deceit' or 'paternity fraud' have raised the awareness of people to the view that men may be supporting a child who is not biologically their own. Additionally, it is not uncommon for men to deny paternity of a child so as to avoid paying financial child support. One of the problems is what Lyn Turney and Paula Wood (2007) refer to as 'the invisible child' in these cases. Children may well consider a man to be their father in a social sense, even if he is not their biological father. In the event of a disputed court case, this relationship seems not to be considered, and the needs of the child are ignored.

Why are families changing?

Most of us live in a family at some time in our lives, and we tend to base our views and assumptions on our own experiences of family relationships. Family life consists of what David Cheal (2002, p. 52) refers to as 'exits and entrances', as families vary in size and composition at different points in our life cycle. In Australia, as in many other countries, the family template of 'Mum, Dad, and the kids'—known as the **nuclear family**—is no longer the standard. By the end of the twentieth century, major demographic changes had affected the formation of families. These were in large part due to the increased life expectancy for both men and women and lower fertility rates. Societies were becoming older, with fewer children and young people.

nuclear family
A household consisting of parents of the opposite sex living with their biological children.

Accompanying these demographic changes have been major social shifts that have challenged traditional models of the family and sexuality. Gender roles and gender divisions are now very different from those of the 1950s and 1960s.

Farah Farouque wrote in *The Age* (24 November 2004) that, in the 1960s, '[t]he script was boy meets girl, fall in love, get married, set up house, woman stops work to have babies, then he retires at 65 and one of them dies.' Of course, the reality was always more complex than that. Today, the structure and composition of families is fluid as many families experience family breakdown and re-partnership. Families may consist of couples, some of whom may be married, while others are cohabiting; they may have co-resident children or can be in their pre- and post-child phases. Some couples remain childless. There are single-parent families, reconstituted families, and a small proportion of same-sex families. Approximately 10 per cent of the Australian population now lives alone (de Vaus 2004, p. 4).

The diversity of families today, as well as the variety of options available to people, makes it very difficult to define '*the* family'. New challenges to concepts of the family have emerged with the legalisation in some countries of same-sex unions, either by marriage or civil partnerships. The availability of new technologies to assist conception, using donor eggs, donor sperm, and surrogacy, has led to new family relationships.

What do we mean by 'family'?

A common definition of families that attempts to encompass diversity is that the family is a group of people who are related by kinship ties—relations of blood, marriage, or adoption—who usually live together. Kinship ties are connections between individuals through lines of descent (that is, blood relatives) or through marriage. Marriage is a socially and legally approved union. In 2004 in Australia, an amendment to the *Marriage Act 1961* (Cwlth) defined marriage as the legal union of a man and a woman. There is now a formal requirement in Australia that wedding vows contain the words 'husband' and 'wife' rather than more a gender-neutral term such as 'partner' (Lindsay & Dempsey 2009).

The legal definition of 'family' has the advantage of being consistently measurable for statistical surveys. Still, it is problematic as it stresses co-residence and does not include family members living apart, same-sex couples, or those people who wish to form families of choice. In order to overcome some of these definitional problems, attempts have been made by some writers to define families in terms of what they *do*.

What do we mean by 'intimate relationships'?

Intimate relationships refer to the close connections between people. As Anthony Giddens points out: '[m]ost people in our society believe that a good relationship is based on emotional communication or intimacy' (2006, p. 205). The term 'intimacy' is not new. Ken Plummer (2003) cites Theodore Zeldin in *An Intimate History of Humanity* (1995), who maintains that there have been three kinds of intimacy over time. The first meaning pertained to space and objects such as 'an intimate room'; the second meaning was more romantic and came to mean sexual intercourse; the third, and most recent, meaning has been 'to signal a partnership in the search for truth, a union of minds'

(Plummer 2003, p. 12). It is this last meaning that Lynn Jamieson explores further in *Intimacy: Personal Relationships in Modern Society* (1998). For Jamieson, intimacy is a close association that is 'loving, caring and sharing' (1998, p. 9). Jamieson (1998, p. 2) suggests four paradigmatic forms of intimacy:

1. couple relationships
2. friend and kin relationships
3. parent–child relationships, and
4. sexual relationships.

The need for good communication and disclosure in intimate relationships is considered to be paramount.

The formation of the modern family

CrossLink: See Chapter 3 for more on Giddens, Beck, Castells, and Bauman.

The rapid rate of change in families has been linked to three periods of major social change. The first of these was the move from a family-based economy, where the household was the unit of consumption and production, to an industrialised economy with a sharp differentiation between home and work. The second of these was the change in the status of women. Following the feminist movement of the 1960s and 1970s, women increased their participation in both education and paid employment. No longer were they dependent on marriage as a means of support; increasingly, they sought a life of their own. The third major change discussed by sociologists Anthony Giddens, Ulrich Beck, and Manuel Castells, among others, is that developed countries have moved to a period of **late modernity** (other terms being post-industrial or **postmodern** societies). By the end of the twentieth century, **globalisation**, urbanisation, and rapid technological change had affected the ways in which people lived and worked, as well as their intimate relationships.

postmodernity
Refers to a new era since the late 1960s in Western societies in which social life is characterised by diversity, consumerism, individualism, and lifestyle choice.

late modernity (or high modernity)
A period reached towards the end of the twentieth century that refers to the advanced state of industrialisation and capitalism.

globalisation
The increased interconnectedness of the cultural, economic, and political aspects of social life: intensified circulation of capital, goods, information, and people across national boundaries; and increased interdependence of countries and regions of the world.

The 'Western' family model

One of the most distinctive features of families in pre-modern or pre-industrial times was that they were units of production or exchange. In this era, kinship and family ties, together with strong links to local communities, provided the basis for social organisation (Reiger 2005). Family units worked on the land, in small businesses or in cottage industries such as spinning and weaving. Men, women and children, young and old (with the exception of the aristocracy), contributed their labour and worked to produce a variety of goods. Men and women did different kinds of work, although men had more social authority than women (Reiger 2005).

There was a common understanding in sociology early in the twentieth century that the main family form in pre-industrial Europe was the extended family; however, research in the 1970s by family historians Louis Flandrin (1979) in France and Peter Laslett (1972) in England, which investigated family life and relationships before the **Industrial Revolution**, contradicts this view. Their work indicates that extended families were rare in pre-industrial western Europe—most were, in fact, nuclear in structure, although often embedded in larger households. In wealthy families, large households consisted of the nuclear family plus some extended kin, domestic servants, apprentices, and labourers; in less affluent households, it was common to have lodgers or boarders. Laslett (1983) concluded that a distinctive **'Western' family** model existed in Britain, northern France, the Netherlands, Belgium, Scandinavia, and parts of Germany and Italy. Importantly, this concept of the pre-industrial 'Western' family model should be qualified, as Flandrin (1979) believes there was considerable diversity, particularly along socioeconomic and regional lines. This 'Western' family form common in pre-industrial times was transplanted to many of the settler societies in North America, New Zealand, and Australia (Coltrane & Collins 2001).

Industrial Revolution
Beginning in England in the late eighteenth century, the Industrial Revolution introduced major changes to work processes and everyday life that resulted in social and political transformations in society. Agrarian economies and lifestyles gave way to a wage-labour system, the separation of home from work, and the urbanisation of the population.

Western family
The model of the family in pre-industrial western Europe. Such families were characterised by a nuclear family embedded in a large household of kin and non-kin.

Industrialisation and the formation of the modern family

The Industrial Revolution brought about major changes to household organisation and families. First, home and work became separated. As a mainly agrarian economy changed to an industrial one, goods were no longer produced in households, workers earned their wages outside of the home, and families were supported by these wages. A family-wage economy developed (Zinn & Eitzen 2005).

The second major change that occurred was the view that marriage should be based on a lifetime of mutual, personal bonds of love. Rather than basing marriage on alliances and property, by the nineteenth century, love and sexual attraction had become the expected basis for marriage. As industrial capitalism forged the gap between home and work, young people expected to be able to make their own choices rather than defer to the views of their family and the community.

The third major change in family life was the exclusion of women from the workforce. In the nineteenth century, there was increasing differentiation between the public and private spheres: women became associated with the private sphere—the home—and men with the public sphere of paid employment, business, and politics. As a new professional and entrepreneurial middle class arose following the reorganisation of jobs and the reallocation of work to different groups of people, so did an ideology about women's place in the home (Davidoff et al. 1999). A new ideal arose regarding the separation of the public and private spheres, in which a man's role was to be family breadwinner and a woman's place was in the home. If women were to be found in the public sphere at all, it was in unpaid work such as involvement in charitable organisations to help the poor and the sick.

Not everyone could achieve this ideal. Women and children from poor or working-class backgrounds had little option but to continue working in order for their families to survive. This, in turn, sharpened class divisions and the 'cult of true womanhood became a class ideology, whereby middle-class women could distinguish themselves from poorer women who were leaving their homes to become factory workers' (Zinn & Eitzen 2005, p. 67).

The fourth major change was the emergence of childhood as a separate sphere of life. From pre-industrial times to the early capitalist period, children were expected to work in family businesses, farms, factories, mills, or mines. Children—some as young as six or seven—were sent away from home to work as servants or apprentices. Historian Philippe Ariès (1965) notes that once children no longer needed constant care they were expected to take their place in society and work, just as adults did. In nineteenth-century England, children were a source of cheap labour; however, by the end of the nineteenth century, laws were introduced to limit the age at which children could work (ten years) and prevent the exploitation of child labour. By the 1870s, compulsory schooling was introduced in many countries. Consequently, children were no longer an economic asset and could no longer contribute to family finances, making them economically dependent on their parents.

family wage
A concept that arose with industrialisation, in which men began to demand wages to support their families. The Harvester Judgment of 1907 established this in Australia.

CrossLink: See Chapters 12 and 20 for further discussion of gender and work.

By the end of the nineteenth century, working-class men and unions in many countries began to demand wages that would support their families. In 1907, the principle of the **family wage**, known as the Harvester Judgment, was established in Australia by a decision of Justice Higgins in the Commonwealth Industrial and Arbitration Court. This judgment established the minimum wages an employer could pay a male worker so that he could support his wife and children. The 'family wage' not only mandated men as the family breadwinner, but reinforced gendered inequalities in the workforce and promoted the domestic ideal of women as wives and homemakers.

Families in colonial Australia

When the British established colonies in Australia, they brought with them ideas about families and family relationships. Certainly there was little regard for Aboriginal family life, where kinship was 'the basic organizing principle' (Tomkinson 1990, p. 57, cited in Gilding 1997, p. 63). The impact of British colonisation was severe, and Indigenous connections to the land and kinship systems were ignored. The establishment of reserves for Aboriginal people dates back to the early nineteenth century, whereby 'remnants of tribes and clans were forcibly removed and placed under the control of either colonial governments or missionary organizations' (Huggins & Blake 1992, p. 43). The convicts of the First Fleet dominated early white settlement. Men outnumbered women almost three to one (Carmichael 1992, p. 103). The colonial administrators saw marriage as a means of promoting stability and were alarmed to see widespread cohabitation rather than the commitment of legal marriage.

By the 1820s, free settlers had begun to outnumber convicts in Australia, and after 1830 free settlement 'began in earnest as assisted passages and land grants to other immigrants were introduced' (Carmichael 1992, p. 103). At this time, the migration of free settlers began to determine family formation patterns in the colonies. Some migrants, such as the Scottish Highlanders, came in large kinship groups; some came alone and then sent for friends and relatives; others came together in groups from the same community (Gilding 1997). Family life established in the Australian colonies was 'typically private, self-contained and inward-looking, because the wider kin group were often in Britain or far away' (Baker 2001, p. 55). Allon Uhlmann (2006 p. 12) writes that, '[u]pon arrival in the colonies, the early settlers did not recreate strong community networks in Australia.' This was not only due to the difficulty in supporting large family groups on the land, but also the isolation of bush families as a consequence of great distances and poor transportation (Uhlmann 2006).

Industrial capitalism arrived in Australia only in the early twentieth century (Uhlmann 2006). Well into the nineteenth century, many rural pioneer families were 'units of production' (as in pre-industrial western Europe). By the late nineteenth century, though, a number of changes had occurred. Compulsory education was introduced in the 1870s, and households that included extended kin, servants (in the case of more affluent families), and lodgers became smaller following the decline of household production (Gilding 1997). In the 1920s, it had become increasingly common for women to go out to work before marriage as domestic servants, in offices and factories, and as schoolteachers. Upon marriage, they withdrew from paid employment—a pattern that continued well into the second half of the twentieth century.

The shaping of the modern nuclear family

Major changes to Australian society occurred following World War II. Migration rates were high in the post-war period, and some of the old cultural attitudes began to change. Times were prosperous. The composition of households changed. The introduction of income support and other welfare measures meant that it was no longer necessary to help out relatives in need and take them in as boarders or lodgers. Only the wealthy continued to employ domestic servants (Gilding 2001). Households became smaller in the 1950s and the traditional nuclear family of 'Mum, Dad, and the kids' became the dominant form. Marriage rates were high and people married young. Generally speaking, women left paid employment to become homemakers at the time of marriage or on the birth of their first child. These were times of full employment. The growth of the welfare state meant that families did not have the financial strain of supporting the old or the sick. Households were small and it seemed that the nuclear family was here to stay.

Families in late modernity

Sociologists such as Anthony Giddens and Ulrich Beck believe that a new form of society emerged at the end of the twentieth century. From the mid-1970s onwards, major changes in family life and relationships were taking place, particularly in Western societies. In summary, marriage rates were falling, divorce was on the rise, cohabitation was increasing, and fertility rates were falling. Sex was no longer harnessed to marriage and gender divisions were crumbling (albeit slowly). More people were single, whether through separation and divorce, or never having found the right partner, or by choice. The concept of 'the family' seemed to have become less central in people's lives. Intimacy and good relationships were seen as important for personal life (Jamieson 1998). There are some who interpret these changes as the end the family. Others would see the changes as a modified continuance of family life and a 'profound commitment to family-type arrangements' (Jamieson 1998, p. 41).

Some theoretical perspectives of the family

CrossLink: See Chapter 3 for more on the theorists discussed here.

Sociologists have provided different theoretical perspectives that offer insights on family formation and family relationships. Theories are a means of answering the 'why' and 'how' questions, and providing explanations about things. James White and David Klein (2008) comment that most family theories have their own historical legacy: some of the earlier theories tried to find the origins of gender inequalities in family life, while others looked at the adaptation of family life to changing social circumstances. More recent theories consider the impact of globalisation and urbanisation on family relationships. The prospect of one over-arching theoretical perspective seems unlikely.

Talcott Parsons: Functionalism and the family

Talcott Parsons (1902–78), an American sociologist, was the chief exponent of what is called **structural functionalism**. According to this perspective, the family performs specific functions that meet the needs of society. In earlier societies, families and kin provided many functions such as caring for the sick and the education and training of the young, whereas in modern societies these functions are provided by governments, 'churches, the larger business firms, universities and professional associations' (Parsons 1956, p. 9). Parsons argues that the nuclear family was the best fit in an industrialised society and provided two major benefits. First, the nuclear family has only one bread-winner, so geographic mobility is achievable. If the husband/father is the sole breadwinner in the family, for Parsons, there is less likelihood of clashes when two people are trying to find jobs in one location (Allan 1985). Second, as occupations in the industrial world require a specialised workforce, they function best when jobs are obtained on 'efficiency and effectiveness' rather than on personal loyalty or via kinship networks (Elliot 1986, p. 36).

According to Parsons (1956), human personalities are 'made', not born, and he maintains that 'the basic and irreducible functions of the family are two: first the primary socialization of children that they truly become members of the society into which they were born, secondly the stabilisation of adult personalities of members of society' (pp. 16–17). Parsons suggests that through stabilisation of adult personalities, it is in the marital relationship that adult personalities are supported and kept healthy. Parsons argues for differentiation of roles within the family, with an **instrumental role** for the husband/ father and an **expressive role** for the wife/mother. He suggests that, given the relative isolation of the nuclear family from the wider kin group, a woman would not receive as much assistance from her mother, sisters, and other kinswomen; therefore, in the absence of the husband/father out in the paid workforce, she would have to take primary responsibility for the care of the children (1956, pp. 22–3).

instrumental role
A term used by Parsons to refer to the role of fathers within families. Their task within the *nuclear family* was to be the primary breadwinner and to mediate between the family and the outside world. See also *expressive role*.

expressive role
A term used by Parsons to describe the nurturing and domestic roles of women within the *nuclear family*.

patriarchy
A system of power through which males dominate households. It is used more broadly by *feminists* to refer to society's domination by patriarchal power, which functions to subordinate women and children.

Parsons' theoretical perspective on the family seems outdated today. Feminists criticised functionalism for reinforcing **patriarchy** and the gendered division of domestic labour. Parson's view of the socialisation of children is now seen as deterministic and passive as it did not recognise children's self-socialisation. It also fails to recognise other socialising agencies such as the media. Functionalist theory fails to account for the diversity of family forms and also ignores many of the problems of family life, such as violence and abuse.

Feminist perspectives

Feminist writing on families represents a variety of perspectives. A major intellectual influence was the work of Simone de Beauvoir in *The Second Sex* (1953), in which she explores women's 'otherness' in terms of their reproductive capacities and the division of labour resulting from those capacities. In 1963, Betty Friedan wrote *The Feminine Mystique*, in which she discusses the dissatisfaction of American women with their lives in the 'problem which had no name'. Friedan attacked Parsons' work for its views on the roles of men and women, highlighting the fact that in the 1950s and 1960s most women were forced to retire from paid work when they married.

In the 1970s and 1980s, many feminist voices arose, providing further impetus for such a critique. Feminist theories treated the family as an 'ideology'—that is, 'a conceptual fabrication used to justify and maintain certain patterns of privilege' (White & Klein 2008, p. 222). Some drew on the work of Friedrich Engels (1820–95), friend and collaborator of Karl Marx (1818–83), in his book *The Origin of the Family, Private Property and the State* (1985). Engels' work suggests that gender inequalities in families reproduce class divisions in society, promote the **sexual division of labour**, and place economic and political power in the hands of men (see Poole 2005). Engels also argues that families sustain patriarchy by controlling the sexuality of women, as men need to know the paternity of their offspring. In a patriarchal system, women are economically and politically subservient to men. In particular, **Marxist** and socialist feminists began to examine inequalities in the workforce and addressed the **domestic division of labour** in the home.

sexual division of labour
Refers to the gender-based division of tasks, with the stereotype being the male breadwinner and the female homemaker.

domestic division of labour
Refers to the gendered division of household work and child-rearing.

Marxist/socialist feminism
Draws on the work of Marx and Engels in order to explain women's inequality, focusing on unpaid labour in the home, wage differentials between women and men, and barriers to women in employment. Since the 1980s, dual systems theory has developed, which argues the necessity to articulate Marxist class theory with *radical feminist* theories of *patriarchy*.

Feminist researchers have argued that gender inequalities begin and are perpetuated in families through the socialisation of children into gender roles. Other researchers have analysed women's unpaid domestic labour of child care and housework. Many women carry the burden of the 'double shift' by undertaking most of the work around the home in addition to being in the paid workforce. Writers such as Jean Duncombe and Dennis Marsden (1995) suggest that women undertake responsibility for the caring and emotional work in families while men pursue the breadwinner role, and that this remains one of the most difficult and relatively unchanging areas of gender inequality. Although caring is based on love and emotion, it is still a form of work.

Despite popular views of egalitarianism, it is still mostly women who are forced to give up work to raise children and who work part time when their children are young. Through this, women's position in the family becomes a major source of disadvantage in the labour market. In the 1970s and 1980s, feminist researchers believed that, given women's increased participation in the labour force and increased awareness of women's unpaid work in the home, men's involvement in domestic labour would improve (Baxter & Gray 2003). This did not happen: 'women do approximately three quarters of household work, a pattern that is evident across all western nations' (Baxter & Gray 2003, p. 10).

Individualisation

A number of sociologists, including Giddens, Beck, and Elisabeth Beck-Gernsheim, believe that the major social and economic transformations, such as globalisation, secularisation, urbanisation, and the liberation movements of the late twentieth century, have had a major impact on people's lives and changed the structure of family life (Lindsay & Dempsey 2009). **Individualisation** refers to the considerable capacity people have today to choose a life of their own, free from the constraints of families and communities. Beck and Beck-Gernsheim (2002) explain individualisation in terms of the historical changes that have taken place in society from pre-industrial times, when people were bound

individualisation
A trend towards the primacy of individual choice, freedom, and self-responsibility.

by obligations to family and community life, to today, when most of us view ourselves as individuals with life as a personal project. According to Beck and Beck-Gernsheim (2002), family life has become a 'balancing act'. In former times, people relied on 'well-functioning rules'; now more things are negotiated and separate decisions made. Beck and Beck-Gernsheim (1995, p. 1) believe that what is happening today is a 'collision between love, family and personal freedom'. Family life involves cooperation, reciprocity, and the constraints of loving and caring for others. There is a contrast and sometimes conflict between life spent in 'living for others' and a 'life of one's own' (Beck & Beck-Gernsheim 2002, p. 74).

Current patterns in family formation and composition

Despite many dire pronouncements to the contrary, the nuclear family remains the dominant family form in Australia. The majority of Australian children still grow up in an intact family (de Vaus 2004, p. 30). Of the 5.2 million families in Australia in 2006, 84 per cent were couple families and 16 per cent were sole-parent families (ABS 2008a). The dominance of couple families with dependant children is changing and represents a 'declining proportion of family types in Australia' (de Vaus 2004, p. 31). The increase in lone-parent families is due to a number of factors, such as the rise in divorce rates, the breakdown of cohabiting relationships (which is higher than that of married couples), and the number of single women having children outside of any relationship (de Vaus 2004).

Most adults (84 per cent) in Australia have been in at least one marriage or de facto relationship. For those under the age of 35 years, women are more likely to have been partnered than men (66 and 55 per cent respectively). For those over 35 years, 95 per cent have been in at least one marriage or de facto relationship. Men with lower levels of education or who are not employed are less likely to have been in such relationships (ABS 2009, p. 9).

There have also been major changes in household composition. In 1911, households commonly consisted of 4.6 persons; by 1965 the number had declined to 3.65 persons; and by 2001 the average number of persons per household had dropped to 2.6 (ABS 2008a). There are some differences when it comes to the Aboriginal and Torres Strait Islander population: at the time of the 2006 Census, they were more likely than other households to be family households (81 per cent compared with 68 per cent) and less likely to be sole-person households (14 per cent compared with 23 per cent) (ABS 2010, (reissued), p. 27).

Marriage and divorce

Marriage rates change according to social and economic conditions. For example, the crude marriage rate (the annual number of registered marriages per 1000 people) fell during the 1930s Depression and increased immediately following World War II. Currently, marriage rates are low and have been declining since 1970, which can be attributed to changing attitudes to marriage and rising rates of cohabitation (ABS 2008b). Table 7.1 shows the differences in median ages of marriage for men and women over a 100-year period. Of great significance is the change in the median age of marriage for women. No longer do they expect to marry in their early twenties, which in turn affects fertility rates.

Table 7.1: Selected summary of marriage rates in Australia, 1901–2005

Year ended 31 December	Crude marriage rate per 1000	Median age at marriage–men	Median age at marriage–women
1901	7.3	Not available	Not available
1921	8.6	27.7	24.5
1933	7.0	27.0	23.7
1947	10.1	26.0	23.0
1954	7.9	25.6	22.6
1966	8.3	24.2	21.5
1976	7.9	24.9	22.2
1986	7.2	27.3	24.9
1995	6.1	29.2	26.8
2000	5.9	30.3	28.3
2005	5.4	32.0	29.7

Source: ABS, *Australian Demographic Statistics* (cat. no. 3101.0), Marriages and Divorces, Australia, cited in ABS (2005); ABS (2008b).

Despite the fluctuations in the marriage rate, marriage remains popular in Australia, with the majority of the population over the age of fifteen (52 per cent) being married, 'even allowing for those who are divorced, cohabiting, widowed or not at a realistic marriageable age' (de Vaus 2004, p. 160). People today are marrying at a later age. The length of time spent in education is certainly a major factor, as well as the time people spend establishing a career, saving for a deposit on a house, travelling, and generally enjoying themselves before 'settling down' in marriage.

Today, many couples live together before they marry: 74 per cent of those marrying in the 2000s have lived together before marriage. Living together is now seen as an alternative arrangement before or instead of marriage, or following separation, divorce, or widowhood. People who had previously married and were in de facto relationships were less likely to marry than those who had never married (ABS 2009, p. 10).

For much of the twentieth century, there were low levels of divorce. Following the introduction of the *Family Law Act 1975* (Cwlth), which introduced no-fault divorce, divorce rates rose rapidly. Once the backlog of divorces had cleared after implementation of this legislation, the divorce rate has remained fairly steady at between 2.4 and 2.9 divorces per 1000 population in a calendar year (ABS 2008b, p. 213). Still, marriages are lasting somewhat longer, with the median duration of marriage before divorce being 12.6 years in 2005 compared with 11.0 years in 1995 (ABS 2008b, p. 214).

Children's living arrangements

The types of families in which children live have not changed greatly over the decade 1997–2007 (AIHW 2009). Most children live in intact families: 88 per cent of young children (aged one to four years) lived in couple families in 2007 compared with five- to nine- and ten- to fourteen-year-olds (82 and 79 per cent respectively). Few children live in **blended families** (6 per cent) and **step-families** (3 per cent). Approximately one in six children lives in a lone-parent family (17 per cent); of these, most live with the mother (ABS 2009).

Table 7.2: Children aged 0–14 years by family structure, 1997, 2003, and 2007 (%)

	1997	*2003*	*2007*
Couple families	81.9	80.7	82.9
Lone-parent families	18.1	19.3	17.1

Source: AIHW (2009, p. 14).

Many people remarry or form new relationships following divorce. As a result, their children spend time in households living with one non-biological parent. Beck and Beck-Gernsheim (2002, p. 96) describe the situation where two family cultures are merged within the one household and thus 'values, rules and routine, different expectations and everyday practices from table manners to pocket money to television viewing and bedtime hours have to be negotiated and agreed'. In addition, some children move between the households of the custodial parent and the non-custodial one, and thus have to negotiate different family worlds. Beck and Beck-Gernsheim (2002) refer to these as 'marriage and divorce chains' or 'multi-parent families', or **patchwork families**. In patchwork families, people have the opportunity to choose potential kin, to activate relationships, and to choose whether relatives from a first marriage remain 'part of the family' (Beck & Beck-Gernsheim 2002). Children and young people are learning about family relationships in a context of divided loyalties, loss, and separation. In a positive light, divorce, separation, and re-partnering mean that kinship boundaries are enlarged and family ties become more of an elective relationship. On the other hand, the balancing act has become more fragile, and an enlarged, 'thinner' kinship network may not be a good substitute for the loss of relations who were closer and had a greater stake in the lives of children and young people (Beck & Beck-Gernsheim 2002). Unfortunately, one of the negative outcomes of divorce and separation of a particular couple is the disruption of 'each member's social networks', and in cases involving children they often 'lose not only a parent but a set of grand-parents, aunts, uncles and other friends they were connected with through the lost parent' (Jamieson 1998, p. 33).

blended families
Families consisting of a couple with one or more children in which at least one child is the biological offspring of the couple, with one or more the step-children of either parent.

step-families
Couple families where one or more children are the biological offspring of only one member of the couple, and there are no jointly conceived or foster children.

patchwork families
A term used by Beck and Beck-Gernsheim to describe multi-parent families resulting from marriage, divorce, and remarriage.

Andrew Cherlin (2008, p. 34) comments that when he began to do research on divorce and remarriage in the 1970s he believed that a 'lone parent's remarriage would improve the well being of the children involved'. His more recent research leads him to comment that children in step-families, on average, do not do better than children in lone-parent households. He goes on to say that the 'greater the number of family living arrangements children experience, the lower, on average, their well being seems to be' (Cherlin 2008, p. 35). The greater the number of family transitions, the greater the risk of children's behavioural problems—although this does not apply to all children in this situation.

Lone-parent families

There has been a marked increase since the 1960s in the number of lone-parent (or one-parent) households with dependant children both in Australia and overseas. This increase may be seen as due to the increased divorce rate, but this is not the whole story. It is also due to the increasing rates of cohabitation and separation—which, according to David de Vaus (2004), is higher than for married couples. Lone-parent families also include those who were single at the birth of their child and who do not form couple relationships. Lone-parent households are generally headed by women and are vulnerable to poverty and welfare dependence. Most children in Australia do not live in lone-parent families, and those who do 'only spend part of their childhood in a lone parent family' (de Vaus 2004, p. 43).

Same-sex couples

The legal status of same-sex couple families is a contested area, although there have been recent reforms giving same-sex couples access to the same government entitlements and superannuation benefits as opposite-sex couples. The number of people living in a same-sex couple relationship has increased over the past decade. In 1996, 0.2 per cent of all adults said they were living with a same-sex partner. By 2006, this had increased to 0.4 per cent (to around 50 000 people). There are limitations to these data, as it is very difficult to know exactly how many gay and lesbian couples there are, because some people may be reluctant to identify themselves as being in a same-sex couple relationship (ABS 2009).

Having children: Fertility

In common with other OECD countries, Australia has witnessed significant downward trends in fertility over the past few decades. This was seen as due to late commencement of childbearing followed by low levels of childbearing that reduced the **Total Fertility Rate (TFR)** to below replacement levels of 2.1 (Johnstone & Lee 2009). It is only recently that there has been a rise in the TFR in Australia (although it is still below replacement level). The potential social and

total fertility rate (TFR)
The statistical average number of children a woman is likely to bear in her lifetime at current fertility rates for each age group.

economic consequences of an ageing population with a small proportion of young people has drawn attention to the need for policies to encourage a rise in fertility (Johnstone & Lee 2009).

Fertility rates have been regarded as a major issue in Australia for well over a century. There has been a general decline in fertility in Australia and in most developed countries since the 1870s, although there have been fluctuations that reflect the social and economic conditions of the period. At the time of Federation in 1901, Australia's TFR was about 3.93. From 1901 until the Depression in the 1930s, there was a decline in fertility and in 1934 the TFR was 2.1; it then increased during the latter part of the 1930s as women who had deferred childbearing during the Depression years began to have children (ABS 2009–10, p. 204).

Following World War II, an upward trend in fertility occurred in Australia, New Zealand, Canada, and the United States (ABS 2004). All of these countries were prosperous, had rising living standards and were experiencing labour shortages. Following the war, all welcomed high levels of migration (ABS 2004). These babies—the first peak—were born in 1947 when soldiers returned home from World War II and women gave up their wartime employment. This post-war period, until about the mid-1960s, was when the Baby Boom generation was born (commonly referred to as 'Baby Boomers'). The TFR was at its highest point of 3.5 in 1961 (ABS 2007a) and fell sharply afterwards, possibly due to the acceptance of the use of oral contraceptives (the Pill) introduced in the early 1960s.

Table 7.3: Total fertility rates (TFR), selected countries

Country	1950–55	1970–75	2000–05
Australia	3.2	2.5	1.8
Canada	3.7	2.0	1.5
China	6.2	4.9	1.7
Indonesia	5.5	5.3	2.4
Japan	2.8	2.1	1.3
Malaysia	6.8	5.2	2.9
New Zealand	3.7	2.8	2.0
Sweden	2.2	1.9	1.7
United Kingdom	2.2	2.0	1.7
United States	3.5	2.0	2.0
World	5.0	4.5	2.7

Source: ABS (2007b, p. 15).

The decline in fertility since the 1960s is a reflection of the introduction of effective and readily available contraception and the impact of the feminist movement. The introduction of the Pill meant women could choose whether and when to have children, and this enabled many married women to re-enter the workforce in ever-increasing numbers. As a result of the feminist movement, women became better educated and wished to invest more in their own careers, and consequently became less dependent on men for financial support.

Australia's fertility rate has been rising since 2001. Australia's total fertility rate (TFR) in 2008 was 1.97 babies per woman and the highest since 1977 (TFR 2.01) (ABS 2008c). Almost half (43 per cent) of the births in 2008 were to first-time mothers (ABS 2008c). Between 2006 and 2007, fertility increased by 3.6 per cent, due largely to births to women aged between 25 and 34 years; however, fertility increased for all age groups of women of childbearing age (ABS 2008 (reissued), p. 6). Indigenous women have more children than non-Indigenous women, but their fertility rates fell from around six babies per woman in the 1960s to 2.1 per woman in 2006. Even so, their fertility rate is higher than for the total female population (ABS 2008 (reissued), p. 7). Although the increase may represent a 'blip' rather than a long-term trend, it has been sufficient for the ABS to revise long-term population projections.

There are a number of explanations for this recent increase in fertility. One explanation suggests that older women are halting the birth slide. Women who spent their twenties establishing a career, on reaching their thirties and forties realise that their window of opportunity to have children is drawing to a close and opt for motherhood. Financial incentives such as the 'baby bonus' (means tested from January 2009) provided by the federal government for each birth seem to have had an effect, as well as workplaces becoming more family friendly. It is likely that the increase in fertility is also a reflection of the economic boom times since 2000. It will be interesting to see whether or not this continues following the economic downturn and rising unemployment of 2009. There is also a possibility that media commentary and the publicity surrounding 'celebrity babies' and 'yummy mummies' has had some influence. There has been a long-standing demand for the introduction of a national system of paid maternity leave, and this is to be introduced in 2011. At the moment, many workplaces offer maternity or parental leave to employees. Some of these are relatively generous, others less so.

CrossLink: See Chapter 20 for more detail about gender and work.

7.1: Intimate relationships

In late modernity, our identities have become fragmented and this has led to a quest for intimacy and an 'intense need for intimate relationships' (Zinn & Eitzen 2005, p. 228). Yet this very need carries both great risk and a great burden. Zygmunt Bauman (2003, p. viii) writes: '"Relationship" is these days the hottest talk of the town and ostensibly the sole game in the town worth playing, despite its notorious risks.' We may demand too much of our intimate relationships: '[i]ndividuals burden their relationships with too many expectations. They demand too much of intimacy. A romantic partner must provide all the things that family and community once provided' (Zinn & Eitzen 2005, p. 228).

In modern societies, individuals view their lives as a project, progressively defining and constructing themselves. According to Anthony Giddens (1992), against this quest for self-actualisation comes what he describes as the 'pure relationship'—defined as 'intimate emotionally demanding relationships' (1992, p. 89)—that can be maintained by close friends, and exists purely for its own sake. In an era where the link between sex and reproduction h friendship has become the model of the pure relationship. It is free of necessity and exists purely for the benefits and pleasures it brings. Once these are over, so is the relationship. For Giddens (1992), in pure relationships, individuals negotiate the conditions of the relationship based on free and open communication. Pure relationships are nevertheless risky, as they do not always offer the same benefits to both parties. Pure relationships have no support other than intimacy itself. If this fails or is no longer satisfying, then the relationship may fail. Is this an explanation for why so many marriages and relationships fail? When relationships are not fulfilling, or sexual attraction becomes muted, this may be a good reason for a relationship to end. Bauman (2003, p. viii) comments: 'In our world of rampant "individualization" relationships are mixed blessings. They vacillate between sweet dream and nightmare, and there is no telling when one turns into the other.'

Work/life balance or work/life interference?

Family life and relationships have changed greatly over the last 40 years. Today, most women expect to be employed as part of their life project and they value the recognition, independence, and friendships that such employment offers. This only really emerged as a major problem at the end of the twentieth century as women entered paid employment in unprecedented numbers and dual-income families became common. There has been a dramatic change in the labour-force participation of women since 1966, although many are in part-time employment. 'The rise in dual earnership and sole-parent households means that finding an optimal balance between work and family commitments has become an issue for almost all parents' (Adema & Whiteford 2008, p. 9). According to information from the Australian Work and Life Index of 2009, 'there has been little change in the overall work-life situation of Australian workers between 2007 and 2009' (Pocock, Skinner & Ichii 2009, p. 1).

Although some parents are fortunate and are able to manage the work/life balance of their choosing, many people face major barriers. This may result in postponing having children or having fewer children than they would like (Adema & Whiteford 2008). People seeking a work/life balance find it has become a juggling act, whether it is achieved by working fewer hours, sacrificing a career or not spending enough time with their children or partner. According to Barbara Pocock and her colleagues (2009, p. 4): '[w]omen are more negatively affected by longer hours than men, and many want to work less, whether they have children or not. Men are more likely to be involuntarily working part-time.'

One of the major issues in work/life balance is the time spent on raising children and housework. As more women enter paid work, there are changing expectations regarding responsibilities for household tasks and the rearing of children. Men in full-time employment work longer hours than women do, and they are expressing a great deal of dissatisfaction that this prevents them from spending more time with their partners and children. Overall, the work/life interference for men is worse than that for women because of longer working hours. On the other hand, if differences in work hours are taken into account, women's work/life situation is worse than that of men. Women are more likely than men to feel rushed and pressed for time (Pocock, Skinner & Ichii 2009). Families today suffer from what is referred to as a 'time famine' (Hochschild 1997), and there is increasing concern at the hurried pace of life for both adults and children. 'Time for family and friends is squeezed for both men and women who work full time.' (Pocock, Skinner & Ichii 2009, p. 2). If women work full time, they spend less time on housework (or outsource tasks such as ironing and cleaning). Although men do less around the house and with regard to looking after children than women, the situation is changing.

Lixia Qu (2008) comments that it is not just parents with dependant children who face the struggle of achieving a good work/family balance. She writes that, '[w]ith the ageing of the population and increasing labour force participation of women, an increasing number of people face the competing demands of paid work and caring for elderly parents (and possibly dependent children)' (2008, p. 7). Parents (usually mothers) often find themselves making impossible choices in terms of finding work compatible with child care, or compromising their careers in order to meet their children's needs. Child care can be difficult to obtain as well as expensive, and waiting lists for places are sometimes as long as eighteen months. Many pregnant women put the unborn child on a waiting list at more than one childcare centre, only to find that the best offer is two days a week some months after the child is born. To add to this, there is a national shortage of childcare workers (Halliday & Dunn 2006). Often this means that women stay out of paid work until their children can attend school.

Violence in families and intimate relationships

Families and intimate relationships are supposed to be about loving and caring. It is still something of a shock to realise the extent of family violence as a problem in Australia. The term 'family violence' encompasses violence between intimate partners and family members, and also includes child abuse and neglect. Family violence occurs across all social and ethnic groups, although the level of violence varies from group to group. *The Personal Safety Survey* (ABS 2005) provides some recent data. Overall, the survey found that men were more likely to be victims of violence than women. In the twelve months before the survey, 10.8 per cent of men had been the victims of violence, as had 5.3 per cent of women (Morrison 2006, p. 10). Women and men both experience violence, most often from male perpetrators. Women's and men's experience of violence differs: women are most likely to experience violence in the home and from someone they know, while men are most likely to experience violence in public places, clubs or pubs from men they do not know. *The Personal Safety Survey* found that women in Australia still experience high rates of sexual violence. Since the age of fifteen, 19.1 per cent of women (or nearly one in five) have experienced sexual violence, compared with 5.5 per cent of men (or one in twenty) (ABS 2005).

Research data and analysis in Australia on domestic violence and child abuse are extensive, but adolescent violence against mothers or other parental abuse remains hidden. Although there is little research evidence, anecdotal data suggest there is a problem. The *It All Starts at Home* report (Howard 2008) indicates that such violence is often hidden because of feelings of shame, or feelings of inadequacy as a parent, and because there is no official reporting of adolescent violence in the home. Victoria police identified that '9% of all family violence incidents recorded by the police in 2003–04 involved parents/step parents who reported violence by a child/stepchild aged 12–14 years' (Howard 2008, p. 14). Of these, the Victoria police identified 70 per cent of the perpetrators to be male and 30 per cent female (Howard 2008, p. 15). The most common targets were mothers (particularly lone parents) and step-mothers. Other studies report that '[t]he peak age for violence against parents is between fifteen and seventeen years' (Howard 2008, p. 15). The explanations for adolescent violence towards parents include 'exposure to domestic violence, family disruptions, ineffective and poor parenting, learnt behaviour from witnessing violence and trauma through abuse and neglect' (Howard 2008, p. 16).

Family violence in Indigenous communities is a major concern. Although reliable statistics are difficult to obtain, it is estimated that there is a disproportionate occurrence of violence in Indigenous communities in Australia (Keel 2004). Some of the indirect causes of violence in Indigenous communities include loss of land and traditional culture, the breakdown of community kinship systems and Aboriginal law, entrenched poverty, racism, alcohol and drug abuse, the effects of institutionalisation, and the 'redundancy' of the traditional Aboriginal male role and status (Keel 2004).

Conclusion

There is little doubt that families have changed since the mid-twentieth century. Fifty years ago, most people married for life, rarely cohabited before marriage, and rarely divorced. By the 1990s and 2000s, cohabitation had become the usual way to begin a partnership, with many people deciding never to marry and high rates of separation and divorce. Commentators express their concerns over high divorce rates, people living alone, and couples remaining childless. These views are expressed against a backdrop of nostalgia for the so-called golden age of the nuclear family of the 1950s. The social transformations of the world of work and the status of women have changed family life and relationships irrevocably. Families are not disappearing—they are more diverse than before and perhaps less permanent. People still strive for close and intimate relationships that give meaning to their lives. There is no single model of the family; new family structures exist alongside other, more traditional, family forms.

Summary of main points

▶ While the Western family model—the model of families in pre-industrial western Europe—was characterised by a nuclear family embedded in a large household of kin and non-kin, today the notion of the nuclear family is changing as new family constellations become more common.

▶ The definition of what family is has changed over time, and has been influenced by a range of factors; some of these are political, while others depend on how society has evolved in other areas.

▶ Australia has witnessed significant downward trends in fertility over the past few decades; only recently has there been a rise in the TFR, though it is still below replacement level.

▶ Before the nineteenth century, marriage was often based on alliances and property, but it is now accepted that it should be based on a lifetime of mutual, personal bonds of love.

▶ Marriage is a socially and legally approved union. In Australia, marriage is defined as the legal union of a man and a woman. A Howard government amendment to the *Marriage Act 1961* means there is now a formal requirement that wedding vows contain the words 'husband' and 'wife'.

▶ As more women enter paid work, there are changing expectations regarding responsibilities for household tasks and rearing of children. Many women work full time and carry the burden for most of the household work. Feminist writers have argued that gender inequalities in families reproduce class divisions in society, promote the sexual division of labour, and place economic and political power in the hands of men, and that families sustain patriarchy.

7.1 What constitutes a family?

(a) What constitutes a family? Discuss the following:

▶ A single father with weekend access to his children who live with their mother
▶ A married couple with their two children in their twenties living at home
▶ A couple and their adopted child
▶ A shared household of seven university students
▶ An elderly widow and her dog, Max
▶ A lesbian couple living with the children of previous relationships of both women
▶ Elderly sisters living in the same house
▶ A de facto couple and their two children
▶ A single man in his late twenties living alone
▶ A married couple in their forties with no children.

(b) Whom do you consider to be members of your family? Have you left anyone out? If so, why?

Discussion questions

7.1 Why do you think fertility rates have risen over the last few years?

7.2 Why do you suppose men generally do less housework than women?

7.3 Reproductive technologies have added new permutations to family relationships. What are the most important issues?

7.4 What is your view on the 2004 amendment to the *Marriage Act 1961* (Cwlth) in Australia that defined marriage as the legal union of a man and a woman? What is your view of this change?

7.5 Which of the theories introduced in this chapter did you consider provided answers to the 'how and why' questions concerning the role of families and why they are changing?

7.6 What are the major issues impeding work/life balance?

Further reading

Beck-Gernsheim, E. 2002, *Reinventing the Family: In Search of New Lifestyles*, trans. Patrick Camiller, Polity Press, Cambridge.

Lindsay, J. & Dempsey, D. 2009, *Families, Relationships and Intimate Life*, Oxford University Press, Melbourne.

Poole, M. (ed.) 2005, *Family: Changing Families, Changing Times*, Allen & Unwin, Sydney.

Websites

- Australian Institute of Family Studies (AIFS): <www.aifs.gov.au>. An immensely useful site and an invaluable resource for anyone researching families in Australia.
- Australian Bureau of Statistics (ABS): <www.abs.gov.au>. The ABS website provides access to useful statistics on families and the general community.
- Sociological Tour Through Cyberspace: <www.trinity.edu/~mkearl/index.html>. An interesting website produced by Professor Michael Kearl of Trinity University, San Antonio, Texas. Scroll down to the section 'Exercising the Sociological Imagination' and click on 'Marriage and the Family'.
- The Australian Sociological Association (TASA): <www.tasa.org.au>. There are many links to resources on this site.

Films/documentaries

- *Muriel's Wedding*, 1994, motion picture, directed by P.J. Hogan, CiBy 2000. Australian tragi-comedy of a family of so-called 'useless no-hopers' dominated by a boorish, culturally insensitive bully. Muriel, the 'ugly duckling', eventually finds admirers and her place in the world.
- *Sex and the City*, 1998–2004, television series, Darren Star Productions/HBO. Quirky romantic comedy about four female friends in New York City featuring issues such as sexuality facing the lives of professional women in the 1990s.
- *My Big Fat Greek Wedding*, 2002, motion picture, directed by J. Zwick, IFC Films. A US comedy about the culture clash that occurs when a Greek woman decides to marry a non-Greek man.
- *Brokeback Mountain*, 2005, motion picture, directed by A. Lee, Paramount Pictures. A film that explores gay relationships and masculinity in the 1960s, focusing on the secret relationship between two cowboys.
- *Pride & Prejudice*, 2005, motion picture, directed by J. Wright, Focus Features. Adapted from the novel by Jane Austen, this comedy of manners set in England in the eighteenth century tells the story of five sisters in search of suitable husbands.
- *Sex and the City*, 2008, motion picture, directed by M.P. King, New Line Cinema. Based on the TV series of the same name. A sequel was released in 2010.

Visit the *Public Sociology* book website to access topical case studies, weblinks, YouTube clips, and extra readings.

References

Adema, W. & Whiteford. P. 2008, 'Matching work and family commitments: Australian outcomes in a comparative perspective', *Family Matters*, no. 80, pp. 9–16.

Allan, G. 1985, *Family Life*, Blackwell, Oxford.

Ariès, P. 1965, *Centuries of Childhood: A Social History of Family Life*, Vintage, New York.

Australian Bureau of Statistics 2001, *Year Book, Australia 2001: A Century of Population Change in Australia*, cat. no 1301.0, ABS, Canberra.

——2004, *Australian Social Trends 2004, Echoes of the Baby Boom*, cat. no 4102.0, ABS, Canberra.

——2005, *Year Book, Australia, 2005: Australian Population Marriages, Divorces and De Facto Relationships*, cat. no. 3310.0, ABS, Canberra.

——2006 *Population Characteristics, Aboriginal and Torres Strait Islander Australians, 2006*, cat. no. 4713.0, ABS, Canberra.

——2007a, *Year Book, Australia, 2007: Fertility and its Effect on Australia's Future Population*, cat. no. 1301.0, ABS, Canberra.

—— 2007b, *Australian Social Trends, 2007: International Fertility Comparison*, cat. no. 4102.0, ABS, Canberra.

—— 2008a *Year Book, Australia: Households and Families 2008*, cat. no. 1301.0, ABS, Canberra.

—— 2008b, *Year Book Australia: Marriages, Divorces and De facto Relationships 2008*, cat no. 1301.0, ABS, Canberra.

—— 2008c, *Births Australia*, cat no. 3301.0, ABS, Canberra.

—— 2009, *Australian Social Trends: Couples in Australia*, cat no. 4102.0, ABS, Canberra.

Australian Institute of Health and Welfare (AIHW) 2009, *A Picture of Australia's Children 2009*, cat. no. PHE 112, AIHW, Canberra.

Baker, M. 2001, *Families, Labour and Love*, Allen & Unwin, Sydney.

Bauman, Z. 2003, *Liquid Love on the Frailty of Human Bonds*, Polity Press, Cambridge.

Baxter, J. & Gray, E. 2003, 'For richer or poorer: Women, men and marriage', paper prepared for the Australian Institute of Family Studies Conference, Melbourne.

Beck, U. & Beck-Gernsheim, E. 1995, *The Normal Chaos of Love*, trans. Mark Ritter & Jane Wiebel, Polity Press, Cambridge.

—— 2002, *Individualization: Institutionalized Individualism and its Social and Political Consequences*, Sage, London.

Carmichael, G.A. 1992, 'So many children: Colonial and post-colonial demographic patterns', in K. Saunders & R. Evans (eds), *Gender Relations in Australia: Domination and Negotiation*, Harcourt, Brace Jovanovich, Sydney, pp. 103–43.

Cheal, D. 2002, *Sociology of Family Life*, Palgrave, Basingstoke.

Cherlin, A.J. 2008, 'Multiple partnerships and children's wellbeing', *Family Matters*, no. 80, pp. 33–6.

Coltrane, S. & Collins, R. 2001, *Sociology of Marriage and the Family: Gender, Love and Property*, 5th edn, Wadsworth, Belmont, CA.

Davidoff, L., Doolittle, M., Fink, J. & Holden, K. 1999, *The Family Story: Blood Contract and Intimacy 1830–1960*, Longman, Harlow, Essex.

de Beauvoir, S. 1953 [1949], *The Second Sex*, trans. and ed. H.M. Parshley, Knopf, New York.

de Vaus, D. 2004, *Diversity and Change in Australian Families: Statistical Profiles*, Australian Institute of Family Studies, Melbourne.

Duncombe, J. & Marsden, D. 1995, '"Workaholics" and "whinging women": Theorising intimacy and emotional work—the last frontier of gender inequality?' *The Sociological Review*, vol. 43, no. 1, pp. 150–69.

Elliot, F.R. 1986, *The Family: Change or Continuity*, Macmillan Education, Basingstoke.

Engels, F. 1985 [1884], *The Origin of the Family, Private Property and the State*, Penguin, Basingstoke.

Farouque, F. 2004, News 7, *The Age*, 24 November.

Flandrin, J.L. 1979, *Families in Former Times: Kinship, Household and Sexuality*, Cambridge University Press, Cambridge.

Friedan, B. 1963, *The Feminine Mystique*, Penguin, Harmondsworth.

Giddens, A. 1992, *The Transformation of Intimacy: Sexuality, Love and Eroticism in Modern Societies*, Polity Press, Cambridge.

Giddens, A. with the assistance of Simon Griffiths 2006, *Sociology*, 5th edn, Polity Press, Cambridge.

Gilding, M. 1997, *Australian Families: A Comparative Perspective*, Addison Wesley Longman, Melbourne.

—— 2001, 'Family change in Australia 1901–2001', *Family Matters*, no. 60, pp. 6–11.

Halliday, C. & Dunn, A. 2006, *The Sunday Age Extra*, 29 January, pp. 11–12.

Hochschild, A.R. 1997, *The Time Bind: When Work Becomes Home and Home Becomes Work*, Metropolitan Books, New York.

Howard, J. 2008, *It All Starts at Home: Male Adolescent Violence to Mothers—a Research Report*, Inner South Community Health Service and Child Abuse Research Australia, Monash University, Melbourne.

Huggins, J. & Blake, T. 1992, 'Protection or persecution? Gender relations in the era of racial segregation', in K. Saunders & R. Evans (eds), *Gender Relations in Australia: Domination and Negotiation*, Harcourt, Brace Jovanovich, Sydney, pp. 42–58.

Jamieson, L. 1998, *Intimacy: Personal Relationships in Modern Society*, Polity Press, Cambridge.

Johnstone, M. & Lee, C. 2009, 'Young Australian women's aspirations for work and family', *Family Matters*, no. 81, pp. 5–14.

Keel, M. 2004, 'Family violence and sexual assault in Indigenous communities: "Walking the talk"', Briefing No. 4, September, Australian Centre for the Study of Sexual Assault, Australian Institute of Family Studies, pp. 1–29.

Laslett, P. 1983, 'Family and household as work group and kin group: Areas of traditional Europe compared', in R. Wall, J. Robin & P. Laslett (eds), *Family Forms in Historic Europe*, Cambridge University Press, Cambridge, pp. 513–63.

Laslett, P. (ed.) with the assistance of R. Wall 1972, *Household and Family in Past Time*, Cambridge University Press, Cambridge.

Lindsay, J. & Dempsey, D. 2009, *Families, Relationships and Intimate Life*, Oxford University Press, Melbourne.

Morrison, Z. 2006, 'Results of the Personal Safety Survey 2005', *ACSSA Aware Newsletter*, no. 13, December, Australian Institute of Family Studies, pp. 9–14, <www.aifs.gov.au/acssa> (accessed 22 July 2009).

Parsons, T. 1956, 'The American family: Its relations to personality and the social structure', in T. Parsons & R.E. Bales (eds), *Family Socialization and Interaction Process*, Routledge & Kegan Paul, London.

Plummer, K. 2003, *Intimate Citizenship: Private Decisions and Public Dialogues*, University of Washington Press, Seattle.

Pocock, B., Skinner, N. & Ichii, R. 2009, *Work, Life and Workplace Flexibility: The Australian Work and Life Index 2009*, Centre for Work + Life, University of South Australia, Adelaide, <www.unisa.edu.au/hawkeinstitute/cwl/publications.asp> (accessed July 30 2009).

Poole, M. (ed.) 2005, *Family: Changing Families, Changing Times*, Allen & Unwin, Sydney.

Qu, L.2008, 'Work and family balance: Issues in research and policy', *Family Matters*, no. 80, pp. 6–8.

Reiger, K. 2005, 'History: The rise of a modern institution', in M. Poole (ed.), *Family: Changing Families, Changing Times*, Allen & Unwin, Sydney, pp. 43–65.

Turney, L. & Wood, P. 2007, '"Paternity fraud" and the invisible child', *Australian Journal of Emerging Technologies and Society*, vol. 5, no. 2, pp. 119–31.

Uhlmann, A. J. 2006, *Family, Gender and Kinship in Australia: The Social and Cultural Logic of Practice and Subjectivity*, Antony Rowe, Chippenham, Wiltshire.

White, J.M. & Klein, D.M. 2008, *Family Theories*, 3rd edn, Sage, Thousand Oaks, CA.

Zeldin, T. 1995, *An Intimate History of Humanity*, HarperCollins, New York.

Zinn, M.B. & Eitzen, S. 2005, *Diversity in Families*, 7th edn, Pearson, Boston.

CHAPTER 8

Consumption and lifestyles

Ian Woodward

Consumer society: I see myself in my possessions

Living in a consumer society means that to a significant degree people understand themselves and others through their possessions. Objects become physical, material opportunities for people to 'objectify' themselves and their ideals. This happens in many domains of everyday life, from clothing and footwear to motor vehicles and jewellery. Think about the recent fascination with Apple products among certain consumers, particularly the whole family of 'iPod' music players that appeals to young people and technology enthusiasts. From a range of perspectives, the iPod is sociologically interesting. First, the iPod has become highly fashionable, to the extent that having one seems like it is essential for keeping up. Second, think of how Apple is frequently updating and changing features of the available range within the iPod family. This can relate to superficial aspects of the iPod such as colour or surface finish, or technological aspects such as memory size, or interactive software features such as touch screens. The release of the iPhone integrates iPod functionality within a mobile telephone, allowing Apple to extend its business beyond the digital music player. The purpose of this is to re-stimulate consumer demand so that iPod owners are frequently challenged to upgrade their purchase. Third, think about how the iPod, along with other digital music players, has changed the way people listen to and purchase music and the impact of this on music and the music retail industry more broadly. Fourth, think about the cultural myths and narratives that inform the Apple brand and the iPod music player. Apple is supposedly about creativity, maverick individuality, urban cool, and high design values; in contrast, it likes to paint its competitors in opposite ways. Finally, think about how and when people listen to their iPods. Does it change the way they experience and participate in city life, for example, and does it suggest people would rather cut themselves off from others rather than relate to them?

Seemingly mundane objects, such as the iPod, come to be appropriated by us and be seen to reflect our values, identities and our culture more broadly. How and why is it that such consumer objects become central to people's sense of identity—the social negotiation of who we are and how we understand others? Does this mean desire to have such things makes one materialistic or shallow? Does purchasing consumer goods become not so much a positive symbol of identity and status, but a sign that one has been exploited by the economic logic of the capitalist system? Within the field broadly known as the sociology of consumption, and also as material culture studies, this chapter deals with such questions.

Introduction

Much of classical sociological theory was founded upon fundamental questions relating to what were considered important materialist conditions of modern life. These considerations were invariably centred on the spheres of work and economic production. This tendency gave much of sociology a predisposition towards studying the economy, and particularly the means and modes of production activities, which were seen as the obvious domains for social analysis. As far as individuals and their motives were studied, they were seen as cogs in the wheel of capitalist economic production. Such a preoccupation within sociological theory has been called a 'productionist bias'. Pivotal to this trend of centring the sphere of economic production in understanding society was Karl Marx (1818–83). For Marx, understanding the modes and means of economic production was the crucial task for any social scientist, as it influenced everything else within a society, including its culture, laws, and institutions.

Over 150 years after Marx's seminal text *Capital* (1967) was published, many sociologists interested in various aspects of culture have turned Marx on his head. This is especially the case for sociologists of consumption, who claim it is through the sphere of consumption—not production, as Marx maintained—that sociologists can best understand the nature, processes, and experiences of contemporary society. More than this, some advocates of a consumption-led sociological analysis have argued that the very basis of society has changed, moving from a production-based economy to a consumption-based one; hence, it is often observed that we live in a **consumer culture**. Advocates of this approach argue that sociologists should move beyond old-fashioned productionist accounts of society, which see consumption practices as marginal, or even trivial. While these sociologists do not necessarily endorse consumer culture and its consumption practices, given its centrality to our society, they seek to understand it better. They urge new vocabularies for sociological theorising based upon more 'cultural' modes of analysis, which better suit the era. Frequently employed terms used as the basis for such an analysis—all of which will be discussed further in this chapter—include expressivity, symbolisation, **aestheticisation**, lifestyle, identity, and **individualisation**. This move is part of a larger trend in sociological theory, called the **cultural turn**. Within studies of consumption, the cultural turn suggests that consumption frequently, though not exclusively, serves the purpose of constructing the 'self' through a type of 'consumption play', making distinctions between oneself and others, thus delineating or demarcating cultural beliefs and collectively held values. Sociologists of consumption therefore see it as central to any analysis of society.

consumer culture
Refers to a society where consumption is the dominant mode of social activity and organisation, to the extent that we understand ourselves and others mainly as consumers of particular things.

aestheticisation
The process of depicting or representing something in an artistic manner, sometimes to the point of glorifying and exalting beauty above all other considerations.

individualisation
A trend towards the primacy of individual choice, freedom, and self-responsibility.

cultural turn
Refers to the way cultural objects and cultural life are now seen as central to understanding society, since around the 1960s.

This larger repositioning of consumption as the motor of social life is underpinned by a key change in the nature of Western societies: the move from a subsistence-based economy to one based on the consumerist, individualist principle of abundance and excess. Georges Bataille (1897–1962), an inventive cultural theorist of the early twentieth century, observed that this condition of abundance was crucial to interpreting modern culture. For Bataille (1985), a principal facet of modern life is that people have to operate in a culture where there are in fact too many things, and almost too much of everything. Intuitively, we may observe that Bataille was correct in his early interpretation of capitalist consumer culture: the abundance of goods and services available to most of the populace means that the key social problem is no longer an economic one of ensuring adequate subsistence, or adequate production. For individuals, the key problem now relates to a range of individualised issues: the problem of consumer choice amid abundance, establishing a viable social and self-identity through one's consumption practices, and the politics of selfhood posed through one's own consumption practices. As Peter Miller and Nikolas Rose (1997) argue, it is as if the contemporary self is actually established, or constituted, through consumption practices. What Miller and Rose mean is that consumption is the primary animator of social action, the principal means through which we come to construct and know ourselves, and others. Interrogating the basis of and issues around such claims is the primary goal of this chapter.

This chapter, then, investigates sociological issues related to, and perspectives on, consumption practice and consumer culture. The chapter looks at consumption using a dialectic approach—that is, seeing consumption both as a key practice in relation to individual constructions of self, and in turn the sense of belonging within cultural systems more broadly, and as a product of various larger, social structural changes that prioritise these identity-constructing processes. In all of this, it aims to follow a key sociological dictum, which suggests that individual behaviours, attitudes, and desires are mobilised and expressed within the context of particular social and cultural conditions.

The chapter has three main parts:

1. an introduction to key terms, concepts, and issues in studies of consumption and lifestyles
2. a critical review of key theoretical approaches to studying consumption, and
3. a series of case studies that look at a number of domains of contemporary consumption: fashion, the home, and shopping. Each of these case studies allows us to draw out important ways in which consumption practice reflects other, broader changes in our culture.

Key concepts, terms, and issues

A commonsense definition of consumption emphasises the purchase and use of goods or services, noting that expenditure on such items constitutes the act of consumption.

This is a starting point. The British sociologist of consumption, Colin Campbell (1995), adds a number of other stages to this definition of consumption. Campbell states that consumption involves not just purchasing or using a good or service, but also selecting it, maintaining it, possibly repairing it, and perhaps ultimately disposing of it. One could note that within each of these stages there are a number of complex and potentially fascinating processes, each of which we could study sociologically. For example, the selection of goods is frequently a rather mysterious process, sometimes undertaken largely subconsciously or automatically, but based upon various social norms, cultural learning, emotional factors, prejudices, and even irrationalities. Likewise, disposing of a good may mean literally throwing it away, or it may mean re-selling it, donating it, or passing it on to others. Campbell's definition usefully shows how consumption is a *process over time*, rather than merely the moment when a person pays for something over the counter. Further, it also reminds us that consumption is contextualised by a range of psychological, cultural, and social factors.

There are two other useful definitions of consumption, each from a partisan perspective, which illuminate unique aspects of the consumption process. The first comes from the early writings of French sociologist Jean Baudrillard (1929–2007), later to become a radical **postmodernist** thinker and social theory celebrity. Baudrillard, writing in a **structuralist** vein, states that consumption is best understood as an activity consisting of 'the systematic manipulation of signs' (1981, p. 200). There are two relevant ideas in Baudrillard's summation. The first is that he defines consumption not as a particular act of purchase or decision-making, but as a mode of generic, systematic engagement with things. Such engagements occur across a variety of consumption instances, irrespective of time and space. Second, Baudrillard talks not of goods or services, but of **signs.** Thus he is suggesting it is not important what particular good or service is consumed, because goods and services are not especially important in themselves; rather they serve as signs or symbols of something else. For Baudrillard, then, consumption is a routine practice of manipulating signs and symbols in order to send messages to oneself, and especially to others.

postmodernism
The culture of postmodernity, referring to the plurality of social meanings and the diversity of social experiences that exist within localised contexts and cultures.

structuralism
A theoretical tradition that emphasises the way culture is organised by various underlying codes, symbols, and ideas that function according to linguistic rules.

sign
An object that symbolises something else—for example, a necktie suggests formality.

The anthropologist of the meanings of modern consumption, Daniel Miller, takes a different tack in his definition of consumption. Miller (1987) emphasises the ability of any consumer object to play an important role in forming and delineating cultural meanings that simultaneously create self and culture. He argues that, through the meanings people give to goods and services, they create their identity, social affiliations, and their lived everyday practices. Miller says most of the important work in the consumption act revolves around the process of giving personal meaning to something one has exchanged for money. We can know this feeling when, for example, we have to become used to an object we have recently purchased, like a new pair of shoes or a shirt. Such a process is really one of forming a type of loving relationship with any object: incorporating ourselves into it, and letting it become part of us.

A couple of other terms require clarification. The first is **consumerism**, which refers to a way of life where consuming things is central to experience and identity-formation. A consumerist orientation constantly seeks new consumption experiences, desires novel goods, and seeks more extensive knowledge about consumer goods and experiences in order to cultivate what is perceived as a distinct set of consumption practices. This distinct set of consumption practices possessed and practised by a person is often referred to as a lifestyle. Lifestyle refers to the choices, tastes, and preferences that are assembled into a coherent set of practices and values: a mode of living. Lifestyle is not necessarily strictly consumerist, and can include both choices obsessed with accumulation of goods, and choices that shy away from conventional modes of consumption, such as a 'green lifestyle' or a 'hippie lifestyle'. The pejorative term **materialistic** is often used to describe a person, or sometimes a culture, excessively occupied with the accumulation and display of goods.

consumerism
The cultural drive to procure more and more consumer items, and define oneself in terms of one's possessions.

materialistic
To be concerned with personal wealth and accumulation of goods at the expense of all else.

Theoretical approaches to the study of consumption

Marx and critical theory

Marxists/Marxism
Those who subscribe to Marx's social theory that changes in human activity—for example, labour—are determined by economic and material factors, such as technology, and *class* conflict over material interests.

commodity
In *Marxist* analysis, refers to a consumer object that has been purchased through economic exchange.

alienation
A term used by Marx to denote the estrangement of workers from the products of their labour and the loss of control felt by workers under *capitalism*.

false consciousness
A *Marxist* term referring to beliefs that reinforce and reproduce class inequality, usually by the working class mistakenly supporting or adopting the interests of the upper class.

There are four major theoretical traditions in the study of consumption within sociology and cultural theory. The first tradition originates in the work of Karl Marx (1818–83), and was developed further in the work of **Frankfurt School** scholars, who came to be known in the middle and latter parts of the twentieth century as practising 'critical theory'.

Marx was not interested in consumption practice *per se*, but rather the object of consumption, which for technical reasons consistent with his theoretical model was called a **commodity**. Further, he was not at all interested in how and why people consumed things and what they might get from it, but in the way in which the commodity was central to understanding society. In Marx's account, the commodity was the embodiment of exploited human labour—a concrete manifestation of the sweat, blood, and energy of workers—and it represented the **alienation** and estrangement of workers from their own work. Therefore, consumption was all about unwittingly supporting exploitative systems of labour relations that were central to propping up the capitalist system. Furthermore, Marx argued, the objects people routinely consume encourage them to overlook their own exploited status within the capitalist system, thus engendering a **false consciousness** within the exploited working classes, which focus on the lure of commodity jewels.

Writing nearly a century after Marx, Max Horkheimer and Theodor Adorno (1944) tried to explain why Marx's scientific predictions of capitalism's revolution-led collapse failed to eventuate. In their work, consumption and the obsession with objects are seen as crucial to social conservatism. Objects of consumption have a mythical quality—they promise liberation and utopian possibilities, but deliver domination and a zombie-like ossification. In doing so, consumer objects enslave those who possess them, ultimately denying them autonomy, compromising their human spirit and, through their **fetishisation** by consumers, making people lose sight of the things that matter in life. Horkheimer and Adorno do not specify what the things are that matter in life, though presumably they revolve around some ideal of authentic human relations.

Frankfurt School
The Frankfurt School of Social Research was founded in 1923 as a centre for socialist research. The leading researchers emigrated to the United States with the rise of Hitler in Nazi Germany. It is closely associated with critical theory, a strand of *Marxism*.

fetishisation
In everyday (rather than *Marxist*) terms, this means to have a strong, harmful obsession with a particular thing, or consumer object.

Developing this thesis in the midst of post-World War II consumer expansion, the Marxist psychoanalyst Erich Fromm (1956) maintained that the obsession of voracious Western consumers constituted a type of psychopathology. Fromm argues that any perceived happiness felt from consuming something is merely superficial and fleeting. Moreover, he recommends (Fromm 1976) that Western citizens need to distinguish more clearly between modes of 'having' and 'being', and for their own sake begin to focus more on the latter, centred on positive personal relationships and experiences outside consumption domains.

agency
The ability of people, individually and collectively, to influence their own lives and the society in which they live.

Overall, the benefits of Marxist and critical theory perspectives on consumption are that they allow us to see that unequal social relations are the basis of our consumer culture, and that our own consumption practices could be unethical or obsessive in some ways. On the downside, this body of work can be seen as moralising about consumption rather than trying to understand it. Thus it may fail to see the socially constructive aspects of consumption and downplay the **agency** of individual consumers.

Consumption and social communication: Semiotic theories of consumption

This tradition began principally with the linguist Ferdinand de Saussure (1857–1913). Saussure's book *A Course in General Linguistics* (1966) puts forward a powerful model of the nature of language and communication, which proposes that many aspects of culture are organised like a language in order to communicate to others—for example, clothing, food, rituals and customs, and architecture. **Encoded** in these objects and their relations

encode

The ways in which particular cultural myths and meanings are built into objects.

decode

The ways in which people are able to read or work out the myths and meanings built into objects.

signify (verb), or signifier (noun)

Saussure's terms for how an object (signifier) is able to refer (signify) to something other than itself—for example, red roses signify romantic interest.

of difference with other objects is a range of meanings, which citizens of a culture would **decode** using their knowledge of cultural rules.

Working its way through the influential anthropological studies of Claude Levi-Strauss (1908–2009) in the mid-twentieth century, this idea was famously picked up and applied by French sociologist Roland Barthes (1915–80). Barthes' work is important because he was the first to systematically consider the communicative and symbolic aspects of a range of everyday consumer products and popcultural icons. Rather than seeing things such as soap powder, plastic toys, and motor vehicles as mundane, everyday, and merely functional, in his book *Mythologies* (1973) Barthes shows how such things speak to people about their strongest desires, and the greatest myths of our culture. More than this, encoded in consumer objects like the latest model Citroën DS19 Goddess, about which Barthes writes, are powerful ideological messages that serve to seduce consumers, and ultimately hide the ideological interests of capitalist producers. At the core of this is a consumer object's ability to **signify** qualities consumers desire—for example, up-to-dateness, power, good taste, and wealth.

Barthes' goal was to uncover the ideological basis of consumer culture through a close analysis of the myths and meanings encoded in popular objects. What types of objects would Barthes likely choose to write about today? An iPod digital music and video player, Manolo Blahnik shoes, a Tiffany bracelet, a BMW, or an Eames lounge chair come to mind as being among the most desirable consumer objects around for enthusiastic consumers. The questions Barthes would ask are: What does each of these objects signify? Why do people desire them? And what larger cultural myths do these objects embody?

In his early writings in the tradition of Saussure and Levi-Strauss, Baudrillard (1981) rigorously applies Barthes' ideas in his analysis of consumer society. Baudrillard develops a historical model of different types of value contained in consumer objects. At the base of Baudrillard's hierarchy is *functional value*, meaning the capacity of a consumer object to meet a functional need. For example, a pen imparts ink on to paper in order to communicate through written means, or a car gets a person from point A to point B. Next, Baudrillard talks of *exchange value*, meaning the capacity of a consumer object to measure value. For example, the cost of a new computer may be equivalent to a month's full-time salary. Third, Baudrillard highlights *symbolic value*, referring to the capacity of a consumer object to symbolise important cultural meanings. For example, giving a bunch of red roses may communicate romantic feelings. Finally, and most importantly, Baudrillard focuses on *sign value*. This refers to the capacity of a consumer object literally to reference something completely unrelated to its functional value. So, for example, an expensive European car might signify economic status or personal success. Possessing the prestigious car has nothing to do with getting from A to B, but everything to do with establishing a person's status within society.

Baudrillard argues that in a consumer society, people are obsessed with communicating messages about themselves to others through their consumption practices. The modern consumer becomes a type of 'symbolic technician'—someone who plays with the signs and symbols at hand within consumer culture. While this perspective usefully shows us how consumption has a socially communicative role, a key problem is that it remains unclear how someone can be sure that others perfectly understand their attempts at symbolic communication.

Consumption and the construction of culture: Anthropological perspectives

Anthropology has been the source of key ideas in explaining contemporary consumption patterns in Western societies. According to this perspective, consumer objects are used by people to establish important cultural meanings and are seen to do some sort of 'cultural work'—for example, represent social difference, establish someone's social identity, or manage social status. The basic idea is that consumption objects are culturally embedded: they have social, cultural, and emotive capacities, which people are able to deploy, or utilise. The anthropologist Marcel Mauss (1872–1950) was an early proponent of this perspective. Mauss' (1925) study *The Gift* argues that gift-giving unites parties, forging a moral hold over each party in such a way that receiving a gift carries an obligation of reciprocity. These ties form a type of contract among people, encouraging cooperation, civility, and social solidarity. Along similar lines, in their book *The World of Goods* (1979), Mary Douglas (1921–2007) and Baron Isherwood argue that the most important role for consumption is in demarcating social categories, maintaining relationships with other people, and assigning worth to things and people.

Clearly, goods are not important for their function alone, but rather for helping people to understand themselves, and their place within society. Consumption, then, is about meaning-making, and the opportunity to perform, affirm, and manage the self in relation to others. For example, if you were to choose a new pair of sneakers, working within a particular budget, what style, brand, and colour would you choose, and why? Would you choose a major global brand or one with special subcultural significance, a retro or futuristic style, or go for a no-name, unbranded pair? Would you choose white or black, red or yellow, three stripes or a tick? Perhaps you would not choose sneakers at all. Whatever your choice, it is not just about what type of sneaker is best to protect your feet, but about positioning yourself within the cultural universe that is played out on your neighbourhood streets, and in your local shopping centres, clubs, and cafés. Your choice of sneaker can be an important signal of who you are, your aspirations and lifestyle, and the type of people with whom you are likely to hang out.

Postmodern consumption: The triumph of personal expression, style, and taste

The postmodern perspective on consumption, which dominated the intellectual landscapes of the 1980s and 1990s, took to an extreme the ability of consumption to signify self-identity. In completely turning Marxist and critical perspectives on their head, and developing a rather extreme version of the semiotic study of consumption, post-modern accounts emphasised consumption freedoms, unfettered personal choice, and consumption as a form of play. The gist of the claim is that postmodern consumption exists within a culture of hyper-commodification, where newness, beauty, and status are god-like in the minds of consumers. The contrast made commonplace in commentary on consumption processes is that if consumption could ever be characterised in a historical perspective as strictly utilitarian or functional, then by contrast it is now characteristically self-constructive: identity-forming, reflexive, expressive, and even playful. For a representation of this perspective, this chapter will now look to the work of British sociologist Mike Featherstone (1991).

postmodernity
Refers to a new era since the late 1960s in Western societies in which social life is characterised by diversity, consumerism, individualism, and lifestyle choice.

Featherstone's account of the contours of contemporary consumer culture is principally indebted to the work of early theorists of **postmodernity**, like Fredric Jameson (1934–), and Scott Lash and John Urry (1946–), and the earlier semiotic analyses of Baudrillard and Barthes, though it develops their ideas with greater intensity, and without a strong sense of the influence of social boundaries and barriers on consumption.

Featherstone's (1991) analysis of the move to a postmodern consumer culture finds the concept of lifestyle to have particular salience. He emphasises the role of pleasure and desire in framing recent consumption practices. He argues that the construction of lifestyle in postmodern culture is the main goal of consumers, resting on the capacity of consumer goods to be social communicators of individuals' tastes, style, aesthetic competence, and originality. Featherstone sees this trend as a component of what he has labelled 'the aestheticisation of everyday life', which refers to the increased role of how a consumer object looks in guiding consumer choice, as much as the way the object works.

hedonism
A devotion to pleasure and happiness as a way of life; in the context of consumption, a hedonistic life can be pursued through consumption.

Postmodern consumers are held to be **hedonistic**, continually calculating or assessing the stylistic effect of their choices, and constantly desiring new or better consumer goods or experiences. The increased range of consumer choices means that people develop their sense of individuality through their unique assemblage of consumer goods, which they are able to develop pleasurably into a coherent identity package. Modern consumers, as Featherstone (1991, p. 86) points out, speak with their clothes, home, car, furnishings, and other decorations, which others can read in terms of the presence or absence of taste and personal style.

The postmodern mode of expressive consumption is enabled by a number of large-scale social changes. The first of these is the widespread, frenetic commodification of all spheres of human life so that people are encouraged to purchase the most fundamental human needs of self-worth—love, sex, and happiness—through commodities.

commodified self
Self-identity that is largely shaped and understood through consumption practices: 'I am what I consume.'

Associated with this, the argument goes, we live in an era where our self-identity is created or discovered, and constantly monitored, relatively free from the constraints of social class, family, and work life. Being responsible for our own identities, we use the abundant resources of consumer markets to construct a viable identity, based around the skilful assemblage of certain commodities that assist in building a sort of **commodified self**.

Third, commodities are not desired purely, or even mostly, for their function, but rather have become aestheticised. That is, consistent with Baudrillard's thesis about sign value being paramount, they must look good as well as work. All sorts of consumer goods come to mind to illustrate this dictum: watches, shoes, mobile telephones, domestic lighting, and so on are all resolutely functional consumer objects that have been thoroughly aestheticised.

Finally, there has been a fragmentation of old hierarchies of cultural tastes. This has meant that products easily available to everyday consumers can be seen as 'art', and contribute to a credible personal style. Social status involves the masterly manipulation of symbols in order to establish one's good taste, discernment, or superior cultural style. In our consumer culture, a person does not need a Rolls-Royce and a country estate to manage this. Establishing superior style can now be done through a cool pair of old sneakers, some faux jewellery purchased from a flea market, a retro pair of sunglasses, and a cheap 1980s-style electronic watch. At least that is what the new rules of our consumer culture tell us.

Fashion: How to be an individual when you are an imitator

This section considers three domains of consumption and lifestyle: fashion, the home, and shopping. One of the great sociologists of cultural life, Georg Simmel (1858–1918), was the first to take fashion seriously as an object of sociological inquiry. Writing in the early twentieth century, Simmel (1971) argued that fashion was a basic phenomenon of social life, an institution fundamental to modern society. Simmel suggests that fashion is not just limited to dress and self-presentation, but that cycles of fashion pervade many aspects of our culture, including religion, scientific ideas, food, and manners. Simmel elegantly outlines the fantastic contradictory capacity of fashion. On the one hand, feeling 'in fashion' assists a person to feel at the centre of things, to feel a vital member of culture. Yet, at the same time, Simmel highlights how such feelings are dependent on copying, thoughtlessness, and imitation. Thus fashion allows an individual to feel special or unique, even though she or he is merely copying others with the same fashion sense.

For the 'modern' person, Simmel (1971) argues that such imitation—which is at the core of the fashion phenomenon—is not merely a negative thing, for it does free individuals from the responsibility of maintaining self, and the hard work of generating an authentic individual style; however, in the process of copying in order to be 'fashionable', the modern imitator forfeits creativity and genuine self-purpose. Moreover, he maintains that those who follow fashion are ultimately doomed—stylistically, that is. After all, Simmel claims, fashion is a type of zero-sum game: if you are a dedicated fashion leader you could be ahead of most others for a while, but as the cycle of fashion moves forward the majority eventually will adopt fashion innovations, effectively cancelling out the distinctions of the leading fashion group, the members of which are forced to look elsewhere for their distinctions.

All of this seems as relevant now as it did over a century ago, which is why Simmel is still read extensively as a cultural sociologist; however, one area in which Simmel's views seem a little outdated concerns the source of fashion in our culture. Simmel (1971) argues that the fashion leaders are the elite strata of society: the wealthy and the upper class. In his day, the upper classes led and the middle classes desired to be fashionable, while the lower classes simply dreamt. These days, the idea that the elite drives fashion is no longer relevant. Sure, the members of the elite have their own fashions: large European motorcar marques, extravagant jewellery, major global brands, and so on; however, there is also more choice and eclecticism in fashion, befitting the postmodern style of consumption. Fashion might come from a traditional form of dress worn in a region of Africa, or have working-class origins. Further, most designers are young, creative, and tap into popular culture for their inspiration. Youth street fashions tend to filter upwards, rather than remain relevant to youth only. Likewise, sportswear has been incorporated into high fashion, as have military motifs. Decades come to represent fashion styles: the 1960s, 1970s, and 1980s have all been plundered by designers and enthusiastically (re)embraced by consumers. Almost any symbol is available for appropriation by the fashion industry: the postmodern consumer is encouraged to dabble and play with the symbolic resources available (see Craik 1993; English 2007).

The home: Australians and the desire for a big home, car, and backyard

As a site of consumption, the home stands as an interesting and important special case. It remains the largest single economic investment people are likely to make, and seems to have enduring cultural salience in Australia, where commentators such as Robin Boyd and Hugh Stretton have long suggested the home has potency as a symbol of modernity, middle-class status, and affluence (see Boyd 1978; Stretton 1975).

The saying often goes that the Australian dream is to own a home on a quarter-acre block. Perhaps that dream needs some revision: the cost of housing is very high, especially in Australia's capital cities, and houses have been attacked for being environmentally unfriendly. Yet Australians typically—and increasingly, it seems—desire their houses to be large: four or more bedrooms; dual indoor/outdoor entertaining areas; gourmet kitchen; a media room for internet, large-screen TV, and playing music; and of course at least a double car space. Because of their tendency to be similar in style, and in turn to mimic grand mansions of other times and places, within some circles these homes have been pejoratively labelled 'McMansions'.

This desire for size and space in the family home has also pushed new housing developments further and further away from our city centres, causing a range of environmental and planning problems. For example, it takes an increasing amount of time to commute to work, putting pressure on road infrastructure and public transport systems, and it is costing more money in fuel. Moreover, the desire to have a new house on a large block of land has led to the clearing of native bushland and ecosystems on the fringes of cities. In response, developers have tried in recent years to integrate environmental features into their suburban developments, and green credentials are an increasingly important way for them to market their housing. Of course, the inner urban areas of cities are also increasingly intensively developed, causing the displacement of traditional residents in these areas and fuelling the speculative development of investment properties. In large part, it is the consumptive and lifestyle possibilities afforded by living in Australia's inner cities on the one hand, and the availability of investment credit on the other, that have driven such processes in recent decades. In turn, such processes expose residents and investors to cyclical upswings and downswings in rent and property values, occasionally being affected by extreme credit crises—as we saw in the Global Financial Crisis (GFC) of 2008 and 2009.

As well as considering the 'macro' aspects of consumption processes in relation to homes, let us also consider what goes on inside them from a sociological point of view. When considering the internal space of a home, it can be observed that domestic spaces are not exclusively public or private, as such meanings shift according to the social and familial relationships of visitors to the spatial organisation of the home. Objects within the home, too, serve shifting purposes according to the needs of the situation. Objects sometimes have a public role in the home as a signifier of status, style, or taste—for example, a large vase, painting, or plasma TV. At other times, they serve as a focus for managing self-identity, family relations or self-esteem—for example, framed family photographs, or mementos.

Environmental psychologists typically have emphasised the psychic dimensions of home. Not only are domestic interiors spaces to be played with via a person's environmental preferences, but they are also spaces of familial and friendship-based interaction. At a deeper level, homes are warehouses of personal experience, housing our memories and deepest attachments, and also containing our fears. As Gaston Bachelard (1958) points out, the home is a site that represents a basic and important division in geographical space between the house (self) and non-house (non-self, or Other). People use homes as a type of shield from the public. In the environmental psychology paradigm, homes are sites for the application of resources directed towards the maintenance of self-identity and self-esteem, family relations and notions of insiders/outsiders. In addition to their psychological dimension, homes carry a freight of sociological meaning. Ways of living in the home, and the organisation and selection of the system of objects within its spaces, are circumscribed by moral prescriptions associated with family-, gender-, and class positions. For example, members of a household typically care for different spaces within the home. In traditional households, housework is strictly divided according to gender.

CrossLink: See Chapter 7 for more on the gendered division of labour.

Shops and the sociology of shopping: Malls versus high streets

The shift from a society of production to a society of consumption is probably best identified in how and why we shop. Since at least the 1970s, the shopping mall has dominated Australian cities. Not only do large malls draw tens of thousands of shoppers each day for a whole range of goods and services, and a variety of shopping expeditions from the drop-in to the leisurely browse; malls have come to anchor whole regions within our cities by acting as magnets for people and discretionary spending, leisure time, and social and family agendas. Australia was one of the first Western nations to embrace the contemporary shopping mall, the main premise of which was to have one site—preferably in the middle of a population growth area within the city—where all needs and wants could be satiated. In this sense, the mall mimics the old type of high-street shopping experience, but within a much more tightly controlled environment. Old shopping strips and centres of the first half of the twentieth century would, to many shoppers, seem boring in comparison to today's malls: they were straight lined and single level; they were open-air and relied upon natural light; they had a much smaller range of stores, and consequently a low level of other entertainment activities nearby.

Historical research into the design of malls in Australia (see Woodward 1998), based upon an analysis of articles from the journal *Architecture Australia* from the 1950s to the 1990s, shows that the contemporary mall operates on a completely opposite set of principles: its shopping vistas are curvilinear and multi-level (as opposed to straight and ground floor) in order to create a sense of discovery and mystery; malls are generally fully enclosed to control lighting and temperature (one of the main reasons people like malls is to escape weather extremes); they try to create a rhythm of movement in shoppers through effective lighting, tiling, and barriers rather than letting the shoppers determine the path of their own shopping expeditions; they have a strongly integrated interior concept relying on entertainment, bright colours, clever lighting, and aesthetic features; they regularly place themselves in local or regional mythologies by referencing some special feature of the region in their decoration (for example, a shopping mall on the Gold Coast displays a series of decorative surfboards just to remind people they are near the beach); and malls also become complete family entertainment centres from movies and games arcades, to celebrity events and signings, to cooking demonstrations. Of course, malls are also shared social spaces, in the sense that they cater to the demands of a range of visitors throughout any one week. At weekends and after school, younger people tend to use them as places to hang out, to meet friends, or to 'do leisure'. In this sense, malls are a relatively free 'third space', away from the routines and demands of the home and school. During the week and daytimes, retirees, parents looking after children, and shiftworkers tend to inhabit the mall, often as much for their services like banks, post offices, and medical centres as for shopping.

It is worth noting that, while the mall has become the dominant space for shopping, many younger people are taking to shopping in district high streets such as Chapel and Greville in Melbourne, Oxford and Crown in Sydney, or Ann and Brunswick in Brisbane.

These spaces are generally youth consumption zones. They are seen to be more authentic and relaxed, more strongly associated with energetic or exciting youth cultures, and offer a greater range of associated activities like clubs, bars, and cafés. Furthermore, these zones within our cities often have, or are located near, vibrant music scenes that feed directly into fashion, shopping, and subcultural senses of being 'cool'. The cafés, shops, and bars within these districts feed off youth culture for their inspiration and for their business, but in turn offer young people a haven from what many see as homogenised, sterile, and meaningless mall environments. Yet, even while they do this, they are still just spaces for consumption—albeit spaces based upon different codes, narratives, and symbols.

SOCIOLOGY **SPOTLIGHT**

8.1: Shopping malls—public or private spaces?

Are shopping malls truly public spaces, or are they merely privatised spaces subject to the interests of capital and teams of mall managers and store owners? The classical vision of the public space is associated with the open-air market, an area for cultural mixing of people from all different parts of the city. In these spaces, commerce became the basis for economic exchanges, which in turn formed the basis of social solidarity and shared interests; however, contemporary urban spaces deviate somewhat from these ideals. Malcolm Voyce (2006) charts the redevelopment of the Hornsby shopping mall in Sydney. He shows how the redevelopment led to the consolidation of the owner Westfield's interests and the shift of control of the mall's space largely to Westfield. This meant that, by and large, Westfield could set the rules about who and what types of activities were allowed inside the mall. After all, if the safety and enjoyment of mainstream shoppers could not be guaranteed, then people would stop shopping at the mall and the profitability of the investments of all owners was under threat. For example, the owners disallowed certain types of activities in the mall, such as busking and skateboarding, and limited things like collection by charities. Signage and branding within the mall were painstakingly controlled, meaning nothing looked out of place. The result—one we might feel while wandering any shopping mall—was that, while we might feel safe and mildly enjoy the experience of mall walking, we also might feel somewhat bored and underwhelmed, as if being manipulated by all the mall's tricks, such as mood music, lighting, and conveniently placed coffee shops. Voyce argues that new malls such as Hornsby radically alter the nature of what we understand to be public space. In fact, because they are so strongly governed and surveilled by technological equipment, and promote certain exclusive forms of consumption, they represent a form of public space that erodes classical social spaces, which were based on equal access and equality. Our cities have become increasingly divided up into types of consumption zones, each subject to its own rules and subtle forms of control.

Conclusion

To participate in contemporary Australian society, one cannot avoid being a consumer. The old institutions of social control and patterning are less relevant: schools, social class, and workplaces arguably have less hold over people's construction and performance of identity. In the space that opens up, consumption, consumerism, and lifestyle have become the dominant new ethic. Such an ethic rewards accumulation, individualism, experimentation and identity-play, hedonism and pleasure-seeking, and, above all, cultivates a 'desire to desire'. As Bryan Turner and Chris Rojek (2002) point out, the irony of a consumerist society is that it never actually seeks to satisfy needs, but multiplies scarcities through the stimulation of desire. Whether this is seen as an opportunity to find meanings through such consumption, or as a site of social exploitation, depends on the sociological perspective.

Summary of main points

▶ A simple definition of consumption is that it is the act of purchasing and using up a good or service.

▶ More importantly, consumption involves the meaningful manipulation of signs and symbols for the purpose of social communication.

▶ Consumption typically refers to an act; consumerism refers to a way of life where consumption is central. Lifestyle refers to the package of individuals' consumption habits and preferences.

▶ Marxist and critical theory approaches emphasise the exploitative and degrading aspects of consumption.

▶ Semiotic, cultural, and postmodern approaches emphasise the constructive, affiliative, and meaningful aspects of people's consumption habits.

▶ Consumption practices shape our cities and urban environments as much as they do our identities.

8.1 What type of consumer are you?

▶ Undertake a 24-hour audit of your own consumption practices. Categorise them according to their type, purpose, and effect.

▶ In what ways, if at all, do you resist or challenge the contemporary pressure to be a 'good consumer'?

▶ Is consumption politically 'bad' or problematic? If someone is a 'green consumer', or consumes lots of alternative music, is she or he still being exploited and degraded, as critical accounts of consumption would suggest?

SOCIOLOGICAL **REFLECTION**

Discussion questions

8.1 Is consumption a practice of freedom, identity-play and culturally meaningful activity, or is it a practice that enslaves and degrades people?

8.2 What is more important in framing people's identity: their work or their consumption habits and preferences? Look for research evidence to support your hypothesis.

8.3 What types of shopping experiences are available in your city, town, or suburb? What types of consumption experiences do they offer and encourage? What types of people typically shop in these places, and what types of shopping do they do?

8.4 This chapter has not talked much about the relationship between gender and consumption practices. Can you find any research and anecdotal evidence to show that consumption is a gendered activity?

8.5 Is it possible to 'opt out' of being a consumer in our society? Is 'opting out' just another form of consumption?

8.6 Do you think consumption is a site of relative freedom, or just another form of social control?

Further reading

Bauman, Z. 1988, *Freedom*, Open University Press, Milton Keynes.

Bennett, T., Emmison, M. & Frow, J. 1999, *Accounting for Tastes: Australian Everyday Cultures*, Cambridge University Press, Melbourne.

Campbell, C. 1987, *The Romantic Ethic and the Spirit of Modern Consumerism*, Blackwell, New York.

Corrigan, P. 1997, *The Sociology of Consumption: An Introduction*, Sage, London.

Douglas, M. & Isherwood, B. 1979, *The World of Goods: Towards an Anthropology of Consumption*, Basic Books, New York.

Miles, S. 1997, *Consumerism as a Way of Life*, Sage, London.

Woodward, I. 2007, *Understanding Material Culture*, Sage, London.

Websites

- Adbusters: <http://adbusters.org/home>. Publisher of *Adbusters* magazine, this network of artists and educators promotes social activism against powerful media and corporate groups. This site contains both informative and amusing material, such as spoof advertisements.
- Association for Consumer Research: <www.acrwebsite.org/index.asp>. A United States-based site with links to useful consumer research resources.

- Australian Consumers' Association: <www. choice.com.au>. The producer of *Choice* magazine, this non-profit and non-government organisation is a leading consumer lobby group.
- CorpWatch (USA): <www.corpwatch.org/index.php>. CorpWatch aims to investigate unethical and fraudulent corporate practices.
- CorporateWatch (UK): <www.corporatewatch.org.uk>. An independent United Kingdom-based corporate watchdog group.
- SocioSite—Consumption: <www.sociosite.net/topics/culture.php#CONSUMPTION>. This site contains many links to quality resources on consumption.
- Waste of the World: <www.thewasteoftheworld.org>. A UK research project that looks at the by-products of consumerism.

Films/documentaries

- *Fight Club*, 1999, motion picture, directed by D. Fincher, Fox 2000 Pictures. What has a bunch of men trying to belt one another about got to do with consumerism? This film picks up on (strongly gendered) themes of alienation, anomie, and powerlessness, along the way indicting the emptiness of consumer culture.
- *The Filth and the Fury*, 2000, documentary, directed by J. Temple, FilmFour. This film looks at codes of punk subcultural consumption and the subversive potential of fashion via a documentary about legendary punk band The Sex Pistols. Should be viewed in conjunction with reading Dick Hebdige's classic text *Subculture: The Meaning of Style*.
- *Sideways*, 2004, motion picture, directed by A. Payne, Fox Searchlight Pictures. This film examines how middle-class consumption habits intersect with touring cultures, gourmet food and wine, and human longing, all set in a contemporary haven of consumer culture: California.

Visit the *Public Sociology* book website to access topical case studies, weblinks, YouTube clips, and extra readings.

References

Bachelard, G. 1958, *The Poetics of Space*, trans. M. Jolas, Beacon Press, Boston, MA.

Barthes, R. 1973 [1957], *Mythologies*, trans. A. Lavers, Paladin Grafton, London.

Bataille, G. 1985, *Visions of Excess: Selected Writings, 1927–1939*, ed. A. Stoekl, University of Minnesota Press, Minneapolis.

Baudrillard, J. 1981, *For a Critique of the Political Economy of the Sign*, trans. C. Levin, Telos Press, St Louis, MO.

Boyd, R. 1978, *Australia's Home: Why Australians Built the Way they Did*, 2nd edn, Penguin, Ringwood.

Campbell, C. 1995, 'The sociology of consumption', in D. Mills (ed.), *Acknowledging Consumption: A Review of New Studies*, Routledge, London, pp. 96–126.

Craik, J. 1993, *The Face of Fashion*, Routledge, New York.

Douglas, M. & Isherwood, B. 1979, *The World of Goods: Towards an Anthropology of Consumption*, Basic Books, New York.

English, B. 2007, *A Cultural History of Fashion in the Twentieth Century: From the Catwalk to the Sidewalk*, Berg, Oxford.

Featherstone, M. 1991, *Consumer Culture and Postmodernism*, Sage, London.

Fromm, E. 1956, *The Sane Society*, Rinehart, New York.

—— 1976, *To Have or to Be?*, Harper & Row, New York.

Horkheimer, M. & Adorno, T. 1944, *The Dialectic of Enlightenment*, Continuum, New York.

Marx, K. 1967 [1867], *Capital: A Critique of Political Economy*, Volume I, International Publishers, New York.

Mauss, M. 1925, *The Gift: Forms and Functions of Exchange in Archaic Societies*, trans. I. Cunnison, Cohen and West, London.

Miller, D. 1987, *Material Culture and Mass Consumption*, Blackwell, Oxford.

Miller, P. and Rose, N. 1997, 'Mobilising the consumer: Assembling the subject of consumption', *Theory, Culture and Society*, vol. 14, no. 1, pp. 1–36.

de Saussure, F. 1966, *Course in General Linguistics*, McGraw-Hill, New York.

Simmel, G. 1971 [1904], 'Fashion', in D. Levine (ed.), *Georg Simmel*, University of Chicago Press, Chicago, pp. 294–323.

Stretton, H. 1975, *Ideas for Australian Cities*, 2nd edn, Georgian House, Melbourne.

Turner, B.S. & Rojek, C. 2002, *Society and Culture: Principles of Scarcity and Solidarity*, Sage, London.

Voyce, M. 2006, 'Shopping malls in Australia. The end of public space and the rise of "consumerist citizenship"?', *Journal of Sociology*, vol. 42, no. 3, pp. 269–86.

Woodward, I. 1998, 'The shopping mall, postmodern space and architectural practice: Theorising the postmodern spatial turn through the planning discourse of mall architects', *Architectural Theory Review*, vol. 3, no. 2, pp. 46–58.

CHAPTER 9

Sporting life

Peter Mewett

Ethics in sports: The case of jumps-racing

Victoria and South Australia remain the last two Australian states to retain 'jumps-racing', which has been banned elsewhere in Australia. The sport involves horses jumping over hurdles or other obstacles. Because of the injury and death rates endured by the horses—considerably higher than for flat-racing—its continuation has raised considerable anger within the animal welfare lobby, from the Royal Society for the Prevention of Cruelty to Animals (RSPCA) through to a radical group called Horse Racing Kills.

Over time, many animal sports such as dog-fighting, cock-fighting, bear-baiting, ratting, and (recently in Britain) fox-hunting, have been outlawed because of the undeniable cruelty of animals being savaged and killed by others. Jumps-racing falls into a different category because it is not a 'blood-sport'; rather, it has attracted adverse attention because of the *unwanted* effects of the sport on the animals. In Victoria, twelve horses died in the 2008 jumps-racing season and at the time of writing, thirteen have so far succumbed in the 2009 season.

The death and injury toll on the horses, described by many as 'unacceptable', provides the opponents of jumps-racing with powerful ammunition to support their calls to ban the sport. But what would be the consequences of banning it? Jumps horses are thoroughbreds that have proved too slow for the flat. Most 'reject' thoroughbreds go to the knackery for processing into pet food. Jumps supporters claim that the horses selected for this sport are saved from the slaughterhouse and well looked after by their trainers. Moreover, jumps-racing is a significant employer in rural and regional Victoria, where many of the jumps stables are located and some of the major jumps races are held.

It is not just a simple case of banning jumps-racing to save the horses that die in competition, because they and many of the others taken into this sport would otherwise have been slaughtered. Moreover, banning the sport would throw some trainers out of business and jumps jockeys and stable employees out of work. On the other hand, the deaths and injuries to horses in jumps-racing are appalling; should this mean that the sport should be banned, as the animal-welfare lobby demands, or dismissed as an unfortunate part of racing, as the jumps supporters claim?

The current controversy over jumps-racing provides an interesting window into the ethics of sports. All actions have consequences, in sports as much as in the larger community, and banning jumps-racing would have both positive and negative outcomes. In light of this, is there an ethically clear argument about jumps-racing?

Introduction

Sport is a social activity embedded in many other aspects of society. To understand how people live together and construct their societies, we cannot exclude any area of social activity. Sport is not isolated from other parts of social life; rather, it is strongly influenced by what takes place in non-sport social fields. What occurs in the sports arena is not just a contest, but the playing of a game in a particular way by a specified group of people. Sport ranges widely from activities done singly or with others as a form of leisure pursuit to professional endeavours that pack large stadia with spectators and attract millions more who watch it on television, listen to it on the radio, or read about it in newspapers.

Sport pervades much of what we do in our daily lives: checking the cricket scores in the morning paper, flicking on the television to find out how a tennis competition is proceeding, discussing a football team's chances, and so on. Sporting metaphors are often used in everyday speech—for example, someone tackling a difficult task might be said to be on 'a sticky wicket', while a change of objectives is called 'moving the goalposts' and having an equal chance of achieving something is a 'level playing field'. Even people totally disinterested in sport are, in their rejection of it, influenced by sport. How do sociologists manage to investigate and make sense of something as pervasive and complex as sport?

Jay Coakley and his colleagues (2009) make the important point that sports are **social constructions**. By this they mean that sports are produced as part of people's social activities. Sports are very much the product of the societies in which they are found; they constitute part of these societies. Many features found in a society are also found in sports. Gender, class, race, ethnicity, age, business, media, nationalism, community, and globalisation all have an effect on how sports are constructed. More than this, sports—on the playing field and in their organisational and support structures—**reproduce** those features of the society found in their construction. For example, exclusive golf clubs, by restricting membership to people of sufficient wealth and the appropriate social connections, reproduce in a sporting field some significant aspects of social inequality that permeate society as a whole. This chapter uses sociology to explore this circular relationship between sport and society, showing how sports are socially constructed and how they in turn reproduce aspects of the wider society.

A brief word first on how sport was added to the stable of sociology specialisms. Glimmerings of a sociology of sport were seen in the 1960s, but the movement did not gain momentum until the 1970s and 1980s, when an increasing number of researchers directed attention to it. Books and specialist journals were started as publishing outlets for sports sociology research. Much of the early development of sports sociology occurred in North America, mostly from departments of **kinesiology**, but significant

social construction/ism
Refers to the socially created characteristics of human life based on the idea that people actively construct reality, meaning it is neither 'natural' nor inevitable. Therefore, notions of normality/abnormality, right/wrong, and health/illness are subjective human creations that should not be taken for granted.

reproduce/reproduction
The social activity of doing things in ways that replicate existing patterns and processes of behaviour.

kinesiology
A North-American term for what is usually referred to in Australia as 'human movement studies'.

figurational sociology
Established by Elias, this approach focuses on long-term processes affecting the networks between interdependent groups of people.

contributions were also made from Leicester University in England, using the **figurational sociology** approach developed by Norbert Elias (1897–1990). Several of Elias' students—most notably Eric Dunning—and subsequently their students, immersed themselves in studies of sport to develop a distinctive and mostly United Kingdom-based contribution. On the whole, a similar level of engagement with sport has been lacking among Australian sociologists, although a small number maintain this specialism here (e.g. McKay 1991; Miller et al. 2001; Rowe 2004; Rowe & Lawrence 1990). Three major methodological alignments have come to dominate the sociological study of sport. *Ethnographic* research concentrates on direct observation and contact with people, such as a sports team or a group of spectators (e.g. Hallinan & Hughson 2001; Klein 1993; Mewett 2000, 2002; Wacquant 2000). *Survey-based* research relies on the administering of a questionnaire to a relatively large sample and requires statistical analysis (e.g. Cunningham & Sagas 2004; Margolis & Piliavin 1999). *Content analysis* involves a detailed analysis of textual sources, such as newspapers, to establish the construction of imagery about sporting personalities and events (e.g. Scherer & Jackson 2004; Vincent 2004). These methodological approaches are not mutually exclusive, and more than one may be used in a study.

What you are is what you play!

life chances
A term associated with the work of Weber to refer to different opportunities and differential access to resources, including education, wealth, housing, and health.

habitus
Refers to socially learnt dispositions or taken-for-granted sets of orientations, skills, and ways of acting that shape behaviour. People are the product and creators of their habitus.

dispositions
The tendency to act in particular ways associated with a person's *habitus*. Thus people from similar backgrounds often profess similar attitudes and behave in comparable ways.

upward social mobility
This takes place when a person achieves a higher social position than that of their parents. The opposite, downward social mobility, also occurs.

Max Weber (1864–1920) wrote that people's social origins established their **life chances**. People from privileged backgrounds have a greater chance of securing privilege for themselves than those from impoverished beginnings. Other social theorists have made similar points. Pierre Bourdieu (1930–2002), for example, uses the concept of **habitus** to encompass not just people's material backgrounds but also their **dispositions** —the attitudes and behaviours associated with particular backgrounds. According to Bourdieu, sport constitutes a field of social activity identifiably different from other activities, but participation in a sporting field varies considerably from person to person according to their habitus.

When we look at particular examples, we begin to understand how Bourdieu's (1984) concept of habitus can apply to sports. To start with, think of the connection made in Sydney between Rugby Union, private schools, and upper-class people, compared with the working-class support for Rugby League. Think also of the social origins of boxers compared with polo players. Boxers are typically from relatively poor backgrounds, using sport as a means of gaining wealth and achieving **upward social mobility**, though very few actually succeed (Wacquant 2000). In contrast, polo players usually require considerable money before entering the sport and they play it for social reasons rather than as a means of acquiring wealth. Similarly, until the 1990s, Rugby Union was technically an amateur sport played by economically comfortable people, whereas Rugby League was professional, paying its players. Income has an important effect on the sports that people play. Historically, lower-income earners have concentrated on sports that have relatively small costs for equipment and participation (club memberships, owning or renting playing areas) such as football. At the other end of the scale, considerable wealth is needed to maintain the team of ponies required for polo or an ocean-racing yacht.

People's **social class**, which involves much more than just income (although the higher their class, the more likely it is that people will enjoy a considerable income), influences the sports they play and follow, but the association between social class and some sports is not always clear-cut. In Australia, unlike in England, golf is played widely across the social classes. In such cases we need to go further than a simple association between income and sport, and examine the ways in which a sport is played by different social groups and the meanings that it has for each of them (Bourdieu 1978). Although the formal objective of golf (trying to complete the round in as few shots as possible) remains the same everywhere, golf as it is played by wealthy people in an exclusive club is different from golf as it is played on a public course by members of the working class. This is because of differences between the social significances of the settings where it is played and the degree of social exclusivity associated with the players. Just about anyone is able to pay the green fees and play golf on a public course in Australia. This is not the case for many private clubs: playing on their courses may involve membership (or being a member's guest), which is secured only after paying a considerable joining fee and a high annual subscription. Prospective members often are vetted for their suitability. As Bourdieu (1984) has pointed out, having enough money does not necessarily grant a person access to sporting clubs—it is also necessary to be part of an appropriate social group, to ensure that members conform to required social standards. Some clubs have maintained their exclusivity through a 'blackballing' system of selecting new members. Others have excluded people on ethnic or religious grounds; for example, some golf clubs have been established by Jews because other clubs would not admit them.

class/social class
A central but contested term in sociology that refers to a position in a system of structured inequality based on the unequal distribution of wealth, power, and status.

blackballing
Refers to a method of voting on applicants for club membership. Eligible members drop either a white ball (which indicates support of the applicant) or a black ball (opposition to the applicant) into a container. If the applicant receives more than a set number or proportion of black balls, the application for membership is rejected.

Gender has a marked effect on sports' playing and spectating. At the start of the twentieth century, women played in few sports because they were mostly considered to be too physically demanding for the female body. Women's athletics started in the 1920s, but female athletes' training programs were kept at a low intensity and the supposedly more gruelling track and field events were omitted (Mewett 2003). Indeed, such was the association between gender and physical activity that active women and those with good sporting skills could be referred to in male terms and at times accused of being men masquerading as women (Cahn 1994).

The introduction of the marathon and the longer distance track events to women's athletics has occurred only in the last quarter-century, and the inclusion of the pole vault has been even more recent. Moreover, women's sustained involvement in 'male' team sports has only occurred relatively recently. The physical contact sports of Rugby Union and Australian Rules (AFL) football are not so widely played by women, but soccer has developed a substantial female player base.

An important reason for the gradual acceptance of women's competition in 'tough' events has been the casting aside of the physiological theories that informed both male and female physical exertion, which stated that any feeling of strain while training or competing could affect a person's health (Mewett 2010; Vertinsky 1992, 1994). Strain was believed to occur at lower levels of exertion for females than for men. In addition, strain was thought to compromise women's childbearing and nurturing capacities. As a result, women were pressured to avoid hard training and keep away from the purportedly more taxing sports. As these theories about exertion and strain fizzled away, training intensity increased and it was realised that women were not going to wreck themselves or compromise their reproductive integrity by pushing their bodies harder.

The widespread acceptance of **medicalised** perspectives on female bodies served to limit female sporting involvement for a long time, something that is still witnessed in the relative under-development of women's sport. Attendances at women's sports are generally significantly less than for the male versions. This has numerous implications in terms of securing television coverage and the considerable sponsorship that this attracts. In some sports—such as cricket—which have high-profile men's versions, women struggle to find enough money to compete, especially in international competitions.

In part, the income differences between male and female sports come from the greater interest that spectators have in watching men compete. It is not uncommon to hear from women who are or have been fine sports players that they do not like watching women's sports whereas they eagerly support men's. Without spectator support and the television and business interest this creates, women's sports are unlikely to achieve the finances to match male players.

Women's participation in sports has been blunted by the **essentialised** expectations associated with their gender—summarised in the idea that nature intended women to be carers. Although girls may engage in some form of physical activity during their teenage years, women are far less likely than men to continue playing sports after leaving school. Ken Dempsey (1992), in his study of an Australian country town, notes that girls often are expected by their boyfriends to watch them play football, rather than participate in (or watch) a netball game that is going on at the same time. Women with

---

medicalised/medicalisation
The process by which non-medical problems become defined and treated as medical issues, usually in terms of illnesses, disorders, or syndromes.

---

essentialism/essential/essentialised
A perspective that reduces the complex nature of individual identities and social phenomena to underlying essences or fixed characteristics. These may be innate biological characteristics or 'authentic' cultural practices.

young children, Dempsey continues, find it difficult to sustain their sport because of domestic commitments. While men will continue their weeknight training and weekend competitions, they are reluctant to mind the children so their partners can do likewise.

National data on participation in sports and physical activities demonstrate that younger males from higher socioeconomic groups are the most active. The not so well off, older people, and women tend to be less physically active. Of course, we find older men and women who are very active; the data only show the general trends aggregated from the whole population. We can at least in part account for the lower participation rate of women from the issues listed above, but why does participation decline as people age? Certainly some sports cannot be played to the same level by older people because reaction times increase, visual acuity may decline, and old injuries take their toll. But why not play in age-graded games? Certainly competitions exist for older people in most sports, and as they age some people change sports to less physically demanding ones. Many others simply stop playing; they become 'couch potatoes', possibly to the detriment of their health. The decline in participation with age can only be speculated about: do people stop playing because they think that they are expected to do so when they reach a certain age? Or do they think that other people may think of them as eccentric if they participate in the competitions restricted to older people?

Race and ethnicity are socially constructed categories that are used to differentiate between people on the basis of their appearance or culture. In the way that social class, gender, and age are significant to social relations in the wider society and affect sports' participation, so race and ethnicity also have an impact. A popular view is that people of West African ancestry can sprint faster than people of any other ancestry. This view derives entirely from the successes of black sprinters over the past few decades. Indeed, non-black sprinters are rarely seen in the final rounds of international athletic meets. Is it biology—something in the genetic make-up of black people—that predisposes them to speed, as Jon Entine (2000) suggests, or are there alternative explanations for this phenomenon, as John Hoberman (1997) and others argue?

If genetic reasons underpin the current supremacy of black sprinters, then DNA clustering should characterise particular racial groupings. Yet, other than for skin colour and hair type, no such clustering is present. 'Races' have no place in scientific knowledge about our genetic composition; rather, races are social constructions. It is therefore necessary to seek sociological rather than biological explanations for associations between particular peoples and sporting performance.

The preponderance of people from a particular ethnic or racial background as the top performers in certain sports tells us more about how those groups are positioned within the wider society than it does about their genetic makeup. It is now rare to see a Jewish boxer, yet American boxing was dominated by Jewish fighters in the 1920s (Bodner 1997). Similarly, other groups—Irish, Italians, and currently African-Americans—have dominated this sport in the United States in different periods. The Irish, Italians, and Jews, as migrant minorities, each passed through a period of settlement and stabilisation in American society in which some people from these backgrounds used sport as a means of upward social mobility; however, sport is a difficult and unpredictable way of seeking a way out of poor circumstances (Leonard & Reyman 1988; Wacquant 2000). As Jews, Italians, and the Irish became established in American society, other ways of making a living that were far less risky than sport became available to them.

Persistent racism against African-Americans has smothered their opportunities for upward social mobility in the same way that the life chances of Indigenous Australians have been limited by discrimination and oppression. For a long time, a **colour bar** operated in American sport that stopped African-Americans from competing against whites. Although there were some exceptions—such as the boxer Jack Johnson and the athlete Jesse Owens—the representation of African-Americans in mainstream sport did not become significant until the second half of the twentieth century. The increase in the number of black competitors in gridiron, baseball, basketball, athletics, and boxing has provided opportunities for African-Americans that previously were closed to them. For some with the required abilities, sport provides a possible means of securing an otherwise unattainable income. For these reasons, rather than genetic factors, African-Americans are over-represented in some sports.

colour bar
A colour bar exists when people are not permitted to do something because of the colour of their skin.

In Australia, a similar process has taken place. Boxing appears to have been dominated by Indigenous fighters, such as Lionel Rose and Anthony Mundine, and by men from migrant (Jeff Fenech) and lower-class (Les Darcy) origins. While more Indigenous players are now being recruited by Australian Football League clubs, several of the oldest clubs have fielded very few Indigenous players since they were founded. Sport provides a means for a few athletically gifted Indigenous Australians to realise good incomes and prestige, because other channels of upward social mobility remain largely closed to them in the same way as they have done to African-Americans in the United States.

Race and ethnicity are also significant in terms of the playing positions allotted to people from particular backgrounds. First reported for American sport over 30 years ago, the practice of **positional segregation**—or 'stacking', as it is also called—has also been observed in Australian, New Zealand, and British sports (e.g. Hallinan 1991; Melnick 1996; Smith & Leonard 1997). Stacking involves the over-representation of players from particular racial or ethnic backgrounds in certain playing positions. A distinction is made between 'central' and other positions. Central positions are those considered to be the most important in directing the course of play. Examples are the quarterback in gridiron and the fly-half in Rugby Union; the players occupying these positions have to be able to read the way the game is going and make decisions about how best to place the ball. Non-central positions are those involved in supplying the ball to the central players and in 'finishing' plays to make a score. Wingers in Rugby Union are examples of non-central positions. Minority-group players are over-represented in the non-central playing positions and under-represented in

positional segregation
Also known as 'stacking', positional segregation involves the allocation of sports people to playing positions on the basis of assumptions made about them because of their race or ethnicity.

the main decision-making positions. This occurs because the requirements of the playing positions are matched with the **stereotypes** held about the groups from which the players are drawn. Stereotyping involves people thinking the members of a particular group have specified physical, behavioural, and mental abilities, irrespective of the actual capabilities of individuals in that group. Even though gridiron players are now predominantly African-Americans, the central position of quarterback is most commonly occupied by white players, who are perceived as having the thinking skills and intellect required to direct the play. In Australian Rugby League, Indigenous players—perceived as fast and evasive—tend to be wingers.

stereotype
The assumption that people have certain characteristics because of the group to which they belong, such as their race or ethnic group. Whether such characteristics are held by the group concerned (usually they are not) is irrelevant to the belief by others that they are, which informs some people's behaviour towards members of the subject group.

SOCIOLOGY **SPOTLIGHT**

9.1: Racism and an Aboriginal basketball team

Chris Hallinan and Barry Judd (2007) studied the experiences of the Aboriginal basketball team The Wanderers in the regional Victorian city of Ballarat. The Wanderers were the only Aboriginal team in the Ballarat area, and no Indigenous person played for any other local team. The Wanderers played all their games against non-Aboriginal teams, which enabled Hallinan and Judd to examine racism within local amateur sport. Considerable efforts to eliminate on-field racism by the peak organisations of major professional sports, such as the Australian Football League, have largely been successful, but the experiences of these Aboriginal basketballers point to ongoing racism at the local level. This took the form of abuse from opposing players and from the supporters of the rival teams. It was also manifested more subtly in the form of stereotypical assumptions about Aboriginal behaviour (such as what they might do on losing a game, and then expressing surprise when this behaviour did not occur). To put this into context, local league players are many times more numerous than professional sportspeople. If the experiences of this Aboriginal basketball team are replicated in other sports, and for both Indigenous and other minority peoples, it may mean that the racism in amateur sport constitutes a large, continuing problem.

When we are involved in a sport, as players or spectators, what we play and who we see playing are strongly influenced by gender and by social, economic, and cultural locations. It is difficult to think of a major sport fielding mixed-gender teams in elite competitions—mixed doubles in tennis is one example, but this is probably the lowest-ranked tennis event. The life chances we derive from our social origins also have a strong effect on the sports with which we become involved.

Habitus structures the influences that impact on people's lives in a subtly different way for each person, but with sufficient similarities between people for patterns of social behaviour to emerge and be reproduced. More than that, habitus promotes dispositions that lead people into certain practices. For example, I grew up as a working-class child in English cities. Although many sports were played in England, I had little choice: I played soccer in the winter and cricket in the summer. I also used to fish (mostly in the local canal) and I could go for a swim in a public pool. Not very far from my home there were golf courses and a tennis and squash club, but there was no way that I could have afforded their fees. Moreover, English people of my background were reluctant to play golf, because to do so would signal that they had achieved a higher income and were using this to develop new social contacts and reposition themselves in terms of class and status. Even now, although I have lived in Australia for over a quarter of a century, realise that golf is widely played across the social scale here, and can afford the costs, I will not take it up. Why? It is because of a disposition gained from my habitus that still induces a negative view of golf.

Sport: The bigger picture

In the preceding section, we saw that the sports people play and watch are strongly influenced by their social backgrounds and characteristics, but sport is also significant in other ways. Importantly, it is used as a vehicle for the expression of national identity. Sport is also closely associated with businesses and the media.

Examples of how the media, business, and nationalism come together in sport can be found in mega-events, the biggest of which is the Olympic Games in terms of the number of different sports involved, the number of competitors and spectators who attend, the number of nations represented, the huge television audience, and the businesses that use the games as a means to promote their products. Other multinational competitions, such as the soccer World Cup, are also significant mega-events, but as single-sport events they do not match the Olympics.

The Olympic Games of today differs quite markedly from the event proposed by Pierre de Coubertin and first staged in Athens in 1896. He was heavily influenced by the amateur ethos of English upper-class athletes, and de Coubertin's perspective on the Games was that they should be a competition between individuals drawn from around the world and that competing fairly was more important than winning. But examples such as the Ashes cricket series, originating from the loss by the England cricket team to Australia and symbolised by a trophy in the form of an urn containing a cremated cricket stump or bail, demonstrate that, even before the Athens Olympics of 1896, sporting successes were associated with national prowess. The Olympics, perhaps because it was established as an explicitly international event, soon became a measure of national esteem. Winning at the Games bestowed glory on the victors' nations as well as on the successful athletes themselves. De Coubertin's vision of a competition between individuals quickly acquired another layer—it became a contest between nations.

Although success in the Olympics was taken to extremes by the former East Germany, with its medically supervised, state-sponsored doping of athletes, the Games is used as a benchmark of a nation's vitality. Today, the Olympic Games and many other major international meets produce 'medal tables'—the tally of how many gold, silver, and bronze medals have been won by competitors from each of the competing nations. In Australia, there is considerable pre-meet hype about how many medals Australian competitors can be expected to win and where this will place Australia in the medal count. Following the 2008 Beijing Olympics, there was much crowing in the British media about the UK team surpassing its 'old enemy', Australia, in this tally.

Winning medals is sufficiently important for governments to put considerable funding into the training of elite sportspeople. The Australian Institute of Sport (AIS) was founded by the Commonwealth government following Australia's poor performance at the 1976 Montreal Olympics. Since then, Australia's wins have improved progressively. This focus is entirely on medals and nation; the winning of medals secures national esteem and finishing in a high position on the medals table is taken to mean a healthy and vigorous national population. Yet the resources used to produce these winners tend to be ignored in these evaluations. Elite performers are not just 'born', they are 'made' through rigorous, well-planned, highly focused, and expensive training regimes. In reality, very few people receive this attention, and the accolades that flow from national achievements gloss over the problems associated with physical inactivity within the wider population.

Craig Calhoun (1997) has described nationalism as a **discursive formation**. 'Nation' is an idea originating from modernity that posits an essential unity between people based on their supposed common origins. The social construction of nation comes from how people organise their thoughts, statements, and actions with reference to this idea. Nations do not exist as a tangible object; rather, they exist in our minds in ways that can inform our behaviour—hence they can be conceptualised as discursive formations.

discursive formation
Something that is socially constructed through ways of thinking, talking, and acting (for example, a 'nation').

This short foray into the theory of nationalism is required to understand another way in which mega-events are used to promote national sentiment: the use of opening and closing ceremonies to relate a story about the host nation's founding myths. In countries of colonial origin, which have displaced Indigenous peoples—including Australia—founding myths differ from the type witnessed in European countries. The ceremonies conducted at the Sydney Olympics in 2000 presented a story that melded Indigenous peoples with the coming of settlers from many parts of the world to produce the present-day multicultural Australia. Absent from this story, of course, were issues of invasion, colonisation, genocide, and land theft. A story was told of an Australia made up of many peoples pulling together in a unique, harmonious way in the wider interests of the nation. Certain ideas with links to ideas of 'Australianness', such as bush workers on their horses, wearing iconic coats and hats, served symbolically to link all Australians to their nation, but did so in a way that was able to be consumed by a worldwide television audience.

The ceremonial start and finish to mega-events may seem a long way from sport, but they are an expected part of these occasions and are associated with sport as a spectacle. In a similar way, cheerleaders have nothing to do with the way a game of gridiron or Rugby

League is played, but they have become a part of the overall entertainment. They are not neutral, meaningless additions, though. All non-sport accretions to sporting events constitute symbols that, while they may have little to do with sport, construct meanings from the context in which they appear; they serve to link sport with wider social issues.

One of the reasons why mega-events have become so big is because of their portrayal through the media. Sport has secured widespread media coverage since the first half of the nineteenth century, when sports newspapers were started. Since about the 1930s, radio broadcasts have complemented the print media. A major change occurred with the coming of radio in the 1930s because it enabled people to follow a sporting event in real time, complementing the print media's provision of an account after a match had taken place. More recently, the internet has provided an additional way of following sports.

All forms of media, whether print, radio, or television, provide the consumer with representations of the event. As consumers, we cannot decide what is or is not printed for our attention or sent for us to watch and listen to in our lounge rooms. Camera angles, commentators' perspectives, and journalists' predilections all serve to select what we can access through the media, which may serve to underpin widely held views about gender or racial issues (Bernstein & Blain 2002).

The media also provide us with a link between sport and business. Because sport is popular and because people use media sources to read about it, listen to it, and watch it, businesses use this interest to promote their products. The connection between commercial interests and sport has a long history. From its origins in modernity, sport has had a commercial side to it: promoters have staged sporting events for profit; and, for the competitors, prizemoney and gambling winnings hinged on the outcome. Today, all major sports have to be run as businesses to maintain their popular appeal, but commercial sponsorships and the selling of broadcast rights can now provide a significant amount of income to sporting bodies, which constitutes the loop between business, sport, and the media. In earlier days, the connection was more between the print media and businesses that took advantage of the sports' readership by placing advertisements in the papers. In some cases, this was done by the manufacturers of sports equipment, but businesses that had no connection with sport also placed advertisements. We see a similar practice today: non-sports businesses, such as car companies sponsoring tennis championships, pay considerable sums for naming rights to major sporting events.

The reason why businesses are so attracted to sports is that they can reach a very wide audience with their products. This may involve paying a premium for advertising time during a major sporting attraction. The most expensive advertising time is during the American Super Bowl game (the gridiron grand final), where in 2009 a 30-second slot cost US$3 million, raking in a total of about US$200 million for the broadcaster. Companies make advertisements especially for the Super Bowl at significant cost—for example, Burger King used a cast of 400 in the advertisement that it made for the 2006 game. Moreover, watched by a US audience approaching 100 million people (and undoubtedly more elsewhere), these advertisements are assessed and spoken about and ranked after the game, which gives further, free exposure to the companies and is another reason why they are prepared to spend so heavily in preparing material for showing at this event (ABC News 2006).

Clearly, Australian companies—faced with a much smaller population and market than that in the United States—do not spend such huge sums on advertising at sporting events, but the principle remains the same: sports provide a captive audience both for the 'commercials' and for the passive advertising that comes from product placement, as well as from company names and logos appearing on billboards surrounding sporting fixtures and on sports equipment and clothing. It is now commonplace for football players of all codes to have their club's sponsors' names on their jerseys. The ball used in AFL football carries a sponsor's name. Cricket stumps are no longer just varnished sticks of wood; they too are emblazoned with commercial messages. Even playing surfaces have become advertising sites: major sponsors of a competition often have their insignias painted on to the playing surfaces. Television broadcasts—in real time, as delayed transmissions, or as highlight packages—outside the country where the game is staged provide multinational companies with an opportunity to reach global audiences. Australians can watch soccer played in Europe, Rugby Union from South Africa, cricket from India, basketball from the United States, and much more. Many of the companies paying large sums for their names and logos to be displayed at major sporting venues almost invariably sell products or services that have nothing to do with sport. For example, as one of the 'Grand Slam' tennis events, the Australian Open attracts a large international viewing audience. Its major sponsor for several years has been Kia, a motor car manufacturer. Only one of the fifteen official sponsors of the 2010 Australian Open is a manufacturer of tennis equipment (see <www.australianopen.com>)—major sports are embedded in the global marketing strategies of numerous multinational businesses. Media technology has globalised spectatorship and sport has become an important vehicle promoting commercial products of all types.

Since the value of sports to television companies comes from the advertising revenue that they raise from the businesses using games to promote their products, television companies will vie with one another to secure the broadcasting rights to popular sports. A 'battle' is waged between the Australian commercial television channels when the broadcast rights for Australian Football League competition are made available. Even when confined to a relatively small population—for AFL has a small market outside this country—Channels 7 and 10 combined to pay A$780 million to the Australian Football League to tie up the broadcast rights for five years from 2006 (Schulze 2006). Channels 7 and 10 make their profits from this deal, provided that they have not over-estimated the forward demand for advertising time from the advertising revenue generated from companies who want exposure to the audience watching football on television. The direct sponsorship of sports competitions, organisations, clubs, and stadia occurs for the same purpose. Every time an event is broadcast from Etihad Stadium in Melbourne, for example, the sponsor's company name (Etihad) is mentioned many times. The same applies to Ford's sponsorship of the Geelong Football Club and Toohey's New's sponsorship of the Super 14 Rugby Union competition.

Companies are interested in individual sportspeople too, especially the well-known 'stars'. When the talented golfer Michelle Wie turned professional in 2005, she became the highest paid female golfer by signing endorsement contracts with Nike and Sony estimated to be worth US$10 million a year—prizemoney, of course, is in addition to this (About Golf 2005). Shane Warne, the first bowler to take 700 Test match wickets, for many years sported Nike symbols from his endorsement by that company. Other cricketers may use a certain make of bat because the manufacturer pays them to do so. Cricketers also are seen, in televised matches, taking guard with bats from which they have removed all logos and names; these 'naked' bats are sending a message to equipment companies that there is a space for hire.

Money has been an integral part of modern sports from their inception in the mid-eighteenth century—a connection that often has been at the expense of the sportsperson. Early runners and fighters were often fielded by wealthy sponsors, who bet heavily on the outcome of matches (see Radford 2001). The welfare and financial return to the contestants often was of secondary importance. Although the forms of sporting finance—now embedded with the media—have changed considerably, a considerable load is still put on the individual player. Age, if injury does not intervene, ends careers in most sports by the time players reach their mid-thirties. This means that they must use their few years 'at the top' to make the money and prepare for their post-playing careers. To do this, they have to try to make the first team (or the equivalent in non-team sports), keep their place in it, and ensure that they have sufficient exposure.

One way in which some players do this is by taking drugs that enable them to put on more muscle, or to suppress the injury pain that would otherwise stop them from competing, or to enable them to perform with more composure under competitive pressure. Individual players are not necessarily well situated in the wider commercial interests that exert significant pressures on sports.

Conclusion

Sport affects the lives of very many people, as players, past players, fans, spectators, and even as sport 'haters'. But what we observe in sport is a field of social action that is significantly affected by a number of wide-ranging influences. Sociological analysis shows us how each of these influences contributes to the distinctive patterns of behaviour that constitute sport. So we can establish the effects, singly and together, of gender, ethnicity, class, and age on people's participation in sports. We can understand why people from a particular social background are more likely to be involved in some sports than others.

Though it is important to examine how people play sports, the sociology of sport also involves an investigation of how sports are received by the large number of people—not themselves players—who watch them. At-the-ground spectators often are just a tiny proportion of the total audience. Very many more receive their sports through the media. Sociology enables us to investigate how the reporting of the play constructs particular perspectives on issues wider than those at the ground itself. Moreover, commentaries may be affected by the commercial interests of a major advertiser that the television company does not want to upset. While the sports we play, where we play them, and even how we play them are influenced by our backgrounds, our understandings of the matches we watch are structured by commercial concerns.

Summary of main points

▶ Irrespective of whether or not people like sport, it influences some part of their lives.

▶ Sports are social constructions 'mirroring' the society in which they occur, and sporting practices also serve to reproduce some major social processes within these societies.

▶ The sports in which people participate and those they follow are significantly influenced by their gender, social background, ethnicity, and age.

▶ Many businesses use sporting events as a vehicle for promoting their goods and services, even though these may have nothing to do with sport or physical activities.

▶ Stereotypes held about racial and ethnic minorities promote popular misconceptions about their sporting abilities.

▶ The media are essential to the commercialisation of sports.

SOCIOLOGICAL **REFLECTION**

9.1 Player misbehaviour

Media reports of players misbehaving appear all too commonly. Team sports players especially have been reported to take illicit 'recreational' drugs, been unacceptably rowdy, been very drunk in public places, and engaged in serious sexual misconduct. These are actions that run counter to the view held by many that well-known players are public figures who should act as 'role models' for children. Eric Carter (2009), in a study of American professional gridiron players, claims that their deviant off-field behaviour derives from their almost instant acquisition of large incomes and celebrity status at a relatively young age. Do you think that this is also the reason for the wayward behaviour of some Australian players?

Discussion questions

9.1 Critically examine the view that high-profile sports people should be 'role models'.

9.2 Why is television coverage important to the financial health of major sports?

9.3 Why are women the 'second-class citizens' of sport?

9.4 What do the ceremonies held at the start and finish of sporting mega-events (such as the Olympic Games) tell us about (a) the sport(s) to be contested; and (b) the nation in which they are held?

9.5 Discuss how racial and ethnic stereotypes affect minority participation in sports.

9.6 Using Bourdieu's concepts of 'habitus' and 'disposition', how has your background affected the sports that you play and follow?

Further reading

Coakley, J., Hallinan, C., Jackson, S. & Mewett, P. 2009, *Sports in Society: Issues and Controversies in Australia and New Zealand*, McGraw Hill, Sydney.

Dunning, E. & Sheard, K. 1979, *Barbarians, Gentlemen and Players: A Sociological Study of the Development of Rugby Football*, Martin Robertson, Oxford.

Hylton, K. 2009, *'Race' and Sport: Critical Race Theory*, Routledge, London.

Karen, D. & Washington, R. 2010, *The Sport and Society Reader*, Routledge, London.

Thompson, S.M. 1999, *Mother's Taxi: Sport and Women's Labor*, SUNY Press, Albany.

Wacquant, L. 2004, *Body and Soul: Notebooks of an Apprentice Boxer*, Oxford University Press, New York.

Websites

- Australian Sports Anti-Doping Authority (ASADA): <www.asada.gov.au>. ASADA is the Australian government agency that undertakes testing, education, and advocacy roles.
- Amateur Athletic Foundation: <www.aafla.org>. Established with surplus funds from the 1984 Los Angeles Olympic Games, this very useful website, while specialising on Olympic material, also provides a wide coverage of sports, albeit from a mostly historical perspective.
- The Australian Sports Commission and the Australian Institute of Sport can be accessed at: <www.ausport.gov.au>. This site provides many links to pages about various aspects of Australian sport. A related site is the National Sport Information Centre, which is at: <www.ausport.gov.au/nsic>.

Peak sports' organisations, as well as major sporting events, usually have their own websites. Examples of these are:

- <www.australianopen.com> for the Australian Open tennis tournament.
- <www.afl.com.au> for the Australian Football League.
- <www.bowls-aust.com.au> for the peak organisation for lawn bowls in Australia.

Films/documentaries

- 'Tarnished Gold', 2004, *Four Corners*, television news feature, reported by Q. McDermott, Australian Broadcasting Corporation (ABC). This report explores the Australian climate of drug use in sports, the researchers who race to expose the newest drugs and the technologies used to hide them, and the bureaucratic barriers to reaching that goal. Transcript available online: <www.abc.net.au/4corners/content/2004/s1139122.htm>.
- 'Code of Silence', 2009, *Four Corners*, television news feature, reported by S. Ferguson, Australian Broadcasting Corporation (ABC). In the last decade, Australian Rugby League players have been involved in numerous scandals and have been subject to serious allegations relating to alcohol, women, and sex. This episode discusses what officials are doing to change player behaviour and rehabilitate the image of Rugby League, and whether they are doing enough. It relies on first-hand accounts from women involved in these incidents and raises issues about a football culture that turns a blind eye to antisocial behaviour, raising both moral and legal issues.

Visit the *Public Sociology* book website to access topical case studies, weblinks, YouTube clips, and extra readings.

References

ABC News 2006, 'The Super Bowl's super ads: As ad prices rise, companies push to grab viewers' attention', *ABC News*, 31 January 2006, <www.abcnews.go.com/GMA/Business/story?id=1560561> (accessed, with accompanying ABC News video, 2 February 2006).

About Golf 2005, 'It's official—Michelle Wie turns professional', *About Golf*, 5 October 2005, <http://golf.about.com/od/michellewie/a/wiegoespro.htm> (accessed 2 February 2006).

Bernstein, A. & Blain, N. 2002, 'Sport and the media: The emergence of a major research field', *Culture, Sport, Society*, vol. 5, pp. 1–30.

Bodner, A. 1997, *When Boxing was a Jewish Sport*, Praeger, Westport.

Bourdieu, P. 1978, 'Sport and social class', *Social Science Information*, vol. 17, pp. 819–40.

—— 1984 [1979], *Distinction: A Social Critique of the Judgement of Taste*, Routledge, London.

Cahn, S.K. 1994, *Coming on Strong: Gender and Sexuality in Twentieth-Century Women's Sport*, Harvard University Press, Cambridge.

Calhoun, C. 1997, *Nationalism*, Open University Press, Buckingham.

Carter, E. 2009, *Boys Gone Wild: Fame, Fortune, and Deviance Among Professional Football Players*, University Press of America, Lanham, MD.

Coakley, J., Hallinan, C., Jackson. S. & Mewett, P. 2009, *Sports in Society: Issues and Controversies in Australia and New Zealand*, McGraw Hill, Sydney.

Cunningham, G.B & Sagas, M. 2004, 'Racial differences in occupational turnover: Intent among NCAA Division IA assistant football coaches', *Sociology of Sport Journal*, vol. 21, pp. 84–92.

Dempsey, K. 1992, *A Man's Town: Inequality between Women and Men in Rural Australia*, Oxford University Press, Melbourne.

Entine, J. 2000, *Taboo: Why Black Athletes Dominate Sports and Why We're Afraid to Talk About It*, Public Affairs, New York.

Hallinan, C. 1991, 'Aborigines and positional segregation in Australian Rugby League', *International Review for the Sociology of Sport*, vol. 26, pp. 69–81.

Hallinan, C. & Hughson, J. (eds) 2001, *Sporting Tales: Ethnographic Fieldwork Experiences*, Australian Society for Sports History, Sydney.

Hallinan, C. & Judd, B. 2007, '"Blackfellas" basketball: Aboriginal identity and Anglo-Australian race relations in regional basketball', *Sociology of Sport Journal*, vol. 24, pp. 421–36.

Hoberman, J. 1997, *Darwin's Athletes: How Sport has Damaged Black America and Preserved the Myth of Race*, Houghton Mifflin, Boston.

Klein, A. 1993, *Little Big Men: Bodybuilding Subculture and Gender Construction*, SUNY Press, Albany.

Leonard, W.M. & Reyman, J. 1988, 'The odds of attaining professional athlete status: Refining the computations', *Sociology of Sport Journal*, vol. 5, pp. 162–9.

Margolis, B. & Piliavin, J.A. 1999, '"Stacking" in major league baseball: A multivariate analysis', *Sociology of Sport Journal*, vol. 16, pp. 16–34.

McKay, J. 1991, *No Pain, No Gain? Sport and Australian Culture*, Prentice Hall, Englewood Cliffs, NJ.

Melnick, M. 1996, 'Maori women and positional segregation in New Zealand netball: Another test of the Anglocentric hypothesis', *Sociology of Sport Journal*, vol. 13, pp. 259–73.

Mewett, P. 2000, 'History in the making and the making of history: Stories and the social construction of a sport', *Sporting Traditions*, vol. 17, pp. 1–17.

—— 2002, 'Discourses of deception: Cheating in professional running', *The Australian Journal of Anthropology*, vol. 13, pp. 292–308.

—— 2003, 'Conspiring to run: Women, their bodies and athletics training', *International Review for the Sociology of Sport*, vol. 38, pp. 331–49.

—— 2010, 'When pain = strain = no gain: The "physiology of strain" and exercise intensity, c.1850–1920', in R. Sands & P. Moore (eds), *The Anthropology of Sport and Human Movement: A Biocultural Perspective*, Lexington Books, Lanham, MD.

Miller, T., Lawrence, J., McKay, J. & Rowe, D. 2001, *Globalization and Sport*, Sage, London.

Radford, P. 2001, *The Celebrated Captain Barclay: Sport, Money and Fame in Regency Britain*, Headline, London.

Rowe, D. 2004, *Sport, Culture and the Media*, 2nd edn, Open University Press, Maidenhead.

Rowe, D. & Lawrence, G. (eds) 1990, *Sport and Leisure: Trends in Australian Popular Culture*, Harcourt Brace Jovanovich, Sydney.

Scherer, J. & Jackson, S. 2004, 'From corporate welfare to national interest: Newspaper analysis of the public subsidization of NHL hockey debate in Canada', *Sociology of Sport Journal*, vol. 21, pp. 36–60.

Schulze, J. 2006, 'We won't foot the AFL bill, advertisers warn', *The Australian*, 6 January, <www.theaustralian.news.com.au> (accessed 2 February 2006).

Smith, E. & Leonard, W.M. 1997, 'Twenty-five years of stacking research in major league baseball: An attempt at explaining this re-occurring phenomenon', *Sociological Focus*, vol. 30, pp. 321–31.

Vertinsky, P. 1992, 'Sport and exercise for old women: Images of the elderly in the medical and popular literature at the turn of the century', *International Journal of the History of Sport*, vol. 9, pp. 83–104.

—— 1994, 'The social construction of the gendered body: Exercise and the exercise of power', *International Journal of the History of Sport*, vol. 11, no. 2, pp. 147–71.

Vincent, J. 2004, 'Game, sex, and match: The construction of gender in British newspaper coverage of the 2000 Wimbledon Championships', *Sociology of Sport Journal*, vol. 21, pp. 435–56.

Wacquant, L. 2000, 'Whores, slaves, and stallions: Languages of exploitation and accommodation among prizefighters', *Mana*, vol. 6, pp. 127–46.

CHAPTER 10

Hybrid identities in a globalised world

Vince Marotta

Will the real Barack Obama please stand up?

The election of Barack Obama as the US President has been seen as a significant milestone in race relations in the United States. His election has led to claims that the race ceiling that existed in every election since George Washington is now broken. Does this mean that America is now a post-racial society? Is race no longer an issue in US politics? CNN reporter Abigail Thernstrom (2009) believes that when 43 per cent of white voters cast their vote for an African-American, then race and ethnicity are becoming less important to US politics. This has not meant that race has disappeared from public discourse. Obama's racial identity has been a constant talking point for media commentators and American right-wing nationalists. The latter argue that Obama is not American because he cannot provide an original American birth certificate. Obama's biracial identity (born from a white American mother and a black Kenyan father) has also led to discussions about whether he is 'white', 'black', or biracial (Carroll 2008). He may look black, but he has white roots. In his first memoir, *Dreams from My Father* (2004), Obama acknowledges the tension and constant struggle to negotiate your identity when you are 'trapped between two worlds'. He notes that his life involved 'the constant, crippling fear that I didn't belong somehow, that unless I dodged and hid and pretended to be something I wasn't, I would forever remain an outsider, with the rest of the world, black and white, always standing in judgement' (Obama 2004, p. 111). The public interest in the racial identity of the US President highlights the issue of mixed race, bicultural identity, and multiple identities. Barack Obama's dilemma encapsulates how, in contemporary global societies, identities are difficult to categorise due to their fluid and hybrid nature.

Introduction

Sociology is interested in how identities are constructed and maintained, especially how gender, race, ethnicity, and class impact on self-identity and our life chances. Who we are, how we perceive ourselves, and how others perceive us have increasingly led many social scientists to describe contemporary identities as hybrid. This might be defined at one level as the intermingling or mixture of people from different cultural backgrounds. Sociologists and other social theorists have argued over the last twenty years that individuals have multiple identities that cut across many group allegiances. Nevertheless, there are problems with the use of the term 'hybrid'. For some, the word suggests some kind of a new 'cultural melting pot, one in which crucial cultural differences are effaced and power relations obscured' (Hynes 2000, p. 32). For others, it implies that something pure or authentic and of traditional value has been lost. These debates do not hide the fact that racial and cultural hybrid identities have been fuelled by globalising and transnational processes.

Globalisation and hybridity

Globalisation is reflected in cross-border flows, which can take a variety of forms: economic flows of trade and finance; political flows of ideas such as democracy and good governance; cultural flows of media products; and, finally, the cross-border flows of people (Castles & Miller 2009). The increasing contact of culturally diverse people has led to crossovers, cultural mixing, and new forms of belonging. Sociologists link the concept of hybridity to processes of globalisation and large-scale migration around the world, and point to increasing differentiation in cultural traditions and forms (Giddens 2001). Rather than greater homogeneity of culture we are seeing greater diversity. As Anthony Giddens (2001) states:

> Local traditions are joined to a host of additional cultural forms from abroad presenting people with a bewildering array of lifestyle options from which to choose . . . established identities and ways of life grounded in local communities and cultures are giving way to new forms of 'hybrid identity'. (2001, p. 64)

These new hybrid identities are not fixed, but fluid, and they are strategically used to negotiate life in global and multicultural societies. Over the last two decades, scholars in cultural and ethnic studies have used the term 'hybridity' to explain and interpret the experiences of those who live across two or more cultures. This chapter will examine some of these studies, but first we will take a brief look at the history of the idea of hybridity and how it is manifested in popular culture.

Tracing hybridity

Interest in the concept of the hybrid is not new and has a long history. The word hybridity originated in biology to describe the selective breeding of plants to produce new varieties with improved qualities such as performance, taste, and durability. In its wider cultural use in the nineteenth century, it had a more pejorative connotation. According to Robert Young (1995), the colonial discourse on hybridity raised several issues. First, it addressed the fertility of the hybrid person. Some nineteenth-century scientists believed that there were different biological races and the proof of this rested on the question of whether the product of a union between white and black people was fertile. If the child of a white European male and a black female was infertile, then it proved that there were different species of humans.

Other/Otherness
Refers to those individuals who are treated as objects and have no agency and freedom. In *post-colonialism*, the Other is seen as someone who is different from the European colonial self, while in ethnic and cultural studies the Other is someone from a marginalised minority group within a country of immigration.

colonisation/colonialism
When a nation takes and maintains power over a territory that is outside its boundaries, based on a belief of superiority over those being colonised. See also *imperialism*.

Second, the nineteenth-century theories of race also raised the issue of fear and desire towards the **Other** (Young 1995). This ambiguity is evident in the novels and travel writings of the period. In colonial literature, the cultural Other was a source of revulsion, but also of desire (Jervis 1999). Mixed with this fear of and desire for the racial Other was the horror of 'mixed-bloods'. The hybrid, usually associated with the stigma of being half-breed or half-caste, reinforced colonial ideas about racial purity, a common view in the early days of the **colonisation** of Australia in terms of relations between whites and the Indigenous population. While colonial patriarchal society accepted sexual relations between white men and 'primitive' females, it conveniently refused to consider the possibility of a sexual relationship between white women and black men. It was unthinkable that a white woman could desire a black man. If sex occurred between them, it was considered non-consensual and therefore an act of rape.

There was little scholarly work conducted on the positive experiences of colonial hybrids, and both coloniser and the colonised usually shunned biracial individuals. Consequently, people were ignorant about the formation of their cultural and racial identity and their life experiences. This changed, at least in America, at the turn of the twentieth century. Scholars and social thinkers began to discuss the nature of cross-cultural interaction and the impact that living in between cultures had on the hybrid's self-identity (Marotta 2006).

Hybridity and popular culture

The idea of hybridity has permeated popular culture, and thus can be seen in 'hybrid forms of cuisine, fashion, music and architecture' (Giddens 2001, p. 256). It is also highlighted by the emergence of a 'remix generation' in the fashion industry and the bicultural character in popular 'multicultural films' such as *Looking for Alibrandi* (2000), *Bend it Like Beckham* (2002), *My Big Fat Greek Wedding* (2002) and *Head On* (1999), all of which explore—some in a more sophisticated manner than others—the challenges of living between two cultures.

Bollywood

Globalising and hybrid processes are evident in Bollywood movies in which different styles are appropriated and mixed to produce a new product. Indian movies appropriate Western-style plots and the English language to convey their stories. The recent success of *Slumdog Millionaire* encapsulates the mixture of Indian and Western actors and the mixture of English and Hindi dialogue (Magnier 2009), but the movie has also raised issues about what constitutes an authentic India. Is the movie an Indian or foreign film? To what extent is it an authentic portrayal of the poor in India, particularly the city of Mumbai? Shyamal Sengupta, a Professor of Film Studies in Mumbai, notes: 'It's a white man's imagined India . . . It's not quite snake charmers, but it's close. It's a poverty tour' (cited in Magnier 2009).

Fashion and the 'remix generation'

The media and advertising industries have only recently begun to awaken to multicultural demographics, and today models who are either of mixed ethnicity or ethnically ambiguous are represented more frequently in Australian magazines and on television. According to Sushi Das writing in *The Age*, ethnic hybridity is increasingly popular and 'is reflected in the myriad ethnic looks eagerly adopted by models and other trend setters' (2004, p. 4).

Cherie Ditcham is a 22-year-old Melburnian who is in great demand as a fashion model around the world. Her mother is Chinese Malay, while her father is Australian of English ancestry. Cherie has 'Chinese shaped eyes that are hazel in colour, a square jaw and a European nose and lips. Her thick hair is dark brown and she describes her skin colour as "chameleon"' (Das 2004, p. 4).

Halle Berry, well-known in American films, is the first black woman to receive an Oscar for 'Best Actress'. She has a 'mixed race' heritage in that her father is black and she was brought up by her white mother. Halle Berry is often depicted as 'a sexually appealing blend of black and whiteness' (Matthews 2002).

It is now common for 'top-end brands such as Louis Vuitton, YSL and Lancome to use models with racially indeterminate features' (Das 2004, p. 4). Notably, the situation is complex in that Asian and Eurasian female images are often represented in different ways. While Eurasian women may feature as fashion models, Asian women are more likely to represent 'forms of cosmopolitanism, technological progress and financial success' (Matthews 2002).

'Mixed race', according to Das (2004, p. 4), is now the 'third largest ethnic minority group in Britain' and this proportion likely to increase:

> Cheekily referring to themselves as the 'remix generation', this group of young people sees a future born out of a mixed race heritage. And while models, superstars and pop idols chase the latest 'look' advertisers and marketing teams are frantically pumping out images that they say reflect a multicultural society. (Das 2004, p. 4)

Migrant youth: Transnational and in-between

If globalisation refers to the interconnectedness of the world, then transnationalism alludes to the multiplicity of global and cross-border connections. The idea of living in between cultures is clearly captured in the life of Barack Obama, but this experience is also prevalent among young immigrants who are more likely to be involved in global cross-cultural border flows and thus construct identities that are both here (host society) and there (country of origin). The in-betweenness of migrant youth in Australia is captured in their sense of belonging, which is ambivalent, contradictory and strategic (Butcher & Thomas 2003). The following statements by two young immigrants of Turkish and Lebanese background respectively encapsulate the idea of in-betweenness.

> Well my sort of cultural background it's mix, like can't say I'm Turk because I'm Aussie sort of thing. You know what I mean? (If she were asked?) I'd say I was mixed. I fit in fine. My best friend is an Aussie. I don't feel like I don't belong.

> Well I can't decide what I am. Sometimes I'm like 'what's up bro' and other times I'm like 'g'day mate'. Sometimes I eat woggy food and sometimes I eat meat pies. (both cited in Butcher and Thomas 2003, p. 37)

Although these young immigrants feel comfortable moving between cultures, their sense of difference is heightened in social situations in which they are in the minority. One Turkish-Australian youth felt 'very Turkish' when he went to a friend's birthday party because the guests were all Anglo-Australians, while a Chinese-Australian felt 'Chinese' when he was 'around no Chinese' (Butcher & Thomas 2003, p. 37). These responses illustrate how identity—in this case, cultural identity—is constructed across difference. The participants did not feel 'Turkish' or 'Chinese' until they were placed in social situations where they felt visibly different.

A sense of difference and being in-between is also evident in migrant youth's transnational engagement. Transnationalism is connected to economic, social, and political activities that cross national boundaries, and is a process in which social actors construct and maintain simultaneous multiple relations linking their societies of origins with their societies of settlement. Maintaining connections and communication across national borders has been made possible and easier through the communication revolution. Readily available air transport, satellite TV, internet, email, and mobile phones mean we can now communicate and live beyond our localised worlds. Place no longer confines us. The global economy, fuelled by the information revolution, has generated new social and cultural spaces where cultures mix both within and across nations.

The process of transnationalism fosters cultures that no longer inhabit localised places and are no longer culture bound. Cultures become porous and open to different influences. The formation and negotiation of cultural identity may no longer depend on face-to-face encounters. Transmigrants can now be socially close but physically distant. The cultural identity of transmigrants is not necessarily confined to one place or origin because they may have friends and family scattered over two or three countries.

Younger immigrants are most likely to have an enthusiasm for transnational practices, and perceive themselves to have multiple homes and dual or multiple identities

(Lee 2008). Research on young transnational Arab-Australians has shown how home is a fluid idea when it comes to deciding where one belongs. A female participant in Heba Batainah's (2008, p. 161) research demonstrates the complex and multifaceted nature of a transnational home. In response to a question about whether Australia is home, she states that:

> For me no I don't think it is [but] ... if I was over there [Palestine] I would consider here [Australia] home, because this is where I have grown up and this is what I know, and I don't think I would be able to adapt there as easily as you know as a lot of other people would.

This movement between here and there illustrates that her cultural identity is not confined to a specific place or time. The in-betweenness of her identity makes home a transnational experience.

Australian research on hybridity

The metaphor of hybridity has increasingly informed research on first- and second-generation immigrants in Australia. So ubiquitous has this kind of work been that it is now rare to read papers on ethnicity that do not address and use terms such as hybridity, 'third space', and multiple identities. The early work on migrant women by Jean Martin (1984, 1985), on Greek-Australians by Gillian Bottomley (1976, 1979, 1987), on ethnic subjectivity by Nikos Papastergiadis (1986), and on multiculturalism by Sneja Gunew (1990) signalled a theoretical shift by scholars in the area of ethnic studies. The 1970s and 1980s saw a reconceptualisation of the 'ethnic self' and an emerging discussion on the multiple, hybrid, and **postmodern** ethnic self. Later work by Joy Elley and Christine Inglis (1995) on Turkish-Australians, Maria Pallotta-Chiarolli (1993, 1995) on sexuality and ethnicity, Loretta Baldassar (1999, 2000) on Italian-Australians, and Ien Ang (1996) on being 'Chinese' theorised a new postmodern ethnic self that highlighted the fluid and porous nature of cultural, sexual, and gender boundaries.

postmodernism
The culture of postmodernity, referring to the plurality of social meanings and the diversity of social experiences that exist within localised contexts and cultures.

Recent work by Torika Bolatagici (2004), Takae Ichimoto (2004), and Melissa Butcher (2004) draws on the idea of hybridity to capture the ambiguity and power of living in multiple worlds. Bolatagici (2004) argues that this 'in-between' position allows individuals to resist stereotypical constructions of their ethnic identity. The empirical work by Greg Noble and Paul Tabar (2002) on the lives of young Lebanese-Australians suggests that to be hybrid allows individuals to work against assumptions about what it means to be 'ethnic' in Australia.

Noble and Tabar's (2002) research on the identity formation of young Lebanese-Australian men explores how their experience of marginalisation has affected the construction of their cultural identity. From their study of second-generation Lebanese youth living in the Canterbury/Bankstown area of Sydney, the authors suggest that the young men see themselves as part of two different worlds. This is not just a question of hyphenated identities; rather, it is 'a series of complex processes of what could be called hybridisation' (Noble & Tabar 2002, p. 131). Despite the diversity of their backgrounds in terms of class, religion, and place of origin, the boys in the study identified themselves as Lebanese-Australians—or, as one young man stated: '[i]t means like, inside I'm Lebanese, but I'm Australian-Lebanese because I'm living in Australians' country' (2002, p. 129).

Some of the young men constructed a 'Lebanese' identity that was 'fixed', and associated being Lebanese with qualities such as honour, respect, morality, and the idea of the family (Noble & Tabar 2002). The assumption is that these qualities do not exist within the so-called 'Australian' culture. Furthermore, being Lebanese in the Australian context hides internal differences because young men from other ethnic groups were assumed to be 'Lebo'. According to Noble and Tabar, the idea that one could identify certain characteristics that were uniquely Lebanese allows the young Lebanese men to construct a collective identity, which provides them with unity and moral certainty in the face of racism experienced at school and in the wider community. In this context, constructing a fixed cultural identity is a positive rather than an oppressive experience. Their 'Lebaneseness' is a source of pride and empowerment, feelings they do not experience within the dominant 'Anglo-Australian' community. For example, one participant recounted how at school they were targeted by teachers when they talked in class, while 'it was all right for other people to talk . . . like most of the Australians' (Noble & Tabar 2002, p. 137).

Noble and Tabar's research also highlights how identity is constructed across difference. The young Lebanese men construct an identity in opposition to a narrow version of Australianness—for example, lack of respect for the family and the absence of honour in the Australian culture. The process of constructing identity across difference occurs for both the 'Anglo-Australians' and members of minority cultures. Both groups construct the identity of the other as fixed and homogenous, but the major difference is that members of the 'Anglo-Australian' group do this from a position of power.

The young Lebanese men also draw on their hybrid identities to undermine those who represent authority figures within the host and ethnic communities. They speak Arabic in class in order to undermine the surveillance of the teacher and use a strategic Australian-ness against their parents by subverting their authority at home when they speak English. Being bilingual becomes a source of power and allows these young men to distinguish themselves from both their parents and the host culture. According to these young men, the Lebanese culture constrains their parents and makes them 'typical Lebanese'. These young men occupy that in-between place and are torn between their parents' culture—which is 'too Lebanese'—and what they perceive to be their own Australianness—an Australianness that can also be distinguished from the one experienced by the Anglo-Australian peers at school. A hybrid position places them in a situation in which they find their ethnicity—as expressed through their parents' actions and values—limiting while simultaneously using a representation of 'Australianness' that is empowering.

Australian studies have expanded and broadened our understanding of those who negotiate multiple identities by incorporating gender and sexuality into their analysis.

10.1: 'That's my Australian side'—the role of gender

Zuleyka Zevallos (2003) explores the in-between hybrid position of Australian women from Central and Latin America. She adopts a qualitative approach, and argues that the construction of ethnic boundaries depends on social context. When overseas, these women identify themselves as 'Australian', whereas when they came back they feel less Australian. The reluctance to construct themselves as Australian is associated with negative stereotypes placed on them by 'Anglo-Australians'. The participants in the study exemplified the hybrid nature of their identity by perceiving themselves as both 'Latin-American' and 'Australian', but the 'Australian side' to which these women are attached has less to do with the social and cultural customs of the host society and is more associated with the value of egalitarianism, especially the promotion of equality for women.

Living with contradictions: Sexuality and hybridity

Maria Pallotta-Chiarolli (1995) has found that the contradictions of being Italian-Australian, Greek-Australian, or Asian-Australian intensify when cultural hybrids try to negotiate their ethnic and sexual identity. Gay men from ethnic backgrounds have to explain what it means to be homosexual to their parents who sometimes believe homosexuality does not exist or is a disgusting habit picked up from Australians. On the other side, gay ethnic men's Anglo-Australian lovers cannot comprehend all this 'cultural stuff' and believe their partners should leave home and be more independent. Italian-Australian lesbians have also struggled to deal with their cultural difference within the lesbian community and their sexuality within their ethnic community. The following passage captures this contradiction particularly well:

> Sometimes I go out to women's events and feel I am in a fishbowl, everyone looking at me because I look different, asking me questions and making assumptions about being Italian, as if I'm necessarily a poor victim who needs rescuing from her culture. (Pallotta-Chiarolli 1995, p. 135)

Apart from scholarly studies on hybrid individuals, other media such as movies and literature have raised issues to do with bicultural and multicultural identities.

The problems with hybridity

Floya Anthias (1999) argues that the contemporary literature on hybridity over-emphasises the role of **agency**. Hybridity assumes a free-floating actor who voluntarily chooses

agency
The ability of people, individually and collectively, to influence their own lives and the society in which they live.

between identities and positions; being and representing her- or himself as hybrid, as the 'remix generation' is doing, is seen as one choice among many. Anthias, along with Noble and Tabar (2002), asserts that we should understand the free-floating hybrid self within a system of social and structural constraints. The film *Looking for Alibrandi* tends to minimise these structural constraints, and consequently does not explicitly address the role that the dominant Anglo-Australian group has in defining Josie's ethnicity through the use of racist stereotypes and how this impacts on Josie's reaction to her Sicilian culture.

Second, Anthias (1999) argues that the formation of hybrid identities does not mean the end of ethnic solidarities and a decrease in ethnocentrism and racism. In other words, being hybrid does not necessarily lead to openness to those who are different. Individuals from the dominant culture may also become 'hybrid' by selectively appropriating minority cultural practices, symbols and ideas, but this process does not lead to genuine openness and the abandoning of some of the dominant cultural practices, values, and symbols. Hybridisation as appropriation may not be a progressive, critical process if adopted by members of the dominant cultural group. Furthermore, the remix generation may also be less interested in upsetting the status quo, especially when its members are busy accommodating the demands of advertisers and marketing companies.

Another weakness with the category of hybridity is that it privileges the domain of culture and ignores the roles of gender, class, and sexuality; however, as shown above, Australian feminist scholars such as Pallotta-Chiarolli (1993, 1995) and Zevallos (2003) have implicitly addressed this problem. Others, like Noble and Tabar (2002), tend to ignore the issue of gender in their research, thus marginalising the voices of young women with an immigrant heritage. In addition, what impact does socioeconomic status (SES) have on the experience of cultural hybridity? Would the experiences of the young Lebanese-Australian men differ if they were from a middle-class background and university educated?

In some cases, the use of the category of hybridity depoliticises culture and minimises internal differences, thereby homogenising the hybrid group. The category of 'Lebanese-Australian' hides the fact that 'Lebaneseness' tends to be used as a catch-all category and includes other ethnic groups (Noble & Tabar 2002), while second-generation Asian-Americans disagree on the nature of what it means to be both Asian and American (Pyke & Dang 2003). In addition, the work on hybridity sometimes downplays hybridity as alienation. The participants in Pallotta-Chiarolli's (1995) study experienced bouts of anger, paranoia, and denial when trying to resolve the tension between their sexuality and their ethnicity. For some groups, the feeling of homelessness may turn into a form of identity politics—for example, the young Lebanese-Australians close ranks to compensate for their sense of isolation. An 'us and them' mentality can then appear at the border zones of hybridity. Finally, at times the scholarship on hybridity assumes that it is describing something novel (Anthias 1999), whereas the mixing of cultures is nothing new.

Conclusion

The idea of hybridity has begun to permeate popular culture through cinematic representations of cross-cultural subjects and through the fashion industry's current obsession with ethnic ambiguity as the latest 'look'. Globalising processes have both contributed to and exacerbated hybridisation processes. Globalising processes have led to greater cross-cultural contact and the establishment of multicultural societies. Consequently, we have seen the emergence of individuals who straddle more than one culture. As we have shown, recent Australian research on ethnicity examines the experiences of bicultural or multicultural subjects—especially how they construct and negotiate living in between cultures.

Summary of main points

▶ In the nineteenth century, cultural and racial hybrids were often viewed as less than human.
▶ Globalising processes such as the movement of capital and people have contributed to and further enhanced the mixing of cultures and identities.
▶ Popular culture has become permeated by hybrid practices (Bollywood movies) and ambiguity (mixed-race fashion models).
▶ Hybrid individuals have transnational connections between their host societies and their countries of origin.
▶ Gender and sexuality provide a more complex understanding of the contradictions of hybridity.
▶ 'Multicultural' films and literature demonstrate the fluid nature of hybridity.
▶ An over-emphasis on culture ignores the fact that hybrid individuals are constrained by the power of host-culture members.

`10.1` The cultural hybrid in multicultural films

Consider the following film dealing with multicultural issues and cultural hybridity.

Bend It Like Beckham and 'British Asians'
In a changing-room scene, the girls are discussing the idea of arranged marriages and why Jess—the central character in the movie *Bend It Like Beckham*—has to hide the fact that she is playing football from her parents.
Jess: Indian girls are not supposed to play football.
Girl: That's a bit backward, isn't it?
Jules: It ain't just an Indian thing, is it? I mean how many people come out and support us?
. . .
Jess: My sister is getting married soon, it's a love match.
Girl: What does that mean?

Jess: It's not arranged.

Girl: I don't know how you Indian girls put up with it.

Jess: It's just culture, sort of. It's better than sleeping around with boys . . . What's the point in that?

(a) Has Jess resolved the tension between her Indian and British identity?

(b) How are these identities represented in *Bend It Like Beckham*?

(c) How is the issue of gender identity and its relationship to ethnicity addressed in the movie?

(d) Giardina (2003, p. 76) argues that in some multicultural films there is a 'quasi-utopian world view that sees everyone coming to terms with their differences without so much as the slightest problem or struggle'. Do you agree with this statement?

Discussion questions

10.1 Do you feel you have a hybrid identity? What does it entail?

10.2 Are we all hybrid to some extent?

10.3 What are the key characteristics of living on the margins of two cultures and why did the colonialists fear the hybrid?

10.4 Does living in between two or more cultures allow you to develop a different perspective from those confined by the parent and host culture?

10.5 Is ethnic ambiguity something to fear or embrace?

10.6 How do gender and sexuality influence the experience of a hybrid identity?

10.7 Does religion complicate the experience of bicultural identities?

Further reading

Edwards, P., Ganguly, D. & Lo, J. 2007, 'Pigments of the imagination: Theorising, performing and historicising mixed race', special issue of the *Journal of Intercultural Studies*, vol. 28, no. 1, pp. 1–155.

Fozdar, F., Wilding, R. & Hawkins, M. 2009, *Race and Ethnic Relations*, Oxford University Press, Melbourne.

Guerra, C. and White, R. (eds) 1995, *Ethnic Minority Youth in Australia: Challenges and Myths*, National Clearinghouse for Youth Studies, Hobart.

Hage, G. (ed.) 2002, *Arab-Australians: Citizenship and Belonging*, Melbourne University Press, Melbourne.

Hall, S. 1992, 'The question of cultural identity', in S. Hall, D. Held & T. McGrew (eds), *Modernity and its Future*, Polity Press, Cambridge, pp. 273–326.

Perkins, M. (ed.) 2007, *Visibly Different: Face, Place and Race in Australia*, Peter Lang, Bern, Switzerland.

Websites

- Abdennebi Ben Beya, *Mimicry, Mimicry, Ambivalence and Hybridity*: <www. english. emory.edu/Bahri/IWEBPAGE.HTML>.
- Elizabeth Laragy, 'Hybridity', *The Imperial Archive: Key Concepts in Postcolonial Studies*: <www.qub.ac.uk/en/imperial/key-concepts/Hybridity.htm>.
- Julie Matthews, 2002, 'Deconstructing the visual: The diasporic hybridity of Asian and Eurasian female images', *Intersections: Gender, History & Culture in the Asian Context*, no. 8, <wwwsshe.murdoch.edu.au/intersections/issue8/matthews.html>.
- Pavna Sodhi Kalsim 2003, '"The best of both worlds": Bicultural identity formation of Punjabi women living in Canada', *Canadian Association for the Study of Adult Education—Online Proceedings 2003*, <www.oise.utoronto.ca/CASAE/ cnf2003/2003_papers/psodhiCAS03.pdf>.
- Sociology Central—Culture and Identity: <www.sociology.org.uk/cculture. htm>. An introductory site with resources on a range of topics related to cultural diversity and identity-formation.
- Youth and European Identity: <www.sociology.ed.ac.uk/youth>. The website of a large research project with access to helpful links and research papers.

Films/documentaries

- *Floating Life*, 1996, motion picture, directed by C. Law, Southern Star Films. A film about Chinese diaspora as a family emigrates from Hong Kong to Australia, experiencing culture shock and social ostracism. The film portrays the process of assimilation as complex and one of ongoing negotiation.
- *Head On*, 1998, motion picture, directed by A. Kokkinos, Palace Films. A confronting Australian film about a young Greek boy dealing with his homosexual identity.
- *Looking for Alibrandi*, 2000, motion picture, directed by K. Woods, Village Roadshow. An amusing and endearing film of the widely read novel about the life of seventeen-year-old Josie, an Australian teenager of Italian descent dealing with the culture clash experienced by the children of first-generation migrants.
- *Hybrid Life: A Series of Films on Multicultural Australia*, 2001, videorecording, produced by M. McMurchy, Ronin Films. An award-winning documentary on the migrant experience.
- *Bend It Like Beckham*, 2002, motion picture, directed by G. Chadha, Warner Home Video. A British film about a teenage girl of Sikh descent who rebels against the traditional views of her parents by playing soccer.
- *My Big Fat Greek Wedding*, 2002, motion picture, directed by J. Zwick, IFC Films. A US comedy about the culture clash that occurs when a Greek woman decides to marry a non-Greek man.

Visit the *Public Sociology* book website to access topical case studies, weblinks, YouTube clips, and extra readings.

References

Ang, I. 1996, 'The case of the smile', *Feminist Review*, no. 52, pp. 36–49.

Anthias, F. 1999, 'Beyond unities of identity in high modernity', *Identities*, vol. 6, no. 1, pp. 121–44.

Baldassar, L. 1999, 'Marias and marriage: Ethnicity, gender and sexuality among Italo-Australian youth in Perth', *Journal of Sociology*, vol. 35, no. 1, pp. 1–22.

—— 2000, 'Gender, ethnicity and transnational citizenship: Italian-Australian', *Studies in Western Australian History*, no. 21, pp. 13–31.

Batainah, H. 2008, 'Issues of belonging: Exploring Arab-Australian Transnationalism', in H. Lee (ed.), *Ties of Homeland: Second Generation Transnationalism*, Cambridge Scholars Publishing, Newcastle, UK, pp. 151–67.

Bolatagici, T. 2004, 'Claiming the (n)either/(n)or of "third space": (Re)presenting hybrid identity and the embodiment of mixed race', *Journal of Intercultural Studies*, vol. 25, no. 1, pp. 75–85.

Bottomley, G. 1976, 'Ethnicity and identity among Greek Australians', *Australian New Zealand Journal of Sociology*, vol. 12, no. 2, pp. 118–25.

—— 1979, *After the Odyssey: A Study of Greek Australians*, University of Queensland Press, Brisbane.

—— 1987, 'Cultures, multiculturalism and the politics of representation', *Journal of Intercultural Studies*, vol. 8, no. 2, pp. 1–10.

Butcher, M. 2004, 'Universal processes of cultural change: Reflections on identity strategies of Indian and Australian youth', *Journal of Intercultural Studies*, vol. 25, no. 3, pp. 215–31.

Butcher, M. & Thomas, M. 2003, 'Being in-between', in M. Butcher and M. Thomas (eds), *Ingenious: Emerging Youth Cultures in Urban Australia*, Pluto Press, Melbourne, pp. 31–46.

Carroll, J. 2008, 'Behind the scenes: Is Barack Obama black or biracial?', CNN Politics. com, <http://edition.cnn.com/2008/POLITICS/06/09/btsc.obama.race/index. html> (accessed 19 August 2009).

Castles, S. & Miller, M. 2009, *The Age of Migration: International Population Movement in the Modern World*, Guilford Press, New York.

Das, S. 2004, 'They've got the look', *The Age* (section A3), 19 April, p. 4.

Elley, J. & Inglis, C. 1995, 'Ethnicity and gender: The two worlds of Australian Turkish youth', in C. Guerra & R. White (eds), *Ethnic Minority Youth in Australia: Challenges and Myths*, National Clearinghouse for Youth Studies, Hobart, pp. 193–202.

Giardina, M.D. 2003, '"Bending it like Beckham" in the global culture: Stylish hybridity, performativity, and the politics of representation', *Journal of Sport and Social Issue*, vol. 27, no. I, pp. 65–82.

Giddens, A., with the assistance of Karen Birdsall 2001, *Sociology*, 4th edn, Polity Press, Cambridge.

Gunew, S. 1990, 'Postmodern tensions: Reading for (multi)cultural difference', *Meanjin*, vol. 49, no. I, pp. 21–33.

Hynes, L. 2000, 'Looking for identity: Food, generation & hybridity', in *Looking for Alibrandi, Australian Screen Education*, no. 24, pp. 30–6.

Ichimoto, T. 2004, 'Ambivalent "selves" in transition: A case study of Japanese women studying in Australian universities', *Journal of Intercultural Studies*, vol. 25, no. 3, pp. 247–69.

Jervis, J. 1999, *Transgressing the Modern: Explorations in the Western Experience of Otherness*, Blackwell, Oxford.

Lee, H. 2008, 'Second generation transnationalism', in H. Lee (ed.), *Ties of Homeland: Second Generation Transnationalism*, Cambridge Scholars Publishing, Newcastle, UK, pp. I–32.

Magnier, M. 2009, 'Indians don't feel good about *Slumdog Millionaire*, *Los Angeles Times*, 24 January, <http://articles.latimes.com/2009/jan/24/world/fg-india-slumdog24> (accessed 23 August 2009).

Marotta, V. 2006, 'Civilisation, culture and the hybrid self in the work of Robert Ezra Park', *Journal of Intercultural Studies*, vol. 27, no. 4, pp. 413–33.

Martin, J. 1984, 'Non-English speaking women: Production and social reproduction', in G. Bottomley & Marie M. de Lepervanche (eds), *Ethnicity, Class and Gender in Australia*, Allen & Unwin, Sydney, pp. 109–22.

—— 1985, 'Multiculturalism and women', *Social Alternatives*, vol. 4, no. 3, pp. 56–8.

Matthews, J. 2002, 'Deconstructing the visual: The diasporic hybridity of Asian and Eurasian female images', *Intersections*, no. 8, <http://intersections.anu.edu.au/issue8/matthews.html> (accessed 24 May 2009).

Noble, G. & Tabar, P. 2002, 'On being Lebanese-Australian: Hybridity, essentialism and strategy among Arabic-speaking youth', in G. Hage (ed.), *Arab-Australians: Citizenship and Belonging*, Melbourne University Press, Melbourne, pp. 128–44.

Obama, B. 2004, *Dreams from My Father*, Three Rivers Press, New York.

Pallotta-Chiarolli, M. 1993, 'From "universalism" to "unity in diversity": Feminist responses to the intersections of ethnicity, gender and sexuality', *Lilith: A Feminist History Journal*, no. 8, pp. 41–52.

—— 1995, '"A rainbow in my heart": Negotiating sexuality & ethnicity', in C. Guerra & R. White (eds), *Ethnic Minority Youth in Australia: Challenges and Myths*, National Clearinghouse for Youth Studies, Hobart, pp. 133–44.

Papastergiadis, N. 1986, 'Culture, self and plurality', *Arena*, no. 76, pp. 49–61.

Pyke, K. & Dang, T. 2003, '"FOB" and "whitewashed": Identity and internalized racism among second generation Asian Americans', *Qualitative Sociology*, vol. 26, no. 2, pp. 147–72.

Thernstrom, A. 2009, 'Commentary: Identity politics in the age of Obama', CNN Politics.com, <http://edition.cnn.com/2009/POLITICS/06/04/thernstrom. identity.politics/index.html> (accessed 19 August 2009).

Young, R. 1995, *Colonial Desire: Hybridity in Theory, Culture and Race*, Routledge, London.

Zevallos, Z. 2003, '"That's my Australian side": The ethnicity, gender and sexuality of young Australian women of South and Central American origin', *Journal of Sociology*, vol. 39, no. 1, pp. 81–98.

Module 3
Social differences and inequalities

This module explores the origins of social differences and social inequalities in contemporary Australia. While individuals experience class, gender, ethnicity, race, religion, and deviance in various ways, the chapters highlight the utility of sociology in exposing the social origins and social impacts of these factors.

This module contains the following chapters:

CHAPTER 11

Class and inequality in Australia

Mark Western and Janeen Baxter

The Global Financial Crisis

The Global Financial Crisis (GFC) that began to manifest itself in 2007 resulted in some of the most severe economic consequences for households, organisations, and economies since the Great Depression of the 1930s. Between 2007 and 2008, the global unemployment rate increased from 5.7 per cent to 6.0 per cent—an increase of 10.7 million people (ILO 2009a, p. 8). This twelve-month increase in world unemployment is almost identical to the whole employed population of Australia—10.8 million in October 2009 (ABS 2009, p. 37).

The origins of the GFC are still being assessed, but analysts have pointed to a number of key factors:

- Housing prices in the United States were severely over-valued and people expected prices to continue to rise in the future, leading them to borrow heavily.
- US banks and financial institutions lent extensively, and in particular made risky loans to people with limited capacity to repay their mortgages; banks then bundled these loans together and sold them to other investors, offloading the risk to other financial institutions.
- The high profits associated with these activities led to banks making even riskier loans, and to other financial institutions entering the high-risk mortgage market.
- The complexity of the financial arrangements used to offload risk between financial institutions made it difficult for institutions to assess properly what they were buying.
- Financial institutions did not have the right controls or management in place to manage risk appropriately.
- Credit rating agencies contributed to the problem by rating highly and thus encouraging financial arrangements to offload risky debts between institutions.
- House prices eventually fell and, coupled with rising interest rates, the number of people defaulting on mortgages increased.
- The impact of mortgage defaults was felt across the US financial system, because of the extent to which institutions and investors were exposed to risky loans, either through mortgages or the risky loans of other institutions.
- Banks stopped lending money to one another because they did not know how many bad loans other banks were holding.
- The credit crisis spread beyond the United States because of global connections between financial institutions.
- Central banks intervened to try to encourage lending; however, as financial institutions stopped making money available, economic growth declined, and

unemployment, company failures, mortgage foreclosures, and repossession of property all increased.

- Governments in a number of countries stepped in to nationalise banks, cut interest rates to encourage investment borrowing, and pump billions into the economy to promote spending and investor and consumer confidence (BBC 2009; Baily, Litan & Johnson 2008).

At the time of writing, the perception is that Australia has been less affected by the GFC than some other countries (OECD 2009), maintaining positive economic growth and household consumption with comparatively small increases in unemployment, but the story is not all positive. ACL Bearing is a Tasmanian company that produces parts for the Australian car industry. Over the course of 2008 and 2009, the company struggled to remain viable. Because of its importance as a supplier for major car companies Ford and Toyota, it eventually received A$7 million in federal government loans to enable it to keep operating. During the period, employees also took pay cuts to help lower costs, and workers were assured by the company that both their jobs and their entitlements would be protected. In August 2009, despite the federal government assistance, the company was placed into administration and a company receiver appointed. In September, the receiver indicated that up to 120 workers would potentially lose their jobs in a bid to keep the company afloat. The receiver also indicated that workers who would be made redundant would probably not receive their entitlements as there was no money available to pay them. Approximately $30 million in employee entitlements would be lost. For some workers the lost entitlements would be equivalent to two years' pay. Employee anger over the threatened job losses and lost entitlements was concentrated when the receiver also revealed that two company directors had been receiving redundancy payments for about a year while workers had taken voluntary pay cuts. Between them, the two directors received almost $700 000 in additional payments (ABC 2009a, 2009b).

Introduction

Why are sociologists interested in studying class? What is class? And is there any such thing as class in Australian society? These are some of the questions we address in this chapter. As the vignette above shows, the Global Financial Crisis (GFC) has focused attention on the vulnerability of some social groups, and the likelihood of increased inequality between the rich and the poor. Those in positions of power and privilege may be able to cushion themselves from the worst of the economic fallout from the GFC, but for those who lose their jobs, homes, or businesses, the impact of the crisis is likely to be felt for many years to come. This chapter looks at what sociologists mean by the term 'class', how this helps us understand the implications of events such as the GFC for different social groups, and what some recent Australian research tells us about class inequalities and differences. First, this chapter explores the ways in which sociologists have used the term 'class' theoretically.

Classical and modern theories of class

Classical theories

CrossLink:
See Chapter 2
for more on
Marx and
Weber.

The two most influential classical sociologists to address issues of class were Karl Marx (1818–83) and Max Weber (1864–1920). All of Marx's writings were about class (Bottomore 1965; Hall 1977), and we will only provide a simplified description of one small set of ideas here. Further information on Marx and Weber is provided in Chapter 2 of this book. For Marx, class fundamentally explained two things: the structure of inequality in a society; and the process by which that inequality would be overcome.

To obtain an understanding of Marxism, it is necessary to begin with a discussion of economic activity, especially the production of goods and services. Production is fundamental for societies to survive, but as people learn to produce a surplus—more than they need to survive—classes and class-based inequality become possible (Carling 1991). This happens because people produce things together, not individually; the relationships between people involved in production define classes.

In all capitalist societies, a group of people owns the **means of production**—the equipment and property used to produce things—and another group of people comprises employees who work for the owners of the means of production. In Marxist terms, the owners of the means of production are referred to as the bourgeoisie or capitalists. People without productive property, who have to sell their labour in order to live, are the working class, or the proletariat, and are employed by capitalists to produce goods or services for sale (Marx & Engels 1955).

means of production
The raw materials, tools, equipment, property, and labour used to produce goods in a particular economic system.

Each of these two classes is defined by its relationship to the means of production (owner and worker) and its relationship to the other class (employer and employee). The existence of one class presupposes the existence of the other (Giddens 1981). As outlined in Chapter 2, for Marx, the basic class structure of capitalism consisted of capitalists and workers defined by their economic positions within production. Marx viewed the relationship between capitalists and workers as fundamentally exploitative.

exploitation
A term that is often used generally to mean the misuse of power by one group over another. Marx used the term specifically to refer to the appropriation of surplus value or profits by capitalists.

This was both a moral judgment about the relationship between capitalists and workers and an objective fact. The 'objective fact' of **exploitation** explains where the economic surplus and capitalists' profits come from, according to

Marx (1973; 1976). When a capitalist employs a worker, the worker produces a good or service by turning raw material into something that can be sold. In today's society, the product might be something physical, like a car or a pair of shoes, but it might also be a service, like a haircut. The wages earned by workers must be enough to buy what they need for themselves and their families (food, shelter, clothing, consumer goods, and the like). The value of what workers produce is determined by technology, production methods, the technical organisation of work, and scientific knowledge, or what Marx called the 'forces of production'. They include the means of production (productive property) and scientific and technical knowledge. While workers' wages are determined by the amount of money needed to look after themselves and their families, productivity is determined by how developed the forces of production are.

In general, Marx argues, workers will produce more in a day than is needed for their ongoing livelihood. This surplus value goes to the capitalist. If, in an eight-hour day, it takes a worker two hours to produce goods equivalent to the value of her wages, for the remaining six hours she is creating *surplus value* for her employer. This process, in which workers produce surplus value for capitalists, is what Marx means by exploitation (Edel 1981). Exploitation is associated with inequality—that is, with an unequal distribution of things that people value, like income and leisure (Western 1983)—because capitalists' profits are substantially greater than workers' wages and, more importantly, because capitalists derive profits at the expense of workers. Profits flow directly to capitalists from the things that workers make in production (Wright 2005).

Exploitation also means that capitalists and workers have interests or social objectives that are opposed. Capitalists are interested in maximising profits by increasing exploitation (paying lower wages, working workers harder, and so on). In the short term, workers are interested in improving their circumstances through better pay and working conditions; in the long term, workers would be interested in abolishing the system of class inequality that promotes their disadvantage.

Marx, and his collaborator Friedrich Engels (1820–1895), explained how this should happen in a famous political book, the *Manifesto of the Communist Party* (Marx & Engels 1955), which was written during a time of considerable political and economic unrest in Europe. At the time, nineteenth-century European society was gradually being split 'into two hostile camps' (Marx & Engels 1955, p. 35), comprising the proletariat and the bourgeoisie. The middle class (tradespeople, craft workers, shopkeepers) was disappearing as rapid industrialisation and increased competition between capitalists led to increased exploitation to improve or maintain profits, forcing people into working-class jobs and forcing inefficient capitalists out of business. Eventually, Marx and Engels predicted, society would reach a stage where the two classes could no longer coexist. As industrial development continued, the opposition of interests between capitalists and workers would become more apparent. Under these circumstances, workers would become aware of their class unity, conscious of their opposition to capitalists, and politically organised. A 'class-in-itself' becomes a 'class-for-itself'—that is, a class with a common consciousness and a political organisation. The result is a proletarian revolution in which private ownership of the means of production is abolished, and a new society without classes emerges (Marx & Engels 1955, p. 54).

class consciousness
A subjective perception of a group of people that they belong to a similar social class. For Marx, the key element for a proletarian revolution was the development of class consciousness among workers by their recognition of common interests.

There has never been a working-class revolution of this type. *The Communist Manifesto* was a piece of political writing, rather than a deep analysis, and the story of working-class revolution it contained was a simplistic one. Still, it demonstrates that Marx's own analysis of classes is dynamic, explaining not only class inequality and class division, but economic, social, and political change. Economic breakdown, **class consciousness**, and collective organisation or class struggle are the significant elements of this theory.

Marx's ideas about class inequality in capitalism have remained influential today, even though his predictions about the end of capitalism have been discredited. Even at the time at which he was writing, Marx's ideas were controversial. The other equally influential classical theorist of class, Weber, is often described as writing in dialogue with 'Marx's ghost', because his own writings were, in many ways, a response to Marx's.

Marx defined classes by social relationships in production. As noted in Chapter 2, for Weber, class situation—the class circumstance of an individual—is based in the market. The market is a concept describing the arena in which buyers and sellers come together to exchange goods and services. Individuals' class situation reflects the economic resources they possess, which can be sold in the market to earn rewards such as income, promotional opportunities, and good working conditions. In other words, for Weber, class situation reflects not how individuals relate to the means of production and other people in the production process (as it does for Marx), but what they have, and what they can bargain with for rewards in the market.

Weber called these rewards and social opportunities **life chances**. Like Marx, Weber makes a fundamental distinction between people who own productive property and

life chances
A term associated with the work of Weber to refer to different opportunities and differential access to resources, including education, wealth, housing, and health.

people who do not. In capitalist societies, there are therefore two property classes: the propertied and the non-propertied (Weber 1982a). Unlike Marx, Weber recognised that other kinds of economic resources also generated rewards. The propertyless might have particular 'marketable skills' for which there is a demand. Privileged commercial classes (Weber 1982b)—individuals with sought-after skills, or who provide valued services—include various skilled workers and professionals, such as doctors, lawyers, engineers, and computer experts. Students doing vocational and university courses to improve their chances in the job market are trying to acquire the kinds of marketable skills to which Weber refers.

**CrossLink:
See Chapter 2
for more on
Marx and
Weber.**

Unlike Marx, Weber did not believe that people in similar class situations would necessarily develop a common awareness of class inequality and act in an organised way. Under certain circumstances, this might happen; often, however, it will not

(Weber 1982b). In contrast to Marx, Weber did not believe that the working class eventually had to organise into a collective entity and overthrow capitalism.

To illustrate how a class might become organised, Weber introduced the concept of social class. The class situation of an individual describes the particular combination of property and marketable skills with which the individual can bargain in the market. There are potentially as many market situations as there are people, because each person could differ slightly from others regarding the kinds of property or skills possessed (Giddens 1981); however, some market situations are more similar than others, implying a reasonably high probability of mobility or movement of people between them. Mobility between market situations may take place over a person's lifetime as they move from one job to another. Mobility between class situations may also be intergenerational, linking parents' and children's jobs—for example, when the son of a bank teller becomes a clerk in the public service. Weber defines a social class as the cluster of market situations with high levels of mobility in them (Weber 1982b).

status groups
Communities or groups of people with a common lifestyle, distinguished from others by a particular non-economic social characteristic. Status groupings can be used to include or exclude people with particular social characteristics.

In describing the social class structure of capitalist societies Weber begins to treat classes as separate groups. Social classes are real groups of people; individual market situations are not, but 'groupness', for Weber, is much more a feature of what he terms **status groups** than classes. Unlike classes, status groups are not economically determined. They are typically communities, groups of people with a common lifestyle, who are distinguished from others because of a specific non-economic, social characteristic (Weber 1982a).

Possible criteria for status group formation include age, race, gender, religion, ethnicity, and region. Crucial to Weber's concept of status is his assumption that the status situation of people is determined by estimations of social honour or prestige. Within a status group, certain kinds of behaviour are typically regarded as being appropriate for members of the group, while others are viewed as inappropriate. When status criteria are important elements of social structure, status groups will have different levels of prestige or social honour, according to the kinds of lifestyles and behaviours their members exhibit. In a status group based around neighbourhood residence, for example, lifestyle differences may be evident in the kinds of car(s) people own, what they do in their leisure time, the clubs and organisations to which they belong, whether their children attend private or state schools, and so on. Furthermore, different ways of life may lead to status groups being ranked on some sort of prestige hierarchy by all members of the community, with general consensus about where groups are located.

Class and status are two sources of group formation. For Weber, the group structure of any society reflects the relative importance of economic market factors that give rise to classes, and social status criteria like race, gender, or neighbourhood, which lead to status group formation. In a community, or the wider society, class and status principles may overlap, as when people in the same social class are also in the same status group(s). Class and status may also cross-cut one another in varying ways.

This very brief treatment of Marx's and Weber's ideas illustrates some of the issues that have been taken up by sociologists today. In the remaining sections of the chapter, we look at three contemporary theoretical approaches to class, briefly discuss debates about the relationship between gender and class, and then consider how Australian researchers have addressed these ideas.

Modern theories

There are a number of major theories of class in modern capitalist societies, but we will focus on three (see Figure 11.1). One, drawing on Marx, was proposed by American sociologist Erik Olin Wright (1947–   ). Another draws to some extent on Weber, and was proposed by British sociologist John Goldthorpe (1935–   ). The third is associated with French sociologist Pierre Bourdieu (1930–2002).

One of the common issues for modern class theorists is how to define the class structure, given the complex occupational and industrial structures in capitalist societies today. In particular, class theorists must deal with a number of core groups (e.g. see Savage et al. 1992; Erikson & Goldthorpe 1992; Goldthorpe 1982, 1995; Wright 1985, 1997) in addition to those considered by Marx and Weber. These include the self-employed who own income-generating property such as shares, stocks, farms, businesses, and so on; managers who are employed to run organisations and make decisions about how they should operate; employees in professional and technical occupations, such as lawyers, nurses, accountants, teachers, and computer systems administrators; people in more routine white-collar jobs such as clerks and salespeople; and people in routine blue-collar or manual work, such as truck drivers, machine operators in factories, and labourers, cleaners, and the like.

Wright (1985, 1997) starts with a basic distinction between people who own income-generating property like a farm or a business and live off the income these assets generate, and people who do not and therefore must work for someone else for a wage or a salary. Some property owners will own large enough businesses to be able to hire people to work for them. These are capitalists or employers. Other self-employed people will have to work in their own businesses. These small business owners, such as family farmers, shopkeepers, and self-employed tradespeople, are called the petite bourgeoisie.

Among employees—those who work for somebody else—Wright (1985, 1989) identifies two sets of groups as being particularly important. The first set consists of managers and supervisors on the one hand, who make organisational decisions and supervise other employees, and non-managerial, non-supervisory employees on the other, whose work is controlled and regulated by their superiors. The second set comprises skilled professional and technical employees ('experts', in Wright's terminology), who are distinguished from employees without substantial skills.

These dimensions—managerial authority and occupational skills—cross-cut one another. Some employees have both managerial authority and occupational skill, others have one or the other, and some have neither. This implies four class categories among employees: expert managers (authority and occupational skill); managers (authority

Figure 11.1: A comparison of modern class theorists

Theorist	Definition of class structure	Explanatory objective of class analysis	Other key concepts and ideas
Wright	Ownership of productive property, followed by occupational skills and managerial authority for employees.	Social and economic inequality, individual and collective behaviour, systematic class conflict, historical variations in inequality, human emancipation.	Relations between classes are exploitative, but forms of exploitation are more diverse than described by Marx.
Goldthorpe	Ownership of property, and for employees their relationships with their employers.	Life chances, lifestyles, attitudes and behaviour, social mobility patterns.	Service class is the preeminent class in capitalism and draws class power from its privileged place in capitalist organisations.
Bourdieu	Ownership and amount of economic and cultural capital, and place in life trajectory.	Lifestyles, consumption patterns, and cultural tastes.	Habitus links objective class to lifestyles, consumption, and tastes.

only); experts (skill only); and workers (neither authority nor skill). Together with the two self-employed classes, this definition gives us six class categories in the Australian class structure. While these categories are less familiar than labels like 'middle class' or 'upper class', managers, experts, and the petite bourgeoisie can be thought of as a 'middle class', workers constitute the working class, and employers are the dominant and most privileged class location. Expert managers are 'middle class' but, as they become more senior within the managerial hierarchy, their class circumstances start to resemble those of employers more closely.

There is one more complication. For Wright, the working class includes all non-managerial, non-expert employees, including those in both blue-collar (such as labouring and trades) and white-collar (like clerical and sales) jobs, but blue- and white-collar workers differ in many respects (see Erikson & Goldthorpe 1992; McAllister 1994). In addition, like most other industrialised countries, Australia's occupational structure is also segregated by sex—men and women are found in different occupations, with women concentrated in particular white-collar occupations and hardly found at all in blue-collar jobs, while men are spread much more evenly throughout the occupational structure (Evans 1996). If we introduce a blue-collar/white-collar, or manual/non-manual, distinction into the worker category to get a seven-category classification, we have a concept of class structure that relates better to structures of inequality and behaviours and attitudes—an improvement on Wright's original concept.

For Wright (2005), defining the class structure is only the first step. Class analysis is about analysing how class 'works' by linking the class structure to a number of other outcomes for which class is an important cause. These outcomes include social and economic inequality, individual and collective attitudes and behaviours, systematic conflicts between organised social groups, historical variations in forms of inequality (i.e. understanding not only class inequality associated with capitalist societies, but that linked to other non-capitalist societies too), and, finally, possibilities for human emancipation (that is, eliminating oppression and class exploitation).

Following Weber, Goldthorpe (1987) initially argued that class situation depended upon market situation—particularly source of income and level of reward; however, in addition, he thought that class situation depended upon relationships of authority and autonomy in the workplace, such as whether people can make decisions about how they do their own work, whether they supervise others, are supervised themselves, and so on. More recently, Goldthorpe (1995, 2000; Erikson & Goldthorpe 1992) has modified this argument to focus explicitly on the kinds of employment relations that position individuals, such as whether they own the means of production, or the particular type of relationship employees have with their employer. In some ways, Goldthorpe's ideas are similar to those of Wright, although Wright (1997) links his class theory to exploitation, whereas Goldthorpe identifies eight occupationally based classes.

Unlike Wright's and Goldthorpe's theories, Bourdieu's class theory cannot be traced closely back to either Marx or Weber. Bourdieu, further, does not have a separate 'theory' of class that he described apart from his other work (Weininger 2005). This chapter extracts some of Bourdieu's key ideas from one of the works that first made him famous in English: *Distinction: A Social Critique of the Judgment of Taste* (Bourdieu 1984).

Distinction is a study of lifestyles and consumption in France. The departure point of the book is Weber's analysis of class and status. For Weber, class and status were alternative economic (class) and symbolic (status) bases of group formation. Bourdieu, though, believes that this separation is misplaced; for him, class distinctions can only exist when objective and symbolic differences coincide—that is, when objective differences translate symbolically into social recognition and social practices, or meaningful patterns of behaviour, particularly consumption behaviours and lifestyles. For Bourdieu, classes designate groups with similar objective circumstances, widespread social recognition and similar lifestyles (Bourdieu 1984; Weininger 2005). In this respect, Bourdieu's classes have much in common with Weber's idea of status groups, except that, for Bourdieu, classes are based 'objectively' in different types of 'capital'.

economic capital
Any financial asset, including raw materials, equipment, and workspace, that can be used to generate income and wealth.

In *Distinction* (1984), Bourdieu defines objective circumstances primarily in terms of economic and cultural capital. **Economic capital** refers to income and wealth arising from income-generating property and skills. **Cultural capital** refers to cultural competence, or the ability to draw upon and use culture—particularly aspects of culture that are socially valued and rewarded—in daily life. For Bourdieu, the class structure of objective positions can be thought of as a three-dimensional space. One dimension measures what kind of capital (economic or cultural) individuals have; another dimension measures how much capital they have; and a third dimension broadly indicates time—that is, where individuals are in terms of their life trajectory. One way to think about the time dimension is that it classifies people in terms of the economic and cultural capital of the family in which they grew up, so it is possible to trace how people's circumstances change over their lives (Bourdieu 1984; Weininger 2005). If we think about the three dimensions of class structure as being at right angles to one another, we can see how they define a 'social space' in which individuals can be located in terms of the kinds of capital they have, the amount of each type, and where they are on their life trajectories.

cultural capital
A term to indicate cultural competencies, such as the taste preferences and lifestyle, that differentiate one social class from another and are transmitted through the generations and via the education system.

habitus
Refers to socially learnt dispositions or taken-for-granted sets of orientations, skills, and ways of acting that shape behaviour. People are the product and creators of their habitus.

How do we get from the social space to real social groups in terms of class lifestyles? For Bourdieu (1984), the **habitus** provides this means. Habitus refers to socially learnt 'dispositions' or taken-for-granted sets of orientations, skills, and ways of acting that shape behaviour (practices). Individuals with similar kinds and amounts of economic and cultural capital have similar experiences, leading to the development of similar habituses that shape their lifestyles and consumption patterns, the key practices with which Bourdieu is concerned.

CrossLink: See Chapter 3 for more on Bourdieu.

This is a very simplified and partial account of *Distinction*. Bourdieu later identifies that much social conflict is symbolic conflict, concerned with defining what aspects of culture are seen to be socially legitimate and valued, and what aspects are devalued. He argues that there is a cultural hierarchy of tastes and practices that defines certain cultural forms (for example, high art, classical music, theatre) as more worthy than others (television, popular music, sport), but that these cultural boundaries are always being contested and are changeable. In later work, Bourdieu (2001) also tries to link his class analysis to other social divisions, most notably gender; however, those analyses are outside the scope of this chapter.

Gender and class

One of the problems with the classical approaches to class discussed above is that women were largely ignored in the various class schemas and in research on social stratification (Sørensen 1994). The conventional approach, rigorously and famously defended by Goldthorpe (1983, 1984), is that all members of a family occupy the same class location, a location best determined by the person with the fullest commitment to the labour market—usually the male head. Many feminist researchers reacted to this defence, in part because it rendered women invisible in social stratification research, but also because it assumed that women were somehow outside of, or irrelevant to, class structures and that class processes operated identically across gender. The feminist critique of this approach argued that the unit of analysis for class research should be the individual, regardless of gender or family location, thereby taking account of women's, and particularly married women's, increased involvement in paid work. Moreover, some argued that class inequality was experienced differently by men and women and that it was important to investigate the way in which gender shaped class processes (Stanworth 1984; Heath & Britten 1984; Crompton 1989). Many empirical studies that appeared in the 1980s and 1990s were designed to test the validity of an individual versus a family approach to class analysis, usually by examining whether a class-related outcome, such as class identification or voting behaviour, was best explained by using the individual or the family as the unit of class analysis (Davis & Robinson 1988; Wright 1989; Marshall et al. 1989). The results were equivocal; no clear conclusions emerging. Some researchers suggested a compromise, with individuals occupying either a 'direct' or a 'mediated' class location, the latter describing the relationship an individual has to the system of production via their family relations (Wright 1997). This classification potentially helps to identify the class location of non-earning wives or secondary earners, but also children and other family members whose class interests are shaped not by direct labour market involvement, but via their position in a system of family relationships.

CrossLink: See Chapters 12 and 20 for further discussion on gender and work.

Although there has been no clear resolution to the class and gender debate as narrowly defined by determining the appropriate unit of class analysis, there is undoubtedly increased recognition that it is impossible to ignore the way in which class and gender patterns intersect (Baxter & Western 2001). Not only has the increased participation of married women in paid work drawn attention to the way in which labour market outcomes vary by gender, but all Western societies have witnessed a transformation in patterns of family formation and dissolution, and the increased diversity of household types that have problematised the conventional approach to class analysis. Moreover, women and men tend to cluster in different class locations, with women much more likely than men to cluster in clerical and service occupations, thus further highlighting the need to understand how gender and class intersect in the labour market.

Class in Australia

Between the 1970s and early 1990s, Australian sociologists produced a number of major publications examining class in Australian society. We have described these elsewhere (Western & Western 1988; Western 1993) and will only quickly mention them here. The Australian class research drew mainly on Marx and Weber, and also on developments in US sociology. Much of it was concerned with describing or explaining connections between class and social inequality (e.g. Connell et al. 1982; Daniel 1983; Dempsey 1990; Western 1983; Wild 1974, 1978), social and political attitudes and behaviour (Chamberlain 1983; Dempsey 1990; Wild 1974, 1981; Williams 1981), or with the role played by classes in social change (Connell 1977; Connell & Irving 1980). Other research addressed social mobility—that is, understanding how open the class structure or social structure was to movement by people over their lives. This research often compared the class circumstances of a person's parents with their own situation as an adult (Broom et al. 1977; Broom et al. 1980; Jones & Davis 1986). Australian researchers also participated in a major international study directed by Wright, to investigate class in contemporary industrial societies using large-scale national surveys (Wright 1997). The major report of the Australian team, which used both Wright's and Goldthorpe's conceptualisations to examine class inequality as well as political and social attitudes and behaviours, was published in 1991 (Baxter et al. 1991).

Using the data from a national survey on neo-liberalism and inequality in Australian society conducted in 2005, we can provide relatively up-to-date figures about the Australian class structure using Wright's scheme (Western et al. 2005, 2007). Table 11.1 shows that in 2005, about 21 per cent of the workforce were self-employed (employers and petite bourgeoisie), about 50 per cent were in 'middle-class' employee locations with managerial authority and/or occupational skills (expert managers, managers, and experts), and about 29 per cent were in white- and blue-collar working-class jobs. There is also a class gradient to income, with the highest average incomes being found among expert managers, experts, and employers, followed by managers and the petite bourgeoisie. The lowest weekly incomes are found among white-collar and blue-collar workers. The especially low weekly earnings of white-collar workers reflect the fact that this category is dominated by women in part-time employment. The differences in Table 11.1 would be even sharper if we further differentiated by gender and full-time and part-time work status, and if, among employers, we isolated owners of larger enterprises from small business owners. The Neoliberalism and Inequality Survey (2005) indicates that 74 per cent of white-collar workers are women, while 78 per cent of blue-collar workers are men (data not shown in table). Men also dominate the employer groups, comprising 62 per cent of employers and 73 per cent of the petite bourgeoisie (data not shown in table). Men and women are thus not evenly distributed across class locations, implying differential access to class-related outcomes such as income.

Table 11.1: Class and yearly income in Australia in 2005

Class category	% in workforce	Average yearly income ($)
Employers	10	53 293
Petite bourgeoisie	11	43 703
Expert managers	23	64 027
Managers	9	42 700
Experts	18	53 292
White-collar workers	19	28 577
Blue-collar workers	10	39 584

Source: Authors' compilation based on Western et al. (2005).

Table 11.2 shows the connections between class location and class identification—that is, people's subjective sense of the class to which they 'belong'. Employers and experts are more likely than others to say they are 'upper class', although very few people in all class locations accept this label. Around 60 per cent of expert managers, experts, and managers say they are 'middle class' compared with about half of employers and the petite bourgeoisie. Blue-collar and white-collar workers are least likely to claim the label 'middle class', with less than a third of blue-collar workers describing themselves in this way. In contrast, blue- and white-collar workers are more likely than others to describe themselves as 'working class', with almost three-quarters of blue-collar workers and 52 per cent of white-collar workers claiming this designation. Significantly, only 5 per cent of people overall say they do not belong to any class, with employers more likely to say this than people in other locations (results not shown). This suggests that class is a symbolically meaningful category for an overwhelming majority of people in the workforce. In addition, 'objective' and 'subjective' aspects of class correspond. People in privileged class locations are more likely to identify as upper or middle class than people in working-class locations, while workers are more likely than others to identify with the working class.

Table 11.2: Class and class identification in Australia in 2005

Class	% who say they belong to the:			
	Upper class	Middle class	Working class	No class
Employers	5	49	37	10
Petite bourgeoisie	<1	51	43	5
Expert managers	3	62	26	8
Managers	0	59	41	0
Experts	5	57	33	5
White-collar workers	0	46	52	2
Blue-collar workers	0	29	67	4
Total	2	49	44	5

Source: Authors' compilation based on Western et al. (2005).

While the 1970s and 1980s saw a number of major studies of class in Australia, in the 1990s there were only some narrow studies into specific aspects of class inequality (e.g. Western 1994, 1999). There were no comprehensive attempts to assess the overall role of class in Australian society, as there had been in the 1970s and 1980s (cf. Gilding 2004). There are several reasons for this. First, two major theoretical debates in the 1980s and 1990s helped undermine a view that class was the fundamental source of social inequality and social change in today's societies. The first debate, between class analysts and feminists, had two concerns: how to define the class structure in a way that reflected women's growing involvement in paid work (Goldthorpe 1983, 1984; Stanworth 1984; Crompton 1996); and how to think about connections between class-based inequalities and gender-based inequalities (Walby 1986; Barrett 1988; Delphy & Leonard 1992). The second debate, the 'death of class' debate, was about whether or not class still mattered for understanding inequality, politics, and social change. Proponents of the 'death of class thesis' (Pakulski & Waters 1996; Kingston 2000) argued that social and economic changes, like the growing numbers of people with more education, the collapse of the trade union movement, the emergence of new social and political movements (based on gender, environmental, and ethnic/racial civil rights), and the rise of **consumerism**, all undermined the importance of class as a source of social inequality, political action, and lifestyle differentiation. New political issues and movements are appearing; education, rather than class, increasingly determines inequality; contemporary societies are dominated by a highly individualised consumer culture; and people no longer think of themselves as belonging to collective groupings like classes. This belief in the highly individualised nature of contemporary culture is especially dominant among younger people, as Jan Pakulski and Malcolm Waters (1996) argue. One consequence is that this highly individualistic view of culture linked to a consumerist lifestyle will become more widespread over time as older generations are replaced by younger ones.

consumerism
The cultural drive to procure more and more consumer items, and define oneself in terms of one's possessions.

The debates reflected real changes occurring in the world, such as women's increasing labour force involvement, and society's growing spending on consumer goods. Class researchers tended to argue that the issues raised by feminists and 'death of class theorists' did not mean that class was irrelevant, but that class analysis needed to be 'reconfigured' to recognise new complex realities (Baxter & Western 2001)—although, as we have just seen, most people can still identify as members of a class. In particular, though, the very abstract analyses of class structure associated with Wright and Goldthorpe need to be supplemented with much more finely grained empirical research into how class processes occur in real societal contexts that are shaped by new cultural trends, labour market institutions, social welfare policies, education systems, and diverse types of families and households. Some theorists, for instance, now argue that one of the defining cultural characteristics of contemporary societies is that life is experienced in highly individualised terms (Savage 2000); however, forms of individuality vary in systematic ways with class. For some middle-class, relatively privileged people, individuality means the ability to take advantage of new opportunities for consumption and geographic and social mobility, and to live highly cosmopolitan lives. For others, as we shall see in Sociology Spotlight 11.1, the individualising experience of modern societies can be one in which there are no certainties and life is unstable and unpredictable.

A consequence of these theoretical debates and the new social realities they reflect was that some Australian class researchers moved on to study other things, such as gender and masculinity (Connell 1995) or the connections between gender and class inequality (Baxter & Western 2001). In the remainder of the chapter, we will look at two topics that are informed by class analysis and that give some indications about the current state of contemporary Australian research.

The Australian ruling class? Elites, power, and wealth in Australia

The question of whether or not an Australian 'ruling class' exists that dominates society economically and politically was a feature of early Australian class research (Connell 1977; Connell & Irving 1980). Connell argued that the Australian ruling class consisted of elite business leaders and executives who were able to coordinate activity in different sectors of the economy, and who had political representation through the leadership of the Liberal and (then) Country Parties. More recently, Michael Gilding (1999, 2004, 2005) investigated the characteristics of the wealthiest Australian individuals by interviewing those on the *Business Review Weekly* 'Rich 200', an annual listing of the 200 largest individual and family fortunes in Australia. Of the 201 individuals and families on the 1999 list, the median wealth was A$145 million, with the largest fortune being A$6.8 billion (Kerry Packer) and the smallest A$75 million. The average age was 62, and 95 per cent of individuals on the list were men. Seventy-two per cent of the richest individuals and families were based in Sydney or Melbourne (Gilding 2005). Through his interviews, Gilding examined the role played by the family in accumulating wealth, managing it, and passing it on to offspring, and also examined differences and similarities between 'old' and 'new' money, in terms of attitudes and involvement in elite institutions. The picture that emerges is of an elite group comprising established long-standing business leaders and 'first-generation' or new entrepreneurs, with some divisions of ethnicity, religion, and social background, and varying degrees of involvement in the 'unifying institutions' of the capitalist class, most notably exclusive clubs, elite private schools, and political parties. Gilding (2004) argues that, as new individuals and families enter the very richest group, the old institutions that helped unify the ruling class become less significant. The 'new money' members of the ruling class have new connections with other wealthy families and individuals through new, often international, networks and institutions, such as business organisations.

Being poor in Australia

Australian studies of poverty have not focused directly on drawing connections between class and poverty, but on assessing what is known as income poverty—that is, having an income that falls below a certain level. The poverty line sets the level and is conventionally drawn at either half the average income, or half the median income (the income of the household in the middle of the income distribution) for a family (Saunders 2005). Families below the line are in poverty. Recent estimates by Peter Saunders and Laura Adelman (2005) suggest that if the poverty line is drawn at half of median family income, almost 8.5 per cent of Australian households are in poverty, with poverty being most common among the single, the aged, lone parents, and couples with three or more children. These findings provide a basis for linking class to income poverty, because the risk of becoming unemployed or of having a marginal connection to the labour market is higher for working-class people than those in other class locations.

While income poverty is an important aspect of poverty, researchers are increasingly turning to a more fundamental definition of poverty that reflects an inability to meet certain socially recognised basic needs (Saunders 2005). Being poor, on this definition, means being unable to participate in society in ways that are typically seen as acceptable or customary: 'poverty restricts people's ability to live a decent life because it imposes restrictions on what they can buy or do, and hence be' (Saunders 2005, p. 59). Poverty in this sense identifies both deprivation, or financial hardship (indicated, for instance, by being unable to pay bills associated with basic necessities such as food, clothing, and shelter), and **social exclusion**, or being unable to take part in activities that are accepted as socially valuable. Social exclusion in Australia means things like being unable to take part in consumption, or being excluded from economic participation, such as paid employment, or being unable to interact with family, friends, neighbours, and the broader community. Income poverty may be associated with deprivation and social exclusion, but it may not. Expanding the definition of poverty around deprivation and social exclusion also links class and poverty. For both Marxist and Weberian class analysts, class is linked to material welfare and to life chances. Material welfare and life chances are both related to ideas of deprivation and social exclusion and so, in theory, should provide the basis for a class analysis of poverty, although Australian researchers have not yet pursued this question very comprehensively.

social exclusion

A general term for the social and economic inequality experienced by a range of minority and socially disadvantaged groups, such as lack of access to, and participation in, social institutions.

11.1: Young people, class, and social exclusion

SOCIOLOGY SPOTLIGHT

Kevin McDonald conducted research with 150 young people in urban Melbourne. Some were unemployed, some were dealing with anorexia and bulimia, some were graffiti writers, and some belonged to urban gangs. They had very different experiences and lived in communities that were 'disorganised' through unemployment and violence (McDonald 1999). McDonald argues that their experiences reflect wider processes in which traditional social institutions like schools and families are much less important vehicles for transmitting social rules and expectations than they once were. At the same time, established roles, norms, and values about what is good and bad, right and wrong are also disappearing. Young people thus live in a world where there appears to be no certainty and no order. This can affect women and men differently. For men, interactions with police are primarily competitive and reinforce a sense of masculinity:

Carson: Royce got caught with, what did you say, three pots of leaf? If he never had any drug charges up before that, now they're just gonna pick him up and they're allowed to strip-search him in the street!

. . .

Serge: Last Friday they took me in and strip-searched me. They said 'Come in mate, just for a check.'

. . .

Serge: . . . Anyway if we walk down the street with a bag, we get pulled over . . . Because, fair enough, we're the hoods, and this is Westview! (McDonald 1999, pp. 68–9)

For women, on the other hand, Westview is violent and menacing, and the police are ineffective. This justifies other strategies, such as carrying knives:

Pam (to a police officer attending the research session): Would I be arrested for carrying a knife?

Officer: . . . Do you need to do that?

Pam: This is Westview, mate! What can you say!

Mandy: When my sister was younger, a dirty old filthbag dropped his daks . . . and chased her. I mean! I wonder why they carry knives? (McDonald 1999, p. 69)

McDonald argues that, despite appearing to be very different, these young people all have a common working-class experience—namely, coming to adulthood at a time when institutions and norms that might provide some stability in their lives are disappearing. For some people, this offers new opportunities because they are no longer constrained by traditional ways of thinking and acting. For working-class disadvantaged young people, though, these changes are experienced as chaotic and incoherent. Their lives are concerned with struggling to respond and attempting to bring a sense of order to their world. The working-class experience here is highly individualised and fragmented, but it is a distinctively working-class one, nonetheless.

Conclusion

Since the birth of sociology as a discipline, class has been a key focus of analysis. Debate continues over the salience of class today, particularly in terms of other social factors that structure inequality and influence people's identity, such as gender, ethnicity, and new social movements (see Chapter 18). Yet the persistence of class-based social inequality suggests that class analysis will continue to be important for some time to come.

Summary of main points

▶ Marx and Weber were the two most influential social theorists to address issues of class.

▶ Although there are many similarities in Marxist and Weberian approaches to class, these approaches differ in fundamental ways. For Marx, classes are defined by social relationships in production, whereas for Weber, class is based in the market.

▶ Modern class theories, such as those developed by Wright and Goldthorpe, tend to draw on one or the other approach. Wright's work adopts a Marxist perspective while Goldthorpe draws more heavily on Weberian principles.

▶ Bourdieu's concepts of cultural capital and habitus help explain how class operates in everyday life in terms of lifestyles and consumption practices.

▶ Feminist research has drawn attention to the need to consider the way in which gender and class work together to produce different outcomes for men and women.

▶ A number of key studies of social class in Australia were undertaken from the 1970s to the 1990s, most of which focused on the links between class and inequality.

▶ Since the 1990s, attention has shifted somewhat, primarily as a result of the emergence of two major theoretical debates—one concerned with the links between class and gender, the other concerned with whether class was the major underlying component of social inequality.

▶ A number of key works have appeared in recent years focusing on elites, wealth, poverty, and social exclusion.

SOCIOLOGICAL REFLECTION

11.1 Class identity

(a) If you were asked to identify the class to which you belong, what would you say? Why?

(b) Do you believe class has influenced your beliefs, lifestyle, and life chances?

(c) Which is more important in terms of lifestyle and life chances today—gender, class, or ethnicity/race?

Discussion questions

11.1 Do you think classes exist in modern Australian society? What evidence is there to support your views?

11.2 Do you think class is more or less important in Australia today than in earlier generations?

11.3 Would you say you belong to the same class as your parents? If not, what are the factors that have contributed to your class mobility?

11.4 What do you think is the main cause of inequality in Australia today?

11.5 Do you think inequality in Australia is growing or declining? Why?

11.6 Do you think that inequality is an inevitable feature of society? If not, what steps can we take to eradicate it?

Further reading

Baxter, J.H., Emmison, J.M., Western, J.S. & Western, M.C. (eds) 1991, *Class Analysis and Contemporary Australia*, Macmillan, Melbourne.

Baxter, J.H. & Western, M.C. (eds) 2001, *Reconfigurations of Class and Gender*, Stanford University Press, Stanford, CA.

Crompton, R. 2008, *Class and Stratification*, 3rd edn, Polity Press, Cambridge.

Habibis, D. & Walter, M. 2009, *Social Inequality in Australia: Discourses, Realities & Futures*, Oxford University Press, Melbourne.

Lee, D.J. & Turner, B.S. (eds) 1996, *Conflicts About Class*, Longman, London.

Pakulski, J. & Waters, M. 1996, *The Death of Class*, Sage, London.

Wright, E.O. (ed.) 2005, *Approaches to Class Analysis*, Cambridge University Press, Cambridge.

Websites

- Australian Bureau of Statistics (ABS): <www.abs.gov.au>. This website provides up-to-date Australian statistics on the labour force as well as a range of statistics on other issues relating to class and well-being.
- Households, Income and Labour Dynamics in Australia (HILDA): <www.melbourneinstitute.com/hilda>. This website provides information about a national longitudinal survey of households in Australia funded by the Department of Families, Community Services and Indigenous Affairs and focusing on the subjective and economic well-being of Australians by examining a range of issues relating to labour market involvement, family relationships, wealth, attitudes to various social issues, and well-being.
- Organisation for Economic Co-operation and Development (OECD): <www.oecd.org/home>. This website provides up-to-date statistics, publications, documents, and news releases on over 30 member countries.
- Marxist Internet Archive: <www.marxists.org>. A vast website covering all aspects of Marxism. It contains information on key writers, a digital library of main reference works, and overviews of historical and political aspects of Marxism.
- SocioSite—Sociological Theories and Perspectives: <www.sociosite.net/topics/ theory.php>. This site includes links to many high-quality resources. In particular, it has links to key texts and writings on Marx and Weber, and a whole section devoted to the topic of class.

Films/documentaries

- *The Castle*, 1997, motion picture, directed by R. Sitch, Working Dog Productions. An Australian comedy film that explores the exploits of a working-class family.
- *People Like Us: Social Class in America*, 2001, television documentary, directed by L. Alvarez and A. Kolker, Center for New American Media (CNAM). This documentary depicts the role of class in the United States, using people's real-life experiences to examine the connections between class structures and daily life.
- *Kath & Kim*, 2002–07, television series, directed by T. Emery, Riley Turner Productions. Australian comedy series dealing with the dysfunctional relationships and suburban life of a working-class mother and daughter, their wider family, and friends. <www.kathandkim.com>.

Visit the *Public Sociology* book website to access topical case studies, weblinks, YouTube clips, and extra readings.

References

Australian Broadcasting Corporation (ABC) 2009a, 'Workers dismissed while executives take large payouts', <www.abc.net.au/7.30/content/2009/s2689343. htm> (accessed 30 October 2009).

—— 2009b, 'ACL Bearing placed in administration', <www.abc.net.au/news/ stories/2009/08/26/2667020.htm> (accessed 30 October 2009).

Australian Bureau of Statistics (ABS) 2009, *Australian Labour Market Statistics*, cat. no. 6105.0, Australian Bureau of Statistics, Canberra.

Baily, M., Litan, R. & Johnson, M. 2008, *The Origins of the Financial Crisis*, Initiative on Business and Public Policy at Brookings, The Brookings Institution, Washington, DC.

Barrett, M. 1988, *Women's Oppression Today: The Marxist/Feminist Encounter*, Verso, New York.

Baxter, J.H., Emmison, J.M., Western, J.S. & Western, M.C. (eds) 1991, *Class Analysis and Contemporary Australia*, Macmillan, Melbourne.

Baxter, J.H. & Western, M.C. (eds) 2001, *Reconfigurations of Class and Gender*, Stanford University Press, Stanford, CA.

BBC 2009, 'Timeline: Credit crunch to downturn', BBC website, <http://news.bbc. co.uk/2/hi/7521250.stm> (accessed 30 October 2009).

Bottomore, T.B. 1965, *Classes in Modern Society*, Allen & Unwin, London.

Bourdieu, P. 1984/1979, *Distinction: A Social Critique of the Judgement of Taste*, trans. Richard Nice, Harvard University Press, Cambridge, MA.

—— 2001 [1998], *Masculine Domination*, trans. Richard Nice, Stanford University Press, Stanford, CA.

Broom, L., Duncan-Jones, P., Jones, F.L. & McDonnell, P. 1977, *Investigating Social Mobility*, Department of Sociology, Research School of Social Sciences, Australian National University, Canberra.

Broom, L., Jones, F.L., McDonnell, P. & Williams, T. 1980, *The Inheritance of Inequality*, Routledge & Kegan Paul, London.

Carling, A. 1991, *Social Division*, Verso, London.

Chamberlain, C. 1983, *Class Consciousness in Australia*, Allen & Unwin, Sydney.

Connell, R. 1977, *Ruling Class, Ruling Culture*, Cambridge University Press, Melbourne.

—— 1995, *Masculinities*, Allen & Unwin, Sydney.

Connell, R., Ashenden, D., Kessler, S. & Dowsett, G. 1982, *Making the Difference: Schools, Families and Social Division*, Allen & Unwin, Sydney.

Connell, R. & Irving, T.H. 1980, *Class Structure in Australian History*, Longman Cheshire, Melbourne.

Crompton, R. 1989, 'Class theory and gender', *British Journal of Sociology*, no. 40, pp. 565–87.

—— 1996, 'Women's employment and the "middle class"', in T. Butler & M. Savage (eds), *Social Change and the Middle Class*, UCL Press, London, pp. 58–75.

Daniel, A.E. 1983, *Power, Privilege and Prestige: Occupations in Australia*, Longman Cheshire, Melbourne.

Davis, N. & Robinson, R. 1988, 'Class identification of men and women in the 1970s and 1980s', *American Sociological Review*, no. 53, pp. 103–12.

Delphy, C. & Leonard, D. 1992, *Familiar Exploitation: A New Analysis of Marriage in Contemporary Western Societies*, Polity Press, Oxford.

Dempsey, K. 1990, *Smalltown: A Study of Social Inequality, Cohesion and Belonging*, Oxford University Press, Melbourne.

Edel, M. 1981, 'Capitalism, accumulation and the explanation of urban phenomena', in M. Dear & A. Scott (eds), *Urbanisation and Urban Planning in Capitalist Society*, Methuen, New York, pp. 19–44.

Erikson, R. & Goldthorpe, J.H. 1992, *The Constant Flux: A Study of Class Mobility in Industrial Societies*, Clarendon Press, Oxford.

Evans, M.D.R. 1996, 'Women's labour force participation in Australia: Recent research findings', *Journal of the Australian Population Association*, no. 13, pp. 67–92.

Giddens, A. 1981, *The Class Structure of the Advanced Societies*, Hutchinson, London.

Gilding, M. 1999, 'Superwealth in Australia: Entrepeneurs, accumulation and the capitalist class', *Sociology*, no. 35, pp. 169–82.

—— 2004, 'Entrepreneurs, elites and the ruling class: The changing structure of power and wealth in Australian society', *Australian Journal of Political Science*, 39, pp. 127–43.

—— 2005, 'Families and fortunes: Accumulation, management succession and inheritance in wealthy families', *Sociology*, vol. 41, no. 1, pp. 29–45.

Goldthorpe, J.H. 1982, 'On the service class: Its information and future', in A. Giddens & G. Mackenzie (eds), *Social Class and the Division of Labour: Essays in Honour of Ilya Neustadt*, Cambridge University Press, Cambridge, pp. 162–85.

—— 1983, 'Women and class analysis: In defence of the conventional view', *Sociology*, no. 17, pp. 465–83.

—— 1984, 'Women and class analysis: A reply to the replies', *Sociology*, no. 18, pp. 491–9.

—— 1995, 'The service class revisited', in T. Butler & M. Savage (eds), *Social Change and the Middle Classes*, UCL Press, London, pp. 313–29.

—— 2000, *On Sociology: Numbers, Narratives, and the Integration of Research and Theory*, Oxford University Press, Oxford.

Goldthorpe, J.H., with C. Llewellyn & C. Payne 1987, *Social Mobility and Class Structure in Modern Britain*, 2nd edn, Clarendon Press, Oxford.

Hall, S. 1977, 'The "political" and the "economic" in Marx's theory of classes', in A. Hunt (ed.), *Classes and Class Structure*, Lawrence and Wishart, London, pp. 17–60.

Heath, A., & Britten, N. 1984, 'Women's jobs do make a difference: A reply to Goldthorpe', *Sociology*, no. 18, pp. 475–89.

International Labour Organization (ILO) 2009a, *Global Employment Trends*, International Labour Office, Geneva.

Jones, F.L. & Davis, P. 1986, *Models of Society: Class, Gender and Stratification in Australia and New Zealand*, Croom Helm, Sydney.

Kingston, P. 2000, *The Classless Society*, Stanford University Press, Stanford, CN.

Marshall, G., Rose, D., Newby, H. & Vogler, C. 1989, *Social Class in Modern Britain*, Unwin Hyman, New York.

Marx, K. 1973 [1858], *Grundrisse: Foundations of the Critique of Political Economy*, Allen Lane, London.

—— 1976 [1867], *Capital: A Critique of Political Economy*, Volume I, Penguin, London.

Marx, K. & Engels, F. 1955 [1848], *Manifesto of the Communist Party*, Foreign Languages Publishing House, Moscow.

McAllister, I. 1994, *Political Behaviour: Citizens, Parties and Elites in Australia*, Routledge, Melbourne.

McDonald, K. 1999, *Struggles for Subjectivity: Identity, Action and Youth Experience*, Cambridge University Press, Cambridge.

Organisation for Economic Cooperation and Development (OECD) 2009, *OECD Economic Outlook*, Organisation for Economic Cooperation and Development, Paris.

Pakulski, J. & Waters, M. 1996, *The Death of Class*, Sage, London.

Saunders, P. 2005, *The Poverty Wars*, UNSW Press, Sydney.

Saunders, P. & Adelman, L. 2005, *Income Poverty, Deprivation and Exclusion: A Comparative Study of Australia and Britain*, Social Policy Research Centre, University of New South Wales, Sydney.

Savage, M. 2000, *Class Analysis and Social Transformation*, Open University Press, Buckingham.

Savage, M., Barlow, J., Dickens, P. & Fielding, P. 1992, *Property, Bureaucracy and Culture: Middle-class Formation in Contemporary Britain*, Routledge, London.

Stanworth, M. 1984, 'Women and class analysis: A reply to Goldthorpe', *Sociology*, no. 18, pp. 159–70.

Sørensen, A. 1994, 'Women, family and class', *Annual Review of Sociology*, no. 20, pp. 27–47.

Walby, S. 1986, *Patriarchy at Work: Patriarchal and Capitalist Relations in Employment*, Polity Press, Cambridge.

Weber, M. 1982a, 'Status groups and classes', in A. Giddens & D. Held (eds), *Classes, Power and Conflict*, Macmillan, London, pp. 69–73.

—— 1982b, 'The distribution of power: Class, status, party', in A. Giddens & D. Held (eds), *Classes, Power and Conflict*, Macmillan, London, pp. 60–9.

Weininger, E.B. 2005, 'Foundations of Pierre Bourdieu's class analysis', in E.O. Wright (ed.), *Approaches to Class Analysis*, Cambridge University Press, Cambridge, pp. 82–118.

Western, J.S. 1983, *Social Inequality in Australian Society*, Macmillan, Melbourne.

Western, M.C. 1993, 'Class and stratification', in J.M. Najman & J.S. Western (eds), *A Sociology of Australian Society: Introductory Readings*, 2nd edn, Macmillan, Melbourne, pp. 54–105.

—— 1994, 'Intergenerational class mobility among women and men', *Australian and New Zealand Journal of Sociology*, vol. 30, pp. 303–21.

—— 1999, 'Who thinks what about capitalism? Class consciousness and attitudes to economic institutions', *Journal of Sociology*, vol. 35, pp. 351–70.

Western, M., Baxter, J., Pakulski, J., Tranter, B., Western, J. and van Egmond, M. 2005, *Neoliberalism, Inequality and Politics National Survey*, Data File, University of Queensland Social Research Centre, Brisbane.

Western M., Baxter, J., Pakulski, J., Tranter, B, Western, J., van Egmond, M., Chesters, J., Hosking, A., O'Flaherty, M. & van Gellecum, Y. 2007, 'Neoliberalism, inequality and politics: The changing face of Australia', *Australian Journal of Social Issues*, vol. 42, no. 3, pp. 401–18.

Western, M.C. & Western J.S. 1988, 'Class and inequality: Theory and research', in J.M. Najman & J.S. Western (eds), *Sociology of Australian Society: Introductory Readings*, Macmillan, Melbourne, pp. 50–91.

Wild, R.A. 1974, *Bradstow: A Study of Status, Class and Power in a Small Australian Town*, Angus & Robertson, Sydney.

—— 1978, *Social Stratification in Australia*, Allen & Unwin, Sydney.

—— 1981, *Australian Community Studies and Beyond*, Allen & Unwin, Sydney.

Williams, C. 1981, *Open Cut*, Allen & Unwin, Sydney.

Wright, E.O. 1985, *Classes*, Verso, London.

—— 1989, 'Rethinking, once again, the concept of class structure', in E.O. Wright et al., *The Debate on Classes*, Verso, New York.

—— 1997, *Class Counts: Comparative Studies in Class Analysis*, Cambridge University Press, New York.

—— 2005, 'Conclusion: If "class" is the answer, what is the question?', in E.O. Wright (ed.), *Approaches to Class Analysis*, Cambridge University Press, Cambridge, pp. 180–92.

CHAPTER 12

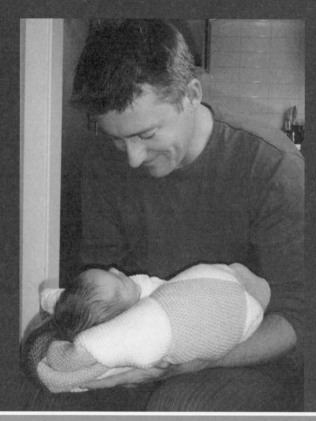

The gender order

Grazyna Zajdow

Is it a boy? Is it a girl? Athletics and the gender question

At the World Athletics Championships in Berlin in August 2009, a young South-African woman, Caster Semenya, won the gold medal in the 800-metre track race in 1:55:45 minutes, beating the previous record for that event by almost two-and-a-half seconds. This was quite a feat, and the furore it caused raises many of the issues that fascinate sociologists when they discuss sex and gender in the world today.

Semenya was eighteen at the time—tall, muscular, and deep-voiced. Concerns had been raised for a number of months before the world championships that perhaps she did not conform to the biological definition of womanhood—in essence, that she was too masculine and it was this masculinity that had contributed to her stunning win. Semenya was not the first female athlete to have her right to compete as a woman questioned. Because of a number of protests about individual athletes and their indeterminate sex, sex testing—both visual and via chromosomal testing—has been undertaken since the 1960s, but in 2000 the International Olympic Committee decided to stop this procedure since such tests have been deemed to be both expensive and difficult to interpret; furthermore, they do not necessarily exclude all imposters and, most interestingly, they discriminate against women since men have never been tested. At the 1996 Olympic Games, for example, eight female athletes failed the initial tests but were subsequently cleared. Indeed, athletes who have undergone sexual reassignment surgery are permitted to compete as their assigned selves after completing all surgical and hormonal procedures.

What this case highlights is that, in an era where equality between men and women in many areas of economic and social life is considered a universal human right, and technology has shown the variability of the human sex/gender distinction, the binary of masculinity and femininity seems as important as ever. It seems that the more we proclaim equality between the sexes, the more we demand that science prove the differences between them. In sport in particular, while women can be athletic, they cannot be too athletic since athleticism is defined in very male terms. As journalist Mary Buckheit (2009) notes, the basketballer Shaquille O'Neal is not criticised for being so very tall, and the swimmer Michael Phelps has physical proportions that make him so suitable for swimming; these are outside the normal proportions of other men, but O'Neal's and Phelps' physical proportions are considered a gift and 'not a laughable genetic blunder'. Even jockeys, who have very feminine bodily proportions, might be laughed at because they are short, but their maleness is not called into question; however, for many women athletes like Semenya, 'their enigmatic strength and athleticism is countered with derisive criticism and gender judgements. Society wants women to be toned, not muscular . . . athletic but not too competitive' (Buckheit 2009, p. 2).

Introduction

Caster Semenya's story illustrates many of the points this chapter will be making about gender and the ways in which it is considered by sociology. Semenya's female-

gender
Refers to the socially constructed categories of feminine and masculine (the cultural values that dictate how women and men should behave), as opposed to the categories of biological *sex* (female or male).

sex
The biological distinction between male and female based on genital organs and physiology. See also *gender*.

(the) self
The reflexive condition of all humans in which they can view themselves objectively as unique individuals by imagining themselves from the standpoint of others.

ness is called into question because of some biological anomalies, but, as pointed out, the biological anomalies of such athletes as Michael Phelps do not call into question their masculinity.

This chapter will discuss one of the major social and structural differences that sociology considers an integral part of society: gender. It will delve into the often contradictory and controversial definitions of **gender** and **sex**. All the chapters in this textbook deal in some larger or smaller way with gender. This chapter argues that, along with race and class differences, gender is fundamental to the way our society (or any society, for that matter) is structured and the way individuals see themselves and act. Gender is also fundamental to an understanding of the **self** and reflexivity. What you will read about in this chapter for the most part will be how gender places all of us within structures of inequality.

Gender inequality in Australia

Gender is one of the major factors in social difference and inequality in all societies. In almost every area of social life, the outcomes for men and women are different, and generally difference means inequality. There are also other factors, of course, that interact in complex ways: race, ethnicity, able-bodiedness, and social class are part of this equation too. These factors are dealt with in other chapters of this book; this chapter concentrates on gender.

In the chapters on families, work, and socialisation, together with many others in this book, you see that women's and men's experiences of the world are different, and often very unequal. As will be discussed below, gender is about power relationships, and with power comes hierarchy and inequality. Inequality means that outcomes for groups and particular individuals are very different, and for some groups decidedly worse than for others. This section outlines some aspects of gender inequality in Australia, but first places Australia within a global setting.

The World Economic Forum has produced an index of gender called the Gender Gap Index (Hausmann et al. 2008). It measures the differences between men and women in each of 128 countries and then compares each country with the others. The index is a composite of such factors as economic participation and wages, educational attainment, health and physical survival, and political representation (measured by how many women are in parliament and serving as ministers). In 2008, Australia sat in twenty-first position behind such countries as Norway, Iceland, Denmark, and New Zealand, but in front of most others in the world. Australia does particularly well in educational attainment, with almost equal male and female ratios in literacy and school finishing rates. Australia also does very well in health and survival, but not as well as other comparable countries in the areas of work and income, and political participation. In political empowerment, if 1.00 is equal (that is, equal numbers of men and women in parliament and as ministers), Australia's ratio is 0.19—a poor outcome indeed.

When we look at work and wages, we see that women and men do different jobs in different industries, and with different outcomes. If we compare full-time wages, for every dollar that a man earns a woman earns 84 cents, and if we look at all earnings, for every dollar a man earns, a woman earns 65 cents (ABS 2008 p. 254). Part of this is explained by many more women working part time than men (because of family responsibilities), but also because women are paid less than men for the same work. Over a working lifetime, men on average will earn one-and-a-half times more than women, and, of those who hold a university degree, men are likely to earn almost twice as much as women (Cassells et al. 2009). Because of this disparity, and because women are more likely to have custody of children after divorce, the lone-parent household is the poorest household type in Australia (Headey, Marks & Wooden 2005). When they retire, women have far less money in superannuation, which means they are much more likely than men to be reliant on the aged pension. In 2009, men between the ages of 55 and 64 held almost twice as much superannuation as women in the same age group (Cassells et al. 2009).

As a variable, gender is important in understanding health and well-being, crime and punishment, and satisfaction and dissatisfaction with life. The difference is not always unidirectional, though. Women live longer than men and in many ways seem more satisfied with their lives. Men are much more likely to commit crimes and be imprisoned, and although women are more likely to be victims of male domestic violence, men are more likely to be victims of other types of violence, almost exclusively perpetrated by men.

CrossLink:
See Chapter 7 on gender and families, Chapter 20 for more on gender and work, Chapter 16 for gendered crime, and Chapter 17 for gendered health.

What is gender?

social structure
The recurring patterns of social interaction through which people are related to each other, such as social institutions and social groups.

Most definitions of gender begin with an understanding of the social distinction between men and women, called masculinity and femininity. This is a distinction that is a part of **social structures** and everyday lived experience. In addition, the distinction made between femininity and masculinity includes notions of difference, hierarchy and power. Gender, according to Stevi Jackson and Sue Scott (2000, p. 1):

> denotes a hierarchical division between women and men embedded in both social institutions and social practices. Gender is thus a social structural phenomenon but is also produced, negotiated and sustained at the level of everyday interaction.

It is important to remember that gender is relational: a gender does not exist on its own, independent of human interaction and relations. Raewyn Connell (2009) adds the dimension of embodiment to the definition. For her, gender is the way that any particular society deals with bodily difference centred on the reproductive arena. But for Connell, as for Jackson and Scott, gender is as much about power, domination, and hierarchy as it is about everyday interaction. One major textbook in the area describes it as follows: 'Gender is not simply a system of classification ... Gender also expresses the universal inequality between women and men' (Kimmel 2004, p. 1).

The most famous phrase in feminist discourses on gender comes from French philosopher and influential feminist Simone de Beauvoir. She wrote in her book *The Second Sex* that 'one is not born, but rather becomes, a woman' (de Beauvoir 1972, p. 295). Women's oppressed status came about, for de Beauvoir, because of their 'otherness' in relation to men, based around the area of biological reproduction.

In sociology, the use of the term 'gender' first made an impact with Ann Oakley's (1985) book *Sex, Gender and Society*. Effectively, she drew the distinction between sex and gender that had become so commonplace. Sex is the biologically based distinction between men and women centring on sexual organs, thus producing male and female, while gender is the cultural and social rendering of masculinity and femininity.

Oakley (1985) points out that the taken-for-granted view in our society is that one's sex and one's gender correspond, but cross-cultural and anthropological studies tell us this is not necessarily so. In her seminal study, Oakley relied heavily on the 1930s anthropological work of Margaret Mead and psychiatrist Robert Stoller, whose interest was in gender identification. In Oakley's work, the biological fact of sex (male or female) is immutable, but the social, cultural and psychological fact of gender (masculinity or femininity) is not; rather, it depends on cultural values and norms, and the differential socialisation that goes along with them. The behaviours and expectations placed on men and women vary according to the culture in which they grew up, and the social expectations inherent in any particular role they may take on.

The sex/gender distinction was groundbreaking, and important for understanding the mutability of gender. Mary Hawkesworth (1997) calls this model the base/superstructure model of gender: sex is the base while gender is the superstructure upon which it is built. The sex/gender distinction undermined what Michael Kimmel (2004) calls the 'just-so' stories of the naturalness of sex and the domination based upon its claimed biological basis, thus allowing women to politically challenge their secondary status. But it does have contemporary critics.

Critics such as Connell (2009) argue that the 'sex = natural' and 'gender = social' distinction is far too simplistic and does not take into account real human interaction in society. The sex/gender distinction is argued to be a form of biological essentialism or determinism. In the sex/gender argument, sociologists point out that the existence of particular genitalia actually provides no indication of a person's likely behaviour with regard to accepted styles of femininity and masculinity.

Doing gender

Socialisation theory in sociology and social psychology has been one of the dominant explanations for the way in which gender is taken on and understood by individuals. Candace West and Don Zimmerman (1987, p. 126) propose an **interactionist** theory of gender in which gender is a 'routine, methodical, and recurring accomplishment'. Individuals 'do gender' during every waking and sleeping moment, because gender is part of all our institutional arrangements, as well as inscribed through our daily social interactions. In fact, West and Zimmerman (1987, p. 137, original italics) ask 'Can we ever *not* do gender?'

socialisation
The process through which the individual learns the culture of a society and internalises its *norms*, values, and perspectives in order to know how to behave and communicate. Socialisation is the process through which we acquire a sense of *self*.

For these sociologists, gender is not fixed or static because it is a product of social interactions. The assumption of a person's gender in any interaction does not come from knowing their primary sexual organs, according to Suzanne Kessler and Wendy McKenna (1978). Our reactions to people are based on our assessment of what they are wearing, how they comb their hair, what sort of language they use, and their non-verbal cues.

symbolic interactionism
A theoretical framework first developed by Mead that places strong emphasis on the importance of language and on social interactions as key components in the development of a sense of *self*.

**CrossLink:
See Chapter 5
for more on
socialisation.**

Kessler and McKenna (1978) argue that **gender attribution** is the most important part of any social interaction, and that most of us have great difficulty with ambiguous gender displays. In their study of transsexualism, they found that at each stage of the change in a person from male to female, they actually had no problem with gender attribution because it was so important to make it clear.

gender attribution
The taken-for-granted attribution of maleness or femaleness based on physical appearance and outward behaviours.

Raine Dozier (2005) found that certain sexual characteristics such as facial hair were more important in gender attribution than others for individuals in the process of gender transformation from women to men: '[w]hen sex is ambiguous or less convincing, there is increased reliance on highly gendered behavior. When sex category is obvious, then there is considerably more freedom in behavior' (Dozier 2005, p. 305).

Some disciplines, such as evolutionary biology, do argue that sex differences are set in our genes and our hormones. Calling on the earlier work of Edward O. Wilson (1978) and Richard Dawkins (1976), David Barash (2002) maintains that human, male violence is an evolutionary adaptation and inherited from our non-human ancestors. He writes that males need to show their dominance by any means possible. Even rape is an evolutionary imperative in Barash's view (2002). Men rape women, according to this logic, because they have otherwise been reproductively unsuccessful and need to spread their genes. This argument does not stand up to scrutiny. Research has shown time and again that male rape is about power, and many rapists are successful in Barash's terms—that is, they are married and have children.

Human societies are also diverse in a way to which many biologists seem to be oblivious. Kimmel (2004, p. 30) provides the example of the Bari in Venezuela who have two forms of fatherhood: the primary and secondary father. Both provide food and shelter for the children of the women with whom they have slept. In this case, it makes more sense for women to be promiscuous during their pregnancy. Female promiscuity is not considered an evolutionary adaptation. Similarly, John Macionis and Ken Plummer (2008) give the example of the Sambia in New Guinea, which takes boys from the ages of seven to ten and places them with older men, where they practise fellatio daily. It is considered essential for their masculinity that they engage in these activities so that when they go back into the wider society they understand the importance of semen to their manhood.

CrossLink: See Chapter 5 for a discussion of the sex/ gender distinction and the nature/ nurture debate.

What, then, of the studies showing that women's and men's brains are structurally different, thus giving rise to differences in male and female behaviour? What of the host of studies that relate male and female hormones to behaviour? For example, does testosterone lead to violence? Since men have higher levels of testosterone than women, perhaps this explains the difference in the violence levels between men and women that Barash (2002) describes. Kimmel (2004, p. 41) presents many studies that show how equivocal this relationship really is, and that there is no straightforward relationship between testosterone and male violence that is not mediated by cultural and social forces.

Similarly with brain studies, definitive conclusions cannot really be made. While men and women may use different sides and parts of their brains to varying degrees, why this is the case is not clear. It may well be, as Ruth Bleier (1997) notes, that the brain is so adaptive it changes with use. Thus, if boys are encouraged to use specific parts of theirs in play, their brains may well develop in this direction (throwing balls to develop good hand–eye coordination and spatial abilities, for example) in comparison to girls, who are directed to play in very different ways. Bleier (1997) strongly argues that human reliance on culture during development, rather than just biology, is both a positive and a negative. Our reliance on culture provides us with an ability to adapt to sudden change and need, but it also works to narrow human abilities. Culture also 'constrains the extraordinary potential our brains offer for a seemingly limitless flexibility of behaviours and relationships' (Bleier 1997, p. 75).

The huge volume of literature dedicated to sex differences in brains and bodies has helped cement the place of **biological determinism** in our everyday life in the twenty-first century. Interestingly, a close look at this literature throws up many more paradoxes and inconclusive findings than are admitted to by the scientists themselves. Meta-analyses of psychological studies on gender have found that gender differences are much smaller than originally thought, and at particular times and in particular circumstances they may almost disappear. As Connell (2009, p. 66) puts it:

biological determinism
A belief that individual and group behaviours are the inevitable result of biology.

biobunk
A term used by Tavris to criticise the biological reductionism inherent in many of the arguments by sociobiologists and evolutionary psychologists.

> We thus get a picture of psychological gender differences and similarities, not as fixed, age-old constants of the species, but as the varying products of the active responses people make to a complex and changing social world . . . psychology has gradually moved towards the way of understanding gender that has also gradually emerged in sociology.

Carol Tavris (2001) calls the biologically determinist argument **biobunk**—or, as Leonore Tiefer (2004, p. 439) puts it, 'Whenever biology enters the scene, it seems that culture becomes invisible.'

The gender order

The first feminists who looked critically at the way women were treated in society and argued for a change used the term **patriarchy** to explain what seemed to be a system of exploitation and oppression across the ages. In general, patriarchy has meant 'the social system of masculine domination over women' (Pilcher & Whelehan 2004, p. 93). The key basis of patriarchal domination differed depending on the philosophical or political tradition of the writer. The radical feminist Shulamith Firestone (1972) claimed it lay in biology and the weak position in which women were placed because of pregnancy and child-rearing. Her formula for overcoming this oppression was to overcome biology. Biology was also the key to understanding de Beauvoir's argument. Other feminists argued that the key institution was capitalism and class inequality (Barrett 1980), the family (Barrett & McIntosh 1980), and rape and male violence (Brownmiller 1976). Sociologist Sylvia Walby (1990) claimed that there were six separate structures that intertwined and combined to produce women's secondary status. These were the state, paid work, household production, male violence, sexuality, and culture.

patriarchy
A system of power through which males dominate households. It is used more broadly by *feminists* to refer to society's domination by patriarchal power, which functions to subordinate women and children.

patriarchal dividend
Refers to the economic and social advantages men gain over women.

The concept of patriarchy has come in for a great amount of criticism since the 1980s. It has been argued that it is a 'homogenising term' (Abbott, Wallace & Tyler 2005, p. 42) that misses many of the complexities of gendered inequality, and the experiences of non-white, non-middle-class women whose racial, ethnic, or embodied experiences differ from those the writers may represent in their work. Patriarchy is not a wholly satisfying term, but it is still very valuable—particularly when we come to what Connell (2009) calls the global **patriarchal dividend**.

gender order

The way in which institutional structures (known as gender regimes) and individual identities intersect to produce the social arrangements that mean one gender can dominate another, politically, socially, and economically.

agency

The ability of people, individually and collectively, to influence their own lives and the society in which they live.

hegemonic masculinity

Connell's term for the dominant form of heterosexual masculinity in Western society that is always constructed against various forms of subordinated masculinities.

In response to the problems with the concept of patriarchy, some sociologists have followed Connell's use of the term **gender order**. Connell (1987) argues that there are three ways in which women's and men's **agency** is constrained by structures of gender inequality. These are structures of labour, structures of power, and structures of cathexis (emotion and sexuality). Unlike the static structure of patriarchy, men and women dynamically create and recreate relationships within historically constructed patterns of power relations. The gender order is the relationship between all of these. Societies such as ours have a particular gender order, but individuals and groups can work to undermine it, thus changing its nature.

Sociologists Mike Donaldson and Scott Poynting (2009) present accounts of the lives of some of Australia's richest and most powerful men. They describe the socialisation processes in their families and schools as the construction of **hegemonic masculinity**. Manliness is presented as powerful, brutal, and unemotional. 'The masculinity of success separates sexuality, emotion and friendship from each other and assigns a low or even negative value to caring and nurturing' (Donaldson & Poynting 2009, p. 89). The authors argue that class and gender are reproduced via familial and educational processes that are 'historically continuous, integrated, networked and impervious to change' (Donaldson & Poynting, 2009, pp. 231–2).

A gender order exists in Australia, but it looks different and operates differently from the way it does in, say, a country like Mali in Africa. There is also a global gender order that involves massive movement of capital to benefit Western countries in general, and particularly those at the pinnacle—mostly men, and a very small group of women. It is the intersection of institutional interests, structures of power and individual gendered identities that produces the outline of the gender order. The next sections will outline how gender is produced in the structures and institutions of our societies, and how individuals also act out and produce gender identities.

12.1: Connell's *Masculinities* (2005)

Raewyn Connell has spent many years analysing and tracking the gender order to construct a relational theory of gender (see Connell 1987, 2009). One aspect of this has been her study called *Masculinities* (Connell 1995). Ten years after its initial publication, a second edition came out with an updated introduction and afterword (Connell 2005).

Masculinities was a large undertaking, as it combined empirical work (long life-story interviews with 31 men) and an exhaustive analysis of existing and historical studies on masculinity and gender construction, power, and identity. Its aim was not just to outline the course of masculinity in modern Western society, but also to outline the sorts of subordinate masculinities that would resist and change the nature of hegemonic masculinity.

The central life-stories are illuminating, since they illustrate how gendered institutions, gendered knowledge, and lived experience produce the gender order as we know it, as well as resist and produce new forms of gender experience and knowledge.

Since masculinity is relational, it can only exist because of the existence of femininity, but there is no single form of masculinity, only types of masculinities. There is one dominant form, though, and Connell (2005) calls this *hegemonic masculinity*. This form may not be the most common, nor does any one male correspond perfectly to its strictures; instead, hegemonic masculinity is the one that is 'culturally exalted', 'it is ... the configuration of gender practice which embodies the currently accepted answer to the problem of the legitimacy of patriarchy, which guarantees ... the dominant position of men and the subordination of women' (Connell 2005, p. 7). Hegemonic masculinity is heterosexual.

While there is only one hegemonic masculinity, there are various subordinated masculinities, the most prominent of which is homosexuality. Other subordinated, but heterosexual, masculinities also exist. In Australia, a prominent example is the intellectual who has no interest in sporting or other such physical activities.

The life-story case histories that Connell (2005) presents are described in roughly four types (although Connell does not set out to present a typology). One chapter, entitled 'Live Fast and Die Young', presents eight men divided into two groups. All eight came from roughly the same background—working class and poor—but took slightly different paths. Five of them had broken work experiences: they were unskilled and often casually employed, if at all. They had experience of law-breaking and even apprehension by the police. They all accept what is called **compulsory heterosexuality** as an abiding theme of life, to the point of homophobia. This group exhibits what Connell (2005, p. 109) calls 'protest masculinity'—that is, in response to the powerlessness they feel, they produce an exaggerated version of physically powerful masculinity. This group is contrasted with the other three men who came from the same background, some even exhibiting the same violence and resistance when children at school. These men had a much more secure attachment to the workforce and one even came out as a cross-dresser. These examples show the way that masculinity from the same background can take divergent forms. It also illustrates resistance, which the next three chapters of *Masculinities* outline further.

compulsory heterosexuality
The dominant cultural norm for sexual orientation that is said to dominate all social institutions, making other sexual orientations deviant. Also known as heterosexism.

The other three life-story chapters present different masculinities. Some, like the group of politically engaged men living with feminist women, actively produce very different and resistant forms of masculinities. Some have renounced well-paid careers for environmental activism. One life-story chapter is devoted to gay men who are actively constructing a different form of gay masculinity based on reciprocity and mutual recognition. Finally, Connell presents middle-class men who seem to embody hegemonic masculinity by being heterosexual, from conventional families and working in career-structured, highly skilled positions—but, even here, the production of masculinities is not straightforward. As Connell (2005, p. 181) notes: '[s]een close up, hegemonic and complicit masculinities are no more monolithic than are subordinated and marginalized masculinities.'

Gender and sexuality

As one sociologist in the field writes: '[a]ll societies have to make arrangements for the organization of erotic life. Not all, however, do it with the same obsessive concerns as the West' (Weeks 2003, p. 28). Sexual expression is one of the most malleable of human activities, with different cultures, societies, and even historical periods in the same culture changing the normative status of many sexual activities, such as premarital sex or homosexual activities.

It has been argued by some sociologists that in advanced capitalist societies such as Australia or Great Britain, sexual activity has been cut free from procreation and has become another identity to be consumed and be used solely for pleasure. Anthony Giddens has written that:

> sexual identity today has been discovered, opened up and made accessible to the development of varying life-styles. It is something each of us 'has' or cultivates, no longer a natural condition which an individual accepts as a preordained state of affairs ... sexuality functions as a malleable feature of self, a prime connecting point between body, self-identity and social norms. (Giddens 1992, p. 15)

The Sex in Australia study (ARCSHS 2003) found that the age at which people have their first sexual experience had fallen from eighteen to sixteen in a generation, but this average age at first experience was slightly older for people who had a homosexual experience. In a national study of secondary school students in 2009, about a quarter of Year 10 students (about sixteen years of age) and a half of Year 12 students were no longer virgins. Oral sex was common among young people, and more were becoming involved with group sex (Jopson & Murray 2009). What was interesting was that the double standard that had existed for generations was still extant. In an article written in response to public outrage at the group sex experiences of some professional footballers, the authors presented the stories of young women who became drunk, took part in group sex, and then found photos of themselves being used as trophies by young men. One young woman described alcohol-fuelled group sex in her university dormitory '"up to nine or 10 guys and two girls ... All scenarios are pretty much imaginable" ... But pride (in the achievements) can turn to shame once their exploits become public knowledge' (Jopson & Murray 2009, p. 19).

Gender and power can be read all the way through these stories, as they can be through the stories of homosexual men and women (Plummer 1995). Connell (2005) argues that the sexual activities and experiences do not exist in a vacuum or a 'featureless world'; the gender order precedes any individual action. Feminist Zillah Eisenstein (2007) argues that biological sex and social gender exist in an uneasy and complex relationship, that the sexual (biological) body constructs gender and gender is used to justify the sexual body as it exists in any given space and time. Still, gender has not always been identified specifically in sociological discussions of sexuality.

The history of sociological interest in sex and sexuality has usually been preceded by a discussion of the nineteenth-century writing of Sigmund Freud and sexologists such as Richard von Krafft-Ebing (Weeks 2003). These writers marked out sexuality as an area of investigation, but did so within a biological perspective. For Freud, babies were born 'polymorphously perverse' (with no defined sexual direction), but the process of repression (or civilisation) meant that the normative direction of their sexuality was imposed on them. In the mid-twentieth century, the American biologist Alfred Kinsey undertook a study of the sexual experiences of men and women and argued that there was no clear-cut distinction between homosexuality and heterosexuality; instead, sexual experience could be seen as a continuum from exclusively heterosexual to exclusively homosexual. For him, sexuality was defined as a physical phenomenon; it seemed to have no subjective meaning. In his studies in the 1940s, he found that 46 per cent of men and 28 per cent of women had had at least one homosexual experience (usually in their youth).

John Gagnon and William Simon (1973) used the symbolic-interactionist perspective to argue that sexual behaviour was organised into various sexual scripts that defined the situations and the actors, and outlined the lines to be used in any encounters. Sexual scripts operated at three levels: as cultural scenarios operating at the level of social institutions; as interpersonal scripts that individuals used in specific contexts with other individuals; and as intrapsychic scripts dealing with the management of desire within individuals. As Walby (1990) points out, this describes the process of becoming sexual as negotiated without an institutional notion of gender, in terms of patterns of social inequality or power differences.

Michel Foucault (1984) has been immensely important for the way in which many sociologists understand sexuality and power. He argues that sexuality is contingent on the discourses produced by the emerging professions of psychiatry and sexology (as illustrated by Freud and von Krafft-Ebing). The nineteenth century was not a period of silence about sexuality; rather, sexuality was increasingly discussed and dissected. Patients needed to talk about their 'sexual perversions' to be cured of them; the psychiatrists needed to identify the perversions to produce their professional discourses. In the incitement to talk and identify perverse homosexual acts, Foucault argues, the modern homosexual identity was born. Women's sexuality does not figure in Foucault's genealogy.

When we use gender theory to understand sexuality, we see a problematising of the institution of heterosexuality—we no longer take it for granted; it becomes visible. American feminist writer Adrienne Rich (1986) coined the term 'compulsory heterosexuality' as the key mechanism used by men as power over women. This compulsory or institutionalised heterosexuality defines women's position as eternally contingent on male desire, denying any authentic or autonomous sexual desire on women's part. It justifies rape as a man's biological and uncontainable sexual urge, and pornography as an extension of this. For Connell (2009), hegemonic masculinity is heterosexual, dominating women and other (homosexual) men. In their descriptions of ruling-class men, Donaldson and Poynting (2009) describe private-school experiences of brutality towards weaker boys by the strongest—often homosexual rape—in a similar way to prison homosexual experience. It is an experience of domination and submission, in the same way that Rich (1986) describes heterosexual experiences between men and women.

Other sociologists (like Giddens, quoted above) have argued that the late modern world has moved beyond perversion to diversity. All sexual relations and identities are culturally and historically specific. Sex 'only attains meaning in social relations, which implies that we can only make appropriate choices around sexuality by understanding its social, cultural and political context' (Weeks 2003, p. 84). Currently in Australia, there are openly gay politicians in federal parliament (one government minister is an openly gay woman), but marriage is still restricted to heterosexual couples. The Sydney Mardi Gras is known and celebrated around the world, but gay men are still beaten and killed for their sexual preference.

Sexual difference is increasingly being recognised and celebrated, but some people consider that there is also an unhealthy increase in the sexualisation of young people. A report from the American Psychological Association (APA) on the commercial sexualisation of all aspects of life for girls and women 'suggests that sexualisation practices may function to keep girls "in their place" as objects of sexual attraction and beauty and significantly limiting their free thinking and movement' (APA Task force on the Sexualization of Girls 2007, p. 22). As noted above, young people are having their first sexual experience younger than in previous generations, and research suggests that up to 30 per cent of young women who are sexually active have experienced unwanted or coerced sex (Smith et al. 2003). Other writers point to the availability of pornography that presents men as predatory and women as inviting abuse. Lauren Rosewarne (2007) claims that much outdoor advertising in Australia of semi-naked women would be considered sexual harassment if it were placed within most workplaces. Thus we see that the arena of sexuality, sexual desire, and representation is still strongly contested.

Gendered institutions

The sociological concept of the institution has been introduced in earlier chapters of this book. For example, Chapter 7 discusses the way in which the modern **nuclear family** is based on a gendered division of labour. If we assume that gender is just a product of the individual, then we miss the gendered nature of institutions— or what Connell (1987) refers to as gender regimes. If we assume that gender is only a matter of socialisation, as many of the writers in the field suggest, then again we miss the variations of gender that exist in social life and the way that it shapes individual lives in different ways.

nuclear family
A household consisting of parents of the opposite sex living with their biological children.

Early writers on gender assumed that gender existed purely as a product of an individual's socialisation and that gendered individuals entered gender-neutral sites or organisations. Feminists saw this as an inadequate explanation of what happened when women entered any male-dominated organisation. Notable feminist scholars like Catherine MacKinnon (1983) argued that the institution of the law was not gender-neutral, but rather deeply misogynist. Rosabeth Moss Kanter (1977), in her seminal work *Men and Women of the Corporation*, recognised the deeply gendered character of the large corporation, with its delineated division of labour between men and women. Regardless of any one woman's talents, most women were placed at the bottom of the hierarchy and given the jobs with the least power and likelihood of advancement. Sociologist Joan Acker (1990) goes further and argues that gender is a fundamental brick in any organisation's social structure:

> To say that an organization, or any other analytic unit, is gendered means that advantage and disadvantage, exploitation and control, action and emotion, meaning and identity, are patterned through and in terms of a distinction between male and female, masculine and feminine. Gender is not an addition to ongoing processes, conceived as gender neutral. Rather, it is an integral part of those processes, which cannot be properly understood without an analysis of gender. (1990, p. 146)

Gender as global: The patriarchal dividend

The Global Gender Gap Index discussed earlier shows us that gender difference and inequality works on a global scale. This does not mean that it operates in the same way and benefits the same groups everywhere. The aim of this chapter has been to impress upon you the very contingent and contextualised nature of gender orders.

Second-wave feminist writers have been accused of ignoring the very different interests of non-white, non-middle-class women in Western societies. In addition, there are global and international differences between women. An example in the twenty-first century is the reliance that middle-class, employed women in many Western economies (and non-Western ones like Singapore) have on importing cheap female labour to look after their families. This has resulted in the movement (legal and illegal) of women from developing countries, leaving their own families to be cared for by others so they are able to care for the families of developed women (Ehrenreich & Hochschild 2003).

Globalisation has also helped create the huge people-trafficking movement in which up to 700 000 people are smuggled from poorer to richer countries. Eighty per cent of these people are women and the bulk of them are forced to work in the sex industry (UNFPA 2006).

Transnational corporations (TNCs) operate beyond national borders, but masculine organisational cultures and gendered divisions of labour ensure that they cannot operate beyond gender lines (Connell 2005). Maria Mies (1998) writes of the 'housewifization' of the new international division of labour, where the housewives of the wealthy West consume the products produced by the women of the poor South.

globalisation
The increased interconnectedness of the cultural, economic, and political aspects of social life; intensified circulation of capital, goods, information, and people across national boundaries; and increased interdependence of countries and regions of the world.

Although we can see one group of women exploiting and gaining the material benefits of the labour of another, the overall effect is a patriarchal dividend nonetheless (Connell 2009). Most of the benefits of globalisation accrue to a relatively small group of men (internationally). Men dominate the global political scene; they form the overwhelming number of executives in global companies, and they also hold the vast number of important religious and cultural positions across the world. Connell (2009) also points out that men are also the victims of the patriarchal dividend, dying in larger numbers as members of armed forces, through workplace accidents, and as victims of homicide and suicide.

Conclusion

Gender is fundamental to understanding structures of inequality, not only in Australian or Western industrial society, but in all societies. This does not mean, though, that gender is a unitary phenomenon that operates in the same way across all historical periods and all societies. Gender is important because it operates in so many diverse ways. This chapter has outlined how the gender order exists across institutional, structural, and individual regimes.

The relationship between the physical body and gender is also complex. We should not dismiss the physical as immaterial; the body has a real materiality, and the sexed body is material as well as social and cultural. To paraphrase a line in Shakespeare's *The Merchant of Venice*, 'if you cut us, do we not bleed?' But the sexed body does not exist outside or beyond the social world. The evidence for sex difference may seem great, but the relationship between outcomes, like differences in violence rates between men and women, cannot solely be explained by hormones or evolutionary imperatives. The very self-consciousness of humans means that we need to explain these differences in nuanced and sophisticated ways.

Summary of main points

▶ Gender is central to an understanding of social inequality.

▶ The structural positions of women and men are often very different in the same society.

▶ The theory that sex is immutable and gender socially constructed has been criticised by many sociologists.

▶ Biological determinist arguments about sex and gender have also been criticised by many sociologists and feminist theorists.

▶ Patriarchy is considered an inadequate explanation, and has been supplanted in many cases by the notion of 'gender order'.

12.1 Gender in the news

Turn to the latest edition of your daily newspaper or view your regular TV news and current affairs shows. Can you see evidence of a gender order in the types of stories presented, the order in which they are presented, and the images used to illustrate the stories? How can you explain this gender order?

Discussion questions

12.1 In what ways do you 'do gender' in your everyday life? Explore your clothing, your attitudes to what is male and female, and the language you use.

12.2 What examples of gender inequality persist today?

12.3 Why is gender socialisation an inadequate explanation of gender inequality?

12.4 Patriarchy and the gender order have been advanced as key concepts in explaining gender inequality. Define these concepts and, using examples from contemporary Australia, justify which concept provides a more persuasive account.

12.5 What does Connell mean by 'hegemonic masculinity' and 'compulsory heterosexuality', and do you agree that many men 'do gender' in this way?

12.6 What social reforms are necessary to address gender inequality?

Further reading

Abbott, P., Wallace, C. & Tyler, M. 2005, *An Introduction to Sociology: Feminist Perspectives*, 3rd edn, Routledge, London.

Chafetz, J.S. (ed.) 2006, *Handbook of the Sociology of Gender*, Springer, New York.

Connell, R. 2009, *Gender*, 2nd edn, Polity Press, Cambridge.

Holmes, M. 2008, *Gender and Everyday Life*, Routledge, London.

—— 2007, *What is Gender? Sociological Approaches*, Sage, London.

Kimmel, M. 2004, *The Gendered Society*, 2nd edn, Oxford University Press, New York.

Pilcher, J. & Whelehan, I. 2004, *50 Key Concepts in Gender Studies*, Sage, London.

Wharton, A.S. 2005, *The Sociology of Gender: An Introduction to Theory and Research*, Blackwell, Malden, MA.

Websites

- Feminist Majority Foundation: <www.feminist.org>. A vast US-based activist-oriented website.
- The Australian Sociological Association (TASA): <www.tasa.org.au>. The TASA website has a resource page that leads to the large gender and sexuality resource. A very useful place to start.
- Intute—Social Sciences, Women's Studies: <www.intute.ac.uk/socialsciences/womensstudies>. A wide variety of international sources on gender and sexuality.
- SocioSite—Sex/Gender and Queer Studies: <www.sociosite.net/topics/gender.php>. This site provides links to a wide range of quality web resources.

Films/documentaries

- *Sex Traffic*, 2004, television mini-series, directed by D. Yates, Big Motion Pictures/Granada Television. Two-part British-Canadian series that presents a fictionalised account of the enforced prostitution of two young sisters in Eastern Europe and the direct involvement and complicity of Western companies and defence forces. Extremely disturbing and powerful.
- *Murderball*, 2005, documentary, directed by H.A. Rubin and D.A. Shapiro, Paramount Pictures. Remarkable story about wheelchair rugby and the intense production of physical masculinity among a group of players. <www.channel14.com/entertainment/tv/microsites/S/sex_traffic>.
- *The Shape of Water*, 2006, documentary, directed by K. Bhavnani, Kum-Kum Bhavnani Productions. Narrated by Susan Sarandon, this documentary is about five women striving for social justice in their developing countries. <www.theshapeofwatermovie.com>.

Visit the *Public Sociology* book website to access topical case studies, weblinks, YouTube clips, and extra readings.

References

Abbott, P., Wallace, C. & Tyler, M. 2005, *An Introduction to Sociology: Feminist Perspectives*, 3rd edn, Routledge, London.

Acker, J. 1990, 'Hierarchies, jobs, bodies: A theory of gendered organizations', *Gender and Society*, vol. 4, no. 2, pp. 139–58.

American Psychological Association 2007, *Report on the APA Task Force on the Sexualization of Girls*, Washington, DC, <www.apa.org/pi/wpo/sexualization.html> (accessed 7 September 2009).

Australian Bureau of Statistics (ABS) 2008, *Year Book Australia 2008*, cat. no. 1301.0, ABS, Canberra.

Australian Research Centre in Sex, Health and Society (ARCSHS) 2003, *Sex in Australia: Summary Findings of the Australian Study of Health and Relationships*, La Trobe University, Bundoora, <www.latrobe.edu.au/ashr> (accessed 7 September 2009).

Barash, D.P. 2002, 'Evolution, males and violence', *Chronicle of Higher Education*, vol. 48, no. 7, pp. B7–9.

Barrett, M. 1980, *Women's Oppression Today*, Verso, London.

Barrett, M. & McIntosh, M. 1980, *The Anti-Social Family*, Verso, London.

Bleier, R. 1997, *Science and Gender: A Critique of Biology and Its Theories on Women*, Teachers College Press, New York.

Brownmiller, S. 1976, *Against Our Will: Men, Women and Rape*, Secker & Warburg, London.

Buckheit, M. 2009, 'Caster Semenya is being treated unfairly', ESPN Online, 28 August, <http://espn.go.com> (accessed 7 September 2009).

Cassells, R., Miranti, R., Nepal, B. & Tanton, R. 2009, *She Works Hard for the Money*, AMP.NATSEM Income and Wealth Report Issue 22, AMP.NATSEM, Sydney.

Connell, R. 1987, *Gender and Power: Society, the Person and Sexual Politics*, Allen & Unwin, Sydney.

—— 1995, *Masculinities*, Allen & Unwin, Sydney.

—— 2009, *Gender*, 2nd edn, Polity Press, Cambridge.

Dawkins, R. 1976, *The Selfish Gene*, Oxford University Press, New York.

de Beauvoir, S. 1972/1949, *The Second Sex*, Penguin, Harmondsworth.

Donaldson, M. & Poynting, S. 2009, *Ruling Class Men: Money, Sex, Power*, Peter Lang, Bern, Switzerland.

Dozier, R. 2005, 'Beards, breasts, and bodies: Doing sex in a gendered world', *Gender and Society*, vol. 19, no. 3, pp. 297–316.

Ehrenreich, B. & Hochschild, A.R. (eds) 2003, *Global Woman: Nannies, Maids and Sex Workers*, Granta, London.

Eisenstein, Z. 2007, *Sexual Decoys: Gender, Race and War in Imperial Democracy*, Spinifex Press, Melbourne.

Firestone, S. 1972, *The Dialectic of Sex: The Case for Feminist Revolution*, Paladin, London.

Foucault, M. 1984, *The History of Sexuality*: *Vol. 1—An Introduction*, trans. Robert Hurley, Penguin, Harmondsworth.

Gagnon, J.H. & Simon, W. 1973, *Sexual Conduct: The Social Sources of Human Sexuality*, Hutchinson, London.

Giddens, A. 1992, *The Transformation of Intimacy: Sexuality, Love and Eroticism in Modern Societies*, Polity Press, Cambridge.

Hausmann, R., Tyson, L.D. & Zahidi, S. 2008, *The Global Gender Gap Report*, World Economic Forum, Geneva.

Hawkesworth, M. 1997, 'Confounding gender', *Signs: Journal of Women in Culture and Society*, vol. 22, no. 3, pp. 649–85.

Headey, B., Marks, G. & Wooden, M. 2005, 'The structure and distribution of household wealth in Australia', *The Australian Economic Review*, vol. 38, no. 2, pp. 159–75.

Jackson, S. & Scott, S. 2000, 'Introduction: The gendering of sociology', in S. Jackson & S. Scott (eds), *Gender: A Sociological Reader*, Routledge, London.

Jopson, D. & Murray, E. 2009, '"Generation sex" as norms shift', *The Age*, 17 May.

Kanter, R.M. 1977, *Men and Women of the Corporation*, Basic Books, New York.

Kessler, S.J. & McKenna, W. 1978, *Gender: An Ethnomethodological Approach*, University of Chicago Press, Chicago.

Kimmel, M.S. 2004, *The Gendered Society*, 2nd edn, Oxford University Press, New York.

Macionis, J.J. & Plummer, K. 2008, *Sociology: A Global Introduction*, 4th edn, Pearson Education, Harlow.

MacKinnon, C. 1983, 'Feminism, Marxism, method and the state: Towards a feminist jurisprudence', *Signs: Journal of Women in Culture and Society*, no. 8, pp. 635–58.

Mies, M. 1998, *Patriarchy and Accumulation on a World Scale: Women in the International Division of Labour*, Spinifex Press, Melbourne.

Oakley, A. 1985 [1972], *Sex, Gender and Society*, Gower, Aldershot.

Pilcher, J. & Whelehan, I. 2004, *50 Key Concepts in Gender Studies*, Sage, London.

Plummer, K. 1995, *Telling Sexual Stories: Power, Change and Social Worlds*, Routledge, London.

Rich, A. 1986, *Blood, Bread and Poetry: Selected Prose, 1979–1986*, W.W. Norton, New York.

Rosewarne, L. 2007, *Sex in Public: Women, Outdoor Advertising and Public Policy*, Cambridge Scholars Publishing, Newcastle, UK.

Smith, P.H., White, J.W. & Holland, L.J. 2003, 'A longitudinal perspective on dating violence among adolescent and college-age women', *American Journal of Public Health*, vol. 93, pp. 1104–9.

Smith, T. & Kimmel, M. 2005, 'The hidden discourse of masculinity in gender discrimination law', *Signs: Journal of Women in Culture and Society*, vol. 30, no. 3, pp. 1827–49.

Tavris, C. 2001, *Psychobabble and Biobunk: Using Psychology to Think Critically About Issues in the News*, 2nd edn, Prentice-Hall, Upper Saddle River, NJ.

Tiefer, L. 2004, 'Biological politics (read: propaganda) remains alive and well in sexology', *Feminism and Psychology*, vol. 14, no. 3, pp. 436–41.

United Nations Population Fund (UNFPA) 2006, *State of World Population, 2006: A Passage to Hope—Women and International Migration*, UNFPA, New York, <www.unfpa.org> (accessed 9 September 2009).

Walby, S. 1990, *Theorising Patriarchy*, Basil Blackwell, Oxford.

Weeks, J. 2003, *Sexuality*, 2nd edn, Routledge, London.

West, C. & Zimmerman, D.H. 1987, 'Doing gender', *Gender and Society*, vol. 1, no. 2, pp. 125–51.

Wilson, E.O. 1974, *Sociobiology: The New Synthesis*, Harvard University Press, Cambridge, MA.

CHAPTER 13

Ethnicity and belonging

Zlatko Skrbis

Ethnicity and identity: Three viewpoints

Ethnicity has chameleon-like characteristics and in real life it plays out in a myriad of ways. The following three examples help us shed some light on this variability:

1. In late 2005, nearly 5000 people took part in a riot at Sydney's popular Cronulla Beach. These people were variously described in the media as 'Aussies', 'Lebs and wogs', and 'young men of Middle-Eastern appearance'. The whole affair received much publicity in the following weeks and months. One of the major Australian newspapers carried photos of purported 'Aussies' who expressed their sentiments through slogans imprinted on their naked skin, posters, or T-shirts. 'Aussies fighting back!' said one. 'We grew here! You flew here!' said another. 'Wog-free zone,' said a third.

2. In the following excerpt from her article 'On Not Speaking Chinese', Ien Ang (1994, p. 10) reflects on her ethnic identity experiences:

    > At the level of everyday experience, the fact of my Chineseness confronted me only occasionally in the Netherlands, for example when passing ten-year-old red-haired boys triumphantly shouting behind my back, while holding the outer ends of their eyes upwards with their forefingers: 'Ching Chong China China', or when, on holiday in Spain or Italy or Poland, people would not believe that I was 'Dutch'. The typical conversation would run like this, as any non-white person in Europe would be able to testify:
    >
    > 'Where are you from?'
    >
    > 'From Holland.'
    >
    > 'No, where are you really from?'

3. Linda, a second-generation Italian born to Northern-Italian parents, has clear views on her second-generation Southern-Italian counterparts (cited in Baldassar 2001, p. 286, original italics):

    > [Guys born to Southern-Italian parents] wear a lot of gold, they're more 'woggy'. They have hotted-up cars. The guys with long hair, pushed back and dark and with lots of gold on and they pull their jeans right up to their waist. The girls with heaps of make-up and gold. They're not like *real* Italians who are much better, especially the guys. Italians here are definitely different to Italians over there.

Introduction: Why ethnicity?

The three aspects in the vignette all relate to ethnicity and attest to the variability of ethnic experience. In the first example, ethnicity and ethnic ascriptions determine ways in which people perceive each other as 'belonging'. The 'Australian' youth take the length of association with Australia as the basis for an assertion of identity that they clearly perceive as being under siege. At the same time, they deny the 'right to belong' to those who have more recent links with Australia. In the second example, the author explains her experiences of living in Holland, where she and her parents migrated from Indonesia when she was a young child. Her Dutchness was regularly contested in more or less subtle ways, and most people saw her Chineseness as irreconcilable with her Dutch identity. In the third example, Linda, a **second-generation** Italo-Australian whose parents were born in Northern Italy, differentiates herself from Italo-Australians born to parents from Southern Italy who, she says, use identity markers that she finds both aesthetically unappealing and un-Italian. Linda's reference to 'real' Italians reminds us that ethnic labels—in this case, 'Italian'—often emphasise a sense of uniformity and shared identity among ethnic groups, yet we also need to be sensitive to contestations of belonging and struggles for symbolic prestige that may be taking place within those ethnic groups. Indeed, Linda's statement is indicative of the 'one-upmanship' that characterises the way Northern Italians often speak about their Southern-Italian counterparts.

second-generation migrants
Children born in Australia who have at least one parent born overseas.

Ethnicity is one of the key sociological categories and an element of human identity that plays an important role in social life. Ethnicity and ethnic cultures loom large in popular culture, as exemplified through film, such as the Australian-based *Looking for Alibrandi* (2000), or the United States-based *My Big Fat Greek Wedding* (2002), and in literature, such as Zadie Smith's *White Teeth* (2000). In real life, though, you may find yourself living next door to a Greek-Australian couple, buying petrol from a 7-Eleven owned by a Fijian Indian, having an evening meal in a Chinese restaurant, taking a taxi driven by a Sudanese refugee, and wearing jeans sewn by a Vietnamese immigrant. Everyday life is a rich source of ethnic experience, but our own ethnic characteristics, or those of others, may have a significant influence on how we look, what we eat, what language we speak, how we worship, and even on whom we marry.

Ethnicity may be a key sociological concept, yet there is much confusion about what it means and represents. Some see ethnicity as inherently negative and hold it responsible for anything from Rwandan genocides and murderous ethnic hatred in the Balkans to clashes on Cronulla Beach. Others see it as something that is completely divorced from their own identity and experience—as if ethnicity is something they do not have—yet they recognise it in others. There are those who are reminded of their ethnic identity and status on a daily basis, either because of the privileges or the disadvantages that it brings them, and those who see it as a straightforwardly positive and enriching aspect of their life experience.

Ethnicity is commonly understood as a cultural identity derived through ancestry, and it gives an essential tone to our identity. This gives credence to an old Chinese saying: 'No ancestors, no identity'. In its broadest sense, ethnicity relates to important aspects of shared cultural heritage and characteristics that include language, tradition, attachment to a specific territory, and social norms. These characteristics are what form the basis of ethnic identity. Adrian Hastings (1997, p. 167) defines ethnicity as 'common culture' through which people share their 'basics of life'—from the ways in which they engage in simple rituals of life, such as birth and marriage, to the way they handle courtship, murder, and robbery, or how they narrate myths and history. In simple terms, one could presume that Hungarians relate to these things differently from Greeks, Germans differently from Poles, and Jews differently from Palestinians. Ethnicity, in other words, relates to 'aspects of relationships between groups which consider themselves, and are regarded by others, as being culturally distinctive' (Eriksen 2002, p. 4).

Because ethnicity concerns aspects of shared cultural heritage, it influences and shapes the configuration of social relations at the level of individuals and social collectivities (from families to nations). It may seem like a truism to most of us, but cultural heritage does matter to people—indeed, denying people the right to express their culture is often perceived as denying and negating their identity and/or existence. Ethnic identity is not just about the recognition of distinct identity and culture; it can have real consequences for people's **life chances**, ranging from jobs to health outcomes.

life chances
A term associated with the work of Weber to refer to different opportunities and differential access to resources, including education, wealth, housing, and health.

Following this brief introduction, this chapter is presented in four parts: the first part explores a number of concepts and definitions; the second takes a brief look at various theories of ethnicity; the third discusses the importance of ethnicity in Australian society by specifically focusing on issues of ethnic diversity in Australia and the question of migrant generations; and the final part provides an insight into contemporary discussions on migrant generations.

Ethnicity: Concepts and definitions

Central as it may be to our daily lives in the early twenty-first century, ethnicity has not always been at the forefront of sociological interest. This is not surprising, considering that the term 'ethnicity' was first mentioned in the English language only in 1953, in the *Oxford English Dictionary* (Glazer & Moynihan 1975). Although the term is relatively new, this does not mean that ethnicity and related phenomena played no part in social life before their introduction into the English language. William McNeill (1986), for example, in his study on ethnicity in world history, shows how ethnic mingling and pluralism played a crucial role in the centres of imperial government, both ancient and mediaeval.

The English adjective 'ethnic' relates to the Greek term *ethnos*, and it was used to label a *gentile*, meaning a non-Christian and non-Jewish pagan (Hutchinson & Smith 1996).

The Greeks used the term in a variety of ways, but what various uses have in common is the idea that people (like animals) share some cultural (or biological) characteristics and 'belong to some group unlike one's own' (Hutchinson & Smith 1996, p. 4). This means that, historically, the term has been used to differentiate between 'us' and 'them', and was used as the basis for various practices of inclusion and exclusion. This basic dichotomy is particularly important in nationalism when ethnic groups attempt to articulate their own interests and points of difference *vis-à-vis* other groups.

There are some important sociological and definitional characteristics of ethnicity that are worth noting:

- First, while ethnicity may be of overwhelming importance for the construction of identity under certain circumstances (for example, when a person's ethnic group is experiencing extreme marginalisation by another dominant ethnic group), sociologically speaking, ethnicity is simply one of the sources of individual and collective identity, along with class, gender and sexuality, age, regional background, occupation, and so on.
- Second, ethnicity is not fixed and unchanging. Instead, ethnic identities continuously evolve and are shaped through a variety of political, cultural, and social forces. Sometimes it takes a migration experience for people to 'discover' how important their ethnic culture is. Thus one may discover Englishness only upon migrating to Australia and after being labelled an 'outsider'. Loretta Baldassar and Ros Pesman (2005) make this point when reporting on the experience of a second-generation Australian-Italian who, before her visit to Italy, always thought of herself as Italian. Once in Italy, she was surprised by the reaction of her relatives and friends who saw her as an Australian: 'I went back [to Italy] thinking, "Oh I'm Italian, I'm Italian" and then I got there and I thought, "I don't know what I am but I'm certainly not Italian"' (Baldassar & Pesman 2005, p. 205). These situational responses to ethnic identity are what Jonathan Okamura (1981) calls situational ethnicity. Richard Jenkins (1996) makes a similar point when he emphasises the importance of a broader historical and political context in the process of ethnic identification. Thus growing up in Denmark in 1994 is not the same as growing up in Northern Ireland in 1994 because: '[e]thnicity, or at least awareness of it, is likely to figure in different ways, with different social costs and benefits attached, in each place' (1996, p. 813).
- Third, ethnic identities do not emerge in a vacuum, even though there has been much debate about the 'invention' of traditions with distinct ethnic undertones (Hobsbawm & Ranger 1997). Ethnic identities tend to evolve through selective appropriation, blending, and discarding of various elements of traditions that a group considers its own.
- Fourth, ethnicity is often used interchangeably with race, and countries as far apart as the United States and Singapore use the term 'race' as one of their

basic tools for classification and diversity management. This is problematic from a conceptual viewpoint, considering that there is no such thing as distinct human 'races' and no evidence that 'racial' groups have a distinct biological underpinning. Humans and chimpanzees share 98.5 per cent of all genes and the genetic differences among members of a particular 'racial' group are often greater than between members of different groups.

Still, many authors argue in favour of retaining both terms—ethnicity and race—in the social science vocabulary. Michael Banton (1967), for example, argues that ethnicity is primarily concerned with the identification of 'us', whereas racism is more about the identification of 'others'. Jenkins (1996, p. 815), in contrast, sees ethnicity as voluntarily embraced while race is something imposed. Others again emphasise that race refers to more physically perceptible differences between groups of people, while ethnicity focuses on cultural distinctiveness between different groups.

Finally, ethnicity is often conflated with nationality and citizenship. These are analytically different concepts and they do not always coincide. One can be ethnically Han Chinese with Dutch citizenship and nationality, or ethnic Malay with Singaporean rather than Malaysian nationality. It is similarly important not to conflate ethnicity and birthplace (one may be ethnic German but born in Kazakhstan), even though social statistics often invite this error.

Theorising ethnicity

The founders of sociology did not pay much specific attention to ethnicity. Karl Marx (1818–83) noted ethnicity-related issues only insofar as they had a capacity to damage the unity of the working class and hinder social progress. It is perhaps not surprising that Max Weber (1864–1920), who was preoccupied with questions of the modernisation and rationalisation of human action, concurred with Marx's argument about the relationship between ethnicity and modernisation; however, Weber went much further and his writing on this topic reads as surprisingly fresh and modern even today. In his posthumously published work *Economy and Society* (1978), he emphasises what we would today call the imagined nature of ethnic ties and ways in which ethnicity facilitates group and community formation. For Weber, a group whose membership is based on believed-in 'blood ties' possesses the fundamental prerequisite for the formation of group consciousness and political community. What makes his account of ethnicity so contemporary is his point that ethnic differences influence the conduct of people's daily lives, thus making us understand ethnicity as something that actually happens in human relationships.

Sociologists do not have a monopoly on research into ethnicity. Due to its complexity and contextual variability, ethnicity represents a truly interdisciplinary topic where various social sciences—most notably sociology and anthropology—can productively engage with one another. What follows is a brief overview of the theories of ethnicity using a rather standard classification, dividing them into two main camps: primordialist and instrumentalist/constructivist approaches.

Primordialist and instrumentalist/constructivist approaches to ethnicity

In general terms, primordialists see ethnicity as an inescapable cultural given, unchanging and unchangeable. **Primordial** attachments, they argue, are the primary drivers of emotional actions, and bind individuals into groups. There are two key proponents of this perspective, although their arguments differ substantially. Clifford Geertz (1973) observes the importance of primordial attachments that, he argues, grow out of congruities of blood, speech, and custom. They are both ineffable and coercive at the same time, but because they are about innate affection and attachment to territory or kin, they generate the sentiments of belonging.

primordialism
A belief that the elements of identity are inborn and relatively independent of cultural context.

Pierre van den Berghe (1981), on the other hand, sees ethnic groups through the perspective of **sociobiology**, which emphasises the links between biological givens and social behaviour. There are two crucial points that help us understand van den Berghe's approach. The first is that he sees ethnic groups as big, inbreeding families and extensions of kinship. The second is that humans behave nepotistically, meaning that they favour kin over non-kin. It is precisely because of this nexus between a sense of family and nepotism that people perceive ethnicity as a 'real' community of related individuals—individuals who perceive themselves as 'bound by preferential endogamy and a common historical experience' (van den Berghe 1995, p. 360). This does not mean, as some authors simplistically like to argue, that van den Berghe sees ethnicity as directly rooted in biology—but it does mean people's perception of biological connectedness encourages them to feel a sense of group membership.

sociobiology
A school of thought in the biological sciences, which argues that all differences in temperament between men and women are a result of evolutionary selection. According to Edward O. Wilson, all behaviour is genetically programmed and resistant to cultural demands.

The idea that social behaviours may be biologically conditioned sits uncomfortably with the dominant view that social life is constructed, but primordialism should be credited for its attempts to help us understand why ethnicity has the capacity to generate intense emotions and a sense of collective belonging. This becomes particularly useful when we try to understand (what most of us would call) the irrational and emotional behaviours of nationalists who make continuing references to blood, national community, sacrifice, and the ethnic purity of their community (Connor 1993). Nationalists often talk about their community as if it were based on blood ties, and see the ethnic group as blood-related family that continually needs protection from the possibility of contaminating influences.

In theory, the instrumentalist/constructivist approach is at the opposite end of the spectrum from primordialism, although the differences between them are often not completely clear-cut. The very terms 'instrumentalism' and 'constructivism' explain the basic premises upon which these perspectives on ethnicity are based: that ethnicity represents a resource for expression of different social, cultural, or political interests, and that it is socially constructed and thus open to change, selective appropriation, expression, and even mixing. For instrumentalists, ethnicity has no natural or objective existence and 'no one can hear, see, smell, taste or touch ethnicity. As an influence upon behaviour it is something we can know only through the things that are taken as signs of it' (Banton 1994, p. 9).

Abner Cohen (1974), whose approach espouses the instrumentalist position, argues that ethnicity can be manipulated to achieve particular political ends. Similarly, Werner Sollors (1989) argues that continuing social changes force ethnic groups to continuously negotiate their boundaries and expressive symbols of ethnicity. Sollors' position, which emphasises both the importance of ethnic boundaries and ethnic symbols, could be seen as combining the insights from two important theorists. The first is Fredrik Barth (1969), one of the most highly influential theorists of ethnicity. For Barth, ethnicity is a feature of social organisation. Even though ethnic groups are defined through culture, the ability to promote the cultural continuity of the group depends on its capacity to delineate and reinforce the boundary that defines it. In this way, the boundary becomes an instrument of identity construction and the basic tool of inclusion, exclusion, and the politics of belonging. The second theorist is Herbert Gans (1979, 1994), who was interested in the question of the visibility of ethnic cultures and introduced the idea of symbolic ethnicity in relation to behaviours of third- and fourth-generation immigrants in the United States. He argues that ethnic identity among the grandchildren and great-grandchildren of Europeans in America may be more visible than in the first and second generations, but this does not mean that it is stronger. Their ethnicity is no longer a part of a practised culture, complete with language and traditions, but instead an assemblage of symbols that they find meaningful and indicative of their ethnic identity: 'ethnicity takes on an expressive rather than instrumental function in people's lives' (Gans 1979, p. 9). The symbols of ethnicity can be represented in the penchant for ethnic foods (Italian pasta), displaying of flags (the Irish), or donations to political regimes associated with ethnic identity (e.g. Jews and Israel). Gans saw symbolic ethnicity as 'an ethnicity of last resort, which could, nevertheless, persist for generations' (1979, p. 1). Arguably, it is impossible to understand contemporary ethnic relations without seriously taking symbolic ethnicity into account.

Theories of ethnic hybridity and choice

Theories of hybridity and choice are an extension of constructionist perspectives. Mary Waters (1990) is one of the exponents of the ethnic choice principle. She argues that

Americans of European descent, such as the Italians or the Irish, are no longer seen as unassimilable and trapped in their ethnic identities. In fact, most of them identify as Americans but they exercise their ethnicity as a voluntary option, very much along the lines of Gans' idea of symbolic ethnicity. For instance, an Irish American may opt to celebrate St Patrick's Day, but this is done voluntarily and largely independently from the sphere of organised Irishness embodied in ethnic groups or associations. David Hollinger (1995), in advocating a 'post-ethnic perspective', argues similarly that ethnicity is a product of people's voluntary affiliation. In contrast—albeit equally utopian—Joseph Raz (1994) argues that people should have the 'right to exit' from an ethnic group. Just how utopian this claim is becomes immediately apparent when we consider situations in which people have ethnic labels imposed upon them. Someone may not feel or identify as Lebanese, for example, but the fact that they are recognised as being 'of Middle-Eastern appearance' may nevertheless result in a particular set of reactions against them.

Obviously, exercising ethnic options is a privilege not granted to everyone. Waters (1990) reminds us that, while Americans of European descent may be able to celebrate their symbolic ethnic identities, others—particularly groups that are racialised by the mainstream—may face a 'socially enforced and imposed racial identity' (p. 449), thus having little if any scope for the voluntaristic celebration of identity. This is an important point, echoing an earlier warning that ethnic and racial ascriptions represent a direct expression of power relations in a broader society. The voluntarism that Waters describes works under external constraints and the choices are not limited: 'One can eat Chinese tomorrow and Turkish the day after; one can even dress in Chinese and Turkish styles. But *being* Chinese or Turkish are not commercially available options' (Billig 1995, p. 139, original italics). Some of the advocates of the ethnic choice approach may be biased towards 'options' at the expense of 'constraints', but they are right to emphasise that individuals are not completely powerless in the ways in which they express or experience ethnicity and that, while ethnicity is always dependent on a social context, there are ways in which choices and identity emphases can be made.

In the age of globalisation, migration and mobility have profoundly affected every corner of the globe. The increasing porousness of national and cultural boundaries encourages travel, human transactions, and cross-cultural exchanges on a global scale, and consequently leads to cultural mixing and hybridisation. We are witnessing an ever-increasing number of individuals who espouse multiple ancestries and loyalties, and who continuously negotiate multiple identity boundaries. Australia provides an interesting context within which to explore these trends.

Ethnicity and identity politics in Australia

The significance of ethnicity in Australia is directly intertwined with immigration and the role it has played in the constitution of Australian society to this day. Ever since the colonisation of the Australian continent—an event of dramatic and tragic consequence to its Indigenous inhabitants—immigration and responses to it have assumed various forms. Here we mention some of them in broad strokes.

The Australian 'immigration story' began with the colonisation of the continent in 1788 and transportation of convicts from Britain in the eighteenth and nineteenth centuries (Hughes 1987). Australian colonial administrators embarked upon a process of building a New Britannia in the Antipodes, a country that was white, Christian, and symbolically, politically, and economically attached to its colonial motherland. Ethnicity played a significant role even in this early period, with the notable tension between the English and the Irish.

**CrossLink:
See Chapter 5
for more
on social
Darwinism.**

Over the nineteenth century, Australian colonialists built the New Britannia, but they simultaneously dispossessed its original inhabitants (Markus 1994) and treated non-European immigrants—particularly the Chinese, who arrived in Australia in relatively large numbers during the gold rush era—with brutality. In 1888, restrictions on Chinese immigration were imposed by all Australian colonies. These practices of dispossession and brutality were justified by the blunt tools of **social Darwinism**, which advocated the superiority of the white race.

In 1901, the newly federated Australian parliament introduced the *Immigration Restriction Act*, a measure that marks the official beginning of the **White Australia policy**. The Act used the bizarre mechanism of a **dictation test**, aimed primarily at restricting the immigration of the 'coloured races'. This tool of ethnic diversity management (removed from the Act in 1958) was indicative of the desperate determination of the government to keep Australia monocultural and white. The dismantling of the White Australia policy began in 1966 (DIMIA 2006a), but its last vestiges were removed only in 1973 (Viviani 1992).

By 1947, Australia was almost completely monocultural and British/European. The non-European population (other than Indigenous) in this period was only 0.25 per cent of the total population (Jupp 2002, p. 9), but the experience of World War II in the Pacific led the government to embark on a radical mass immigration program. The program was introduced by the first Minister for Immigration, Arthur Calwell, under the slogan 'populate or perish' (Calwell 1972). In a relatively short period, Australia became home to 170 000 new residents, largely recruited from refugee camps across Europe. This influx of migrants radically changed the demographic profile of the country, and brought new arrivals from Denmark, Greece, Italy, Germany, and other countries into close contact with the dominant Anglo-Celtic population. It also signalled

social Darwinism
The application of evolutionary laws of natural selection to human societies to 'explain' social processes and behaviours. Spencer coined the term 'survival of the fittest' (often misattributed to Darwin) to describe how Darwin's ideas about natural selection in nature could be used to explain social processes and behaviours.

White Australia policy
A policy of the Australian government associated with the *Immigration Restriction Act 1901*, which prevented the migration of so-called 'coloured' races to Australia.

dictation test
An integral part of the Australian *Immigration Restriction Act 1901* that authorised an immigration officer to administer a dictation test in any European language to a potential immigrant deemed undesirable. It was applied primarily to prevent the immigration of non-white migrants.

assimilation
An idea that diverse groups of people need to adapt to, and be absorbed by, the dominant culture.

multiculturalism
A policy of ethnic management based upon a recognition of difference. Multiculturalism has been a policy framework for the management of ethnic diversity in Australia since the early 1970s.

the beginning of long-term demographic change; however, it was couched in terms of **assimilation**.

Assimilationism is the idea that diverse groups of people need to adapt to a dominant culture. In its radical form, it expects immigrants to turn away radically from their cultures of origin. Assimilationism was a guiding principle of population diversity management in Australia from 1947 until the introduction of **multiculturalism** in 1973, which almost coincided with the official dismantling of the White Australia policy.

Given the changing international circumstances (the dismantling of apartheid in South Africa and the Vietnam War) and changes within Australian society (substantial immigration of non-British people since 1947), multiculturalism has become an economic, political, and social necessity, and has received bipartisan support from government.

While the immigration intake throughout the 1960s was increasingly less European, the end of the Vietnam War and the arrival of Vietnamese refugees in the late 1970s (Viviani 1984) represented a symbolic point of no return for a genuinely multi-ethnic immigration intake.

Multiculturalism is a general label for a progressive, inclusive, and diversity-friendly policy, supported by successive Australian governments since its introduction, but multiculturalism has evolved from its early stages in the Whitlam government era (1972–75), which sensitised government institutions (and the population) to the need to deal with migrant settlement and diversity in the social mainstream, to a series of distinct emphases developed through various government-sponsored reports throughout the 1970s and the 1980s (Jamrozik et al. 1995; Jupp 2002).

Multiculturalism has been under attack from various critics, but here we mention only three. In the early 1980s, historian Geoffrey Blainey (1984) critiqued multiculturalism by arguing that it dictates an Australian immigration policy which privileges Asian migrants at the expense of Europeans. He also warned of the dangers of the emergence of migrant ghettoes and the 'Asianisation' of Australia. Only two years earlier, Frank Knopfelmacher (1982) criticised multiculturalism from the point of view of the threat it represents to 'anglomorphism' (culture as derived by some affiliation with anglomorph societies, such as the United Kingdom, Ireland, and New Zealand) and social cohesion. More recently, and advancing a far more intellectually engaging argument, Ghassan Hage (1998) discussed multiculturalism as a tool for reinforcing white power, saying that Aboriginal people and non-white 'ethnics' represent decorative appendices on a national body that wishes to remain both white and in control.

In terms of political discourse, multiculturalism was a target of Pauline Hanson's and her One Nation party (established in 1997). She saw Australian multiculturalism as chiefly responsible for everything from 'migrant crime' to 'Aboriginal cannibalism' (Jupp 2002). The 1998 election, in which her party attracted 9 per cent of votes, saw the peak of One Nation's influence, but the party and its ideals were soon rejected by the voters and One Nation disintegrated. Hanson's latest attempt at securing a seat came in 2009 in her failed bid to represent Beaudesert in the Queensland state election.

From the point of view of government, multiculturalism as a policy framework came under siege under the Howard Coalition government (1996–2007) and Prime Minister John Howard pointedly avoided any association with multiculturalism. Events such as the racial riots in Cronulla in December 2005 and the incidence of Muslim radicalism in some Australian migrant communities fuelled the anti-multiculturalism arguments of those who saw this policy as chiefly responsible for these developments. With the election of Labor's Kevin Rudd as Prime Minister in 2007, the multicultural agenda was made more visible through initiatives such as the reinstatement of the Australian Multicultural Advisory Council (dismantled by the Howard government), which is charged with advising the government on issues relating to Australia's cultural and religious diversity and overcoming intolerance and racism in Australia (DIAC 2008b). The Labor government's multicultural agenda continues to be heavily associated with broader social debates on population and economic growth, social justice, and illegal migration.

How diverse is Australia today?

This short historical excursion hopefully makes it clear that it is not possible to understand Australian society today without understanding and appreciating the important part that ethnicity-related considerations (mostly linked with migration) have played in the history of Australian society.

According to official statistics, over 6.8 million people have settled in Australia since the end of World War II (ABS 2004), and there has been a continuing increase in ethnic diversity—particularly since the end of the White Australia policy. This trend notwithstanding, there appears to be little possibility that this increasing ethnic diversification will soon erode the dominance of the European-descended population (Jones 2003). According to the most recent 2006 Census, 24 per cent of the population of 19.8 million were born overseas. Furthermore, of those born overseas, 33.1 per cent were born in North-West Europe (primarily the United Kingdom and Ireland), 18.9 per cent in Eastern and Southern Europe, and 12.1 per cent in South-East Asia. Most overseas-born people came from the United Kingdom (23 per cent of the overseas born), New Zealand (10 per cent), and Italy (4.4 per cent) (DIMIA 2006b). Obviously, we must always note that within these broad geographic categories we have considerable heterogeneity of ethnic belonging, and we must always be cognisant of the dangers of the simplistic conflation of ethnicity and birthplace.

Australia as an emigration country?

The 2006 Census statistics support what many of us already know through our daily encounters with a diverse range of people and cultures—that Australia is an immigration country. This focus on immigration, though, often overlooks the fact that Australia is also a country that experiences considerable permanent, long-term, and temporary emigration—that is, outbound migration. This process of outward migration should not be unexpected for at least two reasons. First, Australia is an integral part of a global economic market and people are increasingly likely to pursue economic opportunities in the global arena. Second, because Australia's population is so diverse, many people living in Australia have strong ties with countries overseas. In this way, Australians (of various ancestries) themselves contribute to an increase in global ethnic diversity or—if returning to their ancestral homelands—to an increase in cultural hybridity.

The figures show that the number of people departing Australia permanently, or in the long term, is on the increase: between 1998–99 and 2001–02, Australia experienced an increase in these kinds of departures from 140 281 to 171 446 persons (Hugo, Rudd & Harris 2003, p. 26). For example, the recent data from the Department of Immigration and Citizenship (2008a) show that 76 923 people permanently departed Australia in the 2007–08 financial year alone. To where do Australian residents emigrate? The United Kingdom is a popular destination, with the number of Australian-born citizens emigrating to the United Kingdom increasing from 14 657 persons in 1994–95 to 30 737 persons in 2001–02. In total, 181 924 Australian-born citizens made a permanent or long-term move to the United Kingdom during the period 1994–2002 (Hugo, Rudd & Harris 2003, p. 29). The number of Australians moving to continental Europe also increased during this time, although it remains about one-quarter of the size of the group emigrating to the United Kingdom. Graeme Hugo, Diane Rudd, and Kevin Harris (2003) speculate on the extent to which emigration to continental Europe has been engendered by 'second-generation children of postwar immigrants from Europe who are able to utilise their language skills in the parent's birthplace' (p. 28). No doubt one of the most interesting trends in recent emigration from Australia relates to the numbers of those emigrating long term or permanently to Asian countries—their numbers have increased by 54 per cent since 1997 (Hugo, Rudd & Harris 2003).

13.1: Generations of migrants

According to authors such as Alejandro Portes and Min Zhou (1993), and Portes and Dag MacLeod (1996), the second generation represents a litmus test for the success and viability of ethnic groups. There is more to this question than simply a question of viability. Should, for example, second-generation migrants in Australia be seen as second-generation immigrants or as first-generation Australians? As soon as we pose the question in this manner, we not only make a pertinent empirical point that captures the varied ways in which people may choose to privilege one identity over another, but we are potentially politicising the distinction. It is precisely the questions about belonging, about 'where your loyalties lie', that keep appearing in public debates about immigrants all around the world, be it in Paris, New York, or Sydney.

SOCIOLOGY
SPOTLIGHT

Defining migrants

This section examines the question of migrant generations—the question that goes to the very heart of understanding the place of migrants in a host society. It will specifically focus on the second generation, which has received most attention in the literature on ethnicity and migration. For the purpose of statistics, the second generation is often simply defined as designating persons born in Australia who have one or both parents born overseas. There are other, more sophisticated definitions but if we translate our statistical definition into figures in Australia, then we can say that approximately 20 per cent of the entire population can be classified as second-generation migrants (Khoo, McDonald & Giorgas 2002, p. iv); still, it is important to remind ourselves that being a second-generation migrant is not simply an identity assumed through an accident of birth but a lifelong experiment in navigation across cultures, generations, social environments, and identities (Song 2003).

In Australia, feminist scholars have made an important contribution to shaping our understanding of the second generation. Gillian Bottomley (1991), for instance, emphasised ways in which second-generation individuals negotiate gender, class, culture, and ethnicity—an interest that has been explored extensively in more recent writings (Pallotta-Chiarolli & Skrbis 1994; Baldassar 1999; Zevallos 2003). While these authors emphasise the continuing vibrancy of ethnicity in the second-generation context, another set of authors subscribed to what became known as a straight-line theory of ethnic identity (Baldassar & Skrbis 1998). Charles Price (1994) exemplified this approach by suggesting that ethnic groups in Australia were at risk of diminishing their ethnicity through the 'loss' of their subsequent generations and, by implication, their failure to transmit culture (see also Bertelli 1985). For Price, a keen observer of demographic trends—**intermarriage** in particular—this conclusion may have appeared logical. What he observed was the increased prevalence of marriage outside the ethnic group among the second generation, a process expected to lead towards the dilution of culture. 'Straight-line' theory has been criticised as too simplistic by authors such as Gans (1979, 1994), who observes that ethnicity can transform and assume alternative forms of expression—the earlier mentioned symbolic ethnicity is a case in point.

intermarriage
Marriage across ethnic or religious boundaries.

One of the important features of more recent work on the second generation in Australia is the attempt to link it with the literature on globalisation and **transnationalism**. In her ethnographic research, Baldassar (2001) discusses how individuals of the second generation negotiate ethnicity and a sense of belonging through transnational visits to their parents' place of birth. While going back 'home' is of great emotional importance to first-generation migrants, the same journeys are an important rite of passage for the second generation. There are two important points arising from Baldassar's work: first, that migration does not end with settlement, and returning home is an integral part of

transnationalism
A concept that describes the flows and movements of goods, people, and images across national borders.

migrant identity experience; and second, that second-generation identities are formed not only through the settlement experiences of those individuals' parents and the host society in general, but are also embedded in a transnational context, in a constant dynamic between host and home environments.

The dynamics of the relationship between the home and host environments is also the central theme of my own work on long-distance nationalism (Skrbis 1999). This is a type of **nationalism** that is adapted to the conditions of the modern global system, and that is not limited by territorial considerations. In broad terms, this work links migration and **diaspora** studies with studies of nationalism, and explores the functioning of long-distance nationalist sentiments by drawing on the ethnographic research among second-generation Croatians and Slovenians in Australia. At the forefront of my interest is an attempt to understand ways in which nationalist-coloured sentiments are transmitted across migrant generations, and how these sentiments are manifested among the second generation. The effects of these sentiments are far reaching, and the research demonstrates how they influence a range of behaviours and practices, from the symbolic construction of the 'Other' to marital and partnership choices.

nationalism
Refers to an ideology of patriotic beliefs in support of national sovereignty and independence for an identifiable group of people based on common language, traditions, religion, or ethnicity.

diaspora
A religiously and/or ethnically defined group of people dispersed from their country of origin. The dispersion is often precipitated by political violence.

Although the studies of the second generation are numerous and varied, and it is impossible to provide an exhaustive overview of various approaches, it is important to mention the body of work on 'youth issues', in particular the social stigmatisation of youth of particular ethnic backgrounds and the debates on ethnic 'gangs' (Poynting et al. 2004; White & Perrone 2001). Following a number of violent incidents in Sydney that involved 'ethnic crime' and 'youth of Middle-Eastern appearance', Jock Collins and colleagues (2000) produced an insightful study of the complex interrelationship between youth, ethnicity, and crime. By analysing media presentations and the responses from police, youth, and community leaders, they demonstrated the disturbing way in which the Lebanese community was smeared by the media, thus creating a moral panic among the population. A similar media uproar followed a series of more recent and highly publicised incidents in Melbourne involving members of the Somali and Sudanese communities (Kerbaj 2007).

CrossLink:
See
Chapter 19
for more
discussion on
terrorism.

As the 'War on Terror' expands from the Middle East and the intake of migrants from Africa increases, the discourse of 'Othering' within Australian borders takes on new forms. In the British context, Tariq Modood (2005) refers to this phenomenon as 'cultural racism', arguing that the basis of exclusion is now determined by the extent to which a cultural group is seen as belonging. These types of attitudes have recently been revealed in an Australian study by Kevin Dunn and colleagues (2007), examining contemporary racism in Australia. The study found that, when asked, 736 (66 per cent) of the respondents stated that Islam posed a threat to national security. Only 255 respondents were able to identify what exactly the threat was. In addition, slightly fewer than 50 per cent of respondents stated that some cultural groups simply did not fit into Australian society (Dunn et al. 2007; see also Dunn et al. 2004).

The creation of a scapegoat ethnic group is profoundly problematic in the context of a society that is ethnically heterogenous and that requires the delicate work of bridge-building between various sectors of the community. This is precisely where sociology comes in: its task is to identify and examine factors (structural, institutional, cultural, and political) that lead to ethnic tension in the first place.

Conclusion

Ethnicity is a universal characteristic of all human societies, and consequently also an important characteristic of the Australian social landscape. With the continuing immigration that helps to propel Australia's economic growth, Australia is on a trajectory leading towards more diversity (ethnic, religious, linguistic, cultural, etc.). Given the historical and political circumstances broadly defined by the global 'War on Terror', ethnicity—particularly through its nexus with religion—will continue to be of relevance, globally as well as locally.

Despite the considerable robustness of multiculturalism in Australia, these factors must be taken seriously because diversity needs to be managed in order to maintain social cohesion and the effective functioning of social institutions. Ethnicity has the propensity to intersect with every aspect of society, from the government to the level of families and individuals. This is what makes it an integral element of the sociological enterprise.

Summary of main points

▶ Ethnicity is derived through ancestry and it gives an essential tone to our identities.

▶ Ethnicity concerns aspects of shared cultural heritage—this is why it influences and shapes the configuration of social relations at the individual level as well as the national level.

▶ Ethnicity is not fixed and unchanging. Instead, ethnic identities continuously evolve and are shaped through a variety of political, cultural, and social forces.

▶ Theories of ethnicity can be divided broadly into instrumentalist/constructionist and primordialist approaches.

▶ Population mobility and immigration increase ethnic diversity.

SOCIOLOGICAL REFLECTION

13.1 Ethnicity as identity and practice

(a) Think of somebody whom you know well, but who has a different ethnic background from yours. Answer the following questions:

   – What are the key elements of this person's identity? Consider various identity elements of ethnicity that we identified earlier in this chapter.

– Do you think of this person as an Australian or something else? What exactly do you take to be the characteristics of 'Australianness'?

(b) Select a newspaper article that you consider to be in some way related to ethnicity but that may also contain some elements of 'race/racism' and 'religion'. By reference to this article, try to answer the following questions:

– In what way is this article related to ethnicity?

– Does the article perpetuate positive or negative stereotypes about a particular group of people?

Discussion questions

13.1 Does everyone have an ethnic identity? If so, does this mean everyone is an 'ethnic'?

13.2 In what ways, if at all, is the influx of new immigrants related to changes in Australian culture? Provide examples.

13.3 In what ways are the media responsible for shaping the debate about immigration? Provide specific examples.

13.4 Does immigration undermine social cohesion and weaken Australian national identity?

13.5 Can you identify any changes in the urban landscape that you think may be related to changes in the ethnic composition of your city?

13.6 Why are some immigrant groups more likely to be the target of popular prejudice than others? What makes certain ethnic groups acceptable and others not?

13.7 What are the major stages in Australia's immigration history?

Further reading

Castles, S., Foster, W., Iredale, R. & Withes, G. 1998, *Immigration and Australia: Myths and Realities*, Allen & Unwin in conjunction with the Housing Industry Association Ltd, Sydney.

Fozdar, F., Wilding, R. & Hawkins, M. 2009, *Race and Ethnic Relations*, Oxford University Press, Melbourne.

Hutchinson, J. & Smith, A.D. (eds) 1996, *Ethnicity*, Oxford University Press, New York.

Jupp, J. 2002, *From White Australia to Woomera: The Story of Australian Immigration*, Cambridge University Press, Cambridge.

Song, M. 2003, *Choosing Ethnic Identity*, Polity Press, Cambridge.

Websites

- Australian Bureau of Statistics (ABS): <www.abs.gov.au>. Authoritative information on Australian ethnicity, immigration, and demographic trends.
- Fact Sheet 15—Population Projections: <www.immi.gov.au/media/fact-sheets/15population.htm>. A handy summary of population and immigration data produced by the Australian Government Department of Immigration and Citizenship.
- National Statistics, UK: <www.statistics.gov.uk/focuson/ethnicity>. Source of an up-to-date overview of ethnic groups in the United Kingdom.
- US Census Bureau: <www.census.gov>. Contains data on ethnicity and race categories in the United States.

Films/documentaries

- *Admission Impossible*, 1992, videorecording, directed by A. Morgan, Film Australia/Australian Broadcasting Corporation (ABC). Discusses the origin and development of the White Australia policy from the application of the *Immigration Restriction Act 1901* (Cwlth) to the present.
- *Looking for Alibrandi*, 2000, motion picture, directed by K. Woods, Village Roadshow. An amusing and endearing film adaptation of the widely read novel about the life of seventeen-year-old Josie, an Australian teenager of Italian descent dealing with the culture clash experienced by the children of first-generation migrants.
- *No Man's Land*, 2001, motion picture, directed by D. Tanovic, Noé Productions, distributed in Australia by Madman Cinema. This is a story of a Bosnian and a Serbian soldier during the recent Balkan conflict who find themselves trapped in a trench, surrounded by the two armies, with a comrade lying on a spring-loaded bomb. In this situation, they discover how their lives are intertwined and make the viewer aware of the absurdity and tragedy of an ethnic conflict and war.
- 'Riot and Revenge', 2006, *Four Corners*, television news feature, reported by L. Jackson, Australian Broadcasting Corporation (ABC). Analyses the Cronulla riot and includes interviews with those who were there.

Visit the *Public Sociology* book website to access topical case studies, weblinks, YouTube clips, and extra readings.

References

Ang, I. 1994, 'On not speaking Chinese: Postmodern ethnicity and the politics of diaspora', *New Formations*, vol. 24, pp. 1–18.

Australian Bureau of Statistics (ABS) 2004, *Australian Social Trends*, cat. no. 4102.0, ABS, Canberra.

Baldassar, L. 1999, 'Marias and marriage: Ethnicity, gender and sexuality among Italo-Australian youth in Perth', *Journal of Sociology*, vol. 35, no. 1, pp. 1–22.

—— 2001, *Visits Home: Migration Experiences Between Italy and Australia*, Melbourne University Press, Melbourne.

Baldassar, L. & Pesman, R. 2005, *From Paesani to Global Italians: Veneto Migrants in Australia*, University of Western Australia Press, Perth.

Baldassar, L. & Skrbis, Z. 1998, 'The second generation and the transmission of culture', in M. Alexander, S. Harding, P. Harrison, G. Kendall, Z. Skrbis & J. Western (eds), *Refashioning Sociology: Responses to the New World*, TASA Conference Proceedings, Queensland University of Technology, Brisbane, pp. 454–9.

Banton, M. 1967, *Race Relations*, Tavistock, London.

—— 1994, 'Modelling ethnic and national relations', *Ethnic and Racial Studies*, vol. 17, no. 1, pp. 1–19.

Barth, F. 1969, *Ethnic Groups and Boundaries: The Social Organization of Culture Difference*, Allen & Unwin, Sydney.

Bertelli, L. 1985, 'Italian families', in D. Storer (ed.), *Ethnic Family Values in Australia*, Prentice Hall, Sydney, pp. 33–73.

Billig, M. 1995, *Banal Nationalism*, Sage, London.

Blainey, G. 1984, *All for Australia*, Methuen Haynes, Sydney.

Bottomley, G. 1991, 'Representing the "second generation": Subjects, objects and ways of knowing', in G. Bottomley, M. de Lepervanche & J. Martin (eds), *Intersexions*, Allen & Unwin, Sydney, pp. 92–109.

Calwell, A. 1972, *Be Just and Fear Not*, Lloyd O'Neill, Melbourne.

Cohen, A. (ed.) 1974, *Urban Ethnicity*, Tavistock, London.

Collins, J., Noble, G., Poynting, S. & Tabar, P. 2000, *Kebabs, Kids, Cops and Crime: Youth, Ethnicity and Crime*, Pluto Press, Sydney.

Connor, W. 1993, 'Beyond reasons: The nature of the ethnonational bond', *Ethnic and Racial Studies*, vol. 16, pp. 373–89.

Department of Immigration and Multicultural and Indigenous Affairs (DIMIA) 2006a, *The Evolution of Australia's Multicultural Policy*, <www.immi.gov.au/facts/06evolution.htm> (accessed 9 February 2006).

—— 2006b, *Fact Sheets: Population Projections*. <www.immi.gov.au/facts/15population> (accessed 10 February 2006).

Department of Immigration and Citizenship (DIAC) 2008a, *Permanent Departures Data*, <www.immi.gov.au/media/statistics/statistical-info/oad/perm-dep/permdepa.htm> (accessed 15 November 2009).

—— 2008b, Australian Multicultural Advisory Council (AMAC), <www.immi.gov.au/about/stakeholder-engagement/national/advisory/amac> (accessed 15 November 2009).

Dunn, K.M., Forrest, J., Burnley, I. & Mcdonald, A. 2004, 'Constructing racism in Australia', *Australian Journal of Social Issues*, vol. 39, no. 4, pp. 409–30.

Dunn, K.M., Klocker, N. & Salabay, T. 2007, 'Contemporary racism and Islamaphobia in Australia', *Ethnicities*, vol. 7, no. 4, pp. 564–89.

Eriksen, T.H. 2002, *Ethnicity and Nationalism: Anthropological Perspectives*, 2nd edn, Pluto Press, London.

Gans, H. 1979, 'Symbolic ethnicity: The future of ethnic groups and cultures in America', *Ethnic and Racial Studies*, vol. 2, no. 1, pp. 1–20.

—— 1994, 'Symbolic ethnicity and symbolic religiosity: Towards a comparison of ethnic and religious acculturation', *Ethnic and Racial Studies*, vol. 17, no. 4, pp. 577–92.

Geertz, C. 1973, *The Interpretation of Cultures*, Fontana, London.

Glazer, N. & Moynihan, D.P. (eds) 1975, *Ethnicity: Theory and Experience*, Harvard University Press, Cambridge, MA.

Hage, G. 1998, *White Nation: Fantasies of White Supremacy in a Multicultural Society*, Pluto Press, Sydney.

Hastings, A. 1997, *The Construction of Nationhood: Ethnicity, Religion and Nationalism*, Cambridge University Press, Cambridge.

Hobsbawm, E. & Ranger, T. (eds) 1997, *The Invention of Tradition*, Cambridge University Press, Cambridge.

Hollinger, D. 1995, *Postethnic America: Beyond Multiculturalism*, Basic Books, New York.

Hughes, R. 1987, *The Fatal Shore: A History of the Transportation of Convicts to Australia, 1787–1868*, Collins Harvill, London.

Hugo, G., Rudd, D. & Harris, K. 2003, *Australia's Diaspora: Its Size, Nature and Policy Implications*, CEDA Information Paper No. 80, Canberra.

Hutchinson, J. & Smith, A.D. (eds) 1996, *Ethnicity*, Oxford University Press, Oxford.

Jamrozik, A., Boland, C. & Urquhart, R. 1995, *Social Change and Cultural Transformation in Australia*, Cambridge University Press, Cambridge.

Jenkins, R. 1996, 'Ethnicity etcetera: Social anthropological points of view', *Ethnic and Racial Studies*, vol. 19, no. 4, pp. 807–22.

Jones, G.W. 2003, 'White Australia, national identity and population change', in L. Jayasuriya, D. Walker & J. Gothard (eds), *Legacies of White Australia*, University of Western Australia Press, Perth, pp. 110–28.

Jupp, J. 2002, *From White Australia to Woomera: The Story of Australian Immigration*, Cambridge University Press, Cambridge.

Kerbaj, R. 2007, 'Police say Sudanese a gang threat', *The Australian*, 5 January.

Khoo, S-E., McDonald, P. & Giorgas, D. 2002, *Second Generation Australians: Report for the Department of Immigration and Multicultural and Indigenous Affairs*, Centre for Population and Urban Research, Melbourne.

Knopfelmacher, F. 1982, 'The case against multiculturalism', in R. Manne (ed), *The New Conservatism in Australia*, Oxford University Press, Melbourne, pp. 40–64.

Markus, A. 1994, *Australian Race Relations*, Allen & Unwin, Sydney.

McNeill, W.H. 1986, *Polyethnicity and National Unity in World History*, University of Toronto Press, Toronto.

Modood, T. 2005, *Multicultural Politics: Racism, Ethnicities and Muslims in Britain*. University of Minnesota Press and University of Edinburgh Press, Minneapolis, MN and Edinburgh.

Okamura, J.Y. 1981, 'Situational ethnicity', *Ethnic and Racial Studies*, vol. 4, no. 4, pp. 452–65.

Pallotta-Chiarolli, M. & Skrbis, Z. 1994, 'Authority, compliance and rebellion in second generation cultural minorities', *Australia and New Zealand Journal of Sociology*, vol. 30, no. 3, pp. 259–72.

Portes, A. & MacLeod, D. 1996, 'Educational progress of children of immigrants: The role of class, ethnicity and school context', *Sociology of Education*, vol. 69, no. 4, pp. 255–75.

Portes, A. & Zhou, M. 1993, 'The new second generation: Segmented assimilation and its variants', *The Annals of the American Academy of Political and Social Science*, vol. 530, pp. 74–96.

Poynting, S., Noble, G., Tabar, P. & Collins, J. 2004, *Bin Laden in the Suburbs: Criminalising the Arab Other*, Federation Press, Sydney.

Price, C.A. 1994, 'Ethnic intermixture in Australia', *People and Place*, vol. 2 no. 4, pp. 8–11.

Raz, J. 1994, 'Liberal multiculturalism', *Dissent*, Winter, pp. 67–79.

Skrbis, Z. 1999, *Long-distance Nationalism: Diasporas, Homelands and Identities*, Ashgate, Aldershot.

Sollors, W. (ed.) 1989, *The Invention of Ethnicity*, Oxford University Press, New York.

Song, M. 2003, *Choosing Ethnic Identity*, Polity Press, Cambridge.

van den Berghe, P. 1981, *The Ethnic Phenomenon*, Elsevier, New York.

—— 1995, 'Does race matter?', *Nations and Nationalism*, vol. 1, no. 3, pp. 357–68.

Viviani, N. 1984, *The Long Journey: Vietnamese Migration and Settlement in Australia*, Melbourne University Press, Melbourne.

—— (ed.) 1992, *The Abolition of the White Australia Policy: The Immigration Reform Movement Revisited*, Centre for the Study of Australia-Asia Relations, Griffith University, Brisbane.

Waters, M. 1990, *Ethnic Options*, University of California Press, Berkeley, CA.

Weber, M. 1978/1920, 'Ethnic groups', in G. Roth & C. Wittich (eds), *Economy and Society 1*, University of California Press, Berkeley, pp. 389–95.

White, R. & Perrone, S. 2001, 'Racism, ethnicity and hate crime', *Communal/Plural*, vol. 9, no. 2, pp. 161–81.

Zevallos, Z. 2003, '"That's my Australian side": The ethnicity, gender and sexuality of young Australian women of South and Central American origin', *Journal of Sociology*, vol. 39, no. 1, pp. 81–98.

CHAPTER 14

Race and reconciliation in Australia

Meredith Green and Sherry Saggers

The outstation

It is April 2009 and we are surrounded by Indigenous children and young people aged from a few months to their mid-twenties in the community's youth centre in central Australia. It is a bare-bones, multi-roomed, concrete-block construction covered in graffiti. In one small room there are three computers, a Playstation, and a couch. The computers are highly prized and the kids compete to play *Solitaire* or *Grand Theft Auto* at high volume, or listen to downloaded music. In another room there is a more sophisticated computer and two of the young adults are editing a film they are making about young people in their community. It includes clips of bush trips they have made to traditional country, and also of the local sporting carnival. They are a couple with two young children, and the baby is eagerly minded by the younger children while her parents work. Out in the breezeway, two boys aged about six or seven kick around a soccer ball, while two young girls of about the same age colour in sheets from a drawing book. One picture is of a boy surfing, which seems incongruous as few in this community have ever seen the sea, but this does not seem to faze her. Also present are two young non-Indigenous youth workers who are employed to engage with the young people to divert them from petrol sniffing, alcohol, and other drugs. They are supposed to be focusing on the adolescents, but there are always little kids at the youth centre so they have adapted to this by providing some age-appropriate activities for them. The youth centre is dusty and dilapidated, and I comment to one of the youth workers that it is a pity that this community is not getting funds for a new youth centre, like a nearby community hopes to. 'No,' he says, 'the people are really proud of this. They built it themselves.'

Introduction

Like the children and young people in the vignette above, Indigenous people throughout Australia are making lives for themselves while facing complex challenges, from practical considerations such as trying to stay alive longer and attain a decent standard of living to questions about their identities and relationships with other Australians. Understanding the position of Indigenous people in contemporary Australia requires some knowledge of the past and how the past continues to influence subsequent generations of people.

Race and reconciliation are integral to this understanding. Theories of race, once fixed, have become more complex; invalid biological and 'science'-based frameworks have been replaced by theories focusing on the multiple social meanings of race and race relations. These have implicitly framed the development of policies addressing Indigenous disadvantage, from the earliest attempts to 'protect' Indigenous people by forcing them into missions and reserves to the current mainstreaming of services and challenges to communal land title. The notion of reconciliation—the bringing together of Indigenous and non-Indigenous Australians—encourages us to think about the practical and symbolic dimensions of the past and present, and what is required to address persistent inequality.

Indigenous people and inequity

The disadvantages Indigenous Australians face have come under regular scrutiny over the last decade. In 2000, the Australian government had to appear before the United Nations Committee on the Elimination of Racial Discrimination (Markus 2001). The issues highlighted in this forum included the lack of Indigenous participation in decisions affecting land rights and the high rates of imprisonment of Indigenous Australians. In 2004, Michael Long, a well-known Indigenous AFL player, walked 650 kilometres from Melbourne to Canberra to meet with John Howard and raise his concerns about the poor health, education, and employment status of Indigenous people. In 2007, the 'Close the Gap' campaign was launched, calling for all federal, state and territory governments to close the life-expectancy gap between the Indigenous and non-Indigenous population within 25 years.

Table 14.1 highlights the current state of affairs by showing a selection of health and socioeconomic indicators for Australia's Indigenous and non-Indigenous population as reported in the Productivity Commission report *Overcoming Indigenous Disadvantage: Key Indicators 2009* (SCRGSP 2009).

Table 14.1: Health and social indicators

Indicator	Indigenous	Non-Indigenous	Comparison
Life expectancy	Males: 67 years Females: 73 years	Males: 79 years Females: 83 years	Indigenous people die ten to twelve years earlier.
Weekly income	$398 (gross household)	$612 (gross household)	Non-Indigenous household income is 55% higher.
Unemployment rate	16%	5%	Indigenous unemployment is three times higher.
Year 12 completion	36% of 19-year-olds	74% of 19-year-olds	Double the proportion of non-Indigenous 19-year-olds complete Year 12.
Imprisonment rate	1769 per 100 000 people	13 per 100 000 people	Indigenous people are 136 times more likely to be imprisoned.

While the Steering Committee for the Review of Government Service Provision (SCRGSP) did not deliver a positive report to the government in 2009, according to Jon Altman, Nicholas Biddle and Boyd Hunter (2008), outcomes for Indigenous people have been improving continually since Indigenous people were first included in the Census, with the exception of labour force status and health. The Human Rights and Equal Opportunity Commission (HREOC) also points to improved outcomes in its latest report; however, it highlights the continued gaps between Indigenous and non-Indigenous people and the significant and rapid improvements in the health of non-Indigenous Australians compared with that of Indigenous Australians. For example, for the general population, deaths from cardiovascular disease have decreased by 30 per cent since 1991, while it remains the greatest cause of death for Indigenous people and the area where the largest gap of inequality exists. Alcohol and other drug use also contribute to high rates of violence, child abuse, and neglect in Indigenous communities. In 2007–08, spouse or partner violence contributed to the hospitalisation of 4.8 of every 1000 Indigenous people, compared with 0.2 of every 1000 non-Indigenous people. Children fared particularly badly, with 35 cases of substantiated abuse or neglect for every 1000 Indigenous children, compared with five cases for every 1000 non-Indigenous children (SCRGSP 2009). While these figures are alarming, the issue of child abuse and neglect is too frequently sensationalised—as in the Howard government's response to Patricia Anderson and Rex Wild's (2007) report on child safety in the Northern Territory, *Little Children are Sacred* (cf. Behrendt 2008).

The historical context of contemporary disadvantage

Disadvantage has historical antecedents. To understand the contemporary position of Indigenous people, it is necessary to know something of the societies that flourished in Australia before the European invasion and **colonisation**, and the impact on those societies of subsequent generations of people. As hunter-gatherers, Indigenous people lived in small, semi-nomadic groups in very diverse geographic settings—ranging from the tropical north to the arid centre and temperate south. They were born into complex kinship structures and believed their world was created by mythic beings whose laws must be maintained for society to function well. This way of life had existed for at least 60 000 years, and there is good evidence to suggest that, at the time of first contact, Indigenous Australians were healthier than the average European (Saggers 2003).

colonisation/colonialism
When a nation takes and maintains power over a territory that is outside its boundaries, based on a belief of superiority over those being colonised. See also *imperialism*.

At this time, there were competing philosophical understandings of indigenous peoples of the world. At one extreme, influenced by accounts of Polynesian societies by Jean-Jacques Rousseau, they were seen as 'noble savages', admired for their courage and freedom, living Arcadian lives of simplicity and contentedness. At the other extreme, they were viewed as the lowest form of humankind on the 'Great Chain of Being', a hierarchically ordered scheme of all living things that had Europeans at its apex. Indigenous Australians, in part because of their failure to domesticate their landscape, were ascribed to this latter category. Believed to be biologically inferior, as demonstrated through **phrenology**, they could be violently supplanted by Europeans as an inevitable outcome of social Darwinism. Natural selection, the process proposed by Charles Darwin to explain the evolution of the natural world, had been applied by Herbert Spencer to human societies in the context of the 'survival of the fittest', to use Spencer's term, and this **scientific racism** was used to 'prove' that Indigenous Australians were biologically and culturally inferior to the colonisers (Anderson 2003; Broome 2001; Markus 1994).

phrenology
A pseudo-scientific theory that determined personality traits and intellect on the basis of the shape and size of the head and brain.

scientific racism
The use of scientific research to express and support racist ideologies.

Although there are some accounts of peaceful exchanges at first contact, once it was clear that the invaders meant to stay and control both the land and its people, Indigenous Australians fought back (Attwood 1989; Broome 2001; Reynolds 1989). The impact of this frontier conflict is highly contested, with Henry Reynolds' (1987a) estimates of 20 000 Indigenous deaths compared with 1000 to 3000 European deaths regarded by some as exaggerated 'guess-timates', reflecting a **black armband** view of Australian history designed to fuel national guilt among the non-Indigenous population (Altman 2004; Markus 2001). In what has come to be termed the history wars, a bitter debate rages about how the past should be interpreted (Manne 2003; Windschuttle 2002). This includes a reconsideration of the notion of *terra nullius*, the term popularised by Reynolds (1987b) to describe the 'land belonging to no-one' (p. 12) that the British possessed in 1788. In 1992 the *Mabo* case found 'that common law could recognise the survival of indigenous property rights following the assumption of British sovereignty' (Markus 2001, p. 38). This effectively overturned the notion of *terra nullius* and made pursuing native title claims or compensation possible and a legal right. Recently, the historical origins of the term and its possible misuse in legal decisions about land rights have been raised (Connor 2003).

black armband history
First used by historian Geoffrey Blainey to describe historical accounts highlighting the sadness and shame of Australian history.

terra nullius
Latin term for a land belonging to no one and purportedly used to justify the colonisation of Australia. See also *colonialism* and *imperialism*.

In spite of these vitriolic debates, what is indisputable is that the Indigenous population was decimated within 150 years of European colonisation. In Queensland, for instance, the estimated pre-contact population of 120 000 was reduced to 22 500 by 1927 (Smith 1980). Introduced illnesses such as influenza, smallpox, and tuberculosis killed more people than direct conflict, and international criticism of the devastation to Indigenous populations forced governments to address the question of what was to be done. Indigenous Australians were considered irrelevant to the development of the colony, and 'dispersed' to ensure a swift taking up of land and the establishment of order and productivity. By the beginning of the twentieth century, most Indigenous people had been dispossessed of their land and means of economic independence, and were forced to survive at the margins of the dominant society, where they were discriminated against and excluded socially and economically through the operation of an informal caste system (Broome 2001; Markus 1994; Reynolds 1989).

Policy context of disadvantage

Between the 1830s and the 1970s, Indigenous and non-Indigenous relations were framed by the 'missionary project', which originated out of the government's policy of **protection**. The aim of protectionist policies was to 'smooth the pillow' of these people who were predicted by social Darwinism to be dying out (Attwood 1989; Broome 2001; Markus 1994; Reynolds 1989). Mission and government reserves—so-called 'outback ghettos' (Brock 1993, p. 1)—were established for Indigenous people, who were either forcibly moved there or voluntarily relocated because they were unable to live on their own country. These total institutions (Goffman 1962) controlled every waking moment of the inmates, while missionaries sought to improve the lot of these dispossessed people and 'bring the light' to them (Attwood 1989). Despite the cruelty suffered by many Indigenous people in missions, some maintain a sense of loyalty and warmth towards this way of life, particularly when contrasted with the disorder of much contemporary Indigenous life. These favourable memories are perhaps not surprising as people struggle to represent themselves as survivors, rather than simply victims (Peters-Little 2000).

protection
The separation of Australian Indigenous people into missions and government reserves based on the belief that Indigenous people were a dying race and would not survive in white society alone.

By 1937, as the Indigenous population decline was stemmed, Indigenous people were considered 'Stone-Age' survivors who required a different policy response, and assimilation was implemented in place of protection (Anderson 2003; Broome 2001; Curthoys 2000; Markus 1994). Culturally and biologically, Indigenous people were to be systematically absorbed into white Australian society so as to maintain the moral and aesthetic purity of this proudly white nation. Particular attention was given to the growing population of 'mixed-blood' or 'part-Aboriginal' people, who were seen as trapped between two worlds with no culture (Anderson 2003). It was believed that these people could assimilate into non-Indigenous Australia and take on the rights and responsibilities of non-Indigenous Australians because of their superior white blood (Broome 2001; Curthoys 2000; Markus 1994).

Under this policy, children of mixed descent were forcibly removed from their parents to boarding houses to prevent the transmission of Indigenous cultural knowledge, which was seen as an impediment to their assimilation (Attwood 1989; Broome 2001). Through their European education, Indigenous children were encouraged to scorn their own culture and replace it with Christianity and 'civilised' European notions such as industry and order (Attwood 1989). These children comprise the 'Stolen Generations' documented in the *Bringing Them Home* report (HREOC 1997), a national review of the impact of removal on the lives of contemporary Indigenous people (Haebich 2000). Indigenous people who had exemplary employment and no police records were issued with an Exemption Certificate, which meant they technically were able to keep their children, live in towns freely, and receive welfare, becoming 'honorary whites' (Broome 2001; Markus 1994). Those without such privileges experienced exclusionary practices and continued to be segregated from mainstream society, in a similar way to the apartheid practices of South Africa (Saggers 2003).

Addressing discrimination and disadvantage

In 1972, Indigenous people symbolically expressed their resistance to the oppressive policies and practices discussed above with the establishment of the Aboriginal Tent Embassy in Canberra (Broome 2001; Markus 1994). On a national and international scale, the 1970s witnessed a shift away from overt discriminative policies and towards efforts addressing the disadvantage caused by them. Journalist Nicholas Rothwell describes the late 1960s and early 1970s as a time when 'competing templates for conceiving the indigenous' emerged (Rothwell 2008). In Australia, policy solutions to the inequities and disadvantage are still being searched for, recycled, and consulted on. The timeline in Table 14.2 below lists the key policy changes from the 1970s to 2009 within which the competing paradigms of pro- versus anti-welfare, assimilation versus **self-determination**, and individual responsibilities versus **social determinants** can be identified (Aldrich, Zwi & Short 2007).

self-determination
The right for people, within international law, to have control over their economic, social, and cultural development, and forms and structures of governance.

social determinants
The historical, political, economic, social, and cultural factors that directly and indirectly influence systematic discrimination and inequality.

Table 14.2: Timeline of Indigenous policy changes, 1970s–2009

Era	Events
Self-determination	• The Aboriginal Tent Embassy is established in Canberra in 1972. • The Whitlam Labor government gives Indigenous communities control of their own affairs (Broome 2001; Markus 2001). • The first elected Indigenous advisory body to the government—the National Aboriginal Consultative Committee (NACC)—is established (Altman 2004; Pratt & Bennett 2004).
Self-governance	• In 1990, the Australian and Torres Strait Islander Commission (ATSIC) is established and given power over the management of Indigenous affairs (Hannaford, Huggins & Collins 2003; Pratt & Bennett 2004).
Reconciliation	• The findings of the 1991 Royal Commission into Aboriginal Deaths in Custody recommend a process of reconciliation. The focus for the planned ten-year process is addressing discrimination through measures such as recognising Indigenous Australians and their rights as the first Australians (Altman 2004; Council for Aboriginal Reconciliation 1999; Johnson 1991).

Table 14.2: Timeline of Indigenous policy changes, 1970s–2009 *(continued)*

Era	Events
Mutual obligation	• In 2003, the Howard Liberal/Coalition government establishes shared responsibility agreements (SRAs) with individual communities. Communities can 'voluntarily' enter into these in exchange for essential services (e.g. agreeing to shower once a day in exchange for a petrol bowser) (Office of Indigenous Policy Coordination 2005; Pratt & Bennett 2004). SRAs are considered by the government to be a more legitimate form of engagement with Indigenous people compared with ATSIC and reconciliation (Strakosch 2009). • Policies are strongly influenced by Noel Pearson's (2000) view that a lack of reciprocity between the government (and working taxpayers) and Indigenous people receiving welfare has encouraged passivity and dependence. • The importance of Indigenous political representation is further diminished with the abolishment of ATSIC in 2005. ATSIC is replaced by the National Indigenous Council, which consists of individuals appointed by the government (Altman 2004; Pratt & Bennett 2004).
Intervention	• Based on reports of child sexual abuse in the *Little Children are Sacred* report (Anderson & Wild 2007), the Coalition government announces the Northern Territory Emergency Response (NTER) in 2007. The NTER consists of a range of policy- and service-delivery measures, including income management, child health checks, and changes to the permit system. This comes to be known as the Intervention, and continues in a revised form under the Labor government. There is a mixed response from the Indigenous community to the various measures (Central Land Council 2008; NTER Review Board 2008).
Apology and 'Closing the Gap'	• In 2008, the Rudd Labor government apologises to the Stolen Generations; the apology was originally a recommendation of the 1997 *Bringing Them Home* HREOC report. • There is a commitment of $4.6 billion to initiatives targeting early childhood development, health, housing, economic participation, and remote service delivery in Indigenous communities (Australian Government 2009). • The National Indigenous Council is discontinued after its four-year term at the end of 2007. The Rudd Labor government launches a new national representative body for Indigenous people in May 2010, the National Congress of Australia's First Peoples.

While the Labor government maintains the Coalition government's focus on 'closing the gap' and providing services to address inequalities, it appears to recognise the parallel processes of practical and **symbolic reconciliation**—something the Howard government failed to recognise (Altman 2004). Unless the historical and structural interconnections between disadvantage, dispossession, and racism are dealt with, there will only be short-term reactive solutions rather than longer term **structural and institutional change** (Behrendt 2003; Markus 2001). The introduction of SRAs and the Intervention may have highlighted the re-emergence of paternalism and a focus on individual responsibility rather than social determinants (Central Land Council 2008; McCausland 2005; NTER Review Board 2008; Saggers & Gray 2007), such as improved governance (Cowlishaw 2004) and access to land and resources (Altman, Linkhorn & Clarke 2005).

---

reconciliation

Recognising injustice and making changes in a society to redress human-rights violations and to restore harmony and justice.

---

symbolic reconciliation

A focus on achieving equality in terms of having full rights to citizenship of a nation, and access to the same opportunities, and recognising historic injustice and Indigenous rights.

---

structural and institutional change

Changes to the key institutions in a society and the way a society is organised to address the ways in which it disadvantages a marginalised group.

As well as the paternalism of these policies, they have also impinged upon—or, in the case of the Intervention, suspended—the basic citizenship and human rights of Indigenous people (Altman 2007; Altman & Johns 2008; Behrendt 2008). Government exchanges included in the SRAs—such as a petrol bowser—are generally amenities most non-Indigenous communities enjoy as a right of citizenship. A more overt example is the suspension of the *Racial Discrimination Act 1975* and removal of the anti-discrimination law in relation to the NTER (NTER Review Board 2008).

Furthermore, SRAs (Strakosch 2009) and the Intervention (Altman 2007; Altman & Johns 2008; Behrendt 2008) were based on the ideologies of assimilation and mainstreaming, spurious links between 'passive welfare' and child neglect, and the moral rhetoric of saving the children rather than evidence-based research or recommendations from the *Little Children are Sacred* report. According to Jon Altman (2007), the Intervention was designed to discipline Indigenous people, to reduce land rights in order to be able to expand potential for economic development, and to remove the power of democratic Indigenous organisations and impose external control.

Still, there has been considerable support within Indigenous communities for many of the NTER measures, such as plans to improve the health, safety, and well-being of communities (Central Land Council 2008; NTER Review Board 2008). Following the review of the NTER, changes are planned for some measures in accordance with the feedback provided, which highlighted the paternalism and 'shaming' of some measures. For example, previously income management—which involves the withholding of 50 per cent of a person's welfare payment in managed accounts to be spent at prescribed stores—was compulsory. It is now planned to be a voluntary arrangement or imposed only in response to specific child-protection concerns.

Race relations and identity

Today, race has been largely discredited as a biological concept, and biological discourses of race have been supplanted in educated circles (Goldberg 1990; Omi & Winant 1994); however, race has maintained its potency as a social category around which people think and act. Racism is now organised around and expressed through issues such as immigration, welfare, and dysfunctional families (Goldberg 1990). For example, it has been argued that accusations of inefficiency and corruption directed at Indigenous organisations are disguises for racism. This is referred to as **new racism**, or the 'racism without races'. There is no fixed meaning of what racism is; rather, its meaning changes depending on the social structures and discourses of a particular time and place (Omi & Winant 1994).

new racism
The organisation and expression of racism around economic and sociocultural differences between dominant and marginalised groups.

As discussed earlier, evolutionary theory was central to early understandings of Indigenous people, who were studied as good examples of 'early humankind' (Attwood 1992). In the 1920s, evolutionism was replaced with structural functionalism, which focused on the different parts of a society, the interrelationships between these parts and how they worked to maintain equilibrium within a system (Swingewood 2000). In Australia, this meant a shift away from studying the racial characteristics of 'primitive man' towards studying the cultural characteristics of Indigenous societies (Cowlishaw 1992). A leading figure within this tradition in Australia was A.P. Elkin, whose work was very influential in Indigenous policy development. Still, most attention was paid to 'traditional' culture and 'full-blood' Aboriginal people; changes in Indigenous communities due to the political and economic forces of colonisation were largely ignored.

Towards the 1970s, structural functionalist theories were considered conservative and unable to deal with the changes in Indigenous society, and a range of alternative theories came to the fore. Structural accounts of racism and race relations focus on class-based analyses, including **Marxist** and **Weberian** views (Bradley 1996). **Marxists** view racial divisions as furthering the interests of capitalists through the exploitation of racial groups' labour, while Weberians view society as stratified in multiple ways and consider race as one of these status distinctions. **Neo-Marxist** analyses of political economies in Australia have included the study of pre-capitalist modes of production and the notion of kinship in traditional Aboriginal society (see Godelier 1978). There have also been neo-Marxist accounts of current Indigenous society, such as Mervyn Hartwig's (1978) analysis of the structural features of domination through the dispossession and appropriation of land. An alternative to

Marxists/Marxism
Those who subscribe to Marx's social theory that changes in human activity—for example, labour—are determined by economic and material factors, such as technology and *class* conflict over material interests.

Weberians
Followers of Weber, who view society as stratified according to three main social determinants—*class*, status (such as level of education), and politics—and who analyse the competition and inequalities between these different groups.

neo-Marxism
Theories that derive from Marx but incorporate diverse notions of power and status.

*CrossLink:
See Chapter 2
for more on
Marx and
Weber and
Chapter 3 for
more on post-
modernist
social theory.*

considering class-based power is Michel Foucault's notion of governmentality and the control of people through the everyday power of institutions, which comes to be thought of and promoted as the norm. An example is Tim Rowse's (1998) study on the colonial practice of rationing clothes, food, and other goods to Indigenous people as a form of control.

Structural accounts, such as Marxism, have been criticised for being inadequate to explain the social and psychological processes of race relations. These inadequacies have been addressed by **postmodernist** approaches, which focus on social meanings in local contexts. Postmodernist investigations into race relations include the exploration of different experiences of disadvantage and responses to it, and the political and cultural resistance of marginalised groups. This has been accompanied by analyses of discourses and deconstruction of socially constructed racial categories and meanings. Postmodernism's move away from structural accounts means it is sometimes not well equipped to deal with material factors related to race relations, such as disadvantage and inequality. **Post-colonialism** has also emerged as a critique of relationships and identities within societies with a colonial past. Homi Bhabha's notion of **hybridity** has been used in sociology to describe contemporary ethnic identities that have emerged from the mixing of racial and cultural categories (Bradley 1996). While Bhabha highlights the identity choices available to contemporary ethnic groups, Indigenous Australian identity is both complex and contested (Cowlishaw 1999).

postmodernism
The culture of postmodernity, referring to the plurality of social meanings and the diversity of social experiences that exist within localised contexts and cultures.

post-colonialism
The study of the issues raised in societies with a colonial past, particularly regarding identity and relationships between the colonisers and the colonised.

hybridity
Where two or more cultural forms are combined to form something new that has not existed before—a mutual grafting that creates an original product.

Indigenous identity and authenticity

Constructions of Aboriginality in Australia have been much influenced by the state (Beckett 1988; Dodson 2003; Finlayson & Anderson 2004). Indigenous identity has been manipulated through a range of policies, and at the same time different constructions of Aboriginality have been used to justify oppressive policies. One example is the construction of Indigenous Australians as pristine, exotic, and ancient to justify the assimilation and cultural genocide of Indigenous people who were not considered pure (Dodson 2003). Importantly, Indigenous people have always had an active role in determining their own identities and challenging colonial constructions (Finlayson & Anderson 2004; Peters-Little 2000). For many Indigenous people, survival and resistance have become essential components of Aboriginality (Peters-Little 2000).

For a large part of our history, Indigenous identity has been based on ideas of innate Indigenous characteristics (Finlayson & Anderson 2004). This biological essentialism denies that Aboriginality is shaped by either cultural meanings or social processes. With race discredited as a biological concept, cultural essentialism took on the task of defining a 'real' Aboriginal in terms of 'traditional' cultural practice (Anderson 2003). The more 'traditional' the cultural practices of a person or group seem, the more authentically Indigenous they are considered to be, while contemporary Indigenous cultures are viewed as racially and culturally contaminated (Moreton-Robinson 2000). These views led many non-Indigenous people to regard some Indigenous land claims as inauthentic and opportunistic, because those making claims were not considered 'real' Aboriginal people (Broome 2001; Markus 1994). Many aspects of what is considered 'authentic' culture correspond to the colour continuum, so the blacker your skin the more authentically Aboriginal you are considered to be (Finlayson & Anderson 2004).

SOCIOLOGY SPOTLIGHT

14.1: Whiteness

Over the last decade, the study of race and race relations has widened to include the white subject, rather than simply focusing on the black 'Other' (Frankenberg 1997; Kincheloe & Steinberg 1998; Nakayama & Martin 1999). This has been referred to as **whiteness**, which is the investigation of power, identity, and differences between white and non-white people. A broad definition of whiteness is 'the production and reproduction of dominance rather than subordination, normativity rather than marginality, and privilege rather than disadvantage' (Frankenberg 1993, p. 236). Whiteness plays an important role in determining how people act and interact, and the study of whiteness offers a way of understanding both how white people continue to dominate and how inequalities are reinforced by whiteness (Nakayama & Martin 1999). In Australia, Aileen Moreton-Robinson (2000) has discussed how the power and privilege of whiteness have affected the way white people practise anti-racism.

whiteness
The invisibility and unquestioned norm of white people's dominance and privilege compared with non-white people in societies such as Australia.

Racism and equality

How is it possible to talk about racism in Australia when we are all equal before the law? Gillian Cowlishaw (1997) claims that: '[r]acism can flourish as a hidden discourse because it is hidden behind the assertion of equality which assumes similarity' (1997, p. 178). She analysed educational assistance provided by governments to graziers and Indigenous people in rural New South Wales in the 1980s. While it was widely known that '[t]hey [Indigenous people] get paid to go to school' (p. 183) under the Aboriginal Secondary Grants scheme (ABSEG, now Aboriginal Study Grants Scheme (ABSTUDY)), far fewer people knew of the financial assistance available to children of isolated families. In 1983, in one area, educational subsidies to Indigenous children were estimated at $870.70 per child, while children of isolated families boarding away from home received an average of $1450 per child (see <www.centrelink.gov.au> for details of current Education Payment Rates for ABSTUDY and Isolated Children's Allowance). Despite this, Cowlishaw tells how ABSEG payments were seen as 'pandering to a special interest group' while the subsidy to isolated children was rarely discussed. Many rural people saw the assistance they received as simply equality of opportunity for those forced to live far from educational amenities enjoyed by other Australians. Race-based payments to Indigenous children and their families, on the other hand, were interpreted as a waste of taxpayers' money and seen as encouraging greater welfare dependency. Transient professionals in these rural towns—nurses, teachers, police, and welfare workers—contributed unwittingly to these discourses on race by emphasising the historical deprivation of Indigenous people and their continuing need for government assistance. They were much less likely to know about or discuss how assistance to Indigenous people compared with subsidies to other, more privileged, groups (Cowlishaw 1997).

Conclusion

Thinking about race and reconciliation, and the issues that confront Indigenous people in Australia today, requires us to consider Australia's colonial history and the impact of past and present policies, as well as struggles of identity. Sociology provides a range of structural and post-structural conceptual frameworks for this analysis, which interrogate the basis of current disadvantage and its meanings for Indigenous people. The challenge for all of us is to assess the extent to which these frameworks facilitate or impede more positive Indigenous futures.

Summary of main points

▶ Despite more than three decades of government intervention, Indigenous Australians still experience significant disadvantage on major social indicators such as health, education, employment, income, and housing.

▶ Contemporary disadvantage can be traced to the colonial policies of exclusion and segregation, underpinned by scientific racism ascribing Indigenous people as biologically and culturally inferior to other Australians.

▶ Race has no biological foundation but continues to be a compelling social construct for social theorists and popular culture alike.

▶ Indigenous identity has been negotiated around dominant notions of biological and cultural essentialism, which have attempted to define what constitutes a 'real' Indigenous person.

▶ Whiteness studies redirect attention to the symbolic meanings of whiteness and how they have shaped power relations.

▶ Contemporary Indigenous social policy has been shaped around contested ideas around rights and representation, and the relative importance of so-called practical and symbolic reconciliation.

14.1 Race in contemporary Australia

(a) What did you learn about Indigenous Australians and the colonisation of this country at school, and how did this influence your views on race and racism?

(b) Think about the impact on contemporary Indigenous people whose family members were part of the Stolen Generations. How might those experiences have shaped their views on family life, education, and relationships with the non-Indigenous community?

(c) In your own experience, what part does race play in the construction of identities of individuals and groups?

Discussion questions

14.1 What are the major indicators of contemporary Indigenous disadvantage?

14.2 What is the so-called 'black armband' view of Australian history and how have the different sides in the 'culture wars' interpreted the historical evidence?

14.3 Identify the major policies framing Indigenous development since European colonisation.

14.4 How do different concepts of race contribute to notions of Indigenous authenticity?

14.5 In what ways has the concept of whiteness changed the study of race and race relations?

14.6 What are the differences between practical and symbolic approaches to reconciliation, and how might these approaches be reconciled?

Further reading

Broome, R. 2001, *Aboriginal Australians: Black Responses to White Dominance 1788–2001*, 3rd edn, Allen & Unwin, Sydney.

Cowlishaw, G. & Morris, B. (eds) 1997, *Race Matters: Indigenous Australians and 'Our' Society*, Aboriginal Studies Press, Canberra.

Grossman, M. 2003, *Blacklines: Contemporary Critical Writing by Indigenous Australians*, Melbourne University Press, Melbourne.

Haebich, A. 2000, *Broken Circles: Fragmenting Indigenous Families 1800–2000*, Fremantle Arts Centre Press, Fremantle.

Moreton-Robinson, A. (ed.) 2004, *Whitening Race: Essays in Social and Cultural Criticism*, Aboriginal Studies Press, Canberra.

Websites

- Aboriginal and Torres Strait Islander Social Justice: <www.hreoc.gov.au/social_justice/index.html>. Reports about social justice and human rights issues facing Indigenous Australians.
- Australians for Native Title and Reconciliation (ANTaR): <www.antar.org.au>. Ways to support reconciliation and native title rights for Indigenous Australians.
- Australian Institute of Aboriginal and Torres Strait Islander Studies: <www.aiatsis.gov.au>. Research and information about Indigenous cultures and lifestyles.
- Centre for Aboriginal Economic Policy Research: <www.anu.edu.au/caepr>. Research on Indigenous people's social and economic circumstances, as well as sustainability and governance in relation to Indigenous people.
- Reconciliation Australia: <www.reconciliation.org.au>. Past and present information on reconciliation in Australia.

Films/documentaries

- *Minymaku Way*, 2001, documentary, directed by E. Glynn, CAAMA Productions. A film about an Indigenous Women's Council and how it is addressing problems in remote Indigenous communities, such as petrol sniffing, as well as how they are working together with non-Indigenous women.
- *Yolngu Boy*, 2001, motion picture, directed by S. Johnson, Australian Children's Television Foundation/Beyond Films. A film about three Aboriginal teenagers struggling with questions about identity as they deal with the tensions between being part of today's youth culture and part of Indigenous culture.
- *Rabbit Proof Fence*, 2002, motion picture, directed by P. Noyce, Rumbalara Films. A film set in 1931 that traces the experiences of three young Aboriginal girls who escape from being trained as domestic servants after being taken from their homes.
- *The Tracker*, 2002, motion picture, directed by R. de Heer, Vertigo Productions. Set in 1922, this film tells the story of two white men pursuing a fugitive with the help of an Indigenous 'tracker'.
- *Crossing the Line*, 2005, documentary, directed by K. Harrison, Ronin Films. Deals with the experiences of two young, white medical students who go to work in a remote Aboriginal community and find their personal and professional beliefs challenged.
- *Vote Yes for Aborigines*, 2007, documentary, directed by F. Peters-Little, Ronin Films. This documentary examines the 1967 Referendum and its contemporary relevance for Aboriginal citizenship rights.
- *Why Me? Stories from the Stolen Generations*, 2007, documentary, directed by R. Cavaggion, Ronin Films. A documentary exploring the 'Stolen Generations'

by focusing on how the lives of five children were affected by the government policy to forcibly remove Indigenous children from the families and culture.

Visit the *Public Sociology* book website to access topical case studies, weblinks, YouTube clips, and extra readings.

References

Aldrich, R., Zwi, A.B. & Short, S. 2007, 'Advance Australia fair: Social democratic and conservative politicians' discourses concerning Aboriginal and Torres Strait Islander peoples and their health 1972–2001', *Social Science & Medicine*, vol. 64, pp. 125–37.

Altman, J. 2004, 'Practical reconciliation and the new mainstreaming: Will it make a difference to Indigenous Australians?', *Dialogue: Academy of the Social Sciences*, vol. 23, no. 2, pp. 35–46.

—— 2007, 'The Howard government's Northern Territory Intervention: Are neo-paternalism and Indigenous development compatible?', Topical Issue No. 16/2007, Centre for Aboriginal Economic Policy Research, Australian National University, Canberra, <www.anu.edu.au/caepr/Publications/topical/Altman_AIATSIS.pdf> (accessed 14 April 2010).

Altman, J.C., Biddle, N. & Hunter, B.H. 2008, *How Realistic are the Prospects for 'Closing the Gaps' in Socioeconomic Outcomes for Indigenous Australians?*, Discussion Paper No. 287/2008, Centre for Aboriginal Economic Policy Research, Australian National University, Canberra, <www.anu.edu.au/caepr/Publications/DP/2008DP287.php> (accessed 14 April 2010).

Altman, J.C. & Johns, M. 2008, *Indigenous Welfare in the Northern Territory and Cape York: A Comparative Analysis*, Centre for Aboriginal Economic Policy Research, Canberra.

Altman, J.C., Linkhorn, C. & Clarke, J. 2005, *Land Rights and Development Reform in Remote Australia*, Centre for Aboriginal Economic Policy Research, Canberra.

Anderson, I. 2003, 'Black bit, white bit', in M. Grossman (ed.), *Blacklines: Contemporary Critical Writing by Indigenous Australians*, Melbourne University Press, Melbourne, pp. 43–51.

Anderson, P. & Wild, R. 2007, *Ampe Akelyernemane Meke Mekarle 'Little Children are Sacred': Report of the Northern Territory Board of Inquiry into the Protection of Aboriginal Children from Sexual Abuse Report*, Northern Territory Government, Darwin, <www.inquirysaac.nt.gov.au> (accessed 14 April 2010).

Attwood, B. 1989, *The Making of the Aborigines*, Allen & Unwin, Sydney.

—— 1992, 'Introduction', in B. Attwood & J. Arnold (eds), *Power, Knowledge and Aborigines*, La Trobe University Press, Bundoora, pp. i–xvi.

Australian Government 2009, *Closing the Gap on Indigenous Disadvantage: The Challenge for Australia*, Department of Families, Housing, Community Services and Indigenous Affairs, Canberra.

Beckett, J. 1988, 'The past in the present; the present in the past: Constructing a national Aboriginality', in J. Beckett (ed.), *Past and Present: The Construction of Aborginality*, Aboriginal Studies Press, Canberra, pp. 191–217.

Behrendt, L. 2003, *Achieving Social Justice: Indigenous Rights and Australia's Future*, Federation Press, Sydney.

—— 2008, *Do Indigenous Australians Enjoy Full Citizen Rights Today?*, Manning Clark House, Canberra.

Bradley, H. 1996, *Fractured Identities: Changing Patterns of Inequality*, Polity Press, Cambridge.

Brock, P. 1993, *Outback Ghettos: A History of Aboriginal Institutionalisation and Survival*, Cambridge University Press, Melbourne.

Broome, R. 2001, *Aboriginal Australians: Black Responses to White Dominance 1788–2001*, 3rd edn, Allen & Unwin, Sydney.

Connor, M. 2003, 'Error *nullius*', *The Bulletin*, August.

Central Land Council 2008, *Northern Territory Emergency Response: Perspectives from Six Communities*, Central Land Council, Alice Springs.

Council for Aboriginal Reconciliation 1999, *How Can We Advance Reconciliation?*, Council for Aboriginal Reconciliation, Canberra.

Cowlishaw, G. 1992, 'Studying Aborigines: Changing canons in anthropology and history', in B. Attwood & J. Arnold (eds), *Power, Knowledge and Aborigines*, La Trobe University Press, Bundoora, pp. 20–31.

——1997, 'Where is racism?', in G. Cowlishaw & B. Morris (eds), *Race Matters: Indigenous Australians and Our Society*, Aboriginal Studies Press, Canberra, pp. 177–89.

—— 1999, *Rednecks, Eggheads and Blackfellas: A Study of Racial Power and Intimacy in Australia*, Allen & Unwin, Sydney.

—— 2004, 'Governing cultural difference', *Dialogue*, vol. 23, no. 2, pp. 47–56.

Curthoys, A. 2000, 'An uneasy conversation: The multicultural and the Indigenous', in J. Docker & G. Fischer (eds), *Race, Colour and Identity in Australia and New Zealand*, UNSW Press, Sydney, pp. 21–36.

Dodson, M. 2003, 'The end in the beginning: Re(de)fining Aboriginality', in M. Grossman (ed.), *Blacklines: Contemporary Critical Writing by Indigenous Australians*, Melbourne University Press, Melbourne, pp. 25–42.

Finlayson, J. & Anderson, I. 2004, 'The Aboriginal self', in P. Beilharz & T. Hogan (eds), *Social Self, Global Culture: An Introduction to Sociological Ideas*, 2nd edn, Oxford University Press, Melbourne, pp. 43–54.

Frankenberg, R. 1993, *White Women, Race Matters: The Social Construction of Whiteness*, University of Minnesota Press, Minneapolis.

—— (ed.) 1997, *Displacing Whiteness: Essays in Social and Cultural Criticism*, Duke University Press, Durham, NC.

Godelier, M. 1978, 'The concept of "Asiatic mode of production" and Marxist models of social evolution', in D. Seddon (ed.), *Relations of Production: Marxist Approaches to Economic Anthropology*, Bass, London, pp. 209–57.

Goffman, E. 1962, *Asylums: Essays on the Social Situation of Mental Patients and Other Inmates*, Aldine, Chicago.

Goldberg, D.T. 1990, 'Introduction', in D.T. Goldberg (ed.), *Anatomy of Racism*, University of Minnesota Press, Minneapolis, pp. xi–xxiii.

Haebich, A. 2000, *Broken Circles: Fragmenting Indigenous Families 1800–2000*, Fremantle Arts Press, Fremantle.

Hannaford, J., Huggins, J. & Collins, B. 2003, *In the Hands of the Regions—A New ATSIC: Report of the Review of the Aboriginal and Torres Strait Islander Commission*, Parliamentary Library, Canberra.

Hartwig, M. 1978, 'Capitalism and Aborigines: The theory of internal colonialism and its rivals', in J. Bloomfield (ed.), *Class, Hegemony and Party*, Lawrence & Wishart, London, pp. 119–41.

Human Rights and Equal Opportunity Commission (HREOC) 1997, *Bringing Them Home: Report of the National Inquiry into the Separation of Aboriginal and Torres Strait Islander Children from Their Families*, HREOC, Sydney.

Johnson, Q.C., Commissioner E. 1991, *The Royal Commission into Deaths in Custody: Final Report*, AGPS, Canberra.

Kincheloe, J.L. & Steinberg, S.R. 1998, 'Addressing the crisis of whiteness: Reconfiguring white identity in a pedagogy of whiteness', in J.L. Kincheloe, S.R. Steinberg, N.M. Rodriguez & R.E. Chennault (eds), *White Reign: Deploying Whiteness in America*, Macmillan, Basingstoke, pp. 3–29.

McCausland, R. 2005, 'Shared responsibility agreements: Practical reconciliation or paternalistic rhetoric', *Indigenous Law Bulletin*, vol. 6, no. 12, pp. 9–11.

Manne, R. (ed.) 2003, *Whitewash: On Keith Windschuttle's Fabrication of Aboriginal History*, Black Inc., Melbourne.

Markus, A. 1994, *Australian Race Relations 1788–1993*, Allen & Unwin, Sydney.

——— 2001, *Race: John Howard and the Remaking of Australia*, Allen & Unwin, Sydney.

Moreton-Robinson, A. 2000, *Talkin' Up to the White Woman: Indigenous Women and Feminism*, University of Queensland Press, Brisbane.

Nakayama, T.K. & Martin, J.N. (eds) 1999, *Whiteness: The Communication of Social Identity*, Sage, Thousand Oaks, CA.

Northern Territory Emergency Response Review Board 2008, *Northern Territory Emergency Response Review Board Report*, Australian Government, Canberra.

Office of Indigenous Policy Coordination 2005, *Indigenous Coordination Centres*, Office of Indigenous Policy Coordination, Canberra, <www.indigenous.gov.au/icc/qa> (accessed 10 December 2005).

Omi, M. & Winant, H. 1994, *Racial Formation in the United States: From the 1960s to the 1990s*, Routledge, New York.

Pearson, N. 2000, *Our Right to Take Responsibility*, Noel Pearson and Associates, Cairns.

Peters-Little, F. 2000, *The Community Game: Aboriginal Self-Definition at the Local Level*, AIATSIS, Canberra.

Pratt, A. & Bennett, S. 2004, *The End of ATSIC and the Future Administration of Indigenous Affairs*, Department of Parliamentary Services, Canberra.

Reynolds, H. 1987a, *Frontier*, Allen & Unwin, Sydney.

—— 1987b, *The Law of the Land*, Penguin, Ringwood.

—— 1989, *Dispossession: Black Australians and White Invaders*, Allen & Unwin, Sydney.

Rothwell, N. 2008, 'Indigenous insiders chart an end to victimhood', *Australian Book Review*, September.

Rowse, T. 1998, *White Flour, White Power: From Rations to Citizenship in Central Australia*, Cambridge University Press, Cambridge.

Saggers, S. 2003, 'Indigenous Australians', in R. Jureidini & M. Poole (eds), *Sociology: Australian Connections*, Allen & Unwin, Sydney, pp. 210–31.

Saggers, S. & Gray, D. 2007, 'Social determinants of health: Defining what we mean', in B. Carson, T. Dunbar, R. Chenhall & R. Baillie (eds), *The Social Determinants of Indigenous Health*, Allen & Unwin, Sydney.

Smith, L. 1980, *The Aboriginal Population of Australia*, Australian National University Press, Canberra.

Steering Committee for the Review of Government Service Provision 2009, *Overcoming Indigenous Disadvantage: Key Indicators 2009*, Productivity Commission, Canberra.

Strakosch, E. 2009, 'A reconsideration of the political significance of shared responsibility agreements', *Australian Journal of Politics and History*, vol. 55, no. 1, pp. 80–96.

Swingewood, A. 2000, *A Short History of Sociological Thought*, 3rd edn, Macmillan, Hampshire.

Windschuttle, K. 2002, *The Fabrication of Aboriginal History*, Macleay Press, Sydney.

CHAPTER 15

Religion and spirituality

Andrew Singleton

World Youth Day 2008

Something curious, by Australian standards, happened one afternoon in July 2008. More than 150 000 young Catholics from around the world assembled at Darling Harbour in Sydney to greet the head of the Catholic Church, Pope Benedict XVI, as he arrived by boat for the tenth international Catholic World Youth Day (called WYD08). These youths—WYD08 Pilgrims—had come from 170 countries to participate in the WYD08 week, a series of events including concerts, daily religious teaching, and a Mass (religious service) with the Pope.

It was a sea of colour and movement as they waited for the Pope to arrive at Darling Harbour. Waving flags and banners, most Pilgrims wore WYD08 clothing and distinctive yellow and orange WYD08 backpacks. To get to Darling Harbour, they had walked through the Sydney CBD, singing religious choruses, clapping and shouting out 'Long live the Pope' in various languages. Along the way, they encountered protesters opposing the church's stance on abortion, homosexuality, and contraception.

When the Pope stepped off the boat, he was greeted with cheers and shouts. Pilgrims surged forward, arms raised, flags waving, digital cameras clicking. His reception was not dissimilar to that of a rock star. Once the Pope was on stage, though, it was clear this was no rock concert but a time for religious devotion. The Pope led a traditional service of the Eucharist (Holy Communion) in which the music was solemn and classical. When he delivered his Homily (sermon), the crowd hushed, listening carefully to his message. Thousands of youths from around the world were proudly and publicly celebrating their faith. Australians are not used to this kind of public expression of religious devotion.

Introduction

For many Australians, World Youth Day 2008 was a distant curiosity, while others outside of Sydney were probably unaware of the event. This is not surprising; only about a quarter of the Australian population identify as Catholics, and the majority of those people do not go to Mass regularly. Many Australians have little time for religion, and those who do often practise it differently than in the past. Some examples of religious and spiritual activity we find now include the following:

- Every Sunday, thousands of people pack into 'megachurches' such as Hillsong in Sydney, Paradise Church in Adelaide, and Riverside in Perth. The services are conducted in auditoriums equipped with video screens and thumping sound systems. The music is loud and modern, the preaching fast-paced and lively.

- Every October, scores of Australian Neo-Pagans, Druids, and Wiccans (practitioners of nature religions) gather together to celebrate the traditional Gaelic festival of Beltane.
- Every Friday at noon, Mosques around the country are packed as Muslim worshippers pray together.
- Every Saturday morning, many hundreds of non-religious people go to a yoga class. Yoga has roots in Hinduism, a traditional religion from India.

Religion in Australia is no longer just about Christianity. More religious and spiritual choices are now available to us—many of which demand a high level of commitment. At the same time, however, a greater proportion of the population declare that they have no religion at all and atheism appears to be more popular than ever before. Sociology, perhaps more than any other academic discipline, helps us document and make sense of these changes. This chapter discusses the sociological study of religion and spirituality in contemporary society.

To begin, this chapter defines religion and spirituality and discusses the particular features of the sociological study of religion. Next, it examines various dimensions of recent religious change in Australia: the decline of Christianity, the growth of other religions, and the apparent interest in alternative spiritualities.

What is religion and spirituality?

It is not unusual for an Australian to declare that football is their 'religion'. Football teams certainly have places of 'worship', devoted followers and heroes with glorious past deeds and creeds; there is even music. For the individual supporter, following a team might give life meaning, purpose, and fulfilment. But it seems counter-intuitive to declare that football is a religion. Is religion not about believing in the transcendent—some being, power, or force that is greater than humans?

Many scholars have attempted definitions of religion. Most of these emphasise that religion is about humanity's relationship with the supernatural, the transcendent, or the otherworldly. For example, American sociologists Rodney Stark and Roger Fink declare that religion 'consists of ... general explanations of existence, including the terms of exchange with a god or gods' (Stark & Finke 2000, p. 278). Australian sociologist Gary Bouma (1992, p. 17) defines religion as 'a shared meaning system which grounds its answers to questions of meaning in the postulated existence of a greater environing reality and its related sets of practices and social organisation'. All religions posit some kind of transcendent existence—that is, life beyond our physical being and the material world. Religion also involves activities (prayer, worship services) and teachings (ideas about how to live and what the universe is like). Most religions also have sacred texts, objects, or spaces. Furthermore, religion always has a social dimension. Humans practise religion together, agree on important beliefs together, and have organisations and institutions (like churches or mosques) that assist individuals to encounter the transcendent.

There are major traditional world religions: Islam, Christianity, Hinduism, Judaism, and Buddhism. These are traditional due to their ancient histories and long-established creeds and practices. All have ancient texts or oral traditions that provide guidance to their followers. Each has a global reach: while it originates in one place, substantial groups of followers can be found on every continent. There are many other traditional religions, but these have remained largely confined to one location, culture or people. Examples include Chinese and Japanese religions or various Native American and Australian Aboriginal religions.

All world religions are organised into various doctrinal divisions and branches. Islam, for example, has a fundamental division between the Sunni and Shi'ite traditions. Sociologists have formulated typologies—conceptual maps—for making sense of these divisions. The most well-known typology in the sociology of religion is the Christian-focused 'church-sect typology' (see Johnstone 2004). The Christian religion has basic doctrinal and organisational divisions between Orthodox, Catholic, and Protestant churches, and further denominational (organisational) divisions—Anglican, Baptist, and Presbyterian, for example. Each denomination subscribes to the traditional Christian beliefs, but has a different emphasis in worship or teaching. Beyond this, there are also <u>sects</u>, which are <u>restrictive in their beliefs and practices</u>, and are more likely to demand that followers adhere to specific behaviours and practices (such as the Amish or the Exclusive Brethren) in order to be counted as true members.

sects
Religious groups with orthodox but restrictive views and practices.

cults
Informal and transient groups, usually based on highly unorthodox religious beliefs and practices, often involving devotion to a charismatic leader.

One such example is the Amish people of the United States, a Protestant sect whose radical anti-modern lifestyle was popularised in the film *Witness* (see Stevick 2007). Beyond sects are **cults**, breakaway groups that come to hold new and unorthodox variations of traditional beliefs and have a charismatic leader (Johnstone 2004). Cults maintain rigid boundaries between 'us' (the true believers) and 'them' (the rest), and are often regarded as heretical by mainstream denominations.

New religions also appear all the time. Some are offshoots from a traditional religion. The Church of Jesus Christ and the Latter Day Saints (the Mormons) is one Christian-derived example. Founded in the United States in the 1830s by Joseph Smith, the Mormon Church has sacred texts in addition to the Christian Bible. After much persecution, Mormons have become an accepted (and highly religious) presence in American, and now Australian, life. Some new religions do not have direct foundations in a traditional religion. The two most well-known new religions of the twentieth century are Wicca (contemporary witchcraft) and Scientology. All of these religions, both new and ancient, are formally organised—they have rituals, institutions, and doctrines.

Religion is also something experienced by the individual. A person participating in a religious ritual, such as a communal prayer, meditation, or singing, may well have an experience of transcendence. This might be a moment of ecstasy, an experience of God as real, or a vision. This 'personal, interior dimension' to religion (Singleton et al. 2004,

p. 250) is traditionally described as **spirituality**. Increasingly, though, spirituality is thought of as something that can happen without organised religion. Now, in both academia and public usage, spirituality refers to any enduring experience or awareness of something greater than the self. This kind of spirituality might be achieved through practices such as yoga, tai-chi, astrology, séances, or Tarot, or a strong commitment to beliefs such as reincarnation.

spirituality
Any enduring experience or awareness of something greater than the self.

Sociologists have a rich tradition of studying religions old and new, cults, sects, and spirituality, but with an approach that is often different from that of other academic disciplines. The next section outlines the main features of the sociology of religion.

The sociological study of religion

Sociology is one of many academic disciplines that study religion. History, psychology, political science, literary studies, and anthropology, among others, all have significant sub-branches that consider different aspects of religion. The multidisciplinary fields of religious studies and theology are devoted entirely to religion. Each approaches the study of religion with a particular emphasis. This section describes how the sociological study of religion proceeds.

The sociology of religion dates back to the earliest days of the discipline. Important early sociological thinkers, like Max Weber and Émile Durkheim, had much to say about religion. Sociological studies of religion focus on the interrelationship between religion and the social world—how religion can be explained and understood through reference to sociocultural factors and social theory. Any aspect of religion can be studied: religious change at a societal level; the contours of personal religiosity; or the functioning of religious organisations, institutions, and communities. No matter what aspect of religion is being studied, the sociologist is concerned with the social aspects of religion.

An excellent example of this approach is Lyn Clark's (2003) work on teenagers, the media and the supernatural. Clark's book draws on more than 100 interviews with teens in an effort to understand the current fascination with the supernatural. She argues that the recent interest shown by conservative churches in the supernatural has actually inspired non-religious teens to explore the occult.

Another dynamic example of this approach is Ralph Hood and W. Paul Williamson's (2008) fifteen-year research into the snake-handling (or serpent-handling) churches found in the South of the United States. These churches take literally a sentence in the Christian Bible that says followers of Jesus will pick up snakes with their hands. This practice, done during regular church on a Sunday, results in snake bites, illness, and sometimes death. Why do people participate in this dangerous practice? Hood and Williamson argue that serpent-handling rituals remind the faithful that theirs is a distinctive community favoured by God.

When reading about the curious case of serpent-handling, many questions come to mind. Does God really want these people to handle serpents? Indeed, does God exist? Should believers interpret that passage in the New Testament literally? When a person handles a serpent, do they fall into a trance that enables them to undertake such a dangerous task? Sociologists do not usually try to provide answers to these theological, existential, or philosophical questions. The idea is that we 'check our beliefs at the door'. James McClenon (1994, p. 2), a sociologist who studies the paranormal, notes that social scientific research makes conclusions that are pertinent to the social domain, not the religious or philosophical ones.

CrossLink:
See Chapter 2
for more on
Weber.

Sociologists of religion also examine the ways in which society, groups, and individuals are influenced by religion. One of Weber's most important works was *The Protestant Ethic and the Spirit of Capitalism* (1930). Weber investigated how religion was related to social changes that took place after the **Industrial Revolution**, and in particular why Protestant Christians, more than Catholics, were so active in the rapid expansion of capitalist enterprise. He concluded that aspects of the Protestant faith were conducive to the conduct of business.

Industrial Revolution
Beginning in England in the late eighteenth century, the Industrial Revolution introduced major changes to work processes and everyday life that resulted in social and political transformations in society. Agrarian economies and lifestyles gave way to a wage-labour system, the separation of home from work, and the urbanisation of the population.

This section has described briefly the sociological approach to the study of religion. At the start of this chapter, a snapshot of religious activity in Australia was presented. The observation was made that religion in Australia is now very different from the way it was in the past. A sociological approach can help us to make sense of these changes.

Religious change in Australia I: Religious affiliation

It is commonly thought that Australia is becoming less religious and more secular. The actual situation is more complex, however. One way we can map this change is by examining data on religious affiliation. Every five years, the Australian Census includes a question about religious affiliation. Religious affiliation is about whether a person identifies as 'belonging' to a religious group or not. The data are very reliable, as almost every member of the population is counted in the Census. But this information cannot tell us about the strength of these ties, or even about how religious a person might be (this is better measured by considering religious practices and beliefs). Indeed, we know that the number of people attending religious services regularly is far lower than the number of those identifying with a religion (Mason et al. 2007). Still, data on religious affiliation can provide important clues about what religion means to Australians.

Table 15.1 presents selected Census data on religious affiliation from 1901 to 2006 and illustrates many important changes in Australia's religious composition.

Table 15.1: Religious affiliation among Australians (% of population)

Census year	Anglican	Catholic	Other Christian	Total Christian (inc. Anglican, Catholic, other Christian)	Other religions	No religion	Not stated/ inadequately described
1901	40	23	34	**97**	1	0	2
1933	39	20	28	**87**	1	0	13
1947	39	21	28	**88**	1	0	11
1961	35	25	28	**88**	1	0	11
1971	31	27	28	**86**	1	7	6
1981	26	26	24	**76**	1	11	11
1991	24	27	23	**74**	3	13	11
1996	22	27	22	**71**	4	17	9
2001	21	27	21	**69**	5	16	12
2006	19	26	19	**64**	6	19	11

Note: Percentages may not add up to 100 because of rounding. The column 'Total Christian' adds together Anglicans, Catholics, and other Christian groups.

Sources: Australian Bureau of Statistics Census data for various years. This table is based on one presented in the 2003 *Year Book of Australia*.

This table shows the percentage of the population in any given Census year that identified with a particular group (e.g. in 2006, 19 per cent of the population said they were Anglican, 26 per cent said they were Catholic, 19 per cent said they were other Christian). The best way to read this table is to look down the columns and see how various groups and categories have changed between 1901 and 2006. Here are the major trends:

- In 1901, some 97 per cent of the population affiliated with a Christian denomination. By 2006, only 64 per cent identified as Christian.
- The percentage of the population identifying themselves with the largest Protestant denomination, the Anglican Church, has dropped dramatically. Since 1971, they have declined from 31 per cent of the population to just 19 per cent.
- Other Christian groups have also experienced a notable decline, especially since 1971. More detailed information about specific denominations is not presented in this table, but these groups include the Uniting and Presbyterian Churches.
- Catholics have fared much better than Protestants since 1971. Catholics are now the largest Christian denomination in Australia.
- The category 'Other religions' (which includes Muslims, Hindus, Buddhists, and Jews) has grown dramatically since 1971. According to the Australian Bureau of Statistics (2006, p. 54), since 1986 the number of Muslims increased three-fold, Buddhists five-fold, and Hindus seven-fold.

- Almost 19 per cent of the population in 2006 said they had no religion. In 1901, it was less than 1 per cent.

nature religions
Religious groups, such as Wiccans and Neo-Pagans, who believe in the sacredness of the earth.

The most important changes have taken place over the last 40 years. World religions apart from Christianity and various **nature religions** like Neo-Paganism and Wicca have grown considerably. But these 'other' religions represent about 6 per cent of the population (ABS 2006, p. 54).

The main story is the rapid decline in affiliation with mainstream Protestant Christianity and the increase in the number of those declaring 'no religion'. The majority of the population has always identified as Christian, but we see that increasing numbers of people do not see this religious identity as important or relevant to them. There is a similar pattern in many countries across western Europe (see Berger et al. 2008). Even the United States—always more religious than Australia—has experienced a decline in Protestant affiliation and an increase in those professing no religion (see Pew Forum on Religion and Public Life 2008).

The sociologist's task is to do more than describe patterns of change. We are also interested in explanation. The growth of religions such as Islam, Hinduism, and Buddhism in Australia is almost entirely due to migration, rather than to conversion by former Christians and those with no religion. After World War II, groups of migrants came to Australia, first from Catholic countries like Italy, then from Islamic countries such as Lebanon and Turkey. This was followed by migration from Buddhist and Hindu countries (e.g. Vietnam, China, Sri Lanka, and India) (see Bouma 2006; Bouma & Singleton 2004). According to Bouma (2006, p. 56), 'with the increase in their numbers came the establishment of well-organised communities … these are not just ethnic communities, but religious communities' with centres of worship, schools, and shops with religious supplies (e.g. Halal meat).

Migration patterns also largely explain the growth of the number of Catholics. Large numbers of the post-war immigrants to Australia were Catholic, originating first from Southern Europe and later from Asia (Bouma & Singleton 2004). Bouma (1992) notes that contributing factors include the higher birth rate among Catholics in the 1950s and 1960s.

Although not shown in this table, it is worth mentioning one Protestant 'success story'. **Pentecostals** are one of the few Protestant groups to have grown over the past two decades. The largest congregation in Australia is a Pentecostal church: Hillsong Assemblies of God in Sydney. Why have the Pentecostals grown when other Protestant groups have declined? Data from various National Church Life surveys show that the main source of growth for these churches is from people 'switching in' from other denominations (Kaldor et al. 1999a).

Pentecostals
Christian groups that emphasise dramatic religious experiences such as speaking in tongues and being 'born again' in Jesus.

Why are formerly mainstream Christians joining Pentecostal churches? One of the most influential (and hotly debated) theories to emerge in the recent sociology of religion is **rational choice theory**, which has enjoyed great popularity among some US sociologists (see Stark & Finke 2000; Johnstone 2004). Rational choice theorists treat religion like an economic system, in which religious organisations compete for 'market share' and where individuals actively seek the kind of religion that meets their particular needs. Those religious organisations that offer the most appealing 'product' are the ones most likely to prosper. Pentecostal churches certainly offer an appealing product, especially for youth: loud contemporary music; a church that looks more like an auditorium; extensive use of video during worship; high-quality, topical preaching; and plenty of young faces. This is far different from the traditional Catholic mass or Anglican Eucharist.

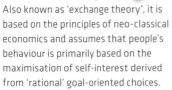

rational choice theory
Also known as 'exchange theory', it is based on the principles of neo-classical economics and assumes that people's behaviour is primarily based on the maximisation of self-interest derived from 'rational' goal-oriented choices.

Notwithstanding the Pentecostal churches' success, people in Australia are moving away from Christianity. Most people who once identified as Christian are not taking up other religions. They are simply not identifying with a religion at all. If identification is declining, is the same true of religious beliefs and practices?

Religious change in Australia II: Religious belief and practice

Several recent national surveys reveal that attendance at religious services in Australia is low. For example, the 2005 World Values Survey (WVS) found that about 20 per cent of the adult population attend services monthly or more often, while about 50 per cent never attend (based on WVS 2005). These are similar to earlier estimates from the 1998 Australian Community Survey (ACS) and the 2002 Wellbeing and Security Survey (see Bellamy & Castle 2004). Not only is attendance at religious services low, it is in decline overall, down from about 44 per cent of the adult population in 1950 to the present figure of about 20 per cent (Kaldor et al. 1999b, p. 21). Most of the decline in attendance has been in the major Christian denominations. Taken together with data about religious affiliation, a clear pattern is emerging: Christianity, the religion of the majority of Australians, is in steady decline. Less is known about attendance levels among other religions, given that Australian social surveys on religion are too small to allow for reliable estimates to be made (Bouma 2006).

What about teenagers? The 2005 Spirit of Generation Y (SGY) survey found that about 25 per cent of teens claim to attend religious services monthly or more often, but this number—like all self-reports of religious observance—is almost certainly an overestimate (Mason et al. 2007, p. 100).

What about religious belief? The 1998 ACS found that 74 per cent of Australians believe in God, but most people see God as being nothing more than 'a life force' (Kaldor et al. 1999a, p. 9). A lower proportion of teens (aged thirteen to eighteen) believe in God. The 2005 SGY survey found that just 49 per cent of teens believed in God; 34 per cent were unsure; and 17 per cent did not believe at all.

What does all this mean for the future of Christianity in Australia? English sociologist Grace Davie (1994) has put forward the idea of 'belief without belonging', the 'persistence of the sacred in contemporary society despite the undeniable decline in churchgoing' (1994, p. 94). While it is tempting to see the widespread belief in God as evidence of the 'persistence of the sacred', having beliefs without religious practice is generally not considered by sociologists to be a particularly meaningful form of religious faith (Mason et al. 2007, p. 55).

secularisation
The process by which religion has come to play less of a role in a society as a whole and in people's lives within that society.

The most commonly cited explanation for this religious decline is that we are witnessing **secularisation**, the process by which religion has come to play less of a role in a society as a whole and in people's lives within that society. Many scholars argue that secularisation is apparent in western Europe, Australia, and even the United States (see Martin 1978; Bruce 2002).

Many theorists see secularisation as linked to the modernisation of society, and the plurality and differentiation that have accompanied modernisation (see Davie 2007). In modern societies, many institutions have emerged, performing roles traditionally done by churches—be it health care, education, or welfare—while alternative meaning systems such as scientific rationalism, consumerism, and humanism have come to the fore (Mason et al. 2007). All of these changes have rendered religion less important in the lives of individuals and society as a whole. A good example of this is the church in the 1950s. At this time, churches—with their associated tennis, cricket, and football teams and regular dances—played a key role in social activities (cf. Evans & Kelley 2004). People now have these needs met in many places apart from church.

Not all sociologists of religion accept the various arguments about the causes or magnitude of secularisation, and it remains the most keenly debated topic in the sociology of religion. Caution is now generally extended when discussing secularisation. Most scholars suggest that it is not an inevitable or totalising process. Indeed, alternative explanations are required to account for the ongoing vitality of some forms of religion in Australia and elsewhere, especially the more conservative and fundamental streams of Christianity, Islam, and Hinduism.

In the previous two sections, we have seen evidence that religion in Australia is clearly not what it was. There is greater religious diversity, but people are also increasingly turning away from religious identification and religious practice, a process we have identified as secularisation. But is there more to the story of contemporary religion in Australia? What about the Neo-Pagans and yoga practitioners discussed in the introduction? It seems that alternative spiritualities have emerged as traditional religion has declined.

Emerging spirituality

A very common idea expressed in recent academic discussion is that exciting new forms of spirituality are emerging as religion in the West declines (Tacey 2003; see also

Heelas & Woodhead 2005; Partridge 2004). Certainly, there are new possibilities and opportunities for spirituality outside traditional religions. Over the past few decades, we have seen the popularisation of **New Age** activities (e.g. Tarot card readings, reiki channelling, crystals, angel cards), the growth in the West of Eastern religions, and the emergence of new religions like Wicca. Other 'mind/body/spirit' options are available, yoga and tai-chi among them. We are now spoilt for spiritual choices, a situation variously described as the 'spiritual marketplace' or the 'spiritual supermarket' (Lyon 2000; Roof 1999). The idea that you can be 'spiritual but not religious' also seems very popular. But how widespread is the emerging spirituality? Is it a legitimate movement, a genuine replacement for religion? It is difficult to measure precisely the extent to which other forms of spirituality are emerging, given that contemporary 'spirituality' appears to be a largely private, self-authenticated phenomenon. We can consider, though, various 'alternatives' to traditional religion and see whether they are indeed thriving.

New Age
Umbrella term for alternative spiritual beliefs and practices popular in the West.

One way in which this interest in contemporary spirituality might find expression is in **alternative religions**. In the 1960s and 1970s, prominent alternative religious groups, such as the Hare Krishnas and Scientology, were either founded or gained significantly in popularity. Recently, nature religions (witchcraft, Druidism, Neo-Paganism, and Wicca) have achieved considerable prominence. In recent years, nature religions have been among the fastest growing religions in Australia (see Mason et al. 2007).

alternative religions
Non-mainstream, new religious movements, such as Scientology or Wicca.

The profile of these religions far exceeds the actual number of adherents, though. The 2006 Australian Census revealed that 0.15 per cent of the population—29 391 people—identify with a nature religion. It is the same in other Western countries: data from the 2001 Census of England and Wales show that only 0.06 per cent of the population identified as a Pagan or Wiccan (based on ONS 2001). Barry Kosmin and Ariela Keysar (2006) estimate that Pagans and Wiccans represent just 0.13 per cent of the US population.

Another way contemporary spirituality might find expression is in various 'spiritual' practices such as yoga, Eastern meditation, tai-chi, and Tarot card reading. Research reveals that these practices are not actually widespread among the general population. The SGY survey (Mason et al. 2007) found that less than 10 per cent of Australian teens and young adults had seriously embraced these activities. Only slightly more adults have done so.

The broader turn away from organised religion may have led to an increase in the acceptance of **supernatural** beliefs. These beliefs might include a belief in ghosts, clairvoyance, astrology, evil spirits, premonitions, and even UFOs. Are people interested in these things? The 1999 AVS found that about 27 per cent of adults believed in reincarnation and about 18 per cent had often or occasionally checked their horoscope (Kaldor et al. 1999a, pp. 9–10). The 2005 SGY

supernatural
Otherworldly, non-religious phenomena, such as ghosts and extra-sensory perception (ESP).

survey collected data about supernatural beliefs among Australian youth. The results are shown in Table 15.2.

Table 15.2: Australians aged 13–24: Selected alternative spiritual beliefs (% of age group)

Believe in	Yes	Maybe	No	Total
Reincarnation	31	22	46	**100**
Communicating with dead	26	19	54	**100**
Astrology	25	18	57	**100**
Psychics and fortune-tellers	21	21	57	**100**

Note: Percentages may not add up to 100 because of rounding or because small proportions of 'Don't know' and 'No answer' responses have been omitted to simplify the table.

Source: The Spirit of Generation Y survey, 2005.

Each row in this table shows the percentage of 13 to 24-year-olds in Australia who definitely, maybe or do not believe in astrology, communicating with the dead, reincarnation, or psychics. By reading down the columns, it is possible to compare levels of belief for these items.

This table shows a substantial level of definite belief among youth and young adults in reincarnation (31 per cent of 13 to 24-year-olds), the possibility of communicating with the dead (26 per cent), and in astrology (25 per cent). Slightly lower is the belief

in fortune-tellers, at 21 per cent. It is also interesting to note the higher percentages of those who do not hold such beliefs (e.g. 57 per cent do not believe in astrology).

But do these beliefs actually amount to anything like a fully realised alternative spirituality? The authors of the SGY survey found that very few of those who firmly hold these beliefs have a strong commitment either to spiritual practices or a clearly articulated alternative spiritual worldview (see Mason et al. 2007). How meaningful is a person's spirituality if it has no basis in serious spiritual practice? Generally, the impact of emerging forms of spirituality is not particularly large in the population as a whole.

15.1: The appeal of Wicca

Wicca—contemporary witchcraft, and a legitimate religion—is growing in countries like Australia, the United Kingdom, the United States, and Germany. It was first popularised by Britain's Gerald Gardner in the late 1950s. Wiccans celebrate significant seasonal and solar changes, while also practising 'magic' by casting spells and preparing potions. Wicca was established in the twentieth century, although its origins are the subject of some debate. Some think that it has roots traceable all the way back to pre-Christian times. Wicca appeals most to younger people—Generations X (born 1966–80) and Y (born 1981–95). Who would be a witch? American Helen Berger and Australian Douglas Ezzy interviewed 90 American, English, and Australian teen witches for their book *Teenage Witches: Magical Youth and the Search for the Self* (2007). Their participants were serious practitioners, and undertook various Wiccan rituals and activities—such as, for example, casting spells. Many had come to witchcraft as part of a general exploration of different kinds of alternative spirituality, and perhaps had their interest piqued by the recent pop-cultural fascination with witches. The particular appeal of Wicca lay in its abiding interest in caring for the self and caring for the environment. Most of these teenage witches did not feel part of the mainstream and many practised the craft alone. The book offers a rare insight into an important new strand of religion in the West.

Conclusion

Sociologists explore the social dimensions of religion. This chapter has made use of various sociological tools to document and explain recent religious change in Australia. Religion in Australia has changed greatly since Federation; we are now a religiously diverse, but also a more secular, nation. Many social factors have caused this change, among them: migration, differentiation, and secularisation. What does the future hold? Religion may not be as important to as many people as it once was, but many religions remain vital, and some are growing, thus ensuring that religion's role in Australian life must continue to be studied.

Summary of main points

▶ Religion and spirituality are now understood to be different from one another.

▶ Sociologists explain and understand religion through reference to sociocultural factors and social theory.

▶ In Australia, we have seen the emergence of greater religious diversity: world religions apart from Christianity and new religions like Neo-Paganism have grown in recent decades.

▶ There has also been a major decline in affiliation with mainstream, Protestant Christianity and an increase in the number of those who have 'no religion'.

▶ While the evidence appears to suggest that Australia is becoming increasingly secular, secularisation theory is still keenly debated by scholars.

▶ We have more spiritual alternatives available to us, but these are not a replacement for religion.

15.1 Religious, spiritual or secular

SOCIOLOGICAL REFLECTION

Think sociologically about your own religious or spiritual beliefs. Consider how what you believe is similar to or different from the beliefs of your peers and your parents.

(a) Are you religious, spiritual, or secular?

(b) What are your religious and supernatural beliefs?

(c) What were your experiences of religion when growing up? How does this influence what you believe now?

Discussion questions

15.1 Census data show that Australian young adults (18 to 35-year-olds) are the age group most likely to declare they have no religion, and yet are those most attracted to alternative religions like Wicca. Why?

15.2 What evidence can you find of secularisation in public life?

15.3 Politicians appear as happy now as at any other time in recent history to declare openly their religious affiliation. Why might this be the case?

15.4 What role do the media play in popularising supernatural beliefs?

15.5 Have movies like *Harry Potter* and TV shows like *Charmed* made witchcraft more popular among teens?

15.6 To what extent are people creating their own 'mix-and-match' spirituality, drawing on eclectic beliefs and practices?

Further reading

Berger, H. & Ezzy, D. 2007, *Teenage Witches: Magical Youth and the Search for the Self*, Rutgers University Press, Piscataway, NJ.

Bouma, G.D. 2006, *Australian Soul: Religion and Spirituality in the 21st Century*, Cambridge University Press, Melbourne.

Carrette, J. & King, R. 2005, *Selling Spirituality: The Silent Takeover of Religion*, Routledge, London.

Heelas, P. & Woodhead, L. 2005, *The Spiritual Revolution: Why Religion is Giving Way to Spirituality*, Blackwell, Oxford.

Mason, M., Singleton, A. & Webber, R. 2007, *The Spirit of Generation Y: Young People's Spirituality in a Changing Australia*, Garratt Publishing, Melbourne.

Smith, C. & Denton, M.L. 2005, *Soul Searching: The Religious and Spiritual Lives of American Teenagers*, Oxford University Press, New York.

Films/documentaries

- *The Root of All Evil*, 2006, television documentary, directed by R. Barnes, Channel 4 Television Corporation, UK. Famous scientist and atheist Richard Dawkins presents a wide-ranging critique of mainstream religions.
- 'The Mormons', *Frontline*, 2007, television series episodes, directed by H. Whitney, Public Broadcasting Service (PBS). Masterful history of the Mormons, regarded by Christians as a heretical group but now part of the mainstream religious landscape. <www.pbs.org/mormons/view>.
- *Y God*, 2008, television documentary, directed by B Lucas, Special Broadcasting Service (SBS). Examines the ways in which young Australians are religious, spiritual, and secular. <http://programs.sbs.com.au/mygeneration/#/ygod/watch>.
- 'The Atheists', *Compass*, 2009, television episode, produced by D. Volaric, Australian Broadcasting Corporation (ABC). *Compass* is ABC TV's religious affairs show. This episode features interviews with prominent atheists. This and many other *Compass* episodes can be viewed online: <www.abc.net.au/compass/s2517600.htm>.

Websites

- Australian Bureau of Statistics (ABS), Census data online: <www.abs.gov.au/websitedbs/d3310114.nsf/home/census+data>. Conduct your own online analysis of religion in Australia using Census data.
- The World Values Survey: <www.worldvaluessurvey.org>. Longitudinal data on religion from many countries. Conduct your own comparative analysis online.
- Social Science Research Council (SSRC), 'Immanent Frame' blog: <http://blogs.ssrc.org/tif>. Blog discussing religion, secularism, and society.

Visit the *Public Sociology* book website to access topical case studies, weblinks, YouTube clips, and extra readings.

References

Australian Bureau of Statistics 2003, *Year Book Australia 2003*, cat. no. 1031.0, ABS, Canberra.

—— 2006, *A Picture of the Nation*, cat. no. 2070.0, ABS, Canberra.

Bellamy, J. & Castle, K. 2004, *2001 Church Attendance Estimates*, NCLS Occasional Paper 3, NCLS Research, Sydney.

Berger, H. & Ezzy, D. 2007, *Teenage Witches: Magical Youth and the Search for the Self*, Rutgers University Press, Piscataway, NJ.

Berger, P., Davie, G. & Fokas, E,. 2008, *Religious America, Secular Europe? A Theme and Variations*, Ashgate, Aldershot.

Bouma, G.D. 1992, *Religion: Meaning, Transcendence and Community in Australia*, Longman, Melbourne.

—— 2006, *Australian Soul: Religion and Spirituality in the 21st Century*, Cambridge University Press, Melbourne.

Bouma, G.D. & Singleton, A. 2004, 'A comparative study of the successful management of religious diversity: Melbourne and Hong Kong', *International Sociology*, vol. 19, no. 1, pp. 5–24.

Bruce, S. 2002, *God is Dead: Secularisation in the West*, Blackwell, Oxford.

Clark, L.S. 2003, *From Angels to Aliens: Teenagers, the Media, and the Supernatural*, Oxford University Press, New York.

Davie, G. 1994, *Religion in Britain Since 1945: Believing Without Belonging*, Blackwell, Oxford.

—— 2007, *Sociology of Religion*, Sage, London.

Evans, M.D.R. & Kelley, J. 2004, *Australian Economy and Society 2002: Religion, Morality and Public Policy in International Perspective 1984–2002*, Federation Press, Sydney.

Heelas, P. & Woodhead, L. 2005, *The Spiritual Revolution: Why Religion is Giving Way to Spirituality*, Blackwell, Oxford.

Hood, R.W. & Williamson, W.P. 2008, *Them That Believe: The Power and Meaning of the Christian Serpent-Handling Tradition*, University of California Press, Berkeley, CA.

Johnstone, R.L. 2004, *Religion in Society*, Pearson, Upper Saddle River, NJ.

Kaldor, P., Dixon, R. & Powell, R. 1999a, *Taking Stock: A Profile of Australian Church Attenders*, Openbook, Adelaide.

Kaldor, P., Bellamy, J., Powell, R., Castle, K. & Hughes, B. 1999b, *Build my Church: Trends and Possibilities for Australian Churches*, Openbook, Adelaide.

Kosmin, B. & Keysar, A. 2006, *Religion in a Free Market*, PMP, Ithaca, NY.

Lyon, D. 2000, *Jesus in Disneyland: Religion in Postmodern Times*, Polity Press, Cambridge.

Martin, D. 1978, *A General Theory of Secularization*, Blackwell, Oxford.

Mason, M., Singleton, A. & Webber, R. 2007, *The Spirit of Generation Y: Young People's Spirituality in a Changing Australia*, Garratt Publishing, Melbourne.

McClenon, J. 1994, *Wondrous Events: Foundations of Religious Beliefs*, University of Pennsylvania Press, Philadelphia, PA.

Office for National Statistics (ONS), 2001, *National Statistics Online: 2001 Census*, ONS, <www.statistics.gov.uk/census2001/access_results.asp> (accessed 21 October 2009).

Partridge, C. 2004, *The Re-enchantment of the West, Vol. 1*, T & T Clark, London.

Pew Forum on Religion and Public Life 2008, *US Religious Landscape Survey: Religious Affiliation: Diverse and Dynamic*, Pew Research Center, Washington, DC.

Roof, W.C. 1999, *Spiritual Marketplace: Baby Boomers and the Remaking of American Religion*, Princeton University Press, Princeton, NJ.

Singleton, A., Mason, M. & Webber, R. 2004, 'Spirituality in adolescence and young adulthood: A method for a qualitative study', *International Journal of Children's Spirituality*, vol. 9, no. 3, pp. 247–61.

Stark, R. & Finke, R. 2000, *Acts of Faith*, University of California Press, Berkeley, CA.

Stevick, R.A. 2007, *Growing Up Amish*, Johns Hopkins University Press, Baltimore, MD.

Tacey, D. 2003, *The Spirituality Revolution: The Emergence of Contemporary Spirituality*, HarperCollins, Sydney.

Weber, M. 1930 [1904–05], *The Protestant Ethic and the Spirit of Capitalism*, trans. T. Parsons, Allen & Unwin, London.

CHAPTER 16

Deviance, crime, and social control

Sharyn Roach Anleu

The social context of deviance

Ambiguity around alcohol use persists in Australian society and permeates public discourse. Sometimes consuming alcohol is deemed deviant, while at other times it is viewed as acceptable. Not everyone agrees about the status of alcohol consumption: some views attract media attention and inform policy, others do not. The point at which alcohol use shifts from acceptable to deviant or from deviant to acceptable is unclear and shifting. A recent magazine cover displays a young white woman dressed in expensive clothes, alone, slumped on the ground holding a champagne bottle to her mouth. The story behind this cover condemns what it labels 'an epidemic of youth binge drinking'. It describes the pervasiveness of binge drinking and suggests causal links with violent assaults and car accidents. The article does not define binge drinking but maintains its problematic status by advising that 'this summer, police [in Melbourne] will deploy a convoy of Hummers to protect its citizens from the bingeing hordes' (Toohey 2008, p. 19). The imagery is that of invasion, the need for security, and a clear-cut distinction between the (abnormal) 'bingeing hordes' and (normal) 'citizens'. The language is emotive: those engaging in binge-drinking behaviour 'are part of a temporarily insane collective, travelling in thirsty, unpredictable swarms' (Toohey 2008, p. 20). A few pages later, in the cooking section, advice is given to readers regarding the appropriate wines to mix with the recipes provided: 'try a pink or light red wine', and 'this refreshing salad needs an equally refreshing liquid accompaniment—a well-chilled 2008 riesling, a glass or two of cold lager . . .' (Herbert 2008, p. 37). There is no intimation that the reader has to be wary of drinking too much, or falling into the binge-drinking category. Alcohol consumption combined with good food is acceptable; it will not result in violence or vomiting, or constitute a threat to others.

Introduction

The term 'deviance' entered the sociological vocabulary in about 1950 and became an umbrella concept encompassing diverse activities and behaviours, including mental illness, crime, juvenile delinquency, drug use, and non-marital sexual relations (Best 2004). This diverse coverage has been a strength as well as a weakness for the sociology of deviance. On the one hand, it allows the same analytic approaches or perspectives to be applied to diverse activities, enabling the identification of similar trajectories and experiences of different rule-breakers—for example, similarities between patients in mental hospitals and prisoners. On the other hand, the parallels between instances of deviance sometimes feel artificial or over-stretched. For example, it may be that the only similarity between someone eating in the library and someone convicted of drug-trafficking is that both have transgressed a rule of some kind, though of course there are significant differences between informal rules of interpersonal behaviour and criminal law. The concept of deviance is a useful tool that can be used to understand and interpret a variety of substantive social issues in many different social settings. The sociology of deviance seeks to understand and explain the process of deviance: who sets the rules, how they are constructed, and why some people deviate from them.

Much of the public attention to deviance is to criminal deviance, rather than to ordinary, everyday examples. Newspaper and television reports often focus on criminal deviance that involves property damage or personal harm. For sociologists, though, the concept of deviance encompasses more than activities that contravene criminal laws and includes any behaviour subject to regulation and control. Deviance and social control are embedded in everyday life.

This chapter provides an overview of the interconnections between deviance and social control by examining two broad theoretical approaches and drawing on contemporary Australian examples. The discussion emphasises that the concept of deviance is broad and does not only encompass criminal deviance or behaviour, or activities assessed by some people as weird, unusual, or exotic. The focus is on the behaviour and activities of individuals or groups, not on the individuals or groups that might be labelled deviant *per se*. The chapter concludes by considering the value and continuing relevance of the concept of deviance.

Often deviance and its management or prevention are built into the social and physical environment, and thus remain unnoticed or normalised. Take the various symbols and signs displayed prominently in public places that indicate acceptable and unacceptable behaviour. Examples include 'no alcohol', 'no smoking', 'no dogs', 'no eating or drinking', and 'turn off mobile phones'. The existence of such signs demonstrates the situational nature of deviance. In other words, all of the prohibited activities can be acceptable—even expected—behaviours in other situations or locations. For example, alcohol use or eating and drinking are certainly not intrinsically deviant, but they are under certain circumstances or in particular locations. Various social norms, including laws, regulate alcohol use. People under eighteen may not purchase alcohol in Australia and it is illegal to sell alcohol to someone under the age of eighteen; illegal to drive a vehicle with more than the prescribed amount of blood alcohol; illegal to consume alcohol in designated dry zones; and unacceptable or inappropriate to consume alcohol in certain social settings. People who consume too much alcohol and become inebriated or those who do not drink alcohol at all are sometimes viewed as deviant by others. Consider what happens when someone declines the offer of a drink at a party or at a bar. Others will likely react by asking why the person is not drinking and seek an explanation for the deviance. Such a question might be followed by joking behaviour as a form of social control. Thus whether an activity or behaviour is considered deviant depends on the rules or expectations that exist in a particular situation.

Deviance can be defined as those activities or behaviours that contravene or break social norms, which can take the form of laws, regulations, guidelines, conventions, expectations, understandings, or other rules. Whenever some people hold others to certain expectations that they do not necessarily share, deviance can emerge. **Norms** vary in the extent to which they are shared or agreed upon, and their existence can be a source of disagreement or conflict. For example, many students might disagree with school rules or university procedures, though they may still comply with them. Deviation from such rules can (though not always) result in some form of sanction or punishment. The analysis of deviance also requires attention to social control; the two concepts go together.

norms
Shared expectations of how people ought to behave or act. They can take the form of laws, regulations, guidelines, conventions, expectations, understandings, or other rules.

Social control

The concept of **social control** refers to all the responses or reactions to deviance that are aimed at reducing or stemming deviance and achieving conformity to particular social norms. Social control can range from a glance or a comment to social exclusion or ostracism. Other concepts, such as discipline, regulation, and governance, point to mechanisms oriented to preventing or circumventing behaviour or activities deemed by some to be inappropriate or deviant. Institutionalised social control is evident in the criminal justice system, which is concerned with the punishment and control of criminal deviance. Social control also occurs within the medical and social welfare systems (see Roach Anleu 2006; Chs 5 and 12).

social control
Refers to all the responses or reactions to deviance that are aimed at reducing or stemming deviance and achieving conformity to particular social norms. Social control can range from a glance or a comment to joking behaviour to social exclusion or ostracism.

It is often assumed that social control follows deviance—that is, deviance occurs and is defined as problematic or disruptive by someone, who then applies negative sanctions with the goal of altering the behaviour to achieve conformity. Social control mechanisms can, however, also anticipate deviance—for example via crime-prevention programs, which seek to deter criminal deviance or inhibit activities defined as anti-social or nuisance before they occur. There are many attempts to attract deviant activity to specific locations which are forms of crime or deviance displacement (Crawford 2003). For example, establishing skate parks is an attempt to move skateboarding away from busy urban streets, used by many people who may consider this activity to be antisocial or a nuisance, to locations where other skateboarders predominate. Skateboarding becomes normal and acceptable behaviour in the skate parks, which usually have codes of conduct, and remains potentially deviant in other locations. Similar observations can be made with regard to graffiti. Many local councils have made specific walls or large surfaces available for graffiti writing in an attempt to channel such activity away from other public and private property.

Social control can take many forms, and sociologists use the term **sanction** to describe the range of informal and formal practices that can be applied. Informal sanctions emerge during social interaction and can include a glance, a comment, joking behaviour, or exclusion from a friendship or other social group, whereas formal sanctions are explicitly articulated in policy and can take the form of a fine or imprisonment issued by the courts. Sanctions can either be positive, in the form of a reward, or negative, in the form of punishment, including deprivation of various kinds. John Braithwaite's (1989) concept of **reintegrative shaming** allows for negative sanctions in the form of shaming to be combined with positive sanctions. The latter seek reintegration to underpin social control strategies.

sanctions
Informal and formal practices applied to individuals (either singly or in groups) and their behaviour as a way of achieving social control and managing or minimising deviance. Sanctions can either be positive, in the form of a reward, or negative, in the form of punishment—including deprivation of various kinds.

reintegrative shaming
A process that attempts to simultaneously shame an offender for their crime and restore them to full participation in society, by making the offender apologise to the victim/s and engage in some form of restitution to the victim/community.

Many new forms of social control and regulation are impersonal and entail sophisticated electronic technology or the contractual form. There is increasing reliance on technologies to regulate individuals and groups. Witness the widespread use of ticket machines and swipe cards that permit access to public transport systems, car parks, and office buildings, and that regulate queue formation in supermarkets, banks, government departments, and other service-oriented enterprises. Bar codes containing the price of an item, passwords or personal identification numbers (PINs) and electronic security gates, X-ray machines and closed-circuit televisions (CCTV) in airports and other locations considered to be at high risk of violent (including terrorist) attack restrict the opportunity for dispute, abuse, and fraud as the user cannot negotiate with the technological system. For the student of deviance, there are at least two things to note in relation to these technological forms of social control:

- The technologies are applied (at least ostensibly) to everyone who comes into contact with the social setting and are not just targeted to potential or actual offenders.
- This type of surveillance is presented as important for all individuals' safety and sense of security and protection, not just for social control purposes.

Other contemporary forms of social control assume an agreement (perhaps subconscious) by a person that she or he will behave or act in the expected manner in exchange for access to certain benefits such as entry to a particular facility. Codes of behaviour or dress that exist at the entrances of cinemas, clubs, hotels, shopping centres, recreational parks, sporting facilities, and so on all assume this contractual form. Entering implies agreement—or at least the agreement to comply—with the code; it involves accepting the terms and forms of regulation, and this applies equally to all who enter. Thus entering implies the choice to accept voluntarily the terms or forms of expected behaviour and the associated regulation in exchange for certain benefits. Complex webs of such informal contracts exist in everyday life that constrain individuals' activity and conduct with the aim of securing social order (Crawford 2003).

Theoretical approaches

Theories in the sociology of deviance attempt to answer two different but related questions:

1. Why are some people motivated to deviate from social norms? Here the attention is on individuals or groups who engage in behaviour that transgresses laws, rules, or conventions.
2. Why are some people motivated to define, designate, and sanction some behaviour or activity as deviant? Here the focus is the individuals or groups that define and sanction behaviour, activities, or individuals as deviant, unacceptable, or inappropriate.

Both questions can be applied to the same behaviour or activities. Everyday life is shaped or constrained—indeed, made possible—by laws, rules, or conventions, and by assumptions about social interactions. Some of these rules are implicit and exist in tradition or convention; others are more explicit and are written down as legislation, regulations, or guidelines. Breaches of implicit rules do not normally amount to criminal or illegal behaviour, but nor are they tolerated as evidence of mere difference or plurality. Take rudeness, for example. Recently, a number of high-profile politicians, judges, authors, and other commentators have lamented what they perceive as a decline in good manners and civility; they attribute this to diminishing deference to people in authority. They cite 'rage' of various kinds—road rage, supermarket rage, loudness, aggression, swearing, and using mobile phones in certain settings as evidence of increasing rudeness (Hope 2005).

On the one hand, we can ask why some people behave in a way others find rude and disrespectful. One answer is that expectations about what constitutes rudeness or appropriate behaviour are not shared. On the other hand, we can ask why some people are offended by certain individuals or groups and label their behaviour and activities as rude and disrespectful, and why they subject them to various forms of social control. We can also ask whether the same behaviour or activity is viewed differently according to who is engaging in the behaviour. One observer interestingly comments: 'It is a fair bet that most rudeness throughout history has flowed from the upper classes to the lower, and has not even counted as rudeness—just the proper way to address inferiors' (Carey 2005).

Why are some people motivated to deviate from social norms?

Theories primarily concerned with answering this question accept the social norms, rules, and regulations as given and assume that individuals are aware of what they are, but that they, for whatever reason, choose or are pressured to transgress those norms. Sociological approaches focus on the social circumstances or influences—such as opportunities, deprivations, and inequalities—on individuals or groups that result in their deviation. Psychological approaches focus more on individuals and their personalities to explain deviance. In an early path-breaking and influential essay, Robert Merton (1938) set out to identify the processes through which social structures generate the circumstances in which infringement of social codes constitutes a 'normal response'. He questions why it is that the frequency of deviant behaviour varies within different social structures and why deviations have different shapes and patterns in different social structures. Merton aimed to discover 'how some social structures *exert a definite pressure* upon certain persons in the society to engage in nonconformist rather than conformist conduct' (1938, p. 672, original italics).

CrossLink:
See Chapter 3
for more
on anomie,
Durkheim,
and Merton.

anomie
A concept used by Durkheim for a societal condition in which individuals feel aimless and lack guidance in social norms. Anomie means to be without laws or norms.

Merton hypothesises that deviant behaviour results from a disjunction between culturally defined goals—such as success—to which most members of society aspire, and institutionalised norms viewed as acceptable or legitimate (as defined by the relevant social system) means for achieving the goals. He termed this disjunction **anomie**, or strain, which individuals must accommodate or manage.

Box 16.1 Robert Merton's typology of modes of adaptation

Merton identified five possible forms of behaviour across the conformity–deviance spectrum:

1. *Conformity* prevails when goals are achievable through legitimate means. This response is the most prevalent, allowing the stability and continuity of the society to be maintained. Most people strive for success (however defined) and do so via hard work and occupational achievement.
2. *Innovation* results when the individual aspires to cultural goals such as financial success, but lacks access to institutional means—for example, appropriate skills or educational qualifications. Merton suggests that higher rates of crime occur among working-class and ethnic minorities, who tend toward deviance because of restricted access to the conventional means for success, such as a good job. Some people might acquire lavish homes, expensive cars, and exotic holidays via drug trafficking or other illegal activities.
3. *Ritualism* occurs when the means are followed but the cultural goals lose their relevance. For example, the bureaucrat who rigidly follows organisational rules

continued over

often loses sight of the purpose of those regulations and the overall goals of the agency. It is not uncommon for experienced bureaucrats or people working in customer courtesy roles to be unhelpful and frustrating because they follow organisational procedures that seem to conflict with assistance and the provision of information.

4. *Retreatism*, the least common adaptation, signifies rejection of both culturally prescribed goals and institutional norms by complete withdrawal from society. This category includes psychotics, problem gamblers, homeless people, chronic alcoholics and drug addicts who seem to have dropped out of mainstream society; still, this does not mean that social norms and conceptions of deviance do not exist in their everyday lives.

5. *Rebellion* involves envisaging and seeking a transformed social structure by replacing existing social goals and means.

One criticism of Merton's theory of anomie is that those engaging in deviance seem to be individuals with few resources and opportunities; therefore, the converse assumption seems to be that those people with access to resources and legitimate opportunities would not be motivated or pressured to engage in deviance. A study of white-collar crime led Edwin Sutherland to disagree strongly with this stance. He proposed that a theory of crime must be able to explain the illegal or deviant activities undertaken by high-status individuals as well as crime pursued by members of other social classes. The finding that disadvantaged individuals are much more likely to come into contact with the criminal justice system for ordinary crimes such as theft and assault than are perpetrators of corporate crime is an empirical—not a theoretical—issue. A theory of criminal deviance must explain the emergence of crime across the social structure. Sutherland's 'differential association theory' stresses the importance of relationships and the learning process in understanding the emergence of deviance.

According to Sutherland, deviant behaviour is learnt in the same way as any other behaviour (Sutherland 1983; Sutherland & Cressey 1978). He explains crime in terms of the learning process, not in terms of personality, poverty, stress, or biological or psychological abnormality. He disagrees that crime is a working-class phenomenon and demonstrates that people in white-collar jobs are not immune from criminological influences or deviant tendencies. When interacting with others, usually in primary groups, individuals confront various definitions of behaviour, some of which are favourable to law violation. An excess of definitions favourable to law violation encourages deviance. The impact of these definitions is affected by the frequency, duration, priority, and intensity of associations, and the consequent exposure to definitions favourable to deviant behaviour.

This is the principle of differential association. Associations, not general needs or values, explain criminal behaviour, and Sutherland maintains that it is the job of empirical research, not theory, to explain the existence or distribution of those associations within the social structure.

White-collar crime

White-collar, or corporate, crime periodically captures the public attention, particularly via media reporting. This can be in the wake of corporate collapses and the search for evidence of fraud, embezzlement, or other crimes of dishonesty such as identity theft (see the online case study), or the discovery of individual businesspeople or corporations suspected of corporate offending. One analysis of news reports covering the Enron and WorldCom bankruptcies demonstrates the extent to which such scandals become media events (Williams 2008). The trial proceedings—especially the prosecution case and the sentencing of individuals convicted of these crimes—are also foci of media reporting and public interest (Brickey 2006). A recent high-profile example of corporate misdeeds in Australia is the cartel arrangement between Visy and Amcor, the cardboard manufacturers who agreed not to deal with each other's customers, thereby constituting anti-competitive behaviour (Beaton-Wells & Haines 2009).

The most recent, widely reported, and large-scale case of individual white-collar crime is that of Bernard Madoff—the New York financier who operated fraudulent investment schemes known as Ponzi schemes, which involve paying investors high dividends that are actually drawn from their own investment or from subsequent investors, rather than from profits. He pleaded guilty to charges of securities fraud and money laundering. The scope of the deception seems vast, with prosecutors seeking more that US$170 billion in forfeiture. According to one newspaper report: 'The scheme robbed a wide range of investors, including charities, hedge funds, trusts and individuals, providing a stark example of corporate greed and of the inability of market regulators to monitor fraud' (Bray & Ef 2009).

Conventionally, white-collar crime is seen as perpetrated by high-status business or professional people in the course of their occupation. It consists principally of trust violation that is aimed at enhancing profit, either of the corporation or the individual. This conception follows Sutherland's (1983) theory of white-collar crime. With the advent of electronic communication, especially the internet, the opportunities for fraud and other cyber crime, or 'computer-based deviance' (Pontell & Rosoff 2009, p. 148) have escalated. This type of crime is not limited to workplaces or high-status employees or professionals, or even to adults. Pontell and Rosoff suggest the term 'white-collar delinquency' to describe the shift from small-scale pranks by computer hackers to major economic crimes:

> What distinguishes white-collar delinquency from computer delinquency, which includes hacking, trespass, and system violations, is that it entails relatively large financial crimes as well as crimes of great cost to society (e.g., server shut-downs and related system costs). (2009, p. 151)

16.1: The oil-for-food scandal

A good example of the fuzzy distinctions between crime and deviance is the so-called oil-for-food scandal in Australia. Following the invasion of Kuwait in 1990, the United Nations imposed sanctions on Iraq that prohibited the payment of hard currency to Iraq directly. In order to preserve the market for Australian wheat in Iraq, in an international context where United Nations' sanctions and government policy prohibited the payment of hard currency to Iraq, the Australian Wheat Board (AWB) made payments to an Iraqi trucking company that were included in the wheat price and sought to cover up these payments. A 2006 inquiry into these arrangements concluded that 'much time and money was spent [by the AWB] trying to determine if arrangements could be formulated in such a way as to avoid breaching the law or sanctions, whether conduct could be protected, by various subterfuges, from discovery or scrutiny, and whether actions were legal or illegal' (Cole 2006, p. xii). Activities that might not amount to crimes but entail unacceptable or immoral behaviour are sometimes termed 'elite deviance'. Considerable systematic research on white-collar and financial crimes has been undertaken by the Australian Institute of Criminology (<www.aic.gov>). Becoming deviant involves learning the techniques of deviance as well as the motives, attitudes, and rationalisations (Sutherland & Cressey 1978). Gresham Sykes and David Matza (1957) develop this point, arguing that much delinquent behaviour is based on justifications or rationalisations that the perpetrators see as valid, thereby not defining their behaviour as deviant. Norm violation does not necessarily mean a rejection of norms, but may involve rationalisations—which Sykes and Matza term 'techniques of neutralisation'—such as denying responsibility, injury, or the existence of a victim, defining the condemners as deviant, or appealing to a higher loyalty. Without damaging self-image, rationalisations neutralise or deflect disapproval arising from a discrepancy between internalised norms and behaviour. Individuals may neutralise being late as acceptable because everyone else arrives late; some may rationalise theft from department stores as reasonable given the high prices of goods; and people may rationalise using illegal drugs as not really criminal because it is a matter of individual choice, not public policy.

Control theory

We can invert the question of why some people are motivated to deviate from social norms and ask: Why are some (perhaps most) people motivated to conform to social norms or comply with others' expectations? Control theory proposes that individuals deviate when they are liberated from the social bonds that constrain their behaviour. All individuals are capable of norm-breaking behaviour. There is nothing special about norm-breakers: the social bonds are what control their behaviour and channel it into conformity. When social constraints weaken, individuals will engage in deviant behaviour. Travis Hirschi, the major proponent of control theory, writes: 'According to *control* or bond theories, a person is free to commit delinquent acts because his [sic] ties to the conventional order have somehow been broken' (1969, p. 3, original italics). Control theory proposes that individuals make rational choices, albeit unconsciously, according to the comparative costs and benefits of conventional and deviant activities. It assumes that individuals pursue activities that maximise benefits and minimise costs. Importantly, other factors—like persuasion, loyalty, and power inequalities—may affect individuals' decisions to engage in high-risk activities. In a sense, it is rational for the individual to do so but then rational choice appears very much like rationalisation, which occurs after the deviance rather than before.

Hirschi (1969) identifies four elements of the bond to conventional society:

1. *Attachment* to others, including parents, school, and peers. To lack these attachments frees an actor from moral restraints. Where these others expect high achievement and an individual has strong attachments to these relationships, then deviance is less likely to occur. This point assumes that those social groups themselves are committed to conformity rather than deviance.
2. *Commitment* to such conventional forms of action as education and occupational success, which involve investments of time and energy, thus rendering deviance costly. Ambition and aspirations play important roles in producing conformity. Career aspirations might inhibit activities that would jeopardise occupational success. For example, a student's incentive to cheat or plagiarise might disappear for fear that discovery would result in fail grades and make the pursuit of a chosen career not possible, or at least more difficult.
3. *Involvement* in conventional activities, which makes a person too busy to engage in deviant behaviour. The opportunity to commit deviant acts rarely arises if a person is tied to appointments, deadlines, schedules, working hours, and family obligations, and has no time for deviant activities.
4. *Belief* in the norms prohibiting deviant activities. A belief in the sanctity of the laws or the value of guidelines and rules will also circumvent the possibility of deviance.

These bonds inhibit deviance because they represent things of value that deviant activities may jeopardise. Their absence 'frees' individuals to maximise their own self-interest, thereby increasing the probability of criminal deviance. The nature or existence of social bonds may change over the life course. The stronger an adult's links to work and family, the lower the levels of crime and deviance, regardless of delinquency as a young person (Sampson & Laub 1990).

Aside from social bonds, changes in the organisation of social life affect opportunities for criminal deviance. The more opportunities for deviance, the more likely that deviation will occur. Though the social world is not neatly divided into opportunities for deviance and opportunities for conformity, we are all confronted every day by opportunities for criminal deviance. There are many opportunities for theft, cheating, lying, harming others, and so on, but most of the time most people do not engage in this behaviour. Why? One explanation is the existence of social controls and surveillance.

Lawrence Cohen and Marcus Felson (1979) argue that changes in the 'routine activities' of everyday life influence deviant behaviour by altering opportunities and social control mechanisms. Specifically, norm-breaking requires a convergence in space and time of motivated offenders, suitable targets, and the absence of capable guardians against a violation.

Changes in routine activities entailing a dispersion of activities away from households and families result in a decrease in social control. One of the most significant changes over the past two decades or so has been women's increased participation in the labour market. The number of households where no adult is present during the day means a reduction in social control, which can increase household burglary rates. To compensate for this shift, many householders install electronic monitoring devices and alarms to deter predatory crime. In addition, technological changes mean that such valuable items as phones, computers, televisions, and other electronic goods are lighter and easier to carry, thus increasing the likelihood of their theft. Moreover, the markets for the sale of such items are not difficult for the layperson to locate—unlike markets for stolen works of art, for example.

Continuing in this vein, many contemporary crime-prevention policies attempt to build social control directly into the physical and spatial environment by affecting the design of buildings and vehicles, and the structure of mass transit stations, shopping malls, central business districts, and other public spaces. For example, much public seating in shopping precincts or train/bus stations is designed in such a way as to make it impossible or very difficult to lie down and sleep, as a way of deterring people who might make these locations their shelter. Garden ledges and other flat surfaces increasingly have large metal clips attached as a deterrent to skateboarding, which is viewed as a nuisance or inappropriate activity in certain locations.

Why are some people motivated to define, designate, and sanction some behaviour or activity as deviant?

Why is heroin use legally prohibited and stigmatised, but alcohol widely available and its consumption an expected behaviour? One answer is that different rules are applied to these activities because particular groups or individuals—including politicians, government officials, social activists, and business elites—have vested interests, informed either by their values or economic concerns, in criminalising some activities. To understand the emergence of deviance, we need to understand who is defining the activity, behaviour, or situation as deviant.

Labelling theory

Labelling theory, sometimes termed symbolic interactionism, focuses on the social reaction—that is, the responses of others who identify and interpret activities or individuals as deviant—rather than just on the person who violates norms (Becker 1963). The reactions depend not only on the violation of a rule but on who breaks the rules, the time and place, and whether she or he is visible to others motivated and with the authority to invoke sanctions. The definition of behaviour as deviant depends on the social audience, not just on the norm-breaking activity. Some types of social audience have more power and authority to enable labels to stick. The forms of behaviour do not themselves activate the processes of social reaction. The application of deviant labels and rule infraction is logically distinct. The consequences of a deviant label for a person's public image, self-identity, and moral career contrast with the actor not so labelled, though both may break the same norms. In other words, individuals may break social norms, but not be noticed or sanctioned. For example, consumption of cannabis or any illegal drug in a private home (unless it and its inhabitants are already known to police) is much less likely to come to the attention of enforcement agents than consumption of cannabis in a public place. Coming to the attention of the police can result in prosecution, conviction, and a criminal record, which will impact negatively on an individual's life chances. Those who do not come to the attention of the criminal justice system, even though they engage in the same norm-breaking activities, obviously will not experience the negative implications of such contact. Put another way, there are unknown numbers of people who engage in activities that offend the criminal law but who are not caught, which means that crime statistics based on police arrests, or other criminal justice system statistics, might under-report the extent of criminal activity in a society.

The labelling perspective reached a high point in the 1960s and early 1970s. Labelling theorists seek to distinguish rule-breaking behaviour from deviance—that is, to separate the objective acts from the identification of an individual or group as deviant and ultimately their subjective view of themselves as such. Howard Becker (1963) formulates the most influential and oft-cited position of the labelling perspective. He writes that:

> deviance is *not* a quality of the act the person commits, but rather a consequence of the application by others of rules and sanctions to an 'offender'. The deviant is one to whom the label has successfully been applied; deviant behavior is behavior that people so label. (1963, p. 9, original italics)

CrossLink: See Chapter 3 for more on symbolic inter-actionism.

Becker suggests reserving the term 'deviant' for those labelled deviant by some segment of society, and concludes that 'whether a given act is deviant or not depends in part on the nature of the act (that is, whether or not it violates some rule) and in part what other people do about it' (1963, p. 33).

For labelling theorists, the focus must be on the social audience that determines whether certain activities are defined as deviation and whether an actor becomes deviant. The concern is not with what 'caused' the individual to engage in specific acts or behaviour, but with the nature of the response and the subsequent definitions of the individual—that is, the processes that produce deviant outcomes.

16.2: Graffiti and changing notions of deviance

Responses to behaviour initially defined as deviant or illegal can change, and this depends on the nature of the audience and shifts in particular markets. While some groups consider graffiti to be highly deviant and anti-social, and graffiti-writing on public property remains illegal, during the 1980s elite New York City art dealers and critics relabelled some (though certainly not all) graffiti as art with economic value at the top end of the art market (Lachmann 1988). Just as importantly, individuals or groups engaging in the behaviour or activity considered deviant by some, place very different definitions and meanings on it, and their conduct is closely linked with their identity and experience.

In Australia, the definition of graffiti is also subject to contest, with some people defining it as attractive and expressive while others consider it to be a signal of community disintegration and demise. Following interviews with graffiti artists and discussions with local government representatives in Victoria and South Australia, Mark Halsey and Alison Young (2002) describe the diverse kinds of graffiti and complex nature of graffiti culture. This empirical research shows that the actual nature of graffiti does not fit within official or stereotypical definitions of graffiti as damage, and its producers as young offenders and troublemakers.

The labelling process

The labelling process operates on at least three levels of social action: interpersonal relations, organisational processing, and collective rule-making (Schur 1971). Everyday interaction and formal agencies of social control, ranging from police departments, courts, and hospitals to government bureaucracies and legislative bodies, constitute different audiences—all of which tend to stereotype, interpret activities retrospectively, bargain and negotiate, producing deviant outcomes.

A large body of research documents how official social agencies identify, classify, and label individuals as deviant and the implications for their careers (Kitsuse & Cicourel 1963). Studies of the criminal justice system, especially the prosecution process, demonstrate that an image of the typical crime emerges during routine interaction with alleged offenders and victims. It entails assumptions about the conditions of the crime, the suspected offender's social characteristics and the role and behaviour of the victim. These descriptions become 'normal crimes' attributable to all people accused of such acts. Questioning becomes not so much an attempt to assess an individual's situation but a process of fitting that person into the stereotyped imagery of the criminal and the crime (Sudnow 1965).

A parallel process occurs in constructing an image of a normal victim so that actual victims are assessed against this typification. For example, in sexual assault cases the 'normal' victim is a woman who can demonstrate that she actively resisted the attack and that she did not contribute in any way to the incident by wearing the 'wrong' clothes, being in the 'wrong' place at the 'wrong' time, or having a previous acquaintance or relationship (including marriage) with the perpetrator (Frohmann 1997). Victims or survivors of the attack who do not fit this picture might not be believed by prosecutors, or prosecutors might decide not to proceed with the allegations in anticipation that the jury or judge might not find the victim or her rendition of events credible.

Moral panics

Sometimes public concern surrounding behaviour or activities identified as deviant reaches a high level and then seems to fade away. There are many examples of concern about certain (though not all) young people and their music, dress, and leisure activities that are characterised as a distinctive youth subculture and their collective interaction often characterised as gangs (not a positive appellation), which can come to symbolise wider social issues or be taken to indicate something negative about the state of contemporary society. The term 'moral panic' is most closely associated with the work of Stanley Cohen (2002), who defines it as 'a condition, episode, person or group of persons [that] emerges to become defined as a threat to societal values and interests; its nature is presented in a stylized and stereotypical fashion by the mass media' (2002, p. I). Following Émile Durkheim (1984, pp. 31–44), moral panics can symbolise (or galvanise) collective consciousness and become important sites for the affirmation or articulation of social norms and emotional expression, including moral outrage (see Smith 2008).

Periodically in Australian society, and elsewhere, there are moral panics, or attempts to initiate them. The release from prison of a person convicted of child sex offences or acts of violence committed by a 'deviantised' group, such as members of a specific ethnic group (cast as illegal migrants or asylum seekers) or motor cycle club (bikie gangs), frequently spark moral panics that are played out in the print and broadcast media. This moral panic can result in political intervention, resulting in changes to legislation that aim to regulate the offensive behaviour, activities, or sometimes groups.

From time to time, members of the public direct moral outrage towards social institutions. For example, sentences handed down in particular cases—especially suspended prison sentences—are sometimes viewed as inappropriate and the sentencing court or judge becomes the focus of public criticism, especially from victims' groups (Freiberg & Moore 2009). In the United Kingdom, a sudden, short, violent attack on an Afro-Caribbean man by a group of white youths in 1993, resulting in his death, led to a public inquiry that concluded: 'Stephen Lawrence's murder was simply and solely and unequivocally motivated by racism' (Macpherson 1999). It also highlighted the pervasiveness of racism and

racially motivated crime, and documented widespread distrust between police and minority ethnic communities; however, this incident failed to materialise into a moral panic. Cohen (2002, p. xi) suggests it lacked three essential elements:

1. a suitable enemy; much of the anger was directed toward the police, which is not a powerless or easily demonised institution

2. a suitable victim, with whom others beyond urban, young black men, would identify and perceive as a risk to their own safety, and

3. a general view that the 'deviant' behaviour is widespread, and that something must be done.

The concept of moral panic does not deny the existence of the incidents, but points to a level of exaggeration which contributes to an impression that a threat or danger is bigger than warranted: 'during moral panics and media frenzies the atypical case is compressed into general categories of crime control (such as "juvenile violence")' (Cohen 2002, p. x). Other concepts, such as risk, point to the pervasiveness of general insecurity, anxiety, and fear (Ungar 2001).

Conclusion

There is some debate about the use or relevance of the concept of deviance both within sociology and generally. Doubt stems from the fact that social norms, as we have seen in this and other chapters, may be shared among some people but are not universally shared (Sumner 1994). In other words, there is no single normative system with which everyone in a society agrees or shares. While we can say that most people agree that theft, murder, rape, and assault are deviant, and accept the criminal law as central for social control, there is little agreement about whether some activities involving consenting adults—for example, homosexuality, abortion, or drug use—including alcohol—are deviant. It is often the language of morality rather than legality that is used to evaluate sexuality and its regulation. Periodically, there are public debates—sometimes acrimonious—about the legal status of some of these activities and their regulation.

Mervyn Bendle further suggests that the crime–deviance–difference continuum tends to polarise. Classifications of behaviour bifurcate either into less tolerance and more punishment for crimes or an increasing valorisation of social difference and acceptance of diverse identities. For example, stronger criminal sanctions can now be applied to corporate crime, domestic violence, and hate crimes than in the past, while homosexuality, abortion, the personal use of some illegal drugs, and prostitution are much less subject to criminal sanctions. 'Caught in the middle, "deviance" threatens to become an increasingly content-less and anachronistic residual category' (Bendle 1999, p. 48). In an institutional sense, this is true: topics that once were investigated and taught primarily within the sociology of deviance—such as mental illness, drug use, sexuality, and crime—have now become more specialised and separate areas of inquiry that are often interdisciplinary, involving social/behavioural and medical scientists and knowledge. Nonetheless, the concepts of deviance, normality, and social control remain viable across a variety of areas of inquiry. Analyses of the body, its presentation, appearance, and emotions provide many examples of deviance, normality, and control.

Summary of main points

▶ Deviance and social control are embedded in everyday life. Social control can take many forms. Many new kinds of social control and regulation are impersonal and entail sophisticated electronic technology or the contractual form.

▶ Theories in the sociology of deviance attempt to answer two different but related questions: 'Why are some people motivated to deviate from social norms?' and 'Why are some people motivated to define, designate, and sanction some behaviour or activity as deviant?'

▶ Control theory proposes that individuals deviate when they are liberated from the social bonds that constrain their behaviour, while the central concern of labelling theorists is to distinguish rule-breaking behaviour from deviance—that is, to separate the objective acts from the identification of an individual or group as deviant, and ultimately their subjective view of themselves as such.

▶ The labelling process operates on at least three levels of social action: interpersonal relations, organisational processing, and collective rule-making.

▶ Coming to the attention of the police can result in prosecution, conviction, and a criminal record, which will negatively impact on an individual's life chances. Those who do not come to the attention of the criminal justice system, even though they engage in the same norm-breaking activities, obviously will not experience the negative implications of such contact.

SOCIOLOGICAL
REFLECTION

16.1 **Normative and deviant bodies**

From your own experiences, reflect on the ways in which the body is subject to normative regulation and sanctions. What are the rules (informal and formal) about body presentation and appearance in a variety of settings? What kinds of sanctions are applied to 'deviant' bodies? Many sociologists point to the ways in which gender—as a normative system—places powerful constraints on men and women in terms of body size and shape. Some suggest that cosmetic surgery—a term that covers a number of procedures—is more expected for women than men, and that intervention conforming to dominant or mainstream definitions of beauty is acceptable, perhaps even normal. The emotions are another area where gendered norms and definitions mean that men and women face expectations of conformity and sanctions for non-conformity.

SOCIOLOGICAL
REFLECTION

16.2 **Contested meanings of deviance**

Many of the examples discussed in the study of deviance point to the constructed and contested nature of deviance. The status of behaviour and activities designated as deviant results from the successful claims and assertions of groups and individuals, which vary in power and persuasion. Is it true that deviance is a matter of definition? In practice, how are these boundaries drawn? How are social norms formed and communicated? What scope is there for disagreement and contest regarding conceptions of deviance and conformity? Are some activities and behaviours inherently unacceptable?

Discussion questions

16.1 Discuss the construction, emergence, persistence, and management or control of deviance in an actual social setting or situation familiar to you. Examples could include an employment setting, a club, a hospital ward, your family, a party, or a group of friends. First, describe the structure and organisation of the setting/situation, and then discuss the formal or informal rules and the explicit or implicit expectations that exist.

16.2 To what extent is the labelling perspective useful in understanding and conducting research on mental health?

16.3 Why are some drugs legally prohibited? What assumptions are made about people who consume drugs (distinguish between legally available drugs and prohibited substances)? To what extent is drug abuse in Australia an urgent social issue?

16.4 Discuss the extent to which current international and national concern about terrorist activities constitutes a moral panic.

16.5 How do gender norms affect cultural representations and political debates surrounding sexuality?

16.6 Discuss recent examples of moral panic in the mass media. For how long did these moral panics continue? How did the moral panic dissipate?

Further reading

Becker, H.S. 1963, *Outsiders: Studies in the Sociology of Deviance*, Free Press, New York.

Best, J. 2004, *Deviance: Career of a Concept*, Wadsworth, Belmont, CA.

Cohen, S. 2002, 'Moral panics as cultural politics: Introduction to the Third Edition', in S. Cohen, *Folk Devils and Moral Panics: The Creation of the Mods and Rockers*, 3rd edn, Routledge, London, pp. vii–xxxvii.

Goffman, E. 1959, *The Presentation of Self in Everyday Life*, Anchor Books, New York.

Roach Anleu, S.L. 2006, *Deviance, Conformity and Control*, 4th edn, Pearson Education, Sydney.

Sumner, C. 1994, *The Sociology of Deviance: An Obituary*, Open University Press, Buckingham.

Sykes, G. & Matza, D. 1957, 'Techniques of neutralization: A theory of delinquency', *American Sociological Review*, no. 22, pp. 664–70.

Websites

- Australian Broadcasting Corporation (ABC): <www.abc.net.au>. Broadcasts television and radio programs covering many topics that can be discussed within the sociology of deviance.

- British Broadcasting Corporation (BBC)—*Thinking Allowed*: <www.bbc.co.uk/podcasts/series/ta>. Radio 4 program hosted by sociologist Laurie Taylor, which explores social research on current issues.
- Australian Bureau of Statistics (ABS): <www.abs.gov.au>. Provides statistical information and research findings on such topics as crime, health, housing, the labour force, mental health, gambling, and the operation of government departments and agencies, including the police, courts, and prisons.
- Australian Institute of Criminology (AIC): <www.aic.gov.au>. Information about crime in Australia, international comparisons, research findings, and commentaries.
- Australian Institute of Health and Welfare (AIHW): <www.aihw.gov.au>. Provides information on health and welfare issues in Australia.
- Australia's National Mental Health Strategy: <www.health.gov.au/internet/main/Publishing.nsf/Content/mental-strat>. Links on policy as well as evaluations and reports on mental health problems in Australia.
- The British Home Office: <www.homeoffice.gov.uk/rds>. Collects statistics on crime, terrorism, policing, justice, immigration, drugs, and race equality.

Films/documentaries

- *One Flew Over the Cuckoo's Nest*, 1975, motion picture, directed by M. Forman, Fantasy Films. A film that deals with human rights, mental illness, and 'total institutions'.
- *Madness*, 1991, television documentary series, hosted by Jonathan Miller, British Broadcasting Corporation (BBC). Traces the history of psychiatry, asylums, and social and scientific reactions to mental illness to the present day.
- *Philadelphia*, 1993, motion picture, directed by J. Demme, Tristar Pictures. Examines issues related to coping with AIDS, discrimination, and the stigmatisation of homosexuality.
- *Bowling for Columbine*, 2002, documentary, directed by M. Moore, Alliance Atlantis Communications. Explores gun violence in the United States by confronting the political and corporate interests that promote gun culture.
- *Brokeback Mountain*, 2005, motion picture, directed by A. Lee, Paramount Pictures. A film that explores gay relationships and masculinity in the 1960s, focusing on the secret relationship between two cowboys.
- 'The Dishonouring of Marcus Einfeld', *Four Corners*, 2009, television news feature, reported by S. Ferguson, Australian Broadcasting Corporation (ABC). This program discusses this former judge's decision to avoid a speeding fine, which ultimately destroyed his reputation and career and resulted in a prison sentence.
- 'Code of Silence', *Four Corners*, 2009, television news feature, reported by S. Ferguson, Australian Broadcasting Corporation (ABC). This report examines

allegations directed towards Rugby League players relating to alcohol, women, and sex.

- 'Who Killed Mr Ward', *Four Corners*, 2009, television news feature, reported by L. Jackson, Australian Broadcasting Corporation (ABC). This program investigates the tragic death of an Aboriginal leader locked in a prison van in heatwave conditions.
- 'The Madoff Hustle', *Four Corners*, 2009, television news feature, reporter unknown, Australian Broadcasting Corporation (ABC). An investigation of the Madoff fraud case.
- 'On the Piss', *Four Corners*, 2009, television news feature, reported by M. Carney, Australian Broadcasting Corporation (ABC). This report examines the federal government's policies regarding binge drinking.
- 'Battling the Booze', *Four Corners*, 2009, television news feature, reported by J. Cohen, Australian Broadcasting Corporation (ABC). An examination of three people with drinking problems and their attempts to stay sober.
- 'Torture', *Four Corners*, 2009, television news feature, reported by S. Neighbour, Australian Broadcasting Corporation (ABC). This program asks whether torture is ever a legitimate weapon in the 'War on Terror'.
- 'Your Money and Your Life', *Four Corners*, 2009, television news feature, reported by Q. McDermott, Australian Broadcasting Corporation (ABC). This program explores cyber-fraud and related con tricks, such as 'phishing' (an email scam that pretends to be from a credible source such as your bank).

Visit the *Public Sociology* book website to access topical case studies, weblinks, YouTube clips, and extra readings.

References

Beaton-Wells, C. & Haines, F. 2009, 'Making cartel conduct criminal: A case study of ambiguity in controlling business behaviour', *Australian and New Zealand Journal of Criminology*, vol. 42, no. 2, pp. 218–43.

Becker, H.S. 1963, *Outsiders: Studies in the Sociology of Deviance*, Free Press, New York.

Bendle, M. 1999, 'The death of the sociology of deviance?', *Journal of Sociology*, no. 35, pp. 42–59.

Best, J. 2004, *Deviance: Career of a Concept*, Wadsworth, Belmont, CA.

Braithwaite, J. 1989, *Crime, Shame and Reintegration*, Cambridge University Press, Cambridge.

Bray, C. & Ef, A. 2009, 'Bernard Madoff pleads guilty to massive fraud', *The Australian*, 13 March.

Brickey, K.F. 2006, 'In Enron's wake: Corporate executives on trial', *Journal of Criminal Law & Criminology*, vol. 96, no. 2, pp. 397–433.

Carey, J. 2005, 'A funny, buoyant, question-begging book', Review of *Talk to the Hand: The Utter Bloody Rudeness of Everyday Life (Or Six Good Reasons to Stay at Home and Bolt the Door)* by Lynne Truss', *Times Online*, <http://entertainment.timesonline.co.uk/tol/arts_and_entertainment/books/non-fiction/article579978.ece> (accessed 18 February 2006).

Cohen, L.E. & Felson, M. 1979, 'Social change and crime rate trends: A routine activity approach', *American Sociological Review*, vol. 44, pp. 588–608.

Cohen, S. 2002, *Folk Devils and Moral Panics: The Creation of the Mods and Rockers*, 3rd edn, Routledge, London.

Cole, Commissioner T.R.H. 2006, *Report of the Inquiry into Certain Australian Companies in Relation to the UN Oil-for-Food Programme*, Commonwealth of Australia, Canberra, <www.oilforfoodinquiry.gov.au> (accessed 14 April 2010).

Crawford, A. 2003, '"Contractual governance" of deviant behaviour', *Journal of Law and Society*, vol. 30, pp. 479–505.

Durkheim, É. 1984 [1893], *The Division of Labour in Society*, trans. W.D. Halls, Macmillan, London.

Freiberg, A. & Moore, V. 2009, 'Disbelieving suspense: Suspended sentences of imprisonment and public confidence in the criminal justice system', *Australian and New Zealand Journal of Criminology*, vol. 42, no. 1, pp. 101–22.

Frohmann, L. 1997, 'Convictability and discordant locales: Reproducing race, class, and gender ideologies in prosecutorial decisionmaking', *Law & Society Review*, no. 31, pp. 531–56.

Halsey, M. & Young, A. 2002, 'The meanings of graffiti and municipal administration', *Australian and New Zealand Journal of Criminology*, vol. 35, no. 1, pp. 165–86.

Herbert, D. 2008, 'Perfect home cooking', *The Weekend Australian Magazine*, 29–30 November, pp. 36–7.

Hirschi, T. 1969, *Causes of Delinquency*, University of California Press, Berkeley, CA.

Hope, D. 2005, 'Rude awakening', *Weekend Australian*, 5–6 November, p. 27.

Kitsuse, J.I. & Cicourel, A.V. 1963, 'A note on the use of official statistics', *Social Problems*, vol. 11, pp. 131–9.

Lachmann, R. 1988, 'Grafitti as career and ideology', *American Journal of Sociology*, vol. 94, pp. 229–50.

Macpherson, W. 1999, *The Stephen Lawrence Inquiry. Report of an Inquiry by Sir William Macpherson of Cluny*, The Stationery Office, London.

Merton, R.K. 1938, 'Social structure and anomie', *American Sociological Review*, vol. 3, pp. 672–83.

Pontell, H.N. & Rosoff, S. 2009, 'White-collar delinquency', *Crime, Law, and Social Change*, vol. 51, pp. 147–62.

Roach Anleu, S.L. 2006, *Deviance, Conformity and Control*, 4th edn, Pearson Education, Sydney.

Sampson, R.J. & Laub, J.H. 1990, 'Crime and deviance over the life course: The salience of adult social bonds', *American Sociological Review*, vol. 55, pp. 609–27.

Schur, E.M. 1971, *Labeling Deviant Behaviour: Its Sociological Implications*, Harper & Row, New York.

Smith, P. 2008, 'Durkheim and criminology: Reconstructing the legacy', *Australian and New Zealand Journal of Criminology*, vol. 41, pp. 333–44.

Sudnow, D. 1965, 'Normal crimes: Sociological features of the penal code in a public defender's office', *Social Problems*, vol. 12, pp. 255–76.

Sumner, C. 1994, *The Sociology of Deviance: An Obituary*, Open University Press, Buckingham.

Sutherland, E. 1983, *White Collar Crime: The Uncut Version*, Yale University Press, New Haven, CN.

Sutherland, E.H. & Cressey, D.R. 1978, *Criminology*, 10th edn, Lippincott, New York.

Sykes, G. & Matza, D. 1957, 'Techniques of neutralization: A theory of delinquency', *American Sociological Review*, vol. 22, pp. 664–70.

Toohey, P. 2008, 'After the binge', *The Weekend Australian Magazine*, 29–30 November, pp. 18–21, 23.

Ungar, S. 2001, 'Moral panic versus the risk society: The implications of the changing sites of social anxiety', *British Journal of Sociology*, vol. 52, no. 2, pp. 271–91.

Williams, J.W. 2008, 'The lessons of "Enron": Media accounts, corporate crimes and financial markets', *Theoretical Criminology*, vol. 12, no. 4, pp. 471–99.

Module 4
Social transformations

This module considers some of the major social processes and social institutions that impact on our lives. Forms of social organisation, such as the healthcare and education systems, as well as workplaces, change over time and vary between countries; what is constant is their significant impact on our lives. In addition, globalisation, threats to our security due to terrorism and the responses to it, along with the mass media, and the urban-rural divide represent some of the major social processes impacting Australian society.

This module contains the following chapters:

CHAPTER 17

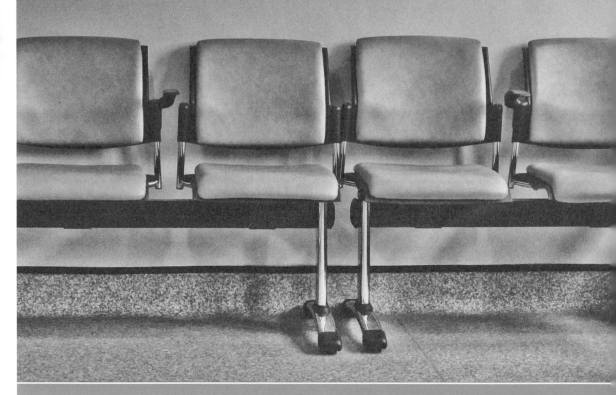

The social basis of
health and illness

Neil Burdess

The social origins of asbestos-related disease

Asbestos has been mined for at least 2000 years. In Australia, blue asbestos mining started at Wittenoom in Western Australia in the 1940s. During the post-war boom, it was widely used in the construction, shipbuilding, and power industries.

Asbestos is highly toxic. Inhaling the microscopic fibres can cause the deadly lung diseases asbestosis and mesothelioma, though symptoms may not appear until decades after exposure. Asbestos victims can experience an agonising death, being slowly suffocated as their lungs gradually cease to function. Even the ancient Romans had some awareness of the risks, and gave slaves crude respirators to wear when working with asbestos. Modern medical concerns led to regulations for dust control, medical surveillance, and workers' compensation in Britain in 1931.

The first medical warning about asbestos at Wittenoom came in 1948 (Hills 1989). By the 1970s, the Wittenoom mine-owner CSR faced the first of many compensation claims from former workers. CSR could have offered compensation to all claimants, but it would have been costly. The cheaper alternative was to use the 'Wall of Flesh' defence, and fight all claims from dying workers. CSR chose the cheaper option. Subsequently, 'many courtrooms saw the spectre of hollow-eyed ex-miners—some sitting day after day in wheelchairs next to oxygen tanks' (Sweeney 1988, p. 66). It was not until 1988, when a court awarded punitive damages against CSR, that the company decided to settle all future claims.

Nearly 30 years on, asbestos still has a high media profile, especially because of similar dubious legal moves by another large Australian company, James Hardie. The company tried to avoid paying compensation to those who had contracted asbestosis and mesothelioma after using asbestos cement products that it manufactured. James Hardie set up a separate compensation fund with a much smaller amount of money than was needed to fund claims, and then moved the James Hardie head office to the Netherlands, and planned to transfer its assets there so they could not be used to meet the claims of asbestos victims. It was only after a high-level New South Wales government inquiry that a deal was signed in December 2005 to commit James Hardie to fund adequate compensation payments. In April 2009, ten former directors and executives were found guilty in the New South Wales Supreme Court of misleading and deceptive conduct in connection with the asbestos compensation fund (see Haigh 2006).

Introduction

'Sociology of *health*?' I can imagine some of you saying, 'Surely that's not right? Health is about what goes on inside people's bodies. How can that be part of sociology?' If I am echoing your thoughts, then congratulations. Your question shows that you are developing your powers of critical thinking. At the very least, you will need some evidence to show that 'sociology of health' is not a contradiction in terms (like 'friendly fire', 'business ethics', or 'political promises').

It is easy to find evidence of the social side of health—simply go to your local general hospital. Sociologists are very interested in the distribution of health across social groups. For example, we know that young men and fast cars are a lethal combination. In contrast, young women seem much less fascinated by speed. Another fascinating area is that of the different groups with different roles interacting with each other in the hospital setting— the professional relationship between doctors and nurses has long been of interest to sociologists.

This chapter focuses on these two social aspects of health: first, the distribution of health across social groups; and second, the relationships between occupational groups in health care. The chapter could include many other possible topics, but these two are sufficient to fulfil the basic aim of this chapter: to show that the sociology of health is definitely not a contradiction in terms, and that sociology has valuable things to say about health issues. First it is worth looking more closely at the underlying concept of health itself.

Ways of understanding health

It is certainly easy to identify those times when you are definitely not healthy. For example, your temperature is sky high, you are covered in sweat, and the only time you get out of bed is to rush to the toilet. The doctor says you have food poisoning. You have an essay to finish—but there is no way you can do it. If you were well enough, you would appreciate the aptness of the World Health Organization's (WHO) long-standing definition: 'Health is a state of complete physical, psychological and social well-being, and not merely an absence of disease or infirmity' (WHO 1946, p. 2). Yet, when you are unwell, the WHO definition offers little comfort.

Although very useful, the WHO definition also raises many questions. For example, as people age they cannot do many of the things they once did. Would you therefore say that they are not healthy? Similarly, are people with physical, sensory, or mental disabilities healthy? And what about people whom doctors consider to be 'in remission' from a potentially fatal disease such as leukaemia, but who feel well and have returned to their normal social activities?

Different groups tend to emphasise different dimensions of health. For example:

- Medical practitioners focus on disease, or the *physical* dimension.

- Psychologists focus on illness, or the *psychological* dimension.
- Sociologists focus on sickness, or the *social* dimension of health.

Which of these is the dominant one is clear from the first paragraph of the chapter. Imagine that I do a word association experiment with you: 'When I say "health" what words first come to mind?' I suspect that 'hospital', 'doctor', or 'medicine' would be somewhere near the top of your list, as we are socialised into thinking about health in this way.

This close association between health and medicine originated less than 150 years ago with the work of Louis Pasteur (1822–95). In the 1870s, he was the first to show that disease was caused by germs entering the body. Others then enthusiastically took up his work. It was during this period that the **biomedical model of health** was established. John Germov (2009a, pp. 10–11) identifies the following elements of the biomedical model:

biomedical model of health
Explanation of health in terms of physical changes to the individual body.

- Specific bacteria cause specific diseases.
- Each disease has specific identifiable physical effects on the body.
- There is a 'view of the body as a machine made up of interrelated parts'.
- The doctor is 'a body mechanic identifying and repairing the broken parts'.
(Germov 2009a, p. 10)

Although much has changed in medicine over the last century, the focus of medicine is still on the diseased individual body, as reflected by the major elements of medicine today: drugs, surgery, and pathology tests. Indeed, the current focus of much medical research is at the molecular level—for example, the Human Genome Project.

The influence of psychology brought about a change in the traditional biomedical model in the 1970s. Behavioural medicine began to study links between personality and illness, and between lifestyle and illness. For example, the approach identified **risk factors** such as cigarette-smoking and lack of exercise, and then attempted to bring about behavioural change, though because this approach still focuses largely on the individual, it simply extends the traditional biomedical model.

risk factors
Physiological states and social behaviours associated with particular illnesses (for example, heavy smokers have a high risk of lung cancer).

The 1970s saw increasing dissatisfaction with the biomedical model. For example, a number of studies questioned the effectiveness of modern medicine. Thomas McKeown (1979) found that the most important factor in reducing deaths in the nineteenth century was not medicine, but public health measures such as piped water, sewerage, and better housing. Similarly, John McKinlay and his colleagues in their paper 'The Questionable Contribution of Medical Measures to the Decline of Mortality in the United States in the Twentieth Century', found that 'medical care has contributed little to the modern decline in mortality' (1977, p. 204). Moreover, developments in behavioural medicine were characterised as victim-blaming (Ryan 1971). By individualising the problem, the biomedical model also individualised the solution.

social model of health

A model that aims to find the causes of inequality between social groups, and to use public policy to improve health-related living and working conditions.

In contrast, the **social model of health** redirects the focus from individuals who are ill to social groups with high illness rates. The aim is to find the causes of inequality and, if they include aspects of people's living and working conditions, to use public policy to change them. Table 17.1 shows a more detailed comparison of the biomedical and social models.

Table 17.1: Biomedical and social models of health

Element	Biomedical model	Social model
Focus	Individuals who are sick	Social groups' living and working conditions
Assumption	Individual responsibility for health	Social responsibility for health
Key indicator	Individual pathology	Health inequalities between social groups
Causes of illness	Gene defects Micro-organisms (e.g. viruses) Lifestyle—risk-taking	Political and economic factors (e.g. poverty) Cultural factors (e.g. discrimination)
Intervention	Cure individuals who are sick Modify behaviour of individuals at risk	State intervention to reduce health inequalities Community participation in health
Goals	Cure disease Reduce risk factors to prevent disease in individuals	Prevent illness Reduce health inequalities between social groups

Source: Based on Germov (2009a).

Of course, the biomedical and social models of health are not either/or choices. Everyone agrees that health care should pay attention to the body of an individual and the wider social system; however, sociologists believe that the social side of health should have much more attention than it currently receives. In part, this requires more attention to be given to 'public health' activities that keep people healthy, such as ensuring food quality and occupational health and safety. Still, total government spending on public health is only 2 per cent of the total recurrent expenditure on health (AIHW 2008a, p. 46).

It is now time to look in more detail at two of the major aspects of the sociology of health mentioned earlier: the distribution of health across social groups, and the relationships between occupational groups in health care.

Distribution of health across social groups

Research by sociologists into the social distribution of health compares very large population groups based on characteristics such as gender (men/women), ethnicity

socioeconomic status (SES)
A statistical measure that classifies individuals, households, or families in terms of their income, occupation, and education.

(e.g. Indigenous/non-Indigenous), and socioeconomic status (e.g. rich/poor). The general aim is to describe the differences in health between each pair of groups, and to explain why they occur. The *describe* part is becoming more straightforward as health statistics improve. The *explain* part is less straightforward, as much depends on which model of health is used. While there is a vast literature on the health differences between social groups, for our purposes it is sufficient to focus on one social characteristic: the health differences between **socioeconomic status (SES)** groups.

SES and health

Studies of death rates usually have to rely on official statistics based on information collected by the funeral director from each deceased's next of kin. One piece of information collected is the area in which the deceased last lived. For each area in Australia, the Australian Bureau of Statistics (ABS) has used Census data to calculate an index of relative socioeconomic disadvantage based on such characteristics as income, employment, and education. The ABS then ranks the areas from that with the lowest index score to that with the highest, and the list is then divided into a small number of equal parts to create status areas. For example, the list can be divided into five equal parts, or quintiles. For example, the 20 per cent of areas with the lowest index scores are grouped into Quintile 1 and the 20 per cent of areas with the highest index scores are grouped into Quintile 5. The socioeconomic status of each deceased person is found by identifying the quintile of the local area in which he or she lived.

Table 17.2 compares the number of deaths caused by cardiovascular disease—diseases of the heart and blood vessels, such as heart attack and stroke. Cardiovascular disease is the biggest cause of death in Australia: the 12 000 deaths shown in Table 17.2 represent over one-quarter of all deaths among people aged 25 to 74. The table shows a remarkably consistent pattern. For both men and women, the highest number of deaths occurred among people living in the poorest areas (Quintile 1). The table then shows a steady fall, with the richest areas (Quintile 5) having the lowest number of deaths. Expressed slightly differently, if the cardiovascular health status of the poorest areas had been as good as the richest areas, there would have been over 1400 (i.e. 3104 minus 1694) fewer deaths from heart attack, stroke, and so on in these areas over the course of the year.

Supporters of the biomedical model point to the very different health behaviours between socioeconomic groups. For example, manual workers smoke more, exercise less, have a less healthy diet, use preventative medical services less, and are more likely to engage in reckless behaviour (Burdess 2004). There are sometimes good reasons why these behaviours occur—for example, low-fat milk and lean meat are more expensive. Statistical analysis shows that risk factors explain only 'between a quarter and a third of the social gradient' in health (Marmot 1998). In other words, for people who have equivalent health behaviours, 'we still find that where you are in the hierarchy is powerfully

Table 17.2: Number of deaths among people aged 25–74 years from cardiovascular disease, by socioeconomic status, Australia, 2002

Sex	Quintile of disadvantage					Total
	Quintile 1 (Poorest)	Quintile 2	Quintile 3	Quintile 4	Quintile 5 (Richest)	
Male	2 121	1 816	1 721	1 518	1 182	8 357
Female	983	885	727	624	512	3 732
TOTAL	3 104	2 701	2 448	2 142	1 694	12 089

Source: Data derived from AIHW (2006, Table A4).

related to your disease risk' (Marmot 1998). What factors explain the remaining two-thirds to three-quarters of these differences?

Working conditions play a major part in determining health. Most obviously, there are deaths at work from falls, burns, explosions, electrocutions, and so on. In addition, there are deaths resulting from exposure to industrial chemicals. Each year in Australia, more people die from these causes than from road accidents. Moreover, nearly half a million Australians—mainly manual workers—suffer a work-related injury or illness each year (Burdess 2004).

These figures are just the tip of the iceberg. Stress at work is now regarded as a major health risk factor. Stress occurs most often among workers doing jobs where there are high demands but low levels of control. These **high-strain jobs** are most likely to be low in status, the archetypal example being assembly-line work. Stress can lead to dangerous physiological changes, referred to as the 'metabolic syndrome'. A British study found that these physiological effects occur almost twice as often among workers in the lowest grade of employment than those in the highest grade (Chandola, Brunner & Marmot 2006).

high-strain jobs
Jobs where demands are high, but the degree of control is low (for example, assembly-line work).

There is, of course, a clear link between job level and income. In turn, the link between income and health applies at a number of levels:

- Most obvious is the link between income and consumer goods. For example, differences in the type, age, and safety features of the cars less affluent road users drive help explain why they are much more likely to be killed or injured in traffic accidents.
- Less obvious is the 'money sickness syndrome'—the lower your income, the less control you have over your life, and thus the higher your general stress level is likely to be (Saunders 1998).
- Least obvious is the 'relative income thesis'. In a classic paper, Wilkinson (1992, p. 167) found 'clear evidence' that in prosperous nations, the wider the income gap between rich and poor, the lower the overall life expectancy. This much-debated idea is underpinned by the concept of social cohesion, which is the degree to which people feel they are part of a wider society largely made up of

people they can trust. It may be that a more trusting society is a less stressful society.

SOCIOLOGY
SPOTLIGHT

17.1: The Whitehall Studies

The Whitehall Studies are some of the largest and most respected research programs in public health, financed by a variety of British government, US government, and private sources. They focus on the health of public servants working in the Whitehall area of London. There are two separate programs, inventively named Whitehall I and Whitehall II.

Whitehall I began in the 1960s, when 17 500 public servants completed a questionnaire and underwent a medical examination. Subsequently, whenever one of the public servants in the study died, the researchers were sent a copy of his death certificate. Eight years after the initial study, there was a distinct step-like pattern in mortality rates: each of the four grades had different rates, with those in the lowest grade having the highest mortality, through to those in the highest grade who had the lowest mortality. Records over a 25-year period show a four-fold difference in mortality rates between the bottom and top public service grades. Because all grades of staff were doing office work, the social gradient in health cannot be explained by different levels of industrial injuries or exposure to industrial chemicals.

Whitehall II was set up to discover the causes of this social gradient in health. It started in 1985 when 10 000 public servants completed a long questionnaire and a screening examination. There have been several further stages, the current one involving approximately 6500 of the original 10 000 participants. In an ABC Radio National interview, expatriate Australian Professor Sir Michael Marmot, the Director of the International Institute for Society and Health, outlined some of the implications of Whitehall II. These include:

1. Stress harms health, and low levels of control at work are of crucial importance to stress levels.

2. What happens to us as infants and young children has a long-standing influence.

3. Poverty creates misery and costs lives.

4. Social support from friends at work and home is crucial to good health.

His overall message is that 'health policy has to run across the whole of society' (Marmot 1998; see also Marmot 2004).

Health status differences based on gender and Indigenous status

There are also differences in health between other major social groups—for example, in terms of gender, and Indigenous status. The next few paragraphs briefly summarise the main issues.

In terms of gender, in virtually every country the life expectancy of women is higher than that of men. In Australia, the life expectancy at birth for girls is almost five years higher than for boys (ABS 2008, p. 206). Surprisingly, illness rates for women are higher than for men. A combination of physical, psychological, and social explanations accounts for these illness differences. For example, every stage of the normal female reproductive life-cycle, from menstruation to menopause, can be subject to medical intervention. Similarly, the health behaviour of males is much riskier than that of females, due to factors such as smoking, heavy drinking, dangerous driving, and so on. It is unclear whether these behaviours owe more to biological factors such as hormone levels or to the different ways in which males and females are socialised. A further issue is domestic violence, which affects one in six women at some time in their adult lives (ABS 2007, p. 201). Other clearly social factors include the traditional employment of men in high-risk occupations, the higher employment of men in the workforce, and the 'double burden' of women who go out to work and do the major share of domestic duties.

There are also major differences between the health of Indigenous and non-Indigenous Australians (AIHW 2008a). Indeed, the life expectancy of Indigenous Australians is an incredible seventeen years less than that of non-Indigenous Australians. There are a number of explanations of these differences, and they should be generally familiar to you by now. The biomedical model stresses high-risk health behaviour among Indigenous Australians, including excessive alcohol consumption, smoking, physical inactivity, and substance abuse. The social model highlights that Indigenous households are often among the poorest on average—an explanation that clearly overlaps with that used to explain differences between SES groups. In addition, there are important issues related to racism, culture, and the remote location of many Indigenous groups.

Occupational groups in health care

This section of the chapter has two main parts. First, by way of background, there is an overview of the Australian healthcare system. The focus then moves to the interaction of doctors with other healthcare workers.

The Australian healthcare system

Let us examine the size of Australia's healthcare system with the help of a few figures (AIHW 2008a).

What we spend:

- total annual expenditure on health—$87 000 million
- average annual expenditure per person—$4200
- proportion of gross domestic product (GDP)—9 per cent
- proportion of health expenditure government funded—68 per cent.

What we get for our money:

- people in health-services industry—750 000
- annual number of hospital separations—7.3 million

- annual number of medical services—250 million
- annual number of prescriptions—237 million.

As you can see, the numbers are huge. For example, the GDP is the market value of all goods and services sold during a year. The third dot point above shows that 90 cents of every $10 spent in Australia goes to health-related goods and services, and the numbers are growing. For example, even after adjusting for inflation, spending on health has increased by nearly 50 per cent over the last ten years (AIHW 2008a, p. 394).

The government plays a major role in health care, with over two-thirds (68 per cent) of health funding coming from government sources. There are two major public healthcare schemes:

1. *Medicare* subsidises payments for medical services provided on a fee-for-service basis by private medical practitioners.
2. The *Pharmaceutical Benefits Scheme* subsidises a high proportion of prescription medicines bought from private pharmacists.

In addition, treatment in public hospitals is free at the point of service, and there is government funding of high-level residential care and medical research.

The remaining one-third of healthcare funding comes largely from individuals, either directly through out-of-pocket payments, or indirectly through private health insurance funds. Ideologically, Liberal-National Party Coalition governments are committed to the notions of individual responsibility, and traditionally have not supported public healthcare schemes; these have been introduced by Labor governments, whose ideological emphasis is more on collective responsibility; however, Medicare is so popular with the public that scrapping it would be electorally disastrous. Instead, the former Coalition federal government supported private health insurance funds with a 30 per cent rebate on premiums, to a total of $3.5 billion a year. The Labor government had to retain it because of its electoral popularity.

About 750 000 people work in the health services industry. These include health occupations, such as doctors, nurses, dentists, and pharmacists, and other occupations, such as clerical workers, cleaners, and kitchen staff. This section focuses on the 480 000 people in health occupations in Australia (AIHW 2008a, p. 431). Figure 17.1 shows the relative size of each sector.

Relations between healthcare workers

It is the 60 000 or so doctors—general practitioners and specialists—who have the lead role in the healthcare industry. For example, your doctor writes your prescription, your doctor's name appears at the top of your bed in hospital, and your doctor discharges you from hospital. Sociologists refer to this leadership role as **medical dominance**. John Germov (2009b, p. 393) defines medical dominance as 'the power

medical dominance
The power of the medical profession to control its own work and the work of others in health care.

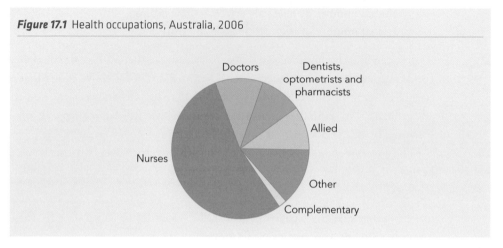

Figure 17.1 Health occupations, Australia, 2006

Notes:
Allied—e.g. physiotherapists, radiographers, psychologists, occupational therapists
Other—e.g. medical technicians, scientists, massage therapists
Complementary—e.g. naturopaths, chiropractors, acupuncturists
Source: Based on statistics in AIHW (2009a, Table A4.6).

of the medical profession in terms of its control over its own work, over the work of other health workers, and over health resource allocation, health policy, and the way that hospitals are run'.

Many people would see this as the best way for health care to be organised. Doctors have an important role. After all, a healthy population is crucial for the smooth running of society, and doctors' use of medical science ensures a healthy population. Access to medical education is highly competitive, and the training is lengthy and rigorous. Once doctors qualify to practise, the work is highly stressful. Not surprisingly, the rewards to medical practitioners are high, both in terms of prestige (Harris Poll 2008) and income (Stinson 2006).

An alternative explanation is that medical dominance came about more through economic and political processes than the effectiveness of medical science. Recall, for example, the studies cited earlier that questioned the effectiveness of modern medicine during both the nineteenth and twentieth centuries. Still, doctors did pursue a very effective social agenda, helped by the fact that they were all men from upper-class backgrounds.

Doctors unified themselves against competitors by establishing associations, membership of which was limited to those who had completed expensive medical training. They also used their social class links with members of the political establishment to curtail the growth of opposing occupational groups. For example, dentists and optometrists were legally limited to practise only on very specific parts of the body, and alternative practitioners such as chiropractors and acupuncturists were legally excluded from state-supported education and treatment subsidies. Until at least the middle of the twentieth century, the vast majority of doctors in Australia were male, and medical specialists and medical organisations were almost exclusively male dominated. It is unsurprising, then, that the medical profession aimed to subordinate occupational groups who were largely female, like nurses, and allied health workers, such as occupational therapists (Willis 1989).

Have recent trends led to any challenges to medical dominance? We can group potentially influential factors in terms of scale. These are listed below, along with some terms commonly used in the literature to describe the processes that may be important:

- doctors—feminisation of medicine
- nurses and allied health workers—competing professionalisation
- patients—deprofessionalisation
- state—bureaucratisation of medicine, and
- global capitalism—proletarianisation of medicine.

First, are there any changes among doctors themselves that may have had an impact on medical dominance? One factor is the **feminisation of medicine**. Recall that the subordination of nursing and allied health occupations owed much to the fact that they were largely female while medicine was almost exclusively male. While nursing and allied health are still very much female occupations, the traditional gender profile of medicine is changing, and the majority of doctors in training are now women (AIHW 2008a). Further, nurses believe that female doctors are less demanding and have a more consultative style (Pringle 1998).

feminisation of medicine
Trend for the medical profession to include an increasing proportion of women.

competing professionalisation
Trend of groups traditionally subordinate to medicine to adopt traits associated with a profession.

Another issue for medical dominance is the **competing professionalisation** of nurses and allied health workers. These occupations have adopted 'the professionalising project of medicine' (Williams 2009, p. 460), and taken on the following traits:

- a scientific body of knowledge
- university-level courses to teach this knowledge
- a professional association, membership of which is limited to course graduates, and
- a code of professional conduct that members must follow.

Still, most sociologists regard the trait approach to defining professions as flawed. Instead, they see professionalism as being about legalised autonomy over work roles—but, in the hospital system at least, you are still the 'doctor's patient', meaning that autonomy for nursing and allied health workers is just not possible. It is only when they work more independently of doctors, in private clinics or in the community, that nurses and allied health workers will achieve more autonomy.

This being so, the recent change in the focus of health care from acute to chronic illness may be much more important than professional traits. Traditionally, the health system focused on *curing* patients with acute illnesses. In contrast, today there is an increasing focus on *caring* for patients with chronic illnesses. This often happens away from a hospital, particularly given the rise of the policy of deinstitutionalisation—caring for people in the community rather than in institutions.

At one time, doctors had an almost god-like status in the eyes of their patients. The phrase 'being under the doctor' clearly indicated the subordinate position of the patient in the relationship. More recently, though, there have been a number of trends that together are referred to as **deprofessionalisation**, such as:

---

deprofessionalisation
A narrowing of the knowledge and authority gap between doctors and patients.

- patients being able to find information about health on the internet
- patients being more aware of problems in medicine, which are widely reported in the media, and
- patients being more likely to voice concerns about what they see as medical negligence or incompetence (AIHW 2009b).

At first glance, it looks as if deprofessionalisation could have a marked impact on medical dominance, but although some people fulfil the role of the knowledgeable and assertive health consumer, the doctor–patient interaction still reflects the traditional relationship of trust and dependence (Germov 2009b), and opinion polls still show medicine as one of the most prestigious and trusted occupations (Harris Poll 2008; Morgan Poll 2008).

Health care consumes about $60 billion of public money per year in Australia, with medical decisions made by private medical practitioners generating most of the costs. Consequently, all governments try to contain costs by placing increasing levels of control on health care. This is known as the **bureaucratisation of medicine**. Cost-containment strategies include:

---

bureaucratisation of medicine
The increasing influence of state bureaucracies on medical practice.

- *Scrutinising referrals from general practitioners (GPs) to specialists:* GPs whose referrals are considerably above average are warned, then pulled in for further investigation, and eventually fined if their referral rates do not come down.
- *Limiting the range of publicly subsidised medicines:* Prescriptions for drugs not in the Pharmaceutical Benefits Scheme are expensive. Medicare (2009) points out that: 'You can ask your doctor to prescribe a less expensive brand, or your pharmacist may be able to supply a less expensive brand.'
- *Scrutinising medical training:* For example, the Australian Competition and Consumer Commission (ACCC) found a 'conflict of interest' in the way the Royal Australasian College of Surgeons (RACS) ran its training program, finding that 'unreasonably high standards inappropriately limit[ed] the size of the surgical profession thereby producing high incomes for surgeons' (ACCC 2003). Subsequently, the College announced that it would 'streamline training … with the intention of reducing the length of training while still maintaining the standards that the Australian community deserves' (RACS 2007).

- *Allowing other occupations to do medical work:* One way to reduce costs is to have medical work done more cheaply by non-medical staff. For example, several state governments have introduced 'nurse practitioners'. In Victoria, their work includes 'assessment and management of clients using nursing knowledge and skills and may include but is not limited to, the direct referral of patients to other health care professionals, prescribing medications and ordering diagnostic investigations' (Victorian Department of Human Services 2009).

Health is a multi-billion dollar business, but the average medical practice in Australia employs just five people (AIHW 2008b, p. 25). There is now a trend for large medical and hospital companies to buy these small businesses. The doctors then become employees—this is where the concept of the **proletarianisation of medicine** stems from. About 12 per cent of Australia's GPs are in these commercial relationships (Kron 2008) and the percentage has increased rapidly in the last few years. Indeed, according to an Australian Medical Association (AMA) spokesperson, there is 'potential for massive majority corporate ownership within our lifetime' (Stevenson, cited in Robertson 2007, p. 32). In terms of medical dominance, these new commercial arrangements could mean that doctors have less autonomy to practise, as their employers require them to tailor their consultations and referrals to maximise group profits.

proletarianisation of medicine
A trend for self-employed doctors in independent practice to be replaced by doctors working for larger companies.

Overall, there is a wide range of interpretations about what these trends mean for the future of medical dominance. Some suggest that we are about to enter a post-physician era. Others see the changes simply as doctors shifting ground to maintain dominance. In Australia, the ever-rising cost of Medicare is probably the most significant issue, leading to an increasing level of bureaucratic involvement in health expenditure, and thus medical decision-making.

In 2008, the federal Labor government established the National Health and Hospitals Reform Commission (NHHRC). Its task was to develop 'a long-term health reform plan to provide sustainable improvements in the performance of the health system' (NHHRC 2009, p. 357). The Commission identified four themes for reform of the health system: (1) 'individual and collective action to build good health and well-being by people, families, communities, health professionals, employers and governments'; (2) 'comprehensive care for people over their lifetime'; (3) 'recognise and tackle the causes and impacts of health inequities'; and (4) 'better use of people, resources, and evolving knowledge' (NHHRC 2009, p. 1). In 2010, the Labor government announced its first response to the Commission's recommendations after what was claimed as a 'historic' agreement was reached between all states and territories (bar Western Australia). It remains to be seen whether the heralded 'landmark' reforms will minimise increases in healthcare costs, improve the quality of services, and ultimately result in greater control of health's biggest cost-generating profession—medical practitioners.

Conclusion

If you went to a leading sociological database, Sociological Abstracts, and did a simple search on 'health', you would get nearly 100 000 hits. In this short chapter, I have just scratched the surface of the very wide range of topics studied by health sociologists, but the aim of the chapter has been to show that to understand health, you need to know much more than just what is going on inside a person's body; you need to know about the social system in which he or she lives. Of course, creating a healthier society by changing parts of a social system is much more difficult than even the most complex surgery. Not everyone would go as far as Lesley Doyal and suggest that 'the demand for a healthier society is, in itself, the demand for a radically different social order' (1979, p. 297), but it is clear from the asbestos story that, at the very least, a healthy society needs to be an extremely vigilant one.

Summary of main points

▶ Health has physical, psychological, and social dimensions. Different groups emphasise different dimensions.

▶ The biomedical model emphasises the physical and psychological dimensions, and focuses on curing sick individuals. The social model emphasises the social dimension, and ways to reduce health inequalities between social groups.

▶ There are major health inequalities between socioeconomic status groups. Health behaviours (such as smoking and diet) play a minor explanatory role. Working conditions are important, both directly (for example, accidents and the impact of chemicals) and, much more importantly, indirectly through work stress and income levels.

▶ Major health differences also occur between men and women, and between Indigenous and non-Indigenous Australians.

▶ The Australian healthcare system is huge, and largely publicly funded, but with private medical practitioners playing a major role in managing health care.

▶ There is debate about why medical dominance happened, and about whether it will continue. Probably the most important factor is the increasing bureaucratisation of health care.

SOCIOLOGICAL
REFLECTION

17.1 Doctor–patient relations

(a) Think back to your last visit to your GP. Did you play the traditional patient role, or were you a knowledgeable and assertive health consumer?

(b) Have you or any of your friends looked up health information on the internet, then used it in a later consultation with a GP?

(c) From conversations with family and friends, do you think older people see their doctor in a different light from younger people?

Discussion questions

17.1 Draw up a table with three columns and eight rows. List the three dimensions of health (physical, psychological, and social) as headings for the three columns. Divide each dimension into just two states: well and ill. Across each row, list all possible combinations, starting with well/well/well and finishing with ill/ill/ill. For example, a person could be physically well, but psychologically and socially ill. Try to give labels to all eight possible combinations.

17.2 Recall the word-association experiment: 'When I say "health" what words first come to mind?' Try this on a few friends. Do 'doctor', 'medicine', or 'hospital' crop up regularly? How are we socialised into thinking about health in this way?

17.3 Were you surprised (or even shocked) by the huge differences in health across SES groups? Why do you think there is so little media comment about this issue?

17.4 Do you think that employers give enough thought to the impact of work-related stress on their employees? In terms of workplace conditions, why is stress more difficult for governments to include in health and safety regulations?

17.5 Describe the basic features of the current Australian healthcare system. Do you think there will be any major changes in the next few years? Why?

17.6 Explain exactly what Lesley Doyal means when she says that 'the demand for a healthier society is, in itself, the demand for a radically different social order' (1979, p. 297). Do you agree with her?

Further reading

There are several excellent recent Australian textbooks on the sociology of health:

Germov, J. (ed.) 2009, *Second Opinion: An Introduction to Health Sociology*, 4th edn, Oxford University Press, Melbourne.

Gray, D.E. 2006, *Health Sociology: An Australian Perspective*, Pearson, Sydney.

Grbich, C. (ed.) 2004, *Health in Australia: Sociological Concepts and Issues*, 3rd edn, Pearson, Sydney.

Australia's Health is the prime source of statistical information. It is published every two years by the Australian Institute of Health and Welfare.

Websites

- Australian Institute of Health and Welfare (AIHW): <www.aihw.gov.au>. The website gives you access to all their publications free of charge.

- The Australian Sociological Association (TASA): <www.tasa.org.au>. The TASA website provides numerous links to health-related sites and topics. From the home page, click on 'web links'.

Films/documentaries

- 'Blue Death', *Four Corners*, 1988, television news feature, reported by P. Barry, Australian Broadcasting Corporation. An award-winning report on the thousands of Australians who have died from asbestos poisoning.
- *The Trouble with Medicine*, 1993, television series, produced by J. West, Australian Broadcasting Corporation/ British Broadcasting Corporation/ WNET-Thirteen. An excellent joint British, Canadian, and Australian series examining a wide range of social and ethical issues.
- *A Dying Shame*, 1997, documentary, directed by P. Roy, Ronin Films. A thought-provoking case study of Indigenous health problems.
- *Too Much Medicine*, 1998, television documentary, Australian Broadcasting Corporation. A three-part series that asks, 'Is there too much medicine?' The three parts look at surgery, drugs, and tests. For example, in the drugs episode, the question is whether drug companies are putting profits before patients.
- *Sicko*, 2007, documentary, directed by M. Moore, The Weinstein Company. This commercially successful documentary compares the American healthcare system with those in France, Britain, and (most provocatively) Cuba.
- 'Sick Around the World', *Frontline*, 2008, television news feature, directed by J. Palfreman, Public Broadcasting Service. A report about how the United Kingdom, Japan, Germany, Taiwan, and Switzerland deliver health care, and what the United States might learn from their successes and failures. <www.pbs.org/wgbh/pages/frontline/sickaroundtheworld>.

Visit the *Public Sociology* book website to access topical case studies, weblinks, YouTube clips, and extra readings.

References

Australian Bureau of Statistics (ABS) 2007, *Australian Social Trends 2007*, cat. no. 4102.0, ABS, Canberra.
—— 2008, *Year Book Australia 2008*, cat. no. 1301.0, ABS, Canberra.
Australian Competition and Consumer Commission 2003, 'ACCC proposes Surgical College reform', <www.accc.gov.au/content/index.phtml/itemId/88308> (accessed 29 January 2006).

Australian Institute of Health and Welfare (AIHW) 2006, *Socioeconomic Inequalities in Cardiovascular Disease in Australia*, cat. no. AUS 74, AIHW, Canberra.

—— 2008a, *Australia's Health 2008*, cat. no. AUS 99, AIHW, Canberra.

—— 2008b, *General Practice Activity in Australia 2007–08*, cat. no. GEP 22, AIHW, Canberra.

—— 2009a, *Health and Community Services Labour Force 2006*, cat. no. HWL 43, AIHW, Canberra.

—— 2009b, *Medical Indemnity National Data Collection Public Sector 2003 to 2004*, cat. no. HSE 39, AIHW, Canberra.

Burdess, N. 2004, 'Class and health', in C. Grbich (ed.), *Health in Australia: Sociological Concepts and Issues*, 3rd edn, Pearson, Sydney.

Chandola, T., Brunner, E. & Marmot, M. 2006, 'Chronic stress at work and the metabolic syndrome: Prospective study', *BMJ Online First*, doi: 10.1136/bmj.38693.435301.80 (published 20 January 2006).

Doyal, L. 1979, *The Political Economy of Health*, Pluto Press, London.

Germov, J. 2009a, 'Imagining health problems as social issues', in J. Germov (ed.), *Second Opinion*, 3rd edn, Oxford University Press, Melbourne, pp. 3–24.

—— 2009b, 'Challenges to medical dominance', in J. Germov (ed.), *Second Opinion*, 3rd edn, Oxford University Press, Melbourne, pp. 392–415.

Haigh, G. 2006, *Asbestos House: The Secret History of James Hardie Industries*, Scribe, Melbourne.

Harris Poll 2008, *Prestige Paradox: High Pay Doesn't Necessarily Equal High Prestige*, Harris Poll, <www.harrisinteractive.com/harris_poll/index.asp?PID=939> (accessed 5 May 2009).

Hills, B. 1989, *Blue Murder*, Sun Books, Melbourne.

Kron J 2008, 'Lifting the corporate lid', *Australian Doctor*, 20 June, pp. 43–6.

Marmot, M. 1998, 'Mastering the control factor, part two', *The Health Report*, Australian Broadcasting Corporation, <www.abc.net.au/rn/talks/8.30/helthrpt/stories/s17092.htm> (accessed 19 January 2006).

—— 2004, *The Status Syndrome: How Social Standing Affects Our Health and Longevity*, Times Books, New York.

McKeown, T. 1979, *The Role of Medicine*, Princeton University Press, Princeton, NJ.

McKinlay, J.B., McKinlay, S.M. & Beaglehole, R. 1977, 'The questionable contribution of medical measures to the decline of mortality in the United States in the twentieth century', *Milbank Memorial Fund Quarterly*, vol. 55, no. 3, pp. 405–28.

Medicare Australia 2009, *Saving You Money on Medicine*, <www.medicareaustralia.gov.au/public/services/scripts/saving-money.jsp> (accessed 5 May 2009).

Morgan Poll 2008, 'Image of Professions Survey: Nurses most ethical (again)', <www.roymorgan.com/news/polls/2008/4283> (accessed 4 May 2009).

National Health and Hospitals Reform Commission 2009, *A Healthier Future for All Australians—Interim Report, December 2008*, Commonwealth of Australia, Canberra.

Pringle, R. 1998, *Sex and Medicine*, Cambridge University Press, Cambridge.

Robertson, J. 2007, 'A big jab in the arm for AMC [Australian Medical Centres]', *Courier-Mail*, 24 September, pp. 31–2.

Royal Australasian College of Surgeons 2007, 'College of Surgeons and the ACCC', <www.surgeons.org/AM/Template.cfm?Section=Home&TEMPLATE=/CM/ContentDisplay.cfm&CONTENTID=15858> (accessed 5 May 2009).

Ryan, W. 1971, *Blaming the Victim*, Pantheon, New York.

Saunders, P.G. 1998, 'Poverty and health', *Australian and New Zealand Journal of Public Health*, vol. 22, no. 1, pp. 11–16.

Stinson, R. 2006, *What Jobs Pay 2006–2007*, Yorkcross, Sydney.

Sweeney, C. 1988, 'The Wall', *Time*, 17 October, pp. 66–8.

Victorian Department of Human Services (VDHS) 2009, 'Nursing in Victoria: Nurse Practitioner', <www.health.vic.gov.au/nursing/furthering/practitioner> (accessed 5 May 2009).

Wilkinson, R.G. 1992, 'Income distribution and life expectancy', *British Medical Journal*, vol. 304, 18 January, pp. 165–8.

Williams, L. 2009, 'Jostling for position: A sociology of allied health', in J. Germov (ed.), *Second Opinion*, 3rd edn, Oxford University Press, Melbourne, pp. 452–75.

Willis, E. 1989, *Medical Dominance*, rev. edn, Allen & Unwin, Sydney.

World Health Organization (WHO) 1946, *Constitution of the World Health Organization*, <www.who.int/governance/eb/who_constitution_en.pdf> (accessed 31 January 2006).

CHAPTER 18

Globalisation, power, and social movements

Jan Pakulski

The globalisation of Isabella

Isabella lives in the city of Newcastle, Australia. Each morning, she goes for a short jog while listening to her iPod (made in China by US company Apple). While having a shower she uses shampoo, cleanser, and moisturiser made in France, and then sits down for breakfast, which consists of Italian espresso coffee (with beans sourced from Brazil), and cereal (made in Australia by the US company Kellogg's). She briefly watches US chat shows on pay TV on a Korean-made LCD TV, while dressing for work in expensive designer clothes (made in China) and Italian leather shoes. Checking her Swiss watch for the time, she drives to work in a German-made VW Golf, chatting hands-free on her Sony Ericsson mobile (half-Swedish, half-Japanese). She arrives just before 9.00 a.m. at the tourism company for which she works, which has offices throughout the Asia-Pacific region. Her week has been spent cancelling clients' holiday bookings to Bali, due to renewed security fears about terrorist threats. During her lunch break, Isabella checks the news headlines on the internet; the latest reports on global warming and the spread of Swine Flu cause her concern, and make her ponder the benefits of global exposure. Recently, Isabella has learnt that her job may fall victim of the global slump in tourism caused by the worldwide recession. She feels a 'collateral damage' of the crisis, to which she has not contributed—or has she?

Introduction

The processes of **globalisation** weaken the regulative powers of individual nation-states. At the same time, they enhance the influence of non-state (global) actors, such as **transnational corporations (TNCs)**, including the powerful media networks, international organisations, transnational **elite** networks and alliances, non-governmental organisations (NGOs), and, last but not least, global social movements, including powerful green, feminist, and anti-globalisation(!) movements. Globalisation has also proven to be movement-friendly by facilitating cross-national flows of information, networking, and collaboration—all facilitating broad mobilisation of mass social movements. By enhancing cross-border information, contacts, and collaboration, globalisation aids both left-libertarian ('new') social movements, such as green and feminist movements, and populist-conservative movements, such as Islamic and

globalisation
The increased interconnectedness of the cultural, economic, and political aspects of social life; intensified circulation of capital, goods, information, and people across national boundaries; and increasing interdependence of countries and regions of the world.

transnational corporations (TNCs)
Business corporations operating in more than one country.

elites
Powerful minorities, such as incumbents of top positions in the state, major corporations, key pressure groups, and social movements, capable of influencing social outcomes in a systematic and significant way. Elites are typically contrasted with the masses.

Christian religious-fundamentalist movements. While the former two promote liberal social reforms, the latter oppose liberal social change and promote traditionalism backed by 'faith politics'. Thus globalisation results in a more complex and less state-organised social and political environment, with more 'stakeholders', more diverse political actors, less certainty about outcomes, and higher risks of unintended consequences.

This chapter first defines globalisation and then discusses pro- and anti-globalisation viewpoints, focusing on the impact of globalisation on the distribution of poverty, the decline of class-based politics, the changing role of the state, the rise of new social movements, and the extent to which these changes pose a challenge to the Western model of liberal democracy.

What is globalisation?

Interest in globalisation—understood as the processes of worldwide economic, informational, and cultural interdependency—grew in the 1960s and 1970s. It was stimulated by the analyses of global media by Marshall McLuhan (who coined the term 'global village') and the analyses of the growth of the world market by Immanuel Wallerstein and the so-called **dependency theorists**. Yet the concept of 'globalisation' only became a buzzword in the 1990s, after being popularised mainly by Roland Robertson (1992), Anthony Giddens (1990), and Malcolm Waters (1995).

dependency theory
The argument developed by *neo-Marxists* that developing (periphery, Southern) societies are locked through trade links in exploitative dependency relations with developed (core, Northern) societies.

Globalisation means increasing interdependence on a world scale. In the most general sense, globalisation implies the continuation of the following key processes of modernisation on a world scale (and not just within 'advanced' societies), largely unrestricted by national boundaries and 'tyrannies of distance':

rationalisation
A tendency to apply reason, to think and act in a calculative manner (as opposed to an emulative or traditional manner). It is seen by *Weberian* scholars as the key aspect of *modernisation* and as the synonym of *detraditionalisation*.

*   **rationalisation** (the standardisation of social life through rules and regulations)
*   **commodification** (the tendency to treat increasing aspects of social life as things that can be bought and sold in the marketplace)
*   **social differentiation** (the increasing specialisation of paid work), and
*   democratisation.

commodification
A tendency for goods and services to be treated primarily as things that are bought and sold on the market.

The key agents of these changes are no longer national governments and elites (as assumed by the theorists of

352 SOCIAL TRANSFORMATIONS

social differentiation

A term coined by Durkheim to refer to the social division of labour, whereby work becomes separated into different social spheres such as the family and the economy, and paid work becomes increasingly specialised into discrete occupations with particular power and status hierarchies.

modernisation

A contested concept that refers to the social changes that agrarian and 'traditional' societies undergo to achieve modernity, such as the development of nation states and associated political institutions based on the rule of law, secularisation, industrialisation, urbanisation, and a reliance on science and reason as the basis for understanding the world.

modernisation), but increasingly non-state organisations, such as TNCs, international agencies, such as the World Bank and the International Monetary Fund (IMF), and supra-national alliances, such as the North American Free Trade Agreement (NAFTA) and the European Union (EU). More specifically, globalisation refers to 'the compression of the world' (Robertson 1992, p. 8) through intensified cross-national circulation of money (capital), goods and services (products), ideas and symbols (information), and people (labour).

Globalisation has three aspects: economic, political, and cultural. The first aspect of globalisation—increasing economic interdependence—is arguably the most important one. It is brought about by:

- the widening networks of investment, production, trade, and consumption, especially after the market reforms in China (after 1978), and the 'opening' *cum* democratisation of Eastern Europe following the collapse of European communist regimes in 1989–90 and the dissolution of the Soviet Union in 1991
- the increasing international mobility of capital, goods, and services, combined with the progressive integration of the financial markets, all facilitated by the new information and communication technologies (ICTs)
- the widening links in production and trade, especially following the 'flow' of manufacturing to the areas of low labour cost (like China), and liberalisation of trade through lowering tariffs and formation of free-trade blocs, such as NAFTA, the European Union, the Association of Southeast Asian Nations (ASEAN), and Mercosur
- the international migrations and circulation of labour, facilitated by the loosening of border controls and improvements in transport and communication, and
- the complex web of international regulation of finance and trade, especially following the 2008–09 economic crisis and its aftermath. Strengthening of the World Bank and coordination of 'anti-crisis measures' laid the foundation for what has been described as a 'new global economic order' (Longworth 2009).

Economic globalisation is accompanied by political globalisation, triggered by the acceleration of cross-national political alliances, the collapse of the politically insulated Soviet bloc, the increasing role of non-state political actors, such as the North Atlantic Treaty Organization (NATO) and al-Qaeda, the rapid expansion of American influence on a global scale, and the rise of the 'other world powers', especially China and India. In line with these developments, contemporary politics has been losing its state-centred and state-controlled character—and with it, its predictability. A new global world politic is in many respects similar to the emerging world economy: increasingly complex, cross-national, multi-polar, and less predictable than the old state-focused and superpower-controlled politic organised into 'power blocs'. The influence of the superpowers, especially the United States, remains considerable, though it has been dented by the United States-triggered economic crisis and messy interventions in Iraq and Afghanistan. Still, in a globalising world even the most powerful nation-state actors, such as the United States, face growing challenges from the rising Asian powers (particularly China and India), and they have to rely on alliances and coalitions—or risk failure.

Finally, **globalising trends** affect contemporary culture, especially popular culture propagated by the global media networks. The key elements of cultural globalisation are the spread of popular culture (especially Hollywood and Bollywood films), diversification of values (increasing 'value polytheism', to use Émile Durkheim's phrase) and progressive individualism (which Ulrich Beck and Giddens refer to as **individualisation**), combined with proliferation of niche subcultures (reflected in specific music, dress, and lifestyle fashions). Under their impact, the formerly insulated cultures are forced to interact; many established traditions crumble, thus producing not only accelerated modernisation but also intensified fear and cultural backlash. Critics fear that such intensified and forced interaction may trigger a 'clash of civilisations'—the intense ethno-religious and inter-communal conflicts—and point to nationalist and conservative movements, often of a religious-fundamentalist-traditionalist nature, as consequences of cultural globalisation. Such movements—Islamist, Hindu-nationalist, and Christian revival—seem to accompany cultural globalisation as popular reactions to a rapid spread through the international media networks of aggressively cosmopolitan, secular, fragmented, and syncretic popular subcultures. These subcultures are also more fickle than traditional national cultures, and change with seasonal regularity. Tastes, consumption patterns, and lifestyles, especially in the metropolitan centres of societies that are most exposed to global trends, change with almost seasonal regularity. The culture industries that produce them are also in constant flux, though they continue to be heavily dominated by the US entertainment industries, the products of which easily adapt to the local tastes and niche demand.

globalising trends

Tendencies in *globalisation* processes. They involve a quantum leap in cross-national interdependencies caused by the intensified circulation of money (capital), goods and services (products), ideas and symbols (information), and people (labour).

individualisation

A trend towards the primacy of individual choice, freedom, and self-responsibility.

Globosceptics versus globoenthusiasts

Clearly, globalisation has integrating and fragmenting, egalitarian and hierarchical, democratic and authoritarian effects. It encourages and promotes a 'global perspective', less affected by local parochialism and national egoisms, but it also undermines national and local cultures, and unleashes global competition that divides nations, regions, ethno-religious collectives, and (sub)cultural groupings. Globalisation facilitates the spread of democratic regimes—since the 1990s, democratic regimes have become the majority form of government, for the first time in history—but also frees corporate elites, especially in TNCs, from state controls. It enhances the 'global village' effect—that is, unrestricted circulation of information combined with increased awareness of global problems—but also exacerbates the marginalisation of isolated regions, such as sub-Saharan Africa. It facilitates coordinated civic actions, especially through the internet and media networks, but also causes the spread of crises (like the 2008 financial crisis), crime (like the international drug and terrorism networks), and infectious diseases (like the 2009 Swine Flu pandemic). The question remains: which effects are more pronounced?

For **globosceptics**, globalisation is economically polarising, exploitative, and corrosive of social bonds. Globosceptics see globalisation as the triumph of exploitative international capitalism, domination by transnational corporations, **economic rationalism**, and environmental degradation—all seen as socially disruptive and unsustainable (see Pusey 1991, 2003; Stiglitz 2002). They see trade liberalisation as causing deindustrialisation and as depressing wages, and thus boosting the ranks of the 'working poor'. Globalisation-triggered migrations, including flows of refugees from marginalised and conflict-torn regions, threaten the social order. According to globosceptics, the deteriorating working conditions among low-skilled or unskilled workers in industrial regions (a trend dubbed 'race to the bottom') cause local impoverishment. The 'export' of manufacturing jobs to the low-cost regions (such as China and India) leaves behind 'rust belts' in the formerly industrialised regions of America and Europe—the 'patches' of high unemployment and urban decay that become breeding grounds for crime, drug abuse, and social dislocation. Similarly, the widening gap between the increasingly affluent 'North' (a term denoting richer, developed countries) and impoverished regions of (mostly sub-Saharan) Africa, South America, and Central Asia cause political instability, which increasingly spills over into the developed world. Globosceptics also blame global competition for deregulatory policies resulting in the unchecked (and untaxed) growth of wealth and influence, especially among corporate elites. Such elites can easily evade state control, including control by democratically elected governments. Sceptics further argue that globalisation weakens **citizenship rights** by eroding the capacity of the state to implement and secure collective rights, especially social (welfare) rights. Internationally, globalisation leads to further centralisation of power, because it involves increased economic, political, military, and cultural domination by the United States (see Stiglitz 2002; Robinson 2004).

Globoenthusiasts, by contrast, emphasise the integrative, pro-developmental, and pro-democratic impact of globalisation,

globosceptics
Those who are critical of *globalisation* because they see it as socially divisive.

economic rationalism
Describes a political philosophy based on small-government and market-oriented policies, such as deregulation, privatisation, reduced government spending, and lower taxation. Used interchangeably with *neo-liberalism*.

citizenship rights
A collection of rights and obligations that determine legal identity and membership of a state, and function to control access to scarce resources.

globoenthusiasts
Those who see *globalisation* as a socially benign process.

especially the liberalising effects of the increasingly free and wide circulation of goods, ideas, and people. They point to the globalisation-induced political and economic integration that has occurred, especially within the European Union and between the developed and developing regions (e.g. the United States–China trade). Globalisation,

civil rights
These form a civil component of modern citizenship, and include liberty of the person, freedom of speech, thought, and faith, the right to own property and to conclude valid contracts, and the right to justice—all safeguarded by independent courts of justice.

globoenthusiasts further argue, is conducive to economic growth that lifts hundreds of million people in China and India out of poverty. It prompts the free movements of people and ideas, facilitates expansion of electoral democracy, and widens freedom of information. Globalisation undermines authoritarian regimes by relaxing censorship and control of migrations, strengthens **civil rights** by increasing the capacity of like-minded citizens to organise, and makes persecution of minorities more difficult by increasing the strength of public opinion and international sanctions. The most authoritarian regimes are those that resist global engagement (e.g. North Korea). Therefore, wherever it occurs, globalisation paves the way for democratic movements and reforms, as illustrated by the successes of the 'peaceful' and 'coloured' liberal-democratic 'revolutions' (i.e. reforms with revolutionary scope) in Central-Eastern Europe in 1989–90, the South African anti-apartheid 'peaceful revolution' in 1994–95, the anti-Milosevic 'Bulldozer Revolution' in Serbia in 2000, the 'Rose Revolution' in Georgia in 2003, the 'Orange Revolution' in Ukraine in 2004, other pro-democratic movements and mobilisations in Kyrgyzstan in 2005 and Lebanon in 2005, and the short-lived 'Twitter' protests in Iran in 2009. Democratisation and liberalisation seem to accompany globalisation.

Globoenthusiasts stress that, as a result of these pro-democratic movements, 121 of the world's 194 national regimes—that is, 62 per cent—were classified by Freedom House in 2008 as electoral democracies; 151 regimes—78 per cent—were classified as 'free' or 'partly free'; and the freedom of the press—a key propellant of democratisation—has increased dramatically since the 1980s (see Table 18.1). Countries embracing globalisation, such as South Korea, Taiwan, and Indonesia, have expanded their civil rights, press freedoms, and democratic practices. Regions that resist globalisation often remain under authoritarian rule or suffer from political instability. Thus the worst forms of political tyranny, typically combined with poverty, have been brought about by isolated regimes, such as the North Korean one, and governments in those regions of Africa, Asia, and South America that shun global trends. Similarly, sweatshops and child labour are not, in the view of globoenthusiasts, products of globalisation, but rather symptoms of isolation and under-development—both symptomatic of *insufficient* globalisation.

The sharp contrast between these two positions—globosceptical and globoenthusiastic—clearly indicates that the effects of globalisation, especially its impact on the distribution of power and wealth, are quite complex and call for an analysis free of partisan selectivity. A convenient starting point for such an analysis is the impact of globalisation on world poverty, and the gap between developing and developed regions.

Table 18.1: 'Free' (democratic), 'partly free', and 'unfree' (non-democratic) countries, 1975–2008 (%)

Period	% free	% partly free	% unfree	% total	No.
1975	25	34	41	100	158
1985	34	34	32	100	167
1995	40	32	28	100	191
2008	47	31	22	100	194

Source: Based on Freedom House (2009) website: <www.freedomhouse.org>.

Globalisation and the developing nations: The poverty and polarisation debate

Is globalisation, as some globosceptics claim, widening the gap between the developed and developing world (global polarisation)? The tentative answer is 'no', though it needs numerous qualifications. Generally, globalisation seems to stimulate economic growth, which in turn helps in reducing poverty. China and India are good examples of these beneficial effects. Both countries cut poverty by embracing globalisation and stimulating economic growth. By contrast, mass deprivations typically accompany isolationism; they affect regions and regimes that either shun globalisation or are recovering from long isolation (e.g. post-communist Eastern Europe and Central Asia).

Poverty typically means cumulative disadvantage—not only economic insufficiency, but also high mortality, high morbidity, and social exclusion. It is correlated with other aspects of disadvantage, such as homelessness, poor health, and illiteracy. At the heart of poverty, however, typically lies inadequate resourcing. Therefore, 'primary poverty' in developing nations is conceptualised as insufficient income, typically living on US$1–2 per day.

The overall trends in world poverty and inequality (measured in disregard of national boundaries) have been well diagnosed, and they seem to contradict the claims of globosceptics. Living standards have been rising in tandem with economic growth. The proportion of extremely poor (those living on less than US$1.25 per day) in the developing countries fell from 52 per cent in 1981 to 25 per cent in 2005. The most spectacular decline occurred in East Asia, where the proportion of extremely poor declined from 78 per cent of the population in 1981 to 17 per cent in 2005—a drop of over 300 million people—mainly due to the fast globalisation, that is 'opening up' to international trade and production in China. Another rapidly globalising region, South Asia, also experienced a sharp fall of poverty between 1981 and 2005: from 60 per cent to 40 per cent of the population (World Bank 2009). Since globalisation and its accompanying economic growth also increase the wealth at the top of the economic hierarchy, the total scope of social inequality—the gap between the wealthy and the poor—remained more or less the same, though the poorest region of the world has shifted from East and South Asia to sub-Saharan Africa—the region that is least integrated with the world network of production and trade. Thus globalisation seems to benefit the poor by stimulating economic growth. Increasing circulation of capital, goods, services, ideas, and people has been accompanied everywhere by growing production, expanding trade, and, generally, a rising standard of living that benefits everyone—the wealthy and the poor alike. The wealthy, it may be noted, seem to benefit from the globalisation-spurred growth earlier and to a larger extent than the poor—hence economic globalisation accompanies the widening of income gaps—but their wealth is also more precarious: the 2008–10 economic recession has decimated the ranks of the 'super-rich'.

How much of this global poverty reduction has been due to globalisation, and how much was caused by the accompanying but contingent factors? This question is hotly debated between globosceptics and globoenthusiasts. Generally, it is accepted that trade liberalisation and economic integration stimulate economic growth, and that increasing growth helps to reduce poverty. It has been estimated that variation in growth explains about half of the variation in poverty levels. Economic stagnation and decline, by contrast, are the key factors in increasing poverty and widening material inequality. Therefore, extreme poverty and deprivation—and their correlates, economic decline combined with social conflicts—are most often diagnosed in countries insulated from global flows (such as North Korea), ravaged by wars (like Afghanistan), or afflicted by both (most of sub-Saharan Africa).

Nevertheless, recent analyses also suggest that the relationship between globalisation, economic growth, and poverty may be more complex. The impact of globalisation-induced growth on poverty, for example, is patchy, and depends on the overall positioning of the country/region within the world economy, as well as the pattern of relative advantage in the 'factors of production'. Thus the poor in the least-affluent developing countries generally benefit from economic integration (the key aspect of globalisation) because this integration boosts demand for low- and medium-skilled labour, which abounds among the poor. It is also noted, though, that in the developed world, the least skilled rural and migrant workers may be adversely affected by economic integration and trade liberalisation because the demand for their labour declines, together with wages. Globalisation also has mixed effects on the poor because it increases unemployment (therefore deepening poverty) in the sectors that are adversely affected by the increasing international competition—for example, in the 'deindustrialising' regions of developed countries: the so-called 'rust belts'. Thus the overall impact of globalisation depends on the labour market supply, and (perhaps more importantly) on governmental policy—especially assistance to the poor. It is this second factor—the policies of governments—that is responsible for the variation in poverty levels.

The globosceptics emphasise these strong links between poverty and policy, and point to the correlation between globalisation on the one hand, and the 'poor-unfriendly' deregulatory, transfer-shy, and welfare-restricting policies on the other. The globoenthusiasts respond by arguing that globalisation and regulatory/welfare policies vary independently, and they point to the examples of China and India, where increasing globalisation has not affected welfare policies and accompanied reductions in poverty levels. So who is right?

It is fair to say that, as far as poverty and material inequality are concerned, the prevailing consensus is that globalisation carries mixed blessings: beneficial opportunities as well as costs and risks (see Pakulski 2004). Globalisation-induced growth benefits all, including the poor, but it tends to benefit the rich far more than the poor. Thus, as far as the overall impact on poverty is concerned, the jury is still out. The decline in the number of poor in the developing regions of East Asia and the Pacific has been counter-balanced by the rises in (mostly rural) poverty in Russia, Central and South Asia, sub-Saharan Africa, and Latin America.

There is also another side to this argument. Globalisation 'opens up' formerly insulated areas (such as Russia and Central Asia) to environmental scrutiny and pollution control, and in that sense it is environmentally friendly. On the other hand, it enhances environmental risks in rapidly developing industrial regions, especially in China and India. The 'risks' and 'costs' attributed to globalisation-spurred growth include both social rifts and ecological degradation—and these costs, critics say, are carried disproportionately by the poor. Hence globalisation is seen by critics as a socially and ecologically polarising force: those prepared to seize opportunities (such as those offered by human capital or mobility) prosper; those who do not—or who are unable to do so—suffer. While trade and financial integration do not increase the vulnerability of the poor to economic breakdown, they can increase the propensity for crises in the developing countries where most of the poor live. When a crisis hits a developing country, the rich migrate or reduce consumption, while the poor starve and die.

Globalisation and the state

The modern states have emerged as centralised administrative machines involved in warfare and welfare—the former securing international position and the latter attenuating internal social conflicts. The three essential functions of the modern state—external defence, internal surveillance, and the maintenance of citizenship rights—have been undermined by the processes of globalisation.

The defensive functions of the state in advanced societies have been undermined by the global proliferation of nuclear/biological weapons, non-state actors (e.g. terrorist groups and organisations), and non-conventional warfare strategies (guerrilla attacks, suicide bombing, and so on). They jointly limit the capacity of state military apparatuses to provide effective protection against 'enemies'. The defensive functions have also been restricted by the declining role of the military elites, and by the global spread of libertarian and pacifistic orientations among the young and educated segments of the population. Military ventures are routinely condemned by the public in affluent democracies unwilling to tolerate the loss of life and the economic costs associated with war.

The role of the state as provider and guardian of citizenship rights and political freedoms has also been eroded by global publicity given to unintended side-effects, such as welfare dependency. Restricting the welfare and other regulative functions of the state became something of the common wisdom of political elites, including the New Labour and neo-conservative regimes. Moreover, an increasing range of rights and freedoms have been depoliticised and thus defined as 'human rights' and 'individual freedoms' located above and beyond the control of the state, while state violations of these rights have been publicised, thus undermining the legitimacy of the state as the principal guardian of citizenship rights.

This shrinking of state regulative functions reflects both the declining willingness and the waning capacities of the state elites to control economy and society. The net result of these declining capacities has been a leaner and more humble state, as well as a shift of power away from the states and towards non-state actors. This shift combines with proliferation of multifarious groups and organisations operating outside and (at least partly) independently of states. According to James N. Rosenau (1997), globalisation facilitates such power shifts, causes political turbulence, and aids the growth of an increasingly powerful network of 'transnational society'; according to David J. Rothkopf (2008), it spawns a powerful 'superclass', a 'global elite without a country'. This elite forms as a result of a rapid concentration of wealth, mergers, and expansion of transnational corporations, widening of information and communication networks, and mobilisation of global movements. Social coalescence of the new, globalisation-spawned 'super-rich' and 'super-powerful'—such as CEOs of the largest transnational corporations, the most influential national political leaders, heads of the most powerful military establishments, leaders of the largest religious movements and organisations, as well as (somewhat surprisingly) heads of the most notorious transnational terrorist and criminal groups—creates, according to Rothkopf, a range of supra-national networks and actors (see Sociology Spotlight 18.1).

SOCIOLOGY
SPOTLIGHT

18.1: Supra-national networks

The networks include, first, transnational structures such as global financial networks, networks of technology and knowledge production, and networks of transnational manufacturing, connected through nodes of TNCs. Second, they include increasingly vocal trans- and international communities based on religion (such as Islamic communities), creeds and lifestyles (such as the Greens), ideology (such as the neo-conservatives), or sexual preferences (such as gay communities). Transnational organisations constitute a third element of the networks. They include the old bodies, such as the Catholic Church, together with the newer, such as the North Atlantic Treaty Organization (NATO) and the United Nations (UN), and very new ones, such as Greenpeace, the World Bank, and the International Monetary Fund (IMF). Last but not least, transnational criminal networks, related to terrorism, drug smuggling, and other forms of organised crime, must be mentioned. The expansion of transnational networks is further prompted by publicity given to transnational problems—that is, problems beyond the control of any single state, such as pollution, global warming, the illegal drug trade, the HIV/AIDS epidemic, and the threat of Swine Flu. Such publicity also generates 'transnational events', such as environmental and pro-democratic movements.

neo-Marxism
Theories that derive from Marx but incorporate diverse notions of power and status.

neo-liberalism
A philosophy based on the primacy of individual rights and minimal state intervention.

A similar argument about power 'leaving the state' has been presented by **neo-Marxist** scholars who see globalisation as spawning a new 'transnational capitalist class' (or, in some versions, class*es*). The professional and executive 'apex' of this class—professional experts, corporate leaders, and their political sponsors—forms a broad elite supporting deregulation and expansion of markets. This 'transnational' class and elite also include the top political executives and bureaucrats in the international associations and alliances, such as the North American Free Trade Agreement (NAFTA) or the Association of Southeast Asian Nations (ASEAN), as well as heads of international regulative and coordinating bodies, such as the World Trade Organization (WTO), the World Bank, and the IMF. All of them support and promote the **neo-liberal** program of deregulation and global expansion of capital, and thus become the global 'management committee' of transnational capitalism. These transnational groupings coexist and interact with national and international organisations. It is a combination of these three types of structures and politics—national, international, and global/transnational—that generates a new power dynamic (Sklair 2001; Robinson 2004; Sassen 2007).

All these arguments should be examined with due scepticism. The claims that political power shifts away from states and into the hands of new 'global' and 'denationalised' elites, classes, and networks, with few national attachments and nation-specific interests, have been heavily criticised as misrepresenting the changes associated with globalisation. As noted by numerous critics (e.g. Stiglitz 2002; Zakaria 2008), globalisation does not necessarily weaken nation states. It weakens *some* states, and strengthens others. Above all, globalisation widens power competition among states—and this competition changes power configurations. Old 'superpowers' wane and new challengers enter the field of competition. Thus the 'Cold War' superpowers, the Soviet Union/Russia and the United States, have declined. This decline, in turn, has changed the power configurations from bipolar (during the 'Cold War', 1945–90), to 'unipolar' (1991–2008), to 'regional-multipolar' (2009+) with China and India entering the ranks of significant regional power-centres.

Similarly, the claims about the alleged denationalisation of popular identities should also be treated with scepticism. In fact, globalisation seems to accompany a rise in nationalism, a 'global political awakening'—Zbigniew Brzezinski's (2008) term—that affects both the elites and the masses. These national 'awakenings' were most apparent in the Balkans and Central Asia following the collapse of the Soviet Union and Yugoslavia. In extreme cases, the 'awakening' combines xenophobic demagogy with militancy and populist mobilisations and nationalistic movements—all facilitated by the information and communication revolution. But the less extreme awakenings are also noticeable in North America, Australia, China, and India, all of which seem to experience resurgences of patriotic zeal and rhetoric. These outbursts of nationalism have been both articulated and seized by political elites. The resurgent American nationalism was harnessed by the neoconservative 'Vulcans' at the inner core of George W. Bush's elite. National pride was promoted by John Howard's elite in Australia. Nostalgic and imperial Russian nationalism has been embraced by a violent Vladimir Putin's elite; the assertive Chinese nationalism found its expression in the tough rhetoric of Hu Jintao, especially in response to the demands for human rights and autonomy in Tibet. National attachments and identities, critics suggest, do not weaken, but are supplemented—and often reinforced—by enhanced regional, gender, racial, and religious identities and commitments.

Thus globalisation—that is, increasing interdependence—does not change the nature of identities or the locus of political power. Instead, it changes the patterns of national identifications, and—more importantly—alters the way power is *exercised*. The increasing interdependence, as the most astute observers note, widens the domains of decisional power, increases the complexity of problems faced by national decision-makers, and amplifies the risks of unintended and adverse consequences. This is reflected in intensifying contacts, coordination, and collaboration among state power elites—all in response to increasing interdependence, growing complexity, declining certainty, widening risks, improved communication, and the multiplication of 'transnational' problems, such as uncontrolled migrations, energy shortages, environmental degradation, pollution, climate change, trade in illegal drugs, terrorism, cyber-crime, and threat of pandemics. Inter-elite contacts, coordination, collaboration, collusion, and competition widen and deepen. National elites have to rely on these widening contacts and coordination in order to maintain the effectiveness of their policies and reducing risks of failures. It is for these same reasons that they create and support transnational coordinative, regulative, collaborative bodies, such as the IMF, the World Bank, and the agencies of the UN. The proliferation of such bodies, however, does not mean that power shifts away from the states. It is simply exercised in a more multilateral manner. The transnational bodies, in other words, rely on political support from, as well as funding/resourcing by, their 'sponsoring' nation states. Thus the IMF and the World Bank rely on US backing, the EU relies on Franco-German support, and the Hezbollah cannot function without Iranian (and Syrian) sponsorship.

class decomposition
According to Ralf Gustav Dahrendorf, the process of declining social formation whereby *social classes* are fragmented and their boundaries weaken.

class/social class
A central but contested term in sociology that refers to a position in a system of structured inequality based on the unequal distribution of wealth, power, and status.

Globalisation and national politics: Dealignment and decomposition of social classes

Much more plausible claims about the impact of globalisation on power distribution have been made by students of national politics. Globalisation, according to them, affects power distribution *within* nation-states, especially by speeding up political dealignment and **class decomposition**. The progression of dealignment—that is, the weakening alliances between **social classes** and political parties ('class parties')—is widely attributed to the declining capacities of national governments to control and regulate national economies, societies, and cultures—a trend reflected in the popularity of neo-liberal strategies. It also reflects the declining capacities of class ideologies to reflect dominant identities and to provide coherent blueprints for change.

The most popular measures of political dealignment, the Alford Index and Thomsen Index of class voting, have declined since the 1960s in all advanced societies for which longitudinal data on voting behaviour are available (see Nieuwbeerta 1997; Charnock 2005). The decline has varied in terms of speed and intensity, but it appears to have been a universal trend throughout the post-World War II period, particularly strong in societies with an initially high level of class voting. It has been accompanied by the rise of various 'third' and 'unallied' forces, including 'single-issue parties', political movements, and the proliferation of 'independents'.

Another aspect of the dealignment process is declining trust in, and loyalty to, the old political organisations, especially class-based parties. The membership of such parties (as well as trade unions) has been declining rapidly in all advanced societies. This results in the collapse of the inter-generational transmission of party loyalties. Taken together, these two trends—dealignment and declining partisanship—mark the waning of stable political constituencies, the ascendancy of temporary alignments, and the proliferation of fickle issue-based voting.

Party programs and platforms, especially those containing strong ideological references (typically polarised along the 'left/right' dimension), are disappearing. Instead, mass political preferences are increasingly focusing on political leaders, particularly on leaders' characters (truthfulness, reliability), and their ability to project a good media image. These become the key factors shaping public opinion and voting behaviour. Leaders, in turn, abandon ideological references, and muster support by responding to current concerns (such as migration, and environmental regulation).

This spells the end of ideologically organised (left/right) party politics. Modern ideologies 'proper'—**liberalism**, **conservatism**, and **socialism**—crystallised in the nineteenth century in the context of deepening national class cleavages. Socialism, in particular, was an ideological child of the industrial class conflict. Modern liberalism and conservatism were reformulated in response to the socialist challenge. The formation of these ideological packages coincided with the formation of the 'left/right' ideological-political dimension, organisational crystallisation of 'class' or 'milieu' parties, and the spread of electoral politics in which references to ideological visions and blueprints were essential for success. The 'imagined communities', especially of nations and classes, relied heavily on these ideological packages for cohesion, legitimacy, and, above all, their identification with political leaders.

Globalisation accompanies a rapid decline in the clarity of the left/right divisions, credibility of ideological creeds, and the

liberalism
An ideology that prioritises the interests of individuals and their freedom in the marketplace.

conservatism
A political philosophy that supports traditional values, cultural homogeneity, social hierarchies, and the status quo.

socialism
A political ideology with numerous variations, but with a core belief in the creation of societies in which private property and wealth accumulation are replaced by state ownership and distribution of economic resources. See also *communism*.

consistency of ideologically organised class politics. The emergence of new movements, the focus on leaders' image and character, the rise of 'life politics', the mobilisation of religious and regional communities, and the appearance of the 'ideologically mixed categories' such as new fiscal populists, progressivists, New Laborists, neo-liberals, and neo-conservatives (neo-cons) may be seen as symptomatic of decomposition of old politics. The place of class/ideological parties is claimed by more ephemeral 'leadership' and 'issue' parties, often allied with mass social movements and/or charismatic leaders. They make political outcomes less predictable and blur the old ideological polarities between political left and right (Giddens 2001; Mair 2007).

Globalisation and civil society: New politics and social movements

Analysts of globalisation point to the growing salience in advanced societies of 'new politics' propelled by leaders' appeals, civic initiatives, and social movements. While parties weaken, social movements and their leaders gather strength, thus making contemporary democratic politics more 'open', personalised, and populist. This also gives the contemporary democratic practices more 'plebiscitary-demagogic' (Weber's term) colouring (McAllister 2007; Dalton & Klingemann 2007).

Such a shift should not be seen as leading towards a less elite-centred politic. Social movements, while seen as a 'voice of the people', are typically led by strong (often charismatic) leaders. In fact, the terms 'charisma' and 'populism' have been applied primarily in studies of leadership in social movements. Therefore the 'new politics', marked by the proliferation of social movements, does not necessarily bring dispersion of power; rather it widens the range of actors influencing political outcomes, thus making political processes more complex and their outcomes less predictable.

Global social movements

Thus globalisation changes the composition and increases the range of actors and stakeholders. It undermines the power of traditional 'class' or 'cleavage' parties, and facilitates the formation of new social movements. Perhaps the most visible and publicised are the *left-libertarian* 'new social movements', such as green, feminist, and minority rights (e.g. gay rights, Indigenous rights) movements. Their rise in the period from the 1970s to the 2000s has been attributed to the spread of 'post-materialist' value priorities. They involve concerns with the quality of life, self-actualisation, and civil liberties, prevalent among the post-World War II ('baby boom') generations raised in the climate of economic prosperity and political stability (Inglehart 1991, 2007).

Partly in response to the successful mobilisation of these left-libertarian movements, almost all advanced societies have experienced strong mobilisations of *right-populist* movements (e.g. One Nation in Australia, the Northern League in Italy) focusing on issues of migration (restricted), minority rights (curbed), and political leadership (authoritarian). Both types of movement differ from the 'old', mainly class-based, movements that dominated in the mid-twentieth century and tend to focus on protest (mobilise against rather than for) and attract diffuse social categories formed along generational divisions, locality, gender, ethnicity, level of education, and lifestyle. Their membership is transient and fluid, and their organisational structure is decentralised, informal, and polymorphous (Offe 1985; Betz 1994; Koopmans 2007). They use innovative tactics and strategies, and aim at influencing the political outcomes directly, through direct action (protest rallies, demonstrations) combined with mobilising public opinion, rather than through the party-parliamentary process, such as systematic lobbying for legislative change.

The third group of movements that contributes to the increasingly complex new politics comprises the largely conservative (if not outright reactionary) *religious-fundamental* movements. Adherents mobilise diverse audiences sharing concerns about social change, especially the erosion of traditional values, orientations, and lifestyles (often considered sacred). Perhaps the best known are the Islamist and Christian revival movements operating globally, but typically with little coordination. While their issue agendas differ from the left-libertarian and right-populist movements, they share the repertoires of protest and publicise their causes through diverse and innovative strategies.

Finally, we have observed in the last two decades the formation and ascendancy of *political reform movements*, especially those spearheading the democratisation and autonomisation of post-communist societies in Eastern Europe and Central Asia: the *Solidarity* movement in Poland, *Rukh* in Ukraine, *Otpor* in Serbia, and *KelKel* in Kyrgyzstan. Most of them have pro-democratic and nationalistic vectors, and they spawn new political elites heading deep reforms of political and economic systems.

We have already mentioned an interpretation of these new social movements in terms of value concerns. According to this interpretation, mass social movements represent reactions to those values that are strongly cherished and at the same time seen as threatened by social change. This helps to account for passions displayed by movement supporters, and for their weak 'anchoring' in the social (especially the class) structure. According to this interpretation, new social movements, and the new politics they shape, are reflective of cultures rather than social structures. Thus the left-libertarian movements can be seen as responses to the (global) proliferation of 'post-material values' in a climate of political stability, security, and prosperity (Inglehart 2007). Their right-populist counterparts reflect concerns with traditional values and lifestyles. The religious-fundamental movements mobilise under the conditions of rapid modernisation, and they attract those most threatened by the erosion of traditional-religious values and mores. Finally, the reformist movements carry on the modern Western value commitments (especially freedom and democracy) ignored by the authoritarian and totalitarian communist rulers.

CrossLink:
See Chapter 3
for more on
Beck and
Giddens.

Another account of new social movements (especially the left-libertarian green and anti-war movements) sees them as responses to risks generated by a new type of 'risk society' (advanced industrialised society). The term 'risk society' has been associated with the work of Beck (1992, 1994). Beck sees highly industrialised Western societies as becoming preoccupied not only with the satisfaction of material needs but also increasingly with the management of risks—that is, unintended consequences of routine human activities, such as pollution and the proliferation of nuclear arms. Beck suggests that preoccupation with risks accompanies a change in the key conflicts: old conflicts over the distribution of goods (including class conflicts) give way to new conflicts over the social distribution of 'bads'—that is, risks of harmful consequences associated with military expansion, pollution, genetic manipulation, and so on. New social movements—primarily the green, pacifist, and anti-development movements— reflect conflicts and antagonisms over the distribution, management, and legitimation of risks. The conflict is primarily over definitions, interpretations, attribution, symbolic representation, and dissemination of information through the media.

Another plausible and influential account of new social movements and new politics has been offered by Giddens (2001, 2002). The new politics, according to Giddens, reflect the key aspects of globalisation:

- *A post-industrial shift from a manufacturing to a service-producing economy.* Giddens stresses the worldwide scope of this shift and the accompanying 'migration' of manufacturing investment and jobs from the high-labour cost areas to the lower-labour cost regions, typically in developing nations such as China and India. This shift generates populist protest mobilisations (anti-globalisation, protectionist, nativist) that unify the old adversaries on the right and left of the political spectrum.

- *A trend towards growing, broadening, and diversifying consumption, and the accompanying differentiation of lifestyles that Giddens calls 'life politics'.* This aspect of global change is fuelled by progressive individualisation—a tendency to value uniqueness and to assert individual selves through stylisation of tastes.

- *A breakdown in the traditional model of family and sexuality.* Gender roles and gender divisions are radically changed so that women are no longer confined to lives of domesticity and child-rearing. In a similar way, the weakening of traditions undermines ethno-racial hierarchies and discriminations, often triggering 'reactive' movements such as religious-fundamentalist, anti-feminist, and pro-traditionalist/family.

- *Reforms of state governance that reduce bureaucratic inefficiencies and welfare dependency.* These lead to a change in the modes of governing by making governing less interventionist and less distributive. Citizenship rights lose their unconditional character, and entitlements are more closely linked with duties and obligations. As a result, the welfare sector shrinks.

- *Revitalisation of civil society in all its diverse forms.* Civic activism and robust civil society increasingly become recognised as the foundations of a prosperous and democratic society.

Finally, the wave of pro-democratic reformist movements in post-communist societies and in South Africa has been seen as a reflection of both cultural globalisation (especially the spread of information through the global media networks) and organised civic initiatives—the revival of 'civil society' (Wnuk-Lipinski 2007).

Conclusion

Giddens' (2002) sanguine assessment of globalisation as strengthening 'civil society' and expanding democracy—contrasting with the much darker vision of risks provided by Beck (1992)—needs some qualifications. The first concerns the corrupt corporate influence on politics. Globalisation may, in fact, facilitate this corrupt influence by freeing the TNCs from governmental controls and by increasing competition for corporate favours—state protection, monopolies and tax privileges, capital investment and jobs, as well as the corporate mobility and power that help them choose and shape their political environments. Corporate contributions and lobbying grow in proportion to the size and power of corporations, and therefore are not features of developing countries alone. They threaten democratic politics in the most advanced societies as much as they do in the developing world. Thus Kevin Phillips (2006) argues that the George W. Bush administration in the United States was 'captured' by powerful 'energy-automotive-military' lobbies that enjoyed not only privileged access, but also strong representation in the state executive. Similarly, the introduction of finance reform legislation in the United States at the beginning of 2002 followed public outrage about astronomical (and highly biased) corporate contributions to the 2000 presidential election campaign, and biased reporting by the corporate media. Similar concerns about corporate influence (especially by resource lobbies) were raised in Australia during the 2007 elections.

There are also other aspects of corporate influence that raise concerns over the health of democracy. Corporations—especially the large TNCs, with their strong stakes in governmental decisions—often show glaring disregard for laws and democratic norms. They fund parties, lobby politicians, are powerfully represented in think-tanks, advisory and consulting groups, and sometimes directly influence legislation. Large business firms maintain permanent lobbyists. The measures taken to curb corporate influence include increasing transparency and instituting disclosure rules in campaigns and candidate funding, restricting political contributions, and providing equitable public funding for parties and candidates.

The second threat to democracy also has a global source: it comes from the global (in scope) mass media and their 'demagogic' impact. The role of 'mass persuaders' has been analysed since the 1940s, but concerns about the role of the mass media in shaping voters' preferences are new. These concerns have been exacerbated by public apathy and low levels of trust in democratic political institutions. The routine and mass character of elections, combined with voters' low and declining trust in political parties and representative institutions—which some diagnose as anti-democratic cynicism—are resulting in a declining turnout in elections, referenda, and plebiscites (Putnam 2000). While compulsory voting mitigates against this trend in Australia, the observers here still note clear signs of political manipulation, disengagement, and apathy.

The third threat comes from what Max Weber (1864–1920) called 'plebiscitary' trends in contemporary democracy. It consists of a tendency for political appeals by leaders to circumvent all forms of scrutiny by parliaments and by 'mediating' political organisations (parties, unions, interest groups, and lobbies). The elites are more responsive to mass demands (which they themselves shape) but less responsible, liberated from considerations of law and long-term political consequences. Populism has been rife among elites in developing countries; recently, however, some symptoms of such plebiscitary/populist practices have been diagnosed among elites in the developed world, including Australia (see Marr & Wilkinson 2003).

Finally, there seems to be a growing 'external' challenge to democratic institutions and liberal order coming from religious-fundamentalist movements, organisations, and regimes, forming mainly in the developing world. Islamic fundamentalism is arguably the most publicised, because of its strength, impact on political regimes, and firm rejection of secular democracy and civil liberties; however, globalisation also facilitates the formation of cross-national religious-fundamentalist movements in the advanced West. The mobilisation of Christian 'evangelicals' in the United States, for example, paved the way for the election of George W. Bush. In Australia, there have been signs of a similar electoral alliance of traditional and fundamental religious groups in support of the Liberal–National Coalition (Maddox 2005).

Summary of main points

- ▶ Globalisation refers to the intensified circulation of capital, goods, information, and people across national boundaries, resulting in the increasing interdependence of countries and regions of the world. It has three main dimensions: economic, political, and cultural.
- ▶ There are widely varying views on globalisation, ranging from 'globoenthusiasts' (those who view it as a socially benign process) to 'globosceptics' (those who are critical of it because it is socially divisive).
- ▶ Globalisation marks an increase in the diversity of political actors—both state and non-state. Supra-national bodies coexist with states as part of a new global and national power dynamic. Globalisation also affects the way in which power is exercised. Contemporary power elites have to act in a more multilateral and coordinated way than their predecessors.
- ▶ Globalisation affects power distribution within nation-states by speeding up the decline of stable political constituencies (particularly class ideologies) and replacing them with a 'new politics' marked by a proliferation of social movements.
- ▶ The above globalising trends represent a significant challenge to democratic institutions.

SOCIOLOGICAL
REFLECTION

18.1 How globalised are you?

Consider examples of how the three dimensions of globalisation—economic, political, and cultural—impact on your life and the community in which you live. Where do you stand in the pro- versus anti-globalisation debate?

Discussion questions

18.1 What are the key features of globalisation?

18.2 List the alleged advantages and disadvantages of globalisation—are you a globosceptic or a globoenthusiast?

18.3 In what ways can globalisation be viewed as not being a new phenomenon?

18.4 Are we witnessing the globalisation of everything?

18.5 What are some examples of the anti-globalisation movement and why has it arisen?

18.6 Is globalisation responsible for the decline of the state? Is this necessarily a 'bad' thing?

18.7 In what ways does globalisation challenge democracy?

Further reading

Beck, U. 2000, *What is Globalisation?*, Polity Press, Cambridge.

della Porta, D. & Diani, M. 2006, *Social Movements: An Introduction*, 2nd edn, Blackwell, Oxford.

Pakulski, J. 2004, *Globalising Inequalities*, Allen & Unwin, Sydney.

Ritzer, G. 2007, *The Globalization of Nothing 2*, rev. edn, Pine Forge Press, Thousand Oaks, CA.

Robertson, R. 2001, 'Globalization theory 2000+: Major problematics', in G. Ritzer & B. Smart (eds), *Handbook of Social Theory*, Sage, London, pp. 458–71.

Stiglitz, J.E. 2002, *Globalisation and Its Discontents*, W.W. Norton, New York.

Tilly, C. & Wood, L.J. 2009, *Social Movements, 1768–2008*, Paradigm, Boulder, CO.

Walby, S. 2009, *Globalization and Inequalities: Complexity and Contested Modernities*, Sage, London.

Waters, M. 2001, *Globalisation*, 2nd edn, Routledge, London.

World Commission on the Social Dimension of Globalization 2004, *A Fair Globalization: Creating Opportunities for All*, International Labour Organization, Geneva, <www.ilo.org/public/english/fairglobalization/origin/index.htm>.

Zakaria, F. 2008, *The Post-American World*, W.W. Norton, New York.

Websites

- Freedom House: <www.freedomhouse.org>. A non-profit, non-partisan organisation that advocates for democratic and economic freedom across the globe.
- 50 Years is Enough: <www.50years.org/about>. An activist network dedicated to critiquing and reforming the World Bank and the IMF.
- Global Exchange: <www.globalexchange.org/index.html>. An activist website that critiques globalisation and global institutions such as the World Bank and the IMF.
- Globalisation Guide: <www.globalisationguide.org>. A student resource site developed by the pro-globalisation Australian APEC Study Centre at Monash University.
- The Globalism Institute—RMIT University: <www.rmit.edu.au/GLOBALISM>. An academic research body aimed at studying global processes of change and continuity.
- Human Development Reports: <http://hdr.undp.org/en>. Produced by the United Nations Development Programme, these annual reports provide a wealth of comparative information on national and global trends.
- International Labour Organization: <www.ilo.org>. A resource-rich site from the United Nations agency that promotes international labour standards and human rights.
- The Runaway World: <http://news.bbc.co.uk/hi/english/static/events/reith_99>. A series of five BBC Reith Lectures delivered by Anthony Giddens in 1999 on various aspects of globalisation. Available online in text, audio, and video form. Revised text versions of the lectures can also be found at: <www.lse.ac.uk/Depts/global/publreithlecturesrev.htm>.
- Whirled Bank: <www.whirledbank.org>. A spoof website on the World Bank with a range of interesting resources.

Films/Documentaries

- *The New Rulers of the World*, 2001, documentary, directed by J. Pilger, Carlton Television. Journalist John Pilger critically examines the impact of globalisation by focusing on economic development in Indonesia.
- *No Logo: Brands, Globalization & Resistance*, 2003, documentary, directed by S. Jhally, Media Education Foundation. Based on journalist Naomi Klein's book, *No Logo*, this documentary presents a critical analysis of the impact of globalisation.

Visit the *Public Sociology* book website to access topical case studies, weblinks, YouTube clips, and extra readings.

References

Beck, U. 1992, *Risk Society*, Verso, London.

—— 1994, 'The reinvention of politics: Towards a theory of reflexive modernization', in U. Beck, A. Giddens & S. Lash, *Reflexive Modernization*, Polity Press, Cambridge, pp. 1–55.

Betz, H.-G. 1994, *Radical Right-Wing Populism in Western Europe*, Macmillan, London.

Brzezinski, Z. (2008) 'The global political awakening', *International Herald Tribune*, 16 December.

Charnock, D. 2005, 'Post-war changes in the influence of social structure on Australian voting: The "decline of social cleavages" revisited', *Australian Journal of Political Science*, vol. 40, no. 3, pp. 343–55.

Dalton, R.J. & Klingemann, H-D. 2007, 'Citizens and political behaviour', in R.J. Dalton & Klingemann, H-D. (eds), *The Oxford Handbook of Political Behaviour*, Oxford University Press, Oxford, pp. 3–28.

Freedom House 2009, Freedom House website, <www.freedomhouse.org>.

Giddens, A. 1990, *The Consequences of Modernity*, Polity Press, Cambridge.

—— (ed.) 2001, *The Global Third Way Debate*, Polity Press, Cambridge.

—— 2002, *Where Now for New Labour?*, Polity Press, Cambridge.

Inglehart, R. 1991, *Culture Shift in Advanced Industrial Society*, Princeton University Press, Princeton, NJ.

—— 2007, 'Postmaterialist values and the shift from survival to self-expression values', in R.J. Dalton & Klingemann, H-D. (eds), *The Oxford Handbook of Political Behaviour*, Oxford University Press, Oxford, pp. 223–40.

Koopmans, R. 2007, 'Social movements', in R.J. Dalton & Klingemann, H-D. (eds), *The Oxford Handbook of Political Behaviour*, Oxford University Press, Oxford, pp. 693–708.

Longworth, R.C. 2009, 'The new global economic order', Encarta, <http://encarta.msn.com/sidebar_1741588055/the_new_global_economic_order.html>.

McAllister, I. 2007, 'The personalization of politics', in R.J. Dalton & Klingemann, H-D. (eds), *The Oxford Handbook of Political Behaviour*, Oxford University Press, Oxford, pp. 571–89.

Maddox, M. 2005, *God Under Howard: The Rise of the Religious Right in Australian Politics*, Allen & Unwin, Sydney.

Mair P. 2007, 'Left–right orientation', in R.J. Dalton & Klingemann, H-D. (eds), *The Oxford Handbook of Political Behaviour*, Oxford University Press, Oxford, pp. 206–23.

Marr, D. & Wilkinson, M. 2003, *Dark Victory*, Allen & Unwin, Sydney.

Nieuwbeerta, P. 1997, *The Democratic Class Struggle in Twenty Countries, 1945–1990*, CIPData KB, The Hague.

Offe, C. 1985, 'New social movements: Challenging the boundaries of institutional politics', *Social Research*, vol. 52, no. 4, pp. 817–68.

Pakulski, J. 2004, *Globalising Inequalities*, Allen & Unwin, Sydney.

Phillips, K. 2006, *American Theocracy*, Viking, New York.

Pusey, M. 1991, *Economic Rationalism in Canberra*, Cambridge University Press, Cambridge.

—— 2003, *The Experience of Middle Australia*, Cambridge University Press, Cambridge.

Putnam, R. 2000, *Bowling Alone: The Collapse and Revival of American Community*, Simon & Schuster, New York.

Robertson, R. 1992, *Globalisation: Social Theory and Global Culture*, Sage, London.

Robinson, W. 2004, *A Theory of Global Capitalism*, John Hopkins University Press, Baltimore, MD.

Rosenau, J. 1990, *Turbulence in World Politics*, Sage, London.

—— 1997, *Along the Domestic–Foreign Frontier*, Cambridge University Press, Cambridge.

Rothkopf, D.J. 2008, *Superclass: The Global Power Elite and the World They are Making*, Farrar Straus & Giroux, New York.

Sassen, S. 2007, *A Sociology of Globalization*, W.W. Norton, New York.

Sklair, L. 2001, *The Transnational Capitalist Class*, Blackwell, Oxford.

Stiglitz, J.E. 2002, *Globalisation and Its Discontents*, W.W. Norton, New York.

Waters, M. 1995, *Globalisation*, Routledge, London.

World Bank 2009, PovertyNet, <http://go.worldbank.org/VL7N3V6F20> (accessed 8 October 2009).

Wnuk-Lipinski E. 2007, 'Civil society and democratisation', in R.J. Dalton & Klingemann, H-D. (eds), *The Oxford Handbook of Political Behaviour*, Oxford University Press, Oxford, pp. 675–93.

Zakaria, F. 2008, *The Post-American World*, W.W. Norton, New York.

CHAPTER 19

Global risk and the surveillance state: A sociology of new terrorism

Maria Freij and John Germov

Terror Australis

Over the past few years, Australia—previously relatively spared of terrorism carried out on its own soil—has been the planned target of some major terrorist attacks. In 2008, Abdul Nacer Benbrika became the first person to be found guilty of running a home-grown terrorist organisation. The jury was told that Benbrika and other members of the group had planned several attacks against civilian targets, among them the 2005 AFL grand final and the Crown Casino building in Melbourne (Perkins & Gregory 2008). Benbrika was sentenced to fifteen years in jail and five other men were sentenced to four and a half and seven and a half years minimum for being members of a terrorist organisation and related terrorist activities (Cooper 2009). The case received a lot of media attention and changed Australia's outlook on terrorism forever: suddenly, terrorism involved a real threat to Australian civilians.

Only a year after the Melbourne trial, the largest Australian terrorism trial came to a close in Sydney in October 2009 (Cummings 2009). In this trial, five men were accused and found guilty of conspiring to plan a devastating terrorist attack, but this time the target of the attack was unknown. In February 2010, the five men received prison sentences of between 23 and 28 years (Brown 2010).

The prosecution was the product of a joint operation between the New South Wales Police Force, the Australian Federal Police, the Australian Security Intelligence Organisation (ASIO), and the New South Wales Crime Commission. It was also supported by other jurisdictions and agencies, in particular the Commonwealth Director of Public Prosecutions (AFP 2009a). The trial, which lasted 181 days, was held in Parramatta, in a specially designed courtroom (Jacobsen 2009). The men were each 'convicted of one count of "conspiring to do an act in preparation/planning for a terrorist act" under Sections 11.5(1) & 101.6(1) *Criminal Code Act 1995* (Cth) which carries a maximum penalty of life imprisonment' (AFP 2009a). Four other men pleaded guilty to related offences before the trial began in 2008.

This case, like the Melbourne trial, attracted enormous media attention. Outside the courtroom, a TV screen streamed live images to family members and waiting media (Catanzariti 2009) and the case was widely reported in the newspapers, on TV, and on web-based media. The emotional responses of the family members of the accused were shown on the news and quoted in the papers.

These two cases certainly shaped the Australian public's relationship to terrorism. For example, Australian laws and policies are being amended to incorporate terror-ism, the public has been encouraged to participate in 'keeping Australia safe' through

continued over

advertisements and television campaigns, and there has been talk about a national identification card. In turn, the relationship between security and human rights has changed. Rights of citizens and detainees, freedoms of speech and religion, and the right to be presumed innocent, are the subject of much public debate in the era of terrorism. Further, while the convictions of the men in these two trials received a large amount of media focus, less attention was given to the fact that four men who had also been detained on suspicion of terrorist activities were found innocent after three years of imprisonment awaiting trial; none of them received any compensation for his wrongful imprisonment (Ingleton & Moore 2009).

Terrorism raises a range of issues and concerns as it resonates widely across society. As we shall see, in a global era, national boundaries are not the only ones being blurred.

Introduction: Terrorism, Australia, and the global risk society

The cases mentioned in the vignette are, to date, the two most prominent cases of confirmed terrorist activity within Australia. There have been many other impacts of the 'War on Terror' in Australia, though (see Box 19.1). Two of the most controversial and public cases of terrorism in Australia involved the protracted detention of Australian David Hicks at Guantanamo Bay and the investigation of Dr Mohammed Haneef (see Clarke 2008), who was accused of terrorist activities (later shown to be unfounded), held without charge for days, and whose visa was cancelled (though it was later reissued). At the time of writing, the most recent case was the arrest of suspects planning an attack on the Holsworthy Army Barracks in Sydney. As in many nations, responses to the real threat of terrorism have involved heated public debate over the underlying causes of terrorism and the appropriate interventions to prevent it. This has involved discussion of areas ranging from the need for national identity cards to the infringement of human rights and civil liberties. For example, the amendment of national security laws and the powers attributed to ASIO, along with Australia's presence in Iraq since 2003, have received much public and media attention.

Sociologists look at the underlying causes of terrorism. As Austin Turk summarises: 'terrorism is to be explained as a product not of discrete causes but rather of systemic processes generated in functional and interactive relationships of inequality' (1982, p. 119). While a multitude of books have been published on the topic of terrorism, violence, and war, the sociology of terrorism remains a relatively new field and an under-studied area (Turk 2004; Ahmad & Sileno 2005; Bergesen & Lizardo 2004), one some sociologists have criticised for its 'absence of any attempt to build systematic, cohesive, and comprehensive theories of terrorism as a social phenomenon' (Ahmad & Sileno 2005, p. 203).

A sociological analysis of terrorism questions who is a terrorist as well as who decides who is a terrorist. The expression, 'One man's terrorist is another man's freedom fighter' (Bergesen & Lizardo 2004; Martin 2003; Mythen & Walklate 2006) illustrates how different perspectives can lead to opposing standpoints. Since terrorist acts are often justified by a perceived notion of social or political oppression, we must recognise the societal structures that create these perceptions, and also the social divides that exist between and within societies—differing political, ideological, cultural, and religious worldviews. As such, it is imperative that we look to the reasons behind terrorism, that we attempt to learn why and how terrorism occurs (Oliverio & Lauderdale 2005). American linguist and political commentator, Noam Chomsky, puts it even more bluntly: '[i]f you don't care if there are further terrorist attacks, then fine, say let's not pay any attention to the reasons. If you're interested in preventing them, of course you'll pay attention to the reasons (Chomsky 2003, p. 15).

Ulrich Beck's (1992) concept of the **risk society**, in which the concept of risk arguably permeates every aspect of our lives, describes how risk calculations have become increasingly important in Western society, so that people's lives are increasingly occupied with 'preventing the worst' (Beck 1992, p. 49). Beck argues that people are negotiating their lives in a context of unanticipated hazards, some of which become central to their individual lives, and to the way society functions. Risk is about the potential future impacting on the present (Boyne 2001). In a **globalised** world, as national borders become decreasingly important to trade, where information technology changes how we communicate, and the global economy has an impact on households everywhere in the world, the notion of risk has also changed. Not only is human responsibility increasingly attached to the causes of risk (Lupton 2006), but the origins of risk exposure have moved beyond the local or national and are increasingly global in nature—particularly the risk of terrorism.

risk society

A term coined by Beck to describe the centrality of risk calculations in people's lives in Western society, whereby the key social problems today are unanticipated (or manufactured) hazards, such as the risks of pollution, food poisoning, and environmental degradation.

globalisation

The increased interconnectedness of the cultural, economic, and political aspects of social life; intensified circulation of capital, goods, information, and people across national boundaries; and increased interdependence of countries and regions of the world.

CrossLink: See Chapter 3 for more on Beck.

Box 19.1: Terrorist acts affecting Australia and its citizens

- **2010:** Five Sydney men received prison sentences of between 23 and 28 years for conspiracy to conduct a major terrorist attack (on an unnamed target).
- **2009:** Holsworthy Barracks terror plot—an alleged Somali-based Islamist terrorist group planned to attack the army barracks in Sydney with automatic weapons and kill as many personnel as possible. They were arrested before they could act.

continued over

- **2008:** Abdul Nacer Benbrika and others were caught and convicted for planned attacks on several civilian targets in Melbourne (see opening vignette).
- **2008:** Mumbai attacks—Pakistani militants killed 166 people, including two Australians, and injured almost 300. Shootings and bombings were focused on four locations, including two international hotels (the Taj Mahal Palace and Tower, and the Oberoi Trident).
- **2006:** Joseph Terrence Thoppil Thomas, an Australian citizen, was initially convicted for receiving funds from al-Qaeda; the conviction was overturned on appeal, after which he was the first person placed on a control order (limiting his movement and certain rights) under the *Australian Anti-Terrorism Act 2005*. Regularly referred to as 'Jihad Jack' in the Australian media, he underwent a retrial after statements made during a media interview on ABC TV program *Four Corners*. In 2008, he was found not guilty of terrorist charges but guilty of passport fraud, though he served no further sentence given he had been in remand for nine months.
- **2005:** The London bombings—a series of bombings on London's public transport system during the morning rush hour. Three bombs exploded on trains on the main lines of the Underground system and one on a double-decker bus. The attacks were carried out by suicide bombers, four British Muslim men. It is estimated that 56 people were killed (including one Australian) and 700 injured, including Australians living and working in London, such as Gill Hicks who lost both her legs in the explosion. In a message broadcast on the al-Jazeera network, al-Qaeda's Ayman al-Zawahiri claimed responsibility for the attacks.
- **2001–07:** David Hicks—an Australian citizen who underwent combat training in Al Qaeda camps and fought for the Taliban regime in Afghanistan—was caught in 2001 and subsequently held by the US government in Guantanamo Bay until 2007, after agreeing to plead guilty, and allowed to return to Australia to serve the remaining nine months of his seven-year sentence in jail.
- **2005:** The Bali Bombings, Kuta, killed 23 people (four Australians) and injured a further 129.
- **2002:** The Bali Bombings, Kuta, killed 202 people (88 Australians) and injured a further 240. Three bombs exploded in Kuta, one inside Paddy's Bar, another outside the Sari Club, and a third outside the American Consulate.
- **1986:** A car bomb exploded in a car park under the Turkish Consulate in Melbourne, killing the bomber who handled the explosive device incorrectly. Levon Demirian, a Sydney resident with links to an Armenian terrorist group, was found guilty of planning the attack and served ten years.

- **1978:** The Sydney Hilton Hotel bomb explosion resulted in two garbage collectors and a police officer being killed and eleven others injured. This was Australia's first domestic terrorist act, and there is continued disagreement regarding who committed the act and for what reason.

What is terrorism?

The word 'terrorism' has its roots in the French Revolution and the word *terreur*—the act of inflicting terror upon an enemy, of making people afraid. The term then referred to governmental oppression such as executions (Tilly 2004), but the phenomenon of terrorism itself existed long before that (Reid 1997). The term has since expanded in scope and it has no one definition—different theorists have found a range of ways to explain the notion, and this is part of the complexity of the issue: how do we discuss terrorism when we bring different connotations to the term, and hence to the phenomenon and its societal impact and/or causes? One of the reasons that it is hard to get accurate data on terrorism is linked to these issues of definition: some researchers may code acts of terrorism as 'political violence', others as 'violent claim-making', and still others as 'heavy violence' (Bergesen & Han 2005, p. 142; Bergesen & Lizardo 2004, p. 40). Since '[t]errorism is violence, but not every form of violence is terrorism' (Laqueur 1999, p. 8), the way data are collated and how acts of terror are described constitute a complicated process, one that will invariably impact on how societies see, interpret, and respond to terrorism.

After the terrorist attacks on New York's World Trade Center on September 11, 2001—referred to as 9/11—observers described the acts as 'criminal' (Black 2004); as Donald Black points out: '[t]o classify terrorism merely as a form of crime ... obscures its sociological identity and obstructs its scientific understanding' (2004, p. 17). Terrorism differs from other violence because of its primary intent, which is 'to show that the cost of opposition is too high even to be risked. Terror is violence intended to deter opposition' (Turk 1982, p. 121).

While many definitions exist, most tend to incorporate similar criteria. For example, Turk defines terrorism as 'the deliberate targeting of more or less randomly selected victims whose deaths and injuries are expected to weaken the opponent's will to persist in a political conflict' (2004, p. 273). Aqueil Ahmad and Michael Sileno define it as 'a planned individual or collective violence against innocent victims or targeted individuals, groups, or property, committed before an audience in order to make a point, create fear, inflict punishment, seek monetary demands' (2005, p. 189). While these two definitions share some points, there are also important differences between them. As the nature of terrorism changes, so do the definitions of the term. There have, in fact, been more than a hundred definitions of terrorism (Laqueur 1999) and there are, presumably, more to come.

Gus Martin (2003, p. 23) has summarised the common features of most formal definitions:

- the use of illegal force
- subnational actors
- unconventional methods
- political motives
- attacks against 'soft' civilian and passive military targets, and
- acts aimed at purposefully affecting an audience.

Terrorism is thus a form of illegal violence, often aimed at civilians, to exert an influence over a wider audience. Through their acts, terrorists aim to scare their target audience into complying with the terrorist group's wishes. These wishes are politically or religiously motivated—terrorists see 'the cause' as justifying the means by which the results are reached. The difference between routine criminal violence and terrorism, then, lies in the motives for the actions (Mythen & Walklate 2006). In short: '[t]errorism is intended to be a matter of perception and is thus seen differently by different observers' (Cronin 2002–03, p. 32).

Different types of terrorism

While there are a multitude of terrorist typologies, this chapter focuses on two in particular because of their relationship with globalisation: *state terrorism* and *dissident terrorism*. We recognise that these two typologies may occur at once and overlap, as shown in Table 19.1.

Table 19.1: State terrorism and dissident terrorism

Type	Description	Practice
Terrorism from above: state terrorism	Committed by governments or quasi-governments against perceived threats to interests or security. State terrorism is government sanctioned, politically and financially.	Warfare violence, such as genocide, assassinations, and torture.
Terrorism from below: dissident terrorism	Committed by non-state actors, such as anti-government movements, ethno-national groups, and religious groups against the national or world order.	Violent attacks of many shapes and forms, including bombings, suicide bombings, destruction of property, and assassinations.

Source: Adapted from Martin (2003).

While state terrorism and dissident terrorism (or terrorism from above and below, respectively) may take similar expressions, they vary in two fundamental aspects: function and sanction. State terrorism is supported and funded, and sometimes carried out, by government/s—the terrorism sponsored by Libya (e.g. the Lockerbie plane bombing), France (the *Rainbow Warrior* bombing), and Sudan (harbouring terrorist groups) belongs to this category, and 'is often characterized by state sponsorship of dissident movements' (Martin 2003, p. 116). Dissident terrorism, on the other hand, is condemned by governments. Most studies of terrorism are concerned with how to handle dissident terrorism—very few studies have been done on how to handle state terrorism (Reid 1997). Dissident terrorism often occurs in the name of the defence of a 'higher cause', and tends to be viewed by perpetrators as a necessary evil. Terrorism of this kind is carried out by, among others, revolutionaries, nationalists, anti-state movements, and organised crime organisations.

Religious terrorism can take both state and dissident forms. For example, violent Christian anti-abortion groups in the United States have committed terrorist acts in the name of their faith by bombing abortion clinics and killing medical staff. Islamic fundamentalists wage a holy war—*jihad*—against those whom they see as a threat to their faith. Depending on perspective, 'there is often debate about whether the perpetrators [of religious violence] should be classified as terrorists or freedom fighters' (Martin 2003, p. 188).

Old and new terrorism

Terrorism is an old phenomenon, but the nature and impact of terrorism have changed in the globalised world, leading many commentators to make a distinction between 'old' and 'new' terrorism. Terrorist acts that take place in the global arena receive much more widespread political and media attention than national acts of terrorism, partly because of the *symbolic value* of their targets. The terrorist strikes of September 11, 2001 not only killed many innocent people; they were intentionally highly symbolic acts. New York's Twin Towers—the World Trade Center—were a symbol of the financial power of the United States, and as such, the West. Another al-Qaeda target was the Pentagon, the US military centre. The other targets remain unclear but speculations include Camp David, the president's holiday dwelling, and the White House. Other high-profile cases of international terrorism include the kidnapping of journalists and assassination of politicians. Acts of international terrorism, as opposed to acts of domestic terrorism, have a 'political-psychological impact [that] goes beyond a domestic agenda' (Martin 2003, p. 219). Other targets with a symbolic international impact include embassies and consulates, and women, tourists, and academics.

As such, it is important to recognise that, for terrorists, the victims are not necessarily the audience; rather, the victims are just a vehicle through which the message is delivered. The symbolism of targets—human or not—conveys a message to an audience. This audience can consist of governments, the media, or onlookers. Martin (2003) outlines the following list of participants in terrorist environments:

- terrorists (who commit the acts)
- supporters (who, by definition, do not commit terrorist acts themselves but who support the cause and encourage the acts)
- victims (these can be targets as well as collateral damage)
- targets (these are often symbolic) and onlookers (people watching the news, reading the papers), and
- analysts (such as sociologists, journalists, political commentators, and academics).

During the era of old terrorism, extremist violence was mainly driven by ethno-nationalist motivations and Cold War ideologies (Martin 2007). It had clearly stated goals and this type of terrorism was, by default, linked to a national geographic location. An example of this type of terrorism is the acts of the Irish Republican Army (IRA), which aimed to get the British out of Ireland (see Table 19.2 for an overview of major terrorist groups and their acts and aims).

New terrorism, or terrorism in a globalised world, has a far wider reach and an international impact. The audience is no longer small and isolated—events are occurring before a worldwide audience. Indeed, terrorism has been likened to theatre and the media its stage (Crelinsten 2008), and it is widely acknowledged that globalisation facilitates the ways in which terrorists communicate (Turk 2004). While some theorists equate new terrorism with the events on and after 9/11, the notion of new terrorism was well established before that (Laqueur 1999). Nevertheless, the events of 9/11, with their high-casualty, high-technology *modus operandi*, and global media impact, made the attacks a quintessential illustration of new terrorism. Further, other novel features of this attack were that it occurred on US soil and that the suicide bombers had lived and trained in the United States and Europe, rather than in some distant place (Martin 2007; Oberschall 2004).

New terrorism differs from old terrorism not only in that it has a global reach, but because of its goals and means of achieving these goals (Ahmad & Sileno 2005); there also seems to be a tendency toward more religiously motivated forms of terrorism (Martin 2007). Weapons of mass destruction (WMDs), chemical warfare, and other high-casualty-causing technologies are part of the risk scenario in a global era, but it must be noted that even the fear of WMDs goes back three decades (Oberschall 2004). The new-generation terrorists, then, are very good at using modern technologies to broadcast their messages worldwide, and are, through globalisation, able to affect a much larger audience. New terrorism has a less straightforward message, though—its aims are more amorphous and its organisational structure less tightly knit (Mythen & Walklate 2006); instead of one group, terrorist organisations now consist of largely independent cells.

For some theorists, globalisation (together with Westernisation) is not just a facilitator of terrorism, and indeed of counter-terrorism, but its root cause (Beck 2002; Bergesen

& Lizardo 2004; Martin 2007). They argue that globalisation 'creates a backlash or resistance that can take the form of terrorist attacks on national powers in the forefront of the globalization processes. In this regard, some see terrorism as a defensive, reactionary, solidaristic movement against global forces of cultural and economic change' (Bergesen & Lizardo 2004, p. 43). Arguably, 'the benefits of globalisation are weighted in favour of the wealthy economies of the West' (Martin 2007, p. 648) and the atrocities we are seeing are 'extensions of longer-running issues rather than a product of new ones' (Mythen & Walklate 2006, p. 382). Turk further states that the:

> regions most likely to generate terrorist threats have a history of colonialist exploitation by Western interests, and more recently of postcolonial economic and cultural penetration. These facts have facilitated identification of the West as the source of global economic and political disadvantage, military weakness, and cultural malaise, which provides a credible focus for resentment and moral outrage in the recruitment of terrorists and the mobilization of supporters and sympathizers. (2004, p. 274)

colonisation/colonialism
When a nation takes and maintains power over a territory that is outside its boundaries, based on a belief of superiority over those being colonised. See also *imperialism*.

hegemony
The operation of one powerful group over others, such that the consensus of the subordinated groups is not achieved by physical force, but rather by convincing people it is in their interests to agree with and follow the dominant group's ideas.

This discussion takes place within the framework of globalisation as another form of **colonialism**: the **hegemony** of globalisation leaves little room for cultures that do not subscribe to the dominant paradigm. As such, terrorism 'is not a plague upon the world-system but something produced by the world system' (Bergesen & Lizardo 2004, p. 51).

Annamarie Oliverio and Pat Lauderdale (2005) point out another aspect of how a taken-for-granted worldview can affect a person's perspective on terrorism: '[a]n example of hegemony as it relates to terrorism can be gleaned from the immediate reaction of the state to the Oklahoma City Federal Building explosion. Without any evidence, the US state blamed the bombing on Middle Eastern terrorists' (2005, p. 157–8). This example shows how terrorism and Middle-Eastern fanaticism have become one and the same—in fact, the Oklahoma City bombings were undertaken by an American white supremacist.

Unfortunately, there are so many terrorist organisations and so many incidents that it is impossible to list them all here. Table 19.2 provides an overview of some of the varied types of terrorism, terrorist groups, and terrorist acts over a period of years.

Responses to terrorism

The impact of international terrorism resonates widely around the world; it has had a major influence on policy-making, laws, and the behaviour of individuals. It has been argued that we now live in a *culture of fear*, shaped by this global risk that posits a constant threat.

Table 19.2: Major terrorist groups, acts, and aims by type

Terrorist/terrorist organisation	Terrorist act(s)	Motivation/aims	Type of terrorism
Al-Qaeda (The Base)	Most infamously the attack on the New York World Trade Center in 2001, where aeroplanes were flown into the two towers killing nearly 3000 people. The attack on the Pentagon the same day killed 125.	Establishing a 'New World Order'—anti-Westernisation, *jihad*, religious fundamentalism. Al-Qaeda is not an organisation but a network of Islamic fundamentalists, under the lead of Osama bin Laden.	International
Anti-abortionists	Bombings of abortion clinics, murders, letters claiming to be infected with anthrax bacteria, arson.	Fundamentalist Christian—religious moralist terrorism.	National
Euskadi Ta Azkatasuna (ETA), formed in 1959.	Kidnappings, assassinations, bombs.	Basque separatist movement.	National
Gavrilo Princip	Assassination of Archduke Ferdinand in 1914. This murder, referred to as 'the shots in Sarajevo', was one of the events that triggered World War I.	Yugoslav nationalist associated with the freedom movement Mlada Bosna, which was committed to the independence of the South Slavic peoples from Austria-Hungary.	International
Hamas (formed in 1987)	Suicide bombings, rocket attacks, shootings.	Islamic resistant movement, ethno-nationalist, wants emancipation for the Palestinian people.	National
Hezbollah (formed in 1982)	Suicide attacks, kidnappings, bombings.	Shi'a Islamic fundamentalists wanting to expel the Americans, the French, and their allies from	International

Terrorist/terrorist organisation	Terrorist act(s)	Motivation/aims	Type of terrorism
		Lebanon, ending colonialism and imperialism; want an Islamic state.	
Jemaah Islamiyah (Islamic Congregation)	A range of bombs and assassinations, including the 2002 and 2005 Bali bombings killing hundreds of people, and the 2004 Australian Embassy bombing, killing nine.	Militant Islamic organisation devoted to the establishment of an Islamic state in Southeast Asia. Linked to al-Qaeda and the Taliban.	International
Ku Klux Klan (KKK) (formed in 1865)	Lynching, rape, cross-burning, assaults, murders.	White supremacist, right-wing, Protestant Christians. There have been several eras of the KKK; all have committed atrocities against black people, Jews, and immigrants. The KKK is a purely American phenomenon.	National
Libya	Lockerbie bombing: in December 1988, a bomb brought down Pan Am Flight 103 in the town of Lockerbie, Scotland, killing 243 passengers, sixteen crew members, and eleven people on the ground.	The motives behind the Lockerbie bombing are thought to be in retaliation for the attack on Iran Air Flight 655, a civilian airliner shot down by a US navy missile in July 1988, killing all 290 passengers and crew. The missile attack was during the military confrontations between the United States and Libya at the time of the Gulf War.	International

continued over

Terrorist/terrorist organisation	Terrorist act(s)	Motivation/aims	Type of terrorism
France	*Rainbow Warrior* bombing: The Greenpeace boat *Rainbow Warrior*, which was protesting the nuclear tests in Mururoa, was sunk by the French government in 1985. One man drowned.	To prevent Greenpeace from interfering with the nuclear tests.	International
Mohammad Sidique Khan, Shehzad Tanweer, Germaine Lindsay, Hasib Hussain, and associates	London terrorist bombings: also referred to as the 7/7 bombings, these 2005 coordinated suicide attacks were carried out in London's public transport system. The four bombs killed a total of 56 people and injured about 700.	Muslim fundamentalists against Britain's involvement in the Iraq War.	International
Fundamentalist Islamic Pakistanis	2008 Mumbai bombings and shootings: a series of coordinated attacks killing a total of 166 and injuring 300.	Religious fundamentalism and anti-Western in terms of targeting hotels and restaurants frequented by foreigners and also an escalation of national disputes between India and Pakistan.	International and national
Liberation Tigers of Tamil Eelam (LTTE) (the Tamil Tigers) (founded in 1976)	Suicide bombings, assassinations.	Ethno-nationalist, want an independent Tamil state.	National
Mujahideen (holy warriors/freedom fighters)	Rape, assassination, bombings, beatings.	Islamic fundamentalists; best known are the Afghan Mujahideen. Linked to al-Qaeda and the Taliban.	International

Terrorist/terrorist organisation	Terrorist act(s)	Motivation/aims	Type of terrorism
Palestine Liberation Organization (PLO) (formed in 1964)	Suicide bombings, paramilitary attacks.	Secular nationalist, Palestinian independence and liberation.	International
Ramzi Yousef	Detonated a bomb in the garage of the World Trade Center in 1993 killing six people and injuring 1000.	Fundamentalist Muslim, supporting Palestine, punishing the United States for its support of Israel. Linked to al-Qaeda.	International
Taliban	Rape, assassination, bombings, beatings.	Islamic fundamentalists, linked to al-Qaeda and the Mujahideen.	International
The Provisional Irish Republican Army (IRA or Provos)	Bombings, assassinations, kidnappings. Ceased violent activity in 1998 (though its offshoot, 'The Real IRA', did not).	Independence for Ireland, a united Ireland. This faction came out of a split from the IRA in 1965. There are also factions of the IRA that continue to carry out violent attacks.	National
The Revolutionary Armed Forces of Colombia (FARC) (founded in 1964)	Kidnappings, such as Columbian presidential candidate Ingrid Betancourt, who was released by FARC on 2 July 2008 after being held since 23 February 2002.	A pluralist-socialist government.	National
Theodore Kaczynski, 'The Unabomber'	Mail bombs, killing three and injuring 22, between 1976 and 1978.	Anti-technology and anti-modernisation.	National
Timothy McVeigh	Oklahoma City bombing in 1995, killing 168 people. McVeigh drove a truck-turned-bomb into a federal building	White supremacist, war against the federal government.	National

Sources: Martin (2003); Turk (2004); Williams (2004).

For example, four levels of counter-terrorism alert were introduced in Australia in 2003—the National Counter-Terrorism Alert level has since remained at medium (AFP 2009b). Indeed, encouraging a climate of fear is often considered one of the explicit aims of terrorists (Mythen 2007). Beck (2002) underlines the fact that it is not that society has become more dangerous, but that the threat has changed: the uncontrollable risk has been de-bounded, de-territorialised, and as such the risks that confront people are different in a global risk society.

In response to terrorism, there have been two main reactions:

- *counter-terrorism*, which involves policy change as a means of proactively preventing terrorism, and
- *anti-terrorism*, which seeks to enhance security and other defence measures (Martin 2003).

In terms of use of force, there are coercive covert operations (this involves extralegal methods such as kidnapping and assassination), suppression campaigns, punitive military strikes, and so-called 'pre-emptive strikes'—a controversial measure that is often considered a euphemism for, and indistinguishable from, initiating an act of war. Pre-emptive strikes have been justified by some political leaders as a form of national self-defence, based on the perceived threat of terrorism. Other responses involve social reform, whereby the grievances of groups are addressed to resolve the underlying societal problems. Law enforcement and international law modifications are also common; the latter entails international tribunals, which bring terrorists to justice (Martin 2003).

There are also punitive attacks, such as the highly criticised (Martin 2007) US invasion of Iraq in the name of anti-terrorism and in response to 'proof' of the harbouring of WMDs, none of which was ever found. Some theorists argue that the escalation of violence is inevitable:

> Often as covert as terrorism itself, counterterrorism may nonetheless include war-like attacks on terrorists and their partisans, illustrated by the American military campaign against the Muslim organization known as al-Qaeda and its supporters in Afghanistan after the attacks of September 11, 2001. Quasi-warfare begets quasi-warfare in a vicious circle, counterterrorism answering terrorism that attracts more terrorism, more counterterrorism and so on. (Black 2004, p. 23)

Counter-terrorism responses can make it seem as if the state is merely reacting to terrorism when in fact it is 'symbiotically related to terrorism' (Oliverio & Lauderdale 2005, p. 163).

There has been widespread concern that counter-terrorism policies and laws are in fact eroding the freedoms they are supposedly protecting, and that civil liberties are being undermined (Turk 2004; Martin 2007). Anthony Oberschall points out that: '[s]ocial control of terrorism tends to burst the limits of legality and, in some cases, escalates to state terrorism' (2004, p. 29). Further, Black states:

[c]ounterterrorism … looks to the future—to what might happen where—guarding potential targets, screening for bombs and other weapons, and restricting entry to vulnerable places. It likewise employs various intelligence techniques (possibly including torture) to locate terrorists before they can launch attacks. (2004, p. 23)

After 9/11, the United States passed the *Patriot Act*, officially known as the *Uniting and Strengthening America by Providing Appropriate Tools Required to Intercept and Obstruct Terrorism (USA Patriot Act) Act of 2001*, which allowed enhanced monitoring of correspondence, use of wire-tapping of phone lines, the detention of US citizens and immigrants without charge for specified periods of time; the creation of military tribunals to hear and sentence people defined as enemy combatants, and relaxation of the prohibition on politically sanctioned assassination to allow for the targeted killing of alleged terrorists (Martin 2003; Turk 2004). The Act was subject to much criticism and a number of subsequent amendments. It is most closely associated with the highly criticised use of Guantanamo Bay, the detention camp in Cuba for terrorist suspects established under the presidency of George W. Bush, in which people were held without being charged and without trial (including Australian David Hicks). As Turk (2004) comments:

> Political pressure to lessen legal restraints on police, and military responses to terrorism have resulted in the, possibly temporary, erosion in the United States and elsewhere of legal protection against intrusive and secret surveillance, arbitrary detention, and hurtful interrogation methods, as well as assassination and extralegal executions. (2004, p. 280)

Beck warns that: '[s]*urveillance states* threaten to use the new power of cooperation to build themselves into fortress states, in which security and military concerns will loom large and freedom and democracy will shrink' (2002, p. 49, original italics). Among the many visible impacts of international terrorism and its responses is the increased level of security in airports, such as restrictions on amounts of fluid allowed on board, restrictions on sharp or pointy objects in hand luggage, and the removal of shoes and other garments as a mandatory requirement (at some airports) before people walk through the metal detectors. In Australia and elsewhere, there has been much discussion of a national identity card, and the right to search 'suspicious' individuals (see Lynch & Williams 2006 for an overview of changes to Australian legislation).

governmentality
The control and regulation of people through practices and knowledges developed within the human sciences and applied to different social institutions, such as schools and prisons.

neo-liberalism
A philosophy based on the primacy of individual rights and minimal state intervention.

Michel Foucault's notion of **governmentality** is one sociological lens through which we can observe the increasing focus on security and control in contemporary society. Foucault's notion of governmentality sees different areas of life as fields subject to governance (Mythen & Walklate 2006). For Foucauldians, risk and control are ways for **neo-liberal** societies to govern, through government surveillance of their populations. Instead of the government having to regulate the population, the population becomes self-policing. An example of a Foucauldian way of looking at governmentality is the anti-terrorism advertisement shown by the Australian government on television. This advertisement shows examples of 'suspicious behaviour'—people taking pictures of buildings, people buying large quantities of fertiliser, and so on—in snapshots that eventually make up a picture of the Australian continent. Citizens are encouraged to report anything suspicious—in essence, to assist in the policing of the population.

CrossLink:
See Chapter 3
for more on
Foucault's
ideas.

Foucault also established the concept of the panopticon—an all-seeing place—as a metaphor for his theories about societal supervision. The idea was based on an eighteenth-century prison with a watchtower in the middle, which made prisoners feel as if they were constantly being observed even though this was not the case. It was about creating the illusion that 'the agents of discipline see everything, without ever being seen' (Foucault 1979, p. 202). Arguably, the panopticon has never been more in play than now, perhaps with the difference that we are, in fact, being watched. There are security cameras in shops, on streets, in garages, elevators, train stations, airports, and the list goes on. If necessary, an individual's movements can be reconstructed through these videotapes and through other information gathered, including mobile phone conversations and text messages, internet activity, electronic correspondence, and much more.

In spite of all this intelligence: '[t]he United States intelligentsia could not predict the simplicity of technique used in the Twin Towers attack' (Oliverio & Lauderdale 2005, p. 165). Similar statements could be heard in the media; indeed, the world reacted with incredulity that something so atrocious, yet so simple, as the 9/11 attacks could occur. In fact, exactly two years before the WTC attacks, an inquiry into the sociology and psychology of terrorism (Hudson 1999) had pointed out that: '[s]uicide bomber(s) belonging to al-Qaida's Martyrdom Battalion could crash-land an aircraft packed with high explosives (C-4 and semtex) into the Pentagon, the headquarters of the Central Intelligence Agency (CIA), or the White House' (1999, p. 7).

19.1: Airline travel—the new panopticon

Airport travellers are subjected to many surveillance techniques as a result of perceived terrorist threats. There is an extensive network of closed-circuit television (CCTV) cameras within airport buildings. CCTV security cameras can monitor airport activity on a 24-hour basis, with just a few people in a central control room to monitor the footage. International travellers may have microchips embedded in their passports to enable the holder to be identified and monitored. Baggage is checked before being loaded in the hold of the plane, passengers go through security checks (some more rigorous than others) before boarding, and their hand luggage is checked both by X-ray and manually for forbidden items. There was a public outcry at the introduction of full-body scans in 2009 at some airports in Europe that show breast enlargements, body piercings, and a clear black-and-white outline of passengers' genitals. After the failed terrorist act of a man who attempted to set off a bomb on a flight in the United States on Christmas Day 2009 (smuggled on board in his underwear), the Australian federal government announced in early

2010 that body scanners would be introduced at all Australian international airports by the end of 2011, and in the 2010 White Paper outlined that the government would assist in the introduction of the 'next generation multi-view X-ray machines', 'bottle scanners capable of detecting liquid-based explosives', and 'X-ray screening, and increased explosive trace detection technology for air cargo' (Australian Government 2010, p. 40). This level of surveillance at airports is in response to past terrorist activity and to protect the security of passengers; it is a panoptic form of surveillance that enables relatively few people to monitor thousands, perhaps millions.

Global risk and terrorism: Where to from here?

Beck's risk society takes into account two types of risk: 'natural hazards' (such as earthquakes and floods) and 'manufactured risks' (e.g. economic and environmental). Natural hazards are risks we cannot predict, but that we still fear: earthquakes happen because of fault lines and floods through extraordinary amounts of rain, for example. Those risks that are manufactured have their causes in society: the Global Financial Crisis (GFC) was caused by over-lending and greed; and global warming is due to the mass consumption of fossil fuels. Beck's risk society thesis has been the subject of criticism because of its division into 'natural' and 'manufactured' risk, as many of the 'natural' hazards 'cannot be freely divested from social processes and human activities' (Mythen 2007, p. 799). Terrorism, though, is clearly a manufactured risk since it has its roots in social structures. Terrorist acts are not random expressions of lunacy, but rather responses to societal structures that these people see as 'wrong'. Indeed, to solve the problem of terrorism we need to turn our sociological imagination to the underlying structures from, or against, which terrorism occurs.

Terrorism in a globalised world means that issues of national security have become global. Since the targets of new terrorism are international, so are its political reverberations and media coverage. Global terrorism has also affected the world in terms of political loyalty and dependability. 'You're either with us or against us,' said George W. Bush when declaring a war on terrorism (CNN 2009); 'In this global campaign against terrorism, no country has the luxury of remaining on the sidelines. There *are* no sidelines,' said Secretary of State Colin Powell in 2002 (State Department 2002, cited in Tilly 2004, p. 5). The United States, when threatened, was desperate for support. While many countries came to its defence, and while many condemned the atrocious terrorist acts of 9/11, arguably, the United States did nothing for 'the free world' by proclaiming that those not siding with the United States, were, in fact, automatically its enemies. While such hegemonic statements are political in nature, and are seen by many—including countries that are neutral—as extremely offensive, it is true that terrorism in some way or other affects most people in a globalised world. Beck, commenting on how terrorism affects us all, says with more eloquence: 'there are no bystanders anymore' (cited in Mythen & Walklate 2005, p. 386). Kellner argues that the 'experience of September 11 points to the objective ambiguity of globalization: that positive and negative sides are interconnected, that the institutions of the open society unlock the possibilities of destruction and violence as well as those of democracy, free trade, and cultural and social exchange' (2002, p. 291).

Conclusion

Throughout history, there have been numerous terrorist attacks against governments, individuals, and organisations. The frameworks of Beck's (global) risk society and Foucault's governmentality lens are two perspectives sociologists can use to make sense of the social phenomenon of terrorism and the ways in which societies react and respond to terrorism. It is necessary to understand its social roots and causes, in order to deal effectively with terrorism and to try to prevent further violence.

Globalisation has led to a range of changes in the world. This chapter has discussed how terrorism is both a product of, and reaction to, globalisation. Terrorism is, somewhat ironically, highly dependent on the very system it opposes: global media attention is one of terrorists' main goals—it is necessary for them to get their message out in order for terror to be spread; and the global media networks are themselves a product of globalisation.

Terrorism and related policy-making and interventions are all highly dependent on perspective. Sociology has a great deal to contribute to the understandings of these perspectives and the analysis of how they ultimately produce and reproduce each other.

Summary of main points

▶ Throughout history, there have been many examples of individual, group, and state terrorism acts. These show us how society shapes and forms leadership, politics, and religion, as well as their responses.

▶ Terrorism differs from other forms of violence in that it aims to inflict fear on a government and population, and because it has politically or religiously founded motives. Terrorism is aimed at military and civilian targets—which are often symbolic—and aims to force change through the infliction of fear.

▶ Terrorism can be national or international. Globalisation has seen an increase in international terrorism, as national boundaries are more easily transgressed because of the global economy, media coverage, and increased impact of nations on each other.

▶ Beck's concept of the global risk society posits that terrorism is now deterritorialised; nation-state boundaries no longer contain terrorism nationally. As such, globalisation implies that the concept of risk is different now that new factors impact on people's negotiation of risk; local or national risk factors no longer have the largest impact on people's lives.

▶ Foucault's notions of governmentality and surveillance are important lenses through which we can understand how increased security measures impact on our lives and change our behavioural patterns.

19.1 Difference of perspective—one person's terrorist is another's freedom fighter

History is full of examples of uprisings—sometimes violent—against the ruling group that have resulted in major societal changes: the suffragette movement, which gave women the right to vote; the Jewish freedom fighters who opposed the British Mandate of Palestine and sought to establish a Jewish state; the African-American Civil Rights Movement, which fought for the out-lawing of racial discrimination and restoring suffrage; the anti-Apartheid movement in South Africa, which fought to overturn white rule; and the Easter rising of 1916, in which Irish Republicans sought to end British rule. Keep these in mind when considering the following points:

(a) Are there occasions when violent uprisings are warranted?

(b) How does violence differ from terrorism?

(c) How does state terrorism differ from non-state terrorism? Are some causes more just than others?

Discussion questions

19.1 Who defines which acts of violence are acts of terrorism?

19.2 What is the role of the media in the global risk society?

19.3 What factors do we need to take into consideration when trying to understand terrorism?

19.4 In your life, can you see any evidence of Foucault's theory of governmentality?

19.5 How do you distinguish a freedom fighter from a terrorist?

19.6 Outline the differences between old and new terrorism. Do you think terrorism will change further?

19.7 When you hear the word 'terrorist', what associations do you get? Compare your responses with those of another student. Are your associations similar or different? In what ways may a person's social, ethnic, and political views shape their views on terrorism?

19.8 What is your view of legislation that impacts on civil rights? Is it worth giving up certain rights in the name of security? When is it acceptable? When is it not?

Further reading

Australian Government 2010, *Counter-Terrorism White Paper: Securing Australia, Protecting our Community*, Australian Government, Department of the Prime Minister and Cabinet, Canberra, <www.dpmc.gov.au/publications/counter_terrorism/docs/counterterrorism_white_paper.pdf> (accessed 14 April 2010).

Collins, R. 2004, 'Rituals and solidarity in the wake of terrorist attack', *Sociological Theory*, vol. 22, no. 1, pp. 53–87.

Cronin, A. 2002–03, 'Behind the curve: Globalization and international terrorism', *International Security*, vol. 27, no. 3, pp. 30–58.

Greenberg, B. (ed.) 2003, *Communication and Terrorism: Public and Media Responses to 9/11*, Hampton Press, Cresskill, NJ.

Gupta, D. 2008, *Understanding Terrorism and Political Violence: The Life Cycle of Birth, Growth, Transformation, and Demise*, Routledge, London.

Laqueur, W. 2003, *No End to War: Terrorism in the Twenty-first Century*, Continuum, New York.

Martin, G. 2003, *Understanding Terrorism: Challenges Perspectives, and Issues*, Sage, Thousand Oaks, CA.

United States Government 2004, *The 9/11 Commission Report: Final Report of the National Commission on Terrorist Attacks Upon the United States*, Official Government edition, <http://govinfo.library.unt.edu/911/report/911Report.pdf> (accessed 14 April 2010).

Wright, L. 2006, *The Looming Tower: Al-Qaeda and the Road to 9/11*, Random House, New York.

Websites

- Australian Government National Security website: <www.nationalsecurity. gov.au>. This website provides a single access point for Australian government national security information.
- Australian terrorism law: <www.aph.gov.au/library/INTGUIDE/law/ terrorism.htm>. This website contains links to internet resources and documents in the area of anti-terrorism law and also provides links to Australian state and territory legislation, as well as overseas resources.
- Australian Institute of International Affairs: <www.aiia.asn.au>. This site provides the latest news items and information on the Australian Institute of International Affairs' activities.
- Australian Strategic Policy Institute: <www.aspi.org.au>. The Australian Strategic Policy Institute website provides independent analysis and policy advice through a library of papers.
- Centre for Policing, Intelligence and Counter Terrorism (PICT, Macquarie University): <www.pict.mq.edu.au>. The Centre for Policing, Intelligence and Counter Terrorism provides postgraduate programs in the areas of policing, intelligence, and counter-terrorism; international security studies; and intelligence. It is a good site for information about upcoming seminars and conferences, new publications, and debates.

- Centre for International Security Studies (University of Sydney): <http://ciss.econ.usyd.edu.au>. The Centre for International Security Studies analyses international and human security challenges facing Australia, Asia, and the world. The Centre focuses on international security and foreign policy issues, particularly in the Asia-Pacific region.
- UN Action to Counter Terrorism: <www.un.org/terrorism>. This website maps the UN's action to counter terrorism and contains a large number of documents for download, webcasts, a news centre, and much more.
- The official website of the European research project Transnational Terrorism, Security, and the Rule of Law (TTSRL): <www.transnationalterrorism.eu/research.php>. This website details European research on terrorism.
- In Good Faith: Sedition Law in Australia: <www.aph.gov.au/library/intguide/law/sedition.htm>. This e-brief provides background on the history of sedition as a commonwealth criminal offence. It provides examples of past sedition prosecutions and outlines proposals for reform in the early 1990s. It also discusses the controversial amendments made during 2005.
- Global Terrorism Research Centre (Monash University): <http://arts.monash.edu.au/politics/terror-research>. This research centre aims to generate globally relevant insights into the threat of terrorism and, through inter-disciplinary research techniques and the development of international research collaboration, strives to foster counter-terrorism practices that strengthen inter-cultural harmony. The site provides access to current research and reports.
- Strategic and Defence Studies Centre (Australian National University): <http://rspas.anu.edu.au/sdsc>. This is the website of Australia's oldest established centre for the study of strategic, defence, and wider security issues. It provides access to contemporary research papers and conference proceedings.

Films/documentaries

- *24*, 2001–10 (ongoing), television series, Imagine Entertainment. A fictional action series dealing with terrorist events and the often morally dubious means of addressing them.
- 'Islamist Terrorism Since 2001: Its Impact on Australia and the World', *Four Corners*, Special Broadband Edition (retrospective of television coverage), 2004, Australian Broadcasting Commission (ABC). An online compilation of a number of years of documentary and news coverage on Islamist terrorism. <www.abc.net.au/4corners/special_eds/20040830>.
- *The Trial*, 2009, documentary, directed by J. Robinson, 360 Degree Films. This documentary follows some of the defence attorneys in the 2008 Melbourne terrorism trial that led to the conviction of six men. It features interviews with the defence team and family members of the accused.

- 'Terror in the Skies', *Panorama*, 2009, television news feature, reported by the British Broadcasting Corporation (BBC). A report on a thwarted terrorist plot to blow up seven airliners using explosives hidden in soft-drink bottles.
- 'Terror in Mumbai', *Four Corners*, 2009, television news feature, reported by D. Reed, Australian Broadcasting Commission (ABC). Examines the 2008 terrorist bombings in Mumbai, India's largest city. <www.abc.net.au/4corners/content/2009/s2642355.htm>.
- 'Conspiracy 7/7: The London Bombings', *Four Corners*, 2009, television news feature, reported by the British Broadcasting Corporation (BBC). The 2005 London transport bombings killed 54 people and injured hundreds. This report examines the many conspiracy theories that arose after the event.

Visit the *Public Sociology* book website to access topical case studies, weblinks, YouTube clips, and extra readings.

References

Ahmad, A. & Sileno, M. 2005, 'Pre- and post–9/11 sociological response to terrorism', *International Journal of Contemporary Sociology*, vol. 42, pp. 189–206.

Australian Federal Police (AFP) 2009a, 'Operation Hammerli/Pendennis Eden', National Media Release, <www.afp.gov.au/media_releases/national/2009/operation_hammerlipendennis_eden> (accessed 17 November 2009).

——2009b, 'Operation Hammerli/Pendennis Eden—Commissioners Press Conference Speech', National Media Release, <www.afp.gov.au/media_releases/national/2009/operation_pendennis_eden_hammerli_-_commissioners_press_conference_speech> (accessed 17 November 2009).

Australian Government 2010, *Counter-Terrorism White Paper: Securing Australia, Protecting Our Community*, Department of the Prime Minister and Cabinet, Canberra, <www.dpmc.gov.au/publications/counter_terrorism/docs/counter-terrorism_white_paper.pdf> (accessed 23 February 2010).

Beck, U. 1992, *Risk society: Towards a New Modernity*, Sage, London.

——2002, 'The terrorist threat: World risk society revisited', *Theory, Culture & Society*, vol. 19, no. 4, pp. 39–55.

Bergesen, A. & Han, Y. 2005, 'New directions for terrorism research', *International Journal of Comparative Sociology*, vol. 46, pp. 133–51.

Bergesen, A. & Lizardo, O. 2004, 'International terrorism and the world-system', *Sociological Theory*, vol. 22, no. 1, pp. 38–52.

Black, D. 2004, 'The geometry of terrorism', *Sociological Theory*, vol. 22, no. 1, pp. 14–25.

Boyne, R. 2001, 'Cosmopolis and risk: A conversation with Ulrich Beck', *Theory Culture Society*, vol. 18, pp. 47–63.

Brown, M. 2010, 'Five Sydney terrorists jailed', *Sydney Morning Herald*, 15 February, <www.smh.com.au/nsw/five-sydney-terrorists-jailed–20100215-o1ca.html> (accessed 15 February 2010).

Cable News Network (CNN) 2009, 'Bush says it is time for action', CNN.com/ US, <http://archives.cnn.com/2001/US/11/06/ret.bush.coalition/index.html> (accessed 8 December 2009).

Catanzariti, K. 2009, 'Muslim terrorists face life jail terms', *Northern Territory News*, 17 October.

Cooper, M. 2009, 'Benbrika jailed for 15 years', *The Age*, 3 February.

Chomsky, N. 2003, *Power and Terror: Post-9/11 Talks and Interviews*, ed. J. Junkerman & T. Masakazy, Seven Stories Press, New York.

Clarke, M. 2008, *Report of the Inquiry into the Case of Dr Mohammed Haneef*, Vol. 1, Commonwealth of Australia, Canberra, <www.haneefcaseinquiry.gov.au/www/ inquiry/rwpattach.nsf/VAP/%283A6790B96C927794AF103ID9395C5C20% 29~Volume+I+FINAL.pdf/$file/Volume+I+FINAL.pdf> (accessed 9 December 2009).

Crelinsten, R. 2008, 'Terrorism, counter-terrorism and the media', in H. Tahiri & S. Pickering (eds), *Counter-Terrorism International Conference 2007: Conference Papers*, Victoria Police and Monash University, Melbourne.

Cronin, A. 2002–03, 'Behind the curve: Globalization and international terrorism', *International Security*, vol. 27, no. 3, pp. 30–58.

Cummings, L. 2009, 'Guilty: Sydney terror strike', *Daily Telegraph*, 17 October 2009.

Dunn, K., Klocker, N. & Salabay, T. 2007, 'Contemporary racism and Islamaphobia in Australia: Racializing religion', *Ethnicities*, vol. 7, pp. 564–89.

Foucault, M. (1979) *Discipline and Punish*, Vintage Books, New York.

Hudson, R. 1999, *The Sociology and Psychology of Terrorists: Who Becomes a Terrorist and Why? A Report Prepared under an Interagency Agreement by the Federal Research Division, Library of Congress*, Washington: Library of Congress, <www.loc.gov/rr/frd/pdf-files/Soc_ Psych_of_Terrorism.pdf> (accessed 8 December 2009).

Ingleton, S. & Moore, J. (Directors), 2009. *The Trial*, 360 Degree Films, Melbourne.

Jacobsen, G. 2009, 'Five guilty in Sydney terrorism trial', *The Age*, 16 October.

Kellner, D. 2002, 'Theorizing globalization', *Sociological Theory*, vol. 20, no. 3, pp. 285–305.

Laqueur, W. 1999, *The New Terrorism: Fanaticism and the Arms of Mass Destruction*, Oxford University Press, Oxford.

Lupton, D. 2006, 'Sociology and risk', in G. Mythen & S. Walklate (eds), *Beyond the Risk Society: Critical Reflections on Risk and Human Security*, Open University Press, Milton Keynes.

Lynch, A. & Williams, G. 2006, *What Price Security? Taking Stock of Australia's Anti-Terror Laws*, UNSW Press, Sydney.

Martin, G. 2003, *Understanding Terrorism: Challenges, Perspectives, and Issues*, Sage, Thousand Oaks, CA.

—— 2007, 'Globalization and international terrorism', in G. Ritzer (ed.), *The Blackwell Companion to Globalization*, Blackwell Publishing, Malden.

Mythen, G. 2007, 'Reappraising the risk society thesis: telescopic sight or myopic vision?', *Current Sociology*, vol. 55, pp. 793–813.

Mythen, G. & Walklate, S. 2005, 'Criminology and terrorism: Which thesis? Risk society or governmentality?', *British Journal of Criminology*, vol. 46, pp. 379–98.

Oberschall, A. 2004, 'Terrorism: The contribution of collective action theory', *Sociological Theory*, vol. 22, no. 1, pp. 26–37.

Oliverio, A. & Lauderdale, P. 2005, 'Terrorism as deviance or social control: Suggestions for future research', *International Journal of Comparative Sociology*, vol. 46, nos. 1–2, pp. 153–69.

Perkins, M. & Gregory, P. 2008, 'Benbrika and five followers found guilty', *The Age*, 16 September, <www.theage.com.au/national/benbrika-and-five-followers-found-guilty—20080915–4h38.html> (accessed 21 December 2009).

Reid, E. 1997, 'Evolution of a body of knowledge: An analysis of terrorism research', *Information Processing & Management*, vol. 33, no. 1, pp. 91–106.

Senechal de la Roche, R. 2004, 'Toward a scientific theory of terrorism', *Sociological Theory*, vol. 22, no. 1, pp. 1–4.

Tilly, C. 2004, 'Terror, terrorism, terrorists', *Sociological Theory*, vol. 22, no. 1, pp. 5–13.

Turk, A. 1982, 'Social dynamics of terrorism', *Annals of the American Academy of Political and Social Science*, vol. 463, pp. 119–28.

—— 2004, 'Sociology of terrorism', *Annual Review of Sociology*, vol. 30, pp. 271–86.

Williams, C. 2004, *Terrorism Explained: The Facts About Terrorism and Terrorism Groups*, New Holland, Sydney.

CHAPTER 20

Working 24/7:
The new work ethic

John Germov

What do you do?

When introduced to someone for the first time, we often ask, 'What do you do?' In today's society, work is seen as a major influence on our lives and a defining characteristic of who we are. What assumptions or expectations would you make if someone answered that she or he was a surgeon, an accountant, a nurse, an engineer, a labourer, a factory worker, or a teacher? Not only do we expect most people to be in paid work, but the type of work we do broadly indicates our income, education level, likely interests, and social status. Those not in paid work are often stigmatised or under-valued, such as the unemployed, retirees, or those responsible for doing domestic work (the vast majority of whom are unpaid women, commonly referred to as house*wives* rather than house*workers*). In fact, work remains highly gendered in both the paid and unpaid spheres, in terms of the type of work performed, the extent of remuneration (if any), and the status attached to particular occupations. There is plenty of material here to which we can apply our sociological imagination.

Introduction

What is considered work, attitudes and motivations towards work, and the way work is experienced are inherently outcomes of social organisation. Economic and technological developments, along with cultural values, public policies, and wider social structures, all set the social context of work. This chapter introduces you to a brief history of work, outlining continuities and changes. It discusses the notion of the 'work ethic' (what motivates us to work) and whether this is changing, given the rise of consumerism and the 24/7 economy. With unsocial work hours, casualisation, and under-employment now increasingly common, this chapter explores whether the contemporary work ethic is primarily governed by consumption preferences. In addition, the chapter covers debates over the persistence of gendered forms of work and its implications for an improved work/life balance for both women and men. The chapter then discusses dominant conceptions of work organisation, examining the ideas of Max Weber, Frederick Winslow Taylor, Henry Ford, and Elton Mayo, before reviewing contemporary theories that suggest we now live in a post-industrial or network society.

CrossLink: See Chapter 7 for a discussion of work/life balance.

A brief history of work

When asked to define work, most people will say that work is something you are paid to do, yet this is only part of what work involves. Defining work as paid employment is a very narrow conception of work and ignores how the meaning of work has changed over time and varied between cultures. The Ancient Greeks and Romans viewed work as a burden, and an interference with intellectual, political, spiritual, and artistic pursuits; they thus relied heavily on slave labour. In many pre-industrial cultures, like the hunter-gatherer societies of Aboriginal Australians, little distinction was made between work and leisure. In feudal Europe, peasants worked the land for their own subsistence, but gave up most of their produce to feudal lords who enforced their land ownership through private armies. The rise of industrial capitalism, which first occurred in Victorian England, resulted in paid work being heralded as the basis of social respectability and social status (Tilgher 1977; Grint 1998).

Our current preoccupation with paid work is a historically recent phenomenon, which owes much to developments stemming from the onset of the Industrial Revolution. Commonly dated between 1760 and 1850, the Industrial Revolution refers to a period of major social, economic, and technological change that first began in Britain and then spread in an uneven fashion during the 1800s and 1900s throughout Europe, the United States, Japan, and Australia. While there has been considerable historical debate over the precise dates and semantics of using the term 'revolution' to refer to such a broad sweep of time, there is general agreement that a new age of work organisation and social life had arisen that was fundamentally different from anything that had come before (O'Brien 1993). The industrialisation process resulted in the dominance of factory-based manufacturing and the widespread use of mechanisation, and marked a move from an agrarian-based subsistence economy to a mass production and mass consumption economy, based on capital investment, profit maximisation, and wage labour.

Profit maximisation and wage labour—the hallmarks of **capitalism**—have existed from classical civilisation onwards, yet it was not until the Industrial Revolution that capitalism would come to dominate social life. In pre-industrial societies, life was centred on subsistence agriculture and/or hunting and gathering. Work was task-oriented and not governed by any sense of time, but rather shaped by the natural rhythm of seasons and available sunlight (Thompson 1982). Once essential tasks to ensure survival were completed, people ceased to work. While work was arduous, it was also irregular and tempered by long periods of rest and idleness. The limited ability to store or transport food, and the lack of commodities to purchase and trade, meant that the pursuit of wealth was unrealistic and thus most people preferred leisure to work once subsistence needs were met (Kumar 1988; Braverman 1974; Weber 2001).

Nonetheless, capitalist forms of production did exist before industrialisation, particularly via cottage industries and **mercantilism**. The origins of capitalism lie in the mercantile period of trading, though pursuit of profit has existed for as long as some form of monetary system has existed, even though it may not have been the dominant form of economic activity.

capitalism
An economic system based on the private ownership of natural resources and the means of production, in which commodities are sold for a profit.

mercantilism
An economic theory and practice, dominant between the sixteenth and eighteenth centuries during the rise of the nation-state that assumes national wealth can be amassed through the accumulation of precious metals (silver and gold), achieved by trade, tariff protection, and conquest.

As Harry Braverman (1974, p. 52) notes, the 'purchase and sale of labor power has existed from antiquity', but the rise to dominance of 'a substantial class of wage-workers did not begin to form in Europe until the fourteenth century, and did not become numerically significant until the rise of industrial capitalism . . . in the eighteenth century'.

The impact of the Industrial Revolution

The Industrial Revolution brought new forms of work organisation and new methods of labour control. Workers congregated in large urban workplaces that housed power-driven machinery, and work was organised via a specialised division of labour. In this way, the concentration and specialisation of labour allowed greater control over how goods were produced. While the division of labour had already existed, factory production provided a more systematic and intensified way for this to occur. Initially, power-driven machinery relied on water turbines and was located next to waterways. These were eventually replaced by steam power, meaning factories could be situated in any geographic location; this helped spread industrialisation. Factory organisation involved a move from task-oriented to time-oriented work; time was now money, and employers had to maximise workers' productivity to ensure a return on capital investment (Thompson 1982). In the words of British historian Edward Palmer (E.P.) Thompson (1982), such 'time-discipline' marked a major change to the way people experienced work. He notes that previously:

> [t]he work pattern was one of alternate bouts of labour and of idleness; wherever men were in control of their working lives. (The pattern persists among some self-employed— artists, writers, small farmers, and perhaps also with students—today, and provokes the question whether it is not a 'natural' human work-rhythm.) (1982, pp. 304–5)

Box 20.1 summarises the enduring changes to the social organisation of work brought by the Industrial Revolution, which still casts a long shadow on the contemporary experience of work.

Box 20.1: Key changes to work brought by the Industrial Revolution

- Creation of distinct public and private spheres of work as work became separated from the household.
- A mass labour market in which workers sold their labour power for a wage.
- The dominance of factory (mass) production and mass consumption.
- Specialised division of labour.
- Sexual division of labour in paid and unpaid work.
- Change in social order from feudalism to capitalism.
- Rapid urbanisation as workers relocated to the cities.

- New class system: industrial working class and an entrepreneurial industrial capitalist class (the power and wealth of the *nouveau riche* overtook that of the land-owning aristocracy).
- Growth of trade unions and industrial conflict.
- Time-oriented production replaced task-oriented work: work was regulated by the clock, the working week, and official holidays, bringing regularity to days, months, and years.
- Clear distinction between work time and non-work time (leisure).

Towards a working definition of work

social construction/ism
Refers to the socially created characteristics of human life based on the idea that people actively construct reality, meaning it is neither 'natural' nor inevitable. Therefore, notions of normality/abnormality, right/wrong, and health/illness are subjective human creations that should not be taken for granted.

An appreciation of the history of work shows that there is no objective or universal definition of work; what is considered 'work' is always historically and culturally contingent. In sociological terminology, work is **socially constructed** and socially organised; it is a by-product of the cultural values and social practices of a particular society at a particular time.

In contemporary societies, the social construction of work is reflected in the primacy given to paid employment, and the social organisation of work is affected by government policies, employer associations, professional bodies and unions, and laws and regulations that define paid work, unemployment, and retirement—all of which have changed over the years and continue to vary between countries; however, this does not mean we cannot arrive at a workable definition that is both inclusive of varieties of work and conceptually meaningful. Work clearly involves some form of productive act—it is human activity that creates or achieves something. In other words, it can be distinguished from mere existence, idleness, rest, and leisure. Yet even non-work can be difficult to define. One person's leisure can be another person's labour, such as gardening or playing sport or music, all of which can either be a career or recreation. We can even speak of a 'leisure industry' where many people work hard at facilitating other people's leisure. Therefore, part of our definition requires a subjective dimension, so that it includes what people themselves perceive as 'work'.

Paid employment is what most people consider to be work. Most of us need to do paid work in order to survive. Yet paid labour is only part of the work that exists in any society (Grint 1998; Hall 1994). For example, there are many forms of unpaid work that are important to social life, such as domestic or household work, voluntary work, unpaid overtime, and self-improvement tasks, such as university study. There is also work in what is often called the informal, underground or black economy—that is, work done 'off the books' for 'cash in hand' (to avoid tax), home renovations involving do-it-yourself (DIY) labour, as well as criminal activity (Gershuny & Pahl 1983; Pahl 1984).

Sociologists were at the forefront of recognising the importance of unpaid housework (see Oakley 1974). What such insights have shown is that unpaid labour underpins much formal economic activity. Indeed, it is difficult to imagine how contemporary societies could function effectively without unpaid housework and voluntary labour. Since these pioneering insights, there have been various attempts to estimate the economic value of domestic (house) work. If unpaid tasks—most of them done by women in the home, such as child care, cleaning, and cooking—were replaced by a paid equivalent, the Australian Bureau of Statistics (ABS) estimates (based on 1997 figures—the most recent available)

gross domestic product (GDP)
The market value of all goods and services that have been sold during a year.

that the economic value would be equivalent to $261 billion, or 48 per cent of Australia's **gross domestic product (GDP)** (ABS 2000). Much of this work concerns what Arlie Hochschild (1983) calls emotional labour (see Chapter 3), an essential feature of many unpaid and paid occupations such as child care, aged care, and nursing.

To sum up the discussion, the most comprehensive and inclusive definition of work is provided by Richard Hall (1994): 'Work is the effort or activity of an individual that is undertaken for the purpose of providing goods or services of value to others and that is considered by the individual to be work' (1994, p. 5, original italics). This definition addresses both the social and subjective meanings of work and is inclusive of manual, intellectual, and emotional labour.

Why work? Motivations and expectations

Work saves us from three great evils: boredom, vice and need.

—**Voltaire (1694–1778)**, *Candide*, **1759**

Many dream of winning the lottery and envisaging a life free from the constraints of work. Yet studies suggest that few people would actually give up work completely if faced with such a choice. The Meaning of Working (MOW 1987) international study surveyed eight countries (Britain, the United States, Germany, Japan, Belgium, the Netherlands, Israel, and the former Yugoslavia). The study found that the majority of respondents would continue to work if they gained independent wealth, but the findings varied by country, with Britain and Germany having the highest number of people who would stop work (over 30 per cent) and Japan the lowest (7 per cent). While the majority of respondents showed a strong commitment to continue working, many stated that they would do so in a different job or under different working conditions. Nonetheless, such findings indicate that people work for more complex reasons than just the money they receive. This has particular implications for the widespread commonsense idea that monetary incentives alone are what motivate people to work harder.

Most of us work because we need an income to survive or to afford a lifestyle we desire. Yet this fact does not explain why we have 'workaholics', why anyone would do unpaid overtime or voluntary labour, why many multi-millionaires continue to work, and why some people dedicate themselves to particular careers irrespective of monetary incentives. The answer lies in the social values and social relations bound up with work, commonly referred to as the 'work ethic'.

The work ethic

The vast majority of people are expected to do paid work. While the welfare state provides a safety net, there is a strong stigma associated with welfare dependency, particularly unemployment. The social pressure on people to work is referred to as the 'work ethic', and represents the moral obligation and social expectation that most adults should do paid work and be diligent at it. The idea of the work ethic gained currency through the writing of Max Weber. In *The Protestant Ethic and the Spirit of Capitalism* (2001), he argues that puritan elements within Protestantism, such as Calvinism, had a substantial influence on the development of capitalism by extolling the virtues of hard work and material gain as the basis of salvation. For Weber, such values legitimised the profit-seeking 'spirit of capitalism' and were the basis for the moral compulsion to work in industrial societies. Much of Weber's thesis has been discredited (Giddens 2001; Hamilton 2000; Green 1973) and a number of authors have also noted that many non-Christian religions promote a work ethic (Noon & Blyton 2002). Despite these criticisms, the importance of Weber's work lay in highlighting the crucial role that cultural practices and values play in shaping meanings and orientations to work.

The status attached to employment compared with the stigma of unemployment helps to explain the centrality of work in people's lives and our orientation or commitment to work. Most studies show that work is central to people's lives, though work commitment varies according to age, gender, and culture, and family commitment is often given primacy (MOW 1987; Noon & Blyton 2002). There is also a gender element to the work ethic, whereby masculinity has long been associated with being 'the breadwinner' in a family unit.

The idea of work as 'virtue' and idleness as 'sin' can be sourced to the Bible. It is no accident that the punishment of criminals was meant to involve 'hard labour'. Thus it is little surprise that work is often viewed as a burden; yet non-work in a life of idleness or unemployment with few resources is hardly liberating. We clearly have ambivalent attitudes to work: some view it as a necessary evil, others as a pleasure through which they achieve self-fulfilment (Tausky 1992). Undoubtedly work can provide people with a sense of purpose in their lives, serve as a relief from boredom, and be an outlet for creativity. As Curt Tausky (1992) notes, most conceptions of work can be categorised into two basic paradigms: optimistic and pessimistic. Optimistic approaches to work focus on the intrinsic benefits of work, whereby the actual process of doing work has inherent value and is an end in itself, often conceived as a means to personal satisfaction and self-actualisation. Pessimistic accounts focus on the extrinsic rewards of work, viewing work as a means to an end, undertaken out of necessity and for monetary reward.

Motivations and orientations to work are contingent on expectations and experiences of work (Hall 1994). People work for both extrinsic and intrinsic reasons. Mike Noon and Paul Blyton (2002) suggest that because people have different and often multiple reasons for working, the unitary notion of a work ethic should be replaced by a plurality of 'work ethics'. Whether singular or plural, the idea of the work ethic exposes a moral underpinning of work that goes beyond the extrinsic rewards of money.

Alienation

**CrossLink:
See Chapters
2 and 11 for
more on
Marx.**

Karl Marx (1818–83) viewed work as the primary human activity—as inherent to humanity and the major way in which humans achieved self-actualisation (self-expression, self-development, fulfilling personal interests and desires). For Marx, the experience of work in capitalist society was inherently alienating because work was based on profit maximisation and exploitation rather than human fulfilment. Alienation could only cease once people were free from control by others and were able to fulfil their potential through productive activity of their choice (Watson 2003). For Marx (1974), as detailed in his *Economic and Philosophical Manuscripts of 1844*, alienation was an objective feature of work organisation under capitalism and comprised four interrelated features:

1. *Product alienation*: Workers are alienated from the products of their labour; they do not own what they make or control the fate of their products.
2. *Activity alienation*: Workers are alienated from the act of production; they are forced to labour for someone else and thus work offers little intrinsic satisfaction.
3. *Species alienation*: Workers are alienated from their 'species being' (that is, their human nature and 'spiritual essence'); they are deprived of their humanity and their bodies become commodities.
4. *Social alienation*: Workers are alienated from each other because capitalism transforms social relations into market relations so that people relate to one another through their market position rather than through their individual human qualities (Marx 1974; Edgell 2006).

While Marx viewed alienation as an evitable and universal experience in capitalist societies, other authors disputed this and focused on the subjective aspects of alienation by studying workers' actual levels of job satisfaction, finding that the experience of alienation was highly varied (cf. Blauner 1964; Goldthorpe et al. 1968). For example, Robert Blauner (1964) found that alienation can vary between different workplaces and industries, and theorised that it may be related to the nature of the work performed. John Goldthorpe and colleagues' (1968) affluent worker study showed that most manufacturing workers were happy with their jobs, even though they considered them to be mundane and unfulfilling, because of the extrinsic rewards the work provided. Their findings showed that manual labour need not automatically be more alienating than other types of work, and that not all workers react to the same work conditions in the same way. Furthermore, alienation is not only a consequence of capitalism: in state-run socialist societies based on the communal ownership of production, worker alienation was not uncommon (Grint 1998). While there is little empirical research on alienation today, the concept has entered popular usage to convey unsatisfying and dehumanising forms of work organisation. Contemporary research tends to focus on the subjective experience of job satisfaction. Findings from the 2005 Australian Survey of Social Attitudes (AuSSA) show that most Australians express reasonably high job satisfaction (7 on a scale of 0–10) (Western, Baxter & Chesters 2007, p. 253), a situation that is comparable with findings from other countries (Martin & Pixley 2005).

The consumer society: From work ethic to consumer ethic?

Work is one of the key factors shaping our self-identity. For example, in answer to the question 'Who am I?', people will invariably list their occupation. Despite popular notions of 'seachange', whereby people opt out of the 'rat race' to lead a more fulfilling life away from the stress of striving for material reward, there is little evidence of it being widespread; still, a number of commentators have suggested that the importance of work for our identities and interests is declining in favour of consumption practices (Ransome 2005).

CrossLink: See Chapter 8 for more discussion about consumption.

Anthony Giddens (1991), among others, has argued that people increasingly choose their lifestyles, rather than follow tradition or class allegiances, and often use consumption choices to express their identity. Such ideas are not new, of course; long ago, Thorstein Veblen (1975) coined the phrase 'conspicuous consumption' to describe the way the wealthy used their consumption practices as markers of social status. The relative affluence of developed societies today allows the majority of people to use consumption in this way. Some authors go so far as to argue that **consumerism** is so rampant that the contemporary era is best characterised as a consumer society dominated by a consumer ethic (Bauman 1998; Baudrillard 1981). While consumption practices do matter, it is important not to divorce them entirely from work, as access to paid employment ultimately underpins the ability of people to consume. Furthermore, social patterns in consumption practices reflecting class, gender, and ethnicity are still prevalent, suggesting that consumption practices should not be treated independently of other social factors.

consumerism
The cultural drive to procure more and more consumer items, and define oneself in terms of one's possessions.

sexual division of labour
Refers to the gender-based division of tasks, with the stereotype being the male breadwinner and the female homemaker.

Gendered work: Paid and unpaid

One of the most significant examples of the social construction and social organisation of work remains the **sexual division of labour**, which refers to the nature of work performed as a result of gender roles, with the stereotype being the male breadwinner and the female homemaker. Within the paid workforce, the sexual division continues, with few women in the senior ranks of management. There are also gendered occupations, such as nursing (predominantly female), and engineering (predominantly male). Despite a range of social reforms—such as equal pay (1972), the *Sex Discrimination Act 1984*, and equal opportunity policies—which have resulted in some gains for women, the sexual division of labour persists. For example, Australian Bureau of Statistics (ABS 2008a, 2006, 2000) figures show the following:

**CrossLink:
See Chapters
3, 7, and 12
for more on
gender.**

- Fifty-eight per cent of all adult women and 72 per cent of adult men were in the paid workforce in 2004–05 (compared with 46 per cent and 76 per cent respectively in 1984–85); of those in paid work, 55 per cent of women and 85 per cent of men were in full-time employment.
- Much of the increase in women's workforce participation has come from a rise in part-time work: women represent 71 per cent of all part-time workers.
- Women earn 84 per cent of the average weekly earnings of men (due to the combined factors of predominantly part-time employment and less access to jobs with paid overtime).
- The most recent available survey of time use (ABS 2000) shows that women do two-thirds of all domestic duties (287 minutes per day compared with men's 170 minutes). Full-time employment makes little difference, with women doing 211 minutes per day compared with 153 minutes for men (hence the notion of the 'double burden'). As Janeen Baxter notes, 'the gender gap' in the home is decreasing 'mainly because women are doing much less, rather than men doing much more' (2002, p. 420).

patriarchal dividend
Refers to the economic and social
advantages men gain over women.

Raewyn Connell (2009) puts it succinctly when she says there is a clear **patriarchal dividend** for most men from current social arrangements.

Many of the jobs women do involve emotional labour (Hochschild 1983), whereby they are expected to 'emote'—use and manage their emotions—as part of their work as nurses and childcare workers, teachers, flight attendants, and restaurant waitstaff. Furthermore, sexual innuendo, explicit jokes, sexual harassment, and overtly masculine and sexist behaviour has been studied by many authors as evidence of the gendered culture of organisations and the importance of informal interactions between men and women (Pringle 1988).

Sylvia Walby (2009, 1986), among others, has highlighted the social construction of gender in the workplace, evidenced by the exclusion of women from some occupations or limits placed on the type of job, hours, pay rates, and promotional opportunities accessible to them. In *Blue, White and Pink Collar Workers in Australia*, Claire Williams (1988) depicts gendered forms of labour control exerted over the appearance of female flight attendants, such as regular inspections of their weight, hair, makeup, and uniforms in a

CrossLink:
*See Chapters
3 and 12
for further
discussion
of feminist
theory and
Chapter 10 for
discussion of
gender and
class.*

manner befitting the military. It is over twenty years since Williams' study was published, and difficult to imagine such a scenario occurring today, though gendered notions of work remain and gendered experiences in the workplace persist.

One explanation offered for the persistence of gender inequality at work, which gained popular support among conservatives, was provided by Catherine Hakim's (2002) 'preference theory'. Embracing a **rational choice** perspective, Hakim suggests women's lower status in the workplace is the result of choice, arguing that many women prefer motherhood and 'women's work', or part-time work with flexible hours and cooperative work environments, rather than competing for career advancement. Based on her research, her argument is that women can be placed into three groups: 'work-centred' (20 per cent), 'home-centred' (20 per cent), or 'adaptive' (a 60 per cent majority). While Hakim's argument highlights the importance of not treating women as a homogenous group, Anne Summers (2003), among others, points out that Hakim's preference theory ignores how preferences are socially, culturally, and historically shaped—it also sheds little insight into the gendered experiences of work for those women who are career oriented (see Sociology Spotlight 20.1). The sexual division of labour is likely to persist until social structures are reformed to alleviate the burden of domestic duties—especially child care—from being primarily 'women's work'. Furthermore, the lack of paid paternity leave, affordable child care, and family-friendly workplaces, along with sex discrimination, underpins and reproduces gendered experiences of work. Only when these aspects are addressed will gender equality be possible, allowing real choice for women and men to pursue the work and home life that they desire.

rational choice theory
Also known as 'exchange theory', it is based on the principles of neo-classical economics and assumes that people's behaviour is primarily based on the maximisation of self-interest derived from 'rational' goal-oriented choices.

20.1: A man's world?

SOCIOLOGY **SPOTLIGHT**

Judy Wacjman's (1999) study of men and women in management found that for women and men in similar managerial positions there were no gender differences in management style, but that gender stereotypes prevailed so that the 'style associated with male management' was dominant (p. 56). If women were to succeed in senior management, they effectively had to conform to masculine values and behaviours—they literally had to 'manage like men'.

Managing work—the first gurus: Weber, Taylor, Ford, and Mayo

Marx's concept of alienation and his theory of capitalist exploitation (see Chapter 2) focused attention on how work was organised and managed. Before industrialisation and mass production, work patterns and organisational structures were highly individualised. Management was based on direct supervision and the exercise of personal authority. The growing complexity and scale of work organisation required systematic forms of management that increasingly involved delegated supervision, prescribed duties, bureaucratic rules, and performance measurement (Clegg, Kornberger & Pitsis 2005).

Max Weber's bureaucratic ideal type

Max Weber (1864–1920), one of sociology's most influential thinkers, is renowned for his theoretical work on bureaucracies. He predicted that bureaucratic administration would become the dominant form of social authority, stating at the time that the 'future belongs to bureaucratisation' (Weber 1968, p. 1401). In defining the major characteristics of bureaucracies to form his **ideal type**, he emphasised their common features as consisting of a pyramidal structure based upon specialisation within a hierarchical division of labour that was bounded by formal rules and regulations (see Weber 1968).

ideal type
A concept originally devised by Weber to refer to the abstract or pure features of any social phenomenon.

Weber correctly predicted the rise of bureaucracies in both the private and public sectors. He viewed bureaucracies as an effective response to dealing with social complexity and as an outcome of democratic processes. The ideal-type bureaucracy encapsulated the development of an administrative structure that attempted to eliminate nepotism, fraud, mismanagement, and inefficiency by focusing on conformity to standardised procedures to avoid arbitrary rule. Employment and promotion within the bureaucracy was based on the merit principle, with security of tenure and training used to maintain the expertise and independence of bureaucratic officials. Weber saw bureaucratic organisation as enhancing democracy because power rested in what he termed 'formal rationality'—that is, the rules and duties prescribed for an official post—rather than from social authority derived from tradition, class affiliation, or charismatic leadership.

CrossLink: See Chapters 2 and 11 for more on Weber.

While Weber viewed the development of bureaucratic organisation as inevitable because of its technical superiority and efficiency, he was nonetheless concerned that bureaucratic authority could threaten individual freedom. He feared humanity would become entrapped by an 'iron cage of rationality', where creativity, innovation, and autonomy would be constrained by the formal rationality of the bureaucratic organisation of work. In Weber's words:

> ... each man becomes a little cog in the machine and, aware of this, his one preoccupation is whether he can become a bigger cog ... it is still more horrible to think that the world could one day be filled with nothing but those little cogs, little men clinging to little jobs and striving towards bigger ones ... This passion for bureaucracy ... is enough to drive one to despair ... That the world should know no men but these: it is in such an evolution that we are already caught up, and the great question is therefore not how we can promote and hasten it, but what can we oppose to this machinery in order to keep a portion of mankind free from this parcelling-out of the soul, from this supreme mastery of the bureaucratic way of life. (cited in Mayer 1944, pp. 96–7)

Weber clearly acknowledged the paradox of bureaucracy: it can simultaneously be democratic and dehumanising, efficient and unresponsive.

Weber recognised that in reality there would be many variations from his ideal type, but his model stressed the key role of formal rationality (rule-governed action) as the basis of bureaucratic domination. Many authors have since proposed a range of alternative ideal types, primarily based on 'substantive rationality' (value-based action), such as Alvin Toffler's (1970) 'adhocracy', Tom Burns and Graham Stalker's (1961) 'organic organisation', and Henry Mintzberg's (1979) **professional bureaucracy**. For example, professional bureaucracies such as hospitals have long been recognised as deviating substantially from Weber's ideal type. They employ professional workers who require a high level of decision-making autonomy because of the specialist, complex, and indeterminate nature of their work, and have also been conceptualised as a **negotiated order** (Strauss 1978), involving the dual power structures of bureaucratic rules (formal rationality) and professionalism (substantive rationality).

professional bureaucracy
Mintzberg's term for an organisation that relies on staff with specialised knowledge and expertise to deliver complex services that require decision-making autonomy at the point of service delivery.

negotiated order
A symbolic interactionist concept that refers to any form of social organisation in which the exercise of authority and the formation of rules are outcomes of human interaction and negotiation.

The search for one best way

One of the earliest management theorists, and regarded by many commentators as the first managerial consultant or guru (as they later came to be popularly known), was Frederick Winslow Taylor (1856–1915) with his theory of 'scientific management' (1947). His 'scientific' theory really only involved 'time and motion studies' that were designed to discover the 'one best way' to perform a certain task; once this was determined, workers could then be trained to work in the 'one best way'. Taylor advocated a greater division of labour in the production process, whereby work tasks were broken down into the smallest repetitive tasks possible so that each worker could be given a simple task to perform. This process, effectively one of deskilling, allowed lower-skilled and cheaper labour to be employed. Individual monetary rewards would be the only incentive to work; workers would be paid by a piece-rate system, so that the more they produced, the more they could earn. Any humanistic concerns for employee participation and job satisfaction were considered subjective, 'unscientific', and unimportant features of the production process.

Taylor's revolutionary idea involved the separation of task conception from execution—that is, it was up to management to conceptualise how work could best be performed and for workers to follow orders to execute management's directives. In other words, management 'thinks' and workers 'do'. Taylor's theory was meant to provide management with complete control over the workplace; but his ideas were not only resisted by unions because of the deskilling and work intensification they entailed, but they were also resisted by management because they challenged traditional managerial authority and discretion (Hill 1981).

While Taylor's ideas were rarely adopted fully and met considerable resistance, they had a widespread influence on work organisation and reinforced the notion of managerial prerogative (Braverman 1974; Rose 1975; Hill 1981; Wright 1995). For example, 'Taylorism', as it became known, had a significant influence on mass production through the development of Henry Ford's (1863–1947) automated assembly line, which extended Taylor's notion of work deskilling in the early 1900s and became dominant after World War II. The automated assembly line allowed management to control the pace of work, and allowed the efficient mass production of cheap and uniform commodities, such as the Model T car that was only available in black. Ford's management style was authoritarian, paternalistic, and anti-union. He combined corporate welfare such as English language classes for migrant workers, together with subsidised schools and food outlets, managed through his so-called Sociology Department, with strict moral codes of worker behaviour both at work and home, often paying workers to spy on one another and using violent vigilantes to oppose attempts at unionisation (Benyon 1975).

A more humanistic conception of work organisation was promoted by Elton Mayo (1880–1949) on the basis of the Hawthorne studies, originally published in 1933, which spawned the human relations movement (Mayo 1949). One of the main findings was that worker productivity increased during their participation in the research: this research-induced factor became known as the 'Hawthorne effect' (Rose 1975). This was interpreted as showing that people were not simply motivated by rational self-interest, but by social solidarity and group association. The development of the human relations movement was a reaction to the dehumanising aspects of Taylorism and Fordism, and instead emphasised the importance of informal social networks within organisations to create humanised work environments. Despite the humanistic orientation, Mayo's prime concern was how to motivate and psychologically manipulate worker behaviour through forms of work organisation such as teamwork, so that productivity could be enhanced.

Contemporary management strategies, such as total quality management (TQM), best practice, business process re-engineering (BPR), and the Learning Organisation, tend to blend both Taylorism/Fordism (performance measurement) with humanistic approaches (teamwork). Debate in the academic literature centres upon whether such strategies should be viewed as intensifying managerial control over the labour process (**neo-Fordism**), or whether they represent a humanisation of the labour process by valuing worker participation and autonomy (**post-Fordism**) (Amin 1994).

neo-Fordism
A term used to describe the refinement of Fordist styles of management and work organisation that intensify control of the labour process.

post-Fordism
A term used to characterise the changing nature of work organisation and management styles in capitalist societies, in which 'flexibility' and worker participation are valued.

CrossLink: See Chapter 3 for more on Foucault.

The 'new' managerial surveillance

Foucauldian analyses (based on the work of Michel Foucault (1926–84)) expose how new managerial strategies use a sophisticated system of surveillance to enhance managerial control over the labour process, through methods such as continual performance monitoring to induce 'anticipatory conformity' in workers. As workers internalise management expectations, they regulate themselves and thus remove the need for bureaucratic regulations, hierarchical control, and direct (human) supervision

just-in-time (JIT)
A system of managing production so that goods are produced as needed to meet market demand by keeping only a minimal amount of stock warehoused.

(see Zuboff 1988; Delbridge & Lowe 1997). Graham Sewell and Barry Wilkinson's (1992) study of the use of **just-in-time (JIT)** and TQM in a Japanese factory describes the use of a 'traffic light system', in which a red card indicates mistakes made by individuals in the production line and is openly displayed for fellow workers to observe. In this way, an individual worker's performance is directly visible to all. Sewell and Wilkinson found that workers' autonomy was limited to the removal, or at least minimisation, of error and waste in the production process. While the performance of most work tasks has always involved varying amounts of shop-floor autonomy, new managerial regimes provide a systematic method for the effective use of worker autonomy in the production process. In this sense, 'participative management' is a thinly veiled attempt to tap into workers' practical knowledge so that once suggestions for improvement are incorporated, they become standardised across the organisation.

Contemporary work trends: Post-industrial, information, or network society?

Daniel Bell (1919–) was one of the first sociologists to argue that an epochal shift was occurring from industrial to post-industrial society due to a range of interrelated social, economic and technological changes (Bell 1973). Influenced by the work of management theorist Peter Drucker (1968), who argued that a 'knowledge society' was emerging based on the wide availability of reliable information, Bell argued that developed societies were moving away from a goods-producing to a service-based economy. He predicted that the majority of the workforce would eventually be employed in white-collar, service-sector work (such as in trade, finance, health, education, recreation, and research). For Bell, a new 'knowledge class' of tertiary-qualified professional and technical workers was emerging, and workers' theoretical (intellectual) knowledge would drive innovation and social change. In post-industrial society, knowledge would indeed be power and, according to Bell, would overtake property as the basis of social inequality. Bell also assumed that work organisation would become more participatory and less bureaucratic in order to accommodate the needs of the new knowledge class (Waters 1996).

Bell correctly anticipated the rise of service work and the importance of information and communication technologies (ICTs) in social, economic, and political life, but his post-industrial society thesis has a number of limitations. He tended to idealise service work and thus under-estimated the extent of routine and mundane white collar jobs. The experience of service work is not uniformly positive, nor does it necessarily involve the need for highly qualified personnel with theoretical knowledge. The 'knowledge class' of workers may have experienced better working conditions, but they are a minority. Moreover, the expansion of professional work has not gone unchecked, and it is increasingly subject to surveillance and control through performance-measurement management systems. Rather than viewing post-industrialism as a radical break with industrial society, it is more accurate to view the rise of service sector work and ICTs as part of a continuum of work in evolving capitalist societies (Edgell 2006). In recent years, the term 'post-industrialism' has been relabelled as the 'information society' or 'information age' by numerous authors. In particular, its central ideas have been developed in a more sophisticated way in the sociological work of Manuel Castells (2000) and his theory of the **network society**.

network society

Castells' term for the combination of economic globalisation and information technology to create a new kind of capitalist economy, based in social networks connected across the world by instant communication.

Castells argues that network-based social structures are the key characteristic of the 'information age' in which we now live, whereby information is the basis of economic activity and wealth creation. ICTs allow the creation and transfer of knowledge with greater speed and precision, and also facilitate networked forms of work organisation (which by definition rely on power-sharing and negotiated decision-making). Castells argues that the 'information revolution' has been as influential as the Industrial Revolution, and maintains that the future is one of a network society. Despite his generally optimistic assessment of the information age and network society, Castells acknowledges that there are detrimental impacts on the organisation and experience of work, notably due to the destandardisation and deregulation of working conditions (May 2002; Edgell 2006).

Crosslink: See Chapter 3 for further discussion of Castells' ideas.

Work intensification, under-employment, and the destandardisation of work

Ulrich Beck (2000) argues that the dominant work trend is that of destandardisation and individualisation, which underpins a growing insecurity regarding paid work. In the 24/7 economy, workers are expected to be 'flexible', and the employment experience is thus characterised by individualisation, whereby working conditions—including hours, times, and rates of pay—are no longer standardised, but rather subject to individual variation. The standard form of paid employment is generally viewed as full-time work, consisting of 35 to 38 daytime hours (such as 9.00 a.m. to 5.00 p.m.), and a range of protected working conditions, such as lunch and tea breaks, annual leave, sickness leave, superannuation, occupational health and safety, and non-discriminatory work practices. Since the 1980s, neo-liberalism and **globalisation** processes have led to the gradual deregulation of working conditions, most notably

globalisation

The increased interconnectedness of the cultural, economic, and political aspects of social life; intensified circulation of capital, goods, information, and people across national boundaries; and increased interdependence of countries and regions of the world.

epitomised in the Howard Liberal-National Coalition government's unpopular *Workplace Relations Amendment (Work Choices) Act 2005*. Work Choices was subsequently repealed and replaced by the Labor government's *Fair Work Act 2009*, marking a shift away from the neo-liberal public policy trend.

Non-standard forms of work have been on the rise; these include casual, temporary, and part-time employment, as well as self-employment and working from home. By 2004, 26 per cent of the Australian workforce was employed on a casual basis, an increase from 23 per cent in 1994, though the number has remained relatively stable since then. Around 55 per cent of casuals have stable employment, having been with the same employer for over twelve months (ABS 2006). Australians are also working longer hours for their full-time work, with the average weekly hours rising 6 per cent from 39 hours in 1984–85 to around 41 hours in 2004–05. A significant number of people work considerably longer than the 35-hour standard, with 37 per cent of all employed men and 13 per cent of employed women working more than 45 hours per week (ABS 2006).

In 2006, unemployment in Australia was at the historically low level of 4.5 per cent (compared with 10.7 per cent in 1993). Yet national averages always mask how unemployment is socially distributed, whereby the highest rates are found among particular social groups, such as youth (around 20 per cent), recent migrants and refugees from non-English-speaking backgrounds (NESB), Indigenous Australians (three times the national average), and those living in rural areas (ABS 2006). Sociologists have often pointed out the existence of 'hidden unemployment', which refers to those people who want to work but who do not appear in official statistics. For example, current estimates of unemployment in Australia exclude all those who have done at least one hour of paid work per week. Furthermore, a person must be actively registered as seeking work and must comply with various government requirements to be included in the statistics.

CrossLink: See Chapter 18 for more on neo-liberalism and globalisation.

Low unemployment has been paralleled by rising under-employment. Using the International Labour Organization (ILO) definition of under-employment as those people willing and available to work additional paid hours and currently below the 'threshold' of 35 hours per week, the ABS (2008b) found that 6 per cent of Australian workers were under-employed, with 51 per cent of part-time workers reporting that they would like to work full time. These figures ignore education and skill-related under-employment, whereby people are doing work for which they are over-qualified (such as university graduates driving taxis) and would rather be doing work commensurate with their qualifications and experience.

The combined rise of non-standard work, under-employment, and the work intensification associated with increasing working hours presents a precarious picture of contemporary employment that is far removed from the ideal of a network society. While ICTs have facilitated the flexible working arrangements that underpin the 24/7 economy, it is important not to over-estimate their benefits and to be wary of **technological determinism**, particularly given that call centres and 'telework' are the prime example of work in the so-called network society.

technological determinism
An assumption that technological innovation is the primary cause of social, political, and economic change.

Conclusion

I don't want to achieve immortality through my work ... I want to achieve it through not dying.

—**Woody Allen**

In the 1970s and 1980s, a number of commentators predicted a future in which the end of work and a leisure society was within reach. The contemporary social organisation of work suggests that such a utopian vision appears as distant as ever. As this chapter has shown, notions of work and its organisation have changed over time, but also reflect continuity with the past—particularly in terms of management of the labour process and the sexual division of labour.

Summary of main points

- ▶ Work is a central human activity, and thus the object of significant sociological interest. What is considered work varies between cultures and over time.
- ▶ Work is more than paid employment and encompasses unpaid and voluntary work.
- ▶ The Industrial Revolution laid the foundations for contemporary conceptions of work.
- ▶ Motivations to work can vary considerably, but most people expect, want, and need paid work.
- ▶ The work ethic refers to the moral compulsion to work and perform work diligently. While work has a major impact on our identity and social status, it is increasingly supplemented by a consumption ethic that allows those with sufficient money to choose particular lifestyles and construct their identities based on their consumption patterns.
- ▶ Marx's concept of alienation focused attention on the organisation and management of the labour process.
- ▶ The ideas of Weber, Taylor, Ford, and Mayo had a major influence on how work should be organised and managed.
- ▶ Contemporary debates over the impact of modern managerial strategies such as TQM focus on their novel blend of Taylorist/Fordist and human relations approaches, with disagreement on the extent to which they are responsible for humanising or dehumanising work.
- ▶ A sexual division of labour persists in paid and unpaid work, reflecting both cultural and structural factors.

SOCIOLOGICAL REFLECTION

20.1 The lotto question

We may yearn for the long weekend and holidays away from 'the daily grind', or even a life of leisure without work. Given the chance, would you give up work completely? Many people play lotteries hoping to win the big jackpot and have enough money to retire early and no longer need to work.

> ▶ What would you do if you won the lottery? Would you no longer work? How would you fill your time?
> ▶ In what way would not working impact on your identity, interests, and social life?
> ▶ Does having sufficient money to engage in various consumption practices supplant the need to work?

Discussion questions

20.1 How would you define work? What does work mean to you?

20.2 Why do people do voluntary work? Why do millionaires continue to work?

20.3 How common is workplace alienation? Have you experienced alienation at work?

20.4 Work ethic or consumer ethic—which is the most influential on our identity, values, and lifestyles?

20.5 Do we live in a post-industrial—or network—society?

20.6 Why does the sexual division of labour persist in paid and unpaid work?

20.7 What examples of gendered work have you experienced?

Further reading

Beck, U. 2000, *The Brave New World of Work*, Polity Press, Cambridge.

Blyton, P. & Jenkins, J. 2007, *Key Concepts in Work*, Sage, London.

Bramble, T. 2008, *Trade Unionism in Australia: A History from Flood to Ebb Tide*, Cambridge University Press, Melbourne.

Crompton, R. 2006, *Employment and the Family: The Reconfiguration of Work and Family Life in Contemporary Societies*, Cambridge University Press, Cambridge.

Grint, K. 2005, *Sociology of Work: An Introduction*, 3rd edn, Polity Press, Cambridge.

Peetz, D. 2006, *Brave New Workplace: How Individual Contracts are Changing our Jobs*, Allen & Unwin, Sydney.

Pocock, B. 2003, *The Work/Life Collision*, Federation Press, Sydney.

Rojek, C. 2010, *The Labour of Leisure*, Sage, London.

Ransome, P. 2005, *Work, Consumption and Culture: Affluence and Social Change in the Twenty-first Century*, Sage, London.

Warhurst, C., Eikhof, D.R. & Haunschild, A. (eds) 2008, *Work Less, Live More? Critical Analysis of the Work-life Boundary*, Palgrave Macmillan, Basingstoke.

Websites

- Australian Council of Trade Unions (ACTU): <www.actu.asn.au>. The peak national body representing worker and union interests has an extensive website with background papers, current campaigns, and a range of other resources.
- Centre for Work + Life (University of SA): <www.unisa.edu.au/hawkeinstitute/cwl/default.asp>. Based at the University of South Australia, the centre has produced some of the key studies on work/life balance.
- Equal Opportunity for Women in the Workplace Agency (EOWA): <www.eowa.gov.au>. EOWA works with employers to improve equal opportunity outcomes for women in the workplace. This site supplies case studies, reports, and other resources.
- Fair Work Australia: <http://www.fwa.gov.au>. The national body responsible for workplace relations, including industrial disputes and the administration of the *Fair Work Act 2009*.
- International Labour Organization (ILO): <www.ilo.org>. A United Nations body that develops and promotes international labour standards; this is a good source of comparative information and analysis.
- LaborNet: <www.labornet.org>. United States-based activist website that provides access to a wide range of resources and links.
- National Institute of Labour Studies (NILS): < http://nils.flinders.edu.au>. Based at Flinders University in Adelaide, the website provides access to a number of papers and reports of ongoing research.
- Organisation for Economic Cooperation and Development (OECD): <www.oecd.org>. A good source for comparative information, analysis, and statistics.
- SocioSite—Sociology of Labor: <www.sociosite.net/topics/labor.php>. One of the best and longest-running sociology portal websites. The section on work includes a vast number of relevant web links.

Films/documentaries

- *Metropolis*, 1927, motion picture, directed by F. Lang, Universum Film (UFA). Fritz Lang's visually stunning classic silent movie portrays a disturbing future of a world divided into two groups: 'thinkers', who lead a luxurious above-ground life, and the 'workers', who labour arduously underground to support the thinkers.
- *Modern Times*, 1936, motion picture, directed by C. Chaplin, Charles Chaplin Productions. This acclaimed and classic film is a savage critique of the alienation and uncertainty caused by the industrialisation process. Highly recommended.

- *People's Century: 1924 On the Line*, 1995, television documentary, produced by A. Holdworth, British Broadcasting Corporation (BBC)/WGBH. An excellent documentary that charts the rise of Fordism, focusing on the rise of the car industry.
- *The Office*, 2001–03, television series, directed by R. Gervais and S. Merchant, British Broadcasting Corporation (BBC). An amusing portrayal of office politics, management double-speak, and corporate restructuring. An equally entertaining and longer-running US remake of the series is also available and recommended.
- *The Corporation*, 2003, documentary feature, directed by M. Achbar and J. Abbott, Big Picture Media Corporation. A fascinating historical and contemporary review of the rise of corporations and the power they wield over our daily lives. Highly recommended.
- *Enron: The Smartest Guys in the Room*, 2005, documentary feature, directed by A. Gibney, Jigsaw Productions/2929 Productions. An entertaining documentary that analyses organisational deviance, corporate corruption, and the ultimate demise of a corporate giant.
- *30 Days, Minimum Wage*, 2005, television documentary, directed by M. Spurlock. As part of the 30 Days documentary series, Morgan Spurlock (of *Super Size Me* fame) and his fiancée Alex try to live for 30 days earning a minimum wage of US$ 5.15 per hour.
- *Capitalism: A Love Story*, 2009, documentary feature, directed by M. Moore, Dog Eat Dog Films/Front Street Productions. An amusing and insightful exposé of US capitalism amidst the GFC. <www.capitalismalovestory.com>.

Visit the *Public Sociology* book website to access topical case studies, weblinks, YouTube clips, and extra readings.

References

Amin, A. (ed.) 1994, *Post-Fordism: A Reader*, Blackwell, Oxford.

Australian Bureau of Statistics (ABS) 2000, *Unpaid Work and the Australian Economy, 1997*, cat. no. 5240.0, ABS, Canberra.

——— 2006, *Year Book Australia, 2006*, cat. no. 1301.0, ABS, Canberra.

——— 2008a, *Australian Social Trends, 2008*, cat. no. 4102.0, ABS, Canberra.

——— 2008b, *Underemployed Workers, Australia*, cat. no. 6265.0, ABS, Canberra.

Baudrillard, J. 1981, *For a Critique of the Political Economy of the Sign*, trans. C. Levin, Telos Press, New York.

Bauman, Z. 1998, *Work, Consumerism and the New Poor*, Open University Press, Buckingham.

Baxter, J. 2002, 'Patterns of change and stability in the gender division of household labour in Australia, 1986–1997', *Journal of Sociology*, vol. 38, no. 4, pp. 399–424.

Beck, U. 2000, *The Brave New World of Work*, Polity Press, Cambridge.

Bell, D. 1973, *The Coming of Post-industrial Society*, Basic Books, New York.

Benyon, H. 1975, *Working for Ford*, E.P. Publishing, Wakefield, CN.

Blauner, R. 1964, *Alienation and Freedom*, Chicago University Press, Chicago.

Braverman, H. 1974, *Labor and Monopoly Capital: The Degradation of Work in the Twentieth Century*, Monthly Review Press, New York.

Burns, T. & Stalker, G.M. 1961, *The Management of Innovation*, Tavistock, London.

Castells, M. 2000, *The Rise of the Network Society*, 2nd edn, Blackwell, Oxford.

Clegg, S., Kornberger, M. & Pitsis, T. 2005, *Managing and Organizations: An Introduction to Theory and Practice*, Sage, London.

Connell, R. 2009, *Gender: In World Perspective*, 2nd edn, Polity Press, Cambridge.

Delbridge, R. & Lowe, J. 1997, 'Manufacturing control: Supervisory systems on the "new" shopfloor', *Sociology*, vol. 31, no. 3, pp. 409–26.

Drucker, P. 1968, *The Age of Discontinuity: Guidelines to our Changing Society*, Harper Business, New York.

Edgell, S. 2006, *The Sociology of Work: Continuity and Change in Paid and Unpaid Work*, Sage, London.

Gershuny, J.I. & Pahl, R.E. 1983, 'Britain in the decade of the three economies', *New Society*, 3 January, pp. 7–9.

Giddens, A. 1991, *Modernity and Self-identity: Self and Society in the Late Modern Age*, Polity Press, Cambridge.

——2001, 'Introduction', in M. Weber 2001, *The Protestant Ethic and the Spirit of Capitalism*, trans. T. Parsons, Routledge, London.

Goldthorpe, J.K., Lockwood, D., Bechhofer, F. & Platt, J. 1968, *The Affluent Worker: Industrial Attitudes and Behaviour*, Cambridge University Press, Cambridge.

Green, R.W. (ed.) 1973, *Protestantism, Capitalism, and Social Science: The Weber Thesis Controversy*, 2nd edn, DC Heath & Co., Lexington, NC.

Grint, P. 1998, *The Sociology of Work*, 2nd edn, Polity Press, Cambridge.

Hakim, C. 2002, *Work–Lifestyle Choices in the 21st Century: Preference Theory*, Oxford University Press, New York.

Hall, R.H. 1994, *Sociology of Work: Perspectives, Analyses, and Issues*, Pine Forge Press, Thousand Oaks, CA.

Hamilton, A. 2000, 'Max Weber's *The Protestant Ethic and the Spirit of Capitalism*', in S. Turner (ed.), *The Cambridge Companion to Weber*, Cambridge University Press, Cambridge, p. 151.

Hill, S. 1981, *Competition and Control at Work*, Gower, Aldershot.

Hochschild, A.R. 1983, *The Managed Heart: Commercialization of Human Feeling*, University of California Press, Berkeley, CA.

Kumar, K. 1988, 'From work to employment and unemployment: The English experience', in R.E. Pahl (ed.), *On Work: Historical, Comparative and Theoretical Approaches*, Basil Blackwell, Oxford, pp. 138–64.

Martin, B. & Pixley, J. 2005, 'How do Australians feel about their work?', in S. Wilson, G. Meagher, R. Gibson, D. Denemark & M. Western (eds), *Australian Social Attitudes: The First Report*, UNSW Press, Sydney, pp. 42–61.

Marx, M. 1974 [1844], *Economic and Philosophical Manuscripts of 1844*, trans. M. Milligan, Progress Press, Moscow.

May, C. 2002, *The Information Society: A Sceptical View*, Polity Press, Cambridge.

Mayer, J.P. 1944, *Max Weber and German Politics: A Study in Political Sociology*, Faber & Faber, London.

Mayo, E. 1949, *The Social Problems of an Industrial Civilisation*, Routledge and Kegan Paul, London.

Meaning of Work (MOW) International Research Team 1987, *The Meaning of Working*, Academic Press, London.

Mintzberg, H. 1979, *The Structuring of Organizations*, Prentice Hall, Englewood Cliffs, NJ.

Noon, M. & Blyton, P. 2002, *The Realities of Work*, 2nd edn, Palgrave, Houndsmills.

Oakley, A. 1974, *The Sociology of Housework*, Martin Robertson, London.

O'Brien, P.K. 1993, 'Introduction: Modern conceptions of the Industrial Revolution', in P.K. O'Brien & R. Quinault (eds), *The Industrial Revolution and British Society*, Cambridge University Press, Cambridge, pp. 1–30.

Pahl, R.E. 1984, *Divisions of Labour*, Basil Blackwell, Oxford.

Pringle, R. 1988, *Secretaries Talk: Sexuality, Power and Work*, Allen & Unwin, Sydney.

Ransome, P. 2005, *Work, Consumption and Culture: Affluence and Social Change in the Twenty-first Century*, Sage, London.

Rose, M. 1975, *Industrial Behaviour: Theoretical Development Since Taylor*, Penguin Books, Middlesex.

Sewell, G. & Wilkinson, B. 1992, '"Someone to watch over me": Surveillance, discipline and the just-in-time labour process', *Sociology*, vol. 26, no. 2, pp. 271–89.

Strauss, A. 1978, *Negotiations: Varieties, Contexts, Processes, and Social Order*, Jossey-Bass, San Francisco.

Summers, A. 2003, *The End of Equality: Work, Babies and Women's Choices in 21st Century Australia*, Random House, Sydney.

Tausky, C. 1992, 'Work is desirable/loathsome: Marx versus Freud', *Work and Occupations*, vol. 19, no. 1, pp. 3–17.

Taylor, F.W. 1947 [1911], *Scientific Management*, Harper & Brothers, New York.

Thompson, E.P. 1982 [1967], 'Time, work-discipline, and industrial capitalism', in A. Giddens & D. Held (eds), *Classes, Power and Conflict: Classical and Contemporary Debates*, Macmillan, Basingstoke, pp. 299–309.

Tilgher, A. 1977 [1930], *Work: What it has Meant to Men Through the Ages*, trans. D.C. Fisher, Arno Press, New York.

Toffler, A. 1970, *Future Shock*, Random House, New York.

Veblen, T. 1975 [1899], *The Theory of the Leisure Class*, Allen & Unwin, London.

Wacjman, J. 1999, *Managing Like a Man*, Allen & Unwin, Sydney.

Walby, S. 1986, *Patriarchy at Work*, Polity Press, Cambridge.

—— 2009, *Globalization & Inequalities: Complexity and Contested Modernities*, Sage, London.

Waters, D. 1996, *Daniel Bell*, Routledge, London.

Watson, T. 2003, *Sociology, Work, and Industry*, 4th edn, Routledge, London.

Weber, M. 1968 [1921], *Economy and Society: An Outline of Interpretive Sociology*, three vols, G. Roth and C. Wittich (eds), Bedminster Press, New York.

—— 2001 [1930], *The Protestant Ethic and the Spirit of Capitalism*, trans. T. Parsons, Routledge, London.

Western, M., Baxter J. & Chesters, J. 2007, 'How are families managing?', in D. Denemark, G. Meagher, S. Wilson, M. Western & T. Phillips (eds) 2007, *Australian Social Attitudes 2: Citizenship, Work and Aspirations*, UNSW Press, Sydney, pp. 241–61.

Williams, C. 1988, *Blue, White and Pink Collar Workers: Technicians, Bank Employees and Flight Attendants*, Allen & Unwin, Sydney.

Wright, C. 1995, *The Management of Labour: A History of Australian Employers*, Oxford University Press, Melbourne.

Zuboff, S. 1988, *In the Age of the Smart Machine, The Future of Work and Power*, Heinemann, London.

CHAPTER 21

Media and popular culture

Timothy Marjoribanks

The election of Barack Obama

One of the great promises of the media has been the idea that it provides a space in which people can connect with each other, discuss critical issues, and build new forms of community and public engagement. Related to this, sociologists, including Manuel Castells and Pierre Bourdieu, have argued that to understand contemporary politics and contemporary society we need to understand the media. Nowhere has this more clearly been demonstrated than in the recent electoral success of President Barack Obama in the United States.

While the media have long been crucial to politics and public life, what was particularly significant about Obama's success was the powerful use made by his campaign team of a diverse range of new media forms. In addition to a website and email, the Obama campaign team developed a YouTube channel, made use of social networking sites—including Facebook and MySpace—and also worked with mobile phone technology, including Twitter (Abroms & Lefebvre 2009). At least two critical lessons emerged from this experience. First, developments in information and communication technologies enabled direct forms of communication between political actors and the public that bypassed the mainstream media. Second, such technologies provided a means for empowering people to participate and to mobilise independently at the local community level.

In seeking to understand these developments from a sociological perspective, it is important not to argue that technology determined particular outcomes. While new technology was clearly important, so, too, was a social context in which participation was seen as important, and in which there was a concern to find alternative means of communicating beyond mainstream media. These factors become even more relevant when we consider that Obama's competitor, John McCain, had access to the same technologies, but was much less effective in using them. In other words, from a sociological perspective, while new media technologies provide the potential for new forms of communication to occur, these technologies do not exist in a vacuum, but rather in a societal context that influences the possibilities associated with technological innovation.

Introduction: What are the media?

The complexity of contemporary media is well captured by Geoffrey Craig:

'The media' is a catch-all term that includes transnational corporations, communication technologies, policy and regulatory frameworks, the practices of journalists, gossip columns, the nightly television news, blockbuster movies, advertisements, business magazines, music radio, the local newspaper and the Internet. The media are businesses and yet they are also ascribed a special function in the democratic health of a society; the media are the *news* media and function as journalism, but they are also the entertainment media and provide escape from the pressures of everyday life. (2004, p. 3, original italics)

Despite the diversity of ways in which the concept of **media** is used, Michael O'Shaughnessy and Jane Stadler (2005) provide a working definition of the media as 'the media industry and the communication technologies involved in transmitting information and entertainment between senders and receivers across space and time' (2005, p. 3). From this, we can identify the media in terms of specific industries, including newspapers, magazines, recordings, movies, broadcast, cable and satellite television, radio, and the internet.

media
Technologically developed forms of human communication, held either in public or private ownership, which can transmit information and entertainment across time and space to large groups of people.

In discussing these media industries, it is critical to recognise that they transform over time. For example, recent technological developments mean previously distinct media forms are now **converging**. Developments in mobile phone technology, for example, mean that the telephone is now a key means by which people can access the internet, and with it television broadcasts, recordings, online newspapers, and the like.

convergence
The process by which previously distinct industries, including media and information and communication technologies (ICTs), come together.

However we define the media, they are a central part of the lives of people in Australia and in societies around the world. To give two examples: an estimated 99 per cent of Australian homes have television, averaging two television sets per household (Australian Government 2003); while a 2008 Australian Bureau of Statistics report indicates that the rate of home internet access in Australia 'has quadrupled in recent years, from 16% of ... households in 1998 to 64% in 2006–07' (ABS 2008).

While such data are important in measuring media use, from a sociological perspective they are only a starting point. A sociological analysis of the media is critically concerned with what goes on behind such numbers. For example, who owns the media, and how are media produced? How are different social groups represented, or not represented, in the media? As consumers, how do we interact with the media, and how do the media affect us? Underlying these questions is the central sociological concern with **power** and how media and society interact. This chapter is primarily concerned with such questions.

power
A capacity, which all groups of people possess to some degree, to exert influence or pursue individual and collective interests.

The media and society

Sociologists have long been interested in the role of the media in society. **Functionalist** theorists in the twentieth century emphasised that the media fulfil a **socialising** role,

functionalism

A theoretical perspective in sociology in which society is seen as consisting of many complex and interdependent parts that contribute to consensus and social stability. Prominent theorists include Durkheim, Merton, and Parsons.

socialisation

The process through which an individual learns the culture of a society and internalises its *norms*, values and perspectives in order to know how to behave and communicate. Socialisation is the process through which we acquire a sense of *self*.

information society

A view that information and its uses have produced a new kind of knowledge-intensive society.

Marxists/Marxism

Those who subscribe to Marx's social theory that changes in human activity—for example, labour—are determined by economic and material factors, such as technology, and *class* conflict over material interests.

social construction/ism

Refers to the socially created characteristics of human life based on the idea that people actively construct reality, meaning it is neither 'natural' nor inevitable. Therefore, notions of normality/abnormality, right/wrong, and health/illness are subjective human creations that should not be taken for granted.

media process

A concept used to analyse the interaction of production, representation, and effects of media, located within a societal context.

providing people with a means of learning how to behave in society, thereby enabling the smooth and consensual functioning of society. In contrast, conflict theories, in particular related to **Marxist** approaches, have understood the media to be a means through which dominant classes in society can exert their rule, both through economic and cultural domination. Recent theorising on the media in society emphasises that the media are now an important—even the central—feature of social and political relations in the emerging **information society**. According to Manuel Castells, 'new information technologies [including media and communications technologies] are transforming the way we produce, consume, manage, live and die' (1989, p. 15). A simple thought experiment to explore the centrality of the media in everyday life involves considering the interactions you have had with media today. Many of you will have listened to the radio or to an iPod, some of you will have watched TV or surfed the internet for fun or for work, maybe through a mobile phone, while others will have read a newspaper. Some of you may have done all of these, and more. In other words, for many of us contemporary life is unimaginable, and would be completely different, without the media.

The media process and power

Given the central significance of the media to contemporary life, questions arise as to how we should analyse the media. The approach taken to understanding the media here is to consider them as a **socially constructed** process. That is, the media we have are the outcome of interactions between people and organisations in societal contexts. More specifically, the **media process** involves the production of media, the content of media, and the effects of media on audiences, together with the connections between these dimensions. It is also vital to consider the social context, including politics, the economy and technology, within which these processes take place (Croteau & Hoynes 2000).

Central to the sociological investigation of the media process is the question of power. The media represent a key location of contested power in contemporary societies. Such contests revolve around a range of issues, from questions of who appears in the media, and who is excluded, through to questions around ways in which the media are used to mobilise political and social struggles and, ultimately, the question of media effects. John Thompson defines power as 'the ability to act in pursuit of one's aims and interests, the ability to intervene in the course of events and to affect their outcome' (1995, p. I3). The key element of this definition is that power is considered as a capacity to do something and to influence outcomes. When a media corporation cuts the price of its newspapers or cable subscription rates, for example, this may result in better short-term deals for consumers, but it may also be an attempt to use economic power to undermine and ultimately destroy competitor corporations. Similarly, when a newspaper publishes an editorial supporting a political party at an election, this is an attempt to exercise political power in a direct way.

CrossLink:
See Chapters 12 and 20 for more on gender and work.

At the same time, it is important to recognise that power is not always exercised openly. In some instances, power may be used to marginalise or silence certain viewpoints or experiences, without overt conflict. In other situations, power can operate because dominated groups in society have come to accept and consent to the ideas of the dominant groups as common sense or as natural. In such cases, dominance occurs without the need for any overt exercise of power (Lukes 1974). The media become a key site through which such processes can occur. For example, media discussion of the work/life debate, where people struggle to balance paid employment, household labour, and family and/or leisure time, routinely assumes that household labour is a female activity, and that achieving work/life balance is a problem for women alone, thereby contributing to the perpetuation of often unspoken but widely accepted assumptions around gendered divisions of labour, which are central to the power dynamics of **patriarchal** societies.

patriarchy
A system of power through which males dominate households. It is used more broadly by *feminists* to refer to society's domination by patriarchal power, which functions to subordinate women and children.

Having explored the ways in which sociologists posit a link between the media and society, and having considered the centrality of power, we can now analyse the dimensions of the media process. In doing so, it is important to remember that, while we can unpack them as separate stages, they are closely connected in practice.

Media production

Sociologists study media production because it is the process through which media content is created. Studying the 'senders' of media messages gives us important insights into how, and with what intention, messages are sent (Cottle 2003). Focusing on news production, which has been a key area of sociological research, a dominant media industry view is that the news is collected and presented by professional journalists who go out into the world with a focus on finding the truth on the important issues of the day, and then report those issues in an objective and impartial fashion, but the process is more complex than this. Simon Cottle (2003) argues that a model of news production needs to engage with:

- the micro-level, including interactions between news workers, and their relations with technologies, professional colleagues, and outside sources

- the meso-level of organisational cultures, corporate strategy, and editorial policy, and
- the macro-context, including regulation, technology, and the competitive environment.

The significance of this approach is that, while it recognises the importance of the role of individual news reporters at the micro-level, it also requires us to investigate the organisational and societal contexts within which news is produced. For example, to understand the way in which news is produced at a major commercial television broadcaster, we need to consider factors including the relations among individual news workers and the news sources to which they have access; the organisational culture of the station, which may be focused on promoting sensationalistic news; and finally, the broader context, which may include the need to develop news content that will attract advertisers.

More recently, it has become important to recognise the significance of newly emerging media technologies for news production. Innovations in digital technology mean that it is now possible for almost anyone to be involved in news production, whether by recording and sending information to mainstream news organisations, by tweeting, or by working as a citizen journalist through an organisational or individual website. Crucial considerations in this context relate to the range and quality of news available. Certainly, many independent and citizen journalism news sites provide diverse and important forms of news not available through mainstream media. At the same time, the sheer volume of information available online makes the judgment of quality a difficult task. The previously clear distinction between producers of news and consumers of news is now being challenged.

Media representations

Another critical issue for sociologists studying the media process concerns the ways in which social relations, including race, ethnicity, gender, sexuality, and disability, are represented in the media. Sociologists are concerned with exploring representations of social relations because it is argued that they are social constructions—that is, they are the outcome of human action and social processes, rather than pre-ordained or natural. As such, it is important to understand the contexts in which these social relations are created, reproduced, and in some instances challenged and transformed. In the contemporary world, the media are a key site for the production of these categories, supplementing and in some cases supplanting other key institutions such as schools, families, and religion. In this context, time and again, sociological research reveals that mainstream commercial media serve to reinforce, and in some cases to exacerbate, stereotypes around these social relations (O'Shaughnessy & Stadler 2005). Here, we will focus on representations of race and gender.

Race in the media

In analysing representations of race in the media, a vital starting point is the work of Stuart Hall (1990). Hall mobilised the notions of overt and inferential racism as a means of exploring representations of race. Overt racism is defined as 'favourable media coverage … granted to what are explicitly or openly racist positions and arguments' (Allan 1999, p. 159). By contrast, inferential racism refers to 'seemingly naturalised representations of situations where racist premises or propositions are being inscribed in the media coverage as a set of unquestioned assumptions' (Allan 1999, p. 159).

CrossLink: See Chapter 9 for more on sport and the media.

By way of example, we can consider media representations of race in sport. While sociological and scientific researchers have revealed that race is a social construction with no biological or genetic basis, media sports commentary often presents race as a biological category—making claims, for example, about supposed innate 'black athletic superiority and white intellectual superiority' (Bruce 2004, p. 861). Such claims tend to be presented as common sense and natural. In so doing, important sections of the media reproduce and reinforce divisive race-based representations of athletes, which have no grounding in scientific evidence but which have profoundly negative social consequences (Brookes 2002; Bruce 2004).

Gender in the media

Media representations of gender have also been a subject of much research, which has explored the ways in which men and women are represented in the media, and how stereotypes are presented, reproduced, and in some cases transformed. For example, Elizabeth van Acker (2003) shows that representations of female politicians in Australia and New Zealand are much more likely to focus on issues such as personal relationships and personal appearance than are representations of male politicians. In another context, Gregory Fouts, Kimberley Burggraf, and Kimberley Vaughan have found that representations of physical appearance, and in particular body weight, continue to be gendered in leading internationally distributed sit-coms (Fouts & Burggraf 2000; Fouts & Vaughan 2002). In particular, their research reveals that female characters below average weight are over-represented, that heavier female characters receive more negative comments from male characters than do thinner characters, and that these negative comments are reinforced by audience reactions such as laughter in a way that does not happen for men. In short, such research reveals how media coverage of gender can reproduce and reinforce gendered stereotypes.

It is also crucial to recognise that people can struggle to engage with, and change, such media representations. In the United States, the Media Action Network for Asian Americans (MANAA) seeks to create a media environment free of racism through the promotion of accurate, balanced and sensitive Asian American images. MANAA is part of the Multi-Ethnic Media Coalition and Asian Pacific American Media Coalition, which regularly meets with the major US television networks to encourage diversity in their programming (see <www.manaa.org>). MANAA is an important example revealing that it is possible for organisations to uncover what are often taken-for-granted assumptions about groups of people, and to then challenge and seek to transform those assumptions and their representation in the media.

Media effects

One of the most controversial areas of sociological research on the media concerns the question of media effects or influence. While the media are central to the experiences of many in contemporary societies, it is quite a different matter to make claims about or measure the specific effects of the media. Through much of the twentieth century, a range of sociological approaches suggested that the media have direct and powerful effects on the population. For functionalists, a key role of the media is their socialising role. In particular, functionalists argue that by consuming media, members of a society are taught appropriate ways to behave to ensure the successful reproduction of society.

From a conflict perspective, members of the **Frankfurt School** understood the media as commodifying culture, through a process by which culture is reduced to the needs of capitalism for profit, and in which people become reduced to being one-dimensional figures seeking more and more commodities. Approaches that propose a direct effect of media on individuals have been critiqued at a number of levels, in particular with the argument that it is very difficult to disentangle the effects of the media from other social factors such as the family, education, religion, and the like. Similarly, in the twenty-first century, the underlying argument of such approaches—that there is a passive audience for the media—is highly contestable (Macionis & Plummer 2002).

Frankfurt School
The Frankfurt School of Social Research was founded in 1923 as a centre for socialist research. The leading researchers emigrated to the United States with the rise of Hitler in Nazi Germany. It is closely associated with critical theory, a strand of *Marxism*.

agency
The ability of people, individually and collectively, to influence their own lives and the society in which they live.

Moving to approaches that seek to return **agency** to audiences, one of the most significant contributions to sociological research into media effects emerged in the work of Hall (1980), Angela McRobbie (2005), David Morley (1992), and others who argue for the need to engage with media effects in the social and cultural contexts of the audience.

The approach of Hall in particular was fundamentally influenced by the work of the Italian Marxist theorist and political activist, Antonio Gramsci, who wrote from the prisons of Fascist Italy in the 1930s, and whose key theoretical contribution was to develop the concept of 'hegemony'. By hegemony, Gramsci (1971) meant that ruling classes in society can never rule by force alone, but need to win the consent of the population to various ideas around the way society should be organised. This can occur, in Gramsci's analysis, through processes such as education and culture, including the media.

Vitally, the notion of hegemony also carries with it the possibility that people can challenge these dominant ideas and overturn their consent. In the context of media, Hall (1980, 1990) and Morley (1992) developed these ideas to argue that processes of encoding and decoding occur in relation to media messages. Encoding refers to the process whereby the media represent certain values and ideas, and intends that these will be accepted by audiences; Hall and Morley make the crucial point that audiences then have to decode these messages, by which they mean to draw attention to the importance of considering how people hear and read messages that are sent out by the media.

Three potential responses on the part of the audience were identified. First, in the dominant or hegemonic decoding process, the viewer accepts the values of the program. Second, in a negotiated decoding response, the viewer recognises the general legitimacy of the message but identifies certain contrasts with their own experiences. Finally, a viewer may challenge the message directly, in an oppositional decoding reading. The significance of this model is that the media become a site of social and political struggle. Unlike earlier approaches, in which audiences were viewed as passive, this model proposes that audience members have some control over how they engage with the media, including the capacity to resist media messages (Allan 1999; Hall 1980; Morley 1992).

Recent approaches to media effects argue for an analysis of the media as being a site of identity construction, relationship formation, and new experiences of social connection (McDonald 2000). In these approaches, the media have influence precisely because they are at the centre of social and political life. For example, a number of researchers have studied the ways in which young people consume shows such as *Gossip Girl* and *The OC*, which focus centrally on the emotional experiences and personal relationships of characters, independent of societal relations. Kevin McDonald (2000) argues that: '[t]hese shows are cultural tools that are used by friendship groups, at school or on the internet, to explore questions of identity and relationship' (2000, p. 565). In other words, this approach stresses that the influence of the media needs to be understood as being central to contemporary creative processes of identity-formation.

The societal context of the media

Having analysed processes of media production, content, and effects, we can now turn our attention to key dimensions of the societal context within which such processes occur. Analysis of this context is critical, as it makes it clear that the media do not exist in a vacuum, but rather are fundamentally influenced by, and in turn can influence, their social, political, and economic context.

Ownership

Major forms of media ownership in Australia are commercial media, public service broadcasting—as exemplified by the Australian Broadcasting Corporation (ABC) and the Special Broadcasting Service (SBS)—and community media. In Australia, commercial media dominate newspapers and broadcasting, and are driven by the need to build mass audiences that will attract advertisers. By contrast, public service broadcasters are, in theory at least, set up to provide quality programming without concern for ratings or commercial support. From the 1970s, societies such as Australia have also witnessed the emergence of a community-based sector, providing a media space for non-government and non-business voices. In recent times, the emergence of various community-based and independent online media sources is a sign of the continuing significance of community media (Louw 2001).

Media regulation

While major media organisations are powerful entities, their activities are influenced by their policy context. For example, in the late 1990s in the United Kingdom, BSkyB—part of News Corporation—sought to buy the English Premier League club Manchester United, one of the most marketable sport brands in the world. At the time, the Labour Party in the United Kingdom had just been voted into office, having been strongly supported by News Corporation's newspapers. As a result, it was widely expected that BSkyB would be allowed to purchase Manchester United. Under intense public pressure, though, the government competition regulator refused to allow the purchase to go ahead, arguing that it would be against the public interest to allow a media corporation to own a club (Boyle & Haynes 2003). This surprising outcome shows that policy-makers at the national level can still influence global processes in certain contexts.

Globalisation

While many important debates exist in the context of media and globalisation, one of the most critical concerns whether global media are carriers of cultural imperialism. In particular, concerns have arisen around whether global media organisations are 'simply vehicles for the global expansion of corporate capitalism and continuing Western dominance' (Rai & Cottle 2007, p. 53), contributing to situations in which local cultures around the world are powerless to resist the imposition of media produced in particular in the United States, to the detriment of local media and local knowledge. Mugdha Rai and Simon Cottle (2007) engage with this issue in their analysis of global 24/7 satellite news channels such as the Cable News Network (CNN), British Broadcasting Corporation (BBC) World, and Fox News. They explore whether these news channels are a new form of cultural imperialism, through which United States- and United Kingdom-based corporations dominate news production, presenting people around the world with a very narrow range of views and perspectives. They find that while global media organisations have a massive reach, it is also important to recognise that, in a number of regions of the world, there is an emerging localisation of satellite news media, so that non-Western and Western news media operate side by side, providing quite different versions of news. Al-Jazeera, headquartered in Qatar, for example, provided very different coverage of the Iraq conflict from that of stations such as CNN and Fox. For Rai and Cottle, while stations such as CNN and Fox are significant players in global media, local cultures are not powerless. While they are not operating on a level playing field, there still exists a capacity for local agency and for contesting voices to emerge, meaning we need to be cautious in making overly deterministic statements about cultural imperialism.

Information and communications technologies

Central to the contemporary societal context of media is the explosion of information and communication technologies (ICTs). Whether through mobile phones, blogs, Twitter, social networking sites, or other examples, newly emerging technologies are contributing not only to the transformation of the media landscape, but to fundamental transformations in how we live our lives. For example, Mark Deuze argues that: '[t]he whole of the world and our lived experience in it can indeed by seen as framed by, mitigated through, and made immediate by pervasive and ubiquitous media' (2007, p. 13). The emergence of social media, whether through websites such as Facebook and MySpace, or through tweeting, adds to the pervasiveness of media in our lives. Whether we are talking about paid employment, personal relationships, or just keeping up to date with news and entertainment, for increasing numbers of people, these processes are managed through the media, and increasingly are incomprehensible without media.

The media as a form of cultural activity

Running through these debates is the argument that the media are a significant part of contemporary culture in Australia and globally. To engage with the significant contribution of the media to contemporary culture, we can consider the example of the interaction of the media, politics, and music as a form of popular culture. For some, music is purely part of the entertainment industry, best represented by shows such as *Australian Idol*, which present themselves as creating opportunities for emerging talent but are principally a means for the recording industry to promote itself, and for advertisers to present their products to consumers. For others, music can raise awareness about social or political issues, either through overt politics—as with the highly influential rap group, Public Enemy, which saw rap as the 'CNN of the black community', a way to give voice to those who would otherwise not be heard in the mainstream media—or more indirectly through songs, such as No Doubt's 'Just a Girl', in which questions around identity and power are explored through personal experiences.

Music can also operate to promote forms of political and social engagement. An example of this form of engagement is when musicians use their celebrity status as a means of pursuing political and social issues. To give one example, Bono, the lead singer of U2, has been significantly involved in ONE, an organisation established to raise awareness about, and to create political and social action in response to, extreme poverty and preventable disease (see <www.one.org/international>). Less frequently, musicians move directly into politics. Perhaps the most celebrated instance in Australia in recent times was when Peter Garrett, the charismatic lead singer of the politically influential Midnight Oil, ran successfully for election for the federal Australian Labor Party (ALP).

In another example of the cultural dimensions of the media, new media technologies also contribute significantly to new forms of personal communication and interaction. For example, research conducted by Australian-based researchers reveals just how quickly mobile phone technologies have become crucial to our lives, in areas including personal relations and work. As one example, fewer than 10 per cent of respondents in their survey indicated 'that they would be unaffected and their lives "would proceed as normal" if they were suddenly without their mobile phones' (Wajcman et al. 2008, p. 639). As with all profound technological innovations, it is also important to recognise the potential downsides of such technology. These include the diminution of spaces of privacy, with individuals feeling they always need to be accessible, and increased opportunities for surveillance, as data on our use of technologies are collected and stored by a range of public and private institutions, often without our knowledge.

Conclusion

As the analysis through this chapter has shown, sociology has a significant contribution to make to our understanding of media. With the ever-increasing significance of media, not just as something that we consume but as a set of practices that we help to produce and that connect to all aspects of our lives, the challenge for us as sociologists is to ensure that we continue to engage critically and constructively with the media, and with the relations between the media and society.

SOCIOLOGY **SPOTLIGHT**

21.1: New media, new relationships

A fundamental part of everyday culture concerns the relationships we form with each other, and the ways in which we create those relationships. For growing numbers of people, online technologies are becoming significant as a means through which to create personal relationships.

In their study of online dating in Australia, Jo Barraket and Millsom Henry-Waring (2008) analysed dating websites and interviewed people who had used such websites. They found that online dating opened up a range of new opportunities for people, including access to a broader network of people than was possible in everyday life. At the same time, online technologies were also being used to reinforce traditional norms of behaviour—for example, with participants looking for people with similar interests and values. In addition, while some participants identified personal reasons such as shyness for using online dating, social factors including social isolation and long and irregular work hours were crucial in explaining the reasons for dating online.

What do you make of online dating? Does it make a difference whether we form relationships online or offline? Is the internet now such a part of our lives that we should reconsider the distinction between the real and the virtual? What does this example suggest about the place of media technology in our lives today?

Summary of main points

▶ While the media have long been a focus of sociological research, recent technological innovations and societal transformations have placed the media at the centre of societal organisation and everyday experience. As a result, there is an urgent need for ongoing sociological research into the media.

▶ Power is a highly contested notion, but also fundamental to analysing the media. Power may be exercised in overt ways in media contexts, but it may exist in indirect ways as well.

▶ Key dimensions of the media process include production, content, and effects—all of which need to be understood in their societal context. That is, the media do not exist independent of society, but are fundamentally influenced by their societal context.

▶ While mass media represent the dominant form of media, technological and societal innovations mean that there are greater possibilities for more people to be involved in media production than ever before. This does not mean that all media are equally powerful, though.

▶ The theoretical models and research tools available to sociology mean that we, as sociologists, are extraordinarily well placed to make a significant contribution to contemporary analyses of the media.

SOCIOLOGICAL
REFLECTION

21.1 What future for news journalism?

The current period is one of immense challenge for news journalists working in mainstream media such as newspapers and broadcast television. The emergence of citizen journalism and online social media mean that people who are not part of the mainstream media can now participate in everyday media as producers as well as consumers. For some, this is liberating as it opens up the space for all to participate in media. For others, concerns arise because the quality of news on the web cannot be controlled in the same way as it can via editorial processes in mainstream media. What do you think?

Discussion questions

21.1 Why should sociologists be interested in studying the media? Are the media really central to contemporary society?

21.2 What contribution can sociology make to our understanding of media representations of social relations such as gender and race?

21.3 Why is the concept of power so important in the context of studying the media?

21.4 Is technology the driver of media transformation? How do social relations influence media technology?

21.5 Do online media provide a real alternative to dominant commercial media, including television and newspapers?

21.6 How do you use the media? What effect do you think they have on you, on your friends, on other people?

Further reading

Balnaves, M., Donald, J. & Donald, S.H. 2001, *The Global Media Atlas*, BFI, London.

Deuze, M. 2007, *Media Work*, Polity Press, Cambridge.

Flew, T. 2007, *Understanding Global Media*, Palgrave, Houndmills.

Holmes, D. 2005, *Communication Theory: Media, Technology, Society*, Sage, London.

Norris, P. 2001, *Digital Divide: Civic Engagement, Information Poverty, and the Internet Worldwide*, Cambridge University Press, Cambridge.

Simons, M. 2007, *The Content Makers: Understanding the Media in Australia*, Penguin, Ringwood.

Websites

- Department of Broadband, Communications and the Digital Economy: <www.dbcde.gov.au/home>. The Australian Federal Government website detailing media and telecommunications policy.
- Media Education Foundation: <www.mediaed.org>. This website contains an array of resources, including documentaries, links, and study guides on a great variety of sociological topics.
- Media Entertainment and Arts Alliance: <www.alliance.org.au>. Website of the professional organisation representing people in the media, entertainment, sports, and arts industries.
- News Corporation: <www.newscorp.com>. Rupert Murdoch's global media empire. An example of a major global commercial media organisation with its origins in Australia.
- *Malaysiakini*: <www.malaysiakini.com>. *Malaysiakini* is an excellent example of an online independent newspaper.
- *Media Watch* <www.abc.net.au/mediawatch>. Television show presented weekly on ABC TV discussing and analysing media performance in Australia.

Films/documentaries

- *Media Rules*, 1996, television documentary, produced and directed by L. Jakubowski and A. Nehl, Special Broadcasting Corporation (SBS). This is still one of the best documentaries on the media and political campaigns, covering the 1996 Australian federal election.
- *Who is Albert Woo?*, 2000, documentary, directed by H. Hoe, National Film Board of Canada. An insightful film revealing interactions of race, ethnicity, sexuality, and gender in a range of contexts, exploring the interactions of the politics of everyday life and media representations.
- *Outfoxed: Rupert Murdoch's War on Journalism*, 2004, documentary, directed by R. Greenwald, Carolina Productions. A significant documentary revealing insights into the ways in which news is produced, and its effects, in the context of a global media organisation. <www.outfoxed.org>.

Visit the *Public Sociology* book website to access topical case studies, weblinks, YouTube clips, and extra readings.

References

Abroms, L.C. & Lefebvre, R.C. 2009, 'Obama's wired campaign: Lessons for Public Health Communication', *Journal of Health Communication*, vol. 14, no. 5, pp. 415–23.

Allan, S. 1999, *News Culture*, Open University Press, Buckingham.

Australian Bureau of Statistics (ABS) 2008, <www.abs.gov.au> (accessed 1 June 2009).

Australian Government, Department of Foreign Affairs and Trade 2003, *Australia Now: The Media in Australia*, <www.dfat.gov.au/facts/media.html> (accessed 5 February 2006).

Barraket, J. & Henry-Waring, M. 2008, 'Getting it on(line): Sociological perspectives on e-dating', *Journal of Sociology*, vol. 44, no. 2, pp. 149–65.

Boyle, R. & Haynes, R. 2003, 'New media sport', in A. Bernstein & N. Blain (eds), *Sport, Media, Culture: Global and Local Dimensions*, Frank Cass, London, pp. 95–114.

Brookes, R. 2002, *Representing Sport*, Arnold, London.

Bruce, T. 2004, 'Marking the boundaries of the "normal" in televised sports: The play-by-play of race', *Media, Culture and Society*, no. 26, pp. 861–79.

Castells, M. 1989, *The Informational City*, Blackwell, Oxford.

Cottle, S (ed.) 2003, *Media Organization and Production*, Sage, London.

Craig, G. 2004, *The Media, Politics and Public Life*, Allen & Unwin, Sydney.

Croteau, D. & Hoynes, W. 2000, *Media Society: Industries, Images and Audiences*, 2nd edn, Pine Forge, Thousand Oaks, CA.

ONE 2009, <www.one.org/international> (accessed 26 July 2009).

Deuze, M. 2007, *Media Work*, Polity Press, Cambridge.

Fouts, G. & Burggraf, K. 2000, 'Television situation comedies: Female weight, male negative comments, and audience reactions', *Sex Roles*, no. 42, pp. 925–32.

Fouts, G. & Vaughan, K. 2002, 'Television situation comedies: Male weight, negative references, and audience reactions', *Sex Roles*, vol. 46, nos. 11/12, pp. 439–42.

Gramsci, A. 1971, *Selections from the Prison Notebooks*, International Publishers, New York.

Hall, S. 1980, 'Encoding and decoding', in S. Hall, Hobson, D., Lowe, A. & Willis, P. (eds), *Culture, Media, Language*, Hutchinson, London, pp. 128–38.

—— 1990, 'The whites of their eyes: Racist ideologies and the media', in M. Alvarado & J.O. Thompson (eds), *The Media Reader*, BFI, London, pp. 7–23.

Louw, E. 2001, *The Media and Cultural Production*, Sage, London.

Lukes, S. 1974, *Power: A Radical View*, Macmillan, London.

Macionis, J. & Plummer, K. 2002, *Sociology: A Global Introduction*, Pearson Education, Harlow.

McDonald, K. 2000, 'Media, identity and globalisation', in R. van Krieken, P. Smith, D. Habibis, K. McDonald, M. Haralambos & M. Holborn (eds), *Sociology: Themes and Perspectives*, Pearson, Sydney, pp. 551–84.

McRobbie, A. 2005, *The Uses of Cultural Studies: A Textbook*, Sage, London.

Media Action Network for Asian Americans 2009, <www. manaa.org> (accessed 1 July 2009).

Morley, D. 1992, *Television, Audiences and Cultural Studies*, Routledge, London.

O'Shaughnessy, M. & Stadler, J. 2005, *Media and Society: An Introduction*, 3rd edn, Oxford University Press, Melbourne.

Rai, M. & Cottle, S. 2007, 'Global mediations: On the changing ecology of satellite television news', *Global Media and Communication*, vol. 3, no. 1, pp. 51–78.

Thompson, J.B. 1995, *The Media and Modernity: A Social Theory of the Media*, Polity Press, Cambridge.

van Acker, E. 2003, 'Media representations of women politicians in Australia and New Zealand: High expectations, hostility or stardom', *Policy, Organisation and Society*, vol. 22, no. 1, pp. 116–36.

Wajcman, J., Bittman, M. & Brown, J. 2008, 'Families without borders: Mobile phones, connectedness and work–home divisions', *Sociology*, vol. 42, no. 4, pp. 635–52.

CHAPTER 22

Educating society: Sociological debates and dilemmas

Julie McLeod

School: A day in the life

It is mid-morning at a state coeducational secondary college serving a working- and lower middle-class community on the edge of a large Australian city. A group of Year 9 girls is struggling with mathematics; their teacher regards them as not very engaged, as not really putting in much of an effort, and tells me that he thinks they will not last the distance at school. The girls themselves do not like the teacher much, as they believe he thinks they are dumb and bad at maths, and that he does not really try to help them understand. When asked why they do not ask more questions, the girls simply shrug their shoulders and say, 'What's the point? He'd just ignore us, or make us feel even dumber', and, 'He doesn't really respect us.' Two of the girls end up leaving school as soon as they turn fifteen; one girl stays on and begins a vocational stream in Year 11 (a course that will not prepare her for university entrance) but leaves early in the year as, 'School is not for her'. Another girl stays on to complete Year 12 and is aiming to enter a university course for nursing but is not sure she will get good enough Year 12 scores; if not, she says she will try for a health-related course at the local TAFE.

In the staffroom, the teachers talk about the kids in this school coming from families that do not really value education: 'They're not your professional background type of parents.' The teachers lament the attitudes of some of their students, wishing they could be more ambitious or adventurous, perhaps even finding ways to get out of the local area—an area that many of the teachers find depressing and from which they hurriedly escape at the end of the working day. The teachers also feel abused and 'put down' by the kids, who do not seem to show much interest in the classes they have been preparing or the assignments they have spent all weekend correcting.

Inside her office, the principal and the Year 9 coordinator are discussing some programs the school could implement to encourage 'at-risk' kids to stay on at school. The school has a bad local reputation for kids leaving early and for truancy, and there has been pressure from parents, the wider community, and the Education Department to turn this situation around. Along with the staff, the principal really does want to make a difference to the lives of her students.

Meanwhile, outside in the schoolyard, a group of Year 9 kids snatch a smoke and complain about the next class.

Introduction

The situation described above could have taken place in any number of schools, but it is based on research that I recently conducted with colleagues in several secondary

class/social class
A central but contested term in sociology that refers to a position in a system of structured inequality based on the unequal distribution of wealth, power, and status.

colleges located in economically disadvantaged outer suburbs. We were investigating young women, schooling, and work (McLeod et al. 2004). This snapshot conveys a number of issues explored by the sociology of education, such as **social class**, the sociogeographic location of schooling, gender and curriculum, young people's pathways through and after leaving school, vocational versus traditional academic programs of study, kids who are 'at risk', and the perspectives and experiences of a range of people directly involved in education: teachers, students, school managers, parents, the community, and education departments and policy-makers. The activities, experiences, and attitudes of all these different players matter when we approach the topic of the sociology of education.

This chapter begins by considering what a sociology of education encompasses, and the kinds of issues it addresses. It then discusses some key concepts and debates within sociology of education, making links to both classic texts and contemporary issues, and to some of the themes raised in the opening vignette.

In increasingly **globalised** times, common trends can be identified across different national educational systems. Australian education historically has had strong links to

globalisation
The increased interconnectedness of the cultural, economic, and political aspects of social life; intensified circulation of capital, goods, information, and people across national boundaries; and increased interdependence of countries and regions of the world.

European and especially British developments, as well as to developments in the United States. This is noticeable, for example, in the recent increase in Australia of standardised student testing and the public ranking of school examination results (Meadmore 2004); nevertheless, there are some distinctive features of the Australian system of education—such as the relationship between government and independent schools (also known as public and private schools) and the

different social status, levels of government funding, and relative cultural authority of the two school systems (Teese 2000; Marginson 1997). In the state of Victoria, for example, approximately 30 per cent of the school-age population attends private schools (which includes elite schools as well as local Catholic schools) and the relative merits of either system are a frequent topic of media, public, and family discussion (see Campbell et al. 2009; Simons 2006).

The ways in which issues of class, or of race and ethnicity, intersect with education in Australia are not identical to the ways in which these matters are played out in the United Kingdom or the United States, even though we could identify some common patterns in social division and hierarchy and in educational outcomes for different social groups. Students from poor and economically disadvantaged families continue, on average, to leave school earlier and to have more troubled educational pathways than students from middle-class families (Gillborn & Youdell 2000; Lamb & McKenzie 2001). Indigenous students, across many countries, report difficulties in having their ways of learning respected by mainstream schools (Malin 1990; McAlpine 1998; Heitmeyer 2004). In relation to gender equity, there is currently widespread policy interest in the education of boys rather than girls, who are now seen to be doing better at school than boys (Collins,

Kenway & McLeod 2000; Ailwood & Lingard 2001; Taylor 2004); however, in each of these examples, we could also find some specific Australian aspect. For example, there are higher rates of participation in education for Aboriginal women compared with Aboriginal men, yet Aboriginal women are proportionally under-represented in formal education in comparison to non-Indigenous women (ABS 2005; McLeod 2004). This chapter attempts to focus on some of the features of Australian education as well as aspects that are connected to wider phenomena and patterns.

The big questions

What, then, is the sociology of education about? If we look at education from a sociological perspective, what are we looking for, what might we see, and what sorts of questions are we asking? What are some of the influential sociological 'ways of seeing' education? And what have been some of the central issues and dilemmas raised by sociological studies of education?

Simply put, sociological studies of education show how educational institutions are part of the social fabric, how what happens in schools, kindergartens, universities, or Technical and Further Education (TAFE) colleges can both reflect and have consequences for social relations and social processes, but the sociology of education is not simply descriptive: it makes strong arguments about these relationships. It sees educational institutions, experiences, and outcomes as major components of social life, and as having a significant impact on the material and cultural conditions that frame a person's **life chances** and experiences.

life chances
A term associated with the work of Weber to refer to different opportunities and differential access to resources, including education, wealth, housing, and health.

meritocratic
An objective measurement by which to assign social positions rather than by means of ascribed positions such as *social class*, age, or *gender*.

Marxists/Marxism
Those who subscribe to Marx's social theory that changes in human activity—for example, labour—are determined by economic and material factors, such as technology, and *class* conflict over material interests.

On the one hand, education is characterised as offering opportunities for social and personal change, as providing the means for social mobility, and as rewarding those who work hard and have talent. This **meritocratic** view of education is discussed below. On the other hand, education—particularly schooling—is seen as reproducing the status quo. In this view, education maintains—if not strengthens—social inequalities through rewarding (via many different subtle and not so subtle practices) those who are already socially advantaged and at the same time converting social disadvantage into educational disadvantage, thereby perpetuating social divisions and inequalities. Understanding education as a form of social reproduction and regulation is typically linked to broader analyses of social relations and power, such as materialist and **Marxist** analyses, or **feminist** and **post-colonial** accounts. For example, schools are analysed as places where conventional gender relations are reproduced, or where **ethnocentric** or class-based assumptions about ability and future occupation are reinforced (Arnot 2002; Dolby & Dimitriadis 2004).

feminism/feminist

A broad social and political movement based on a belief in equality of the sexes and the removal of all forms of discrimination against women. A feminist is one who makes use of, and may act upon, a body of theory that seeks to explain the subordinate position of women in society.

post-colonialism

The study of the issues raised in societies with a colonial past, particularly regarding identity and relationships between the colonisers and the colonised.

ethnocentric

Viewing others from one's own cultural perspective. Implied is a sense of cultural superiority based on an inability to understand or accept the practices and beliefs of other cultures.

agency

The ability of people, individually and collectively, to influence their own lives and the society in which they live.

A perennial 'big question' is thus whether schools remedy social division or whether they work (unintentionally or otherwise) to cement and reproduce social divisions. In between these two contrasting accounts of education there is a great range of different viewpoints. Some people might argue that, on the whole, schools tend to reproduce existing social relations, but that there are some—albeit limited—instances when social change occurs, and this is one reason why education continues to be a focus for social and political reform. Studies of children's gender identities in early childhood education, for example, have shown how educational environments encourage and construct conventional masculine and feminine identities, but also point out how educational practices could be changed to challenge these conventional and constricting expectations—through encouraging children to question or deconstruct the everyday, providing different kinds of reading material and encouraging teachers to question their own gender beliefs and expectations (Davies 1989, 1993; MacNaughton 2000). A very influential strand of research has investigated how students 'resist' the regulating and normalising aspects of schooling. Schools, it is argued, tend to reproduce existing social divisions but students also have a degree of **agency** to resist this process; students are not simply mindless cogs in the schooling factory. Students challenge what happens in schools, act up against discipline, form their own subcultures, and create different worlds for themselves (Hall & Jefferson 1976; see also Chapter 6, this volume). This is sometimes criticised as an overly optimistic or romantic view of youth culture, as it is far from clear whether 'acting up' and resisting the discipline of the school actually challenges the school's role in reproducing inequalities. It is also perhaps more helpful to think of schools as not only about either 'reproduction and inequality' or 'change and opportunity'. This simple opposition is somewhat misleading and inaccurate. We can understand schools as places that contain elements of both these processes.

Whatever position is taken up, there is no doubt, as Rob Moore (2004) argues, that the 'relationship between educational and social inequalities and opportunities is one of the most fundamental issues in the sociology of education' (2004, p. 6). In exploring these matters, sociology of education has historically 'addressed the differences between classes, the sexes and ethnic groups' (2004, p. 7). Educational institutions are places in which patterns of social group difference are starkly evident. Much sociology of education has sought to understand the educational experiences of different social groups and the role education plays in promoting or working against social inequality.

The sociology of education field: Background

The sociological study of education encompasses many different topics, from students' experiences and attitudes to school leadership, educational management, and educational reform, the relationship between schooling, the labour market and future pathways, teachers' professional development and career paths, and young people's values and identities. It includes studies of educational policies to do with curriculum, the gender-related aspects of educating girls and boys, and the use of computer technology, alongside **ethnographic** or case studies of classroom practices. Moreover, 'education' is not confined to schools: it includes pre-schools, kindergartens, post-compulsory education (i.e. that period of education beyond the age at which it is compulsory to attend school—in Australia, education is compulsory to the age of sixteen or seventeen, depending on the state), home schooling, TAFE colleges, universities, various forms of professional and 'on the job' training, and more recently the idea of 'lifelong learning'.

From your own personal experiences of schooling, you will know that simply raising a topic to do with education provokes many different kinds of reaction. Almost everybody has their own view on what constitutes a good school, or what a good education looks like, or what is wrong with the current situation, or whether teachers are being paid enough, or whether standards have declined since 'I was at school'. No matter which side of the political spectrum is being examined—from conservatives to progressives, from parents to policy-makers, and from students to sociologists—there is broad, albeit implicit, agreement that educational institutions are profoundly important in shaping young people's values and life chances and in preparing them for future social life, both during and beyond school. The causes and consequences of this powerful influence, and questions about how well schools do this kind of work, are the subject of intense and ongoing debate.

Within the field of sociology of education itself, there is no single approach or topic, no uncontested argument or policy intervention. As with many types of sociological study, though, there are some clear differences in research approach, and these typically divide along quantitative and qualitative lines. The former has tended to investigate educational outcomes and destinations—the pathways young people follow, the types of occupation they enter, or the fields of further and higher study they pursue. Quantitative studies can provide valuable data—for example, on the correlation between family background (as determined by **socioeconomic status (SES)**) and school success, on rates of participation in post-compulsory education of girls compared with boys, the relative educational participation and performance of Indigenous compared with non-Indigenous students, or changing patterns in school examination results and educational achievement according to gender, class, and ethnicity. Such 'tracking studies' can demonstrate social trends and patterns—for example, the continued under-representation

ethnography/ethnographic
A research method based on the direct observation of the social interaction and culture of a particular social group, involving detailed description and evaluation of behaviours, activities, and events.

socioeconomic status (SES)
A statistical measure that classifies individuals, households, or families in terms of their income, occupation, and education.

of students from working-class backgrounds in high-status university courses—as well as alert us to emerging changes, such as the increasing number of women pursuing higher education (Summers 2003; Teese & Polesel 2003).

Quantitative data have been important in measuring differential outcomes and patterns of these groups and showing patterns of educational inequality and advantage. Major national and international organisations, such as the Organization for Economic Cooperation and Development (OECD) (2006), and the United Nations Educational, Scientific and Cultural Organization (UNESCO) (2006), draw heavily on such findings as they allow comparison of national educational systems. Particular attention is focused on educational outcomes and the ranking of countries' performance in matters such as student achievement in science and mathematics, access to information technology, or rates of literacy—for countries as a whole as well as for particular groups, such as female or rural students. Such studies are sometimes referred to as 'educational sociology', as distinct from 'sociology of education'. Stephen Ball (2004), a British sociologist of education, argues that the 'central concerns of "educational sociology" are descriptive and structural and focus upon patterns of educational opportunity and social mobility within industrial democracy ... That is, the investigation of the relationship between social origins (almost exclusively social class/SES) and educational achievement' (2004, pp. 3–4). These studies, sometimes also called 'black-box sociology', focus upon 'the inputs and outputs of education'; however, as Ball argues, they are usually unable to shed light on the 'processes of educating' (2004, p. 4).

A turn to a more concentrated focus on the 'processes of educating' occurred during the 1970s, a period of major innovation in educational research that saw the emergence of the 'new sociology of education'. This movement is particularly associated with a number of British researchers and studies (Young 1971; Willis 1977; Ball 2004) and was also very influential in Australia, with its influence continuing today. *Making the Difference: Schools, Families and Social Division* (Connell et al. 1982) is perhaps the best-known Australian study emerging from this era. This book, based on case studies of Australian secondary schools, examined the ways in which class and gender differences were mediated in elite and working-class schools. It showed processes of educational and social advantage and disadvantage being worked out in the daily and ordinary practices of schooling. While *Making the Difference* pointed to some of the ways in which social divisions were reproduced, it also showed how some relations and identities were changing. This was the case with middle-class girls, whose lives were changing through the combined impact of **feminism** and the high aspirations of private schooling and ambitions of professional parents for their daughters to be successful and to take on high-status careers.

feminism/feminist
A broad social and political movement based on a belief in equality of the sexes and the removal of all forms of discrimination against women. A feminist is one who makes use of, and may act upon, a body of theory that seeks to explain the subordinate position of women in society.

The new sociology of education, taking off in the early 1970s, had a more self-consciously radical dimension than much of the earlier sociological work on education. It showed the ways in which educational practices, far from ameliorating social divisions, worked to reinforce or reproduce existing social inequalities. Overall, studies within this approach are more likely to be qualitative and to look with a socially critical lens at interactions between micro and macro practices of education, between formal and informal relationships, and at educational experiences and processes, rather than only at the measurable outcomes of education. For example, a number of classic studies influenced by Marxist theories looked at how schooling practices, such as the cultivation of diligence, punctuality, and obedience, prepared young people to develop the right attitudes to enter the workforce, particularly one based in an industrial economy, and to take up class-appropriate working futures, thereby ensuring the reproduction of class-based social divisions (Bowles & Gintis 1976; Bourdieu & Passeron 1977; Willis 1977). Today, with changes in the economy and the labour market, the issues are somewhat different. The more relevant questions for now include whether and how schools are preparing young people to be flexible in their outlook and orientation to jobs, to think of themselves as 'lifelong learners', to adapt to the idea of there being no 'job for life' and to be open to other kinds of career paths (casual, consultancy, or contract-based serial jobs) and to growth areas of employment such as tourism, hospitality, and the communication industries.

Another important strand investigates what happens in classrooms—how teachers interact with students, and how they respond with enthusiasm to some students and with indifference to others. These everyday practices can influence how students see themselves as learners, whether they like the school subject, whether they feel dumb or smart, and whether they go on to be successful in school. Take the girls in the opening scenario, who feel that the teacher thinks they are stupid. It is unlikely that the teacher has ever directly told them that, but these messages can be picked up though the accumulation of seemingly minor incidents—a look of frustration, a shrugging of shoulders when a question is asked, having friends who do not like the subject, and simply not expecting to do well in a so-called hard subject.

During the 1980s, feminist educators identified such 'classroom dynamics' as a major factor in creating or reinforcing gender inequalities. It was strongly argued, based on studies of classroom observations, that teachers repeatedly gave more attention and time to boys rather than girls, and that even if some of this was boys being disciplined for disruptive behaviour, the overall lesson boys learnt was that they could command attention, that their needs mattered (Spender 1982). Girls, in contrast, were more likely to pick up that they were not as important, that the teacher did not really regard what they were doing or their questions as equally important. Similar arguments continue to be raised today, and are especially common in debates about the relative merits of single-sex or coeducational schools, with advocates of the former often arguing that in mixed-sex classrooms boys dominate girls, taking up more teacher time and air space.

Other studies influenced by the new sociology of education looked at the cultural expectations of different curriculum areas and the kind of 'know-how' expected of students if they were to succeed at school, or at the gendered association of curriculum areas (Arnot 2002; Bernstein 1971). There have been some changes since the 1970s, when a major topic was the association of girls with English and the humanities but not with the so-called 'hard areas' of maths and science, which were seen to suit boys more naturally. Related issues continue to be debated today, with some boys' relatively weak performance in language-based areas regarded as a major cause for concern (Gilbert & Gilbert 1998). Additionally, the emergence of new curriculum areas, such as computer technology, communication and media studies, and digital literacy, pose new challenges for investigating curricula, as it is not necessarily so clear-cut how gender is implicated in the social representation of these subjects. Is designing computer hardware 'masculine' while software design and communication are more 'feminine'? Are girls being prepared for the lower-status areas of the computer industry: the help desk and data entry? Or are conventional gendered associations and alignments undergoing some change?

The sociological study of education is thus not only about policy or administration and reform, nor is it only about rates of participation and achievement. These are all important, but one of the main legacies of the new sociology of education was that it showed how attention to everyday and apparently minor practices, such as how teachers talk to students and how kids muck around in playgrounds, could reveal much about how education worked—in other words it could illuminate the 'processes of educating'. It is through such everyday and seemingly benign practices that inequalities and opportunities are (re)created, or cemented, and even potentially transformed.

22.1: Gender and schooling today

The continuing significance of gender for the sociology of education is evident in current government, policy, media, and academic attention to the question of how best to educate girls and boys. Persistent questions remain about whether girls and boys require different types of teaching, or have different learning styles, and whether schools are oriented to suit girls more than boys, or vice versa. These questions have a history. Thirty years ago, educational policy declared that to be 'a girl is an educational disadvantage' and education departments around the country (and internationally) began establishing educational practices that attempted to be 'non-sexist', to expand girls' curriculum and career choices, to stop sex-role socialisation, and to promote equal opportunities (McLeod 2004). Much has changed since then. The question of gender inequality is now more often couched in terms of the disadvantages boys and men experience. The 1997 *National Gender Equity Framework* (a national policy) for schools is currently being reviewed to develop strategies to make education more inclusive and responsive to the educational needs of boys. A Commonwealth government inquiry into the education of boys, *Boys: Getting It Right*, sought to investigate 'the social, cultural and educational factors affecting the education of boys in Australian schools, particularly in relation to their literacy needs and socialisation skills in the early and middle years of schooling' (House of Representatives Standing Committee on Education and Training 2002, p. xi).

In many such discussions about the education of boys (and also of girls), there is a tendency to talk about girls and boys as simple opposing groups. This is done with phrases such as 'the average boy', or 'all girls', or 'most boys', or claims that girls on average perform better in end-of-school examinations than boys. While the latter statement is true, it tells us only one part of a story about gender and educational achievement. As numerous sociological studies have emphasised, we need to interrogate the categories of female and male, girls and boys, and look at the ways in which the category of gender is cut across by other social categories and differences, such as class or ethnicity or disability, and how this in turn influences educational experiences and outcomes (Epstein et al. 1998; Lamb & McKenzie 2001; Walkerdine et al. 2001; Dwyer & Wyn 2001; McLeod & Yates 2006). A fundamental question then becomes 'which girls' and 'which boys' are doing well, or are being disadvantaged, and so forth. Is it all boys, or boys from particular class and cultural backgrounds?

Additionally, some studies have shown that, even though many girls are performing well at school, girls who leave school early and come from poor backgrounds are among the most disadvantaged young people, with low rates of participation in employment or further training. And even though more girls than boys are proceeding to university, there remain some patterns of conventional gender differentiation in choice of course and subsequent employment (Summers 2003; Collins et al. 2000).

In talking of gender and schooling, then, it needs to be recognised that gender is an important category in the sociology of education, but it is also a multi-faceted category—one that is constituted in relation to other social categories and differences, such as class, ethnicity, and religion.

Schooling as meritocratic

Education is charged with many social responsibilities. It has responsibilities not only for teaching literacy, numeracy, and other important skills, but also for instilling sound and desirable civic and social values that will prepare current generations to become productive future citizens. Education—especially schools—is also frequently blamed for a number of social ills: if unemployment rates for young people increase, schools are often seen as failing to prepare them adequately for the workforce; if young people are exhibiting anti-social behaviour—drug-taking, becoming overweight and unfit, or engaging in risky sexual activity—schools are expected to introduce new curricular and teaching strategies. But education is also regarded by some with optimism, held up as offering opportunities for social mobility and individual advancement. In this outlook, schools provide, in the Australian vernacular, a 'fair go for all', with educational success seen as being based upon an individual's efforts and talents. Such beliefs represent a 'meritocratic' view of schooling.

Meritocratic views are linked to the political philosophy of **liberalism**, which developed during the eighteenth and nineteenth centuries. This set of ideas—which remains influential—emphasised the rights and freedoms of individuals, and held that all individuals were born equal and had equal opportunities to succeed. This was in contrast to then very pervasive beliefs that individuals' social background (e.g. whether they were born into a wealthy or poor family) or divine order could determine people's destiny. Hard work and merit, or talent, were for the meritocratic

liberalism
An ideology that prioritises the interests of individuals and their freedom in the marketplace.

theorists the prerequisites for success—in schools, in work, and in life. As Miriam Henry (2000) writes, in a 'well functioning meritocratic society, people would be selected to jobs on the basis of appropriate skills and credentials, not on gender or skin colour; students would succeed at school on the basis of their "ability" and hard work, not hindered by assessment or curriculum practices which, indirectly, discriminate on the basis of cultural background' (2000, p. 48). As many have argued, this notion was more ideal than real. Jeannie Oakes and Martin Lipton (2003) refer to this as the 'merit myth', arguing that in America this takes the form of 'Any child can grow up to be President'. They suggest that many North Americans delight in 'rags-to-riches' stories, and understand their schooling system to be one in which 'individual ability and determination, rather than wealth or personal connections, hold the key to success and upward mobility' (2003, pp. 18–19). Yet, as many social data, as well as personal and group experiences, attest, schools do not simply provide equal opportunities for all, regardless of background. There are strong patterns of achievement and educational and social outcome, and these are linked to social factors such as family social class, gender, and race and ethnic affiliation. We can illustrate this with some examples of summary data on what happens to young people when they leave school.

A recent report on the educational and work pathways of young Australians found that, while 70 per cent of fifteen- to nineteen-year-olds are in full-time education and 14 per cent are working full time, there are significant gender differences within each of these categories: 'More females than males are in full-time study. Males are more often in full-time work' according to the Foundation for Young Australians (FYA) (2009). But what of the 16 per cent of young people who are not engaged in either full-time work or education? Again, on closer inspection we find that there are significant differences according to social groupings, such as those of gender, ethnicity, and race, as well as educational attainment—which is in turn affected by social class background—and residential location (ABS 2005, 2008). More females than males undertake part-time work (7.9 per cent and 6.8 per cent respectively), and this too contributes to a 'gender gap' in income and in likely future employment and income-earning capacity. Significantly, fewer young women than men are registered as part of the labour force; those who are not cannot be counted in social statistics such as unemployment rates. This trend is explained in part by young women undertaking work in the home and/or caring for children or other family members (FYA 2009). This pattern also reveals long-standing gender-based divisions in the primary care of children and families, with females continuing to take up those activities more frequently than males, a situation that makes such young women particularly vulnerable to economic and social disadvantage. Further, the level of school attainment affects people's chances and pathways after school and, as much research shows, there remains a strong correlation between social class and connection to school (Teese & Polesel 2003; Germov 2004). Broader social phenomena also influence school participation and post-school options. The recent Global Financial Crisis is one possible explanation behind the growth in youth unemployment and the sharp increase between 2008 and 2009 of the number of young people not engaged fully in 'learning or earning' (FYA 2009). This is a notable reverse of prior trends that showed a pattern of increasing numbers of fifteen- to nineteen-year-olds engaged in full-time work or study in the previous decade.

Where people live can be a key factor shaping educational participation and work patterns. Reports from the Australian Bureau of Statistics show that young people who leave school before completing Year 10, and who live in remote and very remote areas, are significantly at risk of longer-term economic and social disadvantage: '[i]n 2006, 7% of 15–19 year olds who were no longer attending high school had not completed Year 10. This proportion was considerably higher in Remote (14%) and Very Remote areas (36%)' (ABS 2008, p. 96). Consequently, there is a 'relatively low proportion of the population with non-school qualifications in Remote (43 per cent) and Very Remote (36 per cent) areas' (2008, p. 93), due in part, according to the same ABS report, to 'the higher proportion of Aboriginal and Torres Strait Islander people living in these areas ... and their lower levels of educational attainment' (2008, p. 94). If we look more closely at statistics on Indigenous education, we find a mixture of trends, with some marked improvements in participation alongside some persistent patterns that contribute to wider social inequalities. There remain marked differences in Year 12 completion rates between Indigenous and non-Indigenous students. In the period 2001–06, the proportion of Indigenous people aged fifteen years or over 'who had completed Year 12 increased from 20% to 23%' (HREOC 2008, p. 298). Importantly:

> despite these improvements . . . Indigenous peoples aged 15 years and over were still half as likely as non-Indigenous Australians to have completed school to Year 12 in 2006 (23% compared with 49%). They were also twice as likely to have left school at Year 9 or below (34% compared with 16%). These relative differences have remained unchanged since 2001. (HREOC 2008, p. 299)

This snapshot of data indicates that some groups of young people are more socially vulnerable and more at risk of longer-term unemployment than others, and that educational experiences in interaction with other social factors, such as gender and location, have a profound impact on the kind of futures available to young people. While the dream of individual equality remains powerful, as does the meritocratic promise that hard work will be rewarded, the social data tell us that the reality is far more complex and socially differentiated.

Educational institutions are thus confronted with many challenges. Moore (2004) suggests that what happens in them is never straightforward, in large part because so many different sociocultural factors and relationships need to be taken into account. Schools are frequently faced with contradictory expectations—for example, the 'demand that education promote equality of opportunity may conflict (for some) with the need to preserve standards of academic excellence, or the value placed by liberal educators on developing the 'whole person' with the demand by others that education meet the needs of the economy' (2004, p. 6). Schools, teachers and students are thus often caught in the middle of some very heated debates. This is particularly the case when it comes to discussing the social purposes of schooling: what values do and should schools promote? How do schools respond to social and cultural differences among the student population?

Social values and schooling

It is widely recognised that schools are important in forming the social values of future generations, but there is considerably less agreement about what those values should be. For some, the answer is relatively straightforward: schools should reflect the values of the dominant culture, but for others, even this simple statement is highly problematic. What do we identify as the 'dominant culture' in Australia? Even if we can do that, we still need to consider whether and what are the shared values, and which such values should be fostered. And what of cultural pluralism? Australia is culturally and ethnically diverse, and this raises the basic question of how schools manage to respond to the values of the different communities that might make up their student population.

The *Australian National Framework for Values Education* (2005) identifies nine key values that schools should promote. They are: care and compassion; doing your best; a fair go; freedom; honesty and trustworthiness; integrity; respect; responsibility; and understand-ing, tolerance and inclusion (Department of Education, Science and Training 2005). This framework (which is a set of policy and program guidelines) was developed in the context of considerable debate about whether and how Australian schools were fostering social values.

In early 2004, then Australian Prime Minister John Howard added fire to these debates by announcing that in his view Australian government schools were not doing enough to promote values. Indeed, he charged that government schools were (paradoxically) both devoid of social values and too politically correct. It was for these reasons, he opined, that increasing numbers of Australian families were choosing to send their children to private schools because they saw those schools as offering better and stronger values. There was much media coverage of these comments and ensuing responses, which came from school principals, teachers, and parents, including parents who disputed this assessment.

The election of a new federal Labor government in November 2007 promised an 'education revolution', with pledges for increased expenditure on technology and computing facilities, more testing of student performance, and a national curriculum. Debates about what subjects should be included in a national curriculum have revealed that questions about school knowledge are also bound up in questions about school values: what matters, what it is important to learn, and what kind of people and future citizens should schools be helping to shape?

From these examples alone, we can see that schools are regarded not only as places for the acquisition of formal knowledge and skills and the gaining of credentials, though these are important functions of schooling. Schools do more than teach the disciplines of mathematics or geography, or the skills associated with physical education or computer technology. In Charles Dickens' nineteenth-century novel *Hard Times* (1854), the schoolteacher, Mr Gradgrind, famously insisted that what mattered most in schools was 'facts, facts, facts'. For Gradgrind, and for many actual teachers, children were understood as empty pitchers into which facts would be poured. Schools were simply about conveying information and an established body of knowledge. The sociology of education looks also to what else is learnt and taught, to all the other messages, values, codes, and ways of thinking that influence students and teachers, and shape their identities and ways of being.

Hidden curriculum

A fundamental insight of the sociology of education is that educational institutions do much more than impart a formal set curriculum. They also teach what is called a 'hidden' or informal curriculum. This curriculum can be characterised as social, or implicit and even unintentional or unconscious, learning that takes place in classrooms, but also in schoolyards and corridors, on playing fields, and in gym rooms. It includes the subtle messages, as well as the not so subtle instructions, about what the school values, about what being a good student entails, about whether you are valued, how you should act, and what is socially appropriate. Through the daily practices of schooling, from classroom teaching, teacher expectations, peer interactions, the overall ethos of the school, the school's reputation in the local community (is it regarded as a good school, or a school where discipline is slack, or too authoritarian, is it seen as getting good results, and so forth?), students learn powerful lessons (Kenway & Willis 1997; Groundwater-Smith, Ewing & Cornu 2003; Symes & Preston 1997).

Private schools in Australia are frequently thought of as having tougher discipline and better values, and as encouraging harder work from students than state schools, and this image persists despite what the reality might in fact be in either type of school. Sociologists of education, teachers, parents, and students all take issue with such simple characterisations, but image, reputation, and cultural expectation persist, and can influence how students, as well as teachers and other personnel in schools, view themselves and the education they receive (Campbell et al. 2009; McLeod 2009).

Students pick up **hidden curriculum** messages via a range of practices, including direct comment from teachers and principals, what is talked about in the school newsletter, what students are praised or suspended for, what is tolerated by the peer culture, even the condition of the buildings (is money allocated to the gym or the reading recovery room; are buildings run down or well maintained; is there an informal, low-key reception area or is there a grand wood-panelled entrance?). All these factors influence students' experience of schooling, their sense of self and their confidence—or lack of it—in their capacity and future pathways. The unhappy girls in the opening scenario had learnt many lessons at their school; they knew it was not seen as a good school; they understood that girls

hidden curriculum
Attitudes, values and behaviour learnt in school that are not part of the formal curriculum.

did not usually like maths—and their teacher's expectations confirmed this. They also learnt to stop asking questions, as that just made things worse, and that disengaging from school was one way to stop feeling disrespected. None of this knowledge is part of the formal curriculum. And indeed the girls' teachers, and the principal, would be shocked to think that this was happening, when in their minds they were trying hard to work against such outcomes.

The relationship between the hidden curriculum, the culture of the school, and the family background of students is at the heart of much sociology of education. Whether the culture and values of the school match those of the family is an important factor in shaping students' attitudes to school and their outcomes. The teachers in the opening scenario complained that the kids' parents did not really value education; yet, when we interviewed the mothers of these girls, we found that they took education very seriously, and that they wanted their daughters to stay on and get a good education, but they did not feel confident in dealing with the school, and were unsure how to encourage or help their daughters with their schoolwork or to feel better about school. The mothers themselves had had unhappy experiences at school and expressed some uncertainty about what schooling now required and how to talk to the teachers. We can see here how the relationship between family background and school values and expectations is linked to social divisions and to the role schools play in either strengthening or changing relations of social inequality.

School cultures, habitus, and cultural capital

The work of the French sociologist Pierre Bourdieu and his concepts of **habitus** and **cultural capital** are helpful for deepening our understanding of these relationships. Habitus refers to 'socialised subjectivity' and expresses 'how individuals "become themselves"' and 'the ways in which those individuals engage in practices' (Webb, Schirato & Danaher 2002, p. 11). Habitus does not simply mean that people copy 'role models', or are rewarded or punished for doing certain things (this would be a form of behaviourist socialisation); rather, in quite subtle ways, through discourses, institutional expectations, and social practices, as well as through interactions with others, principles are set up for individuals about what matters, what is noticed, how they comport themselves physically, socially, emotionally, and so on. In Bourdieu's own words, habitus constitutes a 'system of lasting and transposable dispositions which, integrating past experiences, functions at every moment as a matrix of perceptions, appreciations and actions and makes possible the achievement of infinitely diversified tasks' (cited in Bourdieu & Wacquant 1992, p. 18).

Habitus is thus a 'strategy-generating principle' (Bourdieu 1977, p. 72), but it is not only a mentality: it includes

habitus
Refers to socially learnt dispositions or taken-for-granted sets of orientations, skills, and ways of acting that shape behaviour. People are the product and creators of their habitus.

cultural capital
A term used to indicate cultural competencies, such as the taste preferences and lifestyle, that differentiate one social class from another and are transmitted through the generations and via the education system.

embodied responses and ways of being, such as how people act and carry themselves, and the kind of body language they display. It is formed in interaction with 'social fields' or specific social settings, such as schools, family, or workplaces. Bourdieu describes people's interactions with social fields as a matter of learning the 'rules of the game' (Bourdieu & Wacquant 1992). In Bourdieu's theory, individuals form themselves in social situations, which create ways of being that are more often interpreted as individual personality, ability, or choices than as socially shaped dispositions and values. This process of social shaping is not homogenous—it is socially differentiated. Habitus is formed in relation to sociocultural and class positioning, and in relation to specific social fields, and these fields help determine what counts as socially valuable practices and 'cultural capital'.

Cultural capital refers to social and interpersonal resources and the knowledge of how these are culturally valued and how they function as markers of social status. It encompasses tastes, 'consumption patterns, attributes, skills and awards … Within the field of education … an academic degree constitutes cultural capital' (Webb, Schirato & Danaher 2002, p. x). But cultural capital also refers to knowing how to act in certain ways, having an easy familiarity with elite cultural forms, or having the right background and knowing the right people and networks. The girls in the opening scenario would have their own forms of cultural capital and social 'know-how', but it is probably unlikely that they would easily possess the forms of cultural capital that would be valued in other social settings. The point here is not simply that there are different types of cultural capital (all cultural groups will have their own currency), but that in a structurally differentiated and unequal society, some types of cultural capital are more socially valuable than others.

A key sociological issue for education concerns how, whether, and the extent to which schools presume that students possess certain cultural capital and also promote particular types of cultural capital as natural and necessary. Such expectations mean that schooling is not experienced uniformly; if you have the 'right' cultural capital, then school is more likely (though never guaranteed) to be a familiar and self-confirming experience than if you are seen to lack that capital.

Conclusion

This chapter opened with a snapshot of Year 9 girls in a state school in order to suggest some of the different perspectives and issues that come into play when thinking about education. In thinking sociologically about education, we need to recognise the views and interests of various stakeholders—students, teachers, parents, managers, employers, and policy-makers—and understand the impact of these sometimes contradictory expectations on what schools can do. Educational institutions are powerful social agencies, but they are neither simply agents of social change nor agents of social reproduction. This chapter has argued that educational institutions contain elements of both kinds of social processes.

Education is also a dynamic field. It is embedded in broader social, economic, and political changes, such as changes to the funding and management of public institutions. This is evident, for example, in the increasing attention being paid to the 'marketing' and commercialisation of schools and growing discourses of 'parental choice'—between government and non-government, and within the government sector. These shifts in policy and social discourse are happening in other countries too, and are very evident in the United Kingdom and the United States. In this we can see that educational change in Australia is linked to processes of globalisation as well as national political agendas. For many of us, if not most, educational experiences are powerful ones, and they are a significant part of what shapes us and influences our values and our futures. For these reasons alone, the purposes of education, the values schools convey, the curricula they teach, and the opportunities they open up or close down will remain contested topics of widespread and intense social debate—as indeed should be the case.

Summary of main points

▶ There are social dimensions to education, and this means that educational institutions perform much more work than simply conveying a formal curriculum or providing credentials. Schools, kindergartens, and universities are all shaped by social context, and in turn have a profound effect on that context and on social relations.

▶ Education in Australia is characterised by some globalising trends while also having some distinctive features.

▶ The sociology of education has explored the interconnections between education and social groups and social relations, as well as between patterns of inequality and patterns of advantage. Some perennial 'big questions' include debates about whether, or the extent to which, schools and other educational institutions work to remedy or cement social inequalities.

▶ In Australia, as in many other countries, there are identifiable patterns of social difference and inequality in relation to educational experiences and outcomes. These patterns challenge simple notions of schooling as meritocratic.

▶ The purposes of education are hotly debated by many different stakeholders—from parents to policy-makers, teachers, students, and the wider community. This is evident in debates about the kind of social values schools should convey.

▶ The hidden curriculum is a powerful site for learning, and is influential in shaping students' values, sense of themselves, and future orientations and activities. Bourdieu's concepts of habitus and cultural capital offer valuable ways of understanding the hidden curriculum and the relationship between schools, family background, and identity.

SOCIOLOGICAL **REFLECTION**

22.1 School experiences

(a) Looking back on your own schooling experiences, consider some of the 'hidden curriculum' messages you picked up inside and outside of the classroom.

(b)   Return to the opening snapshot of the Year 9 girls. What kinds of educational and social changes do you think would be of most powerful benefit for such young women?

(c)   What do you consider to be some of the main and most important 'purposes of schooling'? In your reflections, distinguish between the purposes or aims of schooling and the (unintended) effects of schooling on different groups of young people.

Discussion questions

22.1. Find examples from the press, from your own experiences, and from discussions with friends and family that express a meritocratic view of schooling. In your view, what are the major limitations, as well as strengths, of a merit-based view of education? For example, is the main problem with meritocratic views that they fall short of their ideal, or are there other flaws?

22.2 Visit one of the recommended websites (or one that you have found yourself) and identify some data on patterns of relative educational participation and achievement. What are some of the dilemmas involved in measuring group differences? Which groups appear not to fare very well and which groups seem to have consistently stronger rates of educational achievement? What explanations can you offer for this?

22.3 What do you recall most about the 'values' you learnt at school? What kind of values do you think should be promoted in schools? Nominate three social values and make your case for why they should be regarded as a central part of the school's mission.

22.4 Hypothetical: A new piece of legislation is to be introduced in state parliament, making it compulsory for all young people to stay at school until the age of eighteen. Make a case for defending and a case for opposing this legislation.

22.5 Why have educational sociologists found the idea of a hidden curriculum such a powerful one? Is it a practice largely confined to schools? Do you think a hidden curriculum operates in universities? If so, provide examples.

22.6 What kind of 'cultural capital' matters most in contemporary life? Do you regard cultural capital and habitus as useful concepts for understanding inequality? Why?

Further reading

Allen, J. (ed.) 2004, *Sociology of Education: Possibilities and Practices*, 3rd edn, Social Sciences Press/Thomson, Melbourne.

Ball, S. (ed.) 2004, *The RoutledgeFalmer Reader in Sociology of Education*, RoutledgeFalmer, London.

Connell, R., Campbell, C., Vickers, M., Welch, A., Foley, D., Bagnall, N. and Hayes, D. 2010, *Education, Change & Society*, 2nd edn, Oxford University Press, Melbourne.

McLeod, J. & Yates, L. 2006, *Making Modern Lives: Subjectivity, Schooling and Social Change*, State University of New York Press, Albany, NY.

Moore, R. 2004, *Education and Society: Issues and Explanations in the Sociology of Education*, Polity Press, Cambridge.

Teese, R. & Polesel, J. 2003, *Undemocratic Schooling: Equity and Quality in Mass Secondary Education in Australia*, Melbourne University Press, Melbourne.

Walkerdine, V., Lucey H. & Melody, J. 2001, *Growing up Girl: Pyscho-social Explorations of Class and Gender*, Palgrave, Basingstoke.

Websites

- Australian Bureau of Statistics (ABS): <www.abs.gov.au>. The main official source for statistical information on Australia.
- Australian Council for Educational Research (ACER): <www.acer.edu.au>. ACER provides research to education policy-makers and professional practitioners.
- Curriculum Corporation: <www.curriculum.edu.au>. An independent education support organisation owned by all Australian education ministers to assist education systems to improve outcomes in student learning.
- Education Network Australia: <www.edna.edu.au/edna/page1.html>. A portal of links and information on key aspects of education in Australia.
- Organization for Economic Cooperation and Development (OECD) <www.oecd.org>. Click on 'Browse–By Topic' in side-bar menu and then 'Education' for access to various reports and programs.
- United Nations Educational, Scientific and Cultural Organization (UNESCO): <www.unesco.org>. Click on Education in the side-bar menu for access to various reports and programs.

Films/documentaries

- *Seven Up!*, 1964–2004, television documentary (ongoing series), directed by M. Apted, Granada Television, DVD distributed by First Run Features (USA, 2004). A series of documentaries beginning in 1964 that traces the lives of fourteen British children. The children were of different socio-economic backgrounds and the documentary was based on the adage, 'Give me a child until he [sic] is seven and I will give you the man.' The participants (those who are still willing and available) are filmed every seven years. The next filming (*56 Up*) is planned for 2011–12.
- *Smokes and Lollies*, 1976; *14's Good, 18's Better*, 1981; *Bingo, Bridesmaids and Braces*, 1988; *Not Fourteen Again*, 1996; *Love, Lust and Lies*, 2009, documentary feature series,

directed by G. Armstrong. This is a series of feature-length documentaries in which Armstrong interviews three girls from working-class families in Adelaide and follows their growing up, schooling, work, and family life. Beginning with the girls at the age of fourteen, the final documentary sees them at age 47.

- *First Day*, 1995, documentary, produced by P. Edgar and G. Glenn, Australian Children's Television Foundation. A documentary about nine families from many parts of Australia, and from diverse cultural and class backgrounds, as they prepare for and experience their child's first day at primary school.

Visit the *Public Sociology* book website to access topical case studies, weblinks, YouTube clips, and extra readings.

References

Australian Bureau of Statistics (ABS) 2005, *Australian Social Trends*, cat. no. 4102.0, ABS, Canberra.

——2009, *Australian Social Trends*, 'Education across Australia', cat. no. 4102.0, ABS, Canberra.

Australian Human Rights Commission 2008, 'A statistical overview of Aboriginal and Torres Strait Islander peoples in Australia', <www.hreoc.gov.au/Social_Justice/sj_report/sjreport08/downloads/appendix2.pdf> (accessed 1 November 2009).

Ailwood, J. & Lingard, B. 2001, 'The endgame for national girls' schooling policies in Australia', *Australian Journal of Education*, vol. 45, no. 1, pp. 9–22.

Arnot, M. 2002, *Reproducing Gender: Essays on Educational Theory and Feminist Politics*, RoutledgeFalmer, London.

Ball, S.J. (ed.) 2004, *The RoutledgeFalmer Reader in Sociology of Education*, RoutledgeFalmer, London.

Bernstein, B. 1971, 'On the classification and framing of educational knowledge', in M.F.D. Young (ed), *Knowledge and Control: New Directions for the Sociology of Education*, Collier Macmillan, London, pp. 47–69.

Bourdieu, P. 1977, *Outline of a Theory of Practice*, Cambridge University Press, Cambridge.

Bourdieu, P. & Passeron, C. 1977, *Reproduction in Education, Society and Culture*, trans. R. Nice, Sage, London.

Bourdieu, P. & Wacquant, L.J.D. 1992, *An Invitation to Reflexive Sociology*, University of Chicago Press, Chicago.

Bowles, H. & Gintis, S. 1976, *Schooling in Capitalist America*, Routledge & Kegan Paul, London.

Campbell, C., Proctor, H. & Sherington, G. 2009, *School Choice: How Parents Negotiate the New School Market in Australia*, Allen & Unwin, Sydney.

Collins, C., Kenway, J. & McLeod J. 2000, *Factors Influencing the Educational Performance of Males and Females at School and Their Initial Destinations After Leaving School*, Department of Education, Training and Youth Affairs (DEETYA), Canberra.

Commonwealth Department of Employment, Education, Training and Youth Affairs 1997, *Gender Equity: A Framework for Australian Schools*, (DEETYA) Canberra.

Connell, R., Ashenden, D.J., Kessler, S. & Dowsett, G.W. 1982, *Making the Difference: Schools, Families and Social Division*, Allen & Unwin, Sydney.

Davies, B. 1989, *Frogs and Snails and Feminist Tales: Pre-school Children and Gender*, Allen & Unwin, Sydney.

——1993, *Shards of Glass: Children Reading and Writing Beyond Gendered Identities*, Allen & Unwin, Sydney.

Department of Education, Science and Training 2005, *Values Education in Perspective*, Report of the 2005 National Values Education Forum, National Museum of Australia, Canberra, 2–3 May, <www.valueseducation.edu.au/values> (accessed 14 April 2010).

Dolby, N. & Dimitriadis, G. (eds) 2004, *Learning to Labor in New Times*, RoutledgeFalmer, New York.

Dwyer, P. & Wyn, J. 2001, *Youth, Education and Risk: Facing the Future*, Routledge, London.

Epstein, D., Elwood, J. & Hey V. 1998, *Failing Boys? Issues in Gender and Achievement*, Open University Press, Buckingham.

Foundation for Young Australians (FYA) 2009, *How Young People are Faring: The National Report on the Learning and Work Situation of Young Australians*, Education Foundation, <www.fya.org.au> (accessed 1 November 2009).

Germov, J. 2004, 'Which class do you teach? Education and the reproduction of class', in J. Allen (ed.), *Sociology of Education: Possibilities and Practices*, 3rd edn, Social Science Press/Thomson Learning Australia, Melbourne, pp. 250–69.

Gilbert R. & Gilbert, P. 1998, *Masculinity Goes to School*, Allen & Unwin, Sydney.

Gillborn, D. & Youdell, D. 2000, *Rationing Education: Policy, Practice, Reform and Equity*, Open University Press, Buckingham.

Groundwater-Smith, S., Ewing, R. & le Cornu, R. 2003, *Teaching Challenges and Dilemmas*, 2nd edn, Thomson, Melbourne.

Hall, S. & Jefferson, T. (eds) 1976, *Resistance through Rituals: Youth Sub-culture in Post-war Britain*, HarperCollins, London.

Heitmeyer, D. 2004, 'It's not a race: Aboriginality and education', in J. Allen (ed.), *Sociology of Education: Possibilities and Practices*, 3rd edn, Social Science Press/Thomson Learning Australia, Melbourne, pp. 220–48.

Henry, M. 2000, ' "It's all up to the individual, isn't it?" Meritocratic practices', in D. Meadmore, B. Burnett & G. Tait (eds), *Practising Education: Social and Cultural Perspectives*, Prentice Hall, Sydney, pp. 47–58.

House of Representatives Standing Committee on Education and Training 2002, *Boys: Getting it Right. Report on the Inquiry into the Education of Boys*, Commonwealth of Australia, Canberra.

Kenway, J. & Willis, S. 1997, *Answering Back: Girls, Boys and Feminism in Schools*, Allen & Unwin, Sydney.

Lamb, S. & McKenzie, P. 2001, *Patterns of Success and Failure in the Transition from School to Work in Australia*, Research Report, Australian Council for Educational Research, Melbourne.

MacNaughton, G. 2000, *Rethinking Gender in Early Childhood Education*, Allen & Unwin, Sydney.

Malin, M. 1990, 'The visibility and invisibility of Aboriginal students in an urban classroom', *Australian Journal of Education*, vol. 324, no. 3, pp. 312–29.

Marginson, S. 1997, *Educating Australia: Government, Economy and Citizen Since 1960*, Cambridge University Press, Melbourne.

McAlpine, L. 1998, 'We can change tomorrow by what we teach today: Aboriginal teacher education in Canada', in K. Sullivan (ed.), *Education and Change in the Pacific Rim: Meeting the Challenges*, Triangle Books, Wallingford, pp. 37–58.

McLeod, J. 2004, 'Which girls, which boys? Gender, feminism and educational reform', in J. Allen (ed.), *Sociology of Education: Possibilities and Practices*, 3rd edn, Social Science Press/Thomson Learning Australia, Melbourne, pp. 165–96.

—— 2009, 'Choice, aspiration and anxiety in the new school markets: Invited Review essay of Craig Campbell, Helen Proctor & Geoffrey Sherington, *School Choice: How Parents Negotiate the New School Market in Australia*', in *Australian Review of Public Affairs*, October, <www.australianreview.net/digest/2009/10/mcleod.html> (accessed 26 November 2009).

McLeod, J., Kenway, J., Mackinnon, A. & Allard, A. 2004, 'Young women negotiating from the margins of education and work: Towards gender justice in education and youth policies and programs', Australian Research Council Discovery Grant 2002–04.

McLeod, J. & Yates. L. 2006, *Making Modern Lives: Subjectivity, Schooling and Social Change*, State University of New York Press, Albany, NY.

Meadmore, D. 2004, 'The rise and rise of testing: How does this shape identity?' in B. Burnett, D. Meadmore & G. Tait (eds), *New Questions for Contemporary Teachers: Taking a Socio-Cultural Approach to Education*, Pearson Education, Sydney, pp. 25–37.

Moore, R. 2004, *Education and Society: Issues and Explanations in the Sociology of Education*, Polity Press, Cambridge.

Oakes, J. & Lipton, M. 2003, *Teaching to Change the World*, McGraw Hill, Boston.

Organization for Economic Cooperation and Development (OECD) 2006, *Education Portal*, <www.oecd.org/topic/0,2686,en_2649_37455_1_1_1_1_37455,00.html> (accessed 5 November 2009).

Simons, M. 2006, 'Different school of thought', *The Age*, Insight, 4 February, p. 7.

Spender, D. 1982, *Invisible Women: The Schooling Scandal*, Writers and Readers, London.

Summers, A. 2003, *The End of Equality: Work, Babies and Women's Choices in 21st Century Australia*, Random House, Sydney.

Symes, C. & Preston, N. 1997, *Schools and Classrooms: A Cultural Studies Analysis of Education*, Addison Wesley Longman, Melbourne.

Taylor, S. 2004. 'Gender equity and education: What are the issues today?', in B. Burnett, D. Meadmore & G. Tait (eds), *New Questions for Contemporary Teachers: Taking a Socio-Cultural Approach to Education*, Pearson Education, Sydney, pp. 87–100.

Teese, R. 2000, *Academic Success and Social Power*, Melbourne University Press, Melbourne.

Teese, R. & Polesel, J. 2003, *Undemocratic Schooling: Equity and Quality in Mass Secondary Education in Australia*, Melbourne University Press, Melbourne.

The Australian 2004, Higher Education Supplement, 3 March, p. 1.

United Nations Educational, Scientific and Cultural Organization (UNESCO) 2006, *Education Portal*, <http://portal.unesco.org/education/en/ev.php-URL_ID=42332&URL_DO=DO_TOPIC&URL_SECTION=201.html> (accessed 5 November 2009).

Walkerdine, V., Lucey, H. & Melody, J. 2001, *Growing Up Girl; Pyscho-social Explorations of Class and Gender*, Palgrave, Basingstoke.

Webb, J., Schirato, T. & Danaher, G. 2002, *Understanding Bourdieu*, Allen & Unwin, Sydney.

Willis, P. 1977, *Learning to Labour: How Working Class Kids Get Working Class Jobs*, Saxon House, Farnborough.

Young, M.F.D. (ed.) 1971, *Knowledge and Control: New Directions for the Sociology of Education*, Collier Macmillan, London.

CHAPTER 23

Urbanisation, community, and rurality

Ian Gray

City and country

There was pushing and shoving on the steps of Flinders Street Station after the crowd of about 2000 refused to move and began pelting the windows above the station entrance with stones and bottles. Up to 60 police, some on horseback, soon restored order and pushed the crowd back on to the streets. Overnight, about 200 students remained in front of Flinders Street Station, but the remaining protesters left by about 5.15 a.m. after a number were detained by police. Yarra Trams said services along Swanston and Flinders streets had been disrupted since 2.30 p.m. the previous day and trams would not run until the area was cleared. Cars were also blocked along Flinders Street. This was reported by Melbourne's *Age* newspaper on 1 June 2009 under the headline: 'Indian Anger Boils Over'. Other media reports were later to examine the situation of many students who had come from India to study in Australian cities, particularly Melbourne.

In November 2004, Sydney commuters were encouraged to protest about the condition of the city's train system by refusing to buy a ticket. Could civil disobedience on a large scale happen in Sydney? The possibility was reported in the British press. When combined with trade unions expressing concern for public safety, the New South Wales government apparently thought it could happen, and declared a fare-free travel day. The condition of the city's infrastructure—the basis for the services that enables Sydney to function—had become a matter of significant public concern. Continuing water shortages were also focusing attention on the systems that enable city life.

Just over a year later, violence occurred in Sydney's beach suburb of Cronulla. It also made international headlines, which focused on the ethnic dimension of the city's fabric just as Melbourne's *Age* newspaper did in 2009. The events in Melbourne and Cronulla brought to public attention the possibility that Australian cities could become sites of serious violence and disruption, as has been seen in the cities of Europe, and earlier in many other cities, notably in the United States.

Rural areas were having their own, but parallel, problems, including transport failures and water shortages. While a three-year drought was easing in many rural areas of southeastern Australia, a range of environmental problems still threatened rural industries, and disparities in wealth and health between resource-rich and resource-poor rural communities continued to grow. Not long after the Cronulla 'riot', the term 'police lockdown', which had become familiar in the wake of Cronulla, was also applied in the regional city of Dubbo. All of these issues have roots in a society constructed through the growth and development of our urban and regional communities.

Introduction

This chapter describes some of the changes that have occurred as our **urban** society has developed. It compares urban and **rural** situations against a background of the empirical

urban
Refers to places of high population density with economies based on industry and commerce.

rural
Areas with economies and societies tied to, and largely dependent on, agriculture.

sustainability
The capacity to provide the resources needed to maintain a standard of living into the long term.

regional
An area separate from the metropolitan areas that dominate national life.

and theoretical issues that have confronted sociologists in their analysis of the problems of our cities, towns, and rural areas, and their estimation of the future for Australian society as we confront the challenges posed by **sustainability**. This topic is very broad. It can be applied to everybody, everywhere in Australia. Ways of life across Australia differ enormously. To help understand and make sense of what is happening in so many different situations, we use the terms 'urban', 'rural', and '**regional**' frequently. 'Urban' clearly encompasses the big cities, but the kinds of sociological analysis carried out with respect to urban areas can be applied to much smaller settlements also, like country towns. 'Rural' is generally used with respect to places that have agricultural economies—that is, places where most of the work is in farming, or in some way supports farming and farm people. The term 'regional' is different. In Australia, a small number of relatively large cities dominate our states, territories, and the nation overall in terms of both population size and government. Regional areas are most usefully considered as those situated away from these metropolitan cities. The cities themselves are sometimes considered to have regions, or at least some parts of them are sufficiently distinctive socially and economically to warrant that label. In this chapter, we look at these areas as socially distinctive, but reserve the term 'regional' for non-metropolitan areas that may or may not be rural.

community
An imprecise term carrying a lot of meanings, all of which in some way refer to positive social relations. Most often used to describe a group of people who live in a geographic area, interact with each other, and share some common interests, if only those related to living space.

Not even the term **community** is clear-cut. It is given a wide range of meanings—all socially positive—that encompass groups of people who interact with each other on almost any basis and can spread across the world. Here, we confine the term to local communities, where people who share living spaces like towns and suburbs have at least an opportunity to interact with each other and form some kind of identification with their locality.

Key debates in urban, community, and rural studies

When do the problems of our cities start to 'bite'? Why do our rural areas cease to offer an attractive alternative to city living, and why do rural ways of life lose their former status and dignity? When do our local communities find themselves incapable of providing safe, healthy, and prosperous lifestyles in which individuality can be expressed?

neo-liberalism
A philosophy based on the primacy of individual rights and minimal state intervention.

globalisation
The increased interconnectedness of the cultural, economic, and political aspects of social life; intensified circulation of capital, goods, information, and people across national boundaries; and increased interdependence of countries and regions of the world.

Or are questions like these just expressions of paranoia, needless worry, and pessimism? The essence of debate about urbanisation, community, and rurality can be distilled into this last question. On one side, supporters of **neo-liberal**, or 'economic rationalist', policies say the changes that have been happening in our cities and rural areas since the 1970s are just the short-term pains that accompany **globalisation** as it brings us ever-greater prosperity. On the other side, those who seek to alter the path of globalisation point to social and environmental problems that, they believe, will only get worse. There is little argument about the existence of problems. There is much debate, though, about how those problems have arisen and what can and should be done about them by governments, communities, and businesses.

Rise of the city: Decline of the rural

By international comparison, Australia's pattern of settlement is heavily dominated by the large metropolitan cities—mostly the state and territory capitals. Following European settlement, Australia's development focused on the capital cities of the colonies and later the state capitals. The settlement of the interior and along the coasts spread away from these metropolitan centres. Transport systems focused trade on them. They became centres of commerce, industry, and administration. Hence they grew into large cities, with few settlements of anything like comparable size and concentration developing anywhere else. Clive Forster (2004, p. 3) describes this as 'metropolitan primacy' in geographical terms. It provided self-generating growth momentum for the metropolitan areas. When manufacturing industry grew in the twentieth century, it concentrated in the state capitals and a few nearby cities, like Geelong, Wollongong, and Newcastle.

Metropolitan primacy also has a strong political element. Other places attracted population, particularly the resource-rich areas along or relatively close to the coast. In the mid-nineteenth century, the possibility of wealth from gold lured many people inland. Later in the nineteenth century, agriculture proved a more stable source of at least occasional prosperity. Neither mining nor agriculture altered the administrative dominance of what became the twentieth century state capital cities. In practical terms, what this has meant is illustrated by Bill Gammage (1986) in a chapter entitled 'The City and the Bush'. It shows how the people of a small country town depended on decisions made in their state capital city, sometimes experiencing great frustration and eventually finding that decisions about development were made for the benefit of the city rather than the country.

Villages, towns, and small cities did grow, though. Many of them were distant from the state capitals. They grew with the expansion of agriculture particularly, but also with the mining and other resource-exploitation industries. Through its first hundred years in Australia, agriculture needed a large labour force, and the labour-intensive system of small farms operated by families was actively promoted by governments. Around the mid-twentieth century, problems in the small farming system and increasing mechanisation, with consequent reduction in the need for labour, started to affect population growth. The people of many regional—meaning non-metropolitan—villages and towns realised that their local communities might never become large cities. The big cities had been growing much more rapidly, thanks to the commerce generated by the agricultural economy and occasional commercial booms from mining, especially the 'gold rushes' of the nineteenth century and the 'mineral booms' of the twentieth century (see Forster 2004).

More recently, the 'fly in, fly out' phenomenon—where corporations fly their employees to remote mining sites to work and fly them out again after a relatively short spell on the job—has become possibly the most profound illustration of the disconnection of workplace from local community living in the village or town, not that mining towns have ever been necessarily permanent features of the pattern of settlement (see Storey 2001), but now mining areas are not necessarily even semi-permanent places of living, raising families, or establishing neighbourhood and community life.

The largest cities continue to grow. In Australia, the growth of Sydney is the most spectacular example, while many rural areas are languishing in terms of population size. At 30 June 2008, 4.4 million of New South Wales' seven million people lived in Sydney. Its population had grown by 1.3 per cent since 30 June 2007. The population of inland New South Wales had grown by about half that figure, 0.7 per cent, during the same period. Nine of New South Wales' ten fastest growing local government areas were in Sydney, though some coastal areas were growing nearly as fast as, and even a little faster than, Sydney (ABS 2009). The capital cities—that is, excluding the larger regional cities like Newcastle and Geelong—are home to about 64 per cent of Australia's population. This percentage has been projected to grow to 67 per cent in 2056 (ABS 2008).

For a while in the early 1990s, the growth of coastal populations was observed as a 'population turnaround': a reversal of the trend toward the cities having increasing and regional areas having decreasing shares of population growth, but the 'turnaround' was found to be largely a coastal phenomenon (see Hugo 1994). Some inland towns and cities are still growing, but many are described as 'sponge cities' because their growth can be attributed to their capacity to attract people from their hinterlands at the expense of smaller towns and rural areas. Recent analysis has shown how the 'sponge cities' phenomenon illustrates the demographic influence of the metropolitan cities (see Argent, Rolley & Walmsley 2008).

Coastal population growth has come to popular attention with the help of the media as well as the expansion of popular recreation sites. The 'seachange' phenomenon, in which middle-aged people seek to escape city life, is now widely recognised, possibly exceeding in the popular mind the well-evidenced movement of older people to northern coastal areas of New South Wales and Queensland in their retirement, not that either retirement or 'seachanging' is necessarily the biggest driver of coastal growth. The expansion of the labour-intensive, people-oriented service industries—including, though not solely focused on, tourism—has created many jobs. While this has been happening, the decline in the agricultural workforce, particularly the small farm sector, has decreased service employment across inland areas.

'Treechanging', the inland counterpart to 'seachanging', may also be occurring but its significance is less certain. This is because a movement of underprivileged people from the big cities to rural areas has been observed for some time. It differs from 'seachanging' in that these people are often poor and frequently unemployed: they are attracted by inexpensive housing and are seeking a cheaper lifestyle, rather than being early retiring professionals seeking a slower lifestyle. This type of 'treechanging' raises concerns when it happens in areas where health and social service provision is in decline at the same time as local populations are ageing. It is also a matter of concern where young families move to non-metropolitan areas, as services for them can be sparse (Healy & Hillman 2008). The increase in the proportion of elderly people can be relatively fast in small inland towns and villages, with older populations suffering net losses of younger people. These communities face growing difficulties servicing the needs of their people at the same time as their own human and economic resources are diminishing.

In all places where populations are changing through the movement of people, there is potential for difficulties in social relations between newcomers and established residents. Sydney and the other metropolitan cities have no monopoly on such problems. Importantly, in all towns and cities, there is also potential for positive change in community life.

Globalisation and restructuring

Much attention is focused on Sydney, which is said to be Australia's 'global city'. Other cities might also have a case for such a title—certainly Melbourne, and possibly also Brisbane. What makes a city 'global' is the extent to which the global economy determines its social and economic structure. In other words, it is said that the global economy, rather than the Australian national economy, is affecting Sydney, its rapid growth, and the distribution of wealth and poverty across its population.

The liberalisation of economic policy since the 1970s, applying the neo-liberal idea that the deregulation and privatisation of production and the lowering of barriers to trade will maximise prosperity and freedom for everyone, has brought great change to our cities and regional areas. This is sometimes described as 'restructuring'. In the metropolitan cities, it has brought a decline in manufacturing employment and growth in service industries, at the same time as immigration has expanded the population into already 'sprawling' suburban areas. While the middle suburbs of western Sydney and Melbourne have lost employment as manufacturing has declined, the inner suburbs have grown with service industries and the outer suburbs have expanded further with people seeking more pleasant living conditions. In contrast to the middle industrial suburbs, some of the older, inner industrial suburbs have become 'gentrified'. Professional and wealthier people have been replacing the older working-class populations.

Poverty has become relatively concentrated in the middle, formerly industrial, suburbs where employment opportunities have diminished, housing costs have decreased, and people with few choices about residential location have become concentrated. These populations include relatively large proportions of immigrants from non-English speaking backgrounds. This is not to say that parts of Australian cities have become ethnic ghettos in the way the term has been applied in the United States and Europe. The concentrations are not that dense and the inequalities are not so profound. But the social inequalities across Sydney, and other Australian cities, have become more pronounced (see Burnley, Murphy & Fagan 1997; Forster 2004).

These issues are not new, but rather are changes in the direction and location of long-standing social phenomena. The rise of neo-liberalism has seen the privatisation of urban spaces, associated with housing developments, which have previously been public assets and open to all. In these 'master-planned estates', which are proliferating on the fringes of metropolitan cities, open space and recreational facilities are provided for and under the collective ownership of those who own housing on the estates, rather than by a local government council. In some cases, these are described as 'gated communities', as they deliberately try to segregate the residents from neighbouring areas. Concerns have been raised about the social exclusivity of these 'communities' and the capacity of their members to maintain the facilities without the support of a local council (see Goodman & Douglas 2008).

Globalisation and restructuring have also been accompanied by an apparent change in the relative significance of production and consumption in both the structure of cities and their sociological analysis. Urban social inequality usually has been analysed in terms of the availability of jobs, housing, and facilities like health and education. The rise of mass consumption has brought cities to light as sites of consumption, as expressions of status and taste, but also as part of a process of transformation (Thorns 2002). 'Gentrification' is an element in this change, involving the adaptation and reconstruction of older industrial and commercial areas into new places of living. Some old industrial areas are also being developed as sites of consumption. This is sometimes seen as cities becoming 'theme parks'—tourist attractions and places of living at the same time. Seeing cities as sites of consumption also opens a window on social exclusion. Is consumption, along with the sites where it is available, equally available or open to all people? It may be no coincidence that the violence at Cronulla occurred at a prominent site of the consumption of leisure.

Restructuring has also affected our rural society. The decline in numbers of small farms has resulted in what has been called 'the disappearing middle'. Small 'hobby' or 'lifestyle' farms have grown in number, as have larger more capital-intensive farming operations. The great majority of farms remain in family ownership and management, even if many are incorporated. The proportion of farms owned by large corporations remains small, although the area they cover is relatively large and corporations are very prominent in some industries, such as beef production. For very many inland regional communities, the basic problem has simply been that fewer people are needed to maintain production and meet local needs for goods and services. Hence those needs are either not being met or are met from other places.

Corporations may be more significant in other ways, because they lock farmers into attempting to maintain high levels of production, which strains their capacities and those of their land, and threatens long-term sustainability. It is reasonable to argue that rural Australia has effectively been globalised since it was settled by Europeans and developed to provide overseas populations with food and overseas industries with primary products. We are now recognising that the kinds of production into which our rural system has been locked are not the kinds that our land and water resources are capable of supporting into the longer term. The problem of over-allocation of irrigation water, arising from a combination of ongoing drought and the previous practices of governments issuing licences to irrigate farms on the basis of rainfall experience during wetter times, is now superseding the problem of soil salinity as the most prominent for Australian agriculture. Restructuring amid continued globalisation have brought poverty to many rural places, where people lack options for employment or migration in ways similar to the experience of many urban residents. In addition, for regional areas the other major factor is the dominance of the metropolitan cities, particularly the wealthier parts of those cities, which has placed the regions in a constant struggle to assert their interests.

Regulating space: Politics in town

The life chances of people are significantly affected by where they live, and where they live is a product of their life chances. Individual prospects for prosperity and development of their individuality are related to their capacity to influence the living conditions that prevail in their locality. Under the ideals of democracy, all people should be able to exert some influence in the process of the decision-making that affects their locality. The system of local government offers, at least in part, opportunities for people to enter those processes. But how democratic are our urban governments? Do all people have equal opportunity to exert influence over the democratic systems? As local government is a relatively small and weak institution in Australia, we should also ask if anything can be achieved by local government or are the important decisions all made in the administrative centres of 'global' cities and the seats of state and federal governments?

There are at least two replies to the last question. Local government in Australia does have some significant responsibilities, even if they are not seen as the most important roles of government. And local government councils are often very important institutions for members of local communities. While their significance can be partly symbolic, they are seen as potentially intervening on behalf of local communities in wider political arenas. This does not mean, though, that local institutions will necessarily be able to exert significant power.

The other questions above are more open to debate. There is a long tradition of research, emanating mostly from the United States, in which towns and cities have been studied to ascertain the extent to which a narrow or single range of interests is able to dominate local affairs. These studies have focused on small country towns at least as often as large cities and areas within them. Most involve some analysis of the affairs of local government councils. In Australia, most studies have been of country towns. One significant exception is Janice Caulfield and John Wanna's (1995) analysis of political processes in Brisbane, the only city in Australia to be covered very largely by just one local government council. The other big cities contain many councils, and many of our smaller towns and rural areas, with relatively small populations, have their own council, despite drastic amalgamations in some states since the 1980s (see Forster 2004).

In general, studies of local politics and the broader arenas of power relations among local-interest groups indicate potential for dominance by a relatively narrow range of interests rather than a more pluralistic system in which there is regular contest for influence across a broad range of interests. For example, the interests of industry have been found to push social issues off the local political agenda, or at least to so dominate debate that there was little room for any other problems to be raised and discussed (Gray 1991). This theme of 'agenda-setting' has provided an important dimension for analysis of local power relations since the publication of Peter Bachrach and Morton Baratz's (1970) American study and Peter Saunders' (1983) work in the United Kingdom. This research showed how the interests and concerns of impoverished urban populations could be left out or kept out of local politics in ways that seriously affected social inequality and social relations. In Australia, the issues have not been so serious, but the principles are the same and the inequalities are not diminishing.

Despite the growing inequalities in our cities, most of the debate about local government surrounds the question of size, confronting inequality only indirectly. Are our relatively small (by international standards) local government areas too economically and politically weak to be able to do enough for local people, or would larger councils remove the opportunities that people now have to make their interests heard? These questions can be applied to both metropolitan and regional local government. Even if councils can obtain greater economic strength by amalgamating into larger entities (a point still debated—see Byrnes, Dollery & Webber 2002), it may be that little strength in local democracy will be lost simply because local democracy is weak anyway. The weakness may be exposed as elitism and agenda-setting, as discussed above. It may also be seen as a difficulty in determining and effectively expressing the interests of local people.

It is very hard to generalise about local government in Australia because of the enormous variations that exist in many important characteristics, including the size of council areas and the different laws and regulations applying among the states; however, weakness and elitism have been revealed by several studies, including those of Ron Wild (1983) and Ian Gray (1991). Wild (1983) documents an attempt by a state government (Victoria) to have a toxic waste dump established near a small town (Heathcote). The study describes how the elected members of the local council agreed to the waste dump, much to the annoyance and concern of some local residents. Those residents successfully overthrew the council plan and changed the mind of the state government. In this case, the council had appeared weak in the face of the state administrative apparatus and failed to represent local interests. It is unwise to generalise about local government in these terms, but elements of tradition have been identified in local government that can make local democracy problematic (Halligan & Paris 1984). State governments have tried to address some of the problems of local democracy, but the fundamentals are hard to change and it is unlikely that any state government would seek to alter the subservience of local councils. Attempts by state governments to form bigger councils by amalgamation are very often opposed by local people, but councils themselves have occasionally agreed to amalgamation when prompted by states.

While local democracy has problems, so do local people when state governments assert their authority over planning and permit developments that are not wanted by local people. This may be in the form of the 'Not in My Backyard' (NIMBY) phenomenon, when people are seen to protest against development that is accepted more widely as in the common good, as has recently been seen in the cases of wind farms and water desalination plants, or it can also be about protecting environment and heritage, as in the case of protests against motorway construction and more recently in Sydney about the destruction of houses with acknowledged heritage value. There have been very well-publicised instances of local government permitting inappropriate development too, and citizens hoping for effective support from their local council on environmental and heritage issues are likely to be disappointed given the relative strength of the higher levels of government.

Dependency and sustainability

The weakness of local interests, particularly as expressed in rural and regional local government in economically declining areas, has been described as 'dependency' (discussed in Gray & Sinclair 2005). This implies that small communities are inherently weak, especially amid globalisation; however, strength and weakness are seldom absolute, as Wild's (1983) findings would suggest, and it is unlikely to be helpful to assume that any community will always be absolutely powerless. The power that communities—urban and rural—have or can obtain has become an important topic of debate. Neo-liberal policies have effectively told communities that they have to find their own pathways towards sustainability, or even find a way to help themselves maintain their own existence without much expectation of help from outside. This approach has been adopted despite the obvious problem that the weakest communities will be those least able to help themselves, and despite the great disparities in the endowment of natural resources across Australia.

There is evidence of some power being exerted by small, relatively isolated regional communities, though. This observation presents an interesting theoretical question. Should we look upon small communities as inherently weak under the conditions imposed by globalisation and metropolitan dominance? Or do we thereby risk assuming that the same forces affect everywhere equally, and all communities share the same problems? Research has warned us that the answer to the latter question may be yes. While globalisation and metropolitan dominance have long historical origins and are ongoing processes which seem unlikely to change, we should be alert to any potential that small communities might have to assert themselves. This point is argued theoretically and empirically by Lynda Herbert-Cheshire (2003) with evidence from regional Queensland.

Neo-liberalism has made any potential for self-sustainability very important among small communities. Analysis of sustainability among regional communities has focused on their possession of 'capitals'. In Chris Cocklin and Margaret Alston's study (2003), several regional communities are subject to assessment of their stocks of human, environmental, institutional, economic, and, importantly, social capital. These concepts refer to, respectively:

- the capacities of people, such as their levels of education (human capital)
- the condition of the local natural environment and its capacity to sustain the population (environmental capital)
- the presence of institutions like local government and hospitals (institutional capital)
- the strength of the local economy as provider of employment and generator of wealth (economic capital), and
- the levels of social interaction and trust detectable in community life (social capital).

Sociologically, social capital is the most interesting. It is also sometimes said to be the most important because it underpins communities' ability to generate activity for their own betterment, including the strengthening of the other capitals, but it also puts the spotlight back on the processes of regulation—the formal and informal ways in which communities organise themselves and come to define the interests to be pursued collectively. Is our town really about supporting agriculture or should we look to tourism and hobby farming? Do we need a new factory or should our suburb or town remain a quiet dormitory and a pleasant environment? This point applies to all communities, metropolitan and regional. The process through which the local interest is defined can involve strong expressions of localism, but the identities that communities accept for themselves can be contested.

Sometimes the problem lies in an absence of contest. As Gray (1991) shows, localism in a country town can lead to acceptance of a narrow expression of local interests. Where localism and strong social capital interact to facilitate particular definitions of local interests, inequality and instability are likely to be longer term results. There is also considerable danger of localism feeding exaggerated estimates of the stocks of the capitals and the capacity for change; nevertheless, the point made by Herbert-Cheshire (2003) still holds. We should not be blinkered by theories that emphasise only the strength of the forces of globalisation and restructuring, and leave out the strengths of local communities—even if it can be argued that they are relatively weak.

Identity, place, and community

The rise of neo-liberalism, alongside the development of broader sociological analyses of urban and rural life, has attracted greater attention to urban and rural cultures. In particular, the notion of identity has been applied. What does it mean to be a city person, a rural person, or a person from an area within a big city? Is everyday life different in the country and in the city? These questions have occupied sociologists from the discipline's inception.

In the nineteenth century, as the growth of cities accompanied the rise of manufacturing industry, people were concerned that life was changing. The close ties of traditional rural life were being replaced by the impersonal relations of the city. This interpretation had some ground in sociology, but close analysis of city life revealed some very close-knit communities, often where people were bound by shared working-class interests, living conditions, and lifestyles, and in some situations shared ethnic or racial origin. This became apparent through studies like those of Michael Young and Peter Willmott (1962) and Herbert Gans (1982). In Australia, Andrew Metcalfe (1988) revealed strong identification with class and locality in a regional coal-mining community. Country towns can be more enigmatic. While people can exhibit a strong sense of attachment to their community and express intense localism, their communities can also present social inequality and exclusion (see Dempsey 1990; Gray 1991). This presents dilemmas for advocates of community action and self-reliance in regional areas, especially where notably disadvantaged groups—often including Indigenous people—suffer exclusion from sites of local production and consumption.

In rural areas—indeed, in most regional areas—metropolitan primacy combined with distinctive traditions and ways of life associated with farming has produced a rural identity. Rural culture is a distinctive part of Australian tradition—or at least, popular belief in the cultural significance of the rural is important. Above all other features, the family farm and the practice of passing it down through the (usually but not always male members of) generations have underpinned rurality. This practice is waning as rural sustainability is under threat and farming becomes increasingly capitalised. Still, rural communities and rural community life are persisting, even if their reality is now removed from the images of traditional farm life. It still provides a foundation for differential identities among country and city people. More importantly, this differentiation retains a political element, despite the apparent decline of the political party (the National, formerly Country, Party), which was formed to represent regional interests.

The idea of virtual communities has become quite popular, though it does depend on the accessibility of technology, which is generally better in cities and towns than in the situations of many rural and remote dwellers. If community members can interact with each other much more readily by using the internet, might community identity and even the potential for collective community organisation be enhanced? Internet-based communication and interaction have been established on a local basis in some communities. There has been scepticism, but research findings are generally positive (Thorns 2002). Hazel Ashton and David Thorns (2007) have raised the prospect of local communities using information technologies for their collective benefit, by way of fostering community networks and organisations. There is some evidence that internet communication can help to foster local community life in very positive ways for members of a community, both individually and collectively.

23.1: Kandos, Rylstone, and 'Bradstow'

Kandos, Rylstone, and 'Bradstow' are small towns in regional New South Wales. Kandos and Rylstone are real names, 'Bradstow' is not. All three were studied by sociologists in the early 1970s. Social life in Kandos and Rylstone was reported by Harry Oxley in the book *Mateship in Local Organization* (1974); 'Bradstow' was reported in a book titled *Bradstow* (1974) by Ron Wild. *Bradstow* became well known, publicised by an ABC television program and subsequent newspaper reports exclaiming that Australia was not the egalitarian society Australians had thought it was. Oxley's work was not publicised and is less well known, but more than 30 years later it has become the more currently relevant of the two.

Wild had analysed the social structure of 'Bradstow', showing that it had class and status divisions related to power. He had tested the theory (derived from the classical sociologist Max Weber) that local social stratification could be analysed in this way. Oxley had been interested in the ways in which social stratification was handled in community life—did it really keep people apart, or did egalitarianism prevail? He explained how class and status differentiation could coexist with egalitarianism in functioning communities. During the 1970s and into the 1980s, Wild was praised for his critical stance, while Oxley occasionally suffered criticism for being functionalist—his work was seen as vindicating social inequality.

Subsequent theoretical developments enable us to see the weaknesses in both studies. In particular, both adopted a narrow view of power that takes little account of ideology, a concept that sociology focused on from the 1970s. Today, Oxley's work prompts us to think critically about 'social capital', a concept adopted enthusiastically by neo-liberal government policymakers as well as social researchers whom one might expect to be more critical of the concept. His interest in local organisations and their social significance was attacked as mundane in the 1970s and 1980s, but the capacity of local communities to organise has become an important element in the analysis of their prospects for survival and any degree of autonomy. In present neo-liberal times, Oxley's work could be reinterpreted as a critical perspective on social capital, a concept some sociologists have attacked for its potential to disguise inequality.

Sustainability, 'Healthy Cities', and 'Slow Cities'

The notion of sustainability has achieved popularity in political and academic circles, and has become a focus for public concern. In cities, it refers to the problem of maintaining an environment conducive to healthy lifestyles. In rural areas, it also has that meaning, but in the context of small towns it can be more about continued existence. As mentioned above, analysis of rural sustainability focuses on agricultural production and the extent to which communities possess 'capitals', including **social capital**.

social capital
A term used to refer to social relations, networks, norms, trust, and reciprocity between individuals that facilitate cooperation for mutual benefit.

In principle, the 'capitals' are important to cities also, but most attention is focused on a range of urban problems—including pollution, but particularly automobile dependence (Newman & Kenworthy 1999). A debate has arisen between those who advocate or surrender to increasingly extensive automobile use and those who advocate more development of public transport.

The pro-public transport groups identify problems associated with automobile dependence, including the economic costs of seemingly endless road construction as well as consequent health and social problems (such as isolation for those without cars). The pro-automobile people see the sprawling suburbs of our cities as inevitable. This debate is very prominent in urban policy. It was described as an 'urban brawl' by a headline in the Melbourne *Age* newspaper (Millar 2005). The motor vehicle is, perhaps more than any other object, an icon of the industrial age. It has provided enormous freedom of movement for people with access to cars and the capacity to use them, but it also has unintended consequences like pollution and congestion, all fuelled by an apparently infinite popular demand for the consumption of motor vehicles and the leisure and other opportunities they provide.

Some governments are tackling the problems of urban sustainability, including automobile dependence, by improving public transport and encouraging people to use it (see House of Representatives Standing Committee on Environment and Heritage 2005). There is also some popular resistance to the apparently deteriorating conditions of life in our cities. The 'Healthy Cities' and 'Slow Cities' movements are relatively minor, but spreading attempts to prompt community action in favour of simpler, less dangerous and less polluted lifestyles, and freedom from dependence on automobiles. Although sometimes led by governments, these movements depend heavily on community organisation and action. Automobile use is at least partly a behaviour of habit, and some writers see potential in community education and action campaigns to alert people to alternatives to the 'fast' lifestyle of the restructured city.

Conclusion

Life in cities differs significantly from life in the country, but the sociological principles used to analyse both situations are the same. Also the same are the forces of globalisation that are restructuring cities and the country. Important questions still remain. Are these changes problems and, if they are, what should be done about them? Although governments seem slow to recognise them, some communities are not. While political debate continues, people can see the problems that inequality causes, even if they do not immediately relate those problems to their underlying causes as they are distracted by more immediate issues like 'law and order'. People are recognising that rural and urban areas have sustainability problems, and they are trying to tackle them. But can local communities make a difference? This chapter has set out some of the conditions that local communities are facing as people search for their own solutions to these problems.

Summary of main points

> ▶ Cities, towns, and rural areas are changing amid globalisation and restructuring, which are increasing social inequalities.

▶ The movement of people from rural to urban areas has become more complex, with some coastal areas growing more quickly and the decline of inland rural areas, including many small towns, persisting.

▶ Community power relations in towns and cities do not always provide pluralistic participation or the expression of a broad range of interests. Policy concerns about local government tend to overlook these problems in favour of economic issues.

▶ Community life remains important and, while often an important site of social interaction, it can contain inequality and exclusion, making collective organisation and action difficult.

▶ The sustainability of our towns and cities is under threat from a range of pollution and planning problems, particularly those related to automobile dependence.

▶ The sustainability of rural areas is under threat from a system of production that ties farmers into exploitation of natural resources and subsumes them under a global economic system.

SOCIOLOGICAL REFLECTION

23.1 Your local community

(a) How did your local community affect your life when you were growing up?

(b) Can you see significant differences between your community and others in your region?

(c) Do you feel you can do anything to help make your local community more sustainable?

Discussion questions

23.1 Does urban and rural social inequality matter?

23.2 Should and can anything be done to change the processes of globalisation and restructuring?

23.3 What interests prevail in your community?

23.4 How can localism and community attachment become socially problematic?

23.5 Is city life more or less impersonal than country life?

23.6 Is your local area, town, or city sustainable?

23.7 What can be done to make it more sustainable?

23.8 Is information technology being used to promote community life in your community?

Further reading

Forster, C. 2004, *Australian Cities: Continuity and Change*, Oxford University Press, Oxford.

Gray, I. & Lawrence, G. 2001, *A Future for Regional Australia*, Cambridge University Press, Cambridge.

Thorns, D. 2002, *The Transformation of Cities: Urban Theory and Urban Life*, Palgrave Macmillan, Basingstoke.

Websites

- Australian Bureau of Statistics (ABS): <www.abs.gov.au>. The ABS provides statistical information at the local as well as state and national levels. The website provides access to statistical tables that allow comparison of parts of states and cities across a wide range of social characteristics.
- Healthy Cities Illawarra: <www.healthycitiesill.org.au>. From an Australian example of the 'Healthy Cities' movement, this site presents the kind of activities that the movement pursues. See also the international website of the Healthy Cities organisation: <www.healthycities.org>.
- Slow Cities: <www.citymayors.com/environment/slow_cities.html>. The 'Slow Cities' movement, and its close relative, the 'Slow Food' movement, are described. As with 'Healthy Cities', values of community, environment, and heritage are emphasised.

Visit the *Public Sociology* book website to access topical case studies, weblinks, YouTube clips, and extra readings.

References

Argent, N., Rolley, F. & Walmsley, J. 2008, 'The sponge city hypothesis: Does it hold water?' *Australian Geographer*, vol. 32, pp. 109–30.

Ashton, H. & Thorns, D.C. 2007, 'The role of information communications technology in retrieving local community', *City and Community*, no. 6, pp. 211–29.

Australian Bureau of Statistics (ABS) 2008, *Population Projections Australia*, cat. no. 3222.0, ABS, Canberra.

——2009, *NSW State and Regional Indicators, June 2009*, cat. no. 1338.1, ABS, Canberra.

Bachrach, P. & Baratz, M.S. 1970, *Power and Poverty*, Oxford University Press, New York.

Burnley, I., Murphy, P. & Fagan, R. 1997, *Immigration and Australian Cities*, Federation Press, Sydney.

Byrnes, J., Dollery, B. & Webber, A. 2002, 'Measuring economies of scale in Australian local government: The case of domestic waste collection', *Australasian Journal of Regional Studies*, vol. 8, pp. 201–18.

Caulfield, J. & Wanna, J. 1995, *Power and Politics in the City: Brisbane in Transition*, Macmillan, Melbourne.

Cocklin, C. & Alston, M. 2003, *Community Sustainability in Rural Australia: A Question of Capital?*, Centre for Rural Social Research, Charles Sturt University, Wagga Wagga.

Dempsey, K. 1990, *Smalltown: A Study of Social Inequality, Cohesion and Belonging*, Oxford University Press, Melbourne.

Forster, C. 2004, *Australian Cities: Continuity and Change*, 3rd edn, Oxford University Press, Melbourne.

Gammage, B. 1986, *Narrandera Shire*, Narrandera Shire Council, Narrandera.

Gans, H. 1982, *The Urban Villagers: Group and Class in the Life of Italian Americans*, Free Press, New York.

Goodman, R. & Douglas, K. 2008, 'Privatised communities: The use of owners corporations in master planned estates in Melbourne', *Australian Geographer*, vol. 39, pp. 521–36.

Gray, I. 1991, *Politics in Place: Social Power Relations in an Australian Country Town*, Cambridge University Press, Cambridge.

Gray, I. & Sinclair, P. 2005, 'Local leaders in a global setting: Dependency and resistance in regional New South Wales and Newfoundland', *Sociologia Ruralis*, vol. 45, pp. 37–52.

Halligan, J. & Paris, C. 1984, 'The politics of local government', in J. Halligan & C. Paris (eds), *Australian Urban Politics*, Longman Cheshire, Melbourne, pp. 58–72.

Healy, K. & Hillman, W. 2008, 'Young families migrating to non-metropolitan areas: Are they at increased risk of social exclusion?', *Australian Journal of Social Issues*, vol. 43, pp. 479–97.

Herbert-Cheshire, L. 2003, 'Translating policy: Power and action in Australia's country towns', *Sociologia Ruralis*, vol. 43, pp. 454–73.

House of Representatives Standing Committee on Environment and Heritage 2005, *Sustainable Cities*, Parliament of the Commonwealth of Australia, Canberra.

Hugo, G. 1994, 'The turnaround in Australia: Some first observations from the 1991 census', *Australian Geographer*, vol. 25, pp. 1–17.

Metcalfe, A. 1988, *For Freedom and Dignity*, Allen & Unwin, Sydney.

Millar, R. 2005, 'Urban Brawl', *The Age*, 24 March, p. 17.

Newman, P. & Kenworthy, J. 1999, *Sustainability and Cities: Overcoming Automobile Dependence*, Island Press, Washington, DC.

Oxley, H. 1974, *Mateship in Local Organization*, University of Queensland Press, Brisbane.

Saunders, P. 1983, *Urban Politics: A Sociological Interpretation*, Hutchinson, London.

Storey, K. 2001, 'Fly-in/fly-out and fly-over: Mining and regional development in Western Australia', *Australian Geographer*, vol. 32, pp. 133–48.

Thorns, D. 2002, *The Transformation of Cities: Urban Theory and Urban Life*, Palgrave Macmillan, Basingstoke.

Wild, R.A. 1974, *Bradstow*, Angus & Robertson, Sydney.

—— 1983, *Heathcote*, George Allen & Unwin, Sydney.

Young, M. & Willmott, P. 1962, *Family and Kinship in East London*, Penguin, Harmondsworth.

Module 5
Future directions

This final section of the book explores the resources and skills necessary to further develop your sociological imagination.

This module contains the following chapters:

24 A sociological toolkit

25 Writing a sociology essay

CHAPTER 24

A sociological toolkit

John Germov

Sociology tricks of the trade to finding information fast

This chapter covers some of the key resources that are available to enable you to expand and enhance your sociological imagination. You will discover information-search shortcuts and sociology-specific websites that will allow you to find relevant and credible sociological material quickly. We provide a list of key websites, including major sociology-dedicated sites, social science research centres, and Australian longitudinal studies, as well as some key general reference sites. The chapter begins by providing some effective tips on finding sociology journal articles and offers guidance on how to evaluate the credibility of websites, particularly information accessed via Wikipedia and Google.

Finding sociology journal articles

Academic journals, such as the *Journal of Sociology*, are a main source of authoritative and up-to-date information in a particular field of study. They are the main publication outlet for new empirical research findings and the discussion of new theories. Journals can be published annually, quarterly, monthly, or bi-monthly.

Academic journals differ from newspapers and magazines in a number of important aspects. Journals contain articles that are peer-reviewed and the material used within them is referenced. Before being published, they are usually sent to three independent academics to review the quality of the article. Most articles submitted for consideration for journal publication will have been revised following reviewers' comments, and many are rejected outright. Therefore, journal articles are considered a source of high-quality scholarly information.

All disciplines have academic journals, and there are literally hundreds of sociology and related social science journals. The best way to search for journal articles is to use specific journal databases that index articles by title, author, and keywords. While your university library catalogue will list journal titles, it will not always give you access to the articles contained within a journal. You will be able to access journal databases online, using your student ID and password, via your university library website. Familiarise yourself with the instructions for using the main social science journal databases offered by your university (as noted in Sociology Spotlight 24.1). It is worth consulting more than one database, as no one database provides access to all the relevant journals available. One further hint is to make use of annual review journals, such as the *Annual Review of Sociology*. These journals publish articles that aim to synthesise research findings and review the key debates on particular topics. They can be an invaluable way to gain an understanding of the major issues and authors in a certain field.

Key Australian social science journals, online journals, and selected journal databases

Australian journals

- *Journal of Sociology*
- *Health Sociology Review*
- *Australian Feminist Studies*
- *Australian Journal of Political Science*
- *Australian Journal of Social Issues*
- *Journal of Australian Political Economy*
- *Labour & Industry*
- *People and Place*
- *The Australian Journal of Anthropology*

Open-access online sociology journals and archives

- *Australian Humanities Review*: <www.australianhumanitiesreview.org>
- *Journal of Australian Political Economy*:
- *Canadian Journal of Sociology*: <http://ejournals.library.ualberta.ca/index.php/CJS/index>
- *Electronic Journal of Sociology*: <www.sociology.org>
- *International Journal of Emerging Technologies and Society*: <www.swinburne.edu.au/hosting/ijets/ijets/about.html>
- DOAJ: Directory of Open Access Journals: <www.doaj.org/doaj?func=home>
- JURN: A curated academic search engine of free e-journals: <www.jurn.org>
- Journal of World-Systems Research: < http://jwsr.ucr.edu/index.php>
- JSTOR: The Scholarly Journal Archive: <http://www.jstor.org>
- *Postmodern Culture*: <http://pmc.iath.virginia.edu>
- Sociological Research Online: <www.socresonline.org.uk>

Selected journal and news databases

- AUSTROM: Australian social science databases
- Statistics: online access to all Australian Bureau of Statistics (ABS) publications (formerly AusStats)
- Australian Public Affairs Full Text (APAFT): an indexing and full text database incorporating the Australian Public Affairs Information Service (APAIS) (subject coverage includes Australian current affairs, economics, law, literature, and politics)

- Factiva: online access to global news and business information, including full-text coverage of Australian newspapers
- NewsBank: full-text content of more than 160 Australian newspapers and around 100 international newspapers. Includes additional sections like literary criticism and editorial pieces
- Social Science Journals (ProQuest): an index of 450 journals, most of which are full-text journals
- Sociofile: sociology and social science index
- Sociological Abstracts: the premier sociological database
- TVNews: index of Australian news, current affairs, and documentary programs; updated daily
- Web of Science: includes social sciences, and incorporates the Current Contents and Journal Citation Reports databases.

Effective web search and evaluation tips

The great advantage of the web is also its greatest disadvantage, virtually instant access to vast amounts of information, meaning that you can be deluged by too much information of dubious quality. Sifting through this information, in terms of finding relevant and reliable material for your assignments, has itself become a significant skill.

Evaluating the credibility of websites

Because anyone can publish anything on the web, it is important to exercise caution when obtaining information from a website. You need to evaluate the credibility of a website before using it as a source of information for assignments. Ask yourself the following questions to help evaluate the credibility of the information on a website:

- Can an author be identified?
- Are the date and title supplied?
- Are contact details for the author or publisher provided?
- How objective is the information provided? Does it represent the interests of a particular organisation, political party, or pressure group? How might this bias the information presented?
- If the source is an academic one, is it properly referenced? Is the material self-published or has it been peer-reviewed like those articles published in online academic journals?

CrossLink:
See Chapter 25
for more on
the shortfalls
of Wikipedia.

Wikipedia is a particular example of why you must critically evaluate information presented on websites. While Wikipedia is a valuable online encyclopedia, and can be a useful starting point for finding information on a topic, it provides no quality assurance of the validity of the information contained within it. It is not a trustworthy academic source of information and should thus not be used as the basis for researching your university assignments.

The general points to remember are not to take anything on the web at face value and to ensure that the source is a credible one.

To save you time when web searching, the following sections provide an overview of the key websites you should consult when searching for sociological information.

Google Scholar: <http://scholar.google.com>

To improve the quality of your web searches, and increase the chances of finding relevant academic sources of information, use Google Scholar instead of regular Google. Google Scholar restricts your search to peer-reviewed journals, books from academic publishers, professional associations, conference abstracts and papers, universities, and various scholarly organisations. The Google Scholar website includes tips for advanced or specific web searching, and it is advisable that you familiarise yourself with these (such as searching only for certain authors or certain types of publications). You can also set a few preferences for how you use Google Scholar, such as automatic formatting of references for importing in referencing programs such as EndNote or Refman (discussed in Chapter 25). A note of caution, though: Google Scholar is not an exhaustive search and only includes access to certain databases with which Google has signed agreements; therefore, it should be used as only one of the possible ways to find relevant sociological information.

Sociology web portals, gateways, web-rings, and virtual libraries

A variety of terms are used to describe websites that provide discipline and subject-specific indexes, such as virtual libraries, gateways, web-rings, web portals, and clearinghouses. SocioSite, <www.sociosite.net>, is one of the longest-running and most comprehensive sites available (see Figure 24.1). It provides an extensive list of links indexed to a range of topics, such as key theorists and fields of sociological interest.

Other recommended general sociology websites are listed below.

- Intute—Sociology: <www.intute.ac.uk/sociology>. A United Kingdom-based site that indexes quality websites and provides short descriptions of what each website contains.
- Social Science Research Council: <www.ssrc.org>. A United States-based site that provides access to a wide range of resources.
- Virtual Library—Sociology: <http://socserv.mcmaster.ca/w3virtsoclib>. As the name implies, this site provides an index to relevant sociology resources. The quality of the content on the sites listed is variable, though it can be a helpful starting place to find the topic you want.

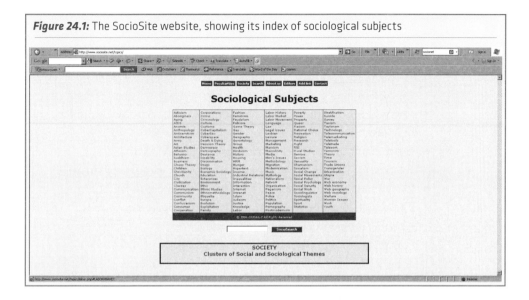

Figure 24.1: The SocioSite website, showing its index of sociological subjects

Professional associations

Professional associations—a selection of which are listed below—can often be sources of free information (working papers, reports, and conference papers), as well as providing access to other topic-based weblinks and discussion groups.

- TASA: The Australian Sociological Association: <www.tasa.org.au>
- APSA: Asia-Pacific Sociological Association: < www.apsa-sociology.org>
- AAS: Australian Anthropological Society: <www.aas.asn.au>
- ASA: American Sociological Association: <www.asanet.org>
- BSA: British Sociological Association: <www.britsoc.co.uk>
- ISA: International Sociological Association: <www.ucm.es/info/isa>
- CHASS: Council for the Humanities, Arts and Social Sciences: <www.chass.org.au>
- DASSH: Deans of Arts, Social Science and Humanities: <www.dassh.edu.au>
- Universities Australia: <www.universitiesaustralia.edu.au>

Australian sites

Australian longitudinal studies

Accessing the websites of the following longitudinal surveys can be a handy way to get the latest information and research findings about Australian society. Most of the websites provide some access to free online articles as well as listings of the latest publications based on survey data.

- Australian Longitudinal Study of Health and Relationships (ALSHR): <www.latrobe.edu.au/alshr/index.htm>
- Australian Longitudinal Study on Women's Health (ALSHW) (also known as Women's Health Australia): <www.alswh.org.au>
- Australian Social Science Data Archive (ASSDA): <http://assda.anu.edu.au>
- Australian Longitudinal Study of Ageing (ALSA): <www.flinders.edu.au/socsci/fcas/alsa/alsa_home.cfm>
- Australian Survey of Social Attitudes (AuSSA): <http://aussa.anu.edu.au>
- Australian Temperament Project (ATP): < www.aifs.gov.au/atp>
- Democratic Audit of Australia: < http://democraticaudit.org.au>
- Household, Income and Labour Dynamics in Australia (HILDA) survey: <http://melbourneinstitute.com/hilda>
- Footprints in Time—The Longitudinal Study of Indigenous Children (LSIC): <www.fahcsia.gov.au/sa/indigenous/progserv/families/lsic/Pages/default.aspx>
- Growing Up in Australia: The Longitudinal Study of Australian Children (LSAC): < www.aifs.gov.au/growingup>
- Life Chances Study: <www.bsl.org.au/main.asp?PageId=67#Lifechances>
- Longitudinal Surveys of Australian Youth (Australian Council for Education Research): <www.acer.edu.au/research/projects/lsay/overview.html>
- Longitudinal Survey of Immigrants to Australia (Department of Immigration & Citizenship): <www.immi.gov.au/media/research/lsia>
- Mater-University of Queensland Study of Pregnancy (MUSP): <www.socialscience.uq.edu.au/musp>
- Negotiating the Life Course Project (Australian National University): <http://lifecourse.anu.edu.au>
- 45 and Up Study in New South Wales (Sax Institute): <www.45andup.org.au>

Australian reference sites

- APL: Australian Parliamentary Library: <www.aph.gov.au/library>. A great source of information on legislation, government inquiries, social research papers, and key economic and social indicators.
- Australian Dictionary of Biography Online: <www.adb.online.anu.edu.au/adbonline.htm>. A valuable resource on key Australian figures.
- Australasian Digital Theses Program: <http://adt.caul.edu.au>. The database provides access to the digitised content of some PhD theses on a wide range of topics. You can search specific university collections by author, keyword or topic, or search the entire database. A good site to see what research has been done on particular topics.
- Australian Government portal: <www.australia.gov.au>. The web entry for all things related to the federal government. A good site to bookmark so that you

can easily find the websites of government departments, many of which produce regular online newsletters, research-based reports, and policy documents.

- Australian Human Rights Commission: <www.humanrights.gov.au>. A national independent statutory body established in 1986 to promote and protect human rights and address discrimination. The site provides access to a wide range of quality reports and briefing papers.
- Australian, state, territory, and local government links: <www.gov.au>. A one-stop site that provides links to all levels of Australian government.
- National Archives of Australia: <www.naa.gov.au>. This site allows you to search for documents of historical significance, some of which are accessible online. The organisation also hosts regular exhibitions, many of which provide supplementary materials online.
- National Library of Australia: <www.nla.gov.au>. All books and journals published in Australia are automatically deposited in the national library. Its online search facility provides access to a very comprehensive collection, which can often be borrowed through your own university library by using its inter-library loan facility.
- National Museum of Australia: <www.nma.gov.au>. A great resource site on Australian social history.
- Trove: <http://trove.nla.gov.au>. The National Library of Australia (NLA) research tool for access to high-quality digitised material.

Australian statistics

The two key sites for statistics on Australia are:

- ABS: Australian Bureau of Statistics: <www.abs.gov.au>. The key website for access to official statistics on all aspects of Australian life, including the latest Census findings.
- AIHW: Australian Institute of Health and Welfare: <www.aihw.gov.au>. This website provides free access to the many publications on all aspects of health, illness, and welfare.

Australian social science research centres and advocacy groups

Most of the following research centres and groups provide access to online working papers, reports, refereed articles, and further helpful links.

- ACSPRI: Australian Consortium for Social and Political Research Incorporated: <www.acspri.org.au>
- ACSR: ACSPRI Centre for Social Research, Australian National University:

<http://acsr.anu.edu.au>
- Australian Council of Social Services: <www.acoss.org.au>
- Australian Consumers' Association: <www.choice.com.au>
- Australian Clearinghouse for Youth Studies: <www.acys.info>
- Australian Youth Research Centre: <www.edfac.unimelb.edu.au/yrc>
- Australian Institute of Aboriginal and Torres Strait Islander Studies: <www.aiatsis.gov.au>
- AHURI: Australian Housing and Urban Research Institute: <http://ahuri.edu.au>
- AIFS: Australian Institute of Family Studies: <www.aifs.gov.au>
- Academy of the Social Sciences in Australia: <www.assa.edu.au>
- ARC Asia Pacific Futures Network: <www.sueztosuva.org.au/index.php>
- ARC Centre of Excellence in Policing and Security: <http://ceps.edu.au>
- ARC Cultural Research Network: <www.uq.edu.au/crn>
- ARC Research Network on Spatially Integrated Social Science: <www.siss.edu.au>
- Australian Council for Educational Research (ACER): <www.acer.edu.au>
- Australia Institute: <www.tai.org.au>
- AIC: Australian Institute of Criminology: <www.aic.gov.au>
- Australian Institute for Social Research (University of Adelaide): <www.aisr.adelaide.edu.au/about>
- Australian Society for the Study of Labour History: <www.asslh.com>
- Australasian Centre on Ageing: <www.uq.edu.au/cfha>
- Centre for Applied Social Research (RMIT): <www.rmit.edu.au/casr>
- Centre for Citizenship, Development and Human Rights (Deakin University): <www.deakin.edu.au/arts-ed/cchr>
- Centre for Critical and Cultural Studies (University of Queensland): <www.cccs.uq.edu.au>
- Centre for Policing, Intelligence and Counter Terrorism (Macquarie University): <www.pict.mq.edu.au/academic>
- Centre for Research on Social Inclusion (Macquarie University): <www.crsi.mq.edu.au>
- Centre for Work + Life (University of South Australia): <www.unisa.edu.au/hawkeinstitute/cwl/default.asp>
- CSAA: Cultural Studies Association of Australasia: <www.csaa.asn.au>
- Evatt Foundation: <http://evatt.labor.net.au>
- Globalism Research Centre (RMIT University) <www.rmit.edu.au/GLOBALISM>
- Hawke Research Institute: <www.unisa.edu.au/hawkeinstitute>
- Institute for Social Research (Swinburne University of Technology): <www.sisr.net>
- Melbourne Institute (University of Melbourne): <http://melbourneinstitute.com>

- NATSEM: National Centre for Social and Economic Modelling (University of Canberra): <www.natsem.canberra.edu.au>
- National Foundation for Australian Women: <www.nfaw.org>
- NILS: National Institute of Labour Studies: <http://nils.flinders.edu.au>
- SPRC: Social Policy Research Centre: <www.sprc.unsw.edu.au>
- The Australian Centre (University of Melbourne): <www.australian.unimelb.edu.au>
- TAISIW: The Australian Institute of Social Inclusion and Wellbeing (University of Newcastle): <www.newcastle.edu.au/institute/australian-institute-for-social-inclusion-and-wellbeing>
- UQSRC: University of Queensland Social Research Centre: <www.uqsrc.uq.edu.au>
- Whitlam Institute (University of Western Sydney): <www.whitlam.org>
- WEL: Women's Electoral Lobby: <www.wel.org.au>
- Workplace Research Centre (University of Sydney): <www.wrc.org.au>

Alternative press

The following publications provide alternative and often critical in-depth commentary on Australian affairs, beyond that found in the mass media. Most of these publications are journalistic in style and are not refereed, and therefore they are not equivalent to academic journals. Nonetheless, they can be useful sources of information.

- AFTINET: Australian Fair Trade and Investment Network: <www.aftinet.org.au>
- *Australian Options*: <www.australian-options.org.au>
- *Australian Prospect*: <www.australianprospect.com.au>
- *Australian Policy Online*: <www.apo.org.au>
- *Australian Review of Public Affairs*: <www.australianreview.net>
- *Bad Subjects*: <http://bad.eserver.org>
- *Dissent Magazine*: <www.dissent.com.au>
- *New Matilda*: <www.newmatilda.com/home/default.asp>
- *Online Opinion*—Australia's e-journal of social and political debate: <www.onlineopinion.com.au>
- *The Nation* (US): <www.thenation.com/about>
- *Southern Perspectives*: <www.southernperspectives.net>

International organisations

International organisations can be good sources of (often) free reports that deal with a range of social and political issues. The various sub-sections of the UN or OECD websites can be particularly good for finding comparative information and statistics. As with all government and non-government agencies, you should exercise reasonable caution in interpreting the information they provide, and should not assume that it is necessarily unbiased.

- APEC: Asia-Pacific Economic Cooperation: <www.apec.org>
- FAO: Food and Agriculture Organization of the United Nations: <www.fao.org>
- ILO: International Labour Organization: <www.ilo.org>
- OECD: Organisation for Economic Cooperation & Development: <www.oecd.org>
- UN: United Nations: <www.un.org/english>
- UNDP: United Nations Development Programme: <www.undp.org>
- UNESCO: United Nations Educational, Scientific and Cultural Organization: <www.unesco.org>
- World Bank: <www.worldbank.org>
- WHO: World Health Organization: <www.who.int/en>

Conclusion

This chapter has provided you with a select list of resources and handy hints for finding information of sociological relevance. The intention has been to equip you with the tools and tricks of the trade you need as a student, and also to provide you with some strategies you can use for lifelong learning. In that regard, the further reading and links at the end of the chapter provide a few final suggestions for enhancing your sociological imagination.

SOCIOLOGY SPOTLIGHT

24.1: Take a library tour

How well do you know your university library? Are you making the most effective use of it? While this chapter has covered a range of websites that can help you find information, one of the best places is still your university library. Not everything is accessible online, and much important information is still contained in books. Therefore, it is important that you familiarise yourself with all the resources your library offers, and learn how to use its electronic catalogue. If you missed the orientation tour at the start of the semester, you will often find self-help online tutorials on your library website, as well as short, printed guides in your library. If all else fails, do not hesitate to ask a librarian for help.

Summary of main points

▶ There is a vast amount of both good-quality and poor-quality information on the web. When making use of web-based information sources, ensure that you evaluate the credibility, reliability, and relevance of the information you intend to use.

▶ If you cannot resist the temptation to Google for information, then at least use Google Scholar, as it will provide you with better-quality hits.

▶ There are many sociology and social science websites available that provide access to high-quality weblinks and resources such as statistics, reports, conference papers, and refereed articles.

▶ It is important to make use of academic journals and learn how to search effectively for relevant articles.

▶ It is recommended that you bookmark the websites you found particularly helpful in this chapter. Alternatively, you can find the entire list of websites discussed here on the *Public Sociology* book website.

Further reading

On being a sociologist

Ballard, C., Gubbay, J. & Middleton, C. (eds) 1997, *The Student's Companion to Sociology*, Blackwell, Malden, MA. This edited book contains some interesting short chapters that cover personal accounts of people who have put their sociological degree to use in a variety of occupational fields, as well as reviews of key issues in sociology, and examples of applying sociological research and analysis to real-world issues.

Becker, H. 1998, *Tricks of the Trade: How to Think About Your Research While You're Doing It*, University of Chicago Press, Chicago, IL. Written in a conversational style, this is an enjoyable review of the research process from a famous sociologist.

Hamilton, P. & Thompson, K. (eds) 2002, *The Uses of Sociology*, Blackwell, Oxford. An introductory text that highlights the relevance and application of sociology to our lives.

Mills, C.W. 1959, *The Sociological Imagination*, Oxford University Press, New York. The appendix 'On Intellectual Craftsmanship' is still a good read, even if you do not agree with all of Mills' prescriptions.

Sociology dictionaries

Some university libraries may provide online access to a range of discipline-related dictionaries; if you are majoring in sociology, it is worth the expense of purchasing a hard copy of any one of the following:

Abercrombie, N., Hill, S. & Turner, B.S. 2006, *The Penguin Dictionary of Sociology*, 5th edn, Penguin, Melbourne.

Bruce, S. & Yearley, S. 2006, *The Sage Dictionary of Sociology*, Sage, London.

Jary, D. & Jary, J. 2006, *Collins Web-linked Dictionary of Sociology*, HarperCollins, Glasgow.

Scott, J. & Marshall, G. (eds) 2005, *A Dictionary of Sociology*, 3rd edn, Oxford University Press, Oxford.

Turner, B.S. 2006, *The Cambridge Dictionary of Sociology*, Cambridge University Press, Cambridge.

Contemporary Sociology

Contemporary Sociology is a journal almost entirely dedicated to book reviews. This can be especially helpful in terms of keeping abreast of the latest publications, and also in terms of finding out how certain books you may be consulting are considered in the professional literature. Each issue of the journal also invites a small number of contributors to debate key issues in the discipline and these debates can often be an insightful and lively read.

Advanced reading

The following books and articles represent a selective list of key resources that aim to stimulate your sociological imagination further.

Connell, R. 1997, 'Why is classical theory classical?', *American Journal of Sociology*, vol. 102, no. 6, pp. 1511–57.

——2007, *Southern Theory: The Global Dynamics of Knowledge in Social Science*, Allen & Unwin, Sydney.

Crook, S. 2003, 'Change, uncertainty and the future of sociology', *Journal of Sociology*, vol. 39, no. 1, pp. 7–14.

Flyvbjerg, B. 2001, *Making Social Science Matter: Why Social Inquiry Fails and How It Can Succeed Again*, Cambridge University Press, Oxford.

Fuller, S. 2006, *The New Sociological Imagination*, Sage, London.

Germov, J. & McGee, T.R. (eds) 2005, *Histories of Australian Sociology*, Melbourne University Press, Melbourne.

McAllister, I., Dowrick, S. & Hassan, R. (eds) 2003, *The Cambridge Handbook of Social Sciences in Australia*, Cambridge University Press, Cambridge.

Ritzer, G. (ed.) 2007, *Blackwell Encyclopedia of Sociology*, Blackwell, Malden, MA.

Saunders, P. & Walter, J. (eds) 2005, *Ideas and Influence: Social Science and Public Policy in Australia*, UNSW Press, Sydney.

Skrbis, Z. & Germov, J. 2004, 'The most influential books in Australian sociology (MIBAS), 1963–2003', *Journal of Sociology*, vol. 40, no. 3, pp. 283–303.

Denemark, D., Meagher, G., Wilson, S., Western, M. & Philips, T. (eds) 2007, *Australian Social Attitudes 2: Citizenship, Work and Aspirations*, UNSW Press, Sydney.

Wilson, S., Meagher, G., Gibson, R., Denemark, D. & Western, M. (eds) 2005, *Australian Social Attitudes: The First Report*, UNSW Press, Sydney.

Websites

- *Public Sociology*: <www.allenandunwin.com/publicsociology>. This book's website provides access to online case studies, YouTube clips, relevant weblinks, and further reading.
- How Stuff Works: <www.howstuffworks.com>. An entertaining site aimed at the general public that claims to provide clear and unbiased explanations of how literally 'everything' works (including genetics and all things electronic and mechanical, to various features of social life).
- Internet Public Library (IPL): <www.ipl.org>. The IPL is run as a global public service by the University of Michigan and provides high-quality resources to find, evaluate, and organise information.
- The Internet Tourbus: <www.internettourbus.com>. A free weekly web and email subscription news service that uses plain English to explain the latest web developments, highlighting interesting websites, tips on effective use of search engines, avoiding spam and computer viruses, and avoiding falling for internet myths.
- Refdesk.com: <www.refdesk.com>. One of the first and most useful indexes of credible web-based resources.
- Search Engine Watch: <http://searchenginewatch.com>. A useful site comparing the performance of various search engines and offering various tips on how to maximise their use.
- The Scout Report: <http://scout.wisc.edu/Reports/ScoutReport/Current>. Published weekly since 1994 on the web and via free email subscription, this report provides short reviews of key web resources and is a helpful way to keep on top of the ever-expanding web.

CHAPTER 25

Writing a sociology essay

John Germov

Getting great marks: Secrets revealed

Despite what some students may initially think, essays are not an attempt by academics to make university life unnecessarily difficult. The essay is a well-established format of communicating knowledge and understanding about a topic in a logical, credible, and persuasive way, within a given timeframe and word limit. That said, there is often very little time in university courses allocated to teaching effective essay-writing skills. While there is no single best way to write a high-quality essay, there are a number of rules that need to be followed. The secret to getting great marks for your essays is to learn the rules of the essay-writing game and adopt a systematic approach—there is no magical way to 'beat the system' by avoiding the necessary hard work. That said, this chapter provides some handy tips on how to plan, research, write, and reference a sociology essay, all of which should save you time and improve your performance.

The essay basics: Expectations and structure

Essay expectations

When writing a university-level sociology essay, you should do the following:

- Use formal expression and avoid emotive phrases such as slang and clichés.
- Read widely so as to be able critically to review the field of sociological literature on a topic.
- Critically analyse a topic by evaluating the strengths and weaknesses of various viewpoints. It is insufficient only to provide descriptive information; you also need to discuss various explanations/theories relevant to the topic.
- Develop a logical argument (also known as your thesis) and use supporting evidence from your reading.
- In making use of supporting evidence, ensure that you draw on authoritative and verifiable sources and, unless you are requested to do so, avoid anecdotal, hypothetical, and personal examples.
- Acknowledge your sources of information by using an accepted system of referencing (lecturers will often provide you with their preferred format). This way you avoid plagiarism (theft of another author's work by claiming it as your own) and you allow readers (including markers) to confirm and follow up on the material you present.

Essay structure

The basic structure of an essay involves the following five parts:

1. The essay *cover sheet*. You may be directed to use a standard cover sheet or include your own with the following information: your name and student number, the subject or course to which your essay applies, your lecturer or tutor (and tutorial time), the essay topic, the due date, and the total number of pages of the essay.

2. The *introduction*. You should clearly state in one paragraph what your essay will cover, concisely state the argument (or thesis) you intend to make, and briefly define any key terms where necessary. In some cases, terms or concepts are contested in the literature, so you may need to devote a part of the body of your essay to discussing definitional disputes.

3. The *body* of your essay. This is a series of logically connected paragraphs where you describe and analyse material relevant to the topic (providing supporting evidence and explanations based on your reading of the literature). Unless otherwise stated, the use of sub-headings in essays is optional. If you do use them, be careful to maintain a logical flow in your essay content from one section to the next.

4. The *conclusion*. A short summary, usually in one paragraph, of the evidence and argument presented throughout the essay. It should only be a summary of what has already been stated and should never include new information.

5. The *reference list*. Sometimes referred to as a bibliography, this is an alphabetical list (by author surname) of all the information sources cited in your essay.

The skills you need

University-level essays, particularly in sociology, require the following skills:

- *Independent thought.* There is often no right answer to a topic and no one will tell you exactly what to write; the essay is a means by which you show how persuasively you can argue your point of view. You do this by drawing on the existing literature on the topic, showing that you can find, comprehend, analyse, and synthesise the appropriate information to answer the question.

- *Library research skills.* You need the ability to find and summarise relevant information sources.

- *Referencing skills.* Use an accepted format for referencing your essay content and compiling a reference list.

- *Professionalism.* It is expected that you will follow any directions (such as word targets and preferred presentation and referencing formats) set by your lecturer, including your ability to produce essays with grammatical sentences and correct spelling, as well as show your capacity to develop time-management skills and work to deadlines so that you submit your essay by the due date.

The time it takes

Essay writing is a skill that gets better and easier with practice, and you should allow yourself sufficient time to produce at least three drafts of any essay before submission. In terms of hours spent on an essay, you should expect a bare minimum of twenty hours for a first-year essay of around 1500 words. An essay likely to receive a high grade would likely reflect double that amount of time. Many students are shocked when they are told this because it highlights just how much time they need to allow before the due date. In short, avoid leaving your essay to the last minute. Next time you write an essay, keep a log of the hours you spend interpreting the topic, doing your library research, taking notes, and writing drafts, and you will be surprised how the hours accumulate. Make sure to proofread your final draft and avoid relying on your computer spell-checker (as this will not pick up correctly spelt words used incorrectly, poor referencing, or poor sentence structure and a lack of logical flow of your essay content).

Interpreting essay topics

Avoid the temptation to Google

When interpreting an essay topic by identifying key words, it is tempting to Google, but you will end up wasting a lot of time this way by getting hundreds of dubious hits of variable quality and relevance. The first thing you need to do is ensure that you understand what the topic is about by doing some preliminary reading. The best places to start are:

- this textbook and your lecture notes
- additional readings or references provided by your lecturer (such as in the course guide)
- other introductory sociological texts found in the library; check their contents and index pages to see whether they have relevant content (start with those recommended at the end of Chapter 1 of this book), and
- a sociological dictionary (a helpful source of definitions, related concepts, authors, and sometimes references).

Such preliminary reading allows you to develop a basic understanding of the topic by identifying key authors, concepts, debates, and relevant sociological theories. You can then use library databases and the web to find more detailed and specific sources of information (such as journal articles and government reports). If you must Google, then at least use Google Scholar (as discussed in Chapter 24), which will give you higher-quality hits (also see Sociology Spotlight 25.1 for a warning about Wikipedia).

25.1: Beware of Wikipedia

If you do a web search on sociological topics, you will often find that on the first page of hits there will be an entry from Wikipedia, the free online encyclopaedia (see <http://en.wikipedia.org/wiki/Main_Page>). Wikipedia began in 2001 and has become a fascinating example of web culture, where users can develop and continually edit any entry in the encyclopaedia. This has allowed it to grow exponentially, and it now covers almost every subject imaginable, from the full gamut of academic disciplines to pop culture references.

Wikipedia can be a good launching point for finding quick information and further weblinks about a topic, but since anyone can put anything up, it relies on a community of scholars to check on the quality and validity of its entries. While many academics contribute to this communal project of democratising knowledge, it can also present biased and sometimes fraudulent information. For example, the initial Wikipedia entry for the term 'public sociology' was primarily authored by one of its most ardent critics. Furthermore, there have been some well-publicised examples of users creating entries about made-up historical figures and events. Thus you must exercise caution when using it and do not reference it in your essays because it is not a trusted academic source of information. Wikipedia itself is very open about its inability to guarantee the quality of information on its website. On its 'General disclaimer' page (see <http://en.wikipedia.org/wiki/Wikipedia:General_disclaimer>), it states:

> Please be advised that nothing found here has necessarily been reviewed by people with the expertise required to provide you with complete, accurate or reliable information . . . Wikipedia cannot guarantee the validity of the information found here.

In summary, information found on Wikipedia is not peer-reviewed and should be treated with great caution. It can be used as a starting point for researching a topic, but you must subsequently verify any information found on Wikipedia through academic sources.

Brainstorming and mind-mapping

After doing some preliminary reading, you should begin to map out an essay plan. By putting your thoughts on paper, you will identify what your essay entails and what information you need to find. While there are a number of ways to draft an essay plan, mind-mapping can be a useful and quick place to begin (see Figure 25.1).

Begin your mind-map by placing your essay topic in the centre of a blank page and then brainstorm everything you know about the topic to date, such as key concepts, authors, facts, and theories, circling and connecting them as appropriate. Once you have something on paper, you can start to organise the points you have noted into some order, perhaps by numbering them or, alternatively, listing them in sequential order. Your plan and order of material are likely to change as you do further research and reading; however, brainstorming and mind-mapping in this way can fill up an empty page fairly quickly (and thus overcome writer's block) and can help you achieve some clarity about what you need to do to complete the essay.

Figure 25.1: A basic essay mind-map

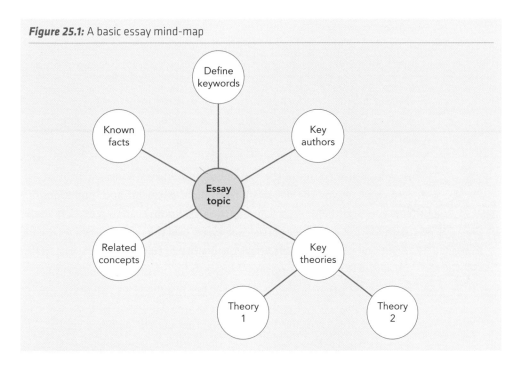

What is academic writing?

Students are often told they need to write in an academic way, but what exactly does this mean? Academic writing aims to be precise and thus uses formal expression rather than slang, clichés, or emotive expression. This involves a clear statement of the author's viewpoint (your argument), critical analysis of the relevant literature on a topic, use of supporting evidence based on reliable and verifiable information sources, and the proper acknowledgment of those sources using an accepted referencing system. This means that, unless otherwise specified, you should avoid using anecdotes, examples drawn from personal experience or the mass media, and hypothetical cases when writing an academic essay. In terms of judging whether your information sources are reliable, ask yourself the following questions:

- Is the material referenced?
- Has the material been peer-reviewed, such as in an academic journal or through a recognised book publisher?
- Is the source authoritative (such as a government report)?
- Has supporting evidence been cited to support the author's argument?

Reviewing the sociological literature

While not all of the sources of information you find will be sociological in origin—for example, reports produced by government and non-government agencies—the majority of your information should come from sociological sources (such as sociology books and journal articles). Once you have identified the relevant sociological literature for your essay topic, you need to review it by considering the following issues and questions:

- *The date and place of publication.* Determine that the information you are seeking is current (if required) and also relevant to the country about which you may be writing.
- *The academic discipline base of the information.* Where relevant, it is best to stick to sociological material as the basis of your academic sources.
- *Key concepts, theories, and methodology.* Consider the benefits and limitations of any key concepts and theories used and, if research findings are reported, note the research methods, the sample of participants used, and the date the data were collected— might any of these factors affect the quality or relevance of the material?
- *The author's argument or perspective.* The introduction and conclusion to an article, book, or report will often convey the key argument or perspective of the author.
- *Evaluate the strengths and weaknesses of your material.* Consider whether the evidence and argument are persuasive by comparing them to the wider sociological literature. In doing this, ask yourself: Could alternative conclusions be drawn? Could the author have approached the topic from another perspective? Are some issues neglected? What assumptions does the author make? What do other authors in the field say? Does the author have a vested interest in presenting a particular viewpoint (such as reports produced by government, non-government, and business organisations)?

Making your argument or thesis

It is not uncommon for students to ask, 'What about my opinion?' in the process of writing their essays. Your opinion is actually your preferred explanation or answer to an essay topic, which is sometimes called your argument or thesis. Therefore, the argument you present in your essay is your *considered* opinion about a topic, supported by detailed evidence and references.

25.2: Essays for sale and plagiarism-detection software

Universities are increasingly making use of plagiarism-detection software that not only compares essays among all students in a class, but also compares them with essays submitted in previous years and from other universities. This can often include essays that are bought from online essay cheat sites. The moral of the story is not to be tempted by shortcuts and avoid purchasing potentially dodgy essays that often have little relevance because they are written by students in other countries. The chance is that you will be caught.

SOCIOLOGY SPOTLIGHT

How to reference

Why reference?

When you use information from sources such as books, journal articles, and government and non-government reports, you are required to reference the sources of your information. You reference material for three basic reasons:

1. to acknowledge where you obtained information and avoid plagiarism (theft of other authors' work by claiming it as your own)
2. to add credibility to your writing by showing the source of the supporting evidence cited in your essay, and
3. to allow essay markers and readers in general to check your information sources.

You must always provide a reference for direct quotes (material used word for word from another author). Direct quotes should be kept to no more than 10 per cent of the word target because you are assessed on your understanding of material, rather than your ability to copy slabs of information correctly. Only use direct quotes as supporting evidence for a particular point you wish to make or because the quote is considered to be a significant one in the field. If you do use a direct quote, use quotation marks, ensure that you use the exact wording and spelling of the original source, and include page number/s with the in-text reference. For direct quotes that are 30 words or longer, drop the quotation marks and instead indent the quote from both the left and right margins of your essay so that it clearly stands out as a direct quote.

The vast amount of referenced information in your essay will be from information you have paraphrased (material that you put into your own words but that is derived from another source, such as research findings, statistics, concepts, and theories). This effectively means that most paragraphs in your essay will have at least one reference.

Be systematic in recording bibliographic details

When you make notes from your information sources, ensure that you record the bibliographic details every time, such as the author/s, date of publication, title, page numbers consulted, publisher, and place of publication. For example, the bibliographic information for this chapter would be:

Germov, J. 2011, 'Writing a sociology essay', in J. Germov & M. Poole (eds), *Public Sociology: An introduction to Australian Society*, 2nd edn, Allen & Unwin, Sydney, pp. 494–508.

This information is needed to compile your essay reference list. Recording it as you make your notes will save you time. When note-taking, be careful to designate clearly where you have written something 'word for word' from the source by placing it in quotation marks, otherwise you may forget to do this when using your notes to write the first essay draft.

Avoid referencing lecture notes in your essay

Given that lecture notes are generally not publicly available and that it is almost impossible to verify that your notes are accurate, you should not reference lecture notes in an essay. Furthermore, part of your essay assessment is based on your ability to conduct effective research on your own, rather than just regurgitate lecture notes in essay form. If you want to use information that was given in a lecture, you will need to find the original source yourself. For the same reasons, you should avoid referencing your course readings.

How to use the Harvard in-text referencing system

There are many types of referencing systems. The preferred method in sociology and the social sciences generally is known as the Harvard in-text referencing system. The Harvard system is very similar to the APA system used by psychology, though it tends to be less prescriptive than the APA format. The Harvard system includes references in the text of the essay—for example, (Germov & Poole 2010, p. 5); this reference tells the reader that the sentence or paragraph came from a source written by Germov and Poole (surnames only) published in 2010 and found on page 5 (this book, in fact). All the other bibliographic details such as the title, publisher, and place of publication appear in a reference list at the end of the essay. Here are a few examples of what in-text references can look like:

- Poole (2007, p. 106) states that . . .
  Here the author's name is part of the sentence. Note the space between the author and the bracket. You may see some variations such as: (2007: 106) or (2007, 106)—choose one and be consistent.
- It can be argued that . . . (Poole 2007, pp. 10–16).
  If the author is not mentioned in the sentence, then the full reference comes at the end, all in brackets, with the full stop after the bracket.
- A number of authors argue that . . . (Kobayashi Maru 2010; Klatuu 2007; Smith & Jones 2000).
  Here a series of sources are referenced at the end of a sentence, with each reference separated by a semi-colon.

When one author quotes another—and you want to use the same direct quote

When one author quotes another and you want to use the same direct quote, there is a simple rule to follow. For example, Poole is the author of the book you are using and she has used a direct quote from Smith, which you also want to use. The rule to follow is always to reference where you got the information—that is, reference Poole. The in-text reference would look as follows:

Smith argues that 'all behaviour has social origins' (cited in Poole 2005, p. 10).

How to reference a website

In the text of your essay, you reference web sources as you would any other information source, noting the author and date. If no author is given, then the organisation that produced the website or the actual title of the website can be used instead. Where the date of web material is unclear (it often appears at the bottom of a web page), state that is has no date (n.d.) and include the date (day, month, and year) that you accessed the website in your reference list (because web material is liable to change) as is customary. With in-text references, do not include the URL (web address) as this is included in the details you provide in your reference list at the end of the essay. Take, for example, the following sentence:

> An essay cheat site says it is okay to pay for an essay and submit it as my own (Essays Anonymous n.d.).

Referencing online journals

For journal articles accessed via websites, there is seldom need to reference them differently from their hard-copy versions if the website provides a pdf version of the article (which by definition is exactly the same as the original hard copy version). The only difference here is how you accessed the journal, and therefore as long as it is also available in hard copy you do not need to provide any web-related details in your reference. Some journals, such as *Sociological Research Online*, only publish in an online format. In this case, while your in-text reference will remain the same (author and year), your reference list entry will need to include the URL and the date you accessed the website. For example:

> Gofton, L. & Haimes, E. 1999, 'Necessary evils? Opening up closings in sociology and biotechnology', *Sociological Research Online*, vol. 4, no. 3, <www.socresonline.org.uk/socresonline/4/3/gofton.html> (accessed 25 April 2007).

How to reference a source without an author

Some sources of information do not have clearly identified authors, particularly reports produced by government and non-government sources. In such cases, it is acceptable to use the publisher of the information (the organisation or department) as the author for the purposes of in-text referencing. For example:

> The report notes that . . . (Department of Health and Ageing 2006)
> The report of the Australian Institute of Health and Welfare (2006) suggests . . .

How to reference newspapers and films

In-text citation of newspapers can be referenced in the same way as a journal article if an author can be identified—that is, cite the author and year of publication (with the reference listed by author surname in the reference list). Where there is no author, it is acceptable to include the title of the newspaper and the year, such as:

... (*The Australian* 2007).

Films and documentaries can be referenced by using their title and the year of production. For example:

... (*Brokeback Mountain* 2005).

The benefits of using referencing software

If you study courses from a number of different academic disciplines, you have no doubt been frustrated by the requirement to reference your material in a different format each time. There are a number of software packages available to help, and it is worth checking with your university whether it provides them free of charge or at a subsidised price. In a nutshell, software such as EndNote and Refman allows you to enter all the bibliographic information of the references you use into a database that can then format your in-text references and reference list automatically to the style required. Beware that these types of software do have bugs and you will still need to make sure your referencing is correct.

Formatting your reference list

Every essay requires a reference list. It includes the full bibliographic details of the information sources referenced in your essay. Only include the actual sources that you referenced in your essay; it is unnecessary to include sources you consulted but did not end up using. A reference list should be formatted consistently and organised in alphabetical order by author surname. See Sociology Spotlight 25.3 for a reference-list template that provides examples of how to list authored books, edited books, journal articles, government reports, films and documentaries, and websites.

25.3: A reference list template

For authored books, provide:

▶ all author surnames and initials of first names

▶ date of publication

▶ book title (italicised or underlined)

▶ edition (where relevant)

- publisher

- place of publication

- Example: Germov, J. 2011, *Get Great Marks for Your Essays, Reports, and Presentations*, 3rd edn, Allen & Unwin, Sydney.

For a chapter in an edited book, provide:

- all author surnames and initials of first names

- date of publication of the book in which the chapter is contained

- chapter title in inverted commas

- initials and surnames of editors, including the abbreviation (ed. or eds)

- book title (italicised or underlined)

- edition (where relevant)

- publisher

- place of publication

- first and last page numbers of the chapter

- Example: Germov, J. & Poole, M. 2011, 'The sociological gaze: Linking private lives to public issues', in J. Germov & M. Poole (eds), *Public Sociology: An Introduction to Australian Society*, 2nd edn, Allen & Unwin, Sydney, pp. 2–18.

For a journal article, provide:

- author surnames and initials of first names

- date of publication of the journal in which the article is contained

- article title in inverted commas

- journal title (italicised or underlined)

- volume and issue numbers (where relevant)

- first and last page numbers of the article

- Example: Skrbis, Z. & Germov, J. 2004, 'The most influential books in Australian sociology, 1963–2003', *Journal of Sociology*, vol. 40, no. 3, pp. 283–302.

For an online-only journal article, provide:

- same as above, but also include the web address of the online journal (URL) and the date you accessed the website

▶ Example: Gofton, L. & Haimes, E. 1999, 'Necessary evils? Opening up closings in sociology and biotechnology', *Sociological Research Online*, vol. 4, no. 3, <www.socresonline.org.uk/socresonline/4/3/gofton.html> (accessed 25 April 2007).

For a web source, provide:

▶ all author surnames and initials of first names where available (sometimes the author is an organisation)

▶ date of publication or last revision/modification (often included at the bottom of a website)

▶ title of the publication and/or particular section of a website (italicised or underlined)

▶ title of the website and the web address (URL)

▶ date you accessed the website (because web information is often subject to change)

▶ Example: Commonwealth of Australia 2002, *Australian Social Trends*, Australian Bureau of Statistics (ABS) <www.abs.gov.au> (accessed 20 January 2007).

For a source without authors (use the publisher where possible):

▶ Australian Institute of Health and Welfare (AIHW) 2008, *Australia's Health*, 11th edn, AIHW, Canberra.

For a newspaper article with and without author:

▶ Tolduso, I. 2007, 'Plagiarism is rife in universities', *The Australian*, 25 April, p. 40.

▶ *The Australian* 2007, 'Plagiarism is rife in universities', 25 April, p. 40.

For a film/documentary:

▶ *Brokeback Mountain*, 2005, motion picture, directed by A. Lee, Paramount Pictures.

Concluding comments: When to ask for help

Sometimes, despite your best-laid plans, you may find yourself confused about how to approach an essay topic or about how to deal with some of the essay content. In such cases, it is always best to ask for help from your tutor or lecturer. Never arrive with a blank page expecting your lecturer to provide a join-the-dots template for how you should do your essay. Always ensure that you have done your preliminary reading and have attempted an essay plan before seeking academic advice. If you are unsure about the standard of work required, ask your tutor whether there are any sample essays from previous years that you may be able to view. Alternatively, ask whether she or he is willing to provide feedback on a detailed essay plan.

Essay writing gets better with practice and feedback. So make sure to collect your marked essays so that you can see where you did well and what still needs improvement. If it is unclear how you could improve your essay, make an appointment with your tutor and bring your essay along so you can both discuss it. If you find that your essay writing is not improving as you would like, consider making use of university support services. Most universities now provide free academic skills workshops and one-on-one help, along with a host of online support materials and guides.

Summary of main points: An essay checklist

- ▶ Have you followed any format requirements or specific guidelines given by your lecturer?
- ▶ Does your introduction define key terms and address what you will cover and argue in the essay?
- ▶ Have you provided sufficient supporting evidence and referenced your essay content in the preferred format?
- ▶ Does your conclusion summarise your content and argument and, where relevant, does it answer the question?
- ▶ Have you proofread your essay?
- ▶ Have you attached a cover sheet?
- ▶ Have you included your essay reference list, and is it in the preferred and consistent format? Do all the sources cited in the essay appear in the reference list?
- ▶ Have you kept a back-up copy of your essay?

SOCIOLOGICAL **REFLECTION**

25.1 Doing better next time

After reading this chapter, and possibly after receiving your first marked essay, reflect on what advice you could apply to your essay writing to improve the planning, writing, and referencing process for next time.

Further reading

Study aids

Germov, J. 2011, *Get Great Marks for Your Essays, Reports, and Presentations*, 3rd edn, Allen & Unwin, Sydney. This book expands on the advice given in this chapter and includes a host of extra practical tips on every aspect of the essay writing process.

Williams, L. & Germov, J. 2001, *Surviving First Year Uni*, Allen & Unwin, Sydney. For students who would like further study skills advice on topics such as time management, effective note-taking, how to do oral presentations, and pass exams, and generally survive their first year of university study unscathed.

Style manual

Snooks & Co. 2002, *Style Manual for Authors, Editors and Printers*, 6th edn, John Wiley & Sons, Brisbane. The definitive Australian reference book, used particularly by government and non-government agencies.

Websites

- InfoSkills: <www.newcastle.edu.au/service/library/tutorials/infoskills>. A very helpful online module that covers effective techniques for finding and evaluating information.
- Online information search tutorials (Monash University): <www.lib.monash. edu.au/vl/howind.htm>. Many universities have established helpful online tutorials, such as this one, for students.
- Online how-to-reference guide by Monash University: <www.lib.monash.edu.au/ tutorials/citing>; Online how-to-reference guide by the University of Newcastle: <www.newcastle.edu.au/service/library/guides/referencing.html>. The two sites above provide online tutorials and links to a variety of referencing formats including the Harvard, APA, and Vancouver systems.
- Surviving First Year Uni: Passing Exams: <www.newcastle.edu.au/teaching-and-learning/surviving-first-year-exams>. An online module covering various aspects of preparing and doing exams, including essay-based exams.

Glossary

aestheticisation The process of depicting or representing something in an artistic manner, sometimes to the point of glorifying and exalting beauty above all other considerations.

agency The ability of people, individually and collectively, to influence their own lives and the society in which they live.

alienation A term used by Marx to denote the estrangement of workers from the products of their labour and the loss of control felt by workers under *capitalism*.

alternative religions Non-mainstream, new religious movements, such as Scientology or Wicca.

anomie A concept used by Durkheim for a societal condition in which individuals feel aimless and lack guidance in social norms. Anomie means to be without laws or norms.

assimilation An idea that diverse groups of people need to adapt to, and be absorbed by, the dominant culture.

atheoretical research Research that does not use a theoretical framework as the starting point for the research.

biobunk A term used by Tavris to criticise the biological reductionism inherent in many of the arguments by sociobiologists and evolutionary psychologists.

biological determinism A belief that individual and group behaviours are the inevitable result of biology.

biomedical model of health Explanation of health in terms of physical changes to the individual body.

black armband history First used by historian Geoffrey Blainey to describe historical accounts highlighting the sadness and shame of Australian history.

blackballing Refers to a method of voting on applicants for club membership. Eligible members drop either a white ball (which indicates support of the applicant) or a black ball (opposition to the applicant) into a container. If the applicant receives more than a set number or proportion of black balls, the application for membership is rejected.

blended families Families consisting of a couple with one or more children in which at least one child is the biological offspring of the couple, with one or more the step-children of either parent.

bureaucratisation of medicine The increasing influence of state bureaucracies on medical practice.

capitalism An economic system based on the private ownership of natural resources and the means of production, in which commodities are sold for a profit.

case study Case study research focuses on one person or group of people as the object of study. The purpose is to gain an in-depth understanding of the concepts under investigation.

citizenship rights A collection of rights and obligations that determine legal identity and membership of a state, and function to control access to scarce resources.

civil rights These form a civil component of modern citizenship, and include liberty of the person, freedom of speech, thought, and faith, the right to own property and to conclude valid contracts, and the right to justice—all safeguarded by independent courts of justice.

class consciousness A subjective perception of a group of people that they belong to a similar social class. For Marx, the key element for a proletarian revolution was the development of class consciousness among workers by their recognition of common interests.

class decomposition According to Ralf Gustav Dahrendorf, the process of declining social formation whereby *social classes* are fragmented and their boundaries weaken.

class/social class A central but contested term in sociology that refers to a position in a system of structured inequality based on the unequal distribution of wealth, power, and status.

collective conscience A term used by Durkheim to refer to the norms and values held by a group or a society.

colonisation/colonialism When a nation takes and maintains power over a territory that is outside its boundaries, based on a belief of superiority over those being colonised. See also *imperialism*.

colour bar A colour bar exists when people are not permitted to do something because of the colour of their skin.

commodification A tendency for goods and services to be treated primarily as things that are bought and sold on the market.

commodified self Self-identity that is largely shaped and understood through consumption practices: 'I am what I consume.'

commodity In *Marxist* analysis, refers to a consumer object that has been purchased through economic exchange.

communism A utopian vision of society based on communal ownership of resources, cooperation, and altruism to the extent that social inequality and the state no longer exist. Sometimes used interchangeably with *socialism* to refer to societies ruled by a communist party.

community An imprecise term carrying a lot of meanings, all of which in some way refer to positive social relations. Most often used to describe a group of people who live in a geographic area, interact with each other, and share some common interests, if only those related to living space.

competing professionalisation Trend of groups traditionally subordinate to medicine to adopt traits associated with a profession.

compulsory heterosexuality The dominant cultural norm for sexual orientation that is said to dominate all social institutions, making other sexual orientations deviant. Also known as heterosexism.

conservatism A political philosophy that supports traditional values, cultural homogeneity, social hierarchies, and the status quo.

consumer culture Refers to a society where consumption is the dominant mode of social activity and organisation, to the extent that we understand ourselves and others mainly as consumers of particular things.

consumerism The cultural drive to procure more and more consumer items, and define oneself in terms of one's possessions.

convergence The process by which previously distinct industries, including media and information and communication technologies (ICTs), come together.

cults Informal and transient groups, usually based on highly unorthodox religious beliefs and practices, often involving devotion to a charismatic leader.

cultural capital A term to indicate cultural competencies, such as the taste preferences and lifestyle, that differentiate one social class from another and are transmitted through the generations and via the education system.

cultural turn Refers to the way cultural objects and cultural life are now seen as central to understanding society, since around the 1960s.

culture The values, assumptions, and beliefs shared by a group of people that influence the behaviour of group members.

decode The ways in which people are able to read or work out the myths and meanings built into objects.

deconstruction An approach that aims to expose the multiple and contradictory interpretations of meaning contained within any text.

deductive research Research that begins with hypotheses based on a theoretical framework and previous empirical literature. The aim of the research process is to test the hypotheses and interpret the research findings in the context of the theory and literature on which the hypotheses were based.

dependency theory The argument developed by *neo-Marxists* that developing (periphery, Southern) societies are locked through trade links in exploitative dependency relations with developed (core, Northern) societies.

deprofessionalisation A narrowing of the knowledge and authority gap between doctors and patients.

detraditionalisation From the 1970s on, old traditions, loyalties, and rituals progressively lost their meanings. People no longer define themselves in traditional terms in the family or in the community. While this is a good thing in some ways, it carries the danger that people can become more confused about their identity, and more isolated, than in previous eras.

deviance Behaviours or activities that violate social expectations about what is normal.

diaspora A religiously and/or ethnically defined group of people dispersed from their country of origin. The dispersion is often precipitated by political violence.

dictation test An integral part of the Australian *Immigration Restriction Act 1901* that authorised an immigration officer to administer a dictation test in any European language to a potential immigrant deemed undesirable. It was applied primarily to prevent the immigration of non-white migrants.

discursive formation Something that is socially constructed through ways of thinking, talking, and acting (for example, a 'nation').

dispositions The tendency to act in particular ways associated with a person's *habitus*. Thus people from similar backgrounds often profess similar attitudes and behave in comparable ways.

DNA (deoxyribonucleic acid) The molecule within cells that transmits hereditary information.

domestic division of labour Refers to the gendered division of household work and child-rearing.

dramaturgical analysis/dramaturgy The term used by Goffman to describe how people take on social roles, just as actors do in the theatre.

dysfunction An institution is dysfunctional when one of its activities impedes the workings of another institution.

economic capital Any financial asset, including raw materials, equipment, and workspace, that can be used to generate income and wealth.

economic rationalism Describes a political philosophy based on small-government and market-oriented policies, such as deregulation, privatisation, reduced government spending, and lower taxation. Used interchangeably with *neo-liberalism.*

elites Powerful minorities, such as incumbents of top positions in the state, major corporations, key pressure groups, and social movements, capable of influencing social outcomes in a systematic and significant way. Elites are typically contrasted with the masses.

emotional dissonance The strain felt by people between the emotions they really feel and those they are supposed to feel.

emotional labour A term used by Hochschild to describe the commodification of feelings experienced by workers in personal service occupations and the use of feelings by employees as part of their paid work (such as nurses caring for patients).

empirical Empirical knowledge is derived from, and can be tested by, the gathering of data or evidence.

encode The ways in which particular cultural myths and meanings are built into objects.

Enlightenment A period in European history that lasted from the seventeenth century to the eighteenth century, also known as the Age of Reason. Enlightenment thinkers advocated the power of reason over the authority of the church to reach a true understanding of nature and society.

essentialism/essential/essentialised A perspective that reduces the complex nature of individual identities and social phenomena to underlying essences or fixed characteristics. These may be innate biological characteristics or 'authentic' cultural practices.

ethnocentric Viewing others from one's own cultural perspective. Implied is a sense of cultural superiority based on an inability to understand or accept the practices and beliefs of other cultures.

ethnography/ethnographic A research method based on the direct observation of the social interaction and culture of a particular social group, involving detailed description and evaluation of behaviours, activities, and events.

ethno-methodology Coined by Garfinkel to refer to the methods people use to describe and understand their everyday life.

eugenics A term coined in 1883 by Francis Galton, who applied the principles of agricultural breeding to humans based on the unproven assumption that selective breeding could improve the intellectual, physical, and cultural traits of a population.

exploitation A term that is often used generally to mean the misuse of power by one group over another. Marx used the term specifically to refer to the appropriation of surplus value or profits by capitalists.

expressive role A term used by Parsons to describe the nurturing and domestic roles of women within the *nuclear family*.

false consciousness A *Marxist* term referring to beliefs that reinforce and reproduce class inequality, usually by the working class mistakenly supporting or adopting the interests of the upper class.

family wage A concept that arose with industrialisation, in which men began to demand wages to support their families. The Harvester Judgment of 1907 established this in Australia.

feminisation of medicine Trend for the medicinal profession to include an increasing proportion of women.

feminism/feminist A broad social and political movement based on a belief in equality of the sexes and the removal of all forms of discrimination against women. A feminist is one who makes use of, and may act upon, a body of theory that seeks to explain the subordinate position of women in society.

fetishisation In everyday (rather than *Marxist*) terms, this means to have a strong, harmful obsession with a particular thing, or consumer object.

field This refers to an area of social activity, for example sport, in which people's dispositions predispose them to construct characteristic social actions that reflect their *habitus*.

figurational sociology Established by Elias, this approach focuses on long-term processes affecting the networks between interdependent groups of people.

Frankfurt School The Frankfurt School of Social Research was founded in 1923 as a centre for socialist research. The leading researchers emigrated to the United States with the rise of Hitler in Nazi Germany. It is closely associated with critical theory, a strand of *Marxism*.

functionalism A theoretical perspective in sociology in which society is seen as consisting of many complex and interdependent parts that contribute to consensus and social stability. Prominent theorists include Durkheim, Merton, and Parsons.

gender Refers to the socially constructed categories of feminine and masculine (the cultural values that dictate how women and men should behave), as opposed to the categories of biological *sex* (female or male).

gender attribution The taken-for-granted attribution of maleness or femaleness based on physical appearance and outward behaviours.

gender order The way in which institutional structures (known as gender regimes) and individual identities intersect to produce the social arrangements that mean one gender can dominate another, politically, socially, and economically.

generalised Other Occurs in the final stage of the development of *self* when a child can take on and understand the roles and attitudes of others.

globalisation The increased interconnectedness of the cultural, economic, and political aspects of social life; intensified circulation of capital, goods, information, and people across national boundaries; and increased interdependence of countries and regions of the world.

globalising trends Tendencies in *globalisation* processes. They involve a quantum leap in cross-national interdependencies caused by the intensified circulation of money (capital), goods and services (products), ideas and symbols (information), and people (labour).

globoenthusiasts Those who see *globalisation* as a socially benign process.

globosceptics Those who are critical of *globalisation* because they see it as socially divisive.

governmentality The control and regulation of people through practices and knowledges developed within the human sciences and applied to different social institutions, such as schools and prisons.

gross domestic product (GDP) The market value of all goods and services that have been sold during a year.

habitus Refers to socially learnt dispositions or taken-for-granted sets of orientations, skills, and ways of acting that shape behaviour. People are the product and creators of their habitus.

hedonism A devotion to pleasure and happiness as a way of life; in the context of consumption, a hedonistic life can be pursued through consumption.

hegemonic masculinity Connell's term for the dominant form of heterosexual masculinity in Western society that is always constructed against various forms of subordinated masculinities.

hegemony The operation of one powerful group over others, such that the consensus of the subordinated groups is not achieved by physical force, but rather by convincing people it is in their interests to agree with and follow the dominant group's ideas.

hidden curriculum Attitudes, values, and behaviour learnt in school that are not part of the formal curriculum.

high culture The cultural products and practices (such as classical music, poetry, opera, ballet, or abstract art) associated with the educated and relatively wealthy elite of society.

high-strain jobs Jobs where demands are high, but the degree of control is low (for example, assembly-line work).

historical materialism A view of society, developed by Marx, which asserts that material conditions of a particular era (ways in which people supply themselves with food, shelter, and clothing) provide the basis for all social arrangements.

hybridity Where two or more cultural forms are combined to form something new that has not existed before—a mutual grafting that creates an original product.

ideal type A concept originally devised by Weber to refer to the abstract or pure features of any social phenomenon.

imperialism A term originally used to describe the political aspirations of Napoleon III of France, and now generally used to describe the domination of developed countries over the developing world. See also *colonialism*.

impression management A concept used by Goffman to describe individuals' presentation of self as they try to create a specific impression in their interactions with others.

individualisation A trend towards the primacy of individual choice, freedom, and self-responsibility.

inductive research Starting with an observation about the social world, this approach then compares this observation with other observations, and eventually leads to the generation of a theory.

Industrial Revolution Beginning in England in the late eighteenth century, the Industrial Revolution introduced major changes to work processes and everyday life that resulted in social and political transformations in society. Agrarian economies and lifestyles gave way to a wage-labour system, the separation of home from work, and the urbanisation of the population.

information society A view that information and its uses have produced a new kind of knowledge-intensive society.

instrumental role A term used by Parsons to refer to the role of fathers within families. Their task within the *nuclear family* was to be the primary breadwinner and to mediate between the family and the outside world. See also *expressive role*.

intermarriage Marriage across ethnic or religious boundaries.

interpretivism A view in sociology that understanding social phenomena cannot be achieved by emulating the natural sciences, but instead requires a focus on the interpretation of people's meanings, reasons, and actions.

intertextuality A term used to describe when one text (written or visual) references or interacts with another text; while still existing in its own right, it also exists in relationship to all other texts. The term is also used to recognise the expectations an audience brings to interpreting a text.

interviews (structured and unstructured) Interviews vary from structured to unstructured. More structured interviews tend to be associated with quantitative research, whereas unstructured interviews are more commonly associated with qualitative research.

just-in-time (JIT) A system of managing production so that goods are produced as needed to meet market demand by keeping only a minimal amount of stock warehoused.

kinesiology A North-American term for what is usually referred to in Australia as 'human movement studies'.

late modernity (or high modernity) A period reached towards the end of the twentieth century that refers to the advanced state of industrialisation and capitalism.

latent functions Functions that may be hidden. See also *manifest functions*.

liberal feminism Liberal feminism maintains that women should have the same citizenship rights as men and focuses on equal rights and anti-discrimination.

liberalism An ideology that prioritises the interests of individuals and their freedom in the marketplace.

life chances A term associated with the work of Weber to refer to different opportunities and differential access to resources, including education, wealth, housing, and health.

liquid modernity A term coined by Zygmunt Bauman to refer to the constantly changing nature of social conditions in contemporary society so that individuals live with uncertainty and flux, undermining the formation of routines and habits to guide actions and beliefs.

manifest functions Functions that are obvious and purposeful. See also *latent functions*.

Marxist/socialist feminism Draws on the work of Marx and Engels in order to explain women's inequality, focusing on unpaid labour in the home, wage differentials between women and men, and barriers to women in employment. Since the 1980s, dual systems theory has developed, which argues the necessity to articulate Marxist class theory with *radical feminist* theories of *patriarchy*.

Marxists/Marxism Those who subscribe to Marx's social theory that changes in human activity—for example, labour—are determined by economic and material factors, such as technology, and *class* conflict over material interests.

materialism A style of sociological analysis that places emphasis on modes of economic production as the key determinant of everything else in society and culture.

materialistic To be concerned with personal wealth and accumulation of goods at the expense of all else.

McDonaldization A term coined by Ritzer to refer to the standardisation of work processes by rules and regulations. It is based on increased monitoring and evaluation of individual performance, akin to the uniformity and control measures used by fast-food chains.

means of production The raw materials, tools, equipment, property, and labour used to produce goods in a particular economic system.

media Technologically developed forms of human communication, held either in public or private ownership, which can transmit information and entertainment across time and space to large groups of people.

media process A concept used to analyse the interaction of production, representation, and effects of media, located within a societal context.

medical dominance The power of the medical profession to control its own work and the work of others in health care.

medicalised/medicalisation The process by which non-medical problems become defined and treated as medical issues, usually in terms of illnesses, disorders, or syndromes.

mercantilism An economic theory and practice, dominant between the sixteenth and eighteenth centuries during the rise of the nation-state that assumes national wealth can be amassed through the accumulation of precious metals (silver and gold), achieved by trade, tariff protection, and conquest.

meritocratic An objective measurement by which to assign social positions rather than by means of ascribed positions such as *social class*, age or *gender*.

meta-narratives The 'big picture' analysis that frames and organises observations and research on a particular topic.

modernisation A contested concept that refers to the social changes that agrarian and 'traditional' societies undergo to achieve modernity, such as the development of nation states and associated political institutions based on the rule of law, secularisation, industrialisation, urbanisation, and a reliance on science and reason as the basis for understanding the world.

modernity The historical period from the mid-eighteenth century until the late twentieth century whereby traditional agrarian societies were transformed into industrialised, urbanised, and secular nation states based on the rule of law, science, and reason.

moral panic An exaggerated reaction by the mass media, politicians, and community leaders to the actions and beliefs of certain social groups or individuals, which are often minor and inconsequential, but are sensationally represented to create anxiety and outrage among the general public.

multiculturalism A policy of ethnic management based upon a recognition of difference. Multiculturalism has been a policy framework for the management of ethnic diversity in Australia since the early 1970s.

nationalism Refers to an ideology of patriotic beliefs in support of national sovereignty and independence for an identifiable group of people based on common language, traditions, religion, or ethnicity.

nature religions Religious groups, such as Wiccans and Neo-Pagans, who believe in the sacredness of the earth.

negotiated order A symbolic interactionist concept that refers to any form of social organisation in which the exercise of authority and the formation of rules are outcomes of human interaction and negotiation.

neo-Fordism A term used to describe the refinement of Fordist styles of management and work organisation that intensify control of the labour process.

neo-liberalism A philosophy based on the primacy of individual rights and minimal state intervention.

neo-Marxism Theories that derive from Marx but incorporate diverse notions of power and status.

network society Castells' term for the combination of economic globalisation and information technology to create a new kind of capitalist economy, based in social networks connected across the world by instant communication.

New Age Umbrella term for alternative spiritual beliefs and practices popular in the West.

new racism The organisation and expression of racism around economic and sociocultural differences between dominant and marginalised groups.

normalising The sociological meaning comes from Foucault, and refers to processes of regulation and surveillance used to normalise (record and treat in standardised forms) persons and populations so they are more easily 'governed'.

norms Shared expectations of how people ought to behave or act. They can take the form of laws, regulations, guidelines, conventions, expectations, understandings, or other rules.

nuclear family A household consisting of parents of the opposite sex living with their biological children.

Other/Otherness Refers to those individuals who are treated as objects and have no agency and freedom. In *post-colonialism*, the Other is seen as someone who is different from the European colonial self, while in ethnic and cultural studies the Other is someone from a marginalised minority group within a country of immigration.

paradigm A paradigm is a framework for understanding the social world. In the context of social research, a paradigm determines what aspects of the social world will be investigated, the types of research questions that will be asked, and how the results of the research will be interpreted.

participant observation Participant observation is a data-collection technique that involves participating at some level in a social environment, while observing and recording experiences in that environment.

patchwork families A term used by Beck and Beck-Gernsheim to describe multi-parent families resulting from marriage, divorce, and remarriage.

patriarchal dividend Refers to the economic and social advantages men gain over women.

patriarchy A system of power through which males dominate households. It is used more broadly by *feminists* to refer to society's domination by patriarchal power, which functions to subordinate women and children.

Pentecostals Christian groups that emphasise dramatic religious experiences such as speaking in tongues and being 'born again' in Jesus.

phrenology A pseudo-scientific theory that determined personality traits and intellect on the basis of the shape and size of the head and brain.

population A population is the group of people about which the researcher is interested in finding more information.

positional segregation Also known as 'stacking', positional segregation involves the allocation of sports people to playing positions on the basis of assumptions made about them because of their race or ethnicity.

positivism A contested view in sociology that social phenomena should be studied in the same way as the natural world, by focusing only on observable and quantifiable events through which causal connections and universal laws can be determined.

post-colonialism The study of the issues raised in societies with a colonial past, particularly regarding identity and relationships between the colonisers and the colonised.

post-Fordism A term used to characterise the changing nature of work organisation and management styles in capitalist societies, in which 'flexibility' and worker participation are valued.

postmodernism The culture of postmodernity, referring to the plurality of social meanings and the diversity of social experiences that exist within localised contexts and cultures.

postmodernity Refers to a new era since the late 1960s in Western societies in which social life is characterised by diversity, consumerism, individualism, and lifestyle choice.

power A capacity, which all groups of people possess to some degree, to exert influence or pursue individual and collective interests.

primary socialisation Refers to the socialisation of babies and young children, and mainly occurs within the family.

primordialism A belief that the elements of identity are inborn and relatively independent of cultural context.

professional bureaucracy Mintzberg's term for an organisation that relies on staff with specialised knowledge and expertise to deliver complex services that require decision-making autonomy at the point of service delivery.

proletarianisation of medicine A trend for self-employed doctors in independent practice to be replaced by doctors working for larger companies.

protection The separation of Australian Indigenous people into missions and government reserves based on the belief that Indigenous people were a dying race and would not survive in white society alone.

questionnaire A data-collection device that includes a set of written questions for the respondent to answer.

radical feminism Radical feminism defines *patriarchy* as the cause of women's oppression and argues that all women are oppressed, focusing on issues such as sexual assault and prostitution.

randomised control trials (RCTs) A research procedure commonly used in health research to evaluate the effectiveness of particular interventions, whereby participants are randomly assigned to an experimental ('trial') group or a control group (which receives a placebo or no treatment and is used for comparison).

rational choice theory Also known as 'exchange theory', it is based on the principles of neo-classical economics and assumes that people's behaviour is primarily based on the maximisation of self-interest derived from 'rational' goal-oriented choices.

rationalisation A tendency to apply reason, to think and act in a calculative manner (as opposed to an emulative or traditional manner). It is seen by *Weberian* scholars as the key aspect of *modernisation* and as the synonym of *detraditionalisation*.

reconciliation Recognising injustice and making changes in a society to redress human-rights violations and to restore harmony and justice.

regional An area separate from the metropolitan areas that dominate national life.

reintegrative shaming A process that attempts to simultaneously shame an offender for their crime and restore them to full participation in society, by making the offender apologise to the victim/s and engage in some form of restitution to the victim/community.

reproduce/reproduction The social activity of doing things in ways that replicate existing patterns and processes of behaviour.

research design A research design is the plan that researchers develop for conducting their research, which includes the rationale for the study, the theoretical framework/s informing the study, the research questions, the methods of data collection and analysis, and the sampling strategy.

resocialisation Part of the socialisation process; it occurs during our adult years.

risk factors Physiological states and social behaviours associated with particular illnesses (for example, heavy smokers have a high risk of lung cancer).

risk society A term coined by Beck to describe the centrality of risk calculations in people's lives in Western society, whereby the key social problems today are unanticipated (or manufactured) hazards, such as the risks of pollution, food poisoning, and environmental degradation.

rural Areas with economies and societies tied to, and largely dependent on, agriculture.

sample (probability and non-probability) The sample is the part of the population that the researcher examines. Samples can be selected from the population using probability and non-probability techniques.

sanctions Informal and formal practices applied to individuals (either singly or in groups) and their behaviour as a way of achieving social control and managing or minimising deviance. Sanctions can either be positive, in the form of a reward, or negative, in the form of punishment—including deprivation of various kinds.

scientific racism The use of scientific research to express and support racist ideologies.

secondary socialisation Refers to the socialisation of children by their peers and by institutions such as schools.

second-generation migrants Children born in Australia who have at least one parent born overseas.

sects Religious groups with orthodox but restrictive views and practices.

secularisation The process by which religion has come to play less of a role in a society as a whole and in people's lives within that society.

(the) self The reflexive condition of all humans in which they can view themselves objectively as unique individuals by imagining themselves from the standpoint of others.

self-determination The right for people, within international law, to have control over their economic, social, and cultural development, and forms and structures of governance.

sex The biological distinction between male and female based on genital organs and physiology. See also *gender*.

sexual division of labour Refers to the gender-based division of tasks, with the stereotype being the male breadwinner and the female homemaker.

signify (verb), or signifier (noun) Saussure's terms for how an object (signifier) is able to refer (signify) to something other than itself—for example, red roses signify romantic interest.

sign An object that symbolises something else—for example, a necktie suggests formality.

social capital A term used to refer to social relations, networks, norms, trust, and reciprocity between individuals that facilitate cooperation for mutual benefit.

social class See *class*.

social closure A term first used by Weber to describe the way power is exercised to exclude outsiders from the privileges of social membership (in *social classes*, professions, or status groups).

social cohesion The degree to which people feel they are part of a wider society made up of people whom they can generally trust.

social construction/ism Refers to the socially created characteristics of human life based on the idea that people actively construct reality, meaning it is neither 'natural' nor inevitable. Therefore, notions of normality/abnormality, right/wrong, and health/illness are subjective human creations that should not be taken for granted.

social control Refers to all the responses or reactions to deviance that are aimed at reducing or stemming deviance and achieving conformity to particular social norms. Social control can range from a glance or a comment to joking behaviour to social exclusion or ostracism.

social Darwinism The application of evolutionary laws of natural selection to human societies to 'explain' social processes and behaviours. Spencer coined the term 'survival of the fittest' (often misattributed to Darwin) to describe how Darwin's ideas about natural selection in nature could be used to explain social processes and behaviours.

social determinants The historical, political, economic, social, and cultural factors that directly and indirectly influence systematic discrimination and inequality.

social differentiation A term coined by Durkheim to refer to the social division of labour, whereby work becomes separated into different social spheres such as the family and the economy, and paid work becomes increasingly specialised into discrete occupations with particular power and status hierarchies.

social exclusion A general term for the social and economic inequality experienced by a range of minority and socially disadvantaged groups, such as lack of access to, and participation in, social institutions.

social facts A term coined by Durkheim to refer to the subject-matter of sociology; social facts are seen as social forces external to the individual.

social identity The idea that people develop an identity, an understanding of themselves, that is conditioned by social processes and becomes key to their own understanding of themselves and how others see them—for example, as an environmentalist, a committed Christian, a *feminist*, an Australian, and so on.

social institutions Formal organisations that address public needs such as education, health care, government, and welfare.

social model of health A model that aims to find the causes of inequality between social groups, and to use public policy to improve health-related living and working conditions.

social structure The recurring patterns of social interaction through which people are related to each other, such as social institutions and social groups.

socialisation The process through which an individual learns the culture of a society and internalises its *norms*, values, and perspectives in order to know how to behave and communicate. Socialisation is the process through which we acquire a sense of *self*.

socialism A political ideology with numerous variations, but with a core belief in the creation of societies in which private property and wealth accumulation are replaced by state ownership and distribution of economic resources. See also *communism*.

sociobiology A school of thought in the biological sciences, arguing that all differences in temperament between men and women are a result of evolutionary selection. According to Edward O. Wilson, all behaviour is genetically programmed and resistant to cultural demands.

socioeconomic status (SES) A statistical measure that classifies individuals, households, or families in terms of their income, occupation, and education.

sociological determinism A view that people's behaviour and beliefs are entirely shaped or determined by the social structure or social processes.

sociological imagination A term coined by Mills to describe the sociological approach to analysing issues. We see the world through a sociological imagination, or think sociologically, when we make a link between personal troubles and public issues.

spirituality Any enduring experience or awareness of something greater than the self.

status groups Communities or groups of people with a common lifestyle, distinguished from others by a particular non-economic social characteristic. Status groupings can be used to include or exclude people with particular social characteristics.

step-families Couple families where one or more children are the biological offspring of only one member of the couple, and there are no jointly conceived or foster children.

stereotype The assumption that people have certain characteristics because of the group to which they belong, such as their race or ethnic group. Whether such characteristics are held by the group concerned (usually they are not) is irrelevant to the belief by others that they are, which informs some people's behaviour towards members of the subject group.

structural and institutional change Changes to the key institutions in a society and the way a society is organised to address the ways in which it disadvantages a marginalised group.

(structural) functionalism A theoretical perspective in sociology in which society is seen as consisting of many complex and interdependent parts that contribute to consensus and social stability. Prominent theorists include Durkheim, Merton, and Parsons.

structuralism A theoretical tradition that emphasises the way culture is organised by various underlying codes, symbols, and ideas that function according to linguistic rules.

structuration A theory developed by Giddens to denote the two-way process by which individuals shape their social world and in turn are shaped by social processes.

structure (or social structure) The recurring patterns that occur in social life, in particular the rules and resources that give similar social practices systematic form.

structure–agency debate A key debate in sociology over the extent to which human behaviour is determined by social structure.

subculture A smaller cultural group of people sharing the same tastes and ideas, nested inside a larger, less well-defined 'culture'. Examples include goths, ferals, and skinheads.

supernatural Otherworldly, non-religious phenomena, such as ghosts and extra-sensory perception (ESP).

sustainability The capacity to provide the resources needed to maintain a standard of living into the long term.

symbolic capital A sub-category of *cultural capital* denoting the honour and prestige accorded to certain individuals.

symbolic interactionism A theoretical framework first developed by Mead that places strong emphasis on the importance of language and on social interactions as key components in the development of a sense of *self*.

symbolic reconciliation A focus on achieving equality in terms of having full rights to citizenship of a nation, and access to the same opportunities, and recognising historic injustice and Indigenous rights.

technological determinism An assumption that technological innovation is the primary cause of social, political, and economic change.

terra nullius Latin term for a land belonging to no one and purportedly used to justify the colonisation of Australia. See also *colonialism* and *imperialism*.

tertiary socialisation Processes of socialisation that occur in adulthood.

theory (social) A theory is a statement that explains the nature of relationships between aspects of the social world.

total fertility rate (TFR) The statistical average number of children a woman is likely to bear in her lifetime at current fertility rates for each age group.

total institutions A term used by Goffman to refer to institutions such as prisons and asylums in which life is highly regulated and subject to authoritarian control to induce conformity.

transnational corporations (TNCs) Business corporations operating in more than one country.

transnationalism A concept that describes the flows and movements of goods, people, and images across national borders.

upward social mobility This takes place when a person achieves a higher social position than that of their parents. The opposite, downward social mobility, also occurs.

urban Refers to places of high population density with economies based on industry and commerce.

variable Any phenomenon with measurable attributes.

Weberians Followers of Weber, who view society as stratified according to three main social determinants—*class*, status (such as level of education), and politics—and who analyse the competition and inequalities between these different groups.

Western family The model of the family in pre-industrial western Europe. Such families were characterised by a nuclear family embedded in a large household of kin and non-kin.

White Australia policy A policy of the Australian government associated with the *Immigration Restriction Act 1901*, which prevented the migration of so-called 'coloured' races to Australia.

whiteness The invisibility and unquestioned norm of white people's dominance and privilege compared with non-white people in societies such as Australia.

youth transitions The sequence of major life events through which full adult social status is achieved.

Index

Also from Allen & Unwin

ALLEN&UNWIN

*Get Great Marks
for your Essays, Reports, and Presentations*
3rd edition

John Germov

ISBN: 978 1 74175 452 0

Not sure how to begin writing? Four assignments and only four weeks to go before the deadline? Then this book is for you.

Find out the rules of the essay writing game: how to muckrake for information, write drafts, handle references, and do analysis. Discover where you win and lose marks. Learn how to take the right shortcuts and make the most of your time.

Get Great Marks for Your Essays, Reports, and Presentations tells you all you need to know to write successful essays and reports, and create attention-grabbing presentations in the social sciences and humanities.

This third edition is fully revised in response to readers' suggestions and includes extensive coverage of online resources, tips for getting the best from your computer tools, and guidance on how to pitch to your audience.

'This guide is great. I had a lot of trouble passing my essays. After reading this book I found I wasn't alone. This book has helped me to understand how to improve my writing ... It's easy to read and it's pretty cool too!'—Student comment

Also from Allen & Unwin

ALLEN&UNWIN

The Sociological Quest:
An introduction to the study of social life
5ᵗʰ edition

Evan Willis

ISBN: 978 1 74237 282 2

What is sociology? How do you 'do' sociology?

Starting sociology can be daunting. This bestselling short introduction takes the reader on a quest towards a sociological understanding of the world we live in.

Using contemporary examples, *The Sociological Quest* asks what is distinctive about the way sociologists view society. Evan Willis shows that they are concerned with the relationship between the individual and society, and that a sociological analysis involves an approach which is historical, cultural, structural and critical.

This fifth edition has been thoroughly revised and incorporates new examples on technology, terrorism, climate change and consumer behaviour. It remains essential preliminary reading for new students of sociology.

Evan Willis is Professor of Sociology at La Trobe University in Melbourne, and one of Australia's leading sociologists. He has published widely and one of his books, *Medical Dominance*, was a winner of the Australian Sociological Association Award for the Ten Most Influential Books in Australian Sociology. *The Sociological Quest* has also been published in North American and Norwegian editions.